ASSESSING POLICE AND OTHER PUBLIC SAFETY PERSONNEL WITH THE MMPI-3

ASSESSING POLICE AND OTHER PUBLIC SAFETY PERSONNEL WITH THE MMPI-3

A Practical Guide

DAVID M. COREY and
YOSSEF S. BEN-PORATH

University of Minnesota Press
Minneapolis
London

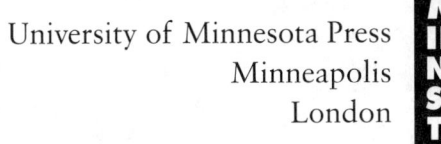

Copyright 2024 by the Regents of the University of Minnesota

All rights reserved. No part of this publication may be reproduced, stored in a retrieval system, or transmitted, in any form or by any means, electronic, mechanical, photocopying, recording, or otherwise, without the prior written permission of the publisher.

Published by the University of Minnesota Press
111 Third Avenue South, Suite 290
Minneapolis, MN 55401-2520
http://www.upress.umn.edu

ISBN 978-1-5179-1263-5 (hc)

A Cataloging-in-Publication record for this book is available from the Library of Congress.

Printed in the United States of America on acid-free paper

The University of Minnesota is an equal-opportunity educator and employer.

33 32 31 30 29 28 27 26 25 24   10 9 8 7 6 5 4 3 2 1

Contents

	List of Tables	vii
	List of Figures	ix
	Preface and Acknowledgments	xi
1	Introduction to the Psychological Assessment of Police and Other Public Safety Personnel	1
2	An MMPI-3 Overview	17
3	Assessing Protocol Validity With the MMPI-3	31
4	Assessing Personality and Psychopathology With the MMPI-3	41
5	Foundational Requirements for Preemployment Assessments	61
6	Empirical Foundations for Using the MMPI-3 in Preemployment Assessments of Public Safety Candidates	79
7	The MMPI-3 Public Safety Candidate Interpretive Reports	105
8	Using the MMPI-3 in Preemployment Assessments of Police and Other Public Safety Candidates: Case Illustrations and Guidance for Evidence-Based Report Writing	153

9	Foundational Requirements for Fitness-for-Duty Evaluations	341
10	Using the MMPI-3 to Assess Fitness for Duty: Case Illustrations	353
	Notes	489
	References	495
	Index	511

Tables

Table 1.1.	Essential Job Functions of Public Safety Positions	5
Table 1.2.	Public Safety Job Performance Problems	6
Table 1.3.	Public Safety Psychological Job Demands	7
Table 1.4.	Attributes Rated as Important for the Four Public Safety Classifications	8
Table 1.5.	Psychological Screening Dimensions for Public Safety Positions	10
Table 1.6.	Aspirational Statements from the Professional Practice Guidelines for Occupationally Mandated Psychological Evaluations (OMPE)	15
Table 2.1.	The MMPI-3 Scales	28
Table 3.1.	MMPI-3 Validity Scales: Threats to Protocol Validity and Confounds	38
Table 4.1.	Recommended Structure and Sources of Information for MMPI-3 Interpretation	58
Table 5.1.	EPPCC Ethical Standards Especially Pertinent to Psychological Screening	67
Table 7.1.	Geographic Distribution of the Police, Correctional, Dispatcher, and Firefighter Candidate Comparison Groups	107
Table 7.2.	Community Origins of the Police, Correctional, Dispatcher, and Firefighter Candidate Comparison Groups	108
Table 7.3.	Race/Ethnicity of the Police, Correctional, Dispatcher, and Firefighter Candidate Comparison Groups	109

Table 7.4.	Age Bands and Means/Standard Deviations of the Police, Correctional, Dispatcher, and Firefighter Candidate Comparison Groups	110
Table 7.5.	Education Levels of the Police, Correctional, Dispatcher, and Firefighter Candidate Comparison Groups	111
Table 7.6.	Means and Standard Deviations for the Police, Correctional, Dispatcher, and Firefighter Candidate Comparison Groups	112
Table 7.7.	Percent Scoring at or Above Designated Cutoffs for the Police, Correctional, Dispatcher, and Firefighter Candidate Comparison Groups	114
Table 7.8.	T-Score Cutoffs for Generating Statements in the Comparison Group Findings Interpretation Section Based on Nonclinically Elevated (and Higher) Scores	130
Table 7.9.	Descriptions of Problem Domains Used as an Organizing Structure in the MMPI-3 Public Safety Candidate Interpretive Reports	132
Table 7.10.	MMPI-3 Scales and T-Score Cutoffs for Generating Statements in the Job-Relevant Correlates Interpretation Section by Problem Domain	133
Table 8.1.	Five-Step Model for Integrating Psychological Screening Data	154
Table 10.1.	Public Safety Fitness-for-Duty Evaluation (FFDE) Descriptive Statistics	357
Table 10.2.	Public Safety Fitness-for-Duty Evaluation (FFDE) Validity Scale Elevation Rates	360
Table 10.3.	Public Safety Fitness-for-Duty Evaluation (FFDE) Substantive Scale Elevation Rates	362

Figures

Figure 7.1.	Police, Correctional, Dispatcher, and Firefighter Candidate Comparison Groups: MMPI-3 Validity Scales Means and Standard Deviations	123
Figure 7.2.	Police, Correctional, Dispatcher, and Firefighter Candidate Comparison Groups: MMPI-3 Higher-Order (H-O) and Restructured Clinical (RC) Scales Means and Standard Deviations	124
Figure 7.3.	Police, Correctional, Dispatcher, and Firefighter Candidate Comparison Groups: MMPI-3 Somatic/Cognitive and Internalizing Scales Means and Standard Deviations	125
Figure 7.4.	Police, Correctional, Dispatcher, and Firefighter Candidate Comparison Groups: MMPI-3 Externalizing and Interpersonal Scales Means and Standard Deviations	126
Figure 7.5.	Police, Correctional, Dispatcher, and Firefighter Candidate Comparison Groups: MMPI-3 PSY-5 Scales Means and Standard Deviations	127
Figure 7.6.	Mr. E's MMPI-3 Police Candidate Interpretive Report	138
Figure 8.1.	Mr. D's MMPI-3 Police Candidate Interpretive Report	158
Figure 8.2.	Ms. Q's MMPI-3 Police Candidate Interpretive Report	179
Figure 8.3.	Mr. G's MMPI-3 Police Candidate Interpretive Report	198
Figure 8.4.	Mr. K's MMPI-3 Correctional Candidate Interpretive Report	220
Figure 8.5.	Mr. B's MMPI-3 Police Candidate Interpretive Report	240
Figure 8.6.	Mr. M's MMPI-3 Police Candidate Interpretive Report	258

Figure 8.7.	Ms. P's MMPI-3 Dispatcher Candidate Interpretive Report	273
Figure 8.8.	Mr. H's MMPI-3 Correctional Candidate Interpretive Report	290
Figure 8.9.	Mr. Z's MMPI-3 Firefighter Candidate Interpretive Report	306
Figure 8.10.	Mr. N's MMPI-3 Police Candidate Interpretive Report	325
Figure 10.1.	Mr. S's MMPI-3 Clinical Settings Interpretive Report	373
Figure 10.2.	Mr. R's MMPI-3 Clinical Settings Interpretive Report	391
Figure 10.3.	Mr. J's MMPI-3 Clinical Settings Interpretive Report	405
Figure 10.4.	Mr. W's MMPI-3 Clinical Settings Interpretive Report (Initial)	426
Figure 10.5.	Mr. W's MMPI-3 Clinical Settings Interpretive Report (Follow-up)	444
Figure 10.6.	Ms. U's MMPI-3 Clinical Settings Interpretive Report	461
Figure 10.7.	Mr. Y's MMPI-3 Clinical Settings Interpretive Report	475

Preface and Acknowledgments

Conducting psychological assessments in applied, high-stakes settings always requires assiduous preparation, particularly when those stakes involve life and death. Police officers, correctional officers, public safety dispatchers, and firefighters/medics perform duties that have potentially catastrophic consequences for the public and themselves. At a time of unprecedented scrutiny of these public safety personnel, accurately assessing their prehire suitability and posthire fitness for duty is equally consequential.

In 2021 alone, state legislators in California, Georgia, Kansas, New Jersey, North Carolina, South Carolina, and Wisconsin introduced bills involving psychological evaluations of police and correctional candidates (National Conference of State Legislators, 2022). Although statutes and regulations related to these evaluations vary greatly (see Corey et al., 2023), the standard of practice or "basic model" requires that psychological testing be used in conjunction with a clinical interview and review of relevant personal history (American Psychological Association [APA], 2018; International Association of Chiefs of Police [IACP], 2020; Mitchell, 2017; Serafino, 2010). It is this combination of high stakes and multimodal assessment requirements that underlies calls for guidance to "help the assessor to cope with the complexities and demands of assessment processes in various contexts of psychological assessment" (Fernández-Ballesteros et al., 2001, p. 187). Answering these calls was our impetus for writing the practical guide for the MMPI-2-RF (Corey & Ben-Porath, 2018) and it remains so for this MMPI-3 version. We are gratified that the initial book was well received as "a unique blend of theory and practice for clinicians who perform psychological evaluations for police and public safety personnel" (Laguna, 2020, p. 624). We have strived to achieve the same blend in this updated edition.

Although the topic of this volume involves the use of the MMPI-3, our focus is on helping test users navigate the "complexities and demands" of conducting suitability and fitness evaluations of police and other public safety personnel. To be sure, proper use of the MMPI-3 requires understanding what it measures, how its scores are used to infer valid meaning, and its hierarchical structure and interpretive framework, which are covered in the first portion of this guide. But the complexities and demands of assessing public safety personnel require an even broader set of knowledge (e.g., legal requirements, professional practice guidelines, job demands, unique stressors, and working conditions) and, just as critical, the ability to *integrate* MMPI-3 data with other assessment findings from the basic model, which we address in the remainder of the book.

This volume is a companion to the *MMPI-3 User's Guide for the Public Safety Candidate Interpretive Reports* (Corey & Ben-Porath, 2022). We have expanded coverage to include use of not only the updated MMPI-3 Police Candidate Interpretive Report (PCIR), but also the newly released Correctional Candidate Interpretive Report (CCIR), Dispatcher Candidate Interpretive Report (DCIR), and Firefighter Candidate Interpretive Report (FCIR). Although the guidelines and recommendations offered in this book are our own, we owe thanks to many who contributed to our work in this area. Indeed, these evidence-based reports would not have been possible without the contributions of an international team of research collaborators, including JoAnne Brewster, Bruce Cappo, Catherine Delsol, Paul Detrick, Laura Sue Elias, Gary Fischler, Matt Guller, Herbert Gupton, David Hill, Catherine Martin-Doto, Heather McElroy, William Menton, Monica Pilarc, Michael Roberts, Ryan Roberts, Jocelyn Roland, Martin Sellbom, Shelley Spilberg, Casey Stewart, Anthony Tarescavage, Ray Turner, Carol Vipari, Elizabeth White, and Megan Whitman.

We are also grateful to Katie Nickerson and Alicia Gomez of the University of Minnesota Press editorial team, whose attention to detail, parsimony, and style is unmatched. Beverly Kaemmer, retired associate director at the University of Minnesota Press, was deeply instrumental in the development of the MMPI-2-RF PCIR, and her wise counsel still influences the updated and newly added reports. The contributions of the late Auke Tellegen, professor emeritus at the University of Minnesota and coauthor of the MMPI-2-RF and MMPI-3, are incalculable. We hope our work pays adequate tribute to his undaunted vision and wisdom.

We remain forever grateful to our families, Denise and Alex (DMC) and Denise, Adam, Rose, and Ella (YBP), for their support and endurance during the 15-year span of this project.

David M. Corey
Yossef S. Ben-Porath

Note to the reader: We have made an earnest effort throughout this book to use inclusive language. Doing so requires language choices that strict grammarians, and some readers, may find awkward. For example, in respecting that gender identity is not exclusively binary, we have used the plural pronoun *they* instead of *he or she* and *themself* rather than *himself or herself.* We believe the endeavor to be more inclusive in our language is a priority over grammar that does not accurately express our meaning or fully convey our intent.

Introduction to the Psychological Assessment of Police and Other Public Safety Personnel

We began our introduction to the earlier, MMPI-2-RF, edition of this book by writing, "perhaps at no other time has the importance of selecting and employing psychologically competent police and other public safety personnel been more self-evident" (Corey & Ben-Porath, 2018, p. 1). We could not have anticipated how much this importance would grow over the ensuing years.

News reports of inexplicable rudeness, indifference, and most concerning, unnecessary and excessive uses of force—often accompanied by video from dashcams, bodycams, or bystanders—by the very persons sworn to "serve and protect" the public have remained pervasive. This has led to mass protests, erosion in public trust of law enforcement officers, and calls for police reform. The need to ensure that individuals in these positions are psychologically suited to carry out the "awesome power at their disposal" (*Duran v. City of Douglas*, 1990, p. 1378) has been emphasized by a long line of special commissions and task forces, beginning with Lyndon Johnson's President's Commission on Law Enforcement and Administration of Justice (1967) and more recently with the Obama-era President's Task Force on 21st Century Policing (2015).

Calls for the increased use of preemployment psychological screening have also included correctional officers. In 1975, the American Bar Association advocated for routine psychological screening of correctional candidates (Goldstein, 1975). In 1983, New York State Department of Correctional Services was among the first statewide penal institutions to require psychological screening of all state correctional officers, with the explicit objective "to identify those individuals displaying psychopathology or other psychological limitations which could significantly impair job performance and effectiveness" (Tatar & Morgenbesser, 1993, p. 1).

But calls for the universal screening of public safety personnel are insufficient without an earnest effort to ensure that these evaluations are evidence based and carried out in a manner consistent with best practices. Two studies conducted 40 years apart—one analyzing the incremental validity of the screening psychologist's suitability determination in evaluations of dispatcher candidates (Weiner, 1997) and the other in evaluations of police and firefighter candidates (Kwaske & Morris, 2015)—report clear evidence of the increased validity of personality tests over individual psychologist judgments in predicting job performance outcomes. Still, the authors of both studies found that the psychologists they observed "rely largely upon information other than test scores (e.g., personal history information and interview) and/or use such scores differently in formulating their suitability determinations" (Weiner, 1997, p. 20) and that "assessor judgments were largely unrelated to standardized test results" (Kwaske & Morris, 2015, p. 25). Our goal in writing this book is to facilitate competent use of the MMPI®-3 (Minnesota Multiphasic Personality Inventory®-3) when conducting assessments of police and other public safety candidates and personnel.

This book is focused on two types of assessments—preemployment and fitness-for-duty evaluations—applied to four public safety job classes with common requirements for emotional and psychological functioning: police officer,[1] correctional officer,[2] dispatcher,[3] and firefighter/medic.[4] A substantial and growing body of research documents associations between preemployment psychological evaluation findings and posthire outcomes (e.g., performance problems, disciplinary actions, citizen complaints, and involuntary termination of employment) in police candidates.[5] Research conducted with the MMPI instruments is reviewed in chapter 6. There is a dearth of literature on the use of all personality and psychopathology measures to predict posthire outcomes for correctional, dispatcher, and firefighter/medic candidates, but considerable evidence (also reviewed in chapter 6) demonstrates that the MMPI-3 predicts job-relevant personality constructs comparably for all four public safety positions. Indeed, along with the consistency in job demands and psychological attributes shared by these positions (discussed next) and comparability in the contexts and settings in which these candidates are evaluated, these validity findings spurred the recent development of the MMPI-3 Public Safety Candidate Interpretive Reports. This is a suite of stand-alone interpretive reports customized for evaluating police, correctional, dispatcher, and firefighter/medic candidates. These reports are described in detail in the *MMPI-3 User's Guide for the Public Safety Candidate Interpretive Reports* (Corey & Ben-Porath, 2022), and case studies illustrating their use are included in chapter 8.

Police officers, correctional officers, dispatchers, and firefighters/medics comprise the first line of public safety defense in modern society. They are tasked with responsibility for a broad array of security functions (e.g., border security, critical infrastructure protection, transportation security, and domestic and international intelligence activities) and to defend local communities from a wide range of threats to life and property. Their effectiveness depends not only on their emotional and psychological ability to perform the job but also on their ability to do so under profoundly stressful and challenging conditions. Failure to identify public safety candidates and personnel who, by virtue of personality or psychopathology, are unable to reliably perform these jobs safely and effectively can have devastating consequences for the community, other public safety personnel, and public trust, as discussed.

The California Commission on Peace Officer Standards and Training (POST) is widely considered the national and international leader in establishing evidence-based practice standards for law enforcement personnel assessment (Mitchell, 2017). Regulations and procedures established by the California POST commission are routinely adopted by parallel commissions throughout the United States.[6] In *Brown v. Sandy City Appeal Board* (2014), a Utah court of appeals ruled that California POST regulations can reasonably be relied on by a psychologist evaluating a police officer in that state. The California POST commission advocated successfully for legislation, California Government Code § 1031(f)(2)(B), that obligates psychologists who conduct evaluations of candidates and incumbent peace officers (e.g., police officers, correctional officers, and probation and parole officers) to have and maintain competencies established by the POST. The requisite competencies, enumerated in the California POST *Peace Officer Psychological Screening Manual* (Spilberg & Corey, 2022, p. 36), consist of the following nine areas of foundational knowledge and skill:

Assessment Competence. The ability to properly gather, analyze, and integrate the full range of pertinent assessment data (personal health records, background investigation and other personal history information, psychological testing, clinical interview, and observations) to reach a determination of psychological suitability for exercising the powers of the position.
Clinical Competence. The ability to assess the impact of a candidate's emotional or mental condition, and normal and abnormal personality traits and adaptation, on psychological suitability for the position.
Communication Competence. The ability to communicate the necessary and appropriate findings, conclusions, and recommendations in a manner that is clear and useful to the hiring agency and others involved in the candidate screening process and conforms to regulatory requirements.
Jurisprudence Competence. Knowledge and application of federal and state statutes, regulations, and case law pertinent to psychological screening for the position, including but not limited to the federal Americans With Disabilities Act and Genetic Information Nondiscrimination Act, as well as related state laws.

Multicultural Competence. The ability to interact effectively with candidates in cross-cultural situations, including the consideration of customs, beliefs, values, and patterns of behavior reflecting disability, sexual orientation, and racial, ethnic, religious, gender, and national identity.

Occupational Competence. Knowledge of the essential job functions, working conditions, chain of command, and the psychological demands and stressors inherent in the public safety position.

Procedural Competence. Knowledge and application of personnel screening procedures and criteria that comply with regulatory requirements and are responsive to the needs and considerations of the hiring authority.

Psychometric Competence. Understanding of psychological test properties, including test score validity, reliability, base rates, test norms, and group differences, and the ability to select appropriate tests for evaluating psychological suitability for a particular position and to make proper, accurate inferences from test scores.

Standards Competence. Knowledge and application of ethical principles, standards, and professional guidelines pertinent to personnel screening (privacy, confidentiality, informed consent, and disclosure).

Before being approved to conduct preemployment evaluations of police candidates, California psychologists must attest to possessing these competencies and provide documentation of having obtained relevant continuing education in support of them. They are also required to maintain their competence through documented biennial continuing education pertinent to these domains. We focus next on two of these competency domains—clinical and occupational competence—that are especially pertinent to using measures of personality and psychopathology to evaluate a candidate's suitability and an employee's fitness for duty.

Clinical competence has a dual focus: one centered on evaluating personality and psychopathology and the other on assessing their impact on an individual's functional abilities related to public safety work. This dual focus requires the evaluator to have expertise both in clinical assessment and in understanding how personality and psychopathology interact ecologically in the real-world work environments of these positions. Consequently, occupational competence—knowledge of the essential job functions, working conditions, and psychological demands of the position—is also needed for the evaluator to assess the impact of clinically relevant findings on an individual's ability to perform public safety functions. Although it is beyond the scope of this book to explicate the full depth of occupational knowledge needed for each of the four positions, Table 1.1 lists the essential job functions typical of each. See also Corey and Zelig (2020) for a discussion of occupational competence necessary for evaluating police suitability and fitness for duty.

TABLE 1.1. Essential Job Functions of Public Safety Positions

Police officers	**Correctional officers**
• Enforce laws • Respond to emergency and nonemergency calls • Conduct interviews with suspects and witnesses • Observe the activities of suspects • Investigate crimes • Obtain warrants and arrest suspects • Write detailed reports and fill out forms • Prepare cases and testify in court • Collect and secure evidence from crime scenes • Use force as authorized, justified and necessary to protect themselves and others and to perform essential functions (e.g., carry out arrests)	• Enforce rules and keep order within jails or prisons • Supervise activities of inmates • Aid in rehabilitation and counseling of offenders • Inspect facilities to ensure that they meet standards • Search inmates for contraband items • Report on inmate conduct • Use force as authorized, justified and necessary to protect themselves and others and to perform essential functions (e.g., carry out searches)

Dispatchers	**Firefighters/medics**
• Answer 911 telephone calls • Determine the type of emergency and its location • Decide the appropriate response based on agency procedures • Relay information to the appropriate first responder agency • Assist people who are in life-threatening situations • Coordinate the dispatch of emergency response personnel to accident scenes • Give over-the-phone medical instructions before emergency personnel arrive • Monitor and track the status of police, fire, and ambulance units • Synchronize responses with other area communication centers • Keep detailed records about calls	• Drive fire trucks and other emergency vehicles • Put out fires using water hoses, fire extinguishers, and pumps • Find and rescue victims in burning buildings or in other emergency situations • Respond to 911 calls for emergency medical assistance, such as cardiopulmonary resuscitation (CPR) or bandaging a wound • Assess a patient's condition and determine a course of treatment • Follow guidelines learned in training or received from physicians who oversee their work • Use backboards and restraints to keep patients still and safe in an ambulance during transport • Help transfer patients to the emergency department of a healthcare facility and report their observations and treatment to the staff • Create a patient care report, documenting the medical care given to the patient • Replace used supplies and check or clean equipment after use • Prepare written reports on emergency incidents • Clean and maintain equipment • Conduct drills and physical fitness training • Provide public education on fire safety

Note. U.S. Department of Labor, Bureau of Labor Statistics.

6 | INTRODUCTION TO THE ASSESSMENT OF PUBLIC SAFETY PERSONNEL

The California POST commission identified the psychologically relevant performance problems and job demands of peace officers as a preliminary step toward isolating the traits and abilities necessary to perform essential functions safely and effectively (Spilberg & Corey, 2022, Tables 4.3 and 4.4, pp. 50–51). Tables 1.2 and 1.3 list the law enforcement officer job performance problems and job demands respectively and indicate, based on our collective experience,

TABLE 1.2. Public Safety Job Performance Problems

Problem	PO	CO	DIS	FF
Excessive/inappropriate use of force	√	√	N/A	N/A
Misuse of authority	√	√	√	√
Partiality in enforcing the law (due to prejudice or dishonesty)	√	√	N/A	N/A
Bias/prejudice/intolerance (reflected in dealing with coworkers, citizens)	√	√	√	√
Substance abuse	√	√	√	√
Theft	√	√	√	√
Dishonesty	√	√	√	√
Law violation	√	√	√	√
Inappropriate reaction to crises/emergencies	√	√	√	√
Reaction to gradual stress buildup over time	√	√	√	√
Panic under stress	√	√	√	√
Disorderliness/sloppy—haphazard work	√	√	√	√
Inattention to detail	√	√	√	√
Failure to carry tasks to completion	√	√	√	√
Inability to work on several concurrent tasks	√	√	√	√
Poor prioritization skills	√	√	√	√
Hostility toward authority	√	√	√	√
Hot-temperedness	√	√	√	√
Failure to take work seriously	√	√	√	√
Impulsiveness	√	√	√	√
Inability to cope with job structure	√	√	√	√
Absenteeism	√	√	√	√
Turnover (due to cost of training)	√	√	√	√
Poor service attitude (officious, sarcastic, rude)	√	√	√	√
Disregard for rules and regulations	√	√	√	√
Recurrent somatic problems	√	√	√	√
Failure to keep up with paperwork	√	√	√	√
Tampering with evidence	√	√	√	√
Going through the motions without attention/vigilance	√	√	√	√
Low activity level	√	√	√	√
Inability to interpret rules	√	√	√	√
Inability to switch "roles" as required by the circumstances	√	√	√	√

Note. PO=Police officer; CO=Correctional officer; DIS=Dispatcher; FF=Firefighter/medic

TABLE 1.3. Public Safety Psychological Job Demands

Job demand	PO	CO	DIS	FF
Discretionary use of force	√	√	N/A	N/A
Verbal abuse from suspects, victims, bystanders, reporters, inmates, witnesses, etc.	√	√	√	√
Willingness to use force	√	√	N/A	N/A
Constant exposure to the worst elements of society; easy to become jaded/cynical	√	√	√	√
Discretionary use of enforcement powers	√	√	N/A	N/A
Access to money and property	√	√	N/A	√
Securing public trust	√	√	√	√
Decision-making under extreme pressure/stress	√	√	√	√
Access to sensitive information	√	√	√	√
Periods of quiet/boredom interrupted by sudden emergency response	√	√	√	√
Responding to tragedies, emergencies, disasters, and highly stressful situations	√	√	√	√
Need to respond to a series of diverse calls and adapt responses ("shift gears" from routine to emergency calls)	√	√	√	√
Exposure to unpleasant/repugnant persons and situations	√	√	√	√
Public contact; communicating with the entire gamut of society; adapting effectively	√	√	√	√
Threats to personal safety, physical attacks	√	√	N/A	√
Serving a diverse community, regardless of culture or socioeconomic status	√	√	√	√
Risk of personal injury, including mortal injury	√	√	N/A	√

Note. PO=Police officer; CO=Correctional officer; DIS=Dispatcher; FF=Firefighter/medic

which of these also apply to the other public safety positions. As Table 1.2 shows, all 32 problem behaviors apply both to law enforcement and correctional officers, and all of the problems (except those involving use of force and enforcement of laws) also apply to firefighters/medics and dispatchers. Similarly, Table 1.3 shows that both law enforcement and correctional officers are subject to all 17 of the psychological job demands. Firefighters/medics experience 14 (all but those related to use of force and enforcement powers), and dispatchers are subject to all but the demands pertaining to use of force, enforcement powers, access to money and property,[7] and risk/threats of personal injury.

The Occupational Information Network (O*NET), functioning under the sponsorship of the U.S. Department of Labor/Employment and Training Administration, is the nation's primary source of occupational information. A central component of this resource is the O*NET database, containing information on hundreds of standardized and occupation-specific descriptors, which is continually updated by surveying a broad range of workers from each occupation. Table 1.4 lists the attributes (skills and work styles) rated in the

TABLE 1.4. Attributes Rated as Important for the Four Public Safety Classifications

Domain	Attribute
INTEGRITY	**Integrity**—Being honest and ethical.
STRESS TOLERANCE AND ADAPTATION	**Stress Tolerance**—Accepting criticism and dealing calmly and effectively with high stress situations.
	Self-Control—Maintaining composure, keeping emotions in check, controlling anger, and avoiding aggressive behavior, even in very difficult situations.
	Adaptability/Flexibility—Being open to change (positive and negative) and to considerable variety in the workplace.
THINKING AND DECIDING	**Judgment and Decision Making**—Considering the relative costs and benefits of potential actions to choose the most appropriate one.
	Critical Thinking—Using logic and reasoning to identify the strengths and weaknesses of alternative solutions, conclusions or approaches to problems.
	Complex Problem Solving—Identifying complex problems and reviewing related information to develop and evaluate options and implement solutions.
	Coordination—Adjusting actions in relation to others' actions.
	Active Learning—Understanding the implications of new information for both current and future problem-solving and decision-making.
	Analytical Thinking—Analyzing information and using logic to address work-related issues and problems.
	Innovation—Using creativity and alternative thinking to develop new ideas for and answers to work-related problems.
CONSCIENTIOUSNESS	**Independence**—Developing one's own ways of doing things, guiding oneself with little or no supervision, and depending on oneself to get things done.
	Dependability—Being reliable, responsible, and dependable, and fulfilling obligations.
	Initiative—Willingness to take on responsibilities and challenges.
	Attention to Detail—Being careful about detail and thorough in completing work tasks.
	Persistence—Persisting in the face of obstacles.
	Monitoring—Monitoring/assessing performance of oneself, other individuals, or organizations to make improvements or take corrective action.
	Achievement/Effort—Establishing and maintaining personally challenging achievement goals and exerting effort toward mastering tasks.
INTERPERSONAL	**Social Perceptiveness**—Being aware of others' reactions and understanding why they react as they do.
	Active Listening—Giving full attention to what other people are saying, taking time to understand the points being made, asking questions as appropriate, and not interrupting at inappropriate times.
	Service Orientation—Actively looking for ways to help people.
	Social Orientation—Preferring to work with others rather than alone, and being personally connected with others on the job.
	Persuasion—Persuading others to change their minds or behavior.
	Leadership—Willingness to lead, take charge, and offer opinions and direction.
	Concern for Others—Being sensitive to others' needs and feelings and being understanding and helpful on the job.
	Cooperation—Being pleasant with others on the job and displaying a good-natured, cooperative attitude.

Note. Adapted from O*NET OnLine Database, 2022.

O*NET database as important for each of the four public safety classifications: Police Patrol Officers/Deputy Sheriffs; Correctional Officers and Jailers; Police, Fire, and Ambulance Dispatchers; and Municipal Firefighters. Although this list corresponds closely with the California POST (CA-POST) Psychological Screening Dimensions discussed next, it is important to keep in mind that there is imperfect synchrony in the weights assigned to all psychologically relevant competencies or traits. For example, "negotiation" (bringing others together to change their minds or behavior) is a skill that the O*NET database weighs as important for police patrol officers (60 on a 100-point scale), deputy sheriffs (72/100), correctional officers (53/100), and emergency communications dispatchers (50/100) but is assigned less weight (i.e., helpful but not important) for municipal firefighters (47/100). The reader should keep in mind that these are average weights across an aggregate of locations across the United States, which may be allotted differently in specific employment contexts and locations. Similarly, each of the selection criteria listed in Table 1.5 does not necessarily carry equal weight for all positions. The hiring agency should be consulted to help ascertain which unique features of the job demands, working conditions, and settings may influence the relative importance of certain screening dimensions.

The CA-POST Psychological Screening Dimensions are generally recognized as the national standard for evaluating the psychological suitability of law enforcement officers, in large part due to the rigor applied to the job analysis and validation procedures that produced them. Mitchell (2017) referred to them as "the most sophisticated and ambitious effort yet to operationally define those psychological qualities" (p. 40). Hough (2016) independently examined the job activities and functions of police officers as well as a large amount of literature identifying characteristics of effective officers in community-oriented law enforcement settings. Hough identified a broad list of necessary personality attributes—conscientiousness, emotional maturity and stability, the ability to influence (persuasiveness), amicability, service orientation, and practical intelligence (judgment and decision making)—and assessed those attributes to be "consistent with" the "more specific characteristics" contained in the CA-POST dimensions (p. 577).

California POST commission regulations require a comprehensive background investigation for all peace officer (a classification that includes law enforcement and correctional officers) and dispatcher positions throughout the state of California based on a common set of background investigation dimensions covering five behavioral domains: moral character, handling stress and adversity, work habits, interactions with others, and intellectually based abilities. Although the CA-POST dimensions (Table 1.5) are mandated only for the evaluation of police and correctional candidates in the state, their close parallel to the attributes listed in Table 1.4 render them a useful starting place for evaluating firefighter/medic candidates as well. Indeed, in its 1997 publication

TABLE 1.5. Psychological Screening Dimensions for Public Safety Positions

Psychological screening dimension	Description
Integrity/Ethics	Maintaining high standards of personal conduct. Consists of attributes such as honesty, impartiality, trustworthiness, and adherence to laws, regulations, and procedures.
Impulse Control/Attention to Safety	Taking proper precautions and avoiding impulsive or unnecessarily risky behavior to ensure the safety of both the public and public safety officers. Includes the ability and inclination to think before acting, to keep one's impulses in control, and behave in conscious regard for the larger situation at hand.
Avoidance of Substance Abuse and Other Risk-Taking Behavior	Avoiding participation in behavior that is inappropriate, self-damaging, and can adversely affect organizational functioning, such as alcohol and drug abuse, domestic violence, sale of drugs, and problem gambling.
Emotional Regulation and Stress Tolerance	Maintaining composure and staying in control, particularly during life-threatening, time-critical events and other stressful situations. Includes taking the negative aspects of the job in stride and maintaining an even temperament as well as accepting criticism rather than becoming defensive or allowing it to hamper job performance.
Conscientiousness/ Dependability	Exhibiting diligent, reliable, and conscientious work patterns, performing in a timely manner in accordance with commitments, rules, regulations and agency policies.
Decision-Making and Judgment	Make sound, common-sense decisions, demonstrated by the ability to size up situations quickly and take appropriate action. Involves the ability to sift through information to glean what's important, and, once identified, to use it effectively.
Social Competence	Communicating in a tactful and respectful manner and showing sensitivity and concern in one's interactions. Includes several facets such as the ability to "read" people and be aware of the impact of words and behavior on others, sensitivity and concern toward the feelings of others, and tact and impartiality in treating all members of society.
Teamwork	Working effectively with others to accomplish goals, as well as subordinating personal interests for the good of the working unit and agency. Involves establishing and maintaining effective, cooperative working relationships with coworkers, supervisors, and other stakeholders. Consists of sharing relevant information, providing assistance and support to coworkers, balancing personal ambitions with work goals, performing one's fair share in a group effort, and not allowing personal differences to affect working relationships. Note: For firefighter/medics, this also includes the ability to tolerate close communal living over a 24-hour shift.
Assertiveness/Persuasiveness	Unhesitatingly taking control of situations in a calm and appropriately assertive manner, even under stressful or adverse conditions. Includes the ability to confront others, act assertively and without hesitation, not be easily intimidated, assert one's ideas and persuade others to adopt a necessary course of action, command respect, and emanate professionalism. Note: For police and correctional officers, this also includes the ability to use force, confront suspects, and engage others physically, as necessary and appropriate. For firefighters/medics, the need for high levels of assertiveness may be substantially lower than for other public safety positions.
Adaptability/Flexibility	Adjusting to the sudden changes and competing demands inherent in public safety work. Consists of adjusting to planned and unplanned work changes, including different types of incidents that must be handled one right after another; prioritizing and working effectively on several very different tasks/projects at the same time; adjusting to differing supervisory styles; adjusting physically and mentally to shift work. Note: For police and correctional officers, this also includes the ability to make sudden adjustments in use of force, as appropriate.

outlining what may have been the first comprehensive proposal for conducting preemployment psychological screening of public safety dispatchers (Weiner, 1997), the California POST commission proposed the use of a criterion standard consisting of 14 personality traits,[8] which a quick inspection will confirm are identical to or contained within the 10 CA-POST dimensions for use in evaluating peace officer candidates. Facets of these dimensions unique to particular public safety positions are noted in italics in Table 1.5. See Spilberg and Corey (2022, chapter 4) for a comprehensive discussion of these dimensions and the positive and counterproductive behaviors that correspond with each. See Corey and Detrick (2022) for a comparison of the CA-POST dimensions to qualifying standards for public safety candidates in Canada and other English-speaking countries.

The relative weight that each of these dimensions will carry in evaluating a candidate or employee for a particular position in a specific agency depends on many factors, including the population context in which the work is carried out (e.g., rural and demographically homogeneous vs. urban and demographically diverse), the volume and intensity of work performed in the agency, and the needs and preferences of the hiring authority.[9] It should also be noted that even in states where use of the psychological screening dimensions listed in Table 1.5 is mandated by law (see Corey, McElroy, & Ben-Porath, 2023), the dimensions are regarded as minimum criteria that can be supplemented with standards reflecting the unique needs of the hiring agency and its constituent community members.

USING THE PSYCHOLOGICAL SCREENING DIMENSIONS IN BOTH PREEMPLOYMENT AND FITNESS-FOR-DUTY EVALUATIONS OF PUBLIC SAFETY PERSONNEL

The original purpose of the CA-POST dimensions—to facilitate preemployment psychological evaluations of *peace officer* candidates—may lead some to regard them, erroneously, as useful only for police candidate screening. As just discussed, the CA-POST dimensions are mandatory minimum criteria for evaluating law enforcement and correctional candidates in California, but they also have strong linkage to the psychological position requirements for dispatchers and firefighters/medics, as demonstrated by the research conducted by Whitman and colleagues (2021; see chapter 6 for a review of this study). For this reason, the CA-POST dimensions can be used to elucidate the psychological qualifications for those candidates as well. Less self-evident is the appropriateness of using these screening dimensions in fitness-for-duty evaluations for police and other public safety evaluations; however, there is a good rational and legal foundation for doing so, as we discuss next.

The CA-POST dimensions were intended originally to provide psychologists with "behaviorally based criteria . . . against which to evaluate the psychological suitability of candidates" (Spilberg & Corey, 2022, p. 159). The need for and practical significance of these criteria result from the fact that, when it is determined that a candidate has a mental health condition or problematic personality trait(s), the relevance of these findings to the candidate's suitability for employment can only be assessed by evaluating how the symptoms (related to emotional, thought, and behavioral functioning) or traits affect these behavioral criteria. As criteria for assessing the job relevance of clinical assessment findings, these dimensions are as important in fitness-for-duty evaluations as they are in preemployment screening. Two state appeals courts (*Brown v. Sandy City Appeal Board*, 2014; *Sager v. County of Yuba*, 2007) have concluded the same.

In *Sager*, the California Court of Appeal ruled in support of a psychologist's reliance on the CA-POST dimensions in evaluating the impact of a deputy sheriff's diagnosed personality disorder on her ability to perform her duties in a safe and effective manner. In *Brown* (cited earlier), the Utah Court of Appeals faced the same question—whether the use of criteria developed for preemployment selection is warranted also in a fitness-for-duty evaluation—and decided similarly. But the *Brown* court also addressed another question: whether it was appropriate for the psychologist evaluating a Utah police officer to rely on California standards. The court decided that it was, noting that the CA-POST dimensions help "flesh out" the Utah standards. The *Brown* court concluded that the Utah psychologist's reliance on the CA-POST dimensions was "analogous to the way that a court might use case law from sister jurisdictions: not as binding authority but as a reference to consider how other courts have analyzed and resolved a particular issue" (para. 14).

TESTING AND ASSESSMENT

This book focuses on the use of the MMPI-3 in both testing and assessment. Tests produce scores, which have inferential meaning for certain uses. The meaning of a test score derives partially from evidence of its validity: the collection of correlations and other statistics that tell us what the scale measures (convergent, construct, and predictive validity) and what it does not measure (discriminant validity). However, determining the meaning of a test score for a particular test taker requires integrating it with information from other sources, such as consideration of cultural factors, personal history questionnaires, employment records, background investigations, health care records, clinical interviews, and other tests. It is this integrative assessment process with which this book is primarily concerned.

When the validated inferences of a test score are in good agreement with information from all other valid assessment sources, conclusions about that test taker, at least with respect to the targeted construct, are easy to make and usually correct. However, in the real world in which assessment occurs, the task is seldom so simple. Throughout this book, we illustrate this integrative assessment process by using redacted and de-identified material from actual cases.

Testing and assessment represent separate but related tasks. Meyer and colleagues (2001) observed that psychological testing "is a relatively straightforward process wherein a particular scale is administered to obtain a specific score. Subsequently, a descriptive meaning can be applied to the score based on normative, nomothetic findings" (p. 143). In contrast, the task of psychological assessment is to integrate test results with historical data, direct observations, interview findings, and information from third parties "to disentangle the competing possibilities" (Meyer et al., 2001, p. 144). This book is intended to provide practical guidance to assist in both tasks.

STANDARDS OF PRACTICE

When describing the standards of practice for preemployment and fitness-for-duty assessments (chapters 5 and 9, respectively), we deliberately rely more heavily on some sources than others, reflecting a hierarchy of authority that also exists in the professional literature. This hierarchy is reflected in a policy statement of the American Board of Police & Public Safety Psychology (ABPPSP, 2014), an affiliated specialty board of the American Board of Professional Psychology (ABPP). The ABPPSP provides a useful description of the sources of authority it relies on when comparing a specialist candidate's work product against the standard of practice. We cite it here in full because it also reflects the hierarchy of sources we considered when articulating the standard of practice in police and public safety assessment. This standard is defined as follows:

> When describing scientific evidence, candidates should gather, analyze, critically evaluate, report, and synthetize the totality of evidence with reference to demonstration of specialty level competence. . . . Several kinds of professional authority are relied upon when defining standards of practice (Heilbrun, DeMatteo, Marczyk, & Goldstein, 2008), in descending order of importance:
>
> 1. The APA Ethics Code and pertinent regulations, laws, and case law, which apply to all psychologists;
> 2. Professional practice guidelines and clinical practice guidelines published by the American Psychological Association linked to scientifically-derived evidence following a rigorous, formal review process with input from multiple stakeholders in professional psychology, and regulatory enforcement guidance (e.g., EEOC guidance for enforcement of ADA and GINA);

3. Publications that articulate broad principles and are developed using multiple sources of authority;
4. An overall description of research and practice as offered in the literature, through a national survey of views or practices, or a meta-analysis of empirical research;
5. Professional practice guidelines prepared through consensus among practitioners (e.g., APA and IACP-PPSS guidelines);
6. Manuals for psychological tests or other assessment instruments that are carefully attentive to reliability and validity and help a reader assess the quality of the instrument and place it in the broader context of specialty practice;
7. The systematic review of what recognized scholars and practitioners in the field have written and taught regarding the elements that comprise competent practice;
8. A single study describing a survey, or offering an empirical description, of some particular aspect of specialty practice. (ABPPSP, 2014, pp. 5–6)

The recommendations and guidance in this book reflect the professional consensus represented in the American Psychological Association's Professional Practice Guidelines for Occupationally Mandated Psychological Evaluations (APA, 2018; OMPE Guidelines). These were developed through deliberation among multiple groups representing several distinct specialties and interests in psychology and law as well as a broad review of the professional literature and input from the public. They were written "for use by psychologists who conduct evaluations for purposes of addressing the needs of the referring party concerning the examinee's suitability, fitness, or eligibility for employment" (APA, 2018) and, as such, apply to the conduct of both preemployment and fitness-for-duty evaluations. Table 1.6 lists the 13 aspirational statements contained in the OMPE professional practice guidelines.

ORGANIZATION OF THE CHAPTERS

In the first part of this book, we include a concise primer on the MMPI-3. Chapter 2 provides a brief overview of the evolution of the MMPI instruments and a description of the MMPI-3's 52 scales. Chapter 3 discusses inherent threats to the validity of scores on self-report measures generally and how the MMPI-3 Validity Scales are used to assess them. Chapter 4 gives an overview of the hierarchical structure of the MMPI-3 Substantive Scales and a more detailed description of the constructs they assess, followed by a description of a recommended interpretive strategy for the inventory. Because our focus is on the nuts and bolts of conducting these evaluations, we occasionally refer the reader to the *MMPI-3 Manual for Administration, Scoring, and Interpreta-*

TABLE 1.6. Aspirational Statements from the Professional Practice Guidelines for Occupationally Mandated Psychological Evaluations (OMPE)

Preparing for an OMPE

1. Psychologists strive to understand the referring party's authority for mandating the evaluation and the legitimacy of a particular referral, prior to conducting the evaluation.
2. In addressing the referral question(s), psychologists endeavor to apply the criterion standard as defined by statutory, regulatory, administrative, or other authoritative sources.
3. Psychologists seek to understand the psychologically relevant demands and working conditions of the examinee's position.
4. Psychologists strive to support conclusions about the job-relevance of a psychological condition with established scientific and professional knowledge.
5. Psychologists endeavor to understand and meet their responsibilities to the referral source, the examinee, and other relevant parties to the evaluation.
6. Psychologists are mindful of the importance of maintaining competence when carrying out all phases of the evaluation.

Conducting an OMPE

7. Psychologists strive to ensure their impartiality when conducting occupationally mandated evaluations and when forming their opinions.
8. Psychologists seek to select and rely on assessment tools validated for use with a population appropriate to the evaluation.
9. Psychologists endeavor to recognize individual and group differences as well as the importance of practicing with cultural competence.
10. Psychologists strive to use multiple sources of relevant and reliable information collected according to established principles and methods.

Communicating OMPE findings

11. Psychologists strive to provide opinions and make recommendations that are directly relevant to the referral question(s).
12. Psychologists seek to document the bases for their opinion(s) in language that is clear and appropriate to the targeted audience.
13. When the referral source or another party is responsible for determining the ultimate issue in a referral, psychologists strive to educate and inform rather than answer the ultimate issue.

Note. Adapted from "Professional practice guidelines for occupationally mandated psychological evaluations," *American Psychologist, 73*(2), pp. 186–197. Copyright 2018 by the American Psychological Association.

tion (Ben-Porath & Tellegen, 2020a), the *MMPI-3 Technical Manual* (Ben-Porath & Tellegen, 2020b), and the *MMPI-3 User's Guide for the Public Safety Candidate Interpretive Reports* (Corey & Ben-Porath, 2022) for more technical details and in-depth treatment of certain topics. In compliance with Standard 9.2 of the *Standards for Educational and Psychological Testing* (American Educational Research Association, American Psychological Association, & National Council on Measurement in Education, 2014), test users are urged to study and evaluate these resource materials prior to the adoption and use of the test. Importantly, the *MMPI-3 Manual for Administration, Scoring, and Interpretation*—which can be accessed only by qualified users—contains test item content that is not included in this publicly accessible book for test security reasons.

The second part of this book is devoted to preemployment psychological evaluations of candidates for the four public safety positions: police officer, correctional officer, dispatcher, and firefighter/medic. Chapter 5 focuses on the common procedural and legal requirements for these evaluations, as well as other foundational knowledge needed to conduct them. Chapter 6 begins with a brief overview of the history of using the MMPI instruments in preemployment evaluations of law enforcement and other public safety personnel, followed by guidance on the adjustment of clinically oriented interpretive guidelines for the MMPI-3. This adjustment is necessary to account for the impact of preselection and selection factors on personality test scores in preemployment screening contexts. Chapter 7 provides descriptive MMPI-3 statistics for each of the four public safety candidate comparison groups and an overview of the four MMPI-3 Public Safety Candidate Interpretive Reports (MMPI-3 PSCIRs), including their rationale, structure, and features. In chapter 8, we describe an integrative strategy for combining MMPI-3 data with information from other elements of the assessment (e.g., background, clinical interview and direct observations, and other psychological tests), and we demonstrate this integrative strategy with case illustrations. Chapter 8 concludes with a discussion of how evidence-based findings from the MMPI-3 can be integrated into a legally defensible written report to the hiring agency.

The third part of this book focuses on psychological fitness-for-duty evaluations of public safety employees. Chapter 9 discusses the foundational knowledge required for these assessments, including relevant federal statutes and regulations in the United States. In chapter 10, we discuss the implications of contextual factors—particularly the motivation to be seen as fit or unfit—on MMPI-3 scores in these evaluations, and we provide descriptive findings for MMPI-3 scores in fitness-for-duty evaluations. Using a variety of case illustrations, we also demonstrate in chapter 10 how MMPI-3 scores can inform the two prongs of the fitness question; namely, whether the person has a mental impairment and, if so, how it interacts with the demands of the position.

An MMPI-3 Overview

The 335-item Minnesota Multiphasic Personality Inventory-3 (MMPI-3; Ben-Porath & Tellegen, 2020a) is the most up-to-date version of the most widely used omnibus measure of personality and psychopathology. In this chapter, we provide a brief description of the evolution of the MMPI instruments and of the 52 scales that make up the MMPI-3.

EVOLUTION OF THE MMPI INSTRUMENTS

The Original MMPI

The original intent of the MMPI's developers, Hathaway and McKinley (1943), was to construct a psychological test that could generate differential diagnoses. Their goal was to develop a measure that could be administered to any new patient presenting for services at the University of Minnesota Hospital to obtain a direct indication of whether that individual was likely to have one or more psychiatric disorders and, if so, which one(s). It is a mistake to attribute a nontheoretical approach to the construction of the original MMPI. Hathaway and McKinley's efforts, particularly the collection of items they used to develop the test, were informed by the then-prevailing descriptive Kraepelinian nosology, other existing surveys of psychiatric symptoms, and their own clinical experience. Thus, the item pool used to derive the MMPI was informed by, and reflected, the prevailing understanding of the symptoms, beliefs, and behaviors associated with commonly occurring forms of psychopathology. In contrast, the assignment of items to the eight original Clinical Scales was strictly empirical, with virtually no consideration given to item content.

The original MMPI Clinical Scales were developed using the method of contrasted groups. This involved administering a large pool of items to members of eight carefully assembled diagnostic groups and contrasting the responses of the members of each group with a sample of nonpatients. Items answered differently by the members of a given diagnostic group when endorsement frequencies were compared with the "normal" nonclinical sample were assigned to a scale designed to detect membership in that diagnostic group. The eight targeted diagnoses correspond to the labels of the eight original Clinical Scales: Hypochondriasis, Depression, Hysteria, Psychopathic Deviate, Paranoia, Psychasthenia, Schizophrenia, and Hypomania.

As detailed by Ben-Porath and Sellbom (2023), soon after the MMPI was put into clinical use, it became evident that the instrument was not performing as intended. Rather than yielding distinctive indications of specific diagnoses to the exclusion of others, Clinical Scale profiles were frequently characterized by multiple and sometimes seemingly contradictory patterns of elevation. However, test users also noticed that certain patterns (i.e., combinations of scores) tended to recur and were associated with common features among the patients who produced them. This sparked empirical research designed to identify commonly occurring score patterns and the features associated with producing such results on the MMPI.

Because of the shift away from diagnosis, and to facilitate identification of test score patterns, the Clinical Scales were assigned numeric codes corresponding to their position on the profiles. By this time (the late 1940s), the eight original Clinical Scales had been augmented by two additional measures: Masculinity-Femininity and Social Introversion. The numeric codes were used to describe patterns of scores on the MMPI Clinical Scale profile and were, therefore, called "code types." For example, a profile in which the first two scales (Hypochondriasis and Depression) had the highest scores would be designated a "12/21" code type. Code types played a pivotal role in MMPI interpretation. As mentioned, Hathaway and McKinley's initial goal to develop scales that would lead directly to psychodiagnoses was not realized. Early MMPI code-type research still focused on attempts to predict diagnoses but was now based on score patterns across the MMPI profiles (e.g., Gough, 1946; Meehl, 1946; Schmidt, 1945). Soon thereafter, investigators began to expand their search to identify nondiagnostic correlates of MMPI code types, including various psychopathology symptoms, behavioral tendencies, and personality characteristics.

With the shift from single-scale scores to code types, the theoretical foundations and interpretation of the MMPI changed dramatically. The rather restricted goal of devising a differential diagnostic test was replaced by a broader, far more ambitious objective: to develop a scheme for classifying patients into meaningful types and detecting clinically meaningful empirical correlates of membership in these classes. Meehl (1954) articulated this goal and marshaled compelling evidence that actuarial interpretation of tests such as the MMPI—that is, interpreting test results based on their known empirical correlates—consistently yielded more accurate information than clinical interpretation based on the user's own experiences with the instrument and impressions of the patient. He later issued his well-known call for a "good cookbook" designed to yield the information needed for actuarial, code-type-based MMPI interpretation (Meehl, 1956).

Following Meehl's (1956) call, several large-scale investigations were conducted, yielding a broad empirical foundation for MMPI code-type interpretation (e.g., Gilberstadt & Duker, 1965; Gynther et al., 1973; Marks & Seeman, 1963). However, while some MMPI authors were implementing Meehl's actuarial scheme, others were beginning to enter what had been largely forbidden territory, capitalizing on item content in MMPI scale construction and interpretation. As discussed, the early history of MMPI scale construction and interpretation was characterized by a strong emphasis on strictly empirical approaches. Some early exceptions to this trend involved the development of content-based subscales for the clinical scales first by Wiener and Harmon (1946) and later by Harris and Lingoes (1955). However, Wiggins (1966) was the first to launch a successful, full-fledged effort to develop content-based scales for the MMPI. In justifying this shift, Wiggins (1966) noted,

> the viewpoint that a personality test protocol represents a communication between the subject and the tester (or institution which he represents) has much to commend it, not the least of which is the likelihood that this is the frame of reference adopted by the subject himself. (p. 2)

Wiggins (1966) began scale construction by examining the internal consistency of 26 content-based groupings of the MMPI item pool described originally by Hathaway and McKinley (1940). He then revised the content categories based on a rational analysis, followed by additional empirical analyses that yielded a set of 15 content dimensions promising enough to warrant further analyses. Eventually, empirical analyses involving the entire item pool of the MMPI yielded a set of 13 internally consistent and relatively independent content scales. The significance of Wiggins's (1966) efforts cannot be overstated. His methods served as the prototype for all subsequent content-based scale development for the MMPI and, later, for other instruments. The psychometric success of his endeavor provided much needed empirical support for the still-fledgling content-based approach to MMPI scale construction and interpretation.

By the 1960s, the MMPI had become the most widely used (Sundberg, 1961) and studied (Welsh & Dahlstrom, 1956) measure of personality and psychopathology.

Nonetheless, Hathaway (1960) expressed significant concern that, after nearly 20 years of research and clinical experience, the test had yet to be updated. He reiterated and more strongly expressed this concern 12 years later (Hathaway, 1972), and a research conference and book (Butcher, 1972) were dedicated to the topic of updating the MMPI. For various reasons, it was not until the early 1980s that the test publisher, the University of Minnesota Press, launched an effort to update the test, which produced its second edition, the MMPI-2 (Butcher et al., 1989).

The MMPI-2

As implied by its name, the MMPI Restandardization Project focused on updating the test's original norms, which were based on a sample of Minnesotans tested in the late 1930s. As the project evolved, several additional goals emerged: exploring the feasibility of developing a separate, adolescent-specific version of the test; replacing nonworking original MMPI items (i.e., ones that were not scored on the basic scales of the instrument) with new ones designed to assess then-contemporary issues not covered adequately by the original item pool (e.g., suicidal ideation); rewriting awkwardly phrased or otherwise problematic items; and developing a new method for deriving standard scores for the scales of the instrument. The project was launched in 1982 and culminated with the publication of a revised adult version of the test, the MMPI-2 (Butcher et al., 1989), and an adolescent-specific version, the MMPI-A (Butcher et al., 1992).

The MMPI-2 consisted of 567 items. Its norms, collected throughout the United States during the mid-1980s, were based on a sample of 1,462 women and 1,138 men. Compared with the original normative sample of the test, the new sample was more representative of the U.S. population in terms of geographic residence and basic demographic features (e.g., race, age, and education). However, the new normative sample was considerably higher in socioeconomic status (SES) as indexed by education level in comparison with the U.S. population. This resulted in some early concerns that the new norms may be skewed owing to the overrepresentation of individuals with higher education levels. Schinka and LaLone (1997) recalculated the MMPI-2 norms based on a reduced sample designed to match national SES distributions and concluded that the resulting norms were not meaningfully different from the MMPI-2 norms. Thus, the relatively high SES standing of the MMPI-2 normative sample did not affect the utility of the revised norms.

At the outset of the Restandardization Project, the committee overseeing its execution decided that the original Clinical Scales would be left essentially intact. This decision was made to ensure continuity between the original and restandardized versions of the test. Consequently, only a very small number of objectionable items (i.e., ones dealing with religious practices and beliefs, sexual orientation, and bowel and bladder movements) were deleted. Other items were slightly modified to correct grammatical errors, improve awkwardly phrased statements, or remove sexist language. Studies by Ben-Porath and Butcher (1989a, 1989b) established that scores on the slightly modified Clinical Scales were essentially interchangeable with their original versions.

An important innovation with the MMPI-2 was the introduction of uniform T (UT) scores (Tellegen & Ben-Porath, 1992). Briefly, these standard scores were developed to correct a long-recognized problem with MMPI T scores. Because the raw score distributions for the Clinical Scales were differentially skewed, when linear T scores were used (as had been done with the original inventory), the same standard score value did not correspond to the same percentile across different scales. The lack of percentile equivalence across scales made direct comparisons of T scores on different scales potentially misleading. The solution adopted for the MMPI-2 was to compute the average distribution of non-K-corrected raw scores on the eight original Clinical Scales for men and women in the normative sample and correct each scale's distribution slightly to correspond to this composite. This was accomplished in the transformation of raw scores to T scores. This approach yielded percentile-equivalent T scores while retaining the skewed nature of the scales' distributions.

As mentioned, a secondary goal of the Restandardization Project was to replace nonworking MMPI items with ones that would introduce new content. These items were incorporated in a new set of scales introduced with the publication of the revised inventory, the MMPI-2 Content Scales (Butcher et al., 1990). The MMPI-2 Content Scales were developed through a series of rational-conceptual and empirical analyses fashioned after the ones used by Wiggins (1966) in developing the original content scales for the MMPI. This process yielded a set of 15 Content Scales. As might be expected, some of these scales were similar in composition to the ones developed by Wiggins (1966). Nearly all included new items; some (e.g., Type A and Negative Treatment Indicators) were composed predominantly of new items.

During the decade following publication of the MMPI-2, research focused initially on comparing Clinical Scale scores based on the MMPI versus MMPI-2 norms. Surveys of practitioners (e.g., Webb et al., 1993) indicated that most were quick to adopt the revised instrument. Consequently, the focus of MMPI-2 research soon shifted to validating the new scales and exploring further scale development based (in part) on the new items added to the inventory. A revised edition of the MMPI-2 manual (Butcher et al., 2001) was published to incorporate these developments. The 2001 manual was designed to update interpretive guidelines for some MMPI-2 scales included in the 1989 manual, formalize the discontinuation of other scales, and provide guidelines for interpreting several new scales developed during the decade following the revision. It did not introduce any changes in the norms or item composition of the MMPI-2 scales included in the 1989 manual.

Of the new scales included in the 2001 manual, the Personality Psychopathology Five (PSY-5) Scales introduced by Harkness and colleagues (1995) were the most influential. Based on a personality model developed and described in detail by Harkness and McNulty (1994), the PSY-5 constructs originated from research conducted by Harkness (1992) using criteria for diagnosing personality disorders. They represented an early attempt to develop a dimensional model of personality-related psychopathology. Harkness and colleagues (1995) used the MMPI-2 item pool to construct scales corresponding to these five constructs, which are described later in the context of the MMPI-3 versions of these scales.

The MMPI-2 PSY-5 Scales were the product of the first effort to link the MMPI-2 to modern constructs that are the focus of personality and psychopathology research. However, the basic source of information on the test, the Clinical Scales, remained essentially unchanged 50 years after their introduction, despite Hathaway's (1960, 1972) earlier cited misgivings. Soon after the revision process was completed, one MMPI-2 Restandardization Committee member, Auke Tellegen, began work on a major research project designed to explore the feasibility of improving the Clinical Scales. A decade later, this work culminated in the publication of the MMPI-2 Restructured Clinical (RC) Scales (Tellegen et al., 2003), described next.

The MMPI-2 RC Scales

Tellegen and colleagues (2003) described in detail the rationale, methods, and results of Tellegen's efforts to restructure the MMPI-2 Clinical Scales. In the following, we briefly summarize this work.

Why Restructure the Clinical Scales?

The Clinical Scales' primary limitation was their weak discriminant validity. Because of unexpectedly (based on the constructs they assess) high correlations between them, amplified by considerable item overlap, MMPI-2 Clinical Scale scores had limited discriminant abilities. This shortcoming was, in part, a product of how the empirical keying technique was applied in assigning items to the Clinical Scales, which was based primarily on their ability to discriminate between a patient group and a common normal comparison sample. Because (essentially) the same normal reference group was used in constructing them, each of the eight scales included items that characterize either the patient group or the difference between being a patient and not being one. Their heterogeneous makeup was another limitation, which diminished the convergent validity of the Clinical Scales. Finally, the near-total absence of theory to guide their interpretation restricted the ability of MMPI users to rely on construct validity in Clinical Scale interpretation.

Goals and Method of Developing the RC Scales

Tellegen's goal in developing the RC Scales was to explore the feasibility of restructuring the Clinical Scales to address the aforementioned limitations, yielding a parsimonious set of scales with improved discriminant and convergent validity that could be linked to contemporary theories and models of personality and psychopathology. Tellegen and colleagues (2003) described in detail the four steps used in developing the RC Scales. The first involved devising a marker of the MMPI common factor, which is overrepresented in the Clinical Scales because of how they were constructed. Tellegen and colleagues (2003) labeled this factor *Demoralization*. Step 2 was designed to identify the major distinctive core component of each Clinical Scale, which was hypothesized to consist of something other than Demoralization. Factor analyses were conducted separately with the items of each Clinical Scale combined with the Demoralization markers identified in Step 1. The first factor that emerged in each case included the Demoralization markers as well as Clinical Scale items that were primarily correlated with this construct. The second (and in some cases third) factor included items representing a core component of the Clinical Scale that was distinct from Demoralization. In step 3, these core markers were refined further to yield a maximally distinct set of "Seed" (S) scales. This step included the removal of all item overlap and retention for the S scales of core items that correlated maximally with a given potential S scale and, minimally, the remaining candidate S scales. Step 4 involved analyses of the entire MMPI-2 item pool. An item was added to a given S scale and included on the final Restructured Clinical Scale if it correlated more highly with that S scale than any other, the correlation exceeded a specified value, and it did not correlate beyond a specified level with any other S scale. The specific criteria varied across scales as detailed by Tellegen and colleagues (2003).

The result of this four-step process was a set of nine nonoverlapping scales representing Demoralization and a major distinctive core component of each of the eight original Clinical Scales. Restructured Scales were not developed for Clinical Scales 5 or 0 because the focus of the RC Scales was on measuring psychopathology. Further development efforts described later included the distinctive core components of these two scales. The 9 MMPI-2 RC Scales were made up of 192 MMPI-2 items.

At the conclusion of the monograph introducing the RC Scales, Tellegen and colleagues (2003) noted,

> The introduction of the RC Scales may stimulate additional MMPI-2 scale development. It may prove worthwhile to search for and measure distinctive core features of important MMPI-2 scales other than the MMPI-2 Clinical Scales, some of which may also be confounded with a strong Demoralization component. Investigations along these lines may lead to additional measures that are incrementally informative beyond the RC Scales. Through such efforts it may be possible eventually to capture the full range of attributes represented by the large body of MMPI-2 constructs with a set of new scales more transparent and effective than those currently available. (pp. 85–86)

Efforts along these lines led to the development and publication of the MMPI-2-RF, to which we turn next.

The MMPI-2-RF

The Minnesota Multiphasic Personality Inventory-2 Restructured Form (MMPI-2-RF; Ben-Porath & Tellegen, 2008/2011; Tellegen & Ben-Porath, 2008/2011) consisted of 338 items scored on 51 scales. Ben-Porath and Sellbom (2023) note that the authors' goal for the MMPI-2-RF was to represent the clinically significant substance of the MMPI-2 item pool with a comprehensive set of psychometrically adequate measures. As described, the nine MMPI-2 RC Scales were designed to assess major distinctive core components of the original MMPI Clinical Scales. These scales were carried over to the MMPI-2-RF in identical form. They were augmented by 33 substantive measures intended to canvass the full range of constructs that could be reliably and validly assessed with the MMPI-2 item pool, as well as nine validity indicators. A central feature of the MMPI-2-RF's development was the linkage of test scores to contemporary concepts and models of personality and psychopathology.

The MMPI-2-RF scales were divided into six sets. The *Validity Scales* included nine MMPI-2-RF measures designed to alert the interpreter to various threats to the validity of an individual test protocol. They included measures of inconsistent responding, overreporting, and underreporting. The remaining 42 Substantive Scales included three *Higher-Order Scales,* which indicated whether and to what extent a test taker was likely experiencing problems in the domains of mood and affect, thought processes, or behavior; the nine aforementioned *Restructured Clinical Scales,* which provided an indication of the individual's standing on the psychological constructs identified by Tellegen and colleagues (2003) as major distinctive core components of the original MMPI Clinical Scales; 23 *Specific Problems Scales,* the most narrowly focused MMPI-2-RF measures, which were subdivided into indicators of somatic and cognitive complaints, internalizing difficulties, externalizing behaviors, and interpersonal functioning; two *Interest Scales,* derived from the original

MMPI Masculinity/Femininity scale; and five *Personality Psychopathology Five (PSY-5) Scales,* which were revised versions of similarly labeled MMPI-2 scales, designed, as noted, to provide a dimensional perspective on features of personality-disorder-related psychopathology.

Except for a transition from gender-specific to nongendered norms, the MMPI-2-RF normative sample was essentially the one used in standardizing the MMPI-2. The practice of reporting and interpreting gendered norms for MMPI scales began with the original test and was maintained with the MMPI-2. However, as detailed in chapter 6, the use of tests in certain areas, particularly in personnel screening, is governed by U.S. laws that prohibit reliance on group-specific norms. To address the resulting need for gender-neutral norms, a set of nongendered standard scores for all scales included in the MMPI-2 test manual (Butcher et al., 2001) was developed by Ben-Porath and Forbey (2003), who reported finding little to no interpretable differences between gender-normed and nongendered MMPI-2 scale scores. Consequently, the MMPI-2-RF standard scores were developed based on a nongendered MMPI-2 normative sample consisting of 1,138 men and 1,138 women. Uniform T scores were used with all but the Validity and Interest Scales.

A substantial peer-reviewed literature was available to guide use of the MMPI-2-RF in a variety of settings. As of this writing, this literature includes more than 570 peer-reviewed publications. A regularly updated reference list with links to peer-reviewed MMPI-2-RF articles is maintained by the MMPI publisher, the University of Minnesota Press (https://www.upress.umn.edu/test-division/MMPI-2-RF/mmpi-2-rf-references), and distributor, Pearson (https://www.pearsonassessments.com/content/dam/school/global/clinical/us/assets/mmpi-3/mmpi-2-rf-reference-list.pdf). The list includes research on general topics, the MMPI-2-RF Validity Scales, studies conducted in forensic and correctional settings, research in mental health and medical settings, publications based on data collected in police and public safety settings, and research conducted in nonclinical settings (e.g., with college students). As discussed in the following section, this literature can also be applied when interpreting the MMPI-3.

A disadvantage of limiting the MMPI-2-RF to the MMPI-2 item pool was that this did not allow the authors to address known shortcomings of these items. For example, although many original MMPI items were rewritten for the MMPI-2, some (old and new) remained awkwardly worded and included overcomplicated content that could have been simplified. The authors were also unable to address concerns from MMPI-2 researchers and users about its item pool's limited coverage of important clinical phenomena such as disordered eating. Moreover, the MMPI-2 norms used to standardize MMPI-2-RF scales are more than 38 years old as of this writing. The population they were intended to represent (U.S. adults) changed substantially over these years, both demographically (e.g., ethnic diversity, education, and age) and experientially (e.g., no member of the MMPI-2/MMPI-2-RF normative sample was likely to have heard of, let alone used, the internet). The MMPI-3 addresses both disadvantages.

The MMPI-3

The primary goals for the MMPI-3 were to expand the item pool and update the test norms. Chapter 2 of the *MMPI-3 Technical Manual* (Ben-Porath & Tellegen, 2020b) describes in detail the procedures used to accomplish these objectives. Data used to construct the MMPI-3 were collected with an expanded version of the MMPI-2-RF, which included the 338 MMPI-2-RF items followed by 95 trial items that were candidates for inclusion in the revised inventory. Of the 338 MMPI-2-RF items, 43 were rewritten to correct awkward language or simplify content. Research described in the *MMPI-3 Technical Manual* had established the psychometric comparability of these items and their MMPI-2-RF counterparts. Placing the 338 MMPI-2-RF items first in the 433-item MMPI-2-RF-EX booklet made it possible to administer the expanded booklet in applied settings, score the MMPI-2-RF, and use the results in actual assessments, including in public safety settings. This facilitated collection of the data reported in this book.

Field data were obtained from over 16,000 individuals who were administered the MMPI-2-RF-EX as part of assessments representing the broad range of settings and populations within which the test is used. These included evaluations conducted in various mental health, medical, forensic, and public safety agencies and practices. As detailed in the *MMPI-3 Technical Manual,* field data were used for three purposes: scale development, scale score validation (using data not used for scale development), and assembly of MMPI-3 comparison groups. Validation data, available for subsets of field data participants, included: clinician ratings and extensive record reviews in mental health settings; clinical ratings and postsurgical outcome data in medical settings; standardized test scores and available outcomes in forensic settings; and job performance outcomes, psychosocial history data, and standardized test results in public safety settings.

The empirical correlate data reported in the *MMPI-3 Technical Manual* are complemented by a growing peer-reviewed literature focusing on applications of the test in a range of settings, including public safety. A regularly updated reference list with links to peer-reviewed MMPI-3 articles is maintained by the MMPI publisher, the University of Minnesota Press (https://www.upress.umn.edu/test-division/MMPI-3/mmpi-3-references), and distributor, Pearson (https://www.pearsonassessments.com/content/dam/school/global/clinical/us/assets/mmpi-3/mmpi-3-reference-list.pdf).

The MMPI-2-RF-EX was also administered by several researchers to over 8,000 students at colleges and universities throughout the United States and in New Zealand. Students were administered a broad range of collateral measures selected to examine in detail the empirical correlates of revised and new MMPI-3 scale scores.

In addition to the validation analyses, MMPI-3 field and college student data were used to examine the comparability of scores on MMPI-3 versions of MMPI-2-RF scales. Although most scale revisions were modest, users may question whether MMPI-2-RF research findings, including those obtained in public safety settings, can be applied when interpreting scores on the updated MMPI-3 scales. The *MMPI-2-RF Technical Manual* (Tellegen & Ben-Porath, 2008/2011) included extensive empirical correlate data for substantive scale scores that served as the foundation for statements in the interpretive guidelines for the test. These data were augmented by findings reported in the over 570 peer-reviewed MMPI-2-RF studies just mentioned. Appendix E of the *MMPI-3 Technical Manual* includes the results of extensive analyses that document the comparability of correlates obtained with the two versions of the inventory in the various settings in which it has been used. These findings support integration of the MMPI-2-RF literature, including correlates reported in the *MMPI-2-RF Technical Manual* and in peer-reviewed research literature, into the body of MMPI-3 research. The interpretive guidelines provided in this book are supported in part by the MMPI-2-RF literature and by the broad range of additional validity data reported in the *MMPI-3 Technical Manual*.

The MMPI-2-RF-EX was also used to collect data for the development of two new MMPI-3 normative samples. To collect the data used to develop English- and Spanish-language norms for the MMPI-3, the University of Minnesota Press hired a social science and market research firm experienced in nationwide data collection and with expertise in recruiting members of difficult-to-reach populations, including Hispanic and other Spanish-speaking populations. Data were collected between September 2017 and December 2018 from 3,423 individuals throughout the United States. Chapter 3 of the *MMPI-3 Manual for Administration, Scoring, and Interpretation* describes the MMPI-3 English-language normative sample, made up of 810 men and 810 women. Chapter 2 of the *MMPI-3 Technical Manual* includes a detailed description of the normative data collection process. The *MMPI-3 Manual Supplement for the U.S. Spanish Translation* (Ben-Porath et al., 2020) describes the Spanish-language MMPI-3 normative sample, composed of 275 men and 275 women.

Table 2.1 provides a brief description of the 52 MMPI-3 scales. Users transitioning from the MMPI-2-RF to the MMPI-3 will notice changes in the location and scoring of some scales. Specifically, the MMPI-2-RF Cynicism scale, originally a Restructured Clinical scale (RC3), is now included among the Externalizing Specific Problems Scales. Family Problems (FML), included among the Interpersonal Scales on the MMPI-2-RF, has also been relocated to the MMPI-3 Externalizing Scales. The MMPI-2-RF scale Interpersonal Passivity

TABLE 2.1. The MMPI-3 Scales

Validity Scales

CRIN	Combined Response Inconsistency—Combination of random and fixed inconsistent responding
VRIN	Variable Response Inconsistency—Random responding
TRIN	True Response Inconsistency—Fixed responding
F	Infrequent Responses—Responses infrequent in the general population
Fp	Infrequent Psychopathology Responses—Responses infrequent in psychiatric populations
Fs	Infrequent Somatic Responses—Somatic complaints infrequent in medical patient populations
FBS	Symptom Validity Scale—Noncredible somatic and cognitive complaints
RBS	Response Bias Scale—Exaggerated memory complaints
L	Uncommon Virtues—Rarely claimed moral attributes or activities
K	Adjustment Validity—Claims of uncommonly high level of psychological adjustment

Higher-Order (H-O) Scales

EID	Emotional/Internalizing Dysfunction—Problems associated with mood and affect
THD	Thought Dysfunction—Problems associated with disordered thinking
BXD	Behavioral/Externalizing Dysfunction—Problems associated with undercontrolled behavior

Restructured Clinical (RC) Scales

RCd	Demoralization (DEM)—General unhappiness and dissatisfaction
RC1	Somatic Complaints (SOM)—Diffuse physical health complaints
RC2	Low Positive Emotions (LPE)—Lack of positive emotional responsiveness
RC4	Antisocial Behavior (ASB)—Rule breaking and irresponsible behavior
RC6	Ideas of Persecution (PER)—Self-referential beliefs that others pose a threat
RC7	Dysfunctional Negative Emotions (DNE)—Maladaptive anxiety, anger, irritability
RC8	Aberrant Experiences (ABX)—Unusual perceptions or thoughts associated with thought dysfunction
RC9	Hypomanic Activation (HPM)—Overactivation, aggression, impulsivity, and grandiosity

Specific Problems (SP) Scales

SOMATIC/COGNITIVE SCALES

MLS	Malaise—Overall sense of physical debilitation, poor health
NUC	Neurological Complaints—Dizziness, weakness, paralysis, loss of balance, etc.
EAT	Eating Concerns—Problematic eating behaviors
COG	Cognitive Complaints—Memory problems, difficulties concentrating

INTERNALIZING SCALES

SUI	Suicidal/Death Ideation—Direct reports of suicidal ideation and recent attempts
HLP	Helplessness/Hopelessness—Belief that goals cannot be reached or problems solved
SFD	Self-Doubt—Lack of self-confidence, feelings of uselessness
NFC	Inefficacy—Belief that one is indecisive and inefficacious
STR	Stress—Problems involving stress and nervousness

WRY	Worry—Excessive worry and preoccupation
CMP	Compulsivity—Engaging in compulsive behaviors
ARX	Anxiety-Related Experiences—Multiple anxiety-related experiences such as catastrophizing, panic, dread, and intrusive ideation
ANP	Anger Proneness—Becoming easily angered, impatient with others
BRF	Behavior-Restricting Fears—Fears that significantly inhibit normal behavior

EXTERNALIZING SCALES

FML	Family Problems—Conflictual family relationships
JCP	Juvenile Conduct Problems—Difficulties at school and at home, stealing
SUB	Substance Abuse—Current and past misuse of alcohol and drugs
IMP	Impulsivity—Poor impulse control and nonplanful behavior
ACT	Activation—Heightened excitation and energy level
AGG	Aggression—Physically aggressive, violent behavior
CYN	Cynicism—Non-self-referential beliefs that others are bad and not to be trusted

INTERPERSONAL SCALES

SFI	Self-Importance—Beliefs related to having special talents and abilities
DOM	Dominance—Being domineering in relationships with others
DSF	Disaffiliativeness—Disliking people and being around them
SAV	Social Avoidance—Not enjoying and avoiding social events
SHY	Shyness—Feeling uncomfortable and anxious in the presence of others

Personality Psychopathology-Five (PSY-5) Scales

AGGR	Aggressiveness—Instrumental, goal-directed aggression
PSYC	Psychoticism—Disconnection from reality
DISC	Disconstraint—Undercontrolled behavior
NEGE	Negative Emotionality/Neuroticism—Anxiety, insecurity, worry, and fear
INTR	Introversion/Low Positive Emotionality—Social disengagement and anhedonia

(IPP) remains in the Interpersonal Scales group; however, it is now labeled Dominance (DOM), and its scoring key was reversed. These changes are discussed in detail in Appendix B of the *MMPI-3 Technical Manual*.

The MMPI-3 can be scored by hand; however, this is a time-consuming and error-prone process (Allard & Faust, 2000; Simons et al., 2002). Computer scoring is available and can be used to produce the MMPI-3 Score Report, which provides scores on the 52 test scales as well as item-response information, and the MMPI-3 Clinical Interpretive Report, which includes all the elements of the Score Report and a computer-generated clinically focused interpretation of the results. A unique feature of this interpretive report is that all of the statements generated are annotated, indicating which scale scores they are based on and whether the statements are empirically or content based. For empirically based statements, the report includes references to the relevant literature, documenting the empirical support for the statement. A user's guide (Ben-Porath & Tellegen, 2020c) is available to guide use and customization of these reports. A third report option, consisting of any of the four MMPI-3 Public Safety Candidate Interpretive Reports (Corey & Ben-Porath, 2022), is described in detail in chapter 7.

In the following two chapters, we provide some brief general guidelines for using the MMPI-3 Validity (chapter 3) and Substantive Scales (chapter 4).

Assessing Protocol Validity With the MMPI-3

Recognizing the inherent vulnerability of self-report measures to misleading responding, Hathaway and McKinley (1943) included Validity Scales, initially termed *validating scores,* in the original MMPI. The availability of these and subsequently introduced measures has enabled MMPI users to gauge, and consider in a comprehensive manner, the implications of potential impediments to the interpretability of individual test protocols. Ben-Porath and Sellbom (2023) describe a conceptual framework that has guided MMPI-2 (Butcher et al., 2001), MMPI-2-RF (Ben-Porath & Tellegen, 2008/2011), and MMPI-3 (Ben-Porath & Tellegen, 2020a) validity scale interpretation for some time. This framework is briefly described in the first part of this chapter; however, the reader is encouraged to consult Ben-Porath and Sellbom's (2023) more detailed treatment of this subject. The current MMPI-3 validity indicators are described in the second part of this chapter. In the final section, we discuss use of the MMPI-3 Validity Scales to assess threats to protocol validity.

THREATS TO PROTOCOL VALIDITY

To provide useful responses to the statements that make up a self-report measure of personality and psychopathology, a test taker must read, comprehend, and respond accurately to the test statements. Failure to do so, intentionally or unintentionally, can compromise the utility of the resulting test scores, in extreme cases rendering them uninterpretable. Therefore, before drawing any substantive inferences from self-report inventory scores, careful consideration must be given to the quality of the information provided by the test taker; that is, to the validity of the individual test protocol. Threats to protocol validity fall broadly into two categories that reflect the role of item content in invalid responding: non-content-based and content-based threats. Important distinctions can be made within each of these categories as well.

Non-Content-Based Invalid Responding

Non-content-based invalid responding occurs when the test taker's responses are not based on an accurate reading and comprehension of the test items. To the extent that a test taker's responses do not reflect their reactions to the actual items, the responses cannot gauge the individual's standing on the constructs of interest. This threat to validity can be divided further into three subtypes: nonresponding, random responding, and fixed responding.

Nonresponding occurs when the test taker fails to provide a scorable response to an item. This typically takes the form of the absence of a response, but if the test taker responds both True and False to a given item, this is also unscorable. Nonresponding may occur for a variety of reasons. Test takers who are uncooperative or defensive may fail to respond to some items, they may be unable to read or understand items, cognitive functioning deficits may result in confusion or obsessing over responses, or they may have limited introspection and insight. To the extent that nonresponding occurs in a given protocol, it has the effect of distorting scores by lowering them artificially. If not identified and considered, nonresponding may lead to underestimation of the individual's standing on the constructs measured by the affected scales.

Random responding is characterized by an unsystematic response pattern that is not based on an accurate reading and comprehension of test items. It may be present to varying degrees in a given test protocol. Two types of random responding can be distinguished. *Intentional random responding* occurs when the individual has the capacity to respond relevantly to test items but chooses to respond irrelevantly in an unsystematic manner. An uncooperative test taker may do this to avoid a confrontation with the examiner over their refusal to participate. In this example, the test taker provides answers to items without reading or considering the content. The individual may do this throughout the test protocol or at various points. *Unintentional random responding* occurs when the individual cannot respond relevantly to test items and responds without understanding their content, often without awareness that they are doing so. This can result from reading or language comprehension difficulties, cognitive deficits or impairment, confusion or disorientation, or something as mundane as a test taker losing their place and mismarking the answer sheet. Regardless of whether it is intentional or unintentional, random responding reduces the validity of the resulting scale scores by adding psychometric noise (unsystematic error variance).

Fixed responding is an invalidating test-taking approach characterized by a systematic response pattern that is not based on an accurate reading and comprehension of test items. If the test taker provides both True and False responses indiscriminately, then they are engaging in random responding. In contrast, when engaging in fixed responding, the test taker provides the same non-content-based responses (e.g., True) to various items without considering their content. In fixed responding, the indiscriminate responses are stereotypic, either True or False, or in the case of a Likert-scale response format, the test taker marks items indiscriminately at the same level without considering their content. Constructing scales with balanced keys or Likert-scale response formats does not make self-report measures less susceptible to this threat to protocol validity. An indiscriminate set of True responses is invalid regardless of whether the scoring key is balanced, and Likert scales provide even more possibilities for stereotypic responses.

Content-Based Invalid Responding

Content-based invalid responding occurs when the test taker skews their responses to items and, as a result, creates a misleading impression. This test-taking approach falls broadly into two classes: overreporting and underreporting.

Overreporting occurs when a test taker reports problems they do not actually have or exaggerates the significance of ones they do. *Intentional overreporting* occurs when the individual knowingly slants their self-report to appear dysfunctional. Intentional overreporting is not synonymous with malingering because, for example, in the absence of an external incentive, it may reflect a factitious disorder. Moreover, intentional overreporting is not in itself an indication that psychopathology is absent. An individual with genuine psychological difficulties may nevertheless amplify their extent or significance or may fabricate others. *Unintentional overreporting* occurs when a test taker is unaware that they are describing themself in an unrealistically negative manner. It is the test taker's self-concept rather than the self-report that is skewed. Individuals who engage in this test-taking approach mistakenly believe that their responses are accurate when, in fact, they are overreporting in comparison with how they are actually functioning.

Underreporting occurs when test takers describe themselves as having less serious or a smaller number of difficulties (or both) than they actually have, or when they claim virtues they do not possess. Here, too, a distinction may be drawn between intentional and unintentional underreporting. In *intentional underreporting*, the individual knowingly denies or minimizes the extent of their psychological difficulties or negative characteristics. They may knowingly make false or exaggerated claims of positive characteristics. This test-taking approach has been studied extensively in the field of industrial/organizational psychology under the label Impression Management (cf. Peck & Levashina, 2017). The resulting test scores underestimate the level of dysfunction. Differentiating denial from minimization is important but difficult. In the former, an individual blatantly denies problems they know exist; in the latter, the test taker may acknowledge some difficulties or negative characteristics but minimizes their extent or impact. *Unintentional underreporting* occurs when the individual unknowingly denies or minimizes difficulties or negative characteristics. When this occurs, objective and subjective indicators of psychological functioning would be at odds; however, in unintentional underreporting, this discrepancy results from the individual's distorted self-concept, rather than from an intentional effort to produce misleading test results. In chapter 8, we provide special guidance for interpreting underreporting in the context of personnel screening.

THE MMPI-3 VALIDITY SCALES

The MMPI-3 includes 11 measures of non-content-based and content-based invalid responding. The indicators are described briefly in this section, followed by a discussion of some important general considerations when using these scales.

MMPI-3 Measures of Non-Content-Based Invalid Responding

Nonresponding is assessed globally with the *Cannot Say* (CNS) raw score, which reflects the number of unscorable responses to the 335 test items. The impact of nonresponding can vary dramatically as a function of the proportion of unscorable responses per scale. Computer scoring enables consideration of the scale-specific impact of nonresponding by providing the *Response%* statistic, which indicates the percentage of scorable responses to the items of each scale. As discussed in detail by Ben-Porath and Sellbom (2023), research findings indicate that if 90% of the responses to a given scale are scorable, it can be interpreted following standard guidelines. If the Response% statistic for a given scale falls below 90, nonelevated scores cannot be interpreted as indicating the absence of the problems the scale is being used to assess. Elevated scores can be interpreted with the understanding that they may provide an underestimate of the problems associated with a scale that has less than 90% scorable responses. These admonishments also apply to use of the MMPI-3 Public Safety Candidate Interpretive Reports.

Random responding is assessed with two MMPI-3 validity scales—the new *Combined Response Inconsistency* (CRIN) scale and the updated *Variable Response Inconsistency* (VRIN) scale. As implied by its label, CRIN combines information from the other two MMPI-3 inconsistent response measures to provide an overall indication of the level of inconsistent responding in a protocol.

The VRIN score is based on the test taker's responses to 53 pairs of items that are similar in content. The raw VRIN score is the number of pairs answered inconsistently in a variable manner (i.e., True–False or False–True). The CRIN and VRIN T scores are used to identify protocols marked by excessive random responding. It is not possible to distinguish between intentional versus unintentional responding based on these scores. Doing so requires consideration of extra-test information, such as the test taker's reading and language comprehension ability and mental status. If potential causes of unintentional random responding can be ruled out, an intentional uncooperative test-taking approach is more likely the cause of a high CRIN or VRIN score. Regardless of intentionality, excessive random responding compromises the interpretability of scores on the other validity scales and on the Substantive Scales of the MMPI-3.

Fixed responding is assessed with the MMPI-3 *True Response Inconsistency* (TRIN) scale. The TRIN score is based on the test taker's responses to 33 pairs of items selected so that the members of each pair are opposite in content. For example, responding True to a pair of items such as "I am happy most of the time" and "I am sad most of the time" would be inconsistent. The scale is scored so that the raw TRIN score equals the number of pairs (inconsistently) answered True–True minus the number of pairs (inconsistently) answered False–False. Thus, higher raw TRIN scores indicate fixed (semantically inconsistent, indiscriminate) True responding, whereas lower scores indicate fixed False responding. The TRIN T scores were derived by first transforming the raw scores into linear T scores and then reflecting all T score values below 50 (i.e., those deviating from the mean in the nonacquiescent direction). For example, an initial T score of 80, indicative of acquiescence, is left unchanged, but a T score of 20, indicating an equally large deviation in the nonacquiescent direction, is reflected and consequently also becomes 80. This was done to ensure that, like all the other validity indicators, only high TRIN T scores indicate possible invalid responding. To distinguish acquiescent from nonacquiescent scores, the former are printed with the letter T (e.g., "80T") and the latter with the letter F ("80F"). Because there are fewer reasons a test taker may unintentionally engage in such a response set (other than possible difficulties with double negatives), an excessive level of fixed inconsistent responding likely indicates an uncooperative test-taking approach. To calculate CRIN, rather than subtracting the number of inconsistent False responses from the number of inconsistent True responses, the two counts are combined and added to the VRIN raw score to provide an overall indication of inconsistent responding in a given MMPI-3 protocol.

There are 5 MMPI-3 *overreporting* scales. The *Infrequent Responses* (F) scale consists of 35 items rarely answered in the keyed direction by members of the MMPI-3 normative sample. Elevated scores on F are associated with overreporting of a broad range of psychological, cognitive, and somatic symptoms.

The *Infrequent Psychopathology Responses* scale (Fp) consists of 21 items rarely answered in the keyed direction by individuals with genuine psychopathology. As a result, Fp scores are less likely to be confounded with severe disorder or distress than are F scores. The scale is therefore particularly helpful in assessing overreporting in settings and populations characterized by high base rates of significant psychological disorders, most notably those marked by psychotic symptoms.

The *Infrequent Somatic Responses* scale (Fs) consists of 16 items with somatic content that are uncommonly endorsed by medical patients. Based on the same rare-symptoms rationale as the other two MMPI-3 infrequent response indicators (F and Fp), the Fs scale is designed to identify test takers who overreport somatic symptoms by endorsing several somatic complaints rarely reported by medical patients. Research reviewed by Ben-Porath and Sellbom (2023) supports this interpretation of elevated MMPI-3 infrequency scale scores.

The *Symptom Validity* scale (FBS) consists of a 30-item subset of the 43 items that comprised the MMPI-2 version of this measure, which was originally developed to complement the MMPI-2 F scale by identifying individuals presenting with noncredible symptoms in civil litigation contexts. The FBS scale has been widely studied and is commonly used by neuropsychologists. As reflected in the respective interpretive recommendations, both Fs and FBS provide information about possible noncredible somatic symptom reporting. The two scales are only moderately correlated (.62 to .63 in the clinical samples reported by Ben-Porath and Tellegen, 2020b), indicating relatedness but not redundancy.

The *Response Bias* (RBS) scale is made up of 28 items designed to detect negative response bias in civil forensic evaluations. These items were selected based on correlations with performance validity measures (e.g., the Word Memory Test; Green et al., 2002) in a sample of disability claimants and personal injury litigants. Research reviewed by Ben-Porath and Sellbom (2023) indicates that the scale is particularly sensitive to noncredible memory complaints.

The MMPI-3 includes two underreporting measures. The *Uncommon Virtues* (L) scale consists of 14 items. Elevated L scores indicate that the test taker presented themselves in a favorable light by denying minor shortcomings that most individuals acknowledge. When L scores indicate excessive underreporting, the absence of elevation on the Substantive Scales is uninterpretable. However, elevated substantive scale scores can be interpreted with the understanding that they may underestimate the magnitude or severity of the problems they assess.

The other underreporting measure, the *Adjustment Validity* (K) scale, also consists of 14 items. Elevated K scores indicate that the test taker presented themselves as well-adjusted, with higher scores representing a higher level of adjustment. This type of self-presentation is associated with underreporting. However, as discussed next, the possibility that the test taker is, in fact, better adjusted than average must also be considered when interpreting an elevated

K score. Extra-test indications that the individual is not well-adjusted would support the conclusion that an elevated K score indicates underreporting, whereas evidence that the individual is well-adjusted would temper this interpretation.

Among the protocol validity threats, underreporting is by far the most common in preemployment evaluations. Moreover, as discussed next, scores on the two MMPI-3 underreporting scales, L and K, are subject to confounds (traditional upbringing for L and good adjustment for K) that are likely more prevalent in public safety candidates than in the general population. This requires special considerations when using these scales in preemployment assessments. In chapter 8, we provide detailed guidance on using L and K scales when assessing public safety candidates.

Assessing Threats to Protocol Validity With the MMPI-3 Validity Scales: Consideration of Confounds

General interpretive guidelines for and illustrations of use of the MMPI-3 Validity Scales are provided in chapter 8 of Ben-Porath and Sellbom (2023). Their use in public safety assessments is discussed and illustrated in chapters 8 and 11 of this book. A critical consideration when interpreting MMPI-3 validity scale findings is that scores on these measures are confounded by factors other than the specific protocol validity threats they are used to assess. Table 3.1 maps the MMPI-3 validity indicators onto the threats to protocol validity discussed earlier while identifying potential confounds that must be considered in their interpretation.

The "X"s in Table 3.1 link each of the MMPI-3 Validity Scales to the specific protocol threat they assess. Plus (+) and minus (–) signs identify confounds. Those denoted with a plus sign are likely to artificially increase scores on a designated scale. Confounds identified with a minus sign are likely to artificially reduce validity scale scores. Two types of confounds are identified in Table 3.1. Shaded cells with a plus or minus sign reflect "internal" confounds. These are protocol validity threats other than the one that a designated validity scale is intended to assess. For example, except for CNS, all the MMPI-3 Validity Scales are marked by minus signs in the nonresponding row, reflecting that this threat can artificially lower scores on all these measures. Unshaded cells with a plus or minus sign reflect "external" confounds. These are extra-test factors that can artificially elevate a validity scale score. For example, the plus sign in the "psychopathology" row under F indicates that genuine psychopathology can artificially elevate the F score.

Turning to the specific confounds identified in Table 3.1, as just noted, *nonresponding* can artificially lower scores on any of the MMPI-3 Validity Scales. Determining which scales may be affected is facilitated by computerized scoring, which provides the Response% statistic for each scale (as discussed

TABLE 3.1. MMPI-3 Validity Scales: Threats to Protocol Validity and Confounds

	CNS	CRIN	VRIN	TRIN	F	Fp	Fs	FBS	RBS	L	K
Threats											
NON-CONTENT-BASED											
Nonresponding	x	−	−	−	−	−	−	−	−	−	−
Random responding		x	x		+	+	+	+	+	+	+
Variable inconsistent responding			x		+	+	+	+	+	+	+
Fixed True responding				x	+	+	+	+	+	−	−
Fixed False responding				x	+	+	+	+	+	+	+
CONTENT-BASED											
Overreporting					x	x	x	x	x		
Underreporting										x	x
Extratest confounds											
Reading/comprehension problems	+	+	+	+							
Psychopathology/ psychological distress					+	+	+	+	+		
Medical conditions							+	+			
Traditional upbringing										+	
Good adjustment											+

Note. x = Scale designed to assess this threat; + = Confound artifactually increases score; − = Confound artifactually lowers score; CNS = Cannot Say; CRIN = Combined Response Inconsistency; VRIN = Variable Response Inconsistency; TRIN = True Response Inconsistency; F = Infrequent Responses; Fp = Infrequent Psychopathology Responses; Fs = Infrequent Somatic Responses; FBS = Symptom Validity Scale; RBS = Response Bias Scale; L = Uncommon Virtues; K = Adjustment Validity
Shaded area identifies confounds that can invalidate scores on the corresponding validity scales.

earlier). Because of the critical role of the Validity Scales in informing the interpreter about threats to the validity of an MMPI-3 protocol, special consideration must be given when more than 10% of responses to a given scale are unscorable (i.e., when Response% falls below 90). To draw the interpreter's attention, any Response% value below 90 is printed in bold in all MMPI-3 reports. If the percentage of scorable items on the CRIN, VRIN, TRIN, F, or Fp scales falls below 90 and responses in the keyed direction to unscorable items would have raised the score up to the cutoff indicating an invalid protocol, the test results should be considered invalid.

A CNS score as low as 1 indicates that scores on some of the shorter MMPI-3 scales may be invalid. For example, the Eating Concerns (EAT) scale is composed of five items. If just one is unanswered, the percentage of scorable responses to the EAT items falls to 80%, rendering a nonelevated score uninterpretable. Consequently, when CNS is greater than 0, the Response% statistic should be examined for all MMPI-3 scales. In such cases, the computer-generated reports will also include a list of the unscorable items with an indication of the scale(s) on which they are scored. This list can provide the interpreter with a sense of the content of the unscorable items and facilitate identification of topics for follow-up with the examinee. For example, if a test taker does not provide scorable responses to several items describing family conflict, this does not necessarily indicate that they experience difficulties in this area, but it does identify an area for follow-up to determine why the examinee chose not to respond to those items.

As depicted in Table 3.1, random and variable inconsistent responding can artificially elevate scores on all the MMPI-3 indicators of content-based invalid responding (i.e., overreporting and underreporting). If the CRIN or VRIN T score reaches 80, indicating an invalid MMPI-3 protocol owing to random or variable inconsistent responding, scores on the scales designated with plus signs in the Random and Variable Inconsistent Responding rows of Table 3.1 are invalid and therefore uninterpretable. As the CRIN and VRIN T scores approach 80, caution should be exercised when drawing inferences from scores on the scales so designated in this row.

As seen in the next row in Table 3.1, fixed True responding can artificially increase scores on the overreporting indicators, whereas it may artificially lower scores on the MMPI-3 underreporting measures. This is because the vast majority of L and K items are keyed False. If a test taker provides a large number of indiscriminate True responses or, in the extreme case, an all-True protocol, low scores on the underreporting scales would not reflect the absence of underreporting. In contrast, fixed False responding can artificially elevate scores on both the overreporting and underreporting scales. Regardless of whether the indiscriminate fixed responding is in the True or False direction, if the TRIN T score reaches or exceeds 80, the protocol is invalid and uninterpretable. This includes scores on both the overreporting and underreporting scales.

Turning to the extra-test confounds depicted in Table 3.1, the presence of genuine psychopathology can, to varying degrees, increase scores on the overreporting indicators. F is the most sensitive to the impact of genuine psychological difficulties or emotional distress. The greater the severity of the psychopathology or degree of emotional distress, the more likely it is to artificially elevate F scores. This is reflected in the interpretive guidelines for F listed in the *MMPI-3 Manual for Administration, Scoring, and Interpretation* (Ben-Porath & Tellegen, 2020a), which indicate that individuals with genuine, severe psychopathology may score as high as 99 on F and that the T score must reach 100 for a protocol to be deemed invalid, even for individuals experiencing severe psychological dysfunction. As discussed, the Fp scale was designed to be less sensitive to genuine psychopathology; however, scores on this overreporting scale can, to a lesser extent, be artificially elevated in individuals experiencing psychological dysfunction.

Scores on the remaining three overreporting indicators, Fs, FBS, and RBS, can also be elevated artificially by genuine psychopathology, though this effect is lowest for Fs. RBS scores, in particular, may be elevated because of internalizing dysfunction. However, T scores exceeding 100 on Fs and 90 on FBS and RBS cannot be attributed solely to genuine psychopathology and likely reflect some degree of the overreporting assessed by these measures.

Medical conditions, particularly if they are severe or affect multiple bodily systems, can, to some extent, increase scores on Fs and FBS, which include items that describe somatic problems. However, as noted in the *Manual for Administration, Scoring, and Interpretation* guidelines, T scores higher than 100 on Fs and 90 on FBS cannot be attributed solely to genuine medical problems and likely reflect some somatic symptom overreporting.

Table 3.1 identifies a traditional upbringing as a potential confound that can artificially elevate L scores. This reflects the content of the L items, which include virtues uncommon in the general population (e.g., never using foul language), to which individuals who grow up in traditional homes are raised to aspire. Research has shown that a traditional upbringing can elevate T scores on the MMPI-2 L scale by about 5 points (Rosen et al., 2016). This also applies to the MMPI-3 L scale, which is similar in composition.

The final confound listed in Table 3.1, good adjustment, can artificially increase K scores. As noted, the items on this scale are keyed to reflect the report of good psychological adjustment, which in clinical settings is unlikely to be valid and reflects underreporting. However, in nonclinical settings, the report of better than average adjustment, which would be reflected in a higher-than-average K score, is not necessarily invalid. This is particularly true in settings where test takers are preselected for factors associated with better-than-average psychological adjustment, such as in preemployment evaluations.

Consideration of these confounds is embedded in the interpretive guidelines for the MMPI-3 Validity Scales listed in the *MMPI-3 Manual for Administration, Scoring, and Interpretation*. However, these guidelines are generic and are most directly applicable to testing in clinical settings, where the base rate for psychopathology is higher than what would be expected in a preemployment context. Special considerations when interpreting the MMPI-3 Validity Scales in public safety contexts, including consideration of these potential confounds, are discussed in chapter 8 for preemployment evaluations and chapter 10 for fitness-for-duty evaluations.

Assessing Personality and Psychopathology With the MMPI-3

The MMPI-3 includes 42 empirically validated measures of conceptually grounded constructs. Ben-Porath and Sellbom (2023) provide a detailed account of the development, conceptual foundations, and empirical support for these Substantive Scales. In this chapter, we provide an overview of the hierarchical structure of the MMPI-3 Substantive Scales along with a description and discussion of the constructs they assess, followed by an overview of the interpretive approach outlined in the *MMPI-3 Manual for Administration, Scoring, and Interpretation* (Ben-Porath & Tellegen, 2020a). The process for updating the Substantive Scales for the MMPI-3 is described in the *MMPI-3 Technical Manual* (Ben-Porath & Tellegen, 2020b). Importantly, Appendix E of the *Technical Manual* includes findings demonstrating that MMPI-3 versions of MMPI-2-RF Substantive Scales have similar to improved validity, indicating that the MMPI-2-RF literature can be used to guide MMPI-3 interpretation. These analyses include results obtained with two police candidate samples.

THE MMPI-3 SUBSTANTIVE SCALES: HIERARCHICAL STRUCTURE AND CONSTRUCTS

The MMPI-3 Substantive Scales are structured into three tiers—the Higher-Order (H-O) Scales, the Restructured Clinical (RC) Scales, and the Specific Problems (SP) Scales, the last representing the lowest, most narrowly focused level of measurement. An exception to this scheme, the MMPI-3 Personality Psychopathology Five (PSY-5) Scales focus respectively on a model of personality-related psychopathology developed independently of the MMPI (Harkness &

McNulty, 1994) for which MMPI-2 scales had been developed (Harkness et al., 1995) and widely studied. Sellbom (2019) reviews evidence linking these scales to current models of psychopathology and personality, including the Hierarchical Taxonomy of Psychopathology (HiTOP; Kotov et al., 2017) and the DSM-5 Alternative Model of Personality Disorders (American Psychiatric Association, 2013). In the following sections, we describe the constructs assessed by the MMPI-3 Substantive Scales and the methods used to develop these measures.

The Higher-Order Scales

Investigators in the fields of personality and psychopathology have long sought to identify meaningful structural models that could provide an organizing descriptive framework for psychological assessment and psychodiagnosis. These efforts to delineate the structure of personality and psychopathology have proceeded along two primary lines of research. In one, nonclinical measures were used to study the structure of "normal" personality. The other focused on demarcating a higher-order structure of psychopathology. Both lines of research led to the development of hierarchical structural models, with broadly defined domains subsuming lower-level constructs. Factor-analytic studies of normal personality measures identified a common higher-order structure exemplified by the Multidimensional Personality Questionnaire (MPQ, Tellegen et al., 2023). The three higher-order factors of the MPQ are labeled *Positive Emotionality, Negative Emotionality,* and *Constraint*. Tellegen and Waller (2008) reported the results of a joint factor analysis of the MPQ, Gough's California Psychological Inventory, and the Eysenck Personality Questionnaire, showing that these three measures yield a highly congruent three-factor, higher-order structure.

In the psychopathology domain, investigators converged on two broad dimensions labeled (following Achenbach & Edelbrock, 1978) *internalizing* and *externalizing*. These broadband constructs have been identified as likely responsible for high rates of comorbidity within the two domains (Krueger et al., 2003; Krueger et al., 2005) and also as playing an etiological role in the development of internalizing and externalizing disorders (Dick, 2007; Hicks et al., 2009; Krueger et al., 2002; Krueger & Markon, 2006; Vaidyanathan et al., 2009). Across the two domains, combinations of internalizing and externalizing dysfunction have been implicated in the development of complex psychiatric disorders such as posttraumatic stress disorder (PTSD; Miller et al., 2008), psychopathy (Blonigen et al., 2005), and borderline personality disorder (James & Taylor, 2008), and gender differences on the internalizing and externalizing dimensions have been found to play a role in gender differences in the prevalence of common mental disorders (Kramer et al., 2008).

A dimension associated with disordered thinking is conspicuously absent from the higher-order dimensions discussed thus far. Although understandable in the context of normal personality inventories, the consistent failure of factor-analytic studies of the MMPI/MMPI-2 and PAI to identify a distinctive dimension related to thought dysfunction was puzzling, given the inclusion of relevant measures on both inventories. MMPI users and investigators have long been cognizant of the need to assess for thought dysfunction with the instrument. Meehl (1946), describing an early system for differential diagnosis based on profile patterns (i.e., code types), distinguished three broad domains of psychopathology assessable with the MMPI, labeled *Psychosis, Psychoneurosis,* and *Conduct Disorder.* His scheme for differentiating between the first two conditions primarily involved examination of the relative elevations of Clinical Scales 7 and 8. Thirty years later, H. A. Skinner and Jackson (1978) proposed an MMPI-based differential diagnostic model derived from existing code-type systems and concluded that the test is most useful in identifying three broad domains of psychopathology: neurotic, psychotic, and sociopathic. Along similar lines, an effort to develop a shorter version of the MMPI informed by "decades of research and clinical lore" (p. 362) prompted Swanson and colleagues (1995) to construct three scales: Subjective Distress, Acting-Out, and Psychosis.

Thus, throughout the test's history, clinicians either explicitly or implicitly used the MMPI to assess three broad types of psychopathology related to emotional, thought, and behavioral dysfunction (with the emotional domain at times bifurcating into emotional dysfunction and somatization), yet factor-analytic studies of the instrument consistently failed to identify a distinctive thought dysfunction dimension. Given the generalizability of this finding to other measures of abnormal and normal personality, the inadequacies of the MMPI Clinical Scales alone are insufficient to explain this failure. However, these shortcomings made an already complicated task of assessment even more difficult.

With this backdrop, Tellegen and Ben-Porath (2008/2011) described their development of the MMPI-2-RF Substantive Scales that, as discussed briefly in chapter 2, began with construction of a set of Restructured Clinical (RC) Scales for the MMPI-2 (Tellegen et al., 2003). The availability of psychometrically improved measures of the nine major distinctive core dimensions embedded within the original Clinical Scales raised the possibility that improvements introduced with the RC Scales might yield a different higher-order structure. Indeed, in two factor-analytic studies of the RC Scales (Hoelzle & Meyer, 2009; Sellbom et al., 2008), the authors found a clearly differentiated thought dysfunction dimension marked by RC6 (Ideas of Persecution) and RC8 (Aberrant Experiences). Sellbom and colleagues also identified higher-order dimensions of internalizing (marked by RCd [Demoralization], RC2 [Low Positive Emotions], and RC7 [Dysfunctional Negative Emotions]) and externalizing (marked by RC4 [Antisocial Behavior] and RC9 [Hypomanic Activation]). Hoelzle and Meyer (2009) identified the same dimensions, as well as two more narrowly focused factors marked by single RC Scales (RC1 [Somatic Complaints] and RC3 [Cynicism]).

Analyses reported in detail by Tellegen and Ben-Porath (2008/2011) also indicated that the RC Scales conform to a higher-order structure reflective of the long-held code-type-based practice of differentiating between emotional, thought, and behavioral dysfunction. Specifically, these analyses pointed to a clear higher-order structure, with the Emotional/Internalizing domain marked by RCd, RC2, and RC7; Thought Dysfunction by RC6 and RC8; and the Behavioral/Externalizing dimension by RC4 and RC9. The combined items of the RC Scales found to be the primary markers of the three higher-order factors (i.e., RCd, RC2, RC4, RC6, RC7, RC8, and RC9) were factor analyzed in the samples used to derive the RC Scales. From each of these item-level analyses, a rotated three-factor solution and corresponding factor scores were obtained. Next, the three factor scores were correlated with each of the 567 MMPI-2 items in each of the derivation samples. Finally, a set of items was identified for each scale by selecting from the MMPI-2 item pool diverse and distinctive item markers associated statistically and conceptually with one, but not the other two, higher-order factors.

The three resulting scales were labeled *Emotional/Internalizing Dysfunction* (EID), a measure of difficulties in the domain of mood and affect; *Thought Dysfunction* (THD), a measure of disordered or unusual thinking; and *Behavioral/Externalizing Dysfunction* (BXD), which assesses problems associated with undercontrolled behavior. These scales were updated for the MMPI-3 by replacing items deleted from the MMPI-2-RF with new items on the basis of empirical analyses described by Ben-Porath and Tellegen (2020b).

The three nonoverlapping Higher-Order (H-O) Scales provide dimensional measures related to the basic categorical distinctions provided by the MMPI 27/72, 68/86, and 49/94 code types, respectively. However, in contrast with the mutually exclusive nature of code-type-based interpretation, a dimensional measurement model allows for the identification of dysfunction in more than one of these broad domains (indicated by clinically elevated scores on more than one of the Higher-Order Scales). This can provide an indication of the relative prominence of problems, as reflected by the relative elevation of the H-O Scales. The scales also provide a link to a rich and expanding literature on internalizing and externalizing psychopathology.

The Restructured Clinical (RC) Scales

The rationale for and method used in developing the MMPI-2 RC Scales were described in chapter 2 as the first step toward development of the MMPI-2-RF. For the MMPI-3, the authors updated the RC Scales, making them no longer than they need to be to maintain their reliability and validity, while adding new item content as described briefly in chapter 2 and detailed in the *MMPI-3 Technical Manual*.

Here, we briefly describe the constructs assessed by the RC Scales. Detailed interpretive guidelines for these measures are provided in chapter 5 of the *MMPI-3 Manual for Administration, Scoring, and Interpretation*.

RCd (Demoralization)

Tellegen (1985) observed that an affect-laden phenomenon he labeled *Demoralization* was the source of problematic excessive intercorrelations between the Clinical Scales. He conceptualized it as the equivalent of the Pleasant/Unpleasant or Happy/Unhappy dimension of self-reported mood. Frank (1974, 1985) had identified amelioration of demoralization as the mechanism underlying the nonspecific effects of psychotherapy. Dohrenwend and colleagues (1980) then linked Frank's demoralization construct to their finding of substantial intercorrelations between scores on psychiatric rating scales and equated its role in the assessment of psychopathology with that of taking a patient's temperature in medicine. Consistent with these views of demoralization, the RCd items reflect the presence of dysphoric affect, distress, self-attributed inefficacy, low self-esteem, and a sense of having given up.

RC1 (Somatic Complaints)

Psychological disorders involving unexplained somatic complaints have been described and diagnosed since at least the civilization of ancient Egypt (Trimble, 2004). Lamberty (2008) provides a detailed historical review of the phenomenon of medically unexplained somatic symptom complaints, recounting that a "wandering uterus" was first implicated as causing unexplained physical symptoms in women in ancient Egypt, a theory later formalized in the label *hysteria*, coined by the Greek physician Hippocrates. British physician Thomas Sydenham subsequently observed that symptoms of hysteria could also be found in men and coined the term *hypochondriasis* to designate hysteria's male counterpart. The similarly labeled MMPI Clinical Scales 1 and 3 are the origin for the MMPI-3 RC1 scale, which is used to identify individuals who report a wide range of somatic concerns with a likely psychological component.

RC2 (Low Positive Emotions)

Tellegen (1985) posited that a lack of positive emotional responsiveness is a core personological risk factor for depression and is related to, but distinguishable from, demoralization (associated with dysphoric affect). Analyses designed to identify the distinctive core of Clinical Scale 2 corroborated this hypothesis when a subset of Scale 2 items with content reflecting low positive emotions emerged as markers of the major distinctive core component of this scale. Tellegen's conceptualization was consistent with a model proposed by Klein (1974), who distinguished acute dysphoria, an acute depressive reaction to situational factors, from Neurotic Depression; he characterized the latter as a chronic emotional or personality disorder related to low self-esteem, overly severe disappointment reactions, feelings of helplessness, and "Endogenomorphic Depression," which Klein postulated was associated with "a sharp, unreactive pervasive impairment of the capacity to experience pleasure or to respond affectively to the anticipation of pleasure" (p. 449). However, a lack or loss of positive emotional responsiveness characterizes other medical and mental health conditions and therefore cannot be considered pathognomonic of depression. Kring and Germans (2000) noted that the French physician T. H. Ribot coined the term "anhedonia" when describing a patient who experienced loss of pleasure secondary to liver damage, and following Rado (1956), Meehl (1962) characterized Anhedonia, which he defined as "a marked, widespread and refractory deficit in pleasure capacity" (p. 829), as "one of the most consistent and dramatic behavioral signs of [Schizophrenia]" (p. 829). The external correlates of RC2 (reviewed by Ben-Porath and Sellbom, 2023) are consistent with a lack of positive emotional responsiveness and corroborate its construct validity.

RC4 (Antisocial Behavior)

Antisocial behavior is a core feature of antisocial personality disorder (ASPD) and, depending on which model one follows, is either a core feature or a consequence of psychopathy. The items of RC4 cover a broad spectrum of conduct, including adult and juvenile criminal behavior, various other manifestations of juvenile misconduct, substance abuse, aggressive behavior, familial conflict, impulsive behavior, and deceit. The RC4 empirical correlates reviewed by Ben-Porath and Sellbom (2023) provide evidence in support of the construct validity of the scale as a measure of antisocial behavior. Across a wide range of settings, scores on RC4 are associated with rule breaking and irresponsible conduct linked empirically and conceptually to ASPD and psychopathy. With regard to ASPD, RC4 correlates include behaviors indicative of failure to conform to social norms, deceitfulness, impulsivity, aggressiveness, and consistent irresponsibility, as well as a history of juvenile misconduct. Strong associations between RC4 and substance abuse are consistent with the high comorbidity rates for the two conditions and the generally higher base rate of substance abuse than of criminal conduct. Higher RC4 scores have robust associations with the acting-out or social deviance facets of psychopathy, as well as the total psychopathy score on the two leading measures of this construct. Higher RC4 scores indicate a strong likelihood of acting-out behaviors that are likely to occur regardless of whether an individual meets diagnostic criteria for antisocial personality disorder or psychopathy.

RC6 (Ideas of Persecution)

The RC6 items describe self-referential beliefs that one is being singled out for mistreatment, ranging from being called names to being poisoned. As expected, scores on this scale are associated with paranoid delusional thought dysfunction; however, as implied by its label, the scale most directly assesses the extent to which a test taker reports experiencing persecutory thoughts. Current conceptualizations of persecutory delusional beliefs postulate that they are the product of unusual experiences that are anxiety inducing and misinterpreted as signs of malevolent intent by others. Efforts to develop measures of persecutory beliefs have produced scales similar in content to RC6. Studies of its empirical correlates support its construct validity and have identified paranoid delusions, less extreme persecutory beliefs, interpersonal suspiciousness and alienation, and mistrust as the strongest correlates of RC6. The possibility that the test taker is, in fact, experiencing some persecution must always be considered when interpreting scores on this scale.

RC7 (Dysfunctional Negative Emotions)

Tellegen (1985) described Negative Emotionality (NEM) as a higher-order personality trait characterized by a tendency to worry, be anxious, feel victimized and resentful, and appraise situations generally in ways that foster negative emotions. He linked the construct to two well-known models: Gray's (1970) emotion-based psychobiological model, relating temperament to psychiatric disorder, and Freud's anxiety-signal system. Tellegen noted that both models included a second system (behavior activation in Gray's and a hope-signal system in Freud's) that closely resembled a construct he labeled *Positive Emotionality* (PEM), which is assessed on the MMPI-3 with RC2. The finding that the major distinctive (from the demoralization) component of MMPI Clinical Scale 7 (a measure of anxiety-related psychopathology) is, in fact, marked by a set of items describing dysfunctional negative emotions provides empirical support for Tellegen's model. Scores on the resulting scale, RC7, are indeed associated with a variety of dysfunctional negative emotions, most notably anxiety and anger, and in expected ways with features of PTSD and psychopathy. They are also associated with measures of Gray's (1970) Behavioral Inhibition System, which is consistent with Tellegen's (1985) conceptualization of Negative Emotionality. Some terminological confusion has been introduced by use of the label *Negative Affectivity* to describe a general mood-related disposition associated with a variety of personality variables related to psychological dysfunction (Watson & Clark, 1984) and responsible for phenotypic comorbidity reflected in measures of anxiety and depression. Used in this manner, the term is synonymous with demoralization rather than with Negative Emotionality or Dysfunctional Negative Emotions.

RC8 (Aberrant Experiences)

RC8 items describe a variety of sensory, perceptual, cognitive, and motor experiences that fall well outside the range of normal experiences. These phenomena have long been associated with thought disturbance, although they are neither unique to this form of psychopathology nor form an exhaustive list of its manifestations. The aberrant experiences assessed by RC8 have been linked with various psychotic disorders and, more broadly, with characteristics of individuals at increased risk for developing thought disorders. The empirical correlates of the scale include expected associations with personality characteristics related to unusual thinking and perceptual processes, well-established measures of psychosis proneness, and a host of clinical phenomena related to nonpersecutory symptoms of thought disorder. At the personality level, Tellegen and Ben-Porath (2008/2011) reported substantial correlations in college students between RC8 scores and the Absorption Scale on Tellegen et al.'s (2023) MPQ. Of the two MPQ Absorption subscales, scores on RC8 were most strongly associated with the one measuring proneness to imaginative and altered states. It is important to consider, however, that there is no reason to assume that the aberrant experiences reported by an individual who scores high on this scale are associated specifically or exclusively with a primary thought disorder. They may, in some instances, be secondary to substance misuse and certain neurological conditions or, as indicated by the MPQ correlates just cited, associated with more benign but idiosyncratic perceptions and beliefs. In addition, Tarescavage and colleagues (2014) reported findings from a longitudinal study of hired police recruits who were administered the MMPI-2-RF during their post-offer psychological evaluation that higher scores on all thought dysfunction scales were related to posthire supervisor ratings indicating a decreased ability to predict situational outcomes. Research reviewed by Ben-Porath and Sellbom (2023) provides good support for the construct validity of RC8 as a measure of psychosis proneness and, at higher levels, nonpersecutory psychotic symptoms.

RC9 (Hypomanic Activation)

The construct targeted by RC9, hypomanic activation, represents a challenge for self-report measures because of the inherently transient nature of some of its core manifestations. Nevertheless, empirical correlates of RC9 reviewed by Ben-Porath and Sellbom (2023) include many of the features of manic and hypomanic states cataloged in Kraepelin's (1921) nosology and captured in subsequent empirical studies, as well as the two core temperamental traits identified by Kraepelin: aggression and overexcitation (i.e., activation). RC9 scores are not associated substantially with the expansive mood component of hypomania, which would instead be reflected in low scores on RC2; this highlights the need to consider scores on multiple MMPI-3 scales in the process of differential diagnosis. Most individuals with hypomanic personality traits do not go on to develop a full-fledged bipolar disorder, although these traits are associated with an increased risk for this diagnosis (cf. Kwapil et al., 2000). Thus, as is the case with all the RC Scales, an elevated score on RC9 indicates a need to consider a *possible* diagnosis of bipolar disorder (by referencing the actual diagnostic criteria). Personality correlates of RC9 include narcissism, manipulativeness, low harm avoidance, sensation seeking, and psychopathy features.

The Specific Problems (SP) Scales

Ben-Porath and Tellegen (2020b) indicate that their goal in developing the Specific Problems Scales for the MMPI-2-RF was to augment the RC and H-O Scales with measures needed to derive a comprehensive instrument that assesses the broad range of constructs measurable with the MMPI-2 item pool. Several types of constructs were targeted in developing these scales. First in the development process, Tellegen constructed a Seed Scale for Clinical Scale 0 (Social Introversion), although a final RC Scale was not derived for this measure because it did not focus on psychopathology. Development of measures of distinctive constructs associated with interpersonal functioning was intended to contribute toward canvassing the full range of domains assessed with the MMPI-2.

A second set of constructs targeted for further scale development emerged from Tellegen's factor analyses of the original Clinical Scales (described briefly in chapter 2). Several of these analyses identified more than one distinctive component in each scale. However, only one was judged the major distinctive component of a scale and was targeted for the restructuring effort. For example, analyses of Clinical Scale 8 identified distinctive demoralization, aberrant experiences, and cognitive complaints components; however, aberrant experiences was designated the major distinctive core component of Scale 8 and therefore was the focus for developing the RC8 scale. The "excess" cognitive complaints component of Scale 8 and excess components of the heterogeneous Clinical Scales were candidates for further scale development and inclusion among the Specific Problems Scales.

A third set of targeted constructs reflected the broader scope of some RC Scales. Although clearly less heterogeneous than the Clinical Scales, some of the restructured scales are multifaceted, suggesting the potential utility of developing more narrowly focused scales targeting subdomains of these measures. For example, RC4 contains items related to juvenile misconduct, substance abuse, and family difficulties, all of which are related conceptually and empirically to the targeted construct of antisocial behavior; however, it may also be helpful to assess each of these constructs separately with more focused scales. RC7 assesses a fairly broad range of dysfunctional negative emotions (related to stress, worry, anxiety, anger, and fear) that are potentially also worthy of separate assessment. Thus, RC Scale facets that may warrant separate, more narrowly focused assessments were also targeted for further scale development.

A fourth set of constructs considered for further scale development represented clinically significant attributes found in the MMPI-2 item pool but not represented (directly) by either the Clinical or RC Scales. For example, the MMPI-2 item pool included several items that describe suicidal ideation or attempts. These items were added to the MMPI-2 as part of the Restandardization Project and therefore are not scored on any of the Clinical Scales. And although current suicidal ideation and recent suicide attempts are correlated with scores on RCd, these items are not scored on this measure either. Tellegen and Ben-Porath (2008/2011) sought to include them on a possible restructured inventory and explored the development of a scale to do so. To identify similar possibilities, the authors examined the content of all the scales included in the MMPI-2 manual, as well as several prominent research scales.

Construction of the Specific Problems Scales for the MMPI-2-RF followed an iterative process using methods similar to those employed in developing the RC Scales. As was the case with the latter, it was not possible to follow a simple recipe in these analyses. Judgment calls were made throughout the process, with an added final step designed to ensure that the resulting measures successfully assessed the targeted constructs. This step examined empirical correlates of the provisional SP Scales with a number of available data sets used later in the validation analyses reported in the *MMPI-2-RF Technical Manual* (Tellegen & Ben-Porath, 2008/2011). Only scales with meaningful empirical correlates were included in the final set of MMPI-2-RF Specific Problems Scales.

The Specific Problems Scales were the primary vehicle for incorporating new content in the MMPI-3. Several new scales were introduced, and several existing SP scales were enhanced for the updated inventory. Ben-Porath and Tellegen (2020b) describe these updates in detail in the *MMPI-3 Technical Manual*. In Appendix B of that document, Sellbom provides the rationale and empirical foundations for a restructuring of the externalizing and interpersonal scales.

The 26 MMPI-3 Specific Problems Scales are organized into four domains. The domains and the scales included in each are described next.

Somatic/Cognitive Scales

As its label implies, scales in this set assess the extent to which a test taker presents with somatic and cognitive complaints. The latter were included in this group based on correlational analyses indicating that cognitive complaints are associated with the reporting of somatic symptoms.

The first scale in this set, *Malaise* (MLS), targets one of the multiple constructs embedded within the item pool of original Clinical Scale 3. The items scored on this scale, all of which were scored on the Harris–Lingoes Lassitude/Malaise (Hy3) scale, describe an overall sense of physical debilitation and poor health. Malaise has been hypothesized and found to play a role in various unexplained medical conditions associated with somatoform psychopathology. The next somatic/cognitive scale, *Neurological Complaints* (NUC), assesses reports of vague neurological symptoms associated with somatic symptoms disorders. The third somatic/cognitive scale, *Eating Concerns* (EAT), is one of the new MMPI-3 scales. It is composed of items that describe various problematic eating behaviors associated with eating disorders. The final scale in this set, *Cognitive Complaints* (COG), was developed by analyzing items scored on two of the Harris–Lingoes subscales for Clinical Scale 8: Lack of Ego Mastery Cognitive and Lack of Ego Mastery Conative. These items describe various cognitive complaints related to memory, attention, and concentration.

Internalizing Scales

The 10 Internalizing Specific Problems Scales can be divided into two subsets: four measures of constructs conceptually and statistically associated with demoralization and six associated similarly with negative emotionality. The first of the demoralization-associated scales, *Suicidal/Death Ideation* (SUI), consists of items directly related to suicide and preoccupation with death. The importance of inquiring about suicide-related thoughts is highlighted by Wingate and colleagues (2004), who concluded, based on a review of the empirical literature, that "patients' own self-report of suicidal symptoms deserves considerable attention within the suicide assessment framework. Unless there are clear reasons to the contrary, self-report regarding suicide potential should be a major source of data" (p. 663). Reflecting this important point, Glassmire and colleagues (2001) found that some individuals willing to endorse suicide-related MMPI-2 items do not acknowledge these experiences in face-to-face interviews, underscoring the importance of incorporating written self-report measures when obtaining information about possible suicidal thoughts.

The second demoralization-related Specific Problems Scale, *Helplessness/Hopelessness* (HLP), includes items keyed to convey pessimism about one's future prospects and the ability to improve them through self-change. The constructs of helplessness and hopelessness have figured prominently in the suicide risk assessment literature. More broadly, hopelessness, specifically negative expectations for the future, has been implicated as a risk factor for depressive and possibly also anxiety disorders (Miranda et al., 2008; Williams et al., 2008).

Also, within the mood disorder domain, hopelessness has been implicated in bipolar disorder in general and in different phases of the disorder (Valtonen et al., 2009). Finally, hopelessness and helplessness have been identified as playing a role in various medical conditions, including hypertension (Stern et al., 2009), other forms of cardiovascular disease (Pedersen et al., 2009), and metabolic syndrome (Valtonen et al., 2008).

The next measure of Internalizing dysfunction within the subset of demoralization-linked scales, *Self-Doubt* (SFD), contains items that describe low self-esteem and a sense of inferiority. The construct assessed by this scale is closely linked to the one measured by the final scale in this subset, *Inefficacy* (NFC), which consists of items keyed to convey an inability to make important decisions or achieve one's goals, particularly when facing crises or difficulties. Focusing specifically on self-doubt or low self-esteem, Orth and colleagues (2009) reported that strong cross-sectional correlations between low self-esteem and depression reflect a vulnerability to depression associated with premorbid self-doubt. Underscoring the importance of assessing self-doubt as part of a comprehensive psychological evaluation, Bhar and colleagues (2008) found that low self-esteem was a risk factor for suicidal ideation when controlling for depressed mood (i.e., demoralization) and hopelessness. Self-doubt has also been implicated as a risk factor for borderline and avoidant personality disorders (Lynum et al., 2008), eating disorders (Dunkley & Grilo, 2007), and PTSD (Kashdan et al., 2006).

Research in self-efficacy distinguishes between general self-efficacy—defined by Bandura (1994) as "people's beliefs about their capabilities to produce designated levels of performance that exercise influence over events that affect their lives" (p. 71), which is the foundation of human agency (Bandura, 2001)—and self-efficacy with respect to more narrowly defined areas of functioning. Wu (2009) evaluated the factorial stability of general self-efficacy in 25 countries and found that a single latent factor best accounted for the data in all. The NFC scale is a measure of general rather than domain-specific efficacy.

The next six Internalizing measures are conceptually and empirically linked to the Negative Emotionality domain, assessed by RC7. The first, *Stress* (STR), includes items that describe experiencing stress and nervousness. Elevated scores on this scale can identify individuals with stress management deficits.

The next scale in this group, *Worry* (WRY), focuses on worry, rumination, and preoccupation with disappointments. Elevations on this scale are associated with internalizing disorders related to excessive worry and rumination.

A conceptually-related scale to WRY, *Compulsivity* (CMP), which is new to the MMPI-3, follows next in this group. The CMP items describe engaging in various compulsive behaviors including repetitive checking and counting. Scores on this scale are associated with obsessive-compulsive disorders.

The next Internalizing measure in the Negative Emotionality domain, *Anxiety-Related* (ARX), has been substantially expanded for the MMPI-3.

The items of this scale describe multiple anxiety-related experiences such as catastrophizing, panic, dread, and intrusive rumination. Reiss and McNally (1985) differentiated between anxiety expectancy, an associative learning process in which the individual learns that a given stimulus arouses anxiety or fear, and anxiety sensitivity, an individual-differences variable involving the belief that anxiety experiences cause illness, embarrassment, or additional anxiety. The ARX items reflect a combination of both the expectation of frequent experiences of anxiety and anticipation that their impact will be pronounced. Anxiety sensitivity has been implicated in PTSD (cf. Marshall et al., 2010).

The next Internalizing measure in the Negative Emotionality cluster, *Anger Proneness* (ANP), consists of items that describe becoming easily angered, irritable, and impatient when interacting with others and being overwhelmed with anger. Drawing from the work of Spielberger and colleagues (e.g., Spielberger et al., 1983) and Novaco (1994), Eckhardt and colleagues (2004) highlighted distinctions between hostility, measured on the MMPI-3 with the externalizing SP scale Cynicism; anger, an affective experience; and aggression, a behavioral construct assessed on the MMPI-3 by an identically named externalizing SP scale. Scarpa and Raine (1997) noted that the affective experience of anger does not always lead to aggressive behavior and that aggression and violence do not always occur within the context of angry affect.

The final Negative Emotionality-related Internalizing scale is *Behavior-Restricting Fears* (BRF), made up of items that describe various fears that inhibit and significantly restrict the individual's normal range of behaviors. Elevations on this scale are associated with features of fear-related disorders, particularly agoraphobia.

Externalizing Scales

The seven Externalizing Specific Problems Scales are divided into two subsets associated with the constructs assessed by RC4 (Antisocial Behavior) and RC9 (Hypomanic Activation). The first of the RC4-related scales, *Family Problems* (FML), is made up of items that describe conflictual family relationships and alienation from family members. Because items do not differentiate between current family and family of origin, FML elevations may indicate dysfunction in either set of relationships or both.

The next SP scale in the RC4 group, *Juvenile Conduct Problems* (JCP), is made up of items that describe a history of juvenile misconduct involving stealing, negative peer group influence, and problematic behavior in school. Diagnostic criteria for adult antisocial personality disorder require a history of juvenile conduct disorder, and numerous studies have demonstrated that such a history is predictive of various negative outcomes in adults.

The next RC4-related scale, *Substance Abuse* (SUB), consists of items that describe problematic alcohol use, drug use, and misuse of prescription medication. Historically, efforts to identify individuals at risk for substance abuse with the MMPI avoided using transparent items for this purpose (e.g., MacAndrew, 1965). However, assessment of substance abuse with transparent items has been accomplished successfully with a number of psychometric devices such as the Addiction Severity Index (ASI; McLellan et al., 1980), the Michigan Alcoholism Screening Test (MAST; Selzer, 1971), and the Drug Abuse Screening Test (DAST; Skinner, 1983). On the MMPI-2, the Addiction Acknowledgment Scale (AAS; Weed et al., 1992) was used successfully in assessing substance abuse, with several studies (e.g., Stein et al., 1999; Weed et al., 1992) indicating the superiority of the AAS over the nontransparent MMPI-2 MacAndrew Alcoholism Scale–Revised in identifying individuals with substance abuse problems.

The remaining MMPI-3 Externalizing SP scales are associated with RC9, *Hypomanic Activation*. The first of these, *Impulsivity* (IMP), is new to the MMPI-3 and focuses on impulsive, nonplanful behavior. Elevations on this scale are associated with features of impulse-control related disorders.

The second Externalizing SP Scale associated with RC9, *Activation* (ACT), contains items that reflect racing thoughts, elated mood, a state of overexcitation, and cycling moods. This content resembles many of the items included in Eckblad and Chapman's (1986) Hypomanic Personality Scale (HYP), although the latter covers a somewhat broader domain than does ACT. Watson and colleagues (2010) examined the utility of MMPI-2-RF scales in differentiating patients diagnosed with bipolar disorder and major depression. ACT scores were the best MMPI-2-RF predictors of this differential diagnosis. This scale's composition is unchanged on the MMPI-3.

The next scale in this group, *Aggression* (AGG), includes items that describe engaging in physically violent behavior toward others, acting violently in response to angry affect, and enjoying thoughts about, or actual infliction of, physical aggression toward others. Like the SUB scale, AGG is a transparent measure of a generally undesirable behavior. However, here too, commonly used measures of aggression have relied successfully on the use of transparent items (e.g., the Buss Perry Aggression Questionnaire; Buss & Perry, 1992).

The final scale in this group, *Cynicism* (CYN), formerly RC3 in the MMPI-2-RF, assesses the degree to which an individual holds misanthropic, negativistic, and mistrusting views of others. Cynicism is nonself-referential; it entails a generalized negative system of beliefs that humans are bad and not to be trusted rather than a belief that one is being singled out for mistreatment. The cynicism construct has been the focus of two distinct bodies of literature in psychology: one, originating in behavioral medicine, focuses on cynicism as a risk factor for cardiovascular disease and other physical health problems; the other, emerging from police psychology, has centered on cynicism as a risk factor for police burnout and misconduct. Although cynicism typically has not been the focus of assessments conducted in mental health settings, the two lines of research have documented significant health and public safety implications of individuals with higher levels of this construct.

Interpersonal Scales

The first scale in this set, *Self-Importance* (SFI), which is new to the MMPI-3, includes items that describe beliefs related to having special talents and abilities that others do not. SFI scores are associated with grandiose features of the narcissistic personality construct.

The second scale in this group, *Dominance* (DOM), consists of items that were scored on the MMPI-2-RF *Interpersonal Passivity* (IPP) scale; however, the scoring key for this scale is reversed on the MMPI-3. DOM elevations are associated with domineering, overbearing, and overly assertive behavior, whereas low scores are associated with submissive and unassertive behavior. Domineering behavior indicated by high DOM scores is associated with manifestations of narcissistic personality disorder, whereas interpersonal passivity and submissiveness reflected in low DOM scores have been linked with features of dependent personality disorder.

The last three MMPI-3 measures of interpersonal functioning, *Disaffiliativeness* (DSF), *Social Avoidance* (SAV), and *Shyness* (SHY), assess various causes and effects of social isolation. The DSF scale consists of items that reflect a lack of interest in being around others and a preference for being on one's own. The SAV items describe a lack of interest in and efforts to avoid social situations, particularly those in which the individual is likely to be the center of attention. Items scored on SHY describe experiences of anxiety and discomfort associated with interacting with others. The three scales assess features of three *DSM-5* disorders marked by social withdrawal: schizoid personality disorder, avoidant personality disorder, and social anxiety disorder. However, the constructs of disaffiliativeness, social avoidance, and shyness are not synonymous with these disorders.

The Personality Psychopathology Five (PSY-5) Scales

Attempts to develop dimensional models of normal personality and psychopathology were discussed earlier in this chapter. As discussed briefly in chapter 2, the Personality Psychopathology Five (PSY-5) Scales of the MMPI-2 were developed to assess a dimensional model of personality disorder proposed by Harkness and McNulty (1994). Harkness (1992) described his initial work in this area, noting that in assembling the item pool he used for this purpose, a list of *DSM-III-R* Axis II criteria was augmented with items reflecting psychopathy and normal personality constructs. Thus, in contrast with other five-factor models, which have been explored ex post facto as dimensional models of personality disorders (e.g., Widiger & Costa, 2002), the PSY-5 constructs originated directly from the clinical criteria for diagnosis.

Harkness (1992) administered to a number of samples a set of items written to canvass the *DSM-III-R* criteria, Cleckley's (1941) psychopathy descriptions, and Tellegen's (1982) primary normal personality factors. Through application of a series of data-reduction techniques, Harkness and McNulty (1994) converged on a model composed of five underlying factors: Aggressiveness, Psychoticism, Constraint, Negative Emotionality/Neuroticism, and Positive Emotionality/Extraversion. Recognizing that MMPI-2 measures of the PSY-5 constructs could help provide a conceptually grounded assessment of personality disorders, Harkness and colleagues (1995) developed the original set of PSY-5 Scales using a method they termed "replicated rational selection." They reasoned that because proper functioning of the scales was predicated on test takers' accurate comprehension of their content and its relation to the underlying construct, having laypersons participate in item selection would yield items most likely to be properly understood. Lay judges were provided detailed descriptions of the five constructs and were asked to select MMPI-2 items they deemed pertinent to each. Items selected by the majority of the lay judges were assigned to provisional PSY-5 Scales. Harkness and McNulty (1994) then deleted some items that, based on their expert review, did not conform to the meaning of the PSY-5 construct for which they had been nominated by the majority of the lay judges. In a final step designed to enhance the discriminant validity of the resulting scales, item analyses were conducted, and items that were more highly correlated with a scale other than the one to which they had been assigned provisionally were dropped. In the process of developing the PSY-5 Scales, two constructs, constraint and low positive emotionality/extraversion, were reflected so that higher scores on all the scales would indicate likely dysfunction.

Following their initial publication, a sizable body of empirical research (reviewed by Ben-Porath and Sellbom [2023]) explored and established the psychometric properties of the PSY-5 Scales, providing substantial support for their construct validity. Availability of this literature, coupled with conceptual and empirical links to contemporary models of personality and psychopathology, led to the scales being carried over to the MMPI-2-RF. Harkness and McNulty revised the PSY-5 Scales using the reduced 338-item MMPI-2-RF booklet, a process described in detail by Harkness and colleagues (2012). For the MMPI-3, Harkness and McNulty again updated the PSY-5 scales, incorporating the new item content included in the inventory.

The first of the PSY-5 Scales, *Aggressiveness* (AGGR), assesses a general disposition to engage in offensive, goal-directed behavior or instrumental aggression. Individuals who produce elevated scores on this scale use aggressive (physical or verbal) behavior to achieve a desired outcome rather than in response to frustration or provocation. The second scale, *Psychoticism* (PSYC), assesses the verisimilitude or accuracy of the individual's inner perceptions of their outer social and object world. Individuals who score higher on this scale tend to misperceive others' intent and other important cues in their environment. The third dimension, *Disconstraint* (DISC), assesses a proclivity toward undercontrolled behavior, particularly poor impulse control. Test takers who score high on this scale have difficulties reining in their impulses. How this manifests behaviorally depends on the impulses the individual experiences. Low scores on this scale are associated with overly controlled and inflexible behavior. The fourth scale in this set, *Negative Emotionality/Neuroticism* (NEGE), assesses a broad affective disposition to experience negative emotions, focusing on anxiety and nervousness. It is similar to RC7, though more highly correlated with demoralization. The final PSY-5 scale, *Introversion/Low Positive Emotionality* (INTR), measures a broad disposition to experience low positive affect and avoid social experiences. It represents a combination of the constructs assessed with the interpersonal SAV scale and RC2.

The alternative *DSM-5* model for personality disorders (AMPD) was proposed by the DSM-5 Personality Disorder Workgroup as a replacement for the traditional, categorical approach for diagnosing these disorders. Ultimately not adopted for use in the *DSM-5*, it is described in Section III of the manual, "Emerging Measures and Models," and has received considerable attention in the research literature (Sellbom, 2019). The AMPD includes five broad trait domains: Negative Affectivity, Detachment, Antagonism, Disinhibition, and Psychoticism, which are described as developed from a review of existing trait models and later through structural research on samples of individuals who sought mental health services. These five domains are essentially the same as the constructs assessed by the MMPI-3 PSY-5 Scales.

The actual diagnostic criteria for personality disorders remain essentially unchanged in the *DSM-5*. Although PSY-5 scale scores do not correspond directly to a specific personality disorder, it is possible to link each of the scales to one of the DSM-5 personality disorder clusters and to features of certain specific disorders, as detailed by Ben-Porath and Sellbom (2023). The primary contribution of the PSY-5 Scales to preemployment evaluations is their ability to assist with identifying individuals who manifest features of personality disorder.

THE MMPI-3 SUBSTANTIVE SCALES: INTERPRETATION

Detailed interpretive guidelines for the MMPI-3, including a recommended structure for test interpretation and interpretive statements for each of the 52 scales, are provided in the *MMPI-3 Manual for Administration, Scoring, and Interpretation*. Ben-Porath and Sellbom (2023) elaborate on these guidelines and illustrate them with a series of case studies. As noted, these guidelines

TABLE 4.1. Recommended Structure and Sources of Information for MMPI-3 Interpretation

Topic	MMPI-3 sources
I. Protocol validity	
a. Content nonresponsiveness	CNS, CRIN, VRIN, TRIN
b. Overreporting	F, Fp, Fs, FBS, RBS
c. Underreporting	L, K
II. Substantive Scale interpretation	
a. Somatic/cognitive dysfunction	RC1, MLS, NUC, EAT, COG
b. Emotional dysfunction	EID RCd, SUI, HLP, SFD, NFC RC2 RC7, STR, WRY, CMP, ARX, ANP, BRF NEGE, INTR
c. Thought dysfunction	THD RC6 RC8 PSYC
d. Behavioral dysfunction	BXD RC4, FML, JCP, SUB RC9, IMP, ACT, AGG, CYN DISC
e. Interpersonal functioning	SFI, DOM, DSF, SAV, SHY AGGR
f. Diagnostic considerations	Most Substantive Scales
g. Treatment considerations	All Substantive Scales

are generally intended for clinical use of the MMPI-3. Special considerations when using the test in preemployment assessments of police and public safety candidates are discussed in chapter 6 of this book. Special considerations for fitness-for-duty evaluations are included in chapter 10. In this chapter, we provided a description of the general interpretive guidelines for the inventory.

Table 4.1 provides a recommended framework for organizing and reporting MMPI-3 findings and identifies the sources of information (the MMPI-3 scale scores) relevant to each of the domains assessed with the test. Because of the inherent limitations of self-report-based assessment, the first step in any interpretation is to appraise the test protocol's validity. Therefore, the first part of the recommended framework for MMPI-3 interpretation presented in Table 4.1 is intended to facilitate consideration of scores on the Validity Scales. If the analysis of protocol validity indicates that interpretation of scores on the Substantive Scales is warranted, the substantive scale section of the framework presents the seven domains addressed: Somatic/Cognitive Dysfunction, Emotional Dysfunction, Thought Dysfunction, Behavioral Dysfunction, Interpersonal Functioning, Diagnostic Considerations, and Treatment Considerations.

When writing a narrative report of MMPI-3 findings, the first four domains can be addressed according to their relative prominence in the protocol. For example, when findings indicate that symptoms related to Emotional Dysfunction are likely to be the most prominent in a particular case, this topic would be addressed first, and scores on all the scales listed under this domain in Table 4.1 would be interpreted at this point. Typically, Interpersonal Functioning will be discussed in a report after the first four domains have been addressed. The sixth and seventh domains in the substantive scale section of the framework deal with Diagnostic and Treatment Considerations. This interpretive framework applies broadly to clinical assessments using the MMPI-3 and is described and illustrated in detail in the *MMPI-3 Manual for Administration, Scoring, and Interpretation*. In chapters 8 and 10 of this book, we describe and illustrate the use of integrative models specific to preemployment and fitness-for-duty evaluations, respectively.

5

Foundational Requirements for Preemployment Assessments

When conducting a psychological assessment for personnel selection, it is first necessary to determine the standards or criteria—commonly referred to as the *criterion standard*—for qualifying (or disqualifying) a candidate.[1] Knowledge of this standard is needed both to form an ultimate determination of suitability (that is, to decide whether a particular candidate meets the criterion standard) and, preliminarily, to choose the assessment instruments and procedures for evaluating that suitability.

When assessing public safety candidates, the criterion standard is generally a matter of jurisdictional law (statute and regulation), which most states have enacted for law enforcement officers and, to a lesser but still substantial degree, for correctional officers. For dispatchers and firefighters/medics, the criterion standard can be inferred from job analytic information, such as the attributes listed in Table 1.4, and are also referenced in industry standards (e.g., National Fire Protection Association [NFPA], 2022) and regulatory guidance (e.g., Berner, 1997), respectively.

A recent review of the state statutes and regulations related to preemployment psychological evaluations of law enforcement officer candidates shows, at the time of this writing, that 37 states mandate these evaluations (Corey et al., 2023), with the majority specifying some variation of the minimum requirement that an acceptable candidate be "free from any physical, emotional, or mental conditions which might adversely affect [their] exercising the powers or duties of a peace officer" (Georgia Administrative Rules and Regulations 464-3-.02[1][e]) or that the candidate be "emotionally and mentally fit for the duties of a police officer" (Annotated Code of Maryland 12.04.01.04, E[2]).

What constitutes a disqualifying "condition" or renders a candidate mentally unfit is a question of singular importance in police and public safety screening. Answering it requires consideration of professional practice guidance, including statutory and regulatory law, and the sources of assessment data relevant to the selection criteria for a given position. These topics comprise the focus of this chapter.

THE STANDARD OF PRACTICE IN PERSONNEL SCREENING

Statutory Requirements

Several federal laws and regulations have a controlling influence on preemployment psychological evaluation procedures. Principal among these are the Americans With Disabilities Act, Title I (ADA, 1990), as amended; the Civil Rights Act of 1964, Title VII; the Civil Rights Act of 1991; and the Genetic Information Nondiscrimination Act of 2008, Title II. Case law pertaining to these statutes as they apply to preemployment assessments of police and other public safety candidates is discussed in detail in Corey and Zelig (2020) and Spilberg and Corey (2022). Most states also have versions of these statutes with a similar and sometimes more restrictive impact. A listing of all state-specific requirements is beyond the scope of this book, but psychologists must consult them for the jurisdictions in which they practice. (See Corey et al. [2023] for a comprehensive review of statewide mandates for psychological evaluations of peace officers in the United States.) We next discuss the federal statutes and their effect on the standard of practice for preemployment psychological evaluations of police and public safety candidates.

Americans With Disabilities Act

Title I of the ADA (1990) is a federal statute that sets minimum employment protections for qualified persons with disabilities. But beyond the ADA's broad purpose as an antidiscrimination act, it is also a procedural one. In relation to preemployment psychological evaluations that include an assessment of mental health (what the ADA terms a "medical" evaluation), the ADA addresses the following questions:

- ***What*** *kinds of tests and inquiries are considered medical?*
  The ADA's definition of a medical test or evaluation involves consideration of eight factors, including whether the procedure is "designed to reveal an impairment or physical or mental health" (Equal Employment Opportunity Commission [EEOC], 1995). Although no

one factor alone is determinative in defining what procedures or tests are medical under the ADA, established case law has decided that the MMPI-2 meets this definition (*Karraker v. Rent-A-Center, Inc.*, 2005). Consequently, for purposes of the ADA, the MMPI-3 is a medical test.

- *Who can be required to take a medical test?*

  If any candidate in a particular job category is mandated to submit to a medical test or evaluation as a condition of employment, the ADA requires the same for all candidates in that job category (29 C.F.R. § 1630.14[b]). Therefore, for any position where an employer may desire to have a candidate submit to a medical/psychological evaluation, all candidates must be similarly tested.

- *When in the sequence of hiring can a medical test be given?*

  To ensure that job applicants are first evaluated on their abilities rather than disabilities, the ADA requires a bright line between nonmedical and medical inquiries and evaluations. This demarcation is referred to as the *conditional offer of employment* (COE), because the job offer is conditioned on the candidate satisfactorily completing the medical evaluation. The phase of selection that precedes the COE is referred to as *preoffer*, and the phase that follows it is called *postoffer*. Only after an employer has evaluated the candidate's suitability on the basis of all relevant nonmedical information that could reasonably be gathered and analyzed is a COE considered a bona fide offer of employment (*Leonel v. American Airlines, Inc.*, 2005).[2] At the postoffer stage, information from nonmedical background investigations should be expected to be routinely available to the screening professional to aid in conducting the most valid assessment (Spilberg & Corey, 2022).

- *How is confidential medical information to be protected?*

  The ADA contains strict provisions for protecting the confidentiality of medical information related to applicants and employees, with a short list of exceptions (29 C.F.R. § 1630.14[b][1]). Not included in this list are other prospective employers, including other public safety agencies. Consequently, preemployment psychological and other medical evaluations are employer specific and may not be used to qualify (or disqualify) a candidate who applies to multiple agencies.[3]

- *Who makes decisions about reasonable accommodation?*

  Under the ADA and the ADA Amendments Act of 2008, if a job candidate is deemed to be unqualified as a result of a disability, the employer must show that (1) the exclusionary criterion is "job related for the position in question and is consistent with business necessity"[4] (29 C.F.R. §1630.10[a]) and (2) no reasonable accommodation could be made that would enable the candidate to perform the essential job functions (or to perform them without posing a direct threat) or that such accommodation would pose an undue hardship to the employer (29 C.F.R. § 1630.9[a]). Fulfilling these obligations requires that the screening professional, as an agent of the employer, provide the information necessary for the employer to make that showing. Spilberg and Corey (2022) summarized these mutual duties this way:

- The responsibility for determining and implementing accommodation, when and for whom it is appropriate, rests with the employer; however, it is incumbent on the psychologist to communicate information necessary to make this determination, including the nature and degree of the impairment and what essential functions are impacted. (p. 172)

The four MMPI-3 Public Safety Candidate Interpretive Reports (discussed in chapter 7) are designed to facilitate these mutual duties by providing evidence-based linkages between scale scores and job-relevant functioning in the respective position.

Civil Rights Act of 1964, Title VII

This U.S. statute prohibits discrimination in hiring and employment practices based on race, color, religion, gender, or national origin[5] as a result of disparate treatment (i.e., intentional discrimination) or disparate impact (unintended consequences). Disparate, or adverse, impact occurs when a hiring or employment practice has the effect of disproportionately excluding members of Title VII's protected classes, regardless of intent. The rule of thumb for assessing adverse impact in selection practices is the "four-fifths rule" (EEOC, 1979), which states that a hiring practice has adverse impact if it results in the protected class having a selection rate less than four-fifths (80%) of that of the majority group. For example, if the majority of applicants to a particular police agency are White and 82.4% of them pass the psychological evaluation, then a pass rate less than 65.92% (82.4 x .80) for any minority group would be prima facie evidence of discrimination. This method would be used to assess adverse impact based on sex, religion, age, or any other protected group. Although this analysis is applied at the point of exclusion (e.g., the percentage of candidates in each class deemed psychologically unqualified), if adverse impact is detected, individual components of the assessment process would be subject to scrutiny to determine their contribution to the disparate result. Conversely, in the absence of a disparate selection ratio, the individual components of the assessment process would not normally be subject to analysis, just as a medical examination does not need to be job relevant and consistent with business necessity unless it results in an adverse outcome based on a disability. When adverse impact is proven, it falls to the employer to show that the test is, nonetheless, a valid predictor of performance in the position (i.e., "job-related and consistent with business necessity"), although it may still be found unlawful if it can be shown that an alternative, equally valid test produces less adverse impact. In chapter 7, we discuss adverse impact in relation to the MMPI-3 Public Safety Candidate Interpretive Reports.

Civil Rights Act of 1991

The Civil Rights Act of 1991 prohibits employers in the United States from adjusting the scores of, using different cutoff scores for, or otherwise altering the results of employment-related tests based on race, color, religion, sex, or national origin. For this reason, when scoring the MMPI-3 or any other psychological test for personnel selection, test users should always use nongendered norms.[6] As discussed in chapter 2, enactment of this U.S. federal statute led to the initial development of nongendered norms for the MMPI-2. Nongendered population norms are used with the MMPI-3 and nongendered preemployment candidate comparison groups are used for all four public safety positions in the MMPI-3 Public Safety Candidate Interpretive Reports (i.e., Police Candidate Interpretive Report [PCIR], Correctional Candidate Interpretive Report [CCIR], Dispatcher Candidate Interpretive Report [DCIR], and Firefighter Candidate Interpretive Report [FCIR]).

Genetic Information Nondiscrimination Act of 2008 (GINA), Title II

The implications of the Genetic Information Nondiscrimination Act of 2008 (GINA), Title II, for preemployment psychological evaluations are not immediately evident when reviewing the statute, which is generally intended to prohibit a U.S. employer from acquiring or using genetic information in hiring and employment. However, genetic information, as defined in the statute, includes information about the genetic tests and the manifestations of disease or disorder in an individual or their family members (i.e., family medical history). Congress included family medical history in the prohibition because it can be used to determine whether someone has an increased risk of getting a disease, disorder, or condition in the future. *Family member* is defined broadly and includes dependents as the result of marriage, birth, adoption, or placement for adoption, as well as first-degree, second-degree, third-degree, and fourth-degree relatives. First-degree relatives include parents, siblings, and children. Second-degree relatives include grandparents, grandchildren, uncles, aunts, nephews, nieces, and half-siblings. Third-degree relatives include great-grandparents, great-grandchildren, great-uncles and aunts, and first cousins. Fourth-degree relatives include great-great-grandparents, great-great-grandchildren, and first cousins once-removed (i.e., the children of the first cousins). GINA, then, prohibits the acquisition of family medical history (i.e., information about the manifestation of disease or disorder in a candidate's family members) of any of these far-reaching dependents and relatives by any means (e.g., test, inventory, questionnaire, or interview). GINA allows for the inadvertent acquisition (but not use) of genetic information only if the individual was first warned not to disclose it, using the following or similar language:

> The Genetic Information Nondiscrimination Act of 2008 (GINA) prohibits employers and other entities covered by GINA Title II from requesting or requiring genetic information of an individual or family member of the individual, except as specifically allowed by this law. To comply with this law, we are asking that you not provide any genetic information when responding to this request for medical information. "Genetic information," as defined by GINA, includes an individual's family medical history, the results of an individual's or family member's genetic tests, the fact that an individual or an individual's family member sought or received genetic services, and genetic information of a fetus carried by an individual or an individual's family member or an embryo lawfully held by an individual or family member receiving assistive reproductive services. (29 C.F.R. § 1635.8)

It is not uncommon for candidates to reveal family medical history despite being admonished not to disclose it. As noted, such inadvertent acquisition of a candidate's family medical history does not violate GINA if the information is not used and the individual received an appropriate warning. We recommend documenting that the candidate disclosed GINA-prohibited family medical information but not making note of or using the disclosure.

Professional Standards

Psychologists are expected to adhere to all 89 ethical standards in all 10 categories of the APA's *Ethical Principles for Psychologists and Code of Conduct* (EPPCC; APA, 2017). Spilberg and Corey (2022), however, cite seven categories and 44 standards, listed in Table 5.1, that have particular relevance for psychological suitability. In states in which the EPPCC constitutes the accepted standard of care in licensing board enforcement policies and disciplinary case reviews, these ethical standards are also legal requirements.

Professionals performing preemployment psychological evaluations should also adhere to the *Standards for Educational and Psychological Testing* (American Educational Research Association, APA, and National Council on Measurement in Education, 2014) unless there is a compelling professional reason why adherence to them is inappropriate. These standards, designed to promote

TABLE 5.1. EPPCC Ethical Standards Especially Pertinent to Psychological Screening

Ethical Standard Category	APA Ethical Standards
Resolving Ethical Issues	1.01 Misuse of Psychologists' Work
	1.02 Conflicts Between Ethics and Law, Regulations, or Other Governing Legal Authority
	1.03 Conflicts Between Ethics and Organizational Demands
Competence	2.01 Boundaries of Competence
	2.03 Maintaining Competence
	2.04 Bases for Scientific and Professional Judgments
	2.05 Delegation of Work to Others
Human Relations	3.01 Unfair Discrimination
	3.02 Sexual Harassment
	3.03 Other Harassment
	3.04 Avoiding Harm
	3.05 Multiple Relationships
	3.06 Conflict of Interest
	3.07 Third-Party Requests for Services
	3.08 Exploitative Relationships
	3.09 Cooperation with Other Professionals
	3.10 Informed Consent
	3.11 Psychological Services to or Through Organizations
	3.12 Interruption of Psychological Services
Confidentiality	4.01 Maintaining Confidentiality
	4.02 Discussing the Limits of Confidentiality
	4.03 Recording
	4.04 Minimizing Intrusions on Privacy
	4.05 Disclosures
	4.06 Consultations
	4.07 Use of Confidential Information for Didactic or Other Purposes
Record Keeping	6.01 Documental of Professional and Scientific Work and Maintenance of Records
	6.02 Maintenance, Dissemination, and Disposal of Confidential Records of Professional and Scientific Work
Research and Publication	8.01 Institutional Approval
	8.02 Informed Consent to Research
	8.03 Informed Consent for Recording Voices and Images in Research
	8.04 Client/Patient, Student, and Subordinate Research Participants
	8.05 Dispensing with Informed Consent for Research

(*continued on next page*)

TABLE 5.1, continued

Ethical Standard Category	APA Ethical Standards
Assessment	9.01 Bases for Assessments
	9.02 Use of Assessments
	9.03 Informed Consent in Assessments
	9.04 Release of Test Data
	9.05 Test Construction
	9.06 Interpreting Assessment Results
	9.07 Assessment by Unqualified Persons
	9.08 Obsolete Tests and Outdated Test Results
	9.09 Test Scoring and Interpretation Services
	9.10 Explaining Assessment Results
	9.11 Maintaining Test Security

Note. American Psychological Association. (2017). *Ethical principles of psychologists and code of conduct* (2002, amended effective June 1, 2010, and January 1, 2017). http://www.apa.org/ethics/code/index.html

sound testing practices and a shared basis for evaluating their quality, are intended for professionals who select tests and for those who interpret them. They address a wide range of issues in psychological testing, including foundations (validity, reliability/precision, errors of measurement, and fairness), operations (test design and development; scores, scales, norms, and cutoff scores; test administration, scoring, reporting, and interpretation; supporting documentation for tests; and rights and responsibilities of test takers and test users), and testing applications (including psychological testing and assessment). The standards apply to both test users and publishers, and they contributed to many of the decisions we made when developing the MMPI-3 Public Safety Candidate Interpretive Reports. For example, when linking the interpretive statements in the "Job-Relevant Correlates" section of the reports to published research findings, we were guided by Standard 10.14, which states, "criterion-related evidence of validity should be available when recommendations or decisions are presented by the professional as having an actuarial basis" (p. 167).

Professional Practice Guidelines

The APA (2018) approved a set of professional practice guidelines for Occupationally Mandated Psychological Evaluations (OMPE), which apply to "clinical evaluations[7] of individuals for occupational purposes, regardless of whether the evaluation is intended to obtain employment, to achieve licensure/certification, or to maintain either" (p. 186). The OMPE guidelines describe aspirational practices organized under three phases: (1) preparing for an OMPE, (2) conducting an OMPE, and (3) communicating OMPE findings.

The International Association of Chiefs of Police (IACP, 2020) publishes its own set of Preemployment Psychological Evaluation Guidelines that reflect recommended psychological screening practices for police agencies and psychologists. They encompass evaluations of not only police candidates but also other public safety candidates. For example, the guidelines define a preemployment psychological evaluation as "a specialized examination to determine whether *a public safety candidate* [emphasis added] meets the requirements for psychological suitability mandated by jurisdictional statutes and regulations, as well as any other psychologically relevant criteria established by the hiring agency" (IACP, 2020; Guideline 3.1).

CRITERION STANDARD

A term commonly applied to preemployment psychological assessments of public safety candidates is *psychological screening*. The traditional use of the term *screening* in medicine refers to efforts to identify an unrecognized condition in individuals without apparent signs or symptoms. In the context of preemployment psychological evaluations, the term connotes that these assessments are designed to "screen out" individuals at increased risk of counterproductive behavior if hired rather than to "select in" individuals with the most desirable qualities (Spilberg & Corey, 2022). That these evaluations are intended to screen out rather than select in is largely a consequence of the significant number of preselection and selection efforts, discussed in chapter 6. The efforts produce a candidate pool that, for the most part, has qualities sought by the hiring authority. At the point that a public safety candidate is referred for psychological screening, the employer typically seeks not to know if the candidate is an acceptable choice—that decision was made before the conditional offer of employment (discussed earlier in this chapter) that preceded it—but rather whether the candidate is unacceptable because of an "unrecognized condition" that will give rise to future counterproductive behavior. Under most state statutes and regulations, only conditions that "might adversely affect performance" in the position are disqualifying.[8] Importantly, the law's definition of an emotional or mental "condition" is sometimes more expansive than how this term is used in clinical contexts. For example, California's statutory requirement that peace officer candidates "be found to be free from any physical, emotional, or mental condition" was revised recently to include "bias against race or ethnicity, gender, nationality, religion, disability, or sexual orientation, that might adversely affect the exercise of the powers of a peace officer" (Cal. Gov. Code § 1031[f]). In the state of Washington, the administrative code requires that peace officer candidates be evaluated for "job-relevant mental and emotional impairments *including, but not limited to*, psychopathology, personality disorders, and *inappropriate behavior patterns*" (WAC 139-07-030[2], emphasis added).

In the U.S. federal arena, when public safety employees have access to classified national security information, an individual's initial or continuous eligibility for employment is evaluated, in part, against the *National Security Adjudicative Guidelines* (Office of the Director of National Intelligence, 2017). Until 2005, these guidelines—which date back nearly seven decades and concern behaviors and personal history linked to loyalty, employment suitability, and the maintenance of security of classified information—included "emotional, mental, and personality *disorders* [emphasis added]" as a category giving rise to heightened security concerns. But in the 2005 revision of the guidelines, this category was renamed *psychological conditions*. By making this revision, the criterion was

> broadened and made more neutral, and deleting the term "disorders" avoided having to fit an applicant's behavior into a category defined by the medical or psychiatric communities as a "disorder." It allowed consideration of behavior that raises questions about a person's reliability, trustworthiness, and judgment whether or not it is officially defined as a "disorder." (Herbig, 2011, p. 29)

This revision corresponds with a broader recognition in the professional literature and practice guidelines that the boundaries between normality and abnormality are often unclear and contribute to unreliability in the use of diagnostic criteria for categorical decisions (see, for example, Frances et al., 1991).

The movement away from diagnostic categories as criteria for disqualification and toward reliance on more dimensional constructs is also supported by psychometric evidence (discussed in detail in chapter 6) that personality test scores substantially lower than the traditional clinical significance cutoff (e.g., 65T on the MMPI-3) are predictive of important counterproductive behaviors (Lowmaster & Morey, 2012; Sellbom et al., 2007). For example, Tarescavage and colleagues (2015) demonstrated in a longitudinal study of 136 male police officers in the Portland (Oregon) Police Bureau that candidates with an MMPI-2-RF score as low as 45T on RC7 had more than six times the risk of exhibiting "restraint and control problems" under stress conditions compared to those with lower RC7 scores. Similar findings have been reported by Tarescavage, Brewster, and colleagues (2015); Tarescavage and colleagues (2016); Tarescavage, Corey, and colleagues (2015); and Tarescavage, Fischler, and colleagues (2015).

Professional practice guidelines also emphasize the importance of relying on nondiagnostic indicators of job-relevant personality constructs when making selection decisions. The Preemployment Psychological Evaluation Guidelines (IACP, 2020) just discussed include the admonishment that, rather than focusing on "clinical diagnoses or psychiatric labeling of candidates," screening psychologists "strive to focus their reports on the individual candidate's ability to safely and effectively perform the essential functions of the position under consideration" (Guideline 11.3). Guidance from the California POST *Peace Officer Psychological Screening Manual* (Spilberg & Corey, 2022) is similar:

> The test of whether the candidate's condition is disqualifying is determined by an individualized assessment of its impact on the candidate's emotional regulation/stress tolerance, assertiveness/persuasiveness, and/or other POST Dimensions, rather than based on stereotypical symptoms or course of the condition. (p. 160)

It is incumbent on the screening professional to determine what, if any, statutes, regulations, administrative rules, or institutional policies may govern the public safety candidate evaluation in a particular jurisdiction and for a specific public safety position. As discussed in chapter 1, in the absence of an established criterion standard or as a minimum standard, the 10 CA-POST Psychological Screening Dimensions listed in Table 1.5 are appropriate for use with any of the four public safety positions, with adjustments to the weight given to certain dimensions based on factors unique to a particular position or agency. Detrick and Chibnall (2013) noted that these selection criteria resulted from a large-scale research project that was "arguably the most sophisticated undertaking of its kind to date" (p. 373). In an unpublished study based on a national survey of mostly experienced police psychologists (more than 85% of the 56 respondents had conducted more than 1,000 evaluations), Corey (2016) reported that 78.6% of the experts relied on the CA-POST dimensions as a principal component of their selection criteria.

When no suitability criteria are mandated for a particular position in a jurisdiction, case law can provide useful guidance, as can standards developed by industry authorities. For example, in the absence of jurisdictional regulations that establish the criterion standard for psychological suitability of firefighters/medics, a federal district court noted in *McKenna v. Fargo* (1978) that firefighting "is a life-endangering profession in which psychological elements play a crucial role" (p. 1368). The court found credible testimony indicating that

> [f]ighting a fire places [firefighters] in situations beyond their control and frequently beyond their expectations. Unlike simulated exercises in the training program, real fires are often neither controlled nor controllable. The unknown quality of the danger and the threat to life occasion emotional demands which can cause errors at crucial moments. The nature of [firefighters'] lives in the fire station also makes special emotional demands on them not found in the working day of most people. (p. 1367)

The court held that "because of the unique psychological factors which are crucial to the life-endangering occupation of firefighting, a psychological and emotional assessment of applicants has an importance that would be found in very few other occupations" (p. 1377), and it deemed the city's use of six psychological suitability criteria permissible:

1. Be able to adjust well to close community living;
2. Be able to follow orders explicitly;
3. Be able to withstand substantial stress and tension as generated by life-endangering circumstances encountered in fire-fighting situations, where circumstances beyond the control of the individual are operative;
4. Be able to make decisions under stress;
5. Be able to take calculated but not any unnecessary risks;
6. Be free of abnormal fears related to fire-fighting duties such as fear of heights or enclosed spaces.

Similarly, New York State Department of Correctional Services has required psychological screening of all state correctional officers since 1983 with the objective "to identify those individuals displaying psychopathology or other psychological limitations which could significantly impair job performance and effectiveness" (Tatar & Morgenbesser, 1993, p. 1). Thus, in addition to assessing impaired functioning, these evaluations focus on "the candidate's demonstrated ability to function effectively under stress, to relate effectively to a wide range of people, to relate appropriately to authority and to rules and regulations, and to use sound judgment, especially under pressure" (p. 5).

Other hiring agencies may take a different approach and rely instead on standards produced by industry authorities. One example of this approach is the Preemployment Psychological Evaluation Guidelines (IACP, 2020) discussed earlier, which state,

> In most jurisdictions, the minimum requirements for psychological suitability are that the candidate be free from any psychological impairment that might adversely affect the performance of safety-based duties and responsibilities and be capable of withstanding the psychological demands inherent in the prospective position (Guideline 3.2).

An internationally recognized body that develops consensus codes and industry standards for the fire profession is the National Fire Protection Association (NFPA). Standard 1582, the *Standard on Comprehensive Occupational Medical Program[s] for Fire Departments,* includes the recommendation that firefighter candidates be evaluated to determine that they are "free of any psychiatric condition" (NFPA, 2022, 6.21.1[1]) and that they have "no history of a psychiatric condition or substance use problem" (6.21.2) that would prevent them from performing essential job tasks. Whether based on legal requirements, job analysis, or agency policy, identifying the suitability criterion is a foundational task for a screening psychologist. As Corey and Zelig (2020) observed, "without knowing the criterion, the examiner cannot identify the methodology needed to conduct the evaluation or how to analyze the assessment data, select the relevant findings, formulate opinions, and communicate the results of the evaluation" (p. 116).

ASSESSMENT METHODOLOGY

The tests and other components used in a preemployment evaluation of a public safety candidate may also be determined by law, regulation, administrative rule, or agency policy. In the absence of local requirements, the "basic model" (Mitchell, 2017; Serafino, 2010) of assessment methodology in these evaluations consists of no fewer than two psychological tests (one a broadband measure of abnormal personality functioning and the other a measure of normal-range personality), a clinical interview, and a review of available background information. This basic model is also reflected in the IACP (2020) Preemployment Psychological Evaluation Guidelines, which recommend that psychological suitability evaluations for police and other public safety candidates include both an "assessment of mental or emotional impairment" (Guideline 3.3) and an "assessment of normal-range personality traits, behaviors and characteristics" (Guideline 3.4). Next, we briefly review important considerations concerning each of these assessment components.

Psychological Testing

The choice to use the MMPI-3 as an omnibus measure of personality and psychopathology is consistent with the general admonition to select tests for which (a) access is restricted by the publisher to qualified professionals, (b) a comprehensive test manual is available, (c) adequate reliability and validity for its intended use are demonstrated through peer-reviewed research, (d) measured constructs are conceptually linked to the selection criteria (e.g., those listed in Tables 1.4 and 1.5), and (e) measures of test-taking orientation or protocol validity are included (Ackerman, 2010; Corey & Zelig, 2020; Melton et al., 2007; Otto et al., 2000; Spilberg & Corey, 2022). Based on the national survey just discussed, Corey (2016) reported that, four years before the MMPI-3's publication, the MMPI-2-RF was the most frequently used (44.6%) measure of abnormal psychological functioning in preemployment psychological evaluations of police candidates, in contrast to 37.5% each for the MMPI-2 and Personality Assessment Inventory (PAI; some respondents reported using more than one test of psychopathology). It is important to note that 100% of the respondents reported using at least one omnibus written measure of psychopathology.

The choice of which test of normal-range personality to use in conjunction with the MMPI-3 should rest on these same criteria. Preferably, there would also exist evidence demonstrating a relationship between the chosen test's scale scores and posthire behavior in one or more of the four public safety positions, pertinent to the problem behaviors listed in Table 1.2. Selection of a normal-range personality test should also be based on its potential to augment interpretation of the MMPI-3 by means of complementary and divergent findings. In other words, interpretations of both tests are optimized when there is some overlap in the constructs they measure; however, users should be mindful that variations in item content can result in meaningfully different facets of a construct being measured, even among similarly named scales (e.g., Low Positive Emotions [RC2] and the Positive Emotions subscale from the Revised NEO Personality Inventory [NEO PI-R]).

Collateral Background Information

The IACP (2020) Preemployment Psychological Evaluation Guidelines state, "evaluators are encouraged to collect and integrate information regarding the candidate's relevant history (e.g., school, work, interpersonal, family, legal, financial, substance use, mental health) in a standardized manner" (Guideline 10.1). Corey (2016) reported that 57.1% of screening psychologists obtain this history from the formal background investigation report provided by the prospective hiring agency, 66.1% obtain it from a written personal history questionnaire, and 83.9% acquire it during the clinical interview (the majority of psychologists reported using two or all three of these methods). Mitchell (2017) noted the general principle "that the more thorough and comprehensive the background investigation, the lower the psychological disqualification rate" (p. 34).[9]

A psychological assessment that does not integrate background information from collateral sources (e.g., current and former coworkers, supervisors, neighbors, romantic partners, or polygraph examination) inescapably relies heavily, if not solely, on self-report data. However, not all candidates report accurately, sometimes from lack of awareness or naïveté and other times from intentional deception. Without collateral data, one can validly assess neither the reliability of a candidate's self-report nor the degree to which it conflicts with reputation. The assessment of psychosocial functioning is best accomplished through the integration of multiple sources of information, including collateral data. Graham's (2012) cautionary statement about interpreting MMPI-2 scores without the benefit of collateral information applies equally well to the MMPI-3 and all other personality tests:

> The interpretive data will not apply completely and unfailingly to each person with specified MMPI-2 scores. In interpreting MMPI-2 scores, one is

dealing in probabilities. A particular extratest characteristic is more likely than another to apply to a person with a higher score on a scale than a person with a lower [score] on that scale, but there can never be complete certainty that it will. The inferences generated from an individual's MMPI-2 scores should thus be validated against other test and non-test information available about that individual. (p. 283)

Often, public safety agencies do not make background information available to the screening professional because of the mistaken belief that this allows for an unbiased evaluation. However, when an assessment depends exclusively on the candidate's self-report and on observations from the narrow slice of behavior displayed in the interview, critical pieces of information may be missing. Rather than biasing the evaluation, background findings properly integrated with testing and interview data can complement these equally important sources of self-report data. In chapter 8, we illustrate the essential utility of background information to the assessment of public safety candidates and how to integrate personal history with test and interview information. The importance of collateral background data to conducting reliable and valid assessments is recognized in the regulations of the California Commission on Peace Officer Standards and Training (POST), which require that law enforcement agencies provide their screening psychologists and psychiatrists with pertinent information collected from the background investigation (11 C.C.R. § 1955[e][3]). The IACP Preemployment Psychological Evaluation Guidelines (2020; Guideline 10.2) also include this expectation. Indeed, so vital are the collection and clarification of collateral background information to psychological screening that California POST Regulation 1953(d)(2) requires that background investigators, examining physicians, examining psychologists, and others involved in the hiring decision "shall work cooperatively to ensure that each has the information necessary to conduct their respective investigations and/or assessments of the candidate." In the assessment of a candidate's potential for biased behavior, access to a well-conducted background investigation is essential (see Spilberg and Corey [2022] for a comprehensive discussion of the California POST's Bias Assessment Framework).

Clinical Interview

Two aspects of the clinical interview deserve comment: its place in the sequence of the assessment components and its function. Regarding sequencing, we recommend that it always *follow* the administration and review of psychological testing.[10] A candidate's responses to test items frequently raise questions, and the interview offers an opportunity to clarify them. Although we do not recommend reading item content to the candidate verbatim, item-level information contained in the MMPI-3 and other test reports may alert the psychologist to potential problems that warrant follow-up. For example, if candidates were to respond True to this statement on a hypothetical test, "At times I feel commanded to do things I know are wrong," asking them to explain their response is likely to yield little, because once they are made aware of the psychologist's concern, candidates typically reply that they misunderstood the item content or incorrectly recorded their answers (Spilberg & Corey, 2022). Instead, it is generally more useful to construct probing interview questions designed to assess a particular concern. In our example, the psychologist is advised to assess not only for the possibility of delusional thinking and command hallucinations but also for other obsessional preoccupations that may account for the item response. Neither assessment requires an inquiry concerning the specific item response. For example, without referencing the test item, the interviewer may ask, "Have you ever felt directed to do things you knew were wrong?" In the relatively rare instance when a candidate may be experiencing command hallucinations, this is more likely to be acknowledged in answer to a general question than in clarification of a response to a specific item that the candidate is likely to understand was the "wrong" answer. Unless testing precedes the interview, such clarifications are precluded.

Although some practitioners read item content to a candidate verbatim, we believe this is contrary to best practice and risks informing them that they have given the "wrong" response. Rarely will a test taker acknowledge an actual problem in this context, and the resulting discussion is unlikely to be illuminating. More troubling, it can affect how the test taker responds to future administrations of the test, leaving those administrations compromised. When it is necessary to discuss a specific item, we recommend that the screening professional take care not to inform the examinee that the inquiry pertains to their response to a particular test item. This can be done by paraphrasing and asking about the item in the broader context of the clinical interview.

The purpose of the assessment interview is to obtain information necessary for an understanding of the candidate's emotional, interpersonal, and behavioral functioning (relevant to the psychological screening dimensions in Table 1.5 or other qualification criteria) that cannot be ascertained by other means. In general, if the information can be obtained another way (such as in a written questionnaire), it is usually more efficient and economical to do so. What interviews do uniquely well is provide opportunities to observe job-relevant behavior (e.g., emotional and behavioral regulation, social competence, adaptability, and judgment), assess attitudes, and test rival hypotheses generated from a review of both psychological testing and background information gathered from collateral and self-report questionnaires.

Psychological testing in postoffer suitability assessments is focused primarily on identifying problems, not assets or strengths.[11] Yet the challenge in psychological assessment is to evaluate not only the maladaptive aspects of an individual but also the adaptive and compensatory or mitigating features. When assessing for psychopathology, for example, relevant indicators include distress, functional impairment, and behaviors characteristic of the condition. But the presence of these indicators is not proof of pathology without first ruling out indicators of their opposite; namely, indicators of psychological health, including flexibility, self-confidence, productivity, self-esteem, autonomy, efficiency, and stable relationships (Frances et al., 1991). Interviews, like background information, provide an occasion to evaluate the merits of hypotheses that rival those generated by psychological testing.

6

Empirical Foundations for Using the MMPI-3 in Preemployment Assessments of Public Safety Candidates

The MMPI was developed for use in mental health and medical settings. The interpretive guidelines included in the *MMPI-3 Manual for Administration, Scoring, and Interpretation* (Ben-Porath & Tellegen, 2020a) apply primarily to assessments conducted in these settings—although clinically elevated scores (T score 65 and higher) on MMPI-3 Substantive Scales indicate likely significant impairment regardless of setting. For reasons discussed later in this chapter, such elevations are uncommon in public safety candidates. However, a substantial body of research indicates that for many of the substantive scales, nonclinically elevated scores deviating substantially from the mean for police candidates (i.e., T scores in the 53–64 range) are associated with significantly increased risk for negative outcomes, as are more uncommonly occurring clinically elevated scores. This research, which serves as the empirical foundation for the MMPI-3 Public Safety Candidate Interpretive Reports (PSCIRs) described in chapter 7, is reviewed in detail next.

As discussed briefly in chapter 1, there is comparatively less research on the prediction of posthire outcomes for correctional, dispatcher, and firefighter/medic candidates. This is true for all personality and psychopathology measures. Consequently, the public-safety-specific research reviewed in this chapter focuses predominantly on candidates for law enforcement positions. Descriptive MMPI-3 findings (scale-score means, standard deviations, and elevation rates) are available for all four public safety positions that are the focus of this book and are provided in the final section of this chapter. They are also integrated into the four MMPI-3 Public Safety Candidate Interpretive Reports, as illustrated in the case studies in chapter 8.

We begin this chapter with a review of the literature on using the MMPI, the MMPI-2, the MMPI-2-RF, and now the MMPI-3 in assessing police and other public safety candidates. This review focuses on studies identifying predictive validity; readers are referred to Ben-Porath and Sellbom (2023) for a detailed discussion of evidence supporting the construct validity of the MMPI-3.

RESEARCH ON THE ORIGINAL MMPI AND MMPI-2 IN POLICE AND OTHER PUBLIC SAFETY CANDIDATE EVALUATIONS

A substantial body of empirical research on preemployment police candidate evaluations was conducted with the MMPI and later the MMPI-2. This section offers a selective review of the main findings of this research and identifies some issues that remain pertinent to contemporary use of the MMPI-3.

The Original MMPI

Early empirical studies conducted with the original MMPI found that several scales were effective in identifying police candidates at risk for counterproductive behaviors posthire. Marsh (1962) reported the results of a 10-year longitudinal study conducted with the Los Angeles County Sheriff's Department. The participants were 619 male deputy sheriffs hired between 1947 and 1950. The author reported that scores on MMPI Clinical Scales 9 (positively) and 2 (negatively) correlated with preventable auto accidents during an officer's first and second years on the force. Ten years later, Azen and colleagues (1973) conducted a follow-up study of 95 deputies from this cohort. These authors replicated and extended Marsh's (1962) findings, particularly that officers' prehire MMPI Scale 9 scores were associated with an increased risk for involvement in any type of traffic accident over the course of 20 years of service.

In one of the most comprehensive early MMPI studies, Blum (1964) conducted a longitudinal investigation of 87 male police applicants who were subsequently hired by a major metropolitan police agency. Seven years after testing, each officer's personnel records were reviewed for evidence of negative outcomes (charges of misconduct, motor vehicle accidents, sick leave use, and termination) and positive outcomes (career progression and commendations). Blum reported significant correlations (.20 or higher) between MMPI scale scores and various outcomes, with Validity Scale F and Clinical Scale 8 having the largest number of significant correlations (three each) with negative outcomes. Blum concluded that "personality problems loom largest in determining the chances for later misconduct as a policeman; they also play a role in risk for accidents and illness. They seem to play no role in whether or not a man is commended" (p. 131).

Saxe and Reiser (1976) compared MMPI scores of three police candidate groups: 100 who were rejected, 100 who were hired but separated from service within 3 years, and 100 who were hired and served successfully for at least 3 years. They reported significant group differences between rejected and successful candidates as well as between separated and successful officers on most MMPI scales. However, they noted that most candidates scored within normal limits, even on scales that differentiated successful from unsuccessful candidates. The authors viewed the absence of clinically elevated preemployment scores among officers who went on to engage in counterproductive behavior as limiting the MMPI's ability to identify potentially problematic candidates. They recommended that use of "successful officer norms" be explored, and they demonstrated that the separated officers scored approximately one-half of a standard deviation above the mean of successful officers on Clinical Scale 7. Misconceptions about the absence of clinically significant elevations among police candidates have figured prominently in criticisms of the utility of the MMPI in screening law enforcement candidates. We return to this topic later in this section.

Holland and colleagues (1976) conducted cluster analyses of the MMPI profiles of 359 correctional applicants and identified five relatively homogeneous subgroups; although, MMPI findings were not associated with posthire performance measures. In contrast, Knatz and colleagues (1992) analyzed a large group ($N = 8,287$) of diverse, male correctional officers hired by a large urban agency between 1980 and 1985 who were administered the MMPI and Inwald Personality Inventory (IPI; Inwald, 1992) as part of their preemployment psychological evaluations, and they used discriminant function analyses to predict membership in one or more groups of posthire counterproductive behavior (termination, excessive absences, excessive tardiness, and disciplinary interviews). Knatz and colleagues reported that the prediction equations for both the MMPI and IPI alone, and particularly in combination, predicted all four counterproductive behaviors and "showed no consistent bias in identifying those who would later display negative or counterproductive behaviors" (pp. 198–199). Although the authors did not publish their prediction equations, they reported that scales represented in the equations measured constructs reflecting "'bad actor' characteristics such as antisocial, impulsive, counterproductive, [and] sensation-seeking behavior patterns" (p. 200).

Beutler and colleagues (1985) examined the prediction of negative outcomes in officers sampled from a variety of departments, finding that scores on Clinical Scales 1, 2, 4, 6, and 7 were associated significantly with subsequent police supervisor ratings and various measures of posthire counterproductive behavior. The most notable correlations were between Clinical Scale 6 and technical proficiency, Clinical Scales 4 and 7 and at-fault motor vehicle accidents, Clinical Scale 1 and use-of-force reprimands, and Clinical Scale 2 and letters of complaint. Like Saxe and Reiser (1976), Beutler and colleagues commented on the absence of clinically significant elevations among officers who exhibited counterproductive behaviors, but they noted that this resulted from the automatic disqualification of candidates who produced elevated scores on MMPI scales associated with emotional and thought dysfunction. Anticipating future developments, the authors observed that they were able to detect substantial associations between MMPI scale scores and outcomes in spite of the absence of clinically elevated scores.

The MMPI-2

Following publication of the MMPI-2 (Butcher et al., 1989), initial questions were raised about the comparability of scores generated with the original and revised versions of the inventory and whether original MMPI findings such as the ones just reviewed could be assumed to carry over to the MMPI-2. Hargrave and colleagues (1994) administered both versions of the test to a sample of incumbent police officers. When MMPI-2 raw scores were converted to original MMPI T scores, Clinical Scale scores were essentially interchangeable across the two versions, indicating that minor rewording and loss of a few items had no appreciable effect on officers' Clinical Scale scores. When scored using the MMPI-2 norms, scores were appreciably (at least 5 T-score points) lower on Clinical Scales 2, 3, 4, 6, and 9 for both genders, and on Scales 5 and 7 for men. This was consistent with findings obtained from other samples in various settings. The test developers addressed these differences by lowering the cutoff for clinically significant elevation from a T score of 70 on the original MMPI to 65 on the MMPI-2. Hargrave and colleagues concluded that the two versions of the inventory would yield comparable results when used as a component of the preemployment assessment process, but they noted the need for new MMPI-2 validation studies.

Boes and colleagues (1997) studied MMPI and MMPI-2 scores of police officers who had been administered the test as part of their preemployment psychological evaluations. Their sample included 439 known-offender (adjudicated as having committed corrupt acts) officers from 69 police departments and a sample of matched controls (who had not committed these acts) from the same departments. They found few MMPI score differences between the groups, but they did report higher scores on Clinical Scale 4 and on the L scale for integrity violators than the nonviolator control subjects. However, they commented on the relatively modest effect sizes for these differences. This data set and some of the problems with the analyses just mentioned were revisited and addressed in a subsequent MMPI-2-RF study (Tarescavage et al., 2016), discussed in the next section.

Detrick and colleagues (2001) provided descriptive data and reported correlations between MMPI-2 scores and scores on the Inwald Personality Inventory (IPI; Inwald, 1992), an instrument designed specifically to assess police candidates, for a sample of 461 Midwestern law enforcement candidates who were administered these tests as part of a preemployment evaluation. This was one of the first MMPI-2 studies published following the Civil Rights Act legislation discussed in chapter 5, which prohibited the use of gender- and race-based norms in preemployment evaluations. The authors provided the first descriptive findings for police candidates using the MMPI-2 nongendered norms. Consistent with prior studies with the original MMPI, and highlighted by the overall lowering of T scores on the MMPI-2, average Clinical Scale T scores were substantially lower than the general population mean (50). The standard deviations associated with these lower means were also substantially smaller than the general population standard T-score deviations (10). Finally, Detrick and colleagues noted that, whereas correlations between MMPI-2 Clinical Scales and IPI scale scores were generally moderate and in the expected direction, this was true only for non-K-corrected Clinical Scale scores. Applying the standard K correction to the five Clinical Scales with which it was used (1, 4, 7, 8, and 9) substantially attenuated their correlations with relevant IPI scales, in some cases reducing sizable correlations to zero. This study led MMPI-2 experts (e.g., Graham, 2012; Greene, 2011) to recommend that non-K-corrected scores be relied on when the test is used in preemployment evaluations. These data were also revisited in the context of the MMPI-2-RF in a study by Detrick and colleagues (2016), discussed later in this chapter.

A Paradigm Shift

Sellbom and colleagues (2007) conducted the most comprehensive, prospective police candidate study carried out with the MMPI-2. It was the first to include the Restructured Clinical (RC) Scales (Tellegen et al., 2003), which, as discussed in chapter 4, were also part of the MMPI-2-RF and are incorporated in the MMPI-3. The authors examined the ability of prehire MMPI-2 scores of 426 candidates to predict future misconduct of police officers who, at the time of the study, had been employed from 7 to 9 years. In addition to reporting associations between prehire MMPI-2 scores and a host of outcome variables, they sought to address two challenges raised by prior research findings. As noted, descriptive statistics reported for both MMPI and MMPI-2 scores of police candidates indicated that, as a group, they score considerably lower than the general population and they evidence substantially reduced scale-score variability.

Sellbom and colleagues (2007) reasoned that the lower scores with reduced variability observed in police candidates were likely the product of preselection and selection effects. *Preselection effects* limit the range of scores of individuals referred by law enforcement agencies for preemployment psychological evaluation. These include any self-selection that may occur among those who choose to seek employment in law enforcement as well as any exclusions that might apply (e.g., a significant criminal record). The impact of preselection factors likely increased substantially following enactment of the ADA (discussed in chapter 5) and, in particular, the requirement that candidates be evaluated only on the basis of nonmedical factors (e.g., past conduct, reliability, employment, and criminal history) before receiving a conditional offer of employment and being referred for a preemployment psychological evaluation. Whereas prior to the ADA, police agencies could refer potential candidates for a psychological evaluation before determining that they were otherwise prepared to hire them, post-ADA candidates, as discussed in chapter 5, must be given a bona fide conditional offer of employment before being referred for an evaluation.

Selection factors stem from the use of MMPI scores as part of the prehire decision-making process, where it stands to reason that candidates whose scores raise suitability concerns are less likely to be hired. For example, in the aforementioned study by Beutler and colleagues (1985), candidates with clinically elevated scores on any of a number of Clinical Scales were automatically disqualified and, therefore, unavailable for the follow-up part of the study. Similarly, when reporting their results, Boes and colleagues (1997) noted that candidates with the most problematic MMPI protocols were likely not hired.

Sellbom and colleagues (2007) estimated preselection effects in their sample by comparing the means and associated standard deviations of MMPI-2 T scores of the full sample of 426 candidates with the known means and standard deviations of the general population (T scores of 50 and 10, respectively). Mean scores on the Clinical Scales (particularly the more informative non-K-corrected scores) and the RC Scales were generally 5–15 T-score points lower than those of the general population, and standard deviations were generally 2–5 T-score units lower (e.g., a 20% to 50% reduction in scale-score variability). Selection effects were estimated by comparing mean scores and standard deviations of the 426 candidates with the 291 individuals among them who "passed" the psychological evaluation and were hired. Selection effects were considerably smaller than those produced by preselection, but they still resulted in a further lowering of mean scores and their associated standard deviations.

These preselection (in particular) and selection effects have significant research and practice implications. The reduced variability of prehire scale scores attenuates correlations between them and the criteria used in studying their validity as predictors of subsequent counterproductive behaviors. Correlations essentially reflect the extent to which variance in a predictor variable (MMPI score) is associated with variance in a criterion (counterproductive behavior). Reduced variance in the predictor variables (stemming from preselection and selection factors) artificially attenuates their correlations with outcome variables. Sellbom and colleagues (2007) applied a formula derived from the work of Hunter and Schmidt (1990) to estimate the true correlation between MMPI-2 scores and outcome variables in their study:

$$r_c = \frac{r_u \cdot (SD_u \div SD_r)}{\sqrt{(1+r_u^2)+(r_u^2)\cdot(SD_u \div SD_r)^2}}$$

where r_c is the estimated correct correlation between the predictor and criterion variable, r_u is the uncorrected or observed correlation, SD_r is the restricted or observed standard deviation, and SD_u is the unrestricted standard deviation. To correct for preselection factors, Sellbom and colleagues (2007) set SD_r to equal 10 (the standard deviation of T scores in the general population) and inserted the r_u and SD_u values obtained in their analyses to calculate the corrected validity coefficient, r_c.

Boes and colleagues (1997), in the MMPI-2 study just reviewed, assumed incorrectly that by including an equal number of violators and nonviolators in their analyses they were countering the impact of range restriction on their results and alleviating the need to correct for it. They were correct in noting that equal cell sizes could correct for the impact of range restriction stemming from the low base rate of integrity violations among police officers; however, it did not correct for range restriction in the candidates' MMPI scores.

The findings by Sellbom and colleagues (2007) indicated that although they rarely reached clinically significant levels, candidates' prehire MMPI-2 scores were substantially correlated with posthire adverse outcomes. A corollary of this finding is that non-elevated T scores can predict risk for such outcomes. From a practice standpoint, the absence of clinically elevated scores stemming from preselection and selection factors creates a need to identify nonclinically elevated cutoffs associated with an increased risk for subsequent adverse outcomes. To address this need, Sellbom and colleagues (2007) reported relative risk ratios associated with T-score cutoffs of 60 and 55. Relative risk ratios (RRRs) quantify the increased risk for a given outcome associated with scoring at or above the designated cutoff versus scoring below the cutoff. For example, a relative risk ratio of 2.0 for a 55T cutoff on a given scale indicates that those who score at or above 55T are at twice the risk of the associated negative outcome as those who score below 55T. When interpreting RRRs, it is important to pay attention to the absolute risk as well. For example, if 20% of those who score at or above a designated cutoff have substance abuse related problems, and 10% of those who score below the cutoff manifest such difficulties, the RRR is 2.0 but the absolute risk is 20%.

Applying the aforementioned Hunter and Schmidt (1990) correction for range restriction, Sellbom and colleagues (2007) reported for a sample of 291 male police officers uncorrected and range-restriction-corrected correlations between prehire MMPI-2 Clinical, RC, and Substance Abuse scale scores and posthire internal affairs and civilian review authority complaints, termination of employment for cause, and supervisory ratings. The authors found that the RC Scales—particularly RC3 (Cynicism), which on the MMPI-3 is the Externalizing Specific Problems Scale CYN (Cynicism); RC4 (Antisocial Behavior); RC6 (Ideas of Persecution); and RC8 (Aberrant Experiences)—had the best predictive utility among the MMPI-2 scales they examined. For example, higher scores on RC6 were significantly associated with termination for cause; complaints from members of the public; use of excessive force; rude behavior; displaying a bad attitude toward members of the public; being uncooperative toward supervisors; being a defendant in civil litigation; deceptiveness; abuse of authority; failure to take responsibility for mistakes; using position for personal advantage; showing biased attitudes toward others; poor response to constructive feedback; and an indication that, given an opportunity to reconsider the initial hire decision, the officer's supervisor would not rehire them. The uncorrected correlations between prehire RC6 scores and the outcomes just listed ranged from .15 to .29. The range-restriction-corrected correlations were from .35 to .60.

Sellbom and colleagues' (2007) results indicated that even utilizing an interpretive cutoff of 60T yielded low elevation rates for the RC Scales. For example, 1.7% and 0.4% of employed officers scored ≥ 60T on RC3 and RC4, respectively. Furthermore, Sellbom and colleagues (2007) noted that, as a result of various preselection and selection factors, none of the officers in their study scored above 60T on RC6. Thus, as discussed, the empirical correlates reflect associations between nonclinically elevated RC6 scores and the outcome variables. This, in turn, indicates that substantial deviations from the mean RC6 score of police candidates are associated with substantially increased risk for negative outcomes at T-score levels well below 65. To quantify this risk, Sellbom and colleagues calculated RRRs for statistically significant correlations. They reported, for example, that 26.3% of officers who scored at or above 55T on RC6 in the prehire evaluation were identified by their supervisors several years later as having engaged in rude behavior toward members of the public. Only 6.5% of those who scored below 55T on RC6 in the prehire testing were similarly identified, producing a RRR of roughly 4 (26.3/6.5). This indicates that candidates who score at or above this cutoff on RC6 are four times more likely to engage in rude behavior toward civilians compared with those who score below 55.

To conclude, Sellbom and colleagues' (2007) results demonstrated several important considerations pertaining to use of the MMPI in prehire assessments of police candidates. First, they found that, when corrected for range restriction, correlations between prehire scores and subsequent counterproductive behaviors were of a meaningful magnitude, reflecting medium to large effect sizes. Second, they demonstrated the need for and appropriateness of using lower (than the traditional 65T) cutoffs to properly interpret police candidates' MMPI-2 scale scores. Their results also replicated those of Detrick and colleagues (2001) in finding generally stronger validity for non-K-corrected versus K-corrected Clinical Scale scores. Finally, their findings indicated that the MMPI-2-RF RC Scales, developed by Tellegen and colleagues (2003), provided substantial improvements above the non-K-corrected Clinical Scale scores in prospective prediction of police candidates' problematic behavior.

In summary, 50 years of empirical research demonstrated the validity of MMPI and MMPI-2 scale scores as predictors of negative outcomes in police candidates, although studies using different outcome criteria did not necessarily produce consistent findings (i.e., different scales were found to work best across these studies). The substantial improvement resulting from restructuring the Clinical Scales reported by Sellbom and colleagues (2007) was a positive indicator of the prospects for using the MMPI-2-RF, which included the RC Scales complemented by measures constructed with similar methods, in preemployment assessments of police candidates. Their findings also introduced important methodological considerations for future research in this area, including use of range restriction corrections and identification of risk for adverse outcomes associated with subclinical cutoffs.

RESEARCH ON THE MMPI-2-RF IN POLICE AND OTHER PUBLIC SAFETY CANDIDATE EVALUATIONS

After the MMPI-2-RF was published in 2008, Weiss and Weiss (2010) identified the updated inventory as having "considerable promise in the area of preemployment screening" (p. 68). They listed as particular benefits the availability of law enforcement applicant norms in the *MMPI-2-RF Technical Manual* (Tellegen & Ben-Porath, 2008/2011), inclusion of the Restructured Clinical (RC) Scales with their evidence of predictive validity for police officer performance (Sellbom et al., 2007), and the smaller number of items (338 versus 567 in the MMPI-2), which made the test easier to administer as part of the additional testing typically required in a preemployment evaluation (see chapter 5). Weiss and Weiss (2010) also commented on the need for research to support use of the MMPI-2-RF in preemployment assessments of police candidates.

After Weiss and Weiss (2010) issued their call, an extensive body of empirical research was published and helped guide use of the MMPI-2-RF in the assessment of police candidates. Some of this research was conducted with archival MMPI-2 data sets, from which the MMPI-2-RF scales were scored. Use of archival data for this purpose was possible because the 338 MMPI-2-RF items were embedded in the 567-item MMPI-2 booklet and was supported by findings that MMPI-2-RF scores derived from the MMPI-2 and that MMPI-2-RF booklets were essentially interchangeable (Tarescavage et al., 2014; Tellegen & Ben-Porath, 2008/2011; van der Heijden et al., 2010).

We begin our review of this literature by examining the results of an innovative study of the assessment of underreporting in police candidates. We follow with investigations that provide empirical correlates (including post-hire outcomes) of MMPI-2-RF scores produced by men and women undergoing preemployment evaluations for law enforcement and other public safety positions. Altogether, the MMPI-2-RF studies described in this chapter include data obtained from several thousand police candidates tested throughout the United States. The majority of these candidates were men, reflecting the relatively small proportion of female law enforcement officers (10%–20% nationally, depending on agency size); for several of these studies, the small number of female candidates did not allow for meaningful analyses by gender. This underscores the need to follow up with additional research using larger samples of women.

Underreporting Scales

Detrick and Chibnall (2014) examined the impact of the demand characteristics associated with preemployment evaluations of police candidates, which incentivize test takers to present in a favorable manner by underreporting problems—a ubiquitous challenge in this type of assessment. They also investigated the sensitivity of the MMPI-2-RF Validity Scales, Uncommon Virtues (L-r) and Adjustment Validity (K-r), to underreporting. Employing a differential prevalence research design, they compared scores generated by a sample of 62 police candidates (53 men and 9 women) tested twice, first under a high-demand condition and again in a low-demand context. The *high-demand* condition involved completion of the MMPI-2-RF as part of the routine preemployment evaluation. For the *low-demand* condition, participants were administered the MMPI-2-RF a second time after completing 6 months of training in the academy. They were informed that the postacademy assessment results would be used strictly for research purposes, there would be no consequences to them resulting from this testing, and the results would not be shared with any police personnel.

Consistent with the authors' hypothesis that the low-demand condition would result in a greater willingness to acknowledge psychological problems, participants scored higher in the low-demand condition on several MMPI-2-RF substantive scales, with some of the highest effect sizes found on measures of externalizing dysfunction. Participants also had higher scores in the low-demand condition on measures of emotional dysfunction and the interpersonal scales. As expected, participants scored higher on L-r and K-r in the high-demand condition, demonstrating that scores on these scales are sensitive to underreporting. With an innovative set of regression analyses, Detrick and Chibnall (2014) found that higher preemployment L-r scores were associated with a proclivity to underreport behavioral dysfunction and cynicism, whereas higher K-r scores were associated with underreporting of emotional dysfunction and cynicism.

Detrick and Chibnall's (2014) study underscored several important considerations related to using the MMPI-2-RF in police candidate assessments, with implications for the use of the MMPI-3 in this context as well. As noted, participants in their study scored higher on L-r and K-r in the high-demand (preemployment evaluation) when compared with the low-demand (no stake in the evaluation) condition, providing evidence of the sensitivity of the MMPI-2-RF underreporting indicators to this type of threat to protocol validity. However, even in the low-demand condition, officers' mean (and associated standard deviation) scores on L-r and K-r were 57.7 (14.4) and 60.6 (7.8), respectively, likely reflected the potential confounds that complicate interpreting scores on these scales (discussed in chapter 3). That is, law enforcement candidates are more likely than a random sample of the general adult population to have been raised in a traditional home, and as discussed, they are more likely to be better adjusted. Due to the aforementioned preselection and selection factors, these candidates are also more likely than members of the normative sample to exhibit a higher number of moral virtues. Proper consideration of these confounds requires accounting for the base rate of MMPI-3 scores in police candidate assessments, which can be accomplished by using the Police Candidate Comparison Group discussed later in this chapter.

In chapter 9, we discuss the literature on and practice of retesting, with altered instructions, candidates whose underreporting scores indicate the possibility of defensive or deceptive responding. We recommend against the use of altered instructions when administering any standardized test, and we explain our rationale for this recommendation in that chapter.

Substantive Scales

Detrick and colleagues (2016) reported correlations between MMPI-2-RF substantive scale scores and results on the IPI (Inwald et al., 1982), which, as discussed earlier, is a psychological test specifically designed and validated to screen police candidates. Their sample consisted of 277 male police candidates from four Midwestern police agencies varying in size. The authors tested a series of conceptually based hypotheses about correlations between scores on these two measures, which were administered to the sample as part of a postoffer preemployment psychological evaluation.

Findings were largely consistent with the authors' conceptually formed hypotheses, supporting the construct validity of MMPI-2-RF scales in a police candidate sample. For example, as expected, Emotional/Internalizing Dysfunction (EID) scores were primarily associated with IPI measures of internalizing difficulties such as depression and obsessional thoughts, as well as with some IPI measures of interpersonal conflict. Also as expected, BXD scores were most strongly correlated with a range of IPI measures of acting-out and externalizing behavior, such as admission of alcohol and drug use, having been in trouble with the law, and an admitted history of job absenteeism. Thought Dysfunction (THD) had a broader than anticipated range of correlates. As expected, scores on this scale were strongly correlated with results on the IPI Unusual Experiences/Thoughts and Undue Suspiciousness scales. Other correlates included IPI measures of nontraditional, antisocial attitudes and of temperamental acting-out proclivities. Although not linked conceptually with THD, these correlates are consistent with the findings of Sellbom and colleagues (2007), who reported that prehire RC6 and RC8 scores predicted a host of on-the-job conduct problems in police candidates who were hired.

As was the case in that study, mean scores and associated standard deviations in the Detrick and colleagues (2016) study were substantially deflated and restricted when compared with the MMPI-2-RF normative sample. For example, the mean EID T score for the 277 police candidates included in this study was 34 with a standard deviation of 4 (in contrast with the mean and standard deviation on this and all other MMPI-2-RF scales in the normative sample, which, by definition, are 50 and 10, respectively). Almost none of the individuals included in the study produced a clinically elevated EID score ($\geq$ 65T), indicating that scores below 65 but substantially above average for the sample are associated with a range of risk factors assessed by the IPI. Similar findings were reported for most of the MMPI-2-RF substantive scales.

Tarescavage, Brewster, Corey, and Ben-Porath (2015)

Tarescavage, Brewster, and colleagues (2015) examined associations between prehire MMPI-2-RF scores and posthire performance ratings for a sample of 131 male police officers employed in the northeastern United States. After consulting with several police chiefs and supervisory personnel, the study's second author created a supervisor survey of police officer performance. Supervisors completed the survey after they had observed officers' behavior for a time period ranging from a month to 2.5 years ($M = 1.1$, $SD = 0.5$ years). The authors selected 39 survey items that addressed constructs related to the CA-POST screening dimensions (Spilberg & Corey, 2022) as well as one global rating as the criteria in their investigation.

Uncorrected and range-restriction-corrected correlations (see the earlier discussion of Sellbom et al., 2007) between MMPI-2-RF scores and the selected criteria indicated that scales from the emotional dysfunction domain were substantially associated with emotional control and stress problems (problems with anger interfering with job performance), routine task performance problems (difficulties drawing crime or accident scenes), decision-making and judgment problems (overlooking violations), and problem-solving difficulties. Scores on MMPI-2-RF scales from the thought dysfunction domain were associated with marksmanship problems and difficulty predicting situational outcomes. Scores from measures included in the behavioral dysfunction domain were correlated with various outcomes related to acting out, such as integrity problems and alcohol and drug use. Scores on MMPI-2-RF measures of interpersonal functioning were associated with problems such as failing to utilize training under stressful conditions, difficulties with assertiveness and social skills, and shortcomings in oral communication skills. Overall, the corrected correlations were mainly of a medium effect size.

A comparison of the MMPI-2-RF means and standard deviations for the study sample with those found for the MMPI-2-RF Police Candidate Comparison Group (Corey & Ben-Porath, 2014) showed that the two samples produced comparably suppressed and range-restricted scores, indicating that in this investigation (as with Sellbom et al. [2007] and Detrick et al. [2016]), correlations between prehire MMPI-2-RF scores and problematic job-relevant behaviors reflect individual differences that, for the most part, were associated with T scores below 65.

Tarescavage, Corey, and Ben-Porath (2015)

Tarescavage and colleagues (2015) investigated the predictive validity of the MMPI-2-RF in a sample of 136 male police officers hired by the Portland (Oregon) Police Bureau. Supervisor ratings of performance and problem behaviors were obtained during the officers' initial probationary period, when they were closely monitored by a field training officer. Each of the officers had been administered the MMPI-2 (converted for the purpose of this study to the MMPI-2-RF) or MMPI-2-RF as part of their preemployment evaluation and subsequently completed a training academy and a 16-week field training program. The officers were evaluated daily during the field training program, and these evaluations were used by training division personnel to complete the Selection Validation Survey (SVS), a measure developed by this book's first author to assess police officers' performance during their initial probationary period. The SVS is organized into three sections: Problem Behaviors, Field Performance Dimensions, and General Performance Dimensions. Problem Behaviors include items such as academic learning problems, failure to engage subjects as necessary, and rude behavior. Field Performance Dimensions include items such as decision-making, assertiveness/control, and multitasking. General Performance Dimensions include items such as initiative and drive, commitment, integrity, and teamwork. Problem Behaviors were coded as *absent, problem during probation,* or *problem leading to separation.* Field Performance Dimensions items were rated under normal and stress conditions. General Performance Dimensions items were rated as either *absent* or *present.* The SVS also includes two Likert scale ratings for overall performance and potential for hiring similar employees. Except for the latter Likert scale ratings, data for all the other variables were derived from archival records that included daily observation ratings of recruits by their field training officers.

Descriptive analyses indicated that this sample produced deflated means and restricted score ranges on MMPI-2-RF Substantive Scales, comparable to the other study samples described in this section and to the MMPI-2-RF Police Candidate Comparison Group (Corey & Ben-Porath, 2014). Next, the authors reported uncorrected and range-restriction-corrected correlations between prehire MMPI-2-RF scores and SVS ratings of officers' performance during their probationary period. Scores on the MMPI-2-RF emotional domain scales were moderately correlated with various emotional control and stress problems, including decision-making under stress and restraint and control problems under stress, as well as with routine task performance problems, such as learning problems under normal conditions and radio operation problems. Scales in this domain were also associated with subsequent problems in the areas of conscientiousness and commitment, as well as with an overall negative performance evaluation. Scales in the thought dysfunction domain were not correlated substantially with most of the SVS criteria. By contrast, scores on the MMPI-2-RF behavioral dysfunction measures were correlated with problems such as failure to accept feedback and interpersonal difficulties. Scores on the BXD, RC9, and DISC-r scales were negatively correlated with failure to engage subjects, indicating that particularly low scores on these measures were associated with problematic performance. Scales in the somatic domain did not have many meaningful associations with SVS ratings. In contrast, scores on the MMPI-2-RF measures of interpersonal functioning were associated with assertiveness and control problems, interpersonal difficulties, and problems with teamwork.

As is the case in the other studies discussed in this section, the correlations between prehire MMPI-2-RF scores and probationary-period performance ratings reflect scale-score variance that occurs, for the most part, below T score 65. Using the methodology applied in the study by Sellbom and colleagues (2007), Tarescavage and colleagues (2015) reported relative risk ratios associated with various subclinical MMPI-2-RF scores. Substantially increased risk for various negative outcomes was found using cutoffs of 45T and 50T. For example, officers scoring at or above 50T on the Cognitive Complaints (COG) scale were at twice the risk for experiencing multitasking problems under stress, compared with those who scored below 50T.

Tarescavage, Corey, Gupton, and Ben-Porath (2015)

Tarescavage, Corey, and colleagues (2015) used essentially the same methodology as the one described in the previous study to examine the predictive validity of MMPI-2-RF scores of 145 male police officers employed by the Honolulu Police Department. Here, too, the sample of hired police officers produced mean scores and standard deviations substantially lower than the general population. After correcting for range restriction, scores on scales from all the domains assessed by the MMPI-2-RF were correlated with various negative outcomes with medium to large effect sizes. In the emotional domain, some of the strongest correlations were found between scores on RC2 and problems in the areas of emotional control and stress, routine task performance, decision-making and judgment, and social competence and teamwork. Higher scores on scales in the thought dysfunction domain were correlated with learning problems, navigation problems, radio operation difficulties, and problems with multitasking. As was the case in the previous study, scores in the externalizing domain were negatively correlated with a number of variables (assertiveness, social competence and teamwork, and interpersonal problems), indicating that particularly low scores on these scales are associated with negative outcomes. Scores on the MMPI-2-RF measures of interpersonal functioning were also correlated with a number of negative outcomes.

Relative risk ratio analyses were conducted to identify the increase in risk for negative outcomes associated with various MMPI-2-RF scale cutoffs. Overall, these analyses pointed to significantly increased risk for a host of negative outcomes associated with cutoffs ranging from 45T to 65T. For example, compared with individuals who scored below this cutoff, those who scored above were at 8.67 times higher risk for being rated by their supervisors as having difficulties restraining and controlling subjects under stressful conditions.

Tarescavage, Fischler, Cappo, Hill, Corey, and Ben-Porath (2015)

Tarescavage, Fischler, and colleagues (2015) reported descriptive findings and correlations between prehire MMPI-2-RF scores and selected scales from the California Psychological Inventory (CPI; Gough, 1956) and the IPI (described in the study by Detrick et al., 2016) for a sample of police candidates comprised of 711 men and women from two Midwestern states. They also reported correlations with outcome data for 288 of the men who were subsequently hired. The men in this sample were a subset of those included in the MMPI-2 study reported by Sellbom and colleagues (2007). The authors augmented the earlier sample with one obtained in a different state using the same methodology (supervisor ratings obtained after the officer had been employed for several years), and they reported findings for the full range of MMPI-2-RF Substantive Scales, whereas Sellbom and colleagues reported only limited findings for the RC Scales.

Descriptive analyses indicated that the male and female candidates produced very similar means and standard deviations on the MMPI-2-RF scales, with the exception that men who were hired scored approximately 5 T-score points higher on the DISC-r scale than women who were hired. Both genders produced generally lower means and standard deviations on the Substantive Scales when compared with those in the MMPI-2-RF normative samples.

Correlations between prehire MMPI-2-RF and CPI scores were reported for the female candidates. The CPI scales examined in this investigation included special measures developed by Roberts and Johnson (2001) for police candidate evaluations. Several sizable associations were found between females' MMPI-2-RF scores and the special CPI scale indexes. For example, RC7 scores were substantially correlated with a CPI composite predicting a self-reported history of job performance problems; RC1, RC7, MLS, and HPC scores were associated with an index predicting increased risk of being rated poorly by the evaluating psychologist; and RCd, RC3, RC6, and BRF scores were correlated with an indicator of increased risk for being fired for cause. Scores on several externalizing scales also were correlated with a wide range of CPI risk indicators. Of note is that the vast majority of women included in this study scored below 65T on most MMPI-2-RF scales, indicating that, as is the case with male candidates, subclinical deviations from the Police Candidate Comparison Group mean are associated with a wide range of risk factors in female candidates.

Male candidates produced similar patterns of correlations with the CPI risk indicators. Correlations between MMPI-2-RF scales and scores on the IPI were generally consistent with those reported by Detrick and colleagues (2016) for a different sample. Scores on the MMPI-2-RF measures of emotional dysfunction were substantially correlated with IPI measures of anxiety, phobic personality, and depression. Externalizing dysfunction scores were correlated with IPI measures of substance abuse, antisocial attitudes, hyperactivity, and lack of assertiveness. Measures of interpersonal functioning were associated with antisocial attitudes, lack of assertiveness, and sexual concerns.

In the subset of men for whom outcome data were available, higher scores on the Substantive Scales were associated substantially with a broad range of negative outcomes. For example, higher prehire MMPI-2-RF scores on emotional dysfunction measures were correlated with subsequent complaints from members of the public, use of excessive force and inappropriate language, and poor ethics. Scores on the thought dysfunction measures were associated with outcomes such as deceptive behavior, rude behavior, being uncooperative toward peers, missing court appearances, and being fired for cause. Behavioral dysfunction measures were correlated with sustained internal affairs complaints, missing court appearances, and poor response to feedback. Interpersonal functioning measures were correlated with outcomes such as inappropriate sexual attitudes, conduct unbecoming, and poor integrity ratings.

As in several of the previously discussed studies, relative risk ratios were calculated to assist in quantifying the increased risk associated with various subclinical MMPI-2-RF scale-score cutoffs. These analyses demonstrated substantially increased risk for various outcomes associated with cutoffs ranging from 45T to 65T, as well as for low scores on some scales and clinically elevated scores on most substantive scales.

Tarescavage, Corey, and Ben-Porath (2016)

Tarescavage and colleagues (2016) used the archival data set collected by Boes and colleagues (1997), described earlier in the context of a study of the ability of prehire MMPI scores to predict police officers' future serious integrity violations. These authors surveyed more than 2,000 police departments throughout the United States, seeking to locate officers with one of 10 prespecified integrity violations that resulted in termination. They identified 439 officers with at least one of the violations and matched them with 439 officers of the same gender, age, and length of employment who did not have any. These officers were employed by 69 agencies in 29 states spread throughout the country, including departments in the Northeast, South, Midwest, Southwest, and West (Boes et al., 1997).

A potential confound in Boes and colleagues' (1997) study design was that approximately one-third of the nonviolator group had a history of disciplinary infractions that were less serious than the integrity violations that were the focus of the study. The infractions included misconduct such as alcohol abuse, firearms misuse, use of excessive force, falsification of time worked, failure to appear for court testimony, and supervisory problems. In fact, the authors reported that for the entire sample, such subthreshold violations were the best predictors of the more serious integrity violations. Consequently, this subsample was not optimal as a nonviolating contrast group.

Tarescavage and colleagues (2016) analyzed this data set, which included information about all violations as well as responses to the 550 original MMPI items, to examine whether the psychometric refinements introduced with the MMPI-2-RF scales and elimination of the aforementioned confound would result in improved integrity violation prediction. After removal of invalid protocols and data for 40 female police officers, the sample included 417 male officers. The first task was to determine whether it is possible to score the MMPI-2-RF from the original MMPI, which contains 274 of the 338 items of the restructured instrument (the remaining items were added to the MMPI-2). The authors estimated MMPI-2-RF raw scores for scales that were missing items by prorating based on the remaining items. To examine the fidelity of the prorated scores, a similar procedure was applied to three MMPI-2 samples, and the resulting estimated and actual T scores were compared, yielding correlations of .90 or higher for 44 of the 51 MMPI-2-RF scales. The remaining 7 scales were excluded from further analyses. The prorated raw scores for the 44 scales were then converted to MMPI-2-RF T scores. In the three samples used to test the fidelity of the estimation procedure, prorated T scores for the scales included in the investigation were all within 2 T-score points of the actual scale scores.

The first analysis involved a comparison of the MMPI-2-RF mean T scores and associated standard deviations for the Boes and colleagues (1997) sample and those of the 1,037 men included in the MMPI-2-RF Police Candidate Comparison Group (Corey & Ben-Porath, 2014). Mean T scores for the two samples were quite similar, with the vast majority falling within 1 or 2 points of each other and only one comparison (for TRIN-r) exceeding 5 T-score points, the benchmark typically used to identify an interpretable difference (Graham, 2012). The remarkable similarity between Boes and colleagues' sample and the MMPI-2-RF Police Candidate Comparison Group bolstered confidence in the generalizability of the predictive analyses to the MMPI-2-RF.

To examine the predictive validity of MMPI-2-RF scores, Tarescavage and colleagues (2016) identified a subsample of 161 officers who had not committed any of the integrity violations or other disciplinary infractions just discussed and contrasted their scores with those of individuals who committed each violation and infraction. Following the procedures of Sellbom and colleagues (2007) described earlier in this chapter, the authors calculated uncorrected and range-restriction-corrected correlations between the prehire MMPI-2-RF scores and posthire violations and infractions. Scores on several MMPI-2-RF substantive scales were meaningfully correlated (with corrected correlations typically of a small to medium effect size) with future integrity violations and disciplinary infractions. Scales from the emotional, thought, and behavioral domains were positively associated with use of excessive force, supervisory problems, substandard work performance, conduct unbecoming, procedural violations, private use of equipment, failure to attend court, embezzlement/fraud, accidents, dropping cases inappropriately, and off-duty violations.

As is the case with all of the samples used in the studies described in this section, these correlations reflect, by and large, variance that occurs below 65T. To examine the potential utility of lower cutoffs, Tarescavage and colleagues (2016) conducted relative risk ratio analyses and reported finding a substantially increased risk for integrity violations and disciplinary infractions associated with cutoffs ranging from 45T to 60T. For example, of the officers who had a T score at or above 55T on RC4, 28.6% were subsequently disciplined for conduct unbecoming, compared with only 8.8% of those who scored below 55T, which produces a relative risk ratio of 3.3. This indicates a threefold increase in the risk for misconduct in candidates who scored at or above 55T on RC4.

Corey, Sellbom, and Ben-Porath (2018)

Corey and colleagues (2018) observed that early studies of MMPI externalizing scales reported positive correlations with problem behavior in law enforcement officers but that later studies reported mixed findings or no significant correlations (or even negative associations). They designed a study to explore these associations with a large sample ($n = 1,226$) of police candidates. They examined correlations between MMPI-2-RF externalizing scale scores and personal history information (biodata) and found expected positive correlations. They then examined associations between posthire performance measures in a subsample of hired police officers and both MMPI-2-RF externalizing scale scores and biodata. The authors hypothesized and observed an association between problematic job performance and *low* scores on externalizing scales measuring disinhibition (particularly BXD, RC4, and DISC-r) but not antagonism (e.g., AGG, ACT, and AGGR-r). They discussed this finding as being consistent with overcontrolling tendencies leading to maladaptive behavioral constraint and inhibition in situations that appear risky and likely to evoke disturbing emotions. Finally, Corey and colleagues (2018) found that MMPI-2-RF low externalizing scale scores and biodata (the absence of a history of externalizing behavior problems) augmented each other in the prediction of poor performance outcomes, which is likely the result of overcontrolled behavior.

Roberts, Tarescavage, Ben-Porath, and Roberts (2019)

Roberts and colleagues (2019) examined associations between prehire-administered CPI (Gough, 1956) and prorated MMPI-2-RF scores (calculated from MMPI profiles) and supervisor ratings for a police officer sample of 143 men. They applied a statistical correction for range restriction and found meaningful associations between scores on both the CPI and MMPI-2-RF Substantive Scales and posthire supervisor ratings. For the MMPI-2-RF, the strongest associations with counterproductive behaviors were found for scales in the emotional dysfunction and interpersonal functioning domains.

The most notable associations between supervisor ratings and MMPI-2-RF interpersonal functioning scales were found for: (1) Cynicism (RC3 on the MMPI-2-RF; an Externalizing Specific Problems scale on the MMPI-3), which correlated with problems related to verbal communications, problem-solving, and reliability; (2) Family Problems (FML; also an externalizing scale on the MMPI-3), which predicted difficulties associated with verbal communications and problem-solving; and (3) Interpersonal Passivity (IPP), which was negatively correlated with problems in job knowledge, verbal communications, problem-solving, control of conflict, reliability, relations with coworkers, and relations with citizens. Among the externalizing dysfunction scales, Juvenile

Conduct Problems (JCP) scores correlated positively with dishonesty and lack of integrity; Aggression (AGG) and Aggressiveness (AGGR-r) with problems relating to verbal communication, patrol responsibility, officer safety, reliability, and relations with citizens; and Disconstraint (DISC-r) with alcohol problems.

Sellbom, Corey, and Ben-Porath (2021)

Sellbom and colleagues (2021) reported associations between prehire MMPI-2-RF scores and clinician ratings of suitability on the 10 CA-POST screening dimensions in a sample of 1,688 police candidates (including 218 women) as well as posthire performance data in a subsample of 396 of these candidates. Although to some extent likely inflated by criterion contamination, the authors found substantial associations between scores on the Higher-Order and RC Scales (the MMPI-2-RF scales that were the focus of this investigation) and clinician-rated deficiencies on the CA-POST dimensions. Specifically, concerns about emotional regulation and stress tolerance were associated with higher scores on EID, RCd, and RC7. Concerns related to avoiding damaging and excessive risk-taking were correlated with higher RC4 scores. Concerns about impulse control and attention to safety were related to higher BXD, RC4, and RC9 scale scores. Concerns related to candidates' assertiveness and persuasiveness were associated with higher EID and RC2 scores. Social competence concerns were correlated with higher EID scores. Concerns related to conscientiousness/dependability and integrity/ethics were associated with higher BDX and RC4 scores. Higher RC4 scores were also found to predict posthire difficulties related to cognitive adaptation, assertiveness, and stress-reactivity.

Menton, Corey, and Ben-Porath (2022)

Menton and colleagues (2022) compared MMPI-2-RF scores generated by in-person versus remote administration and in-person versus remote proctoring in the context of police candidate preemployment evaluations. The need for such research grew considerably following the onset of the Covid-19 pandemic and resultant increased use of teleassessment technology (see discussion of this topic in the *MMPI-3 User's Guide for the Public Safety Candidate Interpretive Reports* [Corey & Ben-Porath, 2022]; see also Corey & Ben-Porath [2020]). The authors compared data gathered from candidates who completed the test under standard, in-person conditions with data from candidates who completed the test remotely with Pearson's Q-global Remote On-Screen Assessment (ROSA) system, using either in-person or remote proctoring. They found that the standard group ($n = 3,311$), remote administration/in-person proctoring group (ROSA-IPP; $n = 108$), and remote administration/remote proctoring group (ROSA-RP; $n = 90$) all produced very similar score distributions, with group differences in means and standard deviations no greater than 2 T-score points per scale. Examination of the correlations between MMPI-2-RF externalizing scale scores and a set of relevant extratest criteria for the ROSA-IPP and ROSA-RP groups revealed little difference between groups and reflected patterns of convergent and discriminant validity similar to those observed in studies of the MMPI-2-RF under standard administration conditions. Taken together, these findings provided evidence that the MMPI-2-RF's psychometric properties in police candidate preemployment evaluations are equivalent regardless of whether the test is administered or proctored in person or remotely.

Applicability of MMPI-2-RF Findings to Public Safety Assessments With the MMPI-3

The *MMPI-3 Technical Manual* contains extensive empirical evidence supporting the construct validity and detailing the empirical correlates of MMPI-3 substantive scale scores. The MMPI-3 retains most of the substantive scales and roughly 80% of the test items from the MMPI-2-RF. Appendix D provides extensive external correlates of the MMPI-3 Substantive Scales, and Appendix E presents comprehensive comparisons of MMPI-3 external correlates with those of the MMPI-2-RF versions of the Substantive Scales. Chapter 3 of the *Technical Manual* provides correlations between MMPI-2-RF and MMPI-3 validity scale scores, including public safety candidate samples of men and women. These findings demonstrate very high cross-version correlations for the validity indicators. Taken together, the data demonstrate clearly that the empirical correlates of the MMPI-3 Substantive Scales, including correlates found in studies of police candidates, are essentially interchangeable with those of their MMPI-2-RF counterparts, and they provide compelling support for the application of the MMPI-2-RF research base to MMPI-3 interpretation. Findings also indicate that the Validity Scales function comparably across the two versions.

RESEARCH ON THE MMPI-3 IN POLICE AND OTHER PUBLIC SAFETY CANDIDATE EVALUATIONS

Data reported in the *MMPI-3 Technical Manual* include empirical correlates of the MMPI-3 Substantive Scales in two police candidate samples. The 1,513 members of the Pacific Northwest police candidate sample completed the MMPI-2-RF-EX as part of a postconditional offer preemployment psychological evaluation to determine their suitability for a police officer position. The evaluation included additional measures—the CPI and a psychosocial history questionnaire (biodata)—to formulate the examiners' recommendations. For a subset of those individuals who were hired, performance data related to their field training, captured with the SVS described earlier in this chapter, were also available.

CPI scores and biodata were available for a sufficiently large sample to conduct the analyses by gender. For both women and men, scores on the MMPI-3 externalizing scales BXD, RC4, JCP, and DISC were substantially associated with a self-reported history of violations of the law and substance use problems. Scores on the SUB scale were particularly associated with a self-reported history of both alcohol and drug use problems. Similar findings were obtained for both genders with the Roberts and Johnson (2001) CPI-based substance use probability scales. Of the latter, the Poor Psychological Suitability measure was substantially associated with MMPI-3 externalizing scales BXD, RC4, FML, and DISC in both genders. The CPI Involuntary Departure score was meaningfully correlated with MMPI-3 scales BXD, RC4, RC8, STR, FML, PSYC, and DISC for women in the Pacific Northwest police candidate sample. The Anger Problems index was correlated with MMPI-3 BXD, RC4, and DISC scores for both genders and ANP scores for women. Correlations between the MMPI-3 Substantive Scales and CPI scales were generally consistent with those reported for both genders in the Tarescavage, Fischler, and colleagues (2015) MMPI-2-RF study discussed earlier.

CPI data were also available for a sample of 164 Southern California police candidates who completed the MMPI-2-RF-EX as part of a preemployment psychological evaluation to determine their suitability for a police officer position. Owing to the relatively small sample size, these data were analyzed for a combined gender sample. Associations between MMPI-3 substantive scale scores and CPI scores were very similar to those just reported for the Pacific Northwest sample.

SVS outcome data were available in sufficient quantity for only a subsample of 134 men in the Pacific Northwest sample. In this sample, MMPI-3 THD scores were substantially associated with constraint problems and supervisor reports that they would not hire similar recruits. Higher RC8 scores were associated with supervisor reports of academic/learning problems, report-writing problems, not wanting to hire a similar recruit, overall performance problems, cognitive adaptation problems, constraint problems, stress-related problems, general decision-making problems, general learning problems, and multitasking problems. COG scores were correlated with general learning problems, HLP scores with report-writing and general learning problems, NFC with general learning problems, BRF with a negative appraisal of the recruit's overall performance, and FML and ACT with cognitive adaptation problems. Higher DSF scores were correlated with academic/learning problems, failure to control conflict, report-writing problems, a negative overall performance rating, stress-related problems, general learning problems, and general restraint/control problems. Higher AGGR scores were correlated with constraint problems. PSYC scores were associated with supervisor reports of academic/learning problems, not wanting to hire a similar recruit, overall performance problems, constraint problems, stress-related problems, and general decision-making problems. These findings were generally consistent with those reported in MMPI-2-RF studies when SVS data were available.

Use of the MMPI-2-RF-EX (described in chapter 2) to collect the data just described made it possible to compare correlations between MMPI-2-RF and MMPI-3 versions of the Substantive Scales and the available criterion data. These comparisons, provided in Appendix E of the *MMPI-3 Technical Manual,* indicate that the empirical correlates of police candidates' MMPI-3 substantive scale scores are essentially the same as those obtained with the MMPI-2-RF versions, supporting continued reliance on MMPI-2-RF findings when using the MMPI-3 in police candidate evaluations.

Whitman, Elias, Cappo, and Ben-Porath (2021)

Whitman and colleagues (2021) evaluated the criterion validity and practical utility of MMPI-3 scores in preemployment evaluations of 377 police candidates and 276 candidates for other public safety positions (including 48 dispatcher candidates, 44 security officer candidates, 45 firefighter candidates, and 27 correctional candidates). The sample included 110 female candidates. Research assistants reviewed the preemployment evaluation reports for the total sample and rated them on the 10 CA-POST screening dimensions, excluding the MMPI-3 interpretation sections. Mean MMPI-3 T scores generated by the male and female candidates and by the police and other public safety candidates were highly comparable and consistent with data reported in chapter 7.

MMPI-3 scale scores were meaningfully associated with problems reflected in the CA-POST dimension ratings. The patterns of MMPI-3 correlates were consistent with those found previously with the MMPI-2-RF, providing further support for cross-version compatibility of correlates. Relative risk ratio analyses supported the practical utility of the cutoffs used in the initial version of the MMPI-3 Police Candidate Interpretive Report (PCIR; Corey & Ben-Porath, 2020).

Whitman and colleagues (2021) also compared the validity findings across male and female and police and other public safety candidates. Of the 48 comparisons across male and female candidates, 13 were statistically significant—nine of these differences were small in magnitude. Of the remaining four comparisons, three showed larger effect sizes for female candidates and one for male candidates. Of the 48 comparisons across police candidates and candidates for other public safety positions, 14 were statistically significant, all with small effect sizes. Nine of these analyses indicated somewhat stronger validity in the non-police subgroup whereas four favored the police subgroup. Overall, these findings demonstrated the comparability of MMPI-3 scales scores and empirical correlates across gender and public safety position type.

Whitman, Corey, and Ben-Porath (2022)

Whitman and colleagues (2022) evaluated the validity of MMPI-3 scores among police ($n = 1,294$), correctional ($n = 190$), dispatcher ($n = 205$), and firefighter/medic ($n = 237$) candidates using psychosocial history data as the criteria. For the total sample, MMPI-3 scores were meaningfully associated with several aggregated scale scores derived from a standard psychosocial history questionnaire (Johnson et al., 2011), particularly in the behavioral/externalizing domain. To address limited research on preemployment personality testing among female police candidates and among non-police public safety occupations, Cohen's q was used to compare validity coefficients across male ($n = 1,095$) and female ($n = 199$) police candidates, and across police, correctional, dispatcher, and firefighter/medic candidates (ns listed above). Differences were minimal, with all statistically significant effects being small in magnitude, indicating that the MMPI-3 correlates identified with police candidates replicate across gender and to other public safety positions.

Whitman, Corey, and Ben-Porath (2023)

Whitman and colleagues (2023) compared MMPI-3 scores of police candidates with and without prior law enforcement experience to determine whether the stress experienced in the line of duty by the former impacts their psychological functioning as reflected in their test responses during a preemployment evaluation. Data were available for a sample of 400 police candidates (18.5% women) evaluated for positions at several law enforcement agencies. Results showed no practically meaningful differences when comparing MMPI-3 scores of candidates with no prior experience, less than 5 years of experience, and 5 or more years of experience. The authors also compared frequencies at which the three groups produced elevated MMPI-3 scales at cutoffs used in the *MMPI-3 Police Candidate Interpretive Report* and found minimal differences. Together, these findings indicate that MMPI-3 scores can be interpreted consistently with published guidelines regardless of a candidate's law enforcement experience.

Summary of MMPI-2-RF and MMPI-3 Findings

The studies described in this chapter provide a sound empirical foundation for using the MMPI-3 in assessments of police and other public safety candidates. The job-relevant correlates included in the MMPI-3 Public Safety Candidate Interpretive Reports are based on a distillation of these findings, incorporating ones that replicated across samples, criteria, and settings. This research also demonstrates the relevance and utility of using the MMPI-3 in preemployment evaluations of public safety candidates, establishing that the inventory meets federal and state legal and regulatory requirements for use of psychological tests that can predict relevant outcomes. Several general conclusions can be drawn about assessing public safety candidates with the MMPI-3.

The police candidate studies provide descriptive findings for the instrument's Substantive Scales. The reported means and standard deviations are remarkably consistent across studies, including the investigation conducted by Tarescavage and colleagues (2016) that used a police candidate data set compiled mainly in the 1980s with the original MMPI. This consistency points to the stability of police candidate psychological characteristics over time and across geographic regions. Moreover, descriptive findings reported by the various authors are also quite similar to the means and standard deviations on the 51 MMPI-2-RF scales in the MMPI-2-RF Police Candidate Comparison Group, which, as seen in Figures 7.1 to 7.5 in the next chapter, are nearly identical to those in the updated MMPI-3 Police Candidate Comparison Group.

Of particular note, in light of the relative paucity of data available for female police candidates and officers, similarities between male and female mean scores and standard deviations on the MMPI-2-RF scales reported by Tarescavage, Fischler, and colleagues (2015) and in the aforementioned comparison group indicate that outcome findings with the male samples can reasonably generalize to female candidates. This is further supported by the comparability of correlations between MMPI-3 scores and specialized CPI scales designed to predict various risks associated with hiring police candidates.

The samples used in the MMPI-2-RF and MMPI-3 substantive scales validation studies vary in terms of their ethnic and racial group composition, which is generally consistent with demographic characteristics of the populations in the geographic regions where the data were collected. The most diverse samples are available in the studies by Corey and colleagues (2018); Detrick and colleagues (2016); Tarescavage and colleagues (2016); and Tarescavage, Corey, and colleagues (2015). As noted, all of the study samples have very similar scale scores. In addition, there is considerable convergence in the empirical correlates found in these investigations. Along with a long line of research documenting the cross-cultural generalizability of MMPI findings (summarized by Ben-Porath and Sellbom, 2023), these results support use of the MMPI-3 with members of diverse racial and ethnic groups.

7

The MMPI-3 Public Safety Candidate Interpretive Reports

The MMPI-3 Public Safety Candidate Interpretive Reports (MMPI-3 PSCIRs) consist of four computer-generated, evidence-based, and annotated interpretive reports for evaluating candidates for the most common public safety positions: police officer (Police Candidate Interpretive Report [PCIR]), correctional officer (Correctional Candidate Interpretive Report [CCIR]), dispatcher (Dispatcher Candidate Interpretive Report [DCIR]), and firefighter/medic (Firefighter Candidate Interpretive Report [FCIR]). Each report is intended for use by professionals qualified to interpret the MMPI-3 in the context of preemployment psychological evaluations of police and other public safety candidates. The computer-generated narrative in each report focuses on identifying problems; it does not convey potential strengths. Thus, the information it contains should be considered in the context of the test taker's background, the demands of the position under consideration, the clinical interview, findings from supplemental tests, and other relevant information.

In this chapter, we describe the four MMPI-3 public safety candidate comparison groups used throughout the reports, provide an overview of the structure and content of the reports, and illustrate these themes with the PCIR produced in the case of Mr. E, a 27-year-old male police candidate (Figure 7.6). Item numbers and content that would normally be included in the reports are redacted for the purpose of maintaining test security. Each MMPI-3 PSCIR includes all the information provided in the MMPI-3 Score Report (see Ben-Porath & Tellegen, 2020c, for a complete description of this report) augmented by a detailed, automated interpretation of the test scores, focusing on their implications for the test taker's suitability for employment in the respective position.

The PSCIRs are designed to efficiently and consistently integrate the available literature to guide use of the MMPI-3 in preemployment assessments of public safety candidates. This includes the nearly 78,000 empirical correlates listed in the *MMPI-3 Technical Manual* (Ben-Porath & Tellegen, 2020b), the more than 54,000 empirical correlates contained in the *MMPI-2-RF Technical Manual* (Tellegen & Ben-Porath, 2008/2011), and more than 500 peer-reviewed publications, among them the studies described in chapter 6 that focus on assessment of police and other public safety candidates. Indeed, the PCIR alone incorporates from these studies nearly 300 job-relevant correlates involving 37 of the 42 substantive scales of the MMPI-3, including at 14 different T-score levels below 65.

Consideration and integration of this vast quantity of information are possible without use of a PSCIR; however, when properly done, that process could take considerably more than an hour per case and could lead to inconsistent interpretations both across and within examiners. Inconsistency in interpreting MMPI-3 results can occur in two forms: by failing to identify interpretable scores (frequently at levels below 65T) and their evidence-based correlates or by erroneously interpreting scores at levels not warranted by the empirical literature. The PSCIRs avoid these errors and provide this information consistently.

THE MMPI-3 PUBLIC SAFETY CANDIDATE COMPARISON GROUPS

The MMPI-3 PSCIRs rely on both the normative sample (i.e., general population norms, discussed in chapter 2) and representative samples of individuals tested to evaluate their psychological suitability for the same class of public safety position (i.e., police officer, correctional officer, dispatcher, and firefighter/medic). Data derived from these four comparison groups and incorporated in the interpretive reports include means and standard deviations on all 52 MMPI-3 scales, the percentage of individuals in the respective comparison group who scored at or below the test taker on each scale, and the percentage of individuals in the comparison group who responded the same as the test taker to individual items. This setting-specific information complements what can be learned from standard T scores and item-level information included in the standard MMPI-3 Score Report, which characterizes the test taker's scores and responses in reference only to the general population norms.

In this section, we provide detailed information concerning the members of the four comparison groups used in the PSCIRs. Each group is made up of an equal number of female and male candidates, which, as discussed earlier, does not accurately represent the gender distribution of entry-level police officers, correctional officers, dispatchers, or firefighters/medics. However, as discussed

TABLE 7.1. Geographic Distribution of the Police, Correctional, Dispatcher, and Firefighter Candidate Comparison Groups

Region	Men	Women	Total
POLICE CANDIDATES			
Midwest	199	199	398
South and Southeast	374	374	748
West and Northwest	389	389	778
Canada	56	56	112
Total	1,018	1,018	2,036
CORRECTIONAL CANDIDATES			
Southeast	138	138	276
West and Northwest	130	130	260
Total	268	268	536
DISPATCHER CANDIDATES			
Southeast	33	33	66
West and Northwest	95	95	190
Total	128	128	256
FIREFIGHTER/MEDIC CANDIDATES			
Midwest	10	10	20
West and Northwest	52	52	104
Southeast	48	48	96
Total	110	110	220

in chapter 5, this convention allows for use of a single, nongendered comparison group that conforms to the prohibition against using gender-based norms in employment-related testing mandated in the Civil Rights Act of 1991.

The geographic origins of the four comparison groups are listed in Table 7.1. These diverse candidate samples consist of individuals assessed in regions across the United States and, in the case of police candidates, in various Canadian provinces. These regions include ethnically heterogeneous urban areas as well as more rural communities. Agreements with some of the agencies that provided these comparison group data prohibit listing them by name. As shown in Table 7.2, the locations where the candidates spent most of their lives are well distributed across cities, suburbs, and rural areas.

Race/ethnicity for the members of the four comparison groups is reported in Table 7.3. The proportion of White candidates in the Police Candidate Comparison Group is consistent with the makeup of the MMPI-3 normative

TABLE 7.2. Community Origins of the Police, Correctional, Dispatcher, and Firefighter Candidate Comparison Groups

Community origin	N	%
POLICE CANDIDATES		
City	618	35.1
Suburb	777	44.1
Rural area	365	20.7
Total	1,760	100.0
CORRECTIONAL CANDIDATES		
City	199	41.4
Suburb	186	38.7
Rural area	96	20.0
Total	481	100.0
DISPATCHER CANDIDATES		
City	58	27.2
Suburb	98	46.0
Rural area	57	26.8
Total	213	100.0
FIREFIGHTER/MEDIC CANDIDATES		
City	43	24.0
Suburb	99	55.3
Rural area	37	20.7
Total	179	100.0

Note. Data were unavailable for a small number of police (n = 276, 13.6%), correctional (n = 55, 10.3%), dispatcher (n = 43, 16.8%), and firefighter/medic candidates (n = 37, 16.8%).

sample, which was designed to match the 2020 projections of the U.S. Census Bureau. Black candidates are overrepresented, whereas candidates of Hispanic origin are underrepresented in the comparison group when contrasted with the general population normative sample. This likely reflects the geographic distribution reported in Table 7.1. In the most recent report of race/ethnicity for law enforcement candidates, Castaneda and Ridgeway (2010) indicate that the primary race/ethnicity of current police and deputy sheriff recruits is 56% White, 25% Hispanic, 14% Black, 6% multiracial, 3% Asian, and 3% other. The Correctional Candidate Comparison Group contains the smallest proportion of White candidates (45.7%) and the highest percentage of Black candidates (34.6%), whereas the Dispatcher Candidate Comparison Group has the highest percentage of White candidates (73.9%) and the smallest proportion of Black candidates (10.7%).

TABLE 7.3. Race/Ethnicity of the Police, Correctional, Dispatcher, and Firefighter Candidate Comparison Groups

Race/ethnicity	N	%
POLICE CANDIDATES		
Asian	41	2.0
Black	471	23.5
Hispanic	166	8.3
White	1,187	59.2
Other	47	2.3
Mixed Race	92	4.6
Total	2,004	100.0
CORRECTIONAL CANDIDATES		
Asian	7	1.4
Black	175	34.6
Hispanic	65	12.8
White	231	45.7
Other	8	1.6
Mixed Race	20	4.0
Total	506	100.0
DISPATCHER CANDIDATES		
Asian	5	2.0
Black	27	10.7
Hispanic	19	7.5
White	187	73.9
Other	2	0.8
Mixed Race	13	5.1
Total	253	100.0
FIREFIGHTER/MEDIC CANDIDATES		
Asian	1	0.5
Black	27	12.9
Hispanic	21	10.0
White	142	67.9
Other	5	2.4
Mixed Race	13	6.2
Total	209	100.0

Note. A small number of police ($n = 32$), correctional ($n = 30$), dispatcher ($n = 3$), and firefighter/medic candidates ($n = 1$) did not provide this demographic information.

TABLE 7.4. Age Bands and Means/Standard Deviations of the Police, Correctional, Dispatcher, and Firefighter Candidate Comparison Groups

Age bands	N	%	Mean (s.d.)
POLICE CANDIDATES			
18-29	1,249	61.7	
30-39	545	26.9	
40-49	168	8.3	
50+	63	3.1	
Total	2,025	100.0	29.6 (7.8)
CORRECTIONAL CANDIDATES			
18-29	347	64.9	
30-39	126	23.6	
40-49	41	7.7	
50+	21	3.9	
Total	535	100.0	29.3 (8.3)
DISPATCHER CANDIDATES			
18-29	121	47.3	
30-39	83	32.4	
40-49	38	14.8	
50+	14	5.5	
Total	256	100.0	31.9 (9.1)
FIREFIGHTER/MEDIC CANDIDATES			
18-29	145	65.9	
30-39	56	25.5	
40-49	12	5.5	
50+	7	3.2	
Total	220	100.0	28.8 (8.0)

Note. Age information was not reported by $n = 1$ correctional candidate.

Table 7.4 provides the age bands for members of the four comparison groups, with nearly two thirds of the members of the police, correctional, and firefighter/medic comparison groups being between 18 and 29 years old, and fewer than half (47.3%) of the members of the dispatcher comparison group being under 30. The mean age of the police candidate sample (30.1 years) is slightly older than the mean recruit age of 27.4 years reported by Castaneda and Ridgeway (2010).

TABLE 7.5. Education Levels of the Police, Correctional, Dispatcher, and Firefighter Candidate Comparison Groups

N	No high school or GED	High school or GED	Some college	Bachelor's degree or higher
POLICE CANDIDATES				
2,001	0.6%	10.3%	44.1%	45.0%
CORRECTIONAL CANDIDATES				
536	0.2%	24.5%	45.4%	29.9%
DISPATCHER CANDIDATES				
256	0.0%	11.9%	58.0%	30.1%
FIREFIGHTER/MEDIC CANDIDATES				
210	0.0%	15.8%	52.7%	31.5%

Note. A small number of police (*n* = 35, 1.7%), correctional (*n* = 51, 9.5%), dispatcher (*n* = 37, 14.5%), and firefighter/medic candidates (*n* = 36, 16.4%) did not provide this demographic information.

Table 7.5 reports the education levels of the four comparison groups. Members of all four samples are comparatively well-educated, with more than three quarters having completed some college or earned a bachelor's or graduate degree. Based on these combined demographic data, it can be concluded that the four MMPI-3 public safety candidate comparison groups adequately represent the population of individuals assessed for these positions in North America.

Comparison Group Findings

Means and standard deviations of the 52 MMPI-3 scales for the police, correctional, dispatcher, and firefighter candidate comparison groups are reported in Table 7.6. Owing to the effects of the preselection factors discussed earlier in this chapter, these data reflect substantially below-average means (compared with general population norms) on nearly all of the substantive scales and most of the validity scales of the inventory, with the expected exception of the underreporting scales. Standard deviations associated with these means show markedly reduced variability compared with the general population norms, which is also a function of the previously discussed preselection factors. These two features of public safety candidate MMPI-3 scores (substantially attenuated means and standard deviations), coupled with research results reviewed earlier, indicate the need for and utility of using lower than the traditional T-score 65 cutoff when assessing public safety candidates with the inventory. Implications of these features are considered in the Comparison Group Findings and Job-Relevant Correlates sections of each PSCIR, as described later in this chapter.

TABLE 7.6. Means and Standard Deviations for the Police, Correctional, Dispatcher, and Firefighter Candidate Comparison Groups

	Police (N = 2,036)		Correctional (N = 536)		Dispatcher (N = 256)		Firefighter (N = 220)	
	M	SD	M	SD	M	SD	M	SD
CRIN	39	5	41	6	40	6	38	5
VRIN	39	5	41	6	40	6	39	5
TRIN	52F	5	53F	7	53F	6	52F	5
F	42	2	42	2	42	3	42	2
Fp	43	4	44	5	43	5	43	4
Fs	44	4	44	4	44	5	43	4
FBS	45	6	45	6	46	6	46	5
RBS	45	6	46	6	45	6	44	6
L	57	12	61	13	54	11	58	11
K	65	7	64	8	64	9	66	7
EID	37	5	38	5	39	6	37	5
THD	42	6	43	6	41	6	41	5
BXD	41	6	41	6	41	6	41	6
RCd	39	4	39	4	40	6	38	4
RC1	40	5	41	6	41	7	40	5
RC2	42	6	42	6	45	7	42	6
RC4	43	6	42	6	42	6	41	6
RC6	43	5	43	6	43	6	43	6
RC7	39	5	39	5	39	6	39	6
RC8	42	6	43	6	42	6	42	5
RC9	42	7	43	7	42	7	43	7
MLS	36	4	37	5	39	6	36	4
NUC	43	6	44	6	43	7	42	6
EAT	44	3	44	3	45	4	44	4
COG	40	4	40	4	41	4	41	5
SUI	45	2	45	2	45	4	45	4
HLP	42	4	42	4	42	4	41	4
SFD	41	3	42	4	43	6	42	4
NFC	41	5	42	5	41	5	41	5
STR	42	5	42	5	42	6	43	6
WRY	40	5	40	5	41	6	40	5
CMP	47	8	48	8	46	7	47	8
ARX	40	4	41	5	41	6	40	5

	Police (N = 2,036)		Correctional (N = 536)		Dispatcher (N = 256)		Firefighter (N = 220)	
	M	SD	M	SD	M	SD	M	SD
ANP	40	4	40	5	40	5	40	5
BRF	44	4	45	6	45	6	44	5
FML	41	6	42	6	42	7	41	6
JCP	44	7	44	7	43	6	43	6
SUB	42	5	42	4	43	5	43	5
IMP	41	5	41	6	42	6	42	6
ACT	45	8	47	9	44	8	45	8
AGG	43	5	43	5	42	5	42	5
CYN	41	8	44	10	40	8	39	8
SFI	51	8	52	9	49	8	52	10
DOM	49	8	50	8	48	8	48	7
DSF	43	6	44	6	44	6	42	5
SAV	45	7	47	8	47	9	44	7
SHY	42	6	42	6	44	8	42	7
AGGR	47	6	48	6	46	6	46	6
PSYC	42	6	44	7	42	6	42	5
DISC	42	6	42	6	42	6	42	6
NEGE	40	5	40	5	41	6	40	5
INTR	45	7	46	7	47	8	44	6

Table 7.7 reports the percent of MMPI-3 comparison group members who score at or below various T-score cutoffs. As depicted in this table, T scores greater than 65 on the inconsistent response (CRIN, VRIN, and TRIN) and overreporting (F, Fp, Fs, FBS, and RBS) validity scales are extremely rare in public safety candidates. In contrast, scores on MMPI-3 underreporting indicators are commonly elevated, as would be expected considering the demand characteristics of these assessments. L scores at or above 80T are relatively uncommon; however, a K score at or above 70T occurs in 32% or more of all four comparison groups. Elevation rates for substantive scale cutoffs are provided beginning at T score of 55. As reported in Table 7.6, scores at this level often fall more than two standard deviations above the comparison group mean. This is particularly true for MMPI-3 measures of emotional dysfunction. For example, T scores of 55 or higher on Emotional/Internalizing Dysfunction (EID) occur in only 0.2% of police and correctional candidates, 0.9% of firefighter/medic

TABLE 7.7. Percent Scoring at or Above Designated Cutoffs for the Police, Correctional, Dispatcher, and Firefighter Candidate Comparison Groups

	Cutoff	Police (N = 2,036)	Correctional (N = 536)	Dispatcher (N = 256)	Firefighter (N = 220)
CRIN	70	0.1	0.2	0.0	0.0
CRIN	65	0.2	0.6	0.0	0.0
CRIN	60	0.7	1.9	0.8	0.5
CRIN	55	1.1	4.1	2.7	0.5
VRIN	70	0.0	0.4	0.0	0.0
VRIN	65	0.1	0.4	0.0	0.0
VRIN	60	1.0	2.8	1.2	0.2
VRIN	55	2.5	5.6	2.3	2.7
TRIN	70 (T or F)	0.2	0.7	0.4	0.0
TRIN	65 (T or F)	1.4	3.5	2.3	2.3
TRIN	60 (T or F)	6.5	11.2	10.2	8.2
TRIN	55 (T or F)	6.5	11.2	10.2	8.2
F	70	0.0	0.0	0.4	0.0
F	65	0.0	0.0	0.4	0.0
F	60	0.0	0.2	0.4	0.5
F	55	0.1	0.6	1.6	0.5
Fp	75	0.0	0.0	0.0	0.0
Fp	70	0.0	0.0	0.0	0.0
Fp	65	0.2	0.4	1.2	0.5
Fp	60	0.2	0.4	1.2	0.5
Fp	55	2.3	3.7	3.5	2.3
Fs	80	0.0	0.0	0.4	0.0
Fs	75	0.0	0.0	0.4	0.0
Fs	70	0.0	0.0	0.4	0.0
Fs	65	0.1	0.4	1.2	0.5
Fs	60	0.3	0.7	2.3	0.5
Fs	55	1.2	2.6	2.3	1.8
FBS	75	0.0	0.0	0.0	0.0
FBS	70	0.1	0.2	0.0	0.5
FBS	65	0.1	0.2	0.0	0.5
FBS	60	0.4	0.9	3.5	1.4
FBS	55	2.5	3.5	7.0	4.1

	Cutoff	Police (N = 2,036)	Correctional (N = 536)	Dispatcher (N = 256)	Firefighter (N = 220)
RBS	65	0.0	0.6	0.0	0.9
RBS	60	0.6	1.9	0.8	0.9
RBS	55	2.9	5.2	3.5	2.3
L	85	1.8	3.5	1.6	0.0
L	80	5.0	10.1	3.1	3.2
L	75	9.4	16.4	5.9	9.1
L	70	15.9	25.4	10.2	13.2
L	65	32.2	43.1	25.0	32.7
L	60	41.5	54.9	31.6	47.3
L	55	52.9	65.5	42.6	60.0
K	70	36.2	34.0	32.0	42.7
K	65	66.6	61.0	60.2	72.7
K	60	76.8	72.6	69.5	80.0
K	55	89.8	87.3	82.4	91.8
EID	55	0.2	0.2	2.7	0.9
THD	70	0.0	0.0	0.4	0.0
THD	65	0.2	0.6	0.4	0.5
THD	60	1.0	1.9	1.6	0.9
THD	55	3.5	5.2	3.9	3.2
BXD	65	0.0	0.2	0.0	0.0
BXD	60	0.3	0.7	0.4	1.4
BXD	55	1.3	1.9	1.2	2.3
RCd	65	0.0	0.0	0.8	0.0
RCd	60	0.0	0.0	0.8	0.0
RCd	55	0.1	0.2	2.3	0.9
RC1	70	0.1	0.0	0.8	0.0
RC1	65	0.2	0.0	1.2	0.0
RC1	60	0.3	0.2	1.2	0.0
RC1	55	1.8	3.9	5.9	2.3
RC2	75	0.0	0.0	0.4	0.0
RC2	70	0.1	0.0	0.4	0.5
RC2	65	0.2	0.4	2.0	0.5
RC2	60	0.9	0.7	3.5	0.5
RC2	55	2.0	1.9	8.6	1.8

(*continued on next page*)

TABLE 7.7, continued

	Cutoff	Police (N = 2,036)	Correctional (N = 536)	Dispatcher (N = 256)	Firefighter (N = 220)
RC4	70	0.1	0.2	0.0	0.0
RC4	65	0.2	0.4	0.0	0.5
RC4	60	0.6	0.6	0.4	0.9
RC4	55	3.4	3.7	3.1	2.7
RC6	75	0.0	0.0	0.4	0.5
RC6	70	0.2	0.2	0.8	0.9
RC6	65	0.4	0.7	1.2	0.9
RC6	60	2.0	2.6	2.0	2.3
RC6	55	8.0	8.8	6.3	8.2
RC7	65	0.0	0.2	0.4	0.9
RC7	60	0.1	0.6	0.4	0.9
RC7	55	0.5	1.1	1.2	1.4
RC8	80	0.0	0.0	0.0	0.0
RC8	75	0.1	0.0	0.4	0.0
RC8	70	0.2	0.6	0.8	0.0
RC8	65	0.5	0.9	1.2	0.0
RC8	60	0.9	1.7	2.0	0.0
RC8	55	3.7	5.0	3.9	1.8
RC9	85	0.0	0.2	0.0	0.0
RC9	80	0.0	0.2	0.0	0.0
RC9	75	0.0	0.2	0.0	0.5
RC9	70	0.2	0.4	0.4	0.9
RC9	65	0.6	0.7	0.8	1.4
RC9	60	2.1	1.7	1.6	2.7
RC9	55	3.5	4.7	3.1	4.5
MLS	65	0.0	0.0	0.4	0.0
MLS	60	0.0	0.0	0.4	0.0
MLS	55	0.2	0.0	2.0	0.0
NUC	75	0.0	0.0	0.4	0.0
NUC	70	0.2	0.0	0.8	0.0
NUC	65	0.5	0.6	0.8	0.0
NUC	60	1.6	2.6	3.1	1.4
NUC	55	4.3	6.3	7.0	2.7

	Cutoff	Police (N = 2,036)	Correctional (N = 536)	Dispatcher (N = 256)	Firefighter (N = 220)
EAT	85	0.0	0.0	0.0	0.0
EAT	80	0.0	0.0	0.0	0.0
EAT	75	0.0	0.0	0.4	0.0
EAT	70	0.0	0.0	0.4	0.0
EAT	65	0.7	0.4	1.6	1.4
EAT	60	0.7	0.4	1.6	1.4
EAT	55	4.1	5.2	6.6	5.5
COG	70	0.0	0.0	0.0	0.5
COG	65	0.1	0.0	0.0	1.4
COG	60	0.4	0.0	0.8	1.4
COG	55	0.9	0.0	1.2	2.3
SUI	80	0.0	0.0	0.4	0.5
SUI	75	0.0	0.0	0.4	0.5
SUI	70	0.0	0.0	0.4	0.5
SUI	65	0.1	0.4	1.2	1.4
SUI	60	0.1	0.4	1.2	1.4
SUI	55	1.9	1.5	5.9	3.2
HLP	65	0.0	0.2	0.4	0.5
HLP	60	0.0	0.2	0.4	0.5
HLP	55	0.7	1.5	1.2	0.5
SFD	70	0.0	0.0	0.8	0.0
SFD	65	0.0	0.0	2.0	0.0
SFD	60	0.0	0.0	2.0	0.0
SFD	55	1.0	1.1	5.1	2.3
NFC	70	0.0	0.0	0.0	0.0
NFC	65	0.1	0.2	0.0	0.0
NFC	60	0.1	0.2	1.2	1.4
NFC	55	0.7	1.5	2.0	1.4
STR	75	0.0	0.0	0.4	0.5
STR	70	0.0	0.0	0.4	0.5
STR	65	0.1	0.4	0.8	1.4
STR	60	0.1	0.4	0.8	1.4
STR	55	0.7	0.9	1.2	2.3

(continued on next page)

TABLE 7.7, continued

	Cutoff	Police (N = 2,036)	Correctional (N = 536)	Dispatcher (N = 256)	Firefighter (N = 220)
WRY	70	0.1	0.4	1.2	0.0
WRY	65	0.4	0.4	1.2	0.9
WRY	60	0.4	0.7	2.3	0.9
WRY	55	0.4	0.7	2.3	0.9
CMP	75	0.8	0.7	0.4	1.8
CMP	70	0.8	0.7	0.4	1.8
CMP	65	7.3	3.9	1.6	6.8
CMP	60	7.3	10.8	7.0	6.8
CMP	55	14.8	17.5	13.3	14.1
ARX	85	0.0	0.2	0.0	0.0
ARX	80	0.0	0.2	0.0	0.0
ARX	75	0.0	0.2	0.0	0.0
ARX	70	0.0	0.2	0.0	0.0
ARX	65	0.0	0.2	0.4	0.5
ARX	60	0.0	0.6	0.4	0.9
ARX	55	0.4	0.9	1.6	1.4
ANP	70	0.1	0.2	0.0	0.5
ANP	65	0.1	0.4	0.0	0.5
ANP	60	0.2	0.4	0.0	1.4
ANP	55	0.4	0.6	0.8	1.8
BRF	80	0.1	0.2	0.0	0.0
BRF	75	0.1	0.2	0.0	0.0
BRF	70	0.2	0.7	0.4	1.4
BRF	65	0.2	3.5	3.1	1.4
BRF	60	1.0	3.5	3.1	1.8
BRF	55	10.0	15.1	14.5	6.4
FML	85	0.0	0.0	0.0	0.0
FML	80	0.0	0.0	0.4	0.0
FML	75	0.0	0.0	0.4	0.0
FML	70	0.1	0.0	0.4	0.5
FML	65	0.4	0.2	0.8	0.5
FML	60	0.4	0.2	0.8	0.5
FML	55	2.8	4.5	5.9	2.3

	Cutoff	Police (N = 2,036)	Correctional (N = 536)	Dispatcher (N = 256)	Firefighter (N = 220)
JCP	80	0.0	0.0	0.0	0.0
JCP	75	0.0	0.0	0.0	0.0
JCP	70	0.2	0.4	0.0	0.0
JCP	65	0.7	1.5	0.0	0.9
JCP	60	2.8	4.1	2.0	2.3
JCP	55	8.6	9.5	6.3	5.9
SUB	65	0.0	0.2	0.0	0.5
SUB	60	0.0	0.2	0.0	0.5
SUB	55	0.5	0.2	1.2	0.9
IMP	75	0.0	0.0	0.0	0.0
IMP	70	0.0	0.0	0.0	0.0
IMP	65	0.4	0.4	0.0	0.9
IMP	60	0.4	0.4	0.0	0.9
IMP	55	1.7	2.6	3.5	3.2
ACT	80	0.1	0.6	0.4	0.0
ACT	75	0.1	0.6	0.4	0.0
ACT	70	1.0	2.2	1.2	0.0
ACT	65	3.6	6.0	3.5	2.7
ACT	60	3.6	6.0	3.5	2.7
ACT	55	10.2	13.8	7.8	9.5
AGG	75	0.1	0.0	0.0	0.0
AGG	70	0.2	0.6	0.0	0.9
AGG	65	0.2	0.6	0.0	0.9
AGG	60	1.6	1.7	1.6	1.4
AGG	55	5.6	4.9	3.5	6.8
CYN	75	0.0	0.4	0.0	0.0
CYN	70	1.1	1.9	1.2	1.4
CYN	65	2.3	5.8	2.0	2.3
CYN	60	4.4	11.2	3.5	5.5
CYN	55	8.3	15.1	5.9	6.4
SFI	70	5.4	6.5	3.5	10.9
SFI	65	5.4	6.5	3.5	10.9
SFI	60	19.1	24.4	15.6	22.3
SFI	55	19.1	24.4	15.6	22.3

(*continued on next page*)

TABLE 7.7, continued

	Cutoff	Police (N = 2,036)	Correctional (N = 536)	Dispatcher (N = 256)	Firefighter (N = 220)
DOM	65	5.7	7.6	7.8	2.7
DOM	60	5.7	7.6	7.8	2.7
DOM	55	27.5	33.8	23.0	22.3
DSF	75	0.0	0.2	0.4	0.0
DSF	70	0.3	0.4	0.4	0.0
DSF	65	0.8	1.9	1.2	0.0
DSF	60	0.8	1.9	1.2	0.0
DSF	55	5.2	9.0	7.8	0.5
SAV	75	0.0	0.0	0.4	0.0
SAV	70	0.3	1.3	3.1	0.9
SAV	65	1.6	3.0	5.9	0.9
SAV	60	4.6	6.2	10.2	1.4
SAV	55	9.6	14.6	14.5	5.5
SHY	75	0.1	0.2	1.2	0.0
SHY	70	0.1	0.2	1.2	0.0
SHY	65	0.7	0.9	2.3	1.4
SHY	60	1.5	2.4	5.1	4.5
SHY	55	3.6	3.9	11.7	5.0
AGGR	75	0.0	0.2	0.0	0.0
AGGR	70	0.0	0.4	0.0	0.0
AGGR	65	0.7	1.1	0.4	0.9
AGGR	60	2.6	3.0	3.1	1.4
AGGR	55	8.3	11.9	8.6	5.9
PSYC	75	0.0	0.4	0.0	0.0
PSYC	70	0.1	0.4	0.0	0.0
PSYC	65	0.3	0.7	0.8	0.0
PSYC	60	0.7	1.7	1.6	0.0
PSYC	55	4.9	7.8	6.3	2.7
DISC	70	0.0	0.0	0.0	0.0
DISC	65	0.0	0.2	0.0	0.0
DISC	60	0.3	0.4	0.0	0.9
DISC	55	1.6	1.5	2.3	2.7

	Cutoff	Police (N = 2,036)	Correctional (N = 536)	Dispatcher (N = 256)	Firefighter (N = 220)
NEGE	75	0.0	0.0	0.4	0.0
NEGE	70	0.0	0.2	0.4	0.0
NEGE	65	0.0	0.2	0.8	0.5
NEGE	60	0.1	0.2	1.6	0.9
NEGE	55	0.2	0.4	2.0	1.4
INTR	75	0.0	0.2	0.4	0.0
INTR	70	0.0	0.2	1.2	0.0
INTR	65	1.2	2.1	3.9	0.9
INTR	60	3.3	5.4	8.2	1.4
INTR	55	6.3	9.1	12.1	2.7

candidates, and 2.7% of dispatcher candidates. Clinically elevated T scores (at or above 65) are extremely rare for all Substantive Scales in the four comparison groups. By and large, with the exception of the Self-Importance (SFI) scale, less than 10% of any of the public safety candidate comparison group members score at or above 60T on the MMPI-3 Substantive Scales.

The findings reported in Table 7.7 are generally quite comparable across groups; although, correctional candidates are somewhat more likely than members of the other comparison groups to produce T scores of 55 or higher on L, CYN, and DOM. In summary, these groups' largely comparable composition and remarkably similar MMPI-3 descriptive findings are consistent with observations (e.g., Corey & Ben-Porath, 2018; Corey & Detrick, 2022; Knatz et al., 1992) that police, correctional, dispatcher, and firefighter/medic candidates share common criterion standards and produce comparable scores and validity findings (e.g., Whitman et al., 2021; Whitman et al., 2022a).

As noted, the percent of comparison group members scoring at or above cutoffs typically used with the MMPI-3 underreporting scales is relatively high. This reflects the high base rate for underreporting in preemployment candidates, as well as the impact of confounds discussed in chapters 3 and 6 (i.e., a traditional upbringing for L and good adjustment for K) in the context of the Detrick and Chibnall (2014) study. In light of these findings, we do not recommend applying the standard guidelines to these scales when interpreting public safety candidates' MMPI-3 scores. Concern about the possible deleterious effects of underreporting is indicated if a candidate's L score reaches or exceeds 77T, which occurs in as few as 5.9% (dispatcher candidates) and as many as 16.4% (correctional candidates). This is particularly so in cases where it reaches or exceeds 86T, which occurs in no more than 3.5% (correctional candidates) of the four comparison group members. As reflected in Table 7.7, more than two thirds of police candidates score at or above 65T on K, reflecting both the highly preselected (and therefore well-adjusted) nature of this population and the impact of attempting to appear psychologically healthy. Among the other three comparison groups, no fewer than 60.2% (dispatcher candidates) and as many as 72.7% (firefighter/medic candidates) score at or above 65T on K. Consequently, only T scores that reach the highest possible value (74) on this scale can be viewed as indicating a *possibility* of significant underreporting; although, as many as 18.2% of the Police Candidate Comparison Group and as few as 14.5% of the Dispatcher Candidate Comparison Group obtained that score.

Figures 7.1 through 7.5 provide a visual comparison of the means and standard deviations of the 52 MMPI-3 scales for the four PSCIR comparison groups. By convention, group mean differences must reach or exceed 5 T-score points to be considered meaningful. Among the Validity Scales, only L shows a mean difference greater than 5 points, with dispatcher candidates having the lowest mean score of 54T and correctional candidates having the highest mean score of 61T. With the exception of the CYN scale, on which the dispatcher candidate mean also falls 5 points lower than the correctional candidate mean, none of the comparison group differences exceed 5 points on any of the substantive scales, and most means fall within 2 to 3 points of each other, with comparable standard deviations. This remarkable similarity across the four comparison groups reflects commonalities in the selection process leading to a conditional offer of employment for all four positions (e.g., passing a background investigation), as well as common demand characteristics to appear well-adjusted.

In summary, these groups' largely comparable composition and remarkably similar MMPI-3 descriptive findings are consistent with our observations in chapter 1 that the essential job functions of police officers, correctional officers, dispatchers, and firefighters/medics (Table 1.1), and the psychological demands for these positions (Table 1.3), share considerable commonalities. Because the potential problems that public safety employers seek to avoid (Table 1.2) are also similar, and a common set of attributes rated as important for all four positions can be identified (Table 1.4), these similarities are also consistent with our discussion in chapter 1 of the likely applicability of findings from police candidate research to preemployment assessments for all four public safety positions. Use of the descriptive findings reported here and available in the MMPI-3 PSCIRs is illustrated with case studies in chapter 8.

STRUCTURE AND CONTENT OF THE MMPI-3 PUBLIC SAFETY CANDIDATE INTERPRETIVE REPORTS

The first seven pages of any PSCIR are identical to those of the standard MMPI-3 Score Report, with the exception that any score interpreted in a PSCIR is bolded on page 7 of the report, which provides scores on the 52 MMPI-3

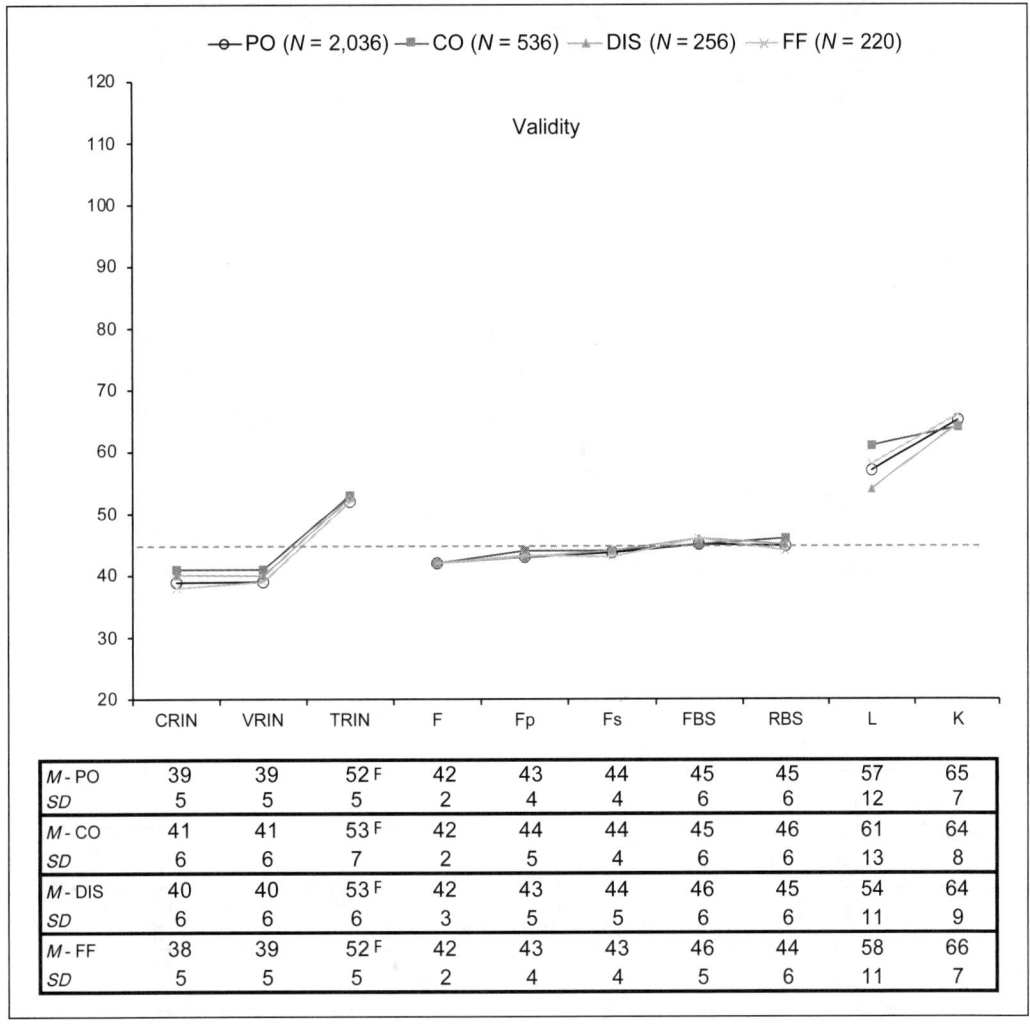

FIGURE 7.1. Police, Correctional, Dispatcher, and Firefighter Candidate Comparison Groups: MMPI-3 Validity Scales Means and Standard Deviations

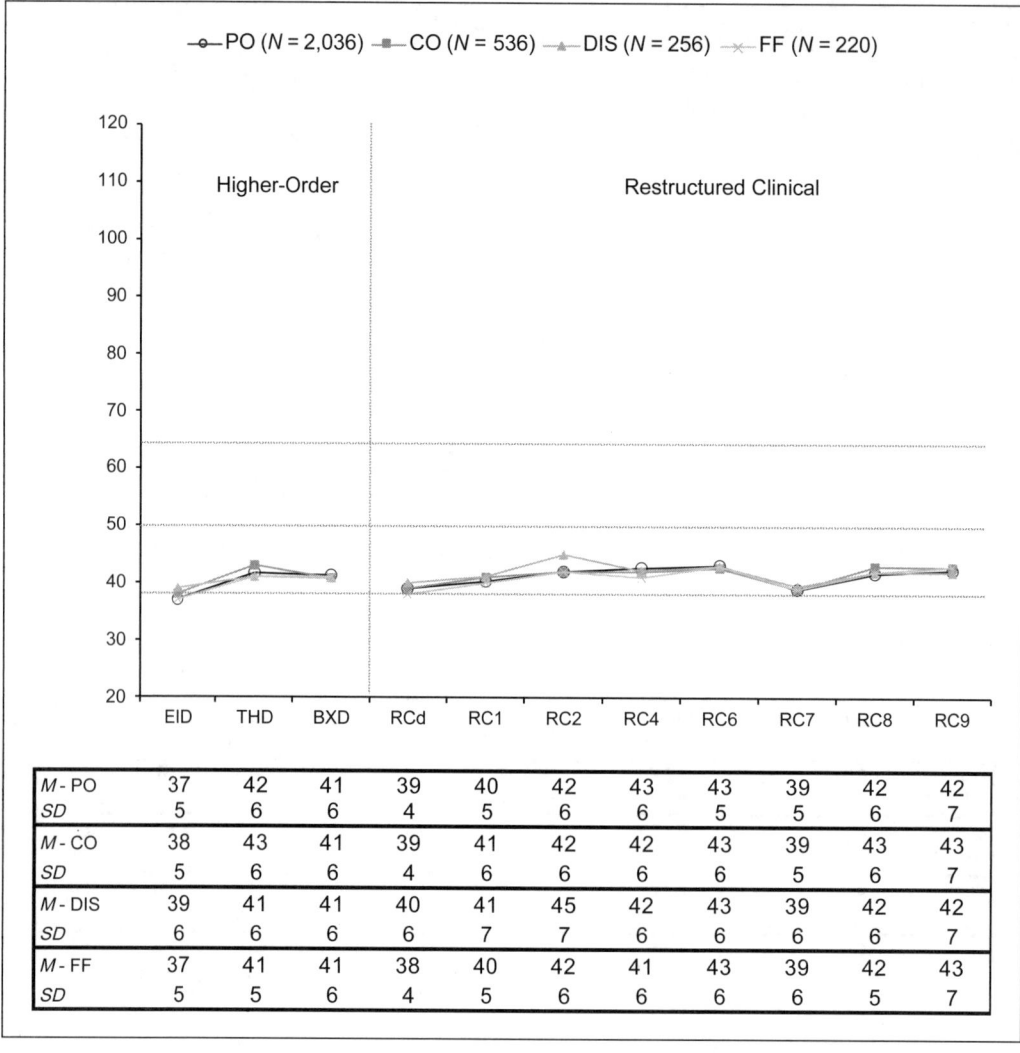

FIGURE 7.2. Police, Correctional, Dispatcher, and Firefighter Candidate Comparison Groups: MMPI-3 Higher-Order (H-O) and Restructured Clinical (RC) Scales Means and Standard Deviations

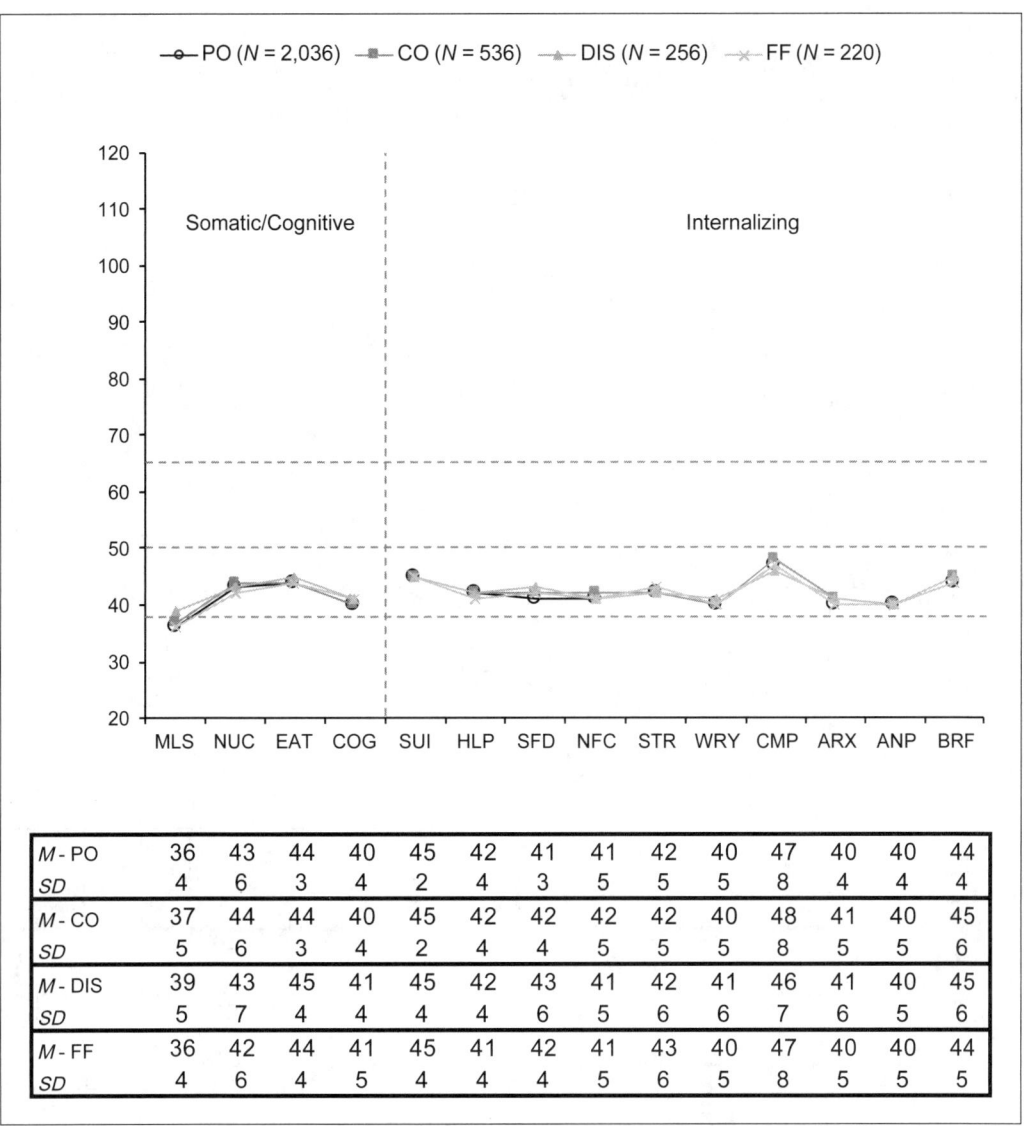

FIGURE 7.3. Police, Correctional, Dispatcher, and Firefighter Candidate Comparison Groups: MMPI-3 Somatic/Cognitive and Internalizing Scales Means and Standard Deviations

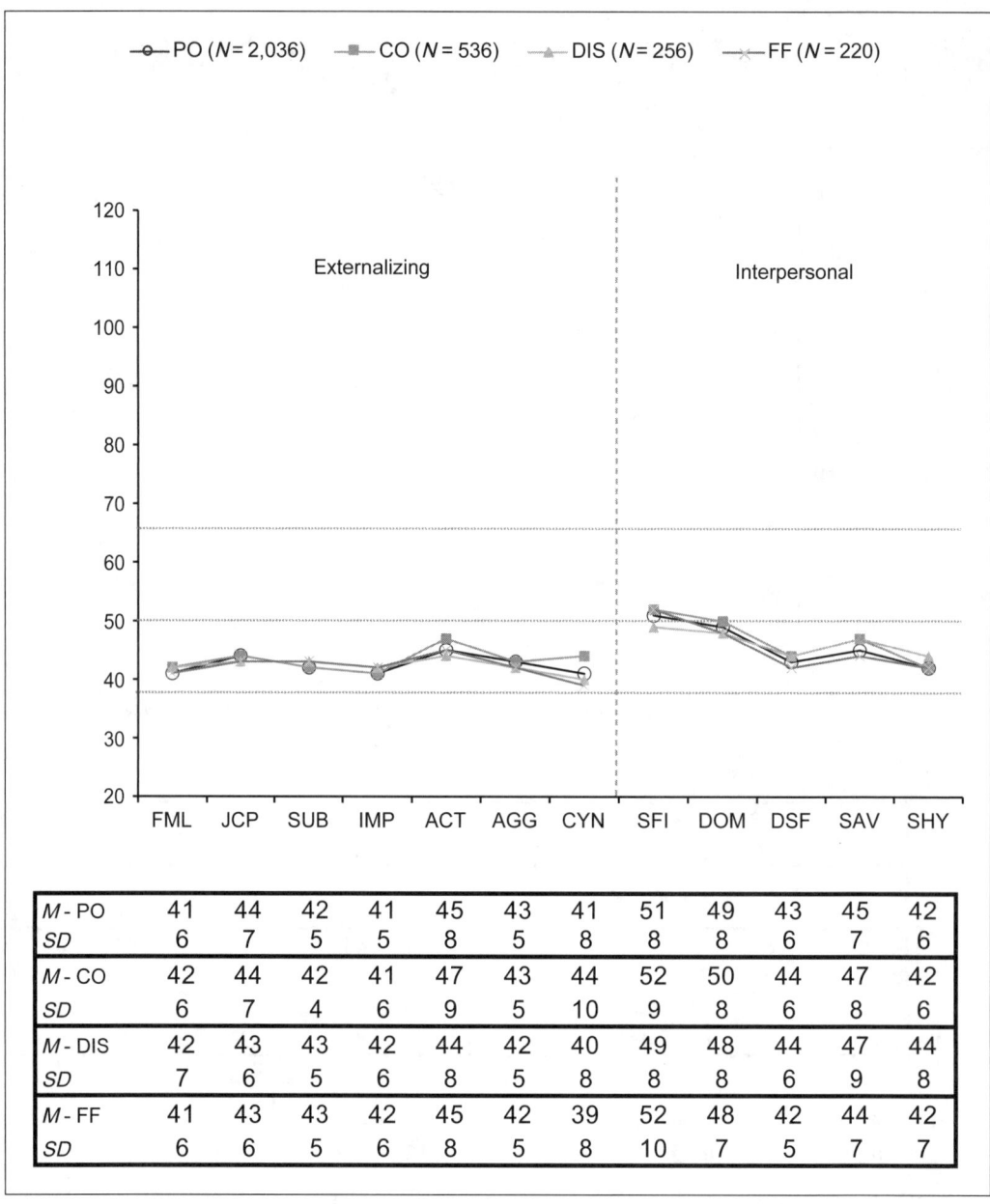

FIGURE 7.4. Police, Correctional, Dispatcher, and Firefighter Candidate Comparison Groups: MMPI-3 Externalizing and Interpersonal Scales Means and Standard Deviations

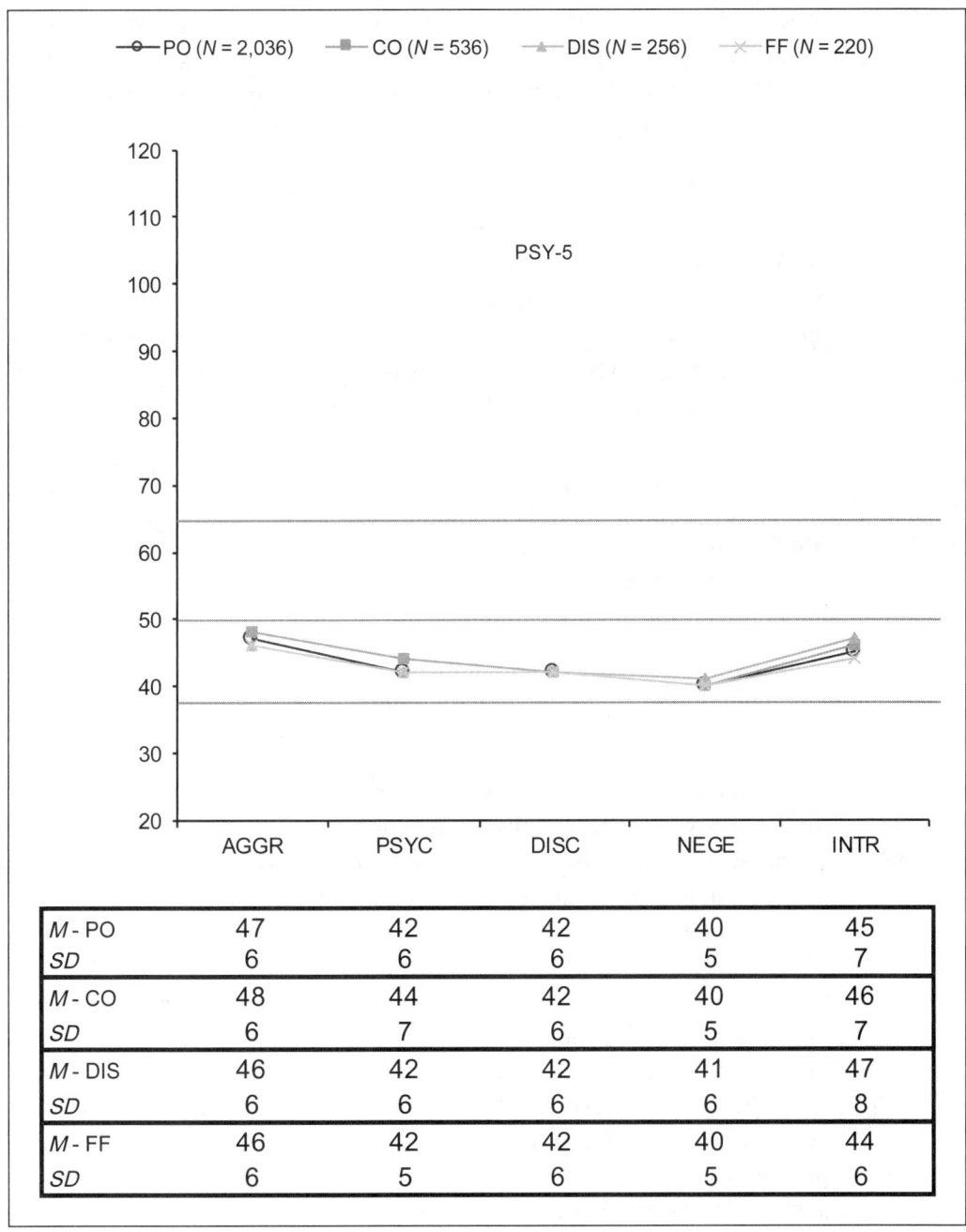

FIGURE 7.5. Police, Correctional, Dispatcher, and Firefighter Candidate Comparison Groups: MMPI-3 PSY-5 Scales Means and Standard Deviations

scales organized by the applicable interpretive domains. In Mr. E's case (Figure 7.6), for example, scores on THD, RC6, RC8, DOM, AGGR, and PSYC are printed in bold, indicating that these findings are interpreted in the report. The automated interpretation begins on page 8 of the PCIR and consists of seven major sections: Synopsis, Protocol Validity, Clinical Findings, Diagnostic Considerations, Comparison Group Findings, Job-Relevant Correlates, and Item-Level Information. All interpretive statements in the report are annotated with Endnotes (on page 12 in Mr. E's case), indicating for each statement whether it is based on empirical correlates, test item content, or inference of the report authors. Any statement identified as based on empirical correlates includes reference numbers associated with the Research Reference List, which appears immediately following the Endnotes section.

Synopsis

The Synopsis section provides a brief overview of the major findings pertaining to the interpretability of the results, any substantive scale scores in the clinically interpretable range (T score 65 or higher), comparison group findings, and job-relevant correlates.

Protocol Validity

The Protocol Validity section provides information about three types of threats to the validity of the test results: content nonresponsiveness (unscorable or inconsistent responses), overreporting, and underreporting. For cases in which possible validity threats are indicated, the prevalence of these scores in the respective comparison group is reported.

For cases in which no protocol validity concerns are indicated by scores on the Validity Scales, a brief statement to that effect will appear in this section. Underreporting, the most common threat to protocol validity in public safety candidate evaluations (Detrick & Chibnall, 2014; Whitman et al., 2021), is addressed with special PSCIR features designed to assist examiners in the inferential task of differentiating candidates who, consistent with their self-presentation, are, in fact, morally virtuous and well-adjusted from those who are actively engaged in deceptive efforts.

In cases where L is substantially elevated, the report prints MMPI-3 items with potentially verifiable historical content to aid the examiner in detecting discrepancies from other self-report or background information. The report authors selected these items on the basis of their review of the entire MMPI-3 booklet. When evaluating what inferences to draw from elevated underreporting scores, responses to these items, considered in the context of collateral information, can aid test users in differentiating naïve responses (often occurring in individuals with a background stressing traditional values) from intentionally deceptive ones, as reflected by discrepancies between a test taker's responses and available extratest information. An illustration using these item responses is provided in the next chapter with the case of Mr. D (Figure 8.1).

Clinical Findings

The interpretation provided in this section of the report is divided into five areas, each described in a separate paragraph (but without a subheading): Somatic/Cognitive Dysfunction, Emotional/Internalizing Dysfunction, Thought Dysfunction, Behavioral/Externalizing Dysfunction, and Interpersonal Functioning. Findings on the Substantive Scales are interpreted in these paragraphs if clinically elevated cutoffs (T score 65 or higher, except for EAT, SUI, and CMP, which are 75T, 58T, and 62T, respectively) are reached. In Mr. E's case, on page 9 of the report, this involves interpretation of a clinically elevated DOM score.

Diagnostic Considerations

This section can be suppressed at the user's option before generating the report (see *MMPI-3 User's Guide for the Public Safety Candidate Interpretive Reports*, Corey & Ben-Porath, 2022, for details). Diagnostic considerations are listed under four possible subheadings: Emotional/Internalizing Disorders, Thought Disorders, Behavioral/Externalizing Disorders, and Interpersonal Disorders. If none of the possibilities listed under any of these subheadings is indicated by the test scores, that subheading is not printed in the report. In Mr. E's case, on page 9 of the report, diagnostic considerations are listed for Interpersonal Disorders.

Comparison Group Findings

Construct-based statements that describe implications of clinically elevated substantive scale scores, as well as statements about possible implications of uncommonly high (but not clinically elevated) scores for public safety candidates, are included in this section of the PSCIR. Base-rate information (derived from the comparison group for the respective position) is provided for both clinically elevated scores and moderately elevated scores that generate interpretive statements.[1] If scores on the Validity Scales indicate the need for caution in interpreting the results of the Substantive Scales, a cautionary statement to this effect is printed in bold.

Interpretation is organized by the same five themes described in the Clinical Findings section. These statements are included only if the candidate's score falls at or above the cutoffs listed in Table 7.8 of this book—although, as seen in this table, two combinations of substantive scales (BXD/RC9 and RC9/DISC)

TABLE 7.8. T-Score Cutoffs for Generating Statements in the Comparison Group Findings Interpretation Section Based on Nonclinically Elevated (and Higher) Scores

Subsection	Scales
Somatic/Cognitive Complaints	RC1 (55), MLS (59), NUC (60), EAT (75), COG (53)
Emotional/Internalizing Problems	EID (53), RCd (53), SUI (58), HLP (58), SFD (53[1]), NFC (55), RC2 (57), RC7 (53), STR (53), WRY (54), CMP (65), ARX (54), ANP (53), BRF (63), NEGE (53), INTR (60)
Unusual Thoughts, Perceptions, and Beliefs	THD (55), RC6 (57), RC8 (55), PSYC (59)
Behavioral/Externalizing Problems	BXD (54), RC4 (55), RC9 (57), JCP (61), SUB (54), IMP (58), ACT (65), AGG (55), DISC (55), BXD (33[2])/RC9 (32[2]), RC9 (32[2])/DISC (34[2])
Interpersonal Problems	FML (55), CYN (60), SFI (40[1,2]), DOM (40[1,2]/69[3]), AGGR (63), DSF (58), SAV (60[1]), SHY (55[1])

[1] In the Dispatcher Candidate Interpretive Report (DCIR), cutoffs for generating Comparison Group Findings statements are 65T for scales SAV, SHY, and INTR; 60T for RC2; 55T for SFD; 37T for low SFI; and 38T for low DOM.
[2] Low scores (italicized font) are interpreted at designated cutoffs for SFI and DOM. Configural combinations BXD/RC9 and RC9/DISC are interpreted only when both scale scores are at the designated cutoffs.
[3] Comparison Group Findings statements are generated by high DOM scores only in the Police Candidate Interpretive Report (PCIR).

are interpreted also when they fall at or below the designated cutoffs. The cutoffs were selected to identify scores that are at least two standard deviations above (or below) the respective public safety candidate comparison group mean and that occur in less than 8% of comparison group members. Statements based on clinically elevated scores (T score 65 or higher) emphasize more substantial implications for compatibility with requirements for public safety positions.

If none of the scale scores for a given subsection meets the cutoffs listed in Table 7.8, the associated section heading is not printed. For cases in which scale scores for all five subsections fail to meet or exceed the designated cutoffs, a statement is printed indicating that the candidate scored within normal limits for the general population and comparison group members. An illustration of the comparison group findings included in the PCIR can be found on page 9 of Mr. E's report (Figure 7.6).

Job-Relevant Correlates

This section consists of interpretive statements supported by the empirical studies referenced in chapter 6 as well as correlations listed in appendices of the *MMPI-3 User's Guide for the Public Safety Candidate Interpretive Reports* (Corey & Ben-Porath, 2022) and the *MMPI-3 Technical Manual* (Ben-Porath &

Tellegen, 2020b). Periodic updates of the PSCIRs will include additional statements warranted by future research. As noted in the report's introduction to this section, these statements are organized by both problem domain and correlate source. The 10 problem domains addressed in this section of the report are listed in Table 7.9 and correspond closely to the CA-POST Psychological Screening Dimensions discussed in chapter 1.

When a candidate's test scores meet or exceed the score cutoffs listed in Table 7.10, associated interpretive statements are included in the Job-Relevant Correlates section of the report, along with annotations indicating the candidate's score on the pertinent scale(s) and references to empirical studies supporting the interpretation. When a candidate's scores are not associated with problems in a particular domain, a statement is printed at the end of this section indicating the domain(s) for which no risk of problems was indicated.

Correlate-based interpretive statements are derived from two sources: (a) those in which scores on other self-report measures (e.g., MPQ, CPI, and IPI) obtained in various candidate samples served as the criteria and (b) correlations with performance outcome criteria in studies of hired candidates. Statements derived from correlations with self-report measures begin with "Compared with other [police, correctional, dispatcher, or firefighter/medic] candidates," and statements originating from outcome studies with public safety candidates who were subsequently hired and trained begin with "He [or she or the candidate][2] is more likely than most [police officers, correctional officers, dispatchers, or firefighters/medics]." At the time of initial release of the PSCIRs, the available studies of hired candidates supported the inclusion of job-relevant correlates based on correlations with other self-report measures only for the PCIR. Studies with other public safety positions is currently underway, and as these studies are completed and published, additional job-relevant correlates will be included in updates for the CCIR, DCIR, and FCIR.

As discussed, the studies on which each statement is based are denoted with endnote annotation. Annotations indicate the scale(s) and score(s) associated with each statement and provide reference numbers linked to citations for the supporting research. The selection ratio (that is, the proportion of candidates in the comparison group who meet or exceed the cutoff score) for each scale is 8% or less, with most falling under 4%. Mr. E's job-relevant correlates are included on pages 10–11 of his PCIR (Figure 7.6).

Item-Level Information

The final main section of the PSCIR provides four types of item-level information under the headings: Unscorable Responses, Critical Responses, User-Designated Item-Level Information (which is optional), and Critical Follow-up Items.

TABLE 7.9. Descriptions of Problem Domains Used as an Organizing Structure in the MMPI-3 Public Safety Candidate Interpretive Reports

Domain 1: Emotional Control and Stress Tolerance Problems

This domain involves deficits in the ability to maintain emotional and behavioral control under pressure and other adverse circumstances. Counterproductive behaviors related to this domain include overreaction to provocation or challenge, moodiness and irritability, inaction or excessive hesitancy in emergency or other high-stress conditions, poor stress tolerance or resilience, and failing to properly employ tactics and knowledge under stress conditions. This domain is distinguished from Impulse Control Problems (Domain 10) by its focus on stress conditions, whereas Domain 10 is concerned with impulsive behavior under normal conditions.

Domain 2: Routine Task Performance Problems

This domain pertains to problems in the ability to apply job-relevant knowledge, skills, and abilities in the context of routine demands. Counterproductive behaviors related to this domain include performing with little or no confidence, avoiding challenges, and having difficulty performing routine tasks and job functions (including report writing and navigation).

Domain 3: Decision-Making and Judgment Problems

This domain pertains to problems in the ability to plan, prioritize, take decisive action, and make decisions under normal conditions. Counterproductive behaviors related to this domain include failing to make decisions or take action, not "thinking on one's feet," failing to make midcourse corrections when needed, and not seeing the "big picture."

Domain 4: Feedback Acceptance Problems

This domain involves deficits in the ability to consider one's own role in or contribution to problems and, in the face of constructive criticism, to integrate feedback into a plan for self-improvement. Counterproductive behaviors related to this domain include excessive defensiveness, blaming others, and dismissing or minimizing the credibility of negative feedback.

Domain 5: Assertiveness Problems

This domain involves limitations in the ability to interact confidently with others, act assertively, and, when necessary, exert dominance and control. Counterproductive behaviors related to this domain include failure to engage others, isolating oneself or avoiding interpersonal contact, being overly submissive or timid, lacking "command presence," and communicating unclearly.

Domain 6: Social Competence and Teamwork Problems

This domain pertains to problems in the ability to communicate with tact and sensitivity, work effectively with others, accept authority and direction, and function as an effective member of a team. Counterproductive behaviors related to this domain include generating interpersonal conflict and complaints, showing biased behaviors or attitudes, behaving rudely, resisting authority, denigrating others, failing to cooperate, and alienating service recipients or coworkers.

Domain 7: Integrity Problems

This domain involves failure to maintain high standards of morality and ethics in one's personal and professional conduct. This includes noncompliance with organizational and societal rules and exploiting the privileges and access of one's position for personal or other illegitimate interests. Counterproductive behaviors related to this domain include corruption, exploitation, dishonesty and deception, misrepresentation, boundary violations, and illegal behavior.

Domain 8: Conscientiousness and Dependability Problems

This domain involves problems in the ability to fulfill employment and other obligations diligently and reliably. Counterproductive behaviors related to this domain include taking impermissible shortcuts, disorganization, safety violations and property damage caused by neglect or inattention, missing deadlines, missing court and other mandatory appearances, failing to complete assignments, and a lack of initiative or perseverance.

TABLE 7.10. MMPI-3 Scales and T-Score Cutoffs for Generating Statements in the Job-Relevant Correlates Interpretation Section by Problem Domain

Problem domain	Scales
Emotional Control & Stress Tolerance	EID (53), BXD (54), RCd (53), RC1 (65), RC2 (57[1]), RC4 (55), RC7 (53), RC8 (55), RC9 (57), MLS (59), NUC (65), SFD (53[1]), STR (53), WRY (54), ANP (53), BRF (63), FML (55), CYN (65), DOM (<40[1]), DSF (58), SAV (60[1]), SHY (55[1]), AGGR (63), PSYC (59), NEGE (53), INTR (60[1])
Routine Task Performance	EID (53), BXD (54), RC2 (57[1]), RC4 (55), RC8 (55), COG (53), HLP (58), NFC (55), FML (55), ACT (65), DOM (<40[1]), DSF (58), SHY (55[1]), NEGE (53), INTR (60[1])
Decision-Making & Judgment	EID (53), THD (55), RC7 (53), RC8 (55), HLP (58), NFC (55), ARX (54), ACT (65), DOM (<40[1]), SHY (55[1]), PSYC (59), INTR (60[1])
Feedback Acceptance	EID (53), AGG (55), CYN (60), DOM (65[2]), DISC (55), NEGE (53), INTR (60[1])
Assertiveness	EID (53), RC2 (57[1]), RC7 (53), HLP (58), NFC (55), DOM (<40[1]), DSF (58), SAV (60[1]), SHY (55[1]), PSYC (59), INTR (60[1])
Social Competence & Teamwork	EID (53), BXD (54), RC2 (57[1]), RC4 (55), RC7 (53), RC8 (55), RC9 (57), HLP (58), WRY (54), FML (55), ACT (65), AGG (55), CYN (65), DOM (65[2]), DSF (58), SAV (60[1]), AGGR (63), PSYC (59), INTR (60[1])
Integrity	BXD (54), RCd (53), RC4 (55), RC6 (57), RC8 (55), RC9 (57), JCP (61), SUB (54), CYN (65), PSYC (59), DISC (55)
Conscientiousness & Dependability	EID (53), THD (55), BXD (54), RCd (53), RC2 (57[1]), RC4 (55), RC8 (55), MLS (59), NFC (55), WRY (54), ARX (54), JCP (61), ACT (65), AGG (55), DSF (58), SAV (60[1]), SHY (55[1]), PSYC (59), NEGE (53), INTR (60[1])
Substance Use	BXD (54), RC4 (55), RC7 (53), RC9 (57), SUB (54), DISC (55)
Impulse Control	EID (53), BXD (54), RC4 (55), RC9 (57), JCP (61), ANP (53), IMP (58), DISC (55), NEGE (53)

[1] In the Dispatcher Candidate Interpretive Report (DCIR), cutoffs for generating Job-Relevant Correlates statements are 65T for scales SAV, SHY, and INTR; 60T for RC2; 55T for SFD; 38T for low DOM; and 37T for low SFI.

[2] Job-Relevant Correlates statements are generated by high DOM scores only in the Police Candidate Interpretive Report (PCIR).

Unscorable Responses

A list of items to which the candidate did not provide scorable answers appears under the heading Unscorable Responses. Unscorable responses occur when the test taker either fails to mark an answer or responds both True and False to an item. Unscorable items are listed in the order in which they appear in the MMPI-3 protocol. The scale(s) on which each item is scored appears in parentheses following the item number and content. This makes it possible to examine the content of the unscorable items to detect possible themes to explore during the clinical interview. As seen at the top of page 11 of his PCIR, Mr. E produced scorable responses to all of the MMPI-3 items.

Critical Responses

A second type of item-level information appears under the heading Critical Responses. It relies on scale-level data to identify a candidate who reports experiencing difficulties that may warrant immediate attention. If the candidate generates an elevated score on one or more of the scales designated as having critical content, then item-level data can be used to identify the specific difficulties being reported by the test taker. Ben-Porath and Tellegen (2020a) designated seven MMPI-3 substantive scales as having critical item content that might require immediate attention and follow-up: Suicidal/Death Ideation (SUI), Helplessness/Hopelessness (HLP), Anxiety-Related Experiences (ARX), Ideas of Persecution (RC6), Aberrant Experiences (RC8), Substance Abuse (SUB), and Aggression (AGG). Items answered by the candidate in the keyed direction on a critical scale are listed if their T score on that scale is 65 or higher. The percentage of the MMPI-3 normative sample (NS) and comparison group (CG) who answered each item listed in the keyed direction is provided in parentheses following the item content. In Mr. E's PCIR (p. 11 of Figure 7.6), no critical responses are listed because he did not produce clinically elevated scores on any of the seven critical scales.

User-Designated Item-Level Information

Pearson software (see PSCIR User's Guide for specific details) provides an option for the user to designate additional scales or alternative cutoff levels for generating a third type of item-level information. Users can select any MMPI-3 scale for inclusion in this part of the report. By default, item-level information for a selected scale will be printed if a candidate's score reaches a level for which interpretive recommendations are provided in the *MMPI-3 Manual for Administration, Scoring, and Interpretation* (excluding interpretive recommendations for low scores; Ben-Porath & Tellegen, 2020a). For the Substantive Scales, the initial default T-score cutoff is 65. The initial default values for the validity indicators vary depending on the interpretive recommendations provided in chapter 5 of the *Manual for Administration, Scoring, and Interpretation*. Once a user has designated a cutoff for a given scale, it is possible to save it as the new default value for that scale. For example, if 60T is selected as the cutoff for RC6, this value can be retained as the new default for generating item-level responses for RC6.

The ability to customize cutoffs can be particularly helpful in assessments such as preemployment screening of public safety candidates in which interpretable deviations from reference group means occur at lower levels. For example, as just described, nonclinically elevated scores are interpreted in both the Comparison Group Findings and Job-Relevant Correlates sections of a PSCIR. The option to select additional scales to generate User-Designated Item-Level Information, in addition to those included in the Critical Responses section, can be used when an initial review of the results identifies areas requiring further attention.

An MMPI-3 PSCIR can be reprinted with different options selected (for example, adding scales to the User-Designated Item-Level Information list) without incurring additional cost. One way to use this option is to begin with a preliminary examination of the report with no scales selected for this section. If the user then identifies additional scales or alternative cutoffs that might provide useful information, these options can be selected and the report reprinted. This is illustrated in Mr. E's case on pages 11–12, which includes items answered in the keyed direction on all six of the substantive scales interpreted in his PCIR. A detailed illustration of how to use the Pearson software to select additional scales and alternative cutoffs for inclusion in this section can be found in the PSCIR User's Guide.

Critical Follow-up Items

This section contains a list of items identified by public safety candidate screening experts as having critical content and warranting follow-up. A list of the items potentially included in this section can be found in the PSCIR User's Guide. Each item is followed by the candidate's response, the percentage of comparison group members who gave this response, and the scale(s) on which the item appears. As seen on page 11 of Figure 7.6, Mr. E responded in the keyed direction to three of these items.

These data, as well as all the item-level information included in a PSCIR, are intended to support and inform the interview portion of a public safety candidate evaluation. However, as we discussed in chapter 5, **we do not recommend reading item content to the candidate verbatim.** A more useful strategy, and one likely to produce more reliable information while maintaining test security, is to use the item content to construct probing interview questions designed to assess the underlying issue.

Annotation

Standard 6.11 of the *Standards for Educational and Psychological Testing* (AERA, APA, & NCME, 2014) states that the sources, rationale, and empirical basis for interpretation should be available. To meet this standard, the annotation feature of each PSCIR identifies the origin of the interpretive statements (that is, attributes the statements to the individual's score[s] on a specific scale or scales); indicates whether the statements are based on the test taker's responses, direct empirical correlates, or construct-based inferences; and provides citations to empirical studies that support the correlate-based statements. Annotation is provided in the Endnotes (see p. 12 of Mr. E's PCIR) and Research Reference List sections (pp. 13–14).

Annotation of the underlying sources of all interpretive statements also provides an important foundation for the legal defensibility of a PSCIR and its admissibility in court proceedings. In *Lindsey v. Costco Wholesale Corporation* (2016), a United States District Court ruled in an employment discrimination case that the testimony of a psychologist who relied on the narrative interpretive text of a proprietary MMPI-2 report "whose basis she does not understand" was inadmissible because "its conclusions . . . cannot be tested on cross-examination, and it is not a proper basis for her testimony" (no pagination).

Endnotes

As a general rule, the construct-based statements appearing in the Comparison Group Findings section will be identified as originating from test responses (i.e., scale item content). Statements in the Job-Relevant Correlates section are based on setting-specific empirical correlates of the MMPI-3 Substantive Scales. Additional statements will be added periodically to each PSCIR as the research base for use of the MMPI-3 in public safety candidate assessments continues to expand. Statements in the Clinical Findings section will, for the most part, be identified as based on test content or empirical correlates. Any PSCIR statement identified as correlate-based includes a list of research references that appear in the next and final section of the report.

Research Reference List

This section includes a list of the empirical studies cited in the report in support of correlate-based statements. With the exception of the *MMPI-2-RF Technical Manual*, the *MMPI-3 Technical Manual*, and the *MMPI-3 User's Guide for the Public Safety Candidate Interpretive Reports*, all of these publications appear in peer-reviewed journal articles. The reference for each article includes a highlighted digital object identifier (doi) number. When viewed on an internet-connected device, the doi numbers provide hyperlinked access to the publisher's website for each article.

THE CASE OF MR. E

Case Description: Mr. E is a 27-year-old, single man who applied for an entry-level police officer position in a large urban agency. Mr. E's background investigation revealed a stable work history as a lead package sorter with no reprimands or legal conflicts. Although several coworkers described him as "entitled," "self-promoting," and "bossy," his supervisor (and best friend since high school) attributed those sentiments to coworker resentment over his comparatively high productivity and associated bonuses. During the interview, Mr. E frequently interrupted and spoke over the psychologist. He denied having any conflicts with coworkers and insisted that he was highly regarded and respected by the other workers on his crew. Mr. E did acknowledge that he frequently needed to reprimand his coworkers, but he viewed this as a reflection of his strong leadership skills. The psychologist's observations noted substantial limitations in Mr. E's capacity for insight, empathy, and accurate reading of his social environment.

A PCIR based on Mr. E's MMPI-3 scores is reproduced in Figure 7.6. As mentioned, the first six pages of the report are identical to what would appear in an MMPI-3 Score Report based on the same set of responses. The first PCIR-specific element appears on page 7 of Mr. E's report, where any score interpreted in the report is printed in bold along with the scale abbreviation. In Mr. E's case, six substantive scale scores are interpreted: all four scales from the Thought Dysfunction domain and two from the Interpersonal Functioning domain. On page 8, the synopsis succinctly summarizes the implications of the one clinically elevated MMPI-3 score as well as comparison group findings or job-relevant correlates associated with Mr. E's substantial deviations from the comparison group mean. A detailed assessment of the validity of Mr. E's protocol also appears on page 8. Clinical findings and diagnostic considerations appear next. The small number of statements in these sections reflects that there is only one clinically elevated score in Mr. E's protocol. Comparison group findings, including statements about the relatively low base rate of these findings in police candidates, appear beginning on page 9. Job-relevant correlates associated with Mr. E's MMPI-3 results are described beginning on page 10, and item-level data are reported on page 11. As mentioned, item numbers and content of items that Mr. E answered in the keyed direction are redacted in Figure 7.6 to maintain test security. Annotation, including the scale scores associated with each of the statements included in Mr. E's PCIR, appears on page 12 of the report. The annotation includes reference numbers for every correlate-based statement, with the citation and hyperlinks to the actual articles appearing on pages 13–14 of Mr. E's PCIR.

IMPORTANT CONSIDERATIONS WHEN USING THE MMPI-3 PUBLIC SAFETY CANDIDATE INTERPRETIVE REPORTS

At the conclusion of chapter 6, we identified some important limitations of the research base available to guide use of the MMPI-3 in preemployment evaluations of public safety candidates. Two such limitations are the insufficiency of

Minnesota Multiphasic Personality Inventory®-3

Yossef S. Ben-Porath
Auke Tellegen

MMPI®-3
Police Candidate Interpretive Report
David M. Corey, PhD, & Yossef S. Ben-Porath, PhD

ID Number:	Mr. E
Age:	27
Gender:	Male
Marital Status:	Not reported
Years of Education:	Not reported
Date Assessed:	10/14/2022

Copyright © 2020 by the Regents of the University of Minnesota. All rights reserved. Distributed exclusively under license from the University of Minnesota by NCS Pearson, Inc. Portions reproduced from the *MMPI-3 English Test Booklet.* Copyright © 2020 by the Regents of the University of Minnesota. All rights reserved. Portions excerpted from the *MMPI-3 Manual for Administration, Scoring, and Interpretation.* Copyright © 2020 by the Regents of the University of Minnesota. All rights reserved. Portions excerpted from the *MMPI-3 Technical Manual.* Copyright © 2020 by the Regents of the University of Minnesota. All rights reserved. Used by permission of the University of Minnesota Press.

Minnesota Multiphasic Personality Inventory and **MMPI** are registered trademarks of the Regents of the University of Minnesota. **Pearson** is a trademark, in the US and/or other countries, of Pearson Education, Inc., or its affiliates.

This report contains copyrighted material and trade secrets. Qualified licensees may excerpt portions of this output report, limited to the minimum text necessary to accurately describe their significant core conclusions, for incorporation into a written evaluation of the examinee, in accordance with their profession's citation standards, if any. No adaptations, translations, modifications, or special versions may be made of this report without prior written permission from the University of Minnesota Press.

[1.4 / RE1 / QG1]

ALWAYS LEARNING   PEARSON

FIGURE 7.6. Mr. E's MMPI-3 Police Candidate Interpretive Report

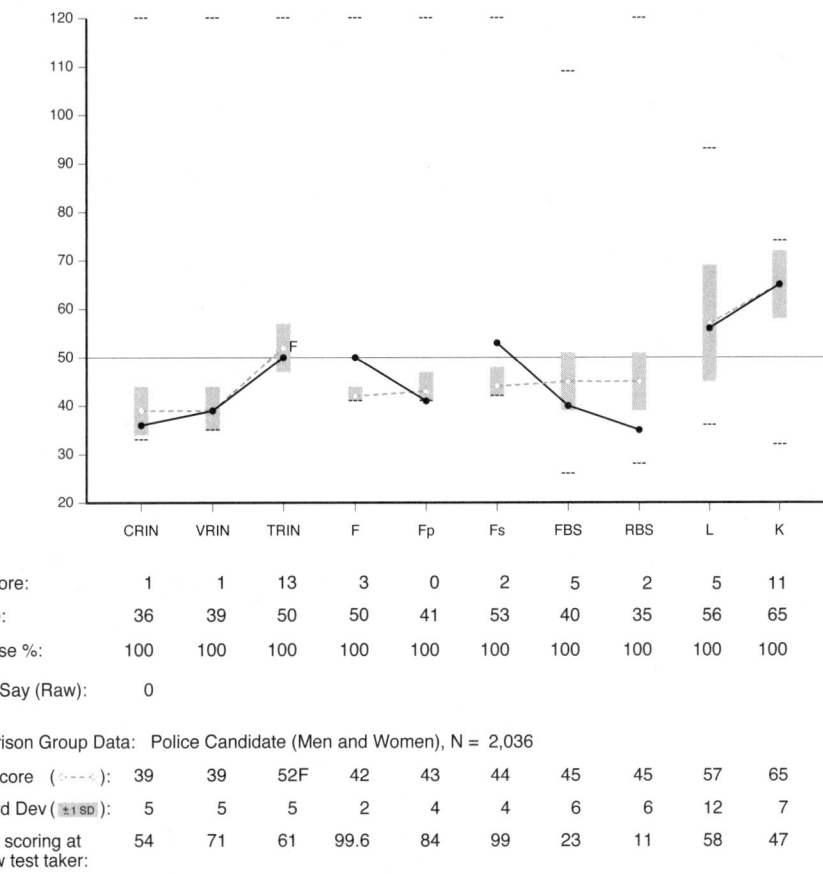

FIGURE 7.6. Mr. E's MMPI-3 Police Candidate Interpretive Report, continued

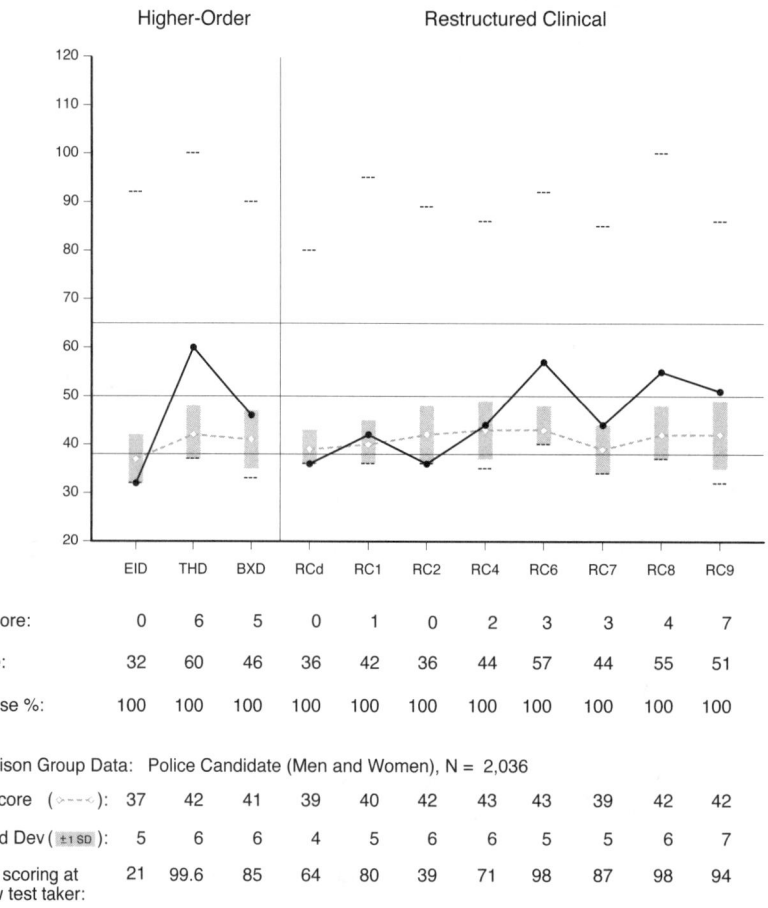

FIGURE 7.6. Mr. E's MMPI-3 Police Candidate Interpretive Report, continued

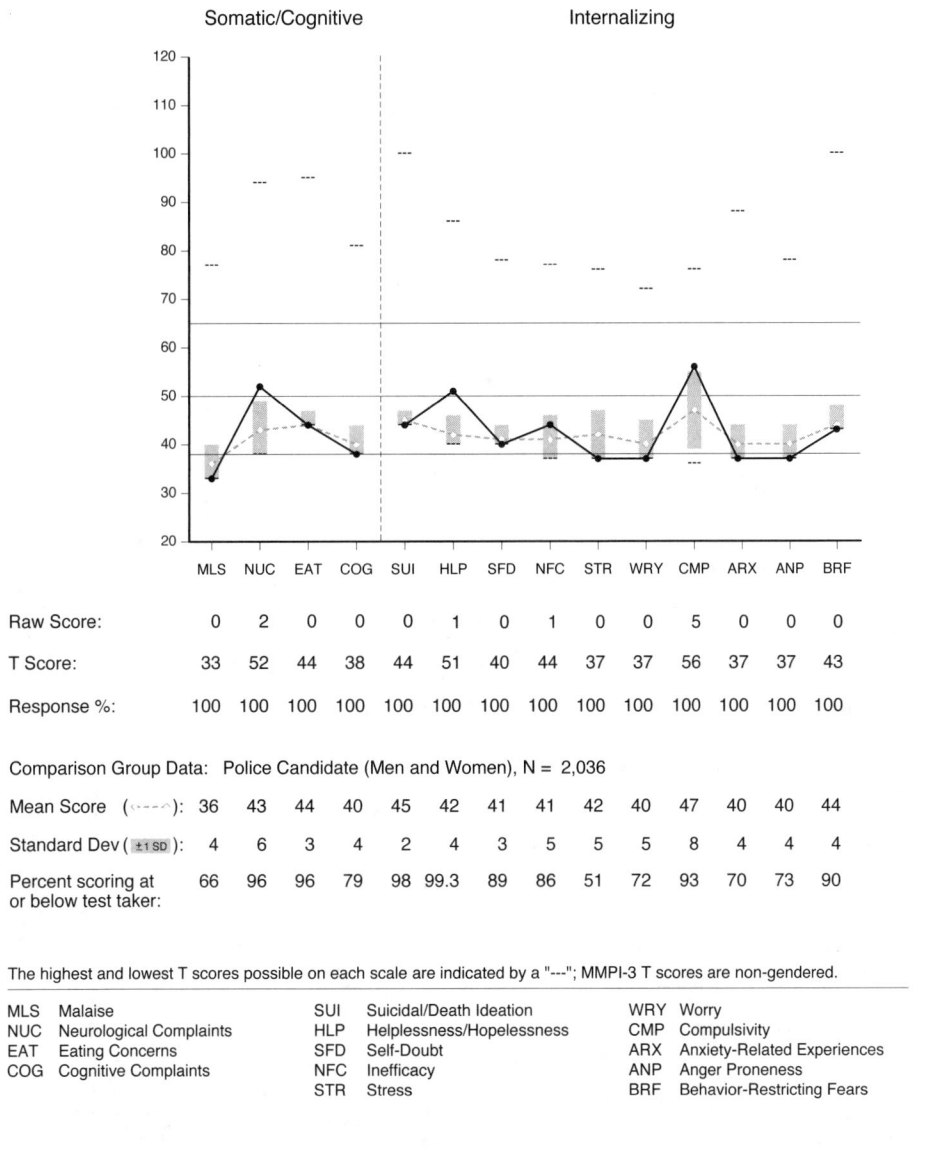

FIGURE 7.6. Mr. E's MMPI-3 Police Candidate Interpretive Report, continued

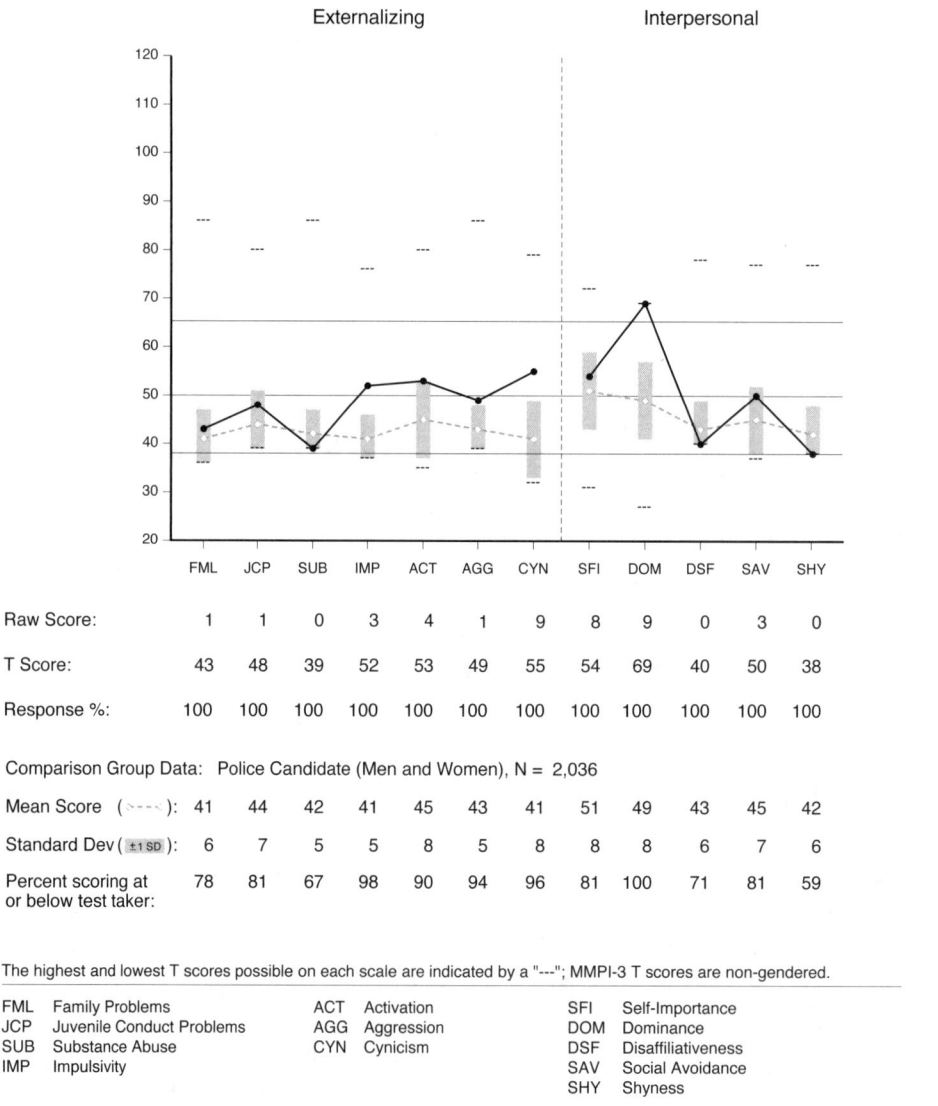

FIGURE 7.6. Mr. E's MMPI-3 Police Candidate Interpretive Report, continued

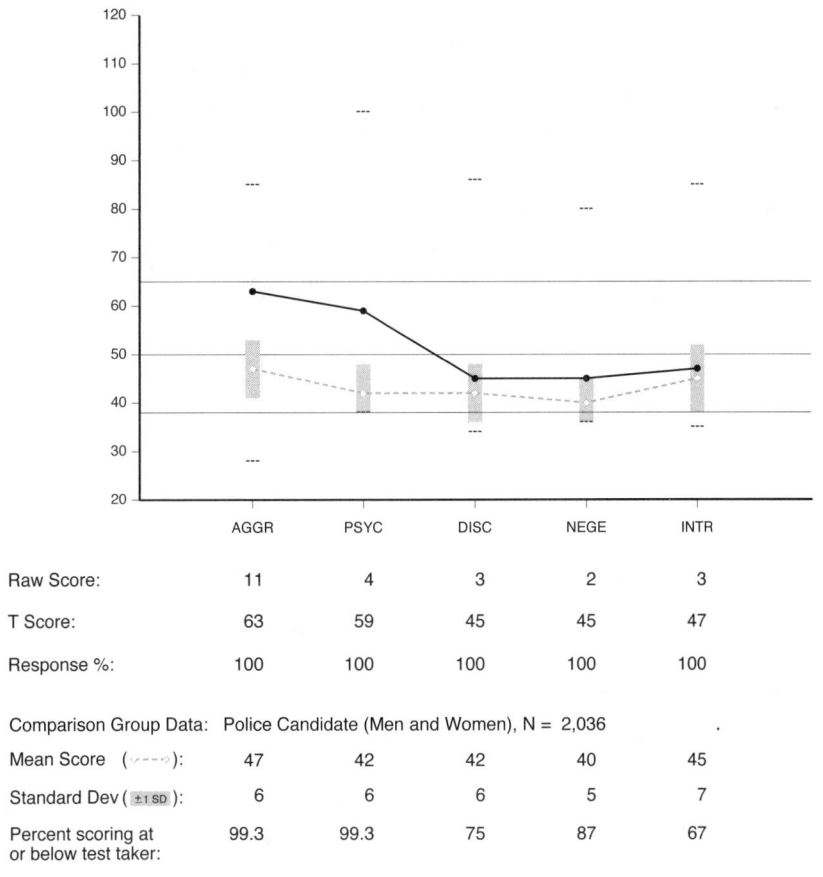

FIGURE 7.6. Mr. E's MMPI-3 Police Candidate Interpretive Report, continued

MMPI-3 T SCORES (BY DOMAIN)

PROTOCOL VALIDITY

Content Non-Responsiveness

0	36	39	50
CNS	CRIN	VRIN	TRIN

Over-Reporting

50	41		53	40	35
F	Fp		Fs	FBS	RBS

Under-Reporting

56	65
L	K

SUBSTANTIVE SCALES

Somatic/Cognitive Dysfunction

42	33	52	44	38
RC1	MLS	NUC	EAT	COG

Emotional Dysfunction

32								
EID								

36	44	51	40	44
RCd	SUI	HLP	SFD	NFC

36	47
RC2	INTR

44	37	37	56	37	37	43	45
RC7	STR	WRY	CMP	ARX	ANP	BRF	NEGE

Thought Dysfunction

60
THD

57
RC6

55
RC8

59
PSYC

Behavioral Dysfunction

46
BXD

44	43	48	39
RC4	FML	JCP	SUB

51	52	53	49	55
RC9	IMP	ACT	AGG	CYN

45
DISC

Interpersonal Functioning

54	**69**	**63**	40	50	38
SFI	**DOM**	**AGGR**	DSF	SAV	SHY

Scale scores shown in bold font are interpreted in the report.

Note. This information is provided to facilitate interpretation following the recommended structure for MMPI-3 interpretation in Chapter 5 of the *MMPI-3 Manual for Administration, Scoring, and Interpretation*, which provides details in the text and an outline in Table 5-1.

FIGURE 7.6. Mr. E's MMPI-3 Police Candidate Interpretive Report, continued

MMPI®-3 Police Candidate Interpretive Report
10/14/2022, Page 8
ID: Mr. E

This interpretive report is intended for use by a professional qualified to interpret the MMPI-3 in the context of preemployment psychological evaluations of police and other law enforcement candidates. **It focuses on identifying problems; it does not convey potential strengths.** The information it contains should be considered in the context of the test taker's background, the demands of the position under consideration, the clinical interview, findings from supplemental tests, and other relevant information.

The interpretive statements in the Protocol Validity section of the report are based on T scores derived from the general MMPI-3 normative sample, as well as scores obtained by the multisite sample of 2,036 individuals that make up the Police Candidate Comparison Group.

The interpretive statements in the Clinical Findings and Diagnostic Considerations sections of the report are based on T scores derived from the general MMPI-3 normative sample. Following recommended practice, only T scores of 65 and higher (with a few exceptions) are considered clinically significant. Scores at this clinical level are generally rare among police candidates.

Statements in the Comparison Group Findings and Job-Relevant Correlates sections are based on comparisons with scores obtained by the Police Candidate Comparison Group. Statements in these sections may be based on T scores that, although less than 65, are nevertheless uncommon in reference to the comparison group.

The report includes extensive annotation, which appears as superscripts following each statement in the narrative, keyed to Endnotes with accompanying Research References, which appear in the final two sections of the report. Additional information about the annotation features is provided in the headnotes to these sections and in the MMPI-3 User's Guide for the Public Safety Candidate Interpretive Reports.

SYNOPSIS

This is a valid MMPI-3 protocol. Scores on the Substantive Scales indicate clinically significant interpersonal dysfunction. Interpersonal difficulties relate to overly domineering behavior.

Comparison group findings point to additional possible concerns about persecutory beliefs, odd perceptions and thoughts, and over-assertiveness.

Possible job-relevant problems are identified in the following domains: Emotional Control and Stress Tolerance, Routine Task Performance, Decision-Making and Judgment, Feedback Acceptance, Social Competence and Teamwork, Integrity, Conscientiousness and Dependability, and Impulse Control.

PROTOCOL VALIDITY

This is a valid MMPI-3 protocol. There are no problems with unscorable items. The test taker responded to the items relevantly on the basis of their content, and there are no indications of over- or under-reporting.

FIGURE 7.6. Mr. E's MMPI-3 Police Candidate Interpretive Report, continued

CLINICAL FINDINGS

Clinical-level symptoms, personality characteristics, and behavioral tendencies of the test taker are described in this section and organized according to an empirically guided framework. (Please see Chapter 5 of the MMPI-3 Manual for Administration, Scoring, and Interpretation *for details.) Statements containing the word "reports" are based on the item content of MMPI-3 scales, whereas statements that include the word "likely" are based on empirical correlates of scale scores. Specific sources for each statement can be viewed with the annotation features of this report.*

The test taker describes himself as having strong opinions, as standing up for himself, as assertive and direct, and as able to lead others[1]. He likely believes he has leadership capabilities, but is viewed by others as overly domineering[2].

There are no indications of clinically significant somatic, cognitive, emotional, thought, or behavioral dysfunction in this protocol.

DIAGNOSTIC CONSIDERATIONS

This section provides recommendations for psychodiagnostic assessment based on the test taker's MMPI-3 results. It is recommended that he be evaluated for the following:

Interpersonal Disorders

- Disorders characterized by excessively domineering behavior[3]

COMPARISON GROUP FINDINGS

This section describes the MMPI-3 substantive scale findings in the context of the Police Candidate Comparison Group. Specific sources for each statement can be accessed with the annotation features of this report. **Job-related correlates of these results, if any, are provided in the subsequent Job-Relevant Correlates section.**

Unusual Thoughts, Perceptions, and Beliefs

The test taker reports a comparatively high level of unusual thinking for a police candidate[4]. Only 1.0% of comparison group members convey such thoughts at this or a higher level. More specifically, he reports a relatively high level of persecutory beliefs for a police candidate[5]. Only 4.0% of comparison group members convey this or a greater level of persecutory thinking.

He reports a comparatively high level of odd perceptions and thoughts for a police candidate[6]. Only 4.0% of comparison group members convey this or a greater level of unusual experiences.

Interpersonal Problems

The test taker's responses indicate a level of dominance that may be incompatible with public safety requirements for good interpersonal functioning[3]. This level of domineering behavior is uncommon among police candidates. Only 6.0% of comparison group members give evidence of this level of dominance. He reports a comparatively high level of over-assertiveness for a police candidate[7]. Only 3.0% of comparison group members convey this or a greater level of interpersonally aggressive behavior.

FIGURE 7.6. Mr. E's MMPI-3 Police Candidate Interpretive Report, continued

JOB-RELEVANT CORRELATES

Job-relevant personality characteristics and behavioral tendencies of the test taker are described in this section and organized according to ten problem domains commonly identified in the professional literature as relevant to public safety candidate suitability. (Please see MMPI-3 User's Guide for the Public Safety Candidate Interpretive Reports *for details.) Statements that begin with "Compared with other police candidates" are based on correlations with other self-report measures obtained in police candidate samples that included individuals who were subsequently hired as well as those who were not. Statements that begin with "He is more likely than most police officers or trainees" are based on correlations with outcome data obtained in samples of hired candidates during academy or field training, probation, and/or the postprobation period. Specific sources for each statement can be accessed with the annotation features of this report.*

Emotional Control and Stress Tolerance Problems

Compared with other police candidates, the test taker is more likely to believe he has been mistreated[8].

He is more likely than most police officers or trainees to exhibit difficulties performing under stressful conditions[9].

Routine Task Performance Problems

The test taker is more likely than most police officers or trainees to exhibit difficulties carrying out tasks under non-stressful conditions[10]; cognitive adaptation problems[11]; and report writing problems[11].

Decision-Making and Judgment Problems

Compared with other police candidates, the test taker is more likely to have thoughts, perceptions, and/or experiences that are rarely reported[12] and to exhibit difficulty with decision-making and judgment[13].

He is more likely than most police officers or trainees to exhibit difficulties prioritizing multiple and essential functions of the job and performing them in quick succession while maintaining good environmental awareness of vital information (in other words, multi-tasking)[11]. He is also more likely to exhibit difficulties with effective decision-making[9] and with seeking assistance in complex situations as needed[14].

Feedback Acceptance Problems

Compared with other police candidates, the test taker is less likely to reflect on his behavior[15] and more likely to brush off criticism and other negative feedback[15].

Social Competence and Teamwork Problems

Compared with other police candidates, the test taker is more likely to be opinionated and outspoken[15]; to be demanding[15]; and to have difficulty trusting others[16]. He is also more likely to feel maligned by others[8]; to have problems with social competence[13]; and to have difficulties with teamwork[17].

He is more likely than most police officers or trainees to exhibit difficulties stemming from rude and/or overbearing behavior that results in complaints from the public[18] and cooperating with peers and/or supervisors[19].

Integrity Problems

The test taker is more likely than most police officers or trainees to exhibit difficulties leading to sustained internal affairs investigations[20]; complaints from the public[21]; and investigations about conduct unbecoming a police officer[21].

Conscientiousness and Dependability Problems

The test taker is more likely than most police officers or trainees to exhibit difficulties with initiative and drive, such as obtaining information and evidence needed to solve crimes and explain incidents[22]. He is also more likely to exhibit difficulties reliably attending court[23]; with punctuality and attendance[24]; and with conscientiousness[25].

FIGURE 7.6. Mr. E's MMPI-3 Police Candidate Interpretive Report, continued

Impulse Control Problems

The test taker is more likely than most police officers or trainees to exhibit problems controlling and de-escalating conflict[14].

The candidate's test scores are not associated with problems in the following domains:
- Assertiveness
- Substance Use

ITEM-LEVEL INFORMATION

Unscorable Responses

The test taker produced scorable responses to all the MMPI-3 items.

Critical Responses

Seven MMPI-3 scales—Suicidal/Death Ideation (SUI), Helplessness/Hopelessness (HLP), Anxiety-Related Experiences (ARX), Ideas of Persecution (RC6), Aberrant Experiences (RC8), Substance Abuse (SUB), and Aggression (AGG)—have been designated by the test authors as having critical item content that may require immediate attention and follow-up. Items answered by the individual in the keyed direction (True or False) on a critical scale are listed below if his T score on that scale is 65 or higher. However, any item answered in the keyed direction on SUI is listed.

The test taker has not produced an elevated T score (≥ 65) on any of these scales or answered any SUI items in the keyed direction.

Critical Follow-up Items

This section contains a list of items to which the test taker responded in a manner warranting follow-up. The items were identified by public safety candidate screening experts as having critical content. Clinicians are encouraged to follow up on these statements with the candidate by making related inquiries, rather than reciting the item(s) verbatim. Each item is followed by the candidate's response, the percentage of Police Candidate Comparison Group members who gave this response, and the scale(s) on which the item appears.

    Item number and content omitted. (True; 5.1%; BXD, RC9, IMP, DISC)
    Item number and content omitted. (True; 0.9%; F)
    Item number and content omitted. (True; 5.0%; VRIN, BXD, RC9, IMP, DISC)

FIGURE 7.6. Mr. E's MMPI-3 Police Candidate Interpretive Report, continued

ENDNOTES

This section lists for each statement in the report the MMPI-3 score(s) that triggered it. In addition, each statement is identified as a <u>Test Response</u>, if based on item content, a <u>Correlate</u>, if based on empirical correlates, or an <u>Inference</u>, if based on the report authors' judgment. (This information can also be accessed on-screen by placing the cursor on a given statement.) For correlate-based statements, research references (Ref. No.) are provided, keyed to the consecutively numbered reference list following the endnotes.

[1] Test Response: DOM=69
[2] Correlate: DOM=69, Ref. 1, 2, 4, 6, 7, 14
[3] Inference: DOM=69
[4] Test Response: THD=60; PSYC=59
[5] Test Response: RC6=57
[6] Test Response: RC8=55
[7] Test Response: AGGR=63
[8] Correlate: RC6=57, Ref. 3
[9] Correlate: RC8=55, Ref. 2; PSYC=59, Ref. 2
[10] Correlate: RC8=55, Ref. 9, 11
[11] Correlate: RC8=55, Ref. 2
[12] Correlate: THD=60, Ref. 13; RC8=55, Ref. 5, 13; PSYC=59, Ref. 5, 13
[13] Correlate: THD=60, Ref. 15; RC6=57, Ref. 15
[14] Correlate: DOM=69, Ref. 8
[15] Correlate: DOM=69, Ref. 2
[16] Correlate: RC8=55, Ref. 2; PSYC=59, Ref. 5, 13
[17] Correlate: RC6=57, Ref. 15
[18] Correlate: AGGR=63, Ref. 8
[19] Correlate: DOM=69, Ref. 8; AGGR=63, Ref. 2, 11
[20] Correlate: RC8=55, Ref. 13; PSYC=59, Ref. 13
[21] Correlate: RC6=57, Ref. 11, 13
[22] Correlate: PSYC=59, Ref. 10, 12
[23] Correlate: THD=60, Ref. 11, 13; RC8=55, Ref. 11; PSYC=59, Ref. 11, 13
[24] Correlate: THD=60, Ref. 2, 8; RC8=55, Ref. 2, 8; PSYC=59, Ref. 2, 8
[25] Correlate: THD=60, Ref. 2; RC8=55, Ref. 2; PSYC=59, Ref. 2

FIGURE 7.6. Mr. E's MMPI-3 Police Candidate Interpretive Report, continued

RESEARCH REFERENCE LIST

The following studies are sources for empirical correlates identified in the Endnotes section of this report.

1. Ayearst, L. E., Sellbom, M., Trobst, K. K., & Bagby, R. M. (2013). Evaluating the interpersonal content of the MMPI-2-RF Interpersonal Scales. *Journal of Personality Assessment, 95*(2), 187–196. https://doi.org/10.1080/00223891.2012.730085

2. Ben-Porath, Y. S., & Tellegen, A. (2020). *The Minnesota Multiphasic Personality Inventory-3 (MMPI-3): Technical manual.* University of Minnesota Press.

3. Corey, D. M., & Ben-Porath, Y. S. (2022). *Minnesota Multiphasic Personality Inventory-3 (MMPI-3): User's guide for the public safety candidate interpretive reports.* University of Minnesota Press.

4. Cox, A., Courrégé, S. C., Feder, A. H., & Weed, N. C. (2017). Effects of augmenting response options of the MMPI-2-RF: An extension of previous findings. *Cogent Psychology, 4*(1), 1323988. https://doi.org/10.1080/23311908.2017.1323988

5. Detrick, P., Ben-Porath, Y.S., & Sellbom, M. (2016). Associations between MMPI-2-RF (Restructured Form) and Inwald Personality Inventory (IPI) scale scores in a law enforcement preemployment screening sample. *Journal of Police and Criminal Psychology, 31,* 81–95. https://doi.org/10.1007/s11896-015-9172-7

6. Kastner, R. M., Sellbom, M., & Lilienfeld, S. O. (2012). A comparison of the psychometric properties of the Psychopathic Personality Inventory full-length and short-form versions. *Psychological Assessment, 24*(1), 261–267. https://doi.org/10.1037/a0025832

7. Menton, W. H., Crighton, A. H., Tarescavage, A. M., Marek, R. J., Hicks, A. D., & Ben-Porath, Y. S. (2019). Equivalence of laptop and tablet administrations of the Minnesota Multiphasic Personality Inventory-2 Restructured Form. *Assessment, 26*(4), 661–669. https://doi.org/10.1177/1073191117714558

8. Roberts, R. M., Tarescavage, A. M., Ben-Porath, Y. S., & Roberts, M. D. (2018). predicting post-probationary job performance of police officers using CPI and MMPI-2-RF test data obtained during preemployment psychological screening. *Journal of Personality Assessment, 101*(5), 544–555. https://doi.org/10.1080/00223891.2018.1423990

9. Tarescavage, A. M., Brewster, J., Corey, D. M., & Ben-Porath, Y. S. (2015). Use of pre-hire Minnesota Multiphasic Personality Inventory-2-Restructured Form (MMPI-2-RF) police candidate scores to predict supervisor ratings of post-hire performance. *Assessment, 22*(4), 411–428. https://doi.org/10.1177/1073191114548445

10. Tarescavage, A. M., Corey, D. M., & Ben-Porath, Y. S. (2015). Minnesota Multiphasic Personality Inventory-2-Restructured Form (MMPI-2-RF) predictors of police officer problem behavior. *Assessment, 22*(1), 116–132. https://doi.org/10.1177/1073191114534885

11. Tarescavage, A. M., Corey, D. M., & Ben-Porath, Y. S. (2016). A prorating method for estimating MMPI-2-RF scores from MMPI responses: Examination of score fidelity and illustration of empirical utility in the PERSEREC police integrity study sample. *Assessment, 23*(2), 173–190. https://doi.org/10.1177/1073191115575070

12. Tarescavage, A. M., Corey, D. M., Gupton, H. M., & Ben-Porath Y.S. (2015). Criterion validity and practical utility of the Minnesota Multiphasic Personality Inventory-2-Restructured Form (MMPI-2-RF) in assessments of police officer candidates. *Journal of Personality Assessment, 97*(4), 382–394. https://doi.org/10.1080/00223891.2014.995800

FIGURE 7.6. Mr. E's MMPI-3 Police Candidate Interpretive Report, continued

13. Tarescavage, A. M., Fischler, G. L., Cappo, B. M., Hill, D. O., Corey, D. M., & Ben-Porath, Y. S. (2015). Minnesota Multiphasic Personality Inventory-2-Restructured Form (MMPI-2-RF) predictors of police officer problem behavior and collateral self-report test scores. *Psychological Assessment, 27*(1), 125–137. https://doi.org/10.1037/pas0000041

14. Tellegen, A., & Ben-Porath, Y. S. (2008/2011). *Minnesota Multiphasic Personality Inventory-2-Restructured Form (MMPI-2-RF): Technical manual.* University of Minnesota Press.

15. Whitman, M. R., Elias, L. S., Cappo, B. M., & Ben-Porath, Y. S. (2021). Criterion validity of MMPI-3 scores in preemployment evaluations of public safety candidates. *Psychological Assessment.* Advance online publication. https://doi.org/10.1037/pas0001042

End of Report

FIGURE 7.6. Mr. E's MMPI-3 Police Candidate Interpretive Report, continued

test scores alone to predict adverse outcomes and the composition of available candidate and employee samples that reflects (1) the very high proportion of men in most public safety positions (dispatchers being the sole exception), with limited availability of data for women, and (2) limited availability of comparative validity studies with persons of color. We noted that the integrative model, which is described in detail in chapter 8, addresses the insufficiency issue by indicating that no single source is sufficiently strong to be solely dispositive and that test findings can, and in some instances should, be mitigated by other findings (from interview, background, or collateral information). We also commented that in the case of women and candidates of color, the relative dearth of empirical research should lead examiners to allow greater leeway for the other aforementioned sources to mitigate test findings. In the following chapter, we describe and illustrate how to integrate MMPI-3 results, including ones obtained with a PSCIR, with other information sources in preemployment assessments of public safety candidates.

POTENTIAL ADVERSE IMPACT AND THE PSCIRS

In chapter 5, we briefly reviewed implications of the Civil Rights Act of 1964, Title VII, for preemployment psychological suitability evaluations, among which is the prohibition against disparate or adverse impact. Adverse impact occurs when a hiring or employment practice has the effect of disproportionately excluding members of Title VII's protected classes (involving race, color, religion, gender, or national origin), regardless of intent. As discussed and illustrated in chapter 5, the rule of thumb for assessing adverse impact in selection practices is the "four-fifths rule" (EEOC, 1979), by which adverse impact is indicated if a hiring practice results in the protected class having a selection rate less than four-fifths (80%) of the majority group's.

In the case of the cutoffs recommended in this book and used in the MMPI-3 PSCIRs, we compared candidates self-identified as man versus woman, White versus Black, and non-Hispanic White versus Hispanic White to determine whether the cutoff scores listed in Tables 7.8 and 7.10 trigger differential proportions of negative statements in these candidate groups. In both the Black and Hispanic groups (the only racial/ethnic minority categories for which we have adequate sample sizes to conduct this analysis), the differential proportions fell above the .80 requirement on all scales, and the median ratio across all 52 scales is higher than .90. In a comparison of men and women, we also found the ratio to exceed .80 on all scales, with a median ratio of 1.00. Thus, the cutoff scores listed in Tables 7.8 and 7.10, which are those used in the PSCIRs, show no evidence of adverse impact on female, Black, and Hispanic candidates.

Using the MMPI-3 in Preemployment Assessments of Police and Other Public Safety Candidates

Case Illustrations and Guidance for Evidence-Based Report Writing

We illustrate in this chapter how MMPI-3 scores can be integrated with personal history and background information, interview findings, and other test data to evaluate the psychological suitability of candidates in all four public safety job categories (police officer, correctional officer, dispatcher, and firefighter/medic) using the MMPI-3 Public Safety Candidate Interpretive Reports (Corey & Ben-Porath, 2022). We begin by describing a model for integrating information from various sources used in psychological assessments of police and other public safety candidates to enhance relevance, validity, consistency, and defensibility.

AN INTEGRATIVE MODEL FOR PSYCHOLOGICAL SCREENING

Spilberg and Corey (2022) proposed a model for systematically integrating information from a psychological assessment of a peace officer candidate to arrive at a suitability determination and "to assist screening psychologists in minimizing reliance on impressionistic judgments and maximizing use of evidence-based methods and strategies" (p. 159). This five-step model, adapted here for use with all public safety candidates, is shown in Table 8.1.

The importance of beginning the integrative process with the consideration of test scores cannot be overemphasized. Indeed, the first two steps in the process involve a review of test data (protocol validity and substantive scales, respectively). This is because the accuracy of assessment judgments is optimized when data from within and across various assessment sources are weighted according to their relevance and reliability (Heilbrun et al., 2009), and the source

TABLE 8.1. Five-Step Model for Integrating Psychological Screening Data

Step	Description
1	**Assess Protocol Validity**
	Evaluate test scores for evidence of content nonresponsiveness, inconsistency, over-reporting, and underreporting. MMPI-2-RF interpretation always begins with an inspection of the Validity Scales to determine whether the substantive test results are interpretable and, if so, whether any interpretive caveats are called for.
2	**Assess Findings From Substantive Scale Scores**
	Identify and interpret relevant findings from the substantive scale scores, first using standard norms and then, if available, position-specific comparison group norms.
3	**Assess Background Findings**
	Evaluate relevant personal history information from all available sources.
4	**Assess Interview Findings**
	Evaluate interview findings to determine how they are convergent with, divergent from, or complementary to relevant test findings and background information.
5	**Identify Relevant Risk Findings**
	Determine whether the weight of the findings (convergent, complementary, and divergent) supports the conclusion that the candidate meets the selection standards: a. Considering all risk-related findings from all sources, what evidence-based inferences can be drawn? Eliminate those that do not map onto the psychological screening dimensions or other selection criteria. b. What divergent findings mitigate these inferences? Eliminate those inferences that are outweighed by divergent findings of sufficient relevance, reliability, and validity. c. Are any surviving risk-related inferences of sufficient relevance and quality to warrant the candidate's disqualification?

Note. Adapted from *Peace Officer Psychological Screening Manual* by S. W. Spilberg and D. M. Corey, 2022. Copyright 2022 California Commission on Peace Officer Standards and Training.

with the greatest *known* relevance and reliability in public safety candidate assessments is psychological testing. The model proceeds to a consideration of background information, for which relevance and reliability are less well-established than for testing but that nonetheless has greater empirical support than interview data, which comprises Step 4. The integrative process takes place at Step 5, when the examiner considers and weighs testing, background, and interview data to determine suitability. We next illustrate these steps in a series of case studies based on actual, redacted screening assessments.

ABOUT THE CASE STUDIES

The cases we have selected for demonstration are not easy ones. Each falls in a gray zone where screening professionals struggle over the interpretation and integration of mixed data—some indicating that the candidate possesses very positive traits and behavioral characteristics and at least one other data source indicating a substantial risk of future counterproductive behavior relevant to the screening dimensions (see chapter 1, Table 1.5). This gray zone is where the challenge of psychological assessment occurs. Corey and Zelig (2020) observed that, in these more opaque assessments, "the data are murky, messy, frustrating, and inconsistent, and result in a head-scratching challenge to combine or integrate these data to answer the referral question(s)" (p. 194). Use of the integrative model makes the task simpler, the process more systematic and reliable, the rationale more transparent, and the outcome more valid, intelligible, and defensible.

The cases involve candidates for all four public safety job categories. Although the facts in each case study reflect the actual material in the assessment record, details that might reveal identities have been altered. None of these alterations meaningfully changes the record.

Owing to space limitations, we have not reproduced the full set of assessment data in each case study (e.g., full results from the test of normal personality, the entire background investigation report, the candidate's complete responses to the personal history questionnaire, the screening psychologist's comprehensive interview notes, and complete medical records). Instead, we have selected data from these various sources as appropriate to illustrate a particular case and to show how that information is integrated with MMPI-3 findings to determine job suitability. Individual readers may disagree with the suitability determinations provided in our case illustrations, just as screening professionals may come to different conclusions about candidates in actual practice. We do not suggest that there is only one possible or "right" determination in any case; rather, our purpose is to guide readers' understanding of how the examiner in each case applied the integrative model to arrive at a determination—and to use the cases as launch points for other related guidance.

Each of the cases in this chapter illustrates the integration of MMPI-3 findings with collateral background information, self-reported history, clinical interview findings, and findings from normal-range personality testing. As discussed in chapter 5, this comprises the "basic model" of psychological screening of public safety candidates. Because this book is focused on use of the MMPI-3 in assessing police and other public safety personnel, and because readers may rely on any of several broadband measures of normal personality validated for use with this population, we summarize the key findings from the normal-range personality test used in the candidate's assessment battery rather than the test scores.

For readers wanting to delve more thoroughly into the process of data integration in public safety candidate assessments, we recommend reading all the cases, not just those from selected job categories. The material in each case is germane to all public safety evaluations and each uses the same assessment components and psychological screening dimensions. In our first case, that of Mr. D, we also orient the reader to the integrative model. Finally, we have included two kinds of case studies: brief reviews, in which we focus on particular findings from the MMPI-3 while summarizing findings from other assessment components to illustrate key points, and comprehensive reviews, in which we provide lengthier, detailed analyses and discussion of the assessment data to illustrate the use of the MMPI-3 in the integrative model.

USING A PSCIR WITH ANOTHER PUBLIC SAFETY POSITION

When deciding whether it is appropriate to use a PSCIR to evaluate a candidate for a position that may be related but not identical to the position named in the report, it is important to consider the degree to which the positions are comparable, including similarities in the essential functions and working conditions. For example, it would be inappropriate to use a PCIR to evaluate an armed security guard or to use the FCIR to evaluate a deputy fire marshal with no first-responder functions, because the duties and working conditions of the positions are too dissimilar. In any instance in which it is contraindicated to use the report, it would also be inadvisable to use the report's comparison group to aid in interpreting scores generated by the Score Report, because members of the comparison group cannot be assumed comparable to incumbents in the position to which the candidate has applied.

The empirical support for the interpretive statements in the four PSCIRs derives from three sources, each with diverse sets of subjects. In the Clinical Findings section, in which statements are generated only for clinically elevated scales, the empirical support comes from the broad literature pertaining to the general adult population and is not specific to any personnel category. In the Comparison Group Findings section, the construct-based statements describe implications of clinically elevated substantive scale scores, as well as statements about possible implications of uncommonly high (but not clinically elevated) scores for candidates in the respective position. Base-rate information (derived from the four public safety candidate comparison groups, described in chapter 7) is provided for both clinically elevated scores and moderately elevated scores that generate interpretive statements. Finally, in the Job-Relevant Correlates section of the reports, empirical support rests on a series of studies, summarized in chapter 6, in addition to updates based on newly published findings.

COMPREHENSIVE REVIEW: MR. D, POLICE CANDIDATE

Assessment Issues Presented

- Orientation to the integrative model
- Interpreting underreporting scores and the inference of deception

- Use of MMPI-3 items with historically verifiable content in conjunction with extratest data (interview and background information) to assess for intentional deception

Referral Summary

Mr. D is a 46-year-old, married, male police candidate who applied to a department with 20 officers, but it borders a much larger community and frequently provides "mutual aid" (i.e., assistance to other emergency responders across jurisdictional boundaries). Nine months before the evaluation, Mr. D was employed by a large police agency in another county but resigned in lieu of termination when he failed to adequately progress during his formal field training program. His training records documented problems with citizen contacts and coworker relationships as well as multitasking, geography, emergency driving, radio control, and decision-making. The background investigation was otherwise positive, including references from the previous job he held for 20 years as a beverage distributor.

Data Integration

Step 1: Assessing Protocol Validity

A review of Mr. D's MMPI-3 scores (Figure 8.1) shows that he provided scorable responses to all 335 test items (CNS = 0) and was consistent in his responding (CRIN = 36T, VRIN = 39T, TRIN = 50T). There is also no evidence of overreporting (F, Fp, Fs, FBS, and RBS are all below their respective score thresholds for interpreting the possibility of overreporting). Possible underreporting, however, is indicated by an elevated score on L (81T). His score on K (56T) is a little more than a standard deviation below the mean score for the Police Candidate Comparison Group, indicating comparatively little effort to present himself as well-adjusted.

As discussed in chapter 3, **evidence of underreporting does not invalidate an MMPI-3 protocol in a personnel screening context.** Owing to the impact of preselection and selection factors, demand characteristics, and other considerations, indications of possible underreporting are commonly found in police and public safety candidate protocols. This underscores the importance of scrutinizing the reliability of a candidate's self-report whenever L reaches or exceeds 77T or there is collateral evidence of inconsistent or deceptive reporting in other assessment components. Mr. D's L score of 81T meets this threshold and highlights the importance of interpreting the substantive scores with caution. This caveat is a function of the asymmetrical impact of underreporting on the Substantive Scales (Ben-Porath & Sellbom, 2023); namely, that nonelevated scores

Minnesota Multiphasic Personality Inventory®-3

Yossef S. Ben-Porath
Auke Tellegen

MMPI®-3
Police Candidate Interpretive Report
David M. Corey, PhD, & Yossef S. Ben-Porath, PhD

ID Number:	Mr. D
Age:	46
Gender:	Male
Marital Status:	Not reported
Years of Education:	Not reported
Date Assessed:	08/21/2022

Copyright © 2020 by the Regents of the University of Minnesota. All rights reserved. Distributed exclusively under license from the University of Minnesota by NCS Pearson, Inc. Portions reproduced from the *MMPI-3 English Test Booklet*. Copyright © 2020 by the Regents of the University of Minnesota. All rights reserved. Portions excerpted from the *MMPI-3 Manual for Administration, Scoring, and Interpretation*. Copyright © 2020 by the Regents of the University of Minnesota. All rights reserved. Portions excerpted from the *MMPI-3 Technical Manual*. Copyright © 2020 by the Regents of the University of Minnesota. All rights reserved. Used by permission of the University of Minnesota Press.

Minnesota Multiphasic Personality Inventory and **MMPI** are registered trademarks of the Regents of the University of Minnesota. **Pearson** is a trademark, in the US and/or other countries, of Pearson Education, Inc., or its affiliates.

This report contains copyrighted material and trade secrets. Qualified licensees may excerpt portions of this output report, limited to the minimum text necessary to accurately describe their significant core conclusions, for incorporation into a written evaluation of the examinee, in accordance with their profession's citation standards, if any. No adaptations, translations, modifications, or special versions may be made of this report without prior written permission from the University of Minnesota Press.

[1.4 / RE1 / QG1]

ALWAYS LEARNING   PEARSON

FIGURE 8.1. Mr. D's MMPI-3 Police Candidate Interpretive Report

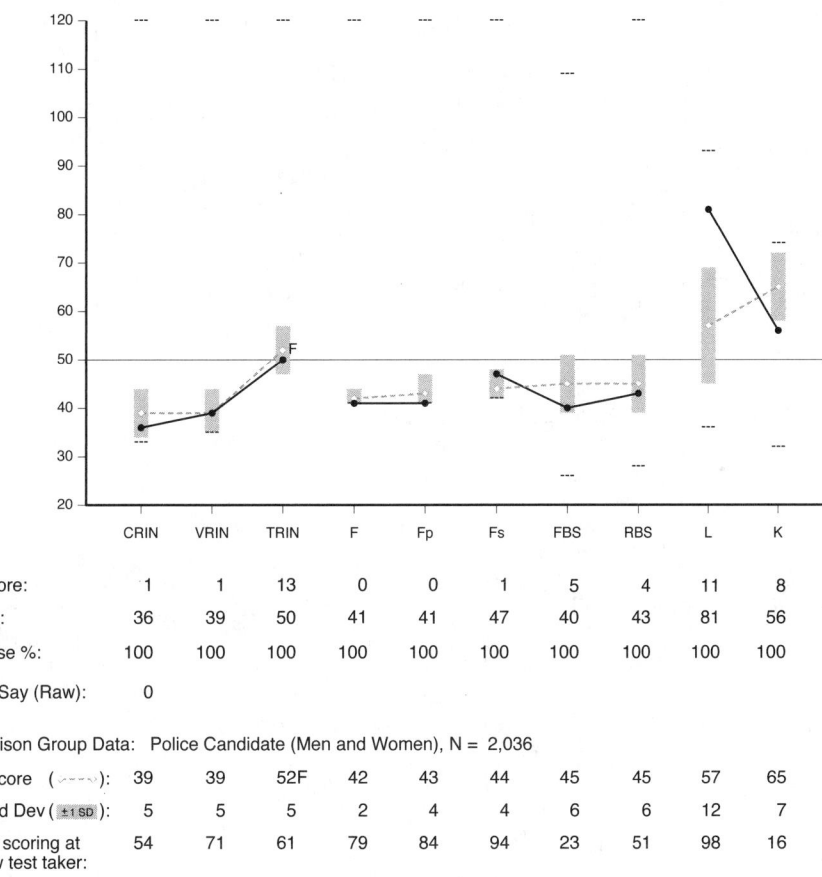

FIGURE 8.1. Mr. D's MMPI-3 Police Candidate Interpretive Report, continued

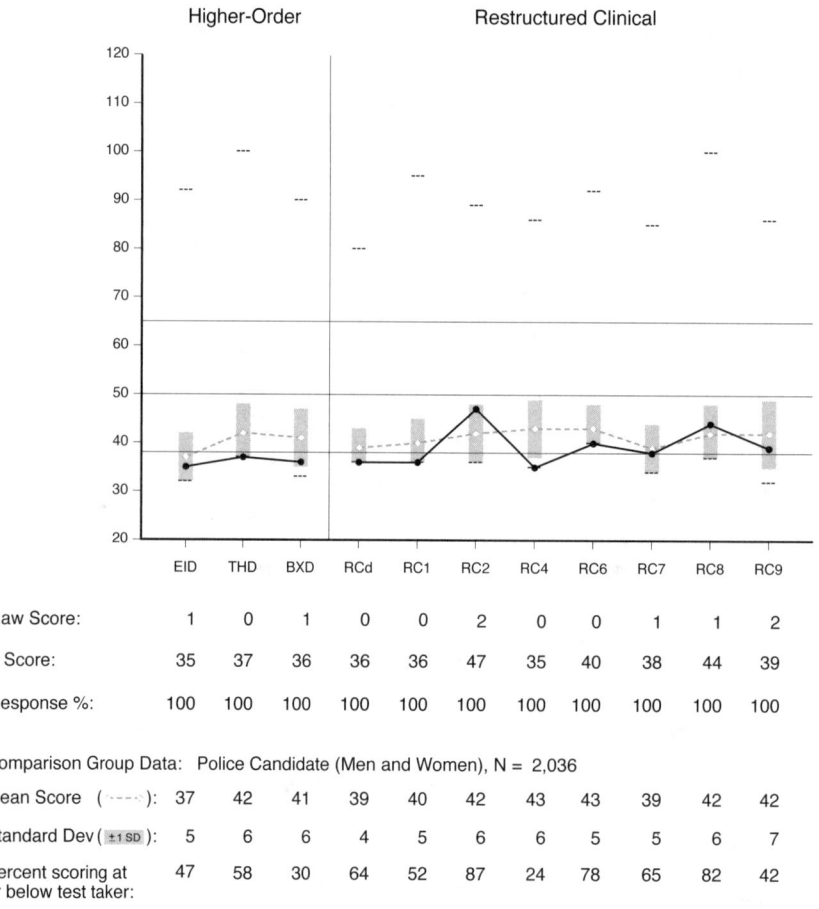

FIGURE 8.1. Mr. D's MMPI-3 Police Candidate Interpretive Report, continued

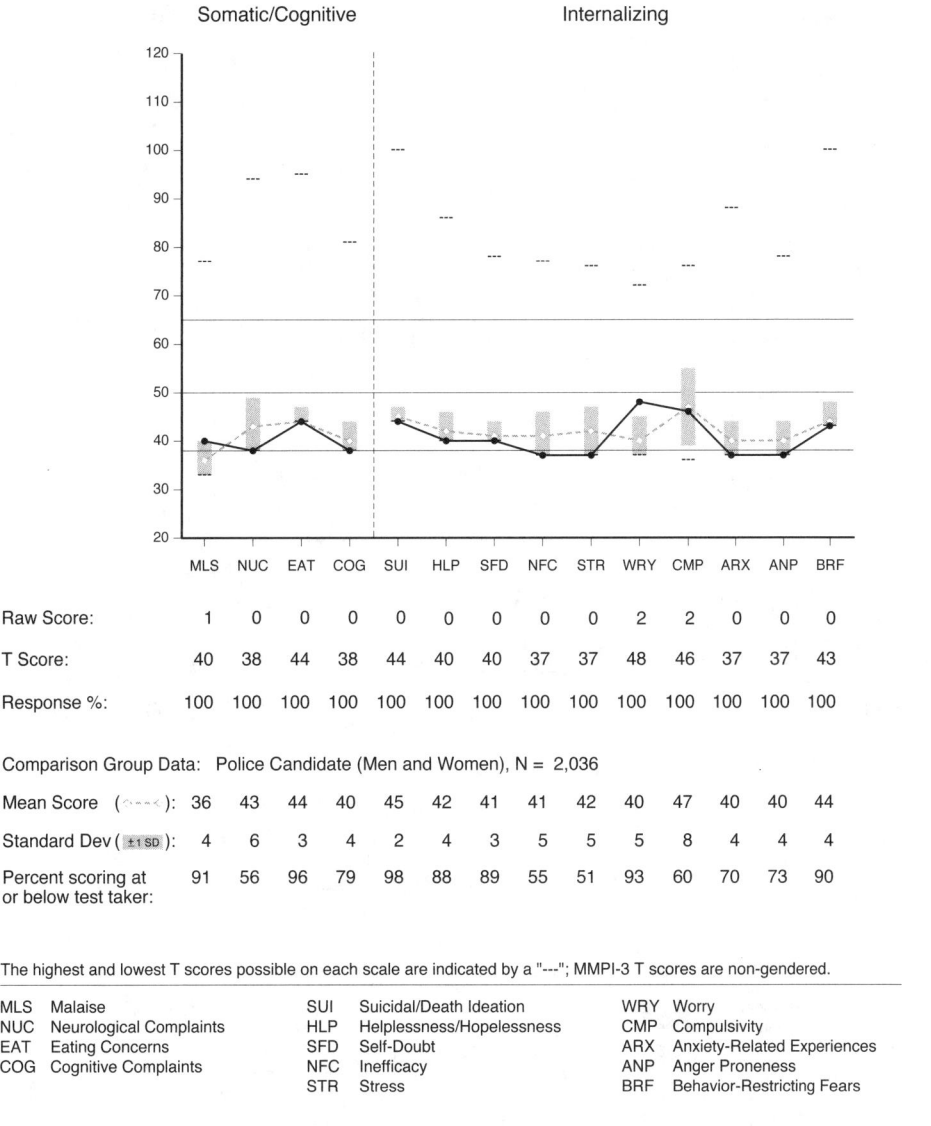

FIGURE 8.1. Mr. D's MMPI-3 Police Candidate Interpretive Report, continued

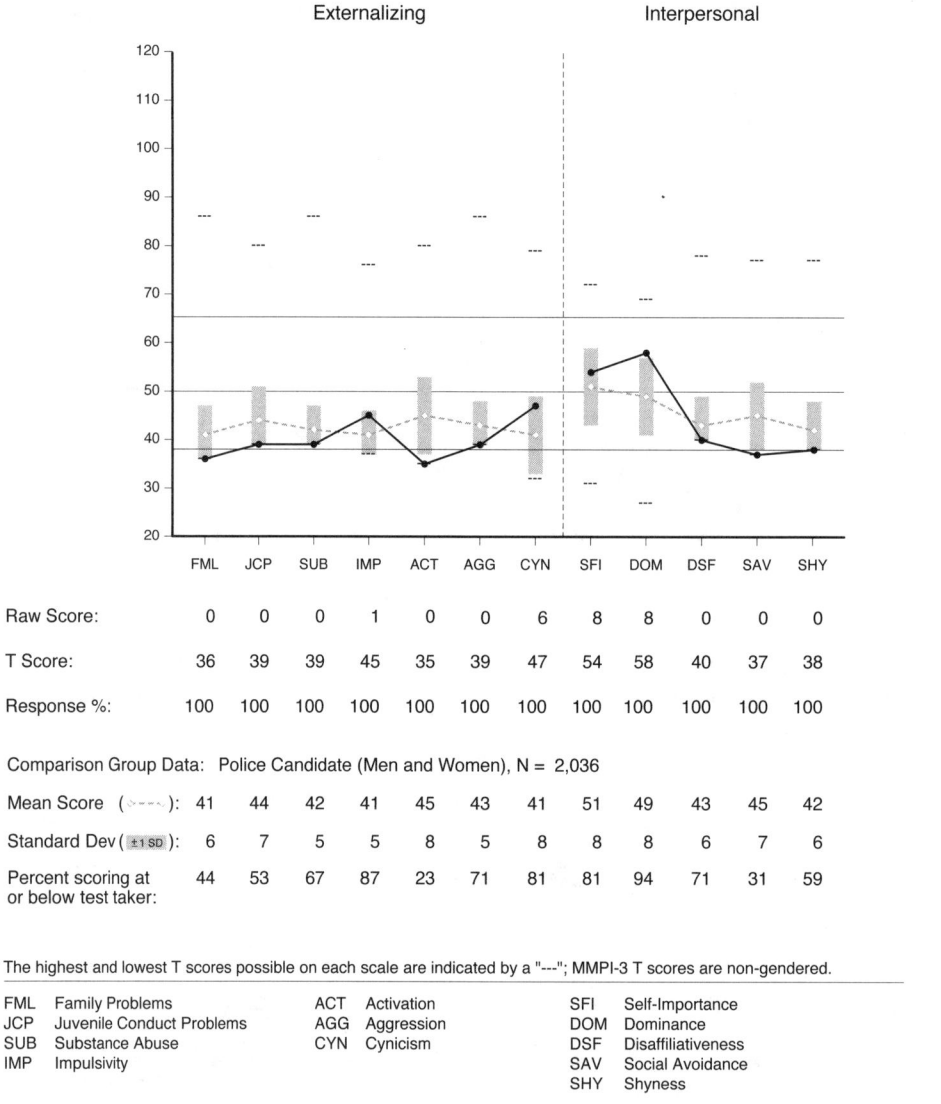

FIGURE 8.1. Mr. D's MMPI-3 Police Candidate Interpretive Report, continued

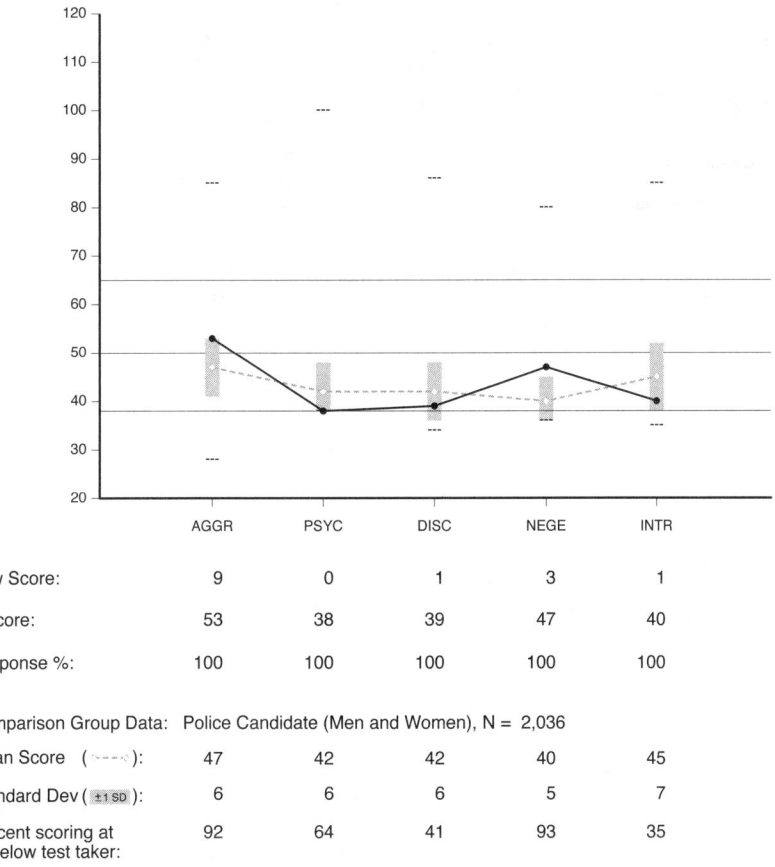

FIGURE 8.1. Mr. D's MMPI-3 Police Candidate Interpretive Report, continued

MMPI-3 T SCORES (BY DOMAIN)

PROTOCOL VALIDITY

Content Non-Responsiveness

CNS	CRIN	VRIN	TRIN
0	36	39	50

Over-Reporting

F	Fp	Fs	FBS	RBS
41	41	47	40	43

Under-Reporting

L	K
81	56

SUBSTANTIVE SCALES

Somatic/Cognitive Dysfunction

RC1	MLS	NUC	EAT	COG
36	40	38	44	38

Emotional Dysfunction

EID							
35							
	RCd	SUI	HLP	SFD	NFC		
	36	44	40	40	37		
	RC2	INTR					
	47	40					
	RC7	STR	WRY	CMP	ARX	ANP	BRF	NEGE
	38	37	48	46	37	37	43	47

Thought Dysfunction

THD	
37	
	RC6
	40
	RC8
	44
	PSYC
	38

Behavioral Dysfunction

BXD					
36					
	RC4	FML	JCP	SUB	
	35	36	39	39	
	RC9	IMP	ACT	AGG	CYN
	39	45	35	39	47
	DISC				
	39				

Interpersonal Functioning

SFI	DOM	AGGR	DSF	SAV	SHY
54	58	53	40	37	38

Scale scores shown in bold font are interpreted in the report.

Note. This information is provided to facilitate interpretation following the recommended structure for MMPI-3 interpretation in Chapter 5 of the *MMPI-3 Manual for Administration, Scoring, and Interpretation*, which provides details in the text and an outline in Table 5-1.

FIGURE 8.1. Mr. D's MMPI-3 Police Candidate Interpretive Report, continued

This interpretive report is intended for use by a professional qualified to interpret the MMPI-3 in the context of preemployment psychological evaluations of police and other law enforcement candidates. **It focuses on identifying problems; it does not convey potential strengths.** The information it contains should be considered in the context of the test taker's background, the demands of the position under consideration, the clinical interview, findings from supplemental tests, and other relevant information.

The interpretive statements in the Protocol Validity section of the report are based on T scores derived from the general MMPI-3 normative sample, as well as scores obtained by the multisite sample of 2,036 individuals that make up the Police Candidate Comparison Group.

The interpretive statements in the Clinical Findings and Diagnostic Considerations sections of the report are based on T scores derived from the general MMPI-3 normative sample. Following recommended practice, only T scores of 65 and higher (with a few exceptions) are considered clinically significant. Scores at this clinical level are generally rare among police candidates.

Statements in the Comparison Group Findings and Job-Relevant Correlates sections are based on comparisons with scores obtained by the Police Candidate Comparison Group. Statements in these sections may be based on T scores that, although less than 65, are nevertheless uncommon in reference to the comparison group.

The report includes extensive annotation, which appears as superscripts following each statement in the narrative, keyed to Endnotes with accompanying Research References, which appear in the final two sections of the report. Additional information about the annotation features is provided in the headnotes to these sections and in the MMPI-3 User's Guide for the Public Safety Candidate Interpretive Reports.

SYNOPSIS

Scores on the MMPI-3 Validity Scales raise substantial concerns about the possible impact of under-reporting on the validity of this protocol.

PROTOCOL VALIDITY

Content Non-Responsiveness

The test taker produced scorable responses to all the MMPI-3 items. He also responded relevantly to the items on the basis of their content.

Over-Reporting

There are no indications of over-reporting in this protocol.

Under-Reporting

The test taker presented himself in an extremely positive light by denying many minor faults and shortcomings that most people acknowledge[1]. This level of virtuous self-presentation is very uncommon even among individuals with a background stressing traditional values[2]. It is also uncommon among police candidates. Only 5% of the comparison group members claimed this many or more uncommon virtues. Any absence of elevation on the Substantive Scales is uninterpretable[3]. Elevated scores on the Substantive Scales may underestimate the problems assessed by those scales[4]. The candidate's responses may be a result of unintentional (e.g., naïve) or intentional under-reporting. One way to distinguish between the two is to compare his responses to items with

FIGURE 8.1. Mr. D's MMPI-3 Police Candidate Interpretive Report, continued

historical content against available collateral information (e.g., background information, interview data). Following are the test taker's responses to items with potentially verifiable historical content:

- Item number and content omitted. (True)
- Item number and content omitted. (False)
- Item number and content omitted. (False)
- Item number and content omitted. (False)
- Item number and content omitted. (False)
- Item number and content omitted. (False)
- Item number and content omitted. (True)
- Item number and content omitted. (False)
- Item number and content omitted. (False)
- Item number and content omitted. (False)
- Item number and content omitted. (False)

Corroborated evidence of intentional under-reporting may be incompatible with the integrity requirements of the position.

CLINICAL FINDINGS

The following interpretation needs to be considered in light of substantial cautions noted about the possible impact of under-reporting (claiming a large number of uncommon virtues) on the validity of this protocol.

There are no indications of clinically significant somatic, cognitive, emotional, thought, or behavioral dysfunction in this protocol. However, because of indications of under-reporting described earlier, such problems cannot be ruled out.

DIAGNOSTIC CONSIDERATIONS

No specific psychodiagnostic recommendations are indicated by this MMPI-3 protocol. However, this finding needs to be considered in light of cautions noted earlier about possible under-reporting.

COMPARISON GROUP FINDINGS AND JOB-RELEVANT CORRELATES

The test taker's scores on the Substantive Scales are all within normal limits for the general population and for police candidates. However, as indicated earlier, in light of evidence of considerable under-reporting, these results do not rule out the possibility that psychological problems will impede the candidate's ability to perform the duties of a police officer.

FIGURE 8.1. Mr. D's MMPI-3 Police Candidate Interpretive Report, continued

MMPI®-3 Police Candidate Interpretive Report
08/21/2022, Page 10

ID: Mr. D

ITEM-LEVEL INFORMATION

Unscorable Responses

The test taker produced scorable responses to all the MMPI-3 items.

Critical Responses

Seven MMPI-3 scales—Suicidal/Death Ideation (SUI), Helplessness/Hopelessness (HLP), Anxiety-Related Experiences (ARX), Ideas of Persecution (RC6), Aberrant Experiences (RC8), Substance Abuse (SUB), and Aggression (AGG)—have been designated by the test authors as having critical item content that may require immediate attention and follow-up. Items answered by the individual in the keyed direction (True or False) on a critical scale are listed below if his T score on that scale is 65 or higher. However, any item answered in the keyed direction on SUI is listed.

The test taker has not produced an elevated T score ($\geq$ 65) on any of these scales or answered any SUI items in the keyed direction.

Critical Follow-up Items

This section contains a list of items to which the test taker responded in a manner warranting follow-up. The items were identified by public safety candidate screening experts as having critical content. Clinicians are encouraged to follow up on these statements with the candidate by making related inquiries, rather than reciting the item(s) verbatim. Each item is followed by the candidate's response, the percentage of Police Candidate Comparison Group members who gave this response, and the scale(s) on which the item appears.

The test taker did not respond to any critical follow-up items in the keyed direction.

FIGURE 8.1. Mr. D's MMPI-3 Police Candidate Interpretive Report, *continued*

ENDNOTES

This section lists for each statement in the report the MMPI-3 score(s) that triggered it. In addition, each statement is identified as a <u>Test Response</u>, if based on item content, a <u>Correlate</u>, if based on empirical correlates, or an <u>Inference</u>, if based on the report authors' judgment. (This information can also be accessed on-screen by placing the cursor on a given statement.) For correlate-based statements, research references (Ref. No.) are provided, keyed to the consecutively numbered reference list following the endnotes.

[1] Test Response: L=81
[2] Correlate: L=81, Ref. 3
[3] Correlate: L=81, Ref. 1, 4, 5, 7, 8, 10
[4] Correlate: L=81, Ref. 2, 6, 8, 9, 10

FIGURE 8.1. Mr. D's MMPI-3 Police Candidate Interpretive Report, continued

RESEARCH REFERENCE LIST

The following studies are sources for empirical correlates identified in the Endnotes section of this report.

1. Bagby, R. M., Onno, K. A., Mortezaei, A., & Sellbom, M. (2020). Examining the "Traditional Background Hypothesis" for the MMPI-2-RF L-r Scores in a Muslim Faith-Based Sample. *Psychological Assessment.* Advance online publication. https://doi.org/10.1037/pas0000941

2. Ben-Porath, Y. S., & Tellegen, A. (2020). *The Minnesota Multiphasic Personality Inventory-3 (MMPI-3): Technical manual.* University of Minnesota Press.

3. Bridges, S. A., & Baum, L. J. (2013). An examination of the MMPI-2-RF L-r scale in an outpatient protestant sample. *Journal of Psychology and Christianity, 32*(2), 115–123. Questia. http://www.questia.com/read/1P3-3083628231/an-examination-of-the-mmpi-2-rf-l-r-scale-in-an-outpatient

4. Brown, T. A., & Sellbom, M. (2020). The utility of the MMPI-2-RF validity scales in detecting underreporting. *Journal of Personality Assessment, 102*(1), 66–74. https://doi.org/10.1080/00223891.2018.1539003

5. Crighton, A. H., Marek, R. J., Dragon, W. R., & Ben-Porath, Y. S. (2017). Utility of the MMPI-2-RF Validity Scales in detection of simulated underreporting: Implications of incorporating a manipulation check. *Assessment, 24*(7), 853–864. https://doi.org/10.1177/1073191115627011

6. Forbey, J. D., Lee, T. T. C., Ben-Porath, Y. S., Arbisi, P. A., & Gartland, D. (2013). Associations between MMPI-2-RF validity scale scores and extra-test measures of personality and psychopathology. *Assessment, 20*(4), 448–461. https://doi.org/10.1177/1073191113478154

7. Marion, B. E., Sellbom, M., Salekin, R. T., Toomey, J. A., Kucharski, L. T., & Duncan, S. (2013). An examination of the association between psychopathy and dissimulation using the MMPI-2-RF Validity Scales. *Law and Human Behavior, 37*(4), 219–230. https://doi.org/10.1037/lhb0000008

8. Sellbom, M., & Bagby, R. M. (2008). Validity of the MMPI-2-RF (Restructured Form) L-r and K-r scales in detecting under-reporting in clinical and non-clinical samples. *Psychological Assessment, 20*(4), 370–376. https://doi.org/10.1037/a0012952

9. Tellegen, A., & Ben-Porath, Y. S. (2008/2011). *Minnesota Multiphasic Personality Inventory-2-Restructured Form (MMPI-2-RF): Technical manual.* University of Minnesota Press.

10. Whitman, M. R., Tylicki, J. L., & Ben-Porath, Y. S. (2021). Utility of the MMPI-3 Validity Scales for detecting overreporting and underreporting and their effects on substantive scale validity: A simulation study. *Psychological Assessment, 33*(5), 411–426. https://doi.org/10.1037/pas0000988

End of Report

FIGURE 8.1. Mr. D's MMPI-3 Police Candidate Interpretive Report, continued

cannot be interpreted as indicating the absence of problems assessed by those scales (because the denial of problems may be an artifact of deception or distortion), and any score elevations that do exist (Mr. D's protocol has none in the clinical range), although interpretable at designated levels, may underestimate the problems measured by those scales (see, e.g., Forbey et al., 2013).

Mr. D's L score (81T) indicates that he reports a very high level of moral virtuousness, with only 2% of Police Candidate Comparison Group members claiming more uncommon virtues (see Figure 8.1, p. 2, identifying the "Percent scoring at or below test taker" on L as 98% of the comparison group members). Note that the narrative in the Under-Reporting subsection of the PCIR (Figure 8.1, p. 8) states that 5% of the comparison group members claimed this many or more uncommon virtues. To clarify, the statistic on page 2 of the PCIR reports the proportion of comparison group members who scored *the same as or lower than* the test taker, whereas the statistic on page 8 reports the proportion who scored *the same as or higher than* the test taker.

As discussed in depth in the *MMPI-3 User's Guide for the Public Safety Candidate Interpretive Reports* (Corey & Ben-Porath, 2022), high underreporting scores present three rival hypotheses that require confirmation from other collateral sources:

1. The candidate is well-adjusted, endowed with positive virtues, and accurately presents these qualities.
2. The candidate is well-adjusted and endowed with positive virtues but exaggerates or otherwise distorts these qualities.
3. The candidate presents as having, but does not actually possess, these qualities.

Collateral evidence to examine when considering these possibilities includes information from the background investigation concerning the candidate's integrity and psychosocial functioning; evidence of consequential or material discrepancies in the self-reported history or between the self-reported history and confirmed background; and evidence from other tests or test items. With respect to this last source, Table 5.6 of the *MMPI-3 User's Guide for the Public Safety Candidate Interpretive Reports* lists 12 MMPI-3 items that contain potentially verifiable historical information. These items can aid test users in differentiating intentionally deceptive responses from naïve ones (i.e., lacking in self-reflection or having a rigidly moralistic self-perception, often seen in individuals with a background stressing traditional values). These items are printed automatically in a PSCIR if a test taker produces elevated scores on L; however, users of the MMPI-3 Score Report will need to manually check for the candidate's responses. Mr. D answered in the keyed direction all the historically verifiable items listed in Table 5.6 of the User's Guide. For reasons of test security, these items are not reprinted in this book, but it should be noted that they pertain to his past experiences and behavior. As we proceed through the remaining steps of the integrative model, it is important to be especially alert for information that might contradict these responses and, more generally, Mr. D's self-report of being uncommonly virtuous.

Notwithstanding the fact that consideration of collateral background information in public safety candidate psychological screening is a recommended best practice (APA, 2018; IACP, 2020; Mitchell, 2017; Serafino, 2010) and a requirement in California (California Code of Regulations, Title 11 § 1953[d][2] and [g][3]), Texas (Texas Administrative Code, Title 37, Part 7, Rule § 217.1[12]), and Ontario, Canada (Ministry of Community Safety & Correctional Services, 2018), some hiring agencies and screening psychologists avoid it for fear that it will somehow contaminate or prejudice the evaluation. Spilberg and Corey (2022) challenged this view directly:

> Although some may believe that background information may bias the psychological evaluation, in fact, just the opposite is true. When an agency deprives the screening psychologist of its findings from the background investigation, the psychologist is forced to rely on personal history information provided by the candidate, and this self-report cannot be solely relied upon as accurate and complete. By providing the psychologist with objective and third-party information, discrepancies can be identified and reconciled, thereby ensuring that the determination of a candidate's psychological suitability is made with maximum reliability and validity. (p. 47)

Corey and colleagues (2018; reviewed in chapter 6) found that MMPI-2-RF scores and biodata augmented one another in the prediction of poor performance outcomes. Sarchione and colleagues (1998) reported similar findings, noting that "prior life history evidence of dysfunctional behaviors (either at work, through drug use, or criminal activity) should be taken very seriously in the personnel selection process" (p. 910). Depending on candidates to honestly report negative life history without access to collateral data needed to verify that self-report reduces the reliability and validity of job suitability evaluations.

Because the "basic model" of psychological screening involves at least one broadband test of personality and psychopathology and another measuring normal-range personality traits, screening examiners whose batteries include a test of normal personality with underreporting measures (e.g., positive impression management, good impression, and defensiveness) have another source for evaluating these hypotheses. This is especially useful because intentionally deceptive candidates are unlikely to be deceptive on just one test or component of the assessment process. In other words, candidates who are actively engaged in a deceptive effort respond in this manner on testing, on personal history questionnaires, and in interviews, and they are often inconsistent in their deceptive reporting.

The measure of normal-range personality used to assess Mr. D also contained a measure of underreporting. The results indicated a level of underreporting that was more than three standard deviations above the normative sample and a standard deviation and a half above the mean for police candidates.

When underreporting scores are high, screening professionals are sometimes tempted to readminister a test, with instructions to respond honestly (i.e., recentering instructions). We advise against this practice for two reasons: it alerts the candidate to respond differently but not necessarily more accurately; and altering standard instructions by inserting a caveat to answer honestly violates test standardization, thereby rendering the results uninterpretable against standardized norms and validation data obtained with standard instructions. A preferred procedure when an evaluator concludes that retesting is warranted is to administer an alternate test measuring similar constructs but still use the test's standard instructions. See chapter 9 for an in-depth discussion of recentering instructions.

Step 2: Assessing Substantive Scale Findings

As discussed in chapter 4, the review of substantive scale scores on the MMPI-3 always begins with an analysis of clinically significant findings ($\geq 65T$), followed by an analysis of moderately elevated or subclinical scores that are uncommon relative to the appropriate personnel comparison group (if available). Mr. D's scores on the MMPI-3 Substantive Scales are all well below 65T and indicate no reports of clinically significant somatic, cognitive, emotional, thought, or behavioral dysfunction. However, given the evidence of possible underreporting, the absence of scale elevations cannot be interpreted as indicating the absence of problems measured by these scales. Mr. D's substantive scale scores also show no moderate-level elevations relative to the Police Candidate Comparison Group, although the interpretive caveat applies here too: owing to underreporting, the absence of comparison group findings cannot be interpreted as indicating the absence of problems they are used to assess.

A feature of the MMPI-3 is the interpretability of several substantive scale scores at both upper and lower cutoffs (Ben-Porath & Sellbom, 2023; *MMPI-3 Manual for Administration, Scoring, and Interpretation* [Ben-Porath & Tellegen, 2020a]). Among these scales is the Hypomanic Activation (RC9) scale. Ben-Porath and Tellegen note that the interpretive caution warranted by underreporting, whether intentional or unintentional, applies specifically to nonelevated (i.e., subclinical) scores and *particularly* to low scores (i.e., 38T or lower). Mr. D's score on RC9 (39T) barely lies above the lower threshold for interpreting the scale ($\leq 38T$) and cannot be interpreted to mean, as it would in a protocol with a lower

RC9 score, that he reports "a low energy level" (Ben-Porath & Tellegen, 2020a, Table 5-23). Consequently, it should not be interpreted at all.

Mr. D's scores on normal personality testing reveal a denial of problems and claims of moral virtues consistent with his scores on the test's measure of underreporting. As with the MMPI-3, the magnitude of underreporting indicated by his test scores also precludes interpreting substantive scale scores from normal-range personality testing to reflect the absence of problems.

Our review so far reveals that Mr. D presents as morally virtuous and free of problems. We now turn to the remaining sources of assessment information in this case to see how their findings converge with or diverge from these test findings.

Step 3: Assessing Background Findings

As noted in the case summary, Mr. D spent nearly a year as a police officer recruit in training with another police department. However, he failed field training and probation due to problematic interactions with citizens and fellow officers as well as problems with geography, emergency driving, radio control, multitasking, and decision-making. Training records at that agency indicated that he had a "know-it-all attitude" when dealing with coworkers and an overly officious, stern, and inflexible approach to citizens. Each of the interviewed references at the former agency stated that they thought he could perform more successfully in a small agency with a low call volume. Except for his performance during field training at the previous agency, all other findings from the background investigation were positive.

Step 4: Assessing Interview Findings

Although Mr. D completed a structured personal history questionnaire during the written testing phase of the evaluation before the interview, we treat that information as a component of the interview because his responses consist of self-reported history given in anticipation of the interview and the interview itself is largely structured around that history (e.g., as a review and clarification of certain historical and behavioral admissions related to the candidate's developmental, educational, occupational/military, substance use, avocational, legal, medical, and psychological history). As noted in chapter 5, one purpose of the interview is to clarify personal history and another is to test hypotheses that derive from the psychological testing and background investigation.

The evaluator reviewed all the material from the testing and background investigation before conducting the interview—which, as we discussed in chapter 5, is an essential procedural practice. On page 9 of Mr. D's PCIR (Figure 8.1) are 12 MMPI-3 items with potentially verifiable historical content. As mentioned, their item numbers and content are redacted from Figure 8.1 for test security, but they are listed in Table 5.6 of the *MMPI-3 User's Guide for the Public Safety Candidate Interpretive Reports* and would be included in an actual report. These items are particularly useful in cases where, as with Mr. D, the background investigation does not reveal deceptive acts or integrity violations, but it nonetheless appears that the candidate's self-report is unreliable. In reviewing Mr. D's background investigation, the screening psychologist noted facts from his juvenile and young adult history that contradicted his answers to eight of the MMPI-3 items with potentially verifiable historical content. The psychologist counted these discrepancies as risk-related findings to be considered at Step 5a of the integrative model (Table 8.1).

In addition to reviewing discrepancies between Mr. D's documented history from the background investigation and his self-reported history in response to the MMPI-3 items with historical content, the evaluator reviewed Mr. D's responses to the structured personal history questionnaire administered earlier. Mr. D reported on this questionnaire that he had never resigned from a job under pressure or negative circumstances. In cases involving such bold dissembling, it may be tempting for a screening psychologist to assume it to be a mere error and to ask the candidate to reconcile his answer with the fact that he resigned during training in lieu of termination. There is usually little to be gained by this approach, because, once alerted to the psychologist's concern over his erroneous answer, he undoubtedly would respond in one of two ways: either he would "double-down" on his answer and argue (no doubt unsuccessfully) that his resignation was not under negative circumstances, or he would say that he "checked the wrong box" and his answer was a mere mechanical error. Following the integrative model, the psychologist evaluating Mr. D counted the discrepancy as another pertinent data point—another *risk-related finding*—to be weighed with findings from all other assessment sources, including possibly mitigating findings.

One of the benefits of a full review of findings from the background investigation and psychological evaluation prior to the clinical interview is that it provides the screening psychologist important information for constructing the interview. Spilberg and Corey (2022) cautioned that "whether the interview adds more validity than error variance hinges on how it is constructed and conducted, and on how the resulting information is analyzed and used" (p. 149). Corey and Zelig (2020) noted that viewing the interview "as something that is *constructed*, rather than passively and unwaveringly carried out in the same way for all candidates, enables evaluators to harness its unique benefits and features" (p. 177). Among these are the opportunities to pursue questions generated by a review of psychological test results and personal history and to observe the candidate's decision-making, judgment, reasoning, self-reflection, interpersonal skills, and other job-relevant aspects of the candidate's functioning. As a cautionary note, it is generally "best to use the interview to clarify what isn't known, not to mitigate what is already known" (Spilberg & Corey, 2022, p. 150).

Discrepancies between facts contained in the background investigation and a candidate's self-report may owe to deception or to legitimate differences in perspectives or recollection about what occurred. However, discrepancies across self-reports are a characteristic marker of integrity problems and are associated with future counterproductive behavior (Cuttler & Muchinsky, 2006). It is also true that police and public safety candidates, like all persons, may lie on occasion, both by omission and commission. But not all lies are equally significant. Intentional and consequential lies (i.e., materially false statements and omissions of significant negative history) are of far greater importance to a screening professional than discrepancies resulting from the candidate's misunderstanding, confusion, or erroneous beliefs about what was being asked (Spilberg & Corey, 2022). In Mr. D's case, the discrepancies between his documented personal history and that which he reported on the MMPI-3 and on the personal history questionnaire are consequential.

As an interview strategy, the evaluator chose to inquire initially about all aspects of the candidate's history without confronting him with these discrepancies. This way, the evaluator could assess Mr. D's positive adjustment more reliably. If the interviewer had begun by confronting him with his omissions and false statements, the remainder of the interview might have been overly influenced by it.

In the interview, Mr. D initially presented as engaging, self-confident (but not cocky), and affable. As the interview progressed through the various domains of his personal history, the screening professional was careful to probe for information that would aid in confirming the candidate's responses to the historically verifiable MMPI-3 items he had answered in the keyed direction (discussed earlier). Both the background information and his interview responses were consistent with four of the 12 items but inconsistent with eight. The evaluator also probed for evidence of good psychological adjustment, and Mr. D appeared to function reasonably effectively in all domains of his life—work (after his resignation, he went back to his job as a beverage distributor), family, and social relationships.

Once the evaluator completed his standard interview, he informed Mr. D that there were several discrepancies in his interview statements and personal history questionnaire compared to information from the background investigation. The examiner went through the discrepancies and asked Mr. D to explain each one. With each successive query, Mr. D's behavior increasingly took on the characteristics ascribed to him by his field training officers: officious, stern, and inflexible. He attributed the discrepancies to normal forgetting and differences of opinion. Regarding his denial of having resigned from a job under pressure or negative circumstances, he said that there was no pressure put on him to resign. When asked if he could have remained in his position if he had not resigned, he acknowledged that he would have been fired, although he insisted that this did not create a negative circumstance.

Step 5: Identifying Relevant Risk Findings

As listed in Table 8.1, Step 5 of the integrative model calls for the psychologist to examine the findings from all data sources (testing, background, and interview) to answer three questions, which we now apply to the findings in Mr. D's case.

    a. *Considering all risk-related findings from all sources, what evidence-based inferences can be drawn?*

    Test Findings. The one risk-related finding from Mr. D's test results involves the inference of intentional deception, which derives from (a) evidence of underreporting on the MMPI-3 (i.e., his score on L) and the measure of normal-range personality testing and (b) multiple discrepancies between objective facts in his background and his responses to MMPI-3 items with verifiable historical content. Although these findings raise two rival hypotheses (i.e., intentional deception vs. unintentional/naïve deception), the integrative model requires that we list at this stage only the risk-related inferences and, moreover, only those that "map onto" or conceptually link to the screening dimensions (see Table 1.5). The inference of intentional deception links directly to the Integrity/Ethics dimension and, therefore, is relevant to our analysis. It also undermines the confidence we can have in the absence of elevations on the MMPI-3 Substantive Scales and in the positive findings from normal-range personality testing. Because there are no other risk-related findings in the psychological test results, we now turn to the other assessment sources.

    Background Findings. Although Mr. D failed a previous training program as a police recruit, it is not unusual for a recruit to fail field training and probation in one agency only to have a successful police career at another, often smaller or more accommodating agency. In this case, however, Mr. D's training failure did not result merely from poor performance on tasks that he could, perhaps, master in a less demanding and stressful training environment of a smaller agency. Rather, he failed, among other reasons, because of how he treated people. This fact underscores the importance of the screening psychologist having reliable information about the candidate's emotional, behavioral, and interpersonal functioning.

Interview Findings. The risk findings in the interview relate to deception (i.e., Integrity/Ethics). It is arguable that Mr. D's officious, stern, and inflexible behavior in the interview in response to being confronted with his various self-report discrepancies is another risk factor, although it is also ultimately implicated in his pattern of deception.

b. *What divergent findings might mitigate these inferences?*

The integrative model requires that we eliminate any identified risk-related inference that is mitigated by divergent findings of sufficient relevance, reliability, and validity. If credible, Mr. D's explanations for his erroneous answers would constitute divergent findings mitigating the inference that his deception was intentional. However, it should be noted that Mr. D's scores on CRIN (36T), VRIN (39T), and TRIN (50T) reflect careful attention to response consistency and item content, and he completed both the personal history questionnaire and the MMPI-3 in the same session. Also, no other reading errors were found in his responses to the personal history questionnaire. Thus, it is not credible that Mr. D misread these items, let alone that he misread only the questions about which his personal history was the most negative and discrepant from known facts.

Mr. D's very positive references from all other sources and a wholly positive 20-year employment history diverge from the inference of intentional deception. However, even if these divergent findings are reliable, they are irrelevant to the findings of deception in the current evaluation. If we accept that Mr. D is nearly always honest in his dealings with employers and others, this does not negate the relevance of lying (consequentially) in this evaluation. Indeed, even if these positive findings are valid, they are valid only for purposes of characterizing his past behavior. Mr. D's behavior in this assessment stands on its own and cannot be mitigated by behavior before or outside it. Thus, we conclude that the inference of intentional deception is not mitigated by any divergent data in the assessment record of sufficient relevance, reliability, and validity and that it therefore survives the analysis.

c. *Are any surviving risk-related inferences of sufficient relevance and quality to warrant the candidate's disqualification?*

In some states (e.g., Arizona, Maine, and Oregon), this is an "ultimate question" that belongs to the employer or training academy. In most jurisdictions, the screening professional is responsible for making this determination (Corey et al., 2023). In either case, the decision maker will necessarily rely on the relevance and quality of the inferences when making it. In Mr. D's case, the inference of deception is relevant both because of its job relatedness and because of its impact on the evaluator's ability to accurately assess the candidate's standing on the other screening dimensions. For a police officer, integrity is a requirement for reliable performance in a sworn position involving the enforcement of laws and regulations, writing official reports, preparing affidavits for use by courts and prosecutors, and giving sworn testimony. Consequently, the screening psychologist determined that Mr. D **does not meet** the criterion standard and is unqualified to be a police officer.[1]

COMPREHENSIVE REVIEW: MS. Q, POLICE CANDIDATE

Assessment Issues Presented

- Interpreting moderately elevated substantive scale scores
- Integrating information from personal history, clinical interview, and psychological testing

Referral Summary

Ms. Q is a 32-year-old, married, female police candidate with a bachelor's degree in criminal justice. At the time of the evaluation, she had three young children and was employed with another police department in an administrative position. She was highly recommended by the administrative personnel at her employing agency for a police officer position at a neighboring agency. All the references were positive except for (a) a report by her direct supervisor that she has difficulty following oral instructions and (b) concerns expressed by several officers at her employing agency that she may have difficulty taking enforcement actions, particularly with resistant and hostile citizens, because of her apparent "need to be liked by everyone."

Data Integration

Step 1: Assessing Protocol Validity

Ms. Q's PCIR (Figure 8.2) includes a narrative interpretation of protocol validity on page 8. As noted, the protocol contained no unscorable items, no indications of response inconsistency, and no indications of over- or underreporting. Nevertheless, page 8 of the report includes the statement, "It's worth noting that the test taker reported being much less well-adjusted than a typical police candidate" (referring to her score [47T] on K). Further, it notes that less than 3% of comparison group members reported such a low level of psychological adjustment and that scores on the Substantive Scales "do indeed raise possible concerns about the test taker's psychological functioning compared with other police candidates." Ms. Q's scores on measures of underreporting from normal-range personality testing presented a similar pattern.

Minnesota Multiphasic Personality Inventory®-3

Yossef S. Ben-Porath
Auke Tellegen

MMPI®-3
Police Candidate Interpretive Report
David M. Corey, PhD, & Yossef S. Ben-Porath, PhD

ID Number:	Ms. Q
Age:	32
Gender:	Female
Marital Status:	Not reported
Years of Education:	Not reported
Date Assessed:	09/18/2022

Copyright © 2020 by the Regents of the University of Minnesota. All rights reserved. Distributed exclusively under license from the University of Minnesota by NCS Pearson, Inc. Portions reproduced from the *MMPI-3 English Test Booklet*. Copyright © 2020 by the Regents of the University of Minnesota. All rights reserved. Portions excerpted from the *MMPI-3 Manual for Administration, Scoring, and Interpretation*. Copyright © 2020 by the Regents of the University of Minnesota. All rights reserved. Portions excerpted from the *MMPI-3 Technical Manual*. Copyright © 2020 by the Regents of the University of Minnesota. All rights reserved. Used by permission of the University of Minnesota Press.

Minnesota Multiphasic Personality Inventory and **MMPI** are registered trademarks of the Regents of the University of Minnesota. **Pearson** is a trademark, in the US and/or other countries, of Pearson Education, Inc., or its affiliates.

This report contains copyrighted material and trade secrets. Qualified licensees may excerpt portions of this output report, limited to the minimum text necessary to accurately describe their significant core conclusions, for incorporation into a written evaluation of the examinee, in accordance with their profession's citation standards, if any. No adaptations, translations, modifications, or special versions may be made of this report without prior written permission from the University of Minnesota Press.

[1.4 / RE1 / QG1]

ALWAYS LEARNING   PEARSON

FIGURE 8.2. Ms. Q's MMPI-3 Police Candidate Interpretive Report

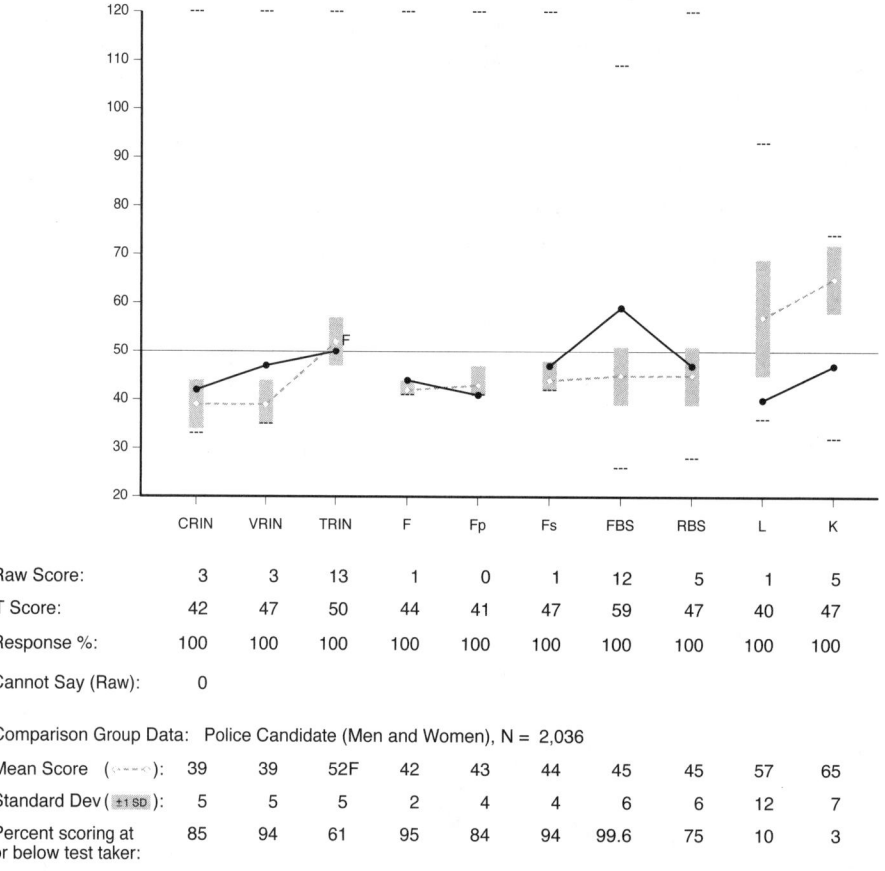

FIGURE 8.2. Ms. Q's MMPI-3 Police Candidate Interpretive Report, continued

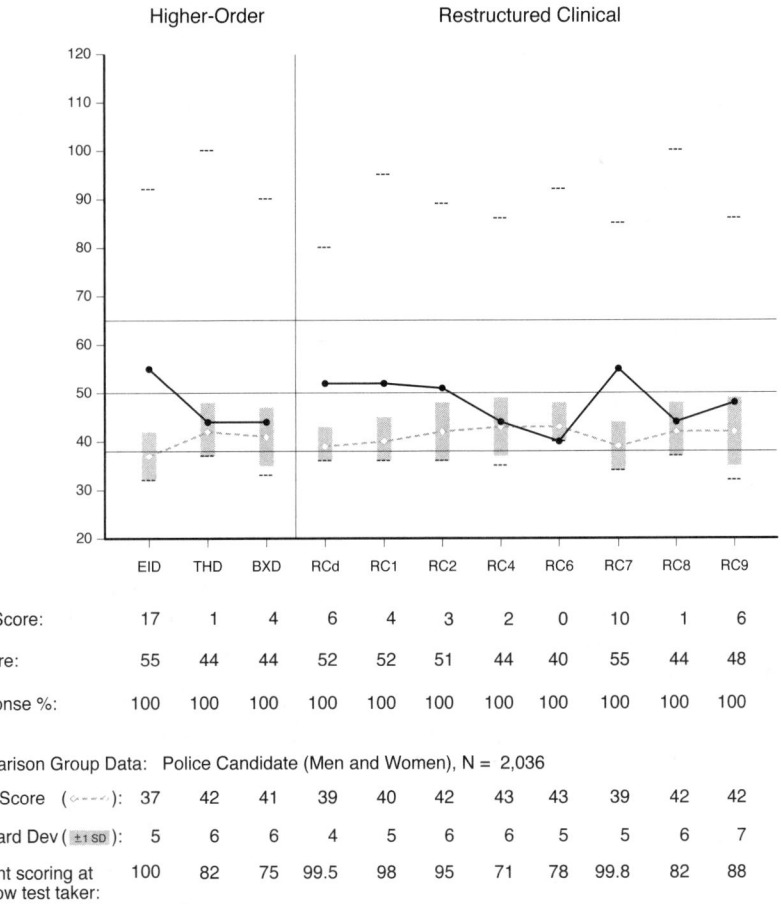

FIGURE 8.2. Ms. Q's MMPI-3 Police Candidate Interpretive Report, continued

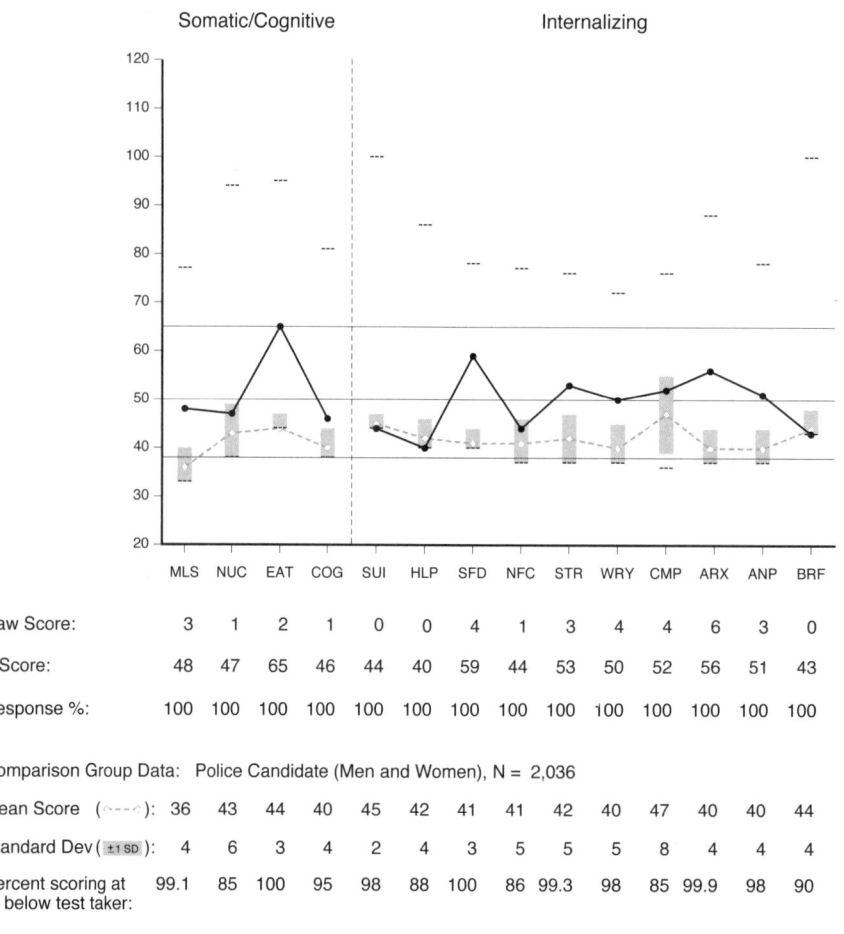

FIGURE 8.2. Ms. Q's MMPI-3 Police Candidate Interpretive Report, continued

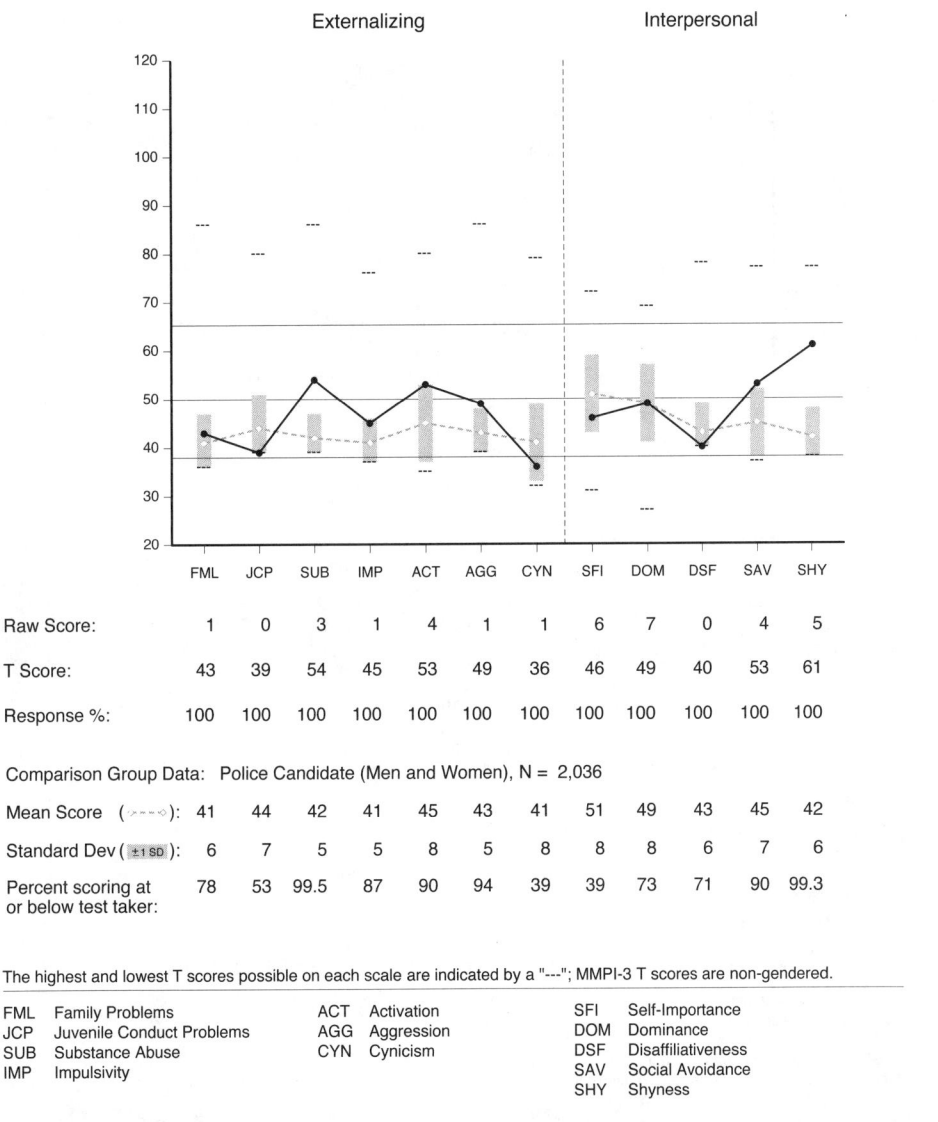

FIGURE 8.2. Ms. Q's MMPI-3 Police Candidate Interpretive Report, continued

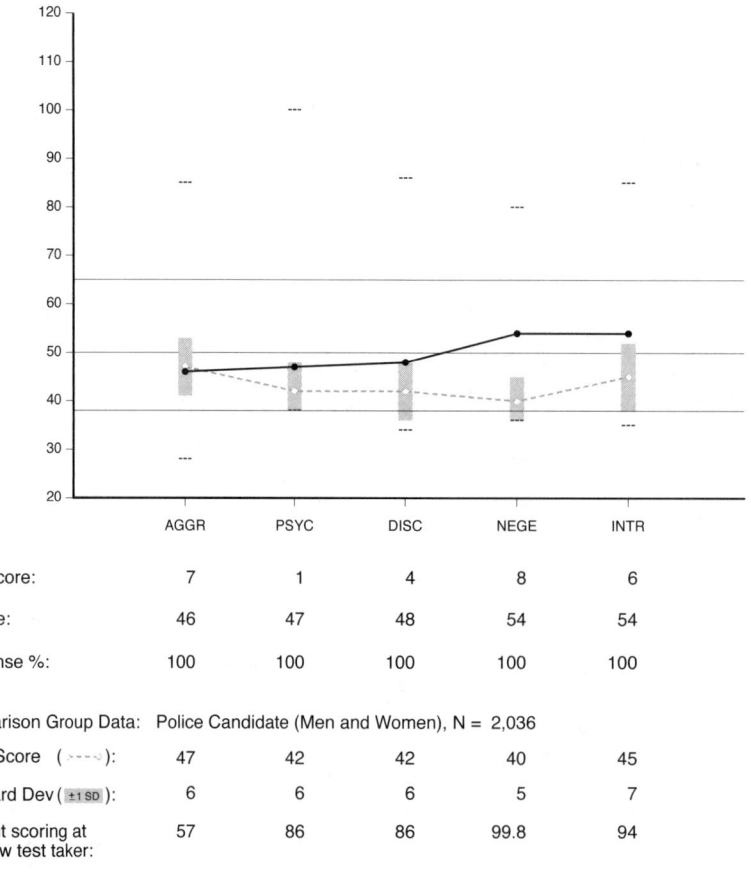

FIGURE 8.2. Ms. Q's MMPI-3 Police Candidate Interpretive Report, continued

MMPI-3 T SCORES (BY DOMAIN)

PROTOCOL VALIDITY

Content Non-Responsiveness

0	42	47	50
CNS	CRIN	VRIN	TRIN

Over-Reporting

44	41		47	59	47
F	Fp		Fs	FBS	RBS

Under-Reporting

40	**47**
L	**K**

SUBSTANTIVE SCALES

Somatic/Cognitive Dysfunction

52	48	47	65	46
RC1	MLS	NUC	EAT	COG

Emotional Dysfunction

55
EID

52	44	40	**59**	44
RCd	SUI	HLP	**SFD**	NFC

51	54
RC2	INTR

55	**53**	50	52	**56**	51	43	**54**
RC7	**STR**	WRY	CMP	**ARX**	ANP	BRF	**NEGE**

Thought Dysfunction

44
THD

40
RC6

44
RC8

47
PSYC

Behavioral Dysfunction

44
BXD

44	43	39	**54**
RC4	FML	JCP	**SUB**

48	45	53	49	36
RC9	IMP	ACT	AGG	CYN

48
DISC

Interpersonal Functioning

46	49	46	40	53	**61**
SFI	DOM	AGGR	DSF	SAV	**SHY**

Scale scores shown in bold font are interpreted in the report.

Note. This information is provided to facilitate interpretation following the recommended structure for MMPI-3 interpretation in Chapter 5 of the *MMPI-3 Manual for Administration, Scoring, and Interpretation*, which provides details in the text and an outline in Table 5-1.

FIGURE 8.2. Ms. Q's MMPI-3 Police Candidate Interpretive Report, continued

MMPI®-3 Police Candidate Interpretive Report
09/18/2022, Page 8

ID: Ms. Q

This interpretive report is intended for use by a professional qualified to interpret the MMPI-3 in the context of preemployment psychological evaluations of police and other law enforcement candidates. **It focuses on identifying problems; it does not convey potential strengths.** *The information it contains should be considered in the context of the test taker's background, the demands of the position under consideration, the clinical interview, findings from supplemental tests, and other relevant information.*

The interpretive statements in the Protocol Validity section of the report are based on T scores derived from the general MMPI-3 normative sample, as well as scores obtained by the multisite sample of 2,036 individuals that make up the Police Candidate Comparison Group.

The interpretive statements in the Clinical Findings and Diagnostic Considerations sections of the report are based on T scores derived from the general MMPI-3 normative sample. Following recommended practice, only T scores of 65 and higher (with a few exceptions) are considered clinically significant. Scores at this clinical level are generally rare among police candidates.

Statements in the Comparison Group Findings and Job-Relevant Correlates sections are based on comparisons with scores obtained by the Police Candidate Comparison Group. Statements in these sections may be based on T scores that, although less than 65, are nevertheless uncommon in reference to the comparison group.

The report includes extensive annotation, which appears as superscripts following each statement in the narrative, keyed to Endnotes with accompanying Research References, which appear in the final two sections of the report. Additional information about the annotation features is provided in the headnotes to these sections and in the MMPI-3 User's Guide for the Public Safety Candidate Interpretive Reports.

SYNOPSIS

This is a valid MMPI-3 protocol. There are no indications of clinically significant somatic or cognitive complaints, or of clinically significant emotional, thought, behavioral, or interpersonal dysfunction.

Comparison group findings point to possible concerns about self-doubt, negative emotions, stress, anxiety, past or current substance use, and shyness.

Possible job-relevant problems are identified in the following domains: Emotional Control and Stress Tolerance, Routine Task Performance, Decision-Making and Judgment, Feedback Acceptance, Assertiveness, Social Competence and Teamwork, Integrity, Conscientiousness and Dependability, Substance Use, and Impulse Control.

PROTOCOL VALIDITY

This is a valid MMPI-3 protocol. There are no problems with unscorable items. The test taker responded to the items relevantly on the basis of their content, and there are no indications of over- or under-reporting.

It is worth noting that the test taker reported being much less well-adjusted than a typical police candidate[1]. Only 3% of members of the Police Candidate Comparison Group reported this or a lower level of psychological adjustment. As detailed later in this report, her scores on the Substantive Scales do indeed raise possible concerns about the test taker's psychological functioning compared with other police candidates.

FIGURE 8.2. Ms. Q's MMPI-3 Police Candidate Interpretive Report, continued

CLINICAL FINDINGS

There are no indications of clinically significant somatic, cognitive, emotional, thought, or behavioral dysfunction in this protocol.

DIAGNOSTIC CONSIDERATIONS

No specific psychodiagnostic recommendations are indicated by this MMPI-3 protocol.

COMPARISON GROUP FINDINGS

This section describes the MMPI-3 substantive scale findings in the context of the Police Candidate Comparison Group. Specific sources for each statement can be accessed with the annotation features of this report.
Job-related correlates of these results, if any, are provided in the subsequent Job-Relevant Correlates section.

Emotional/Internalizing Problems
The test taker reports a comparatively large number of emotional problems for a police candidate[2]. Only 0.2% of comparison group members convey this or a greater level of emotional difficulties. More specifically, she reports a relatively high level of negative emotions for a police candidate[3]. Only 0.5% of comparison group members convey this or a greater level of negative emotionality. In particular, she reports a comparatively high level of anxiety for a police candidate[4]. Only 0.4% of comparison group members convey this or a greater level of anxiousness. She also reports a relatively high level of problems with stress for a police candidate[5]. Only 3.0% of comparison group members convey this or a greater level of stress.

She reports a comparatively high level of self-doubt for a police candidate[6]. Only 0.3% of comparison group members convey this or a greater lack of confidence.

Behavioral/Externalizing Problems
The test taker reports a comparatively large number of problems with substance use for a police candidate[7]. Only 2.0% of comparison group members convey this or a greater level of misusing substances.

Interpersonal Problems
The test taker reports a comparatively high level of social anxiety for a police candidate[8]. Only 2.0% of comparison group members convey this or a greater level of shyness and inhibition.

JOB-RELEVANT CORRELATES

Job-relevant personality characteristics and behavioral tendencies of the test taker are described in this section and organized according to ten problem domains commonly identified in the professional literature as relevant to public safety candidate suitability. (Please see MMPI-3 User's Guide for the Public Safety Candidate Interpretive Reports *for details.) Statements that begin with "Compared with other police candidates" are based on correlations with other self-report measures obtained in police candidate samples that included individuals who were subsequently hired as well as those who were not. Statements that begin with "She is more likely than most police officers or trainees" are based on correlations with outcome data obtained in samples of hired candidates during academy or field training, probation, and/or the postprobation period. Specific sources for each statement can be accessed with the annotation features of this report.*

FIGURE 8.2. Ms. Q's MMPI-3 Police Candidate Interpretive Report, continued

Emotional Control and Stress Tolerance Problems

Compared with other police candidates, the test taker is more likely to become easily discouraged[9]; to have difficulty coping with stress[10]; and to worry about problems and be uncertain about how to deal with them[11]. She is also more likely to behave in a self-defeating fashion[12]; to have trouble tolerating ambiguous, confusing, and unstructured environments[13]; and to develop physical symptoms in response to stress and worry about her health[14]. In addition, she is more likely to experience negative emotions[15].

She is more likely than most police officers or trainees to exhibit difficulties applying instructions appropriately under stressful conditions[16] and performing under stressful conditions[16].

Routine Task Performance Problems

Compared with other police candidates, the test taker is more likely to be lacking in confidence in her own abilities[12]; to avoid, when she can, seemingly complex challenges[17]; and to have a difficult time making use of her talents[17].

She is more likely than most police officers or trainees to exhibit difficulties carrying out tasks under non-stressful conditions[16] and cognitive adaptation problems[18].

Decision-Making and Judgment Problems

Compared with other police candidates, the test taker is more likely to avoid making decisions, fail to take action, or do anything that may prompt scrutiny from others[19]. She is also more likely to be made anxious by change and uncertainty[12].

She is more likely than most police officers or trainees to exhibit difficulties prioritizing multiple and essential functions of the job and performing them in quick succession while maintaining good environmental awareness of vital information (in other words, multi-tasking)[20].

Feedback Acceptance Problems

The test taker is more likely than most police officers or trainees to exhibit difficulties accepting and responding to constructive performance feedback[21].

Assertiveness Problems

Compared with other police candidates, the test taker is more likely to avoid situations that others generally view as benign and non-intimidating[17]; to be ill at ease in dealing with others[22]; and to feel inadequate[23]. She is also more likely to be unsure and act hesitantly[24] and to lack assertiveness[25].

Social Competence and Teamwork Problems

Compared with other police candidates, the test taker is more likely to have difficulty creating and sustaining mutually satisfying relationships[26].

Integrity Problems

The test taker is more likely than most police officers or trainees to exhibit difficulties leading to integrity violations[27] and sustained internal affairs investigations[27].

Conscientiousness and Dependability Problems

Compared with other police candidates, the test taker is more likely to give up easily and not persevere in the face of challenges[28].

She is more likely than most police officers or trainees to exhibit difficulties with punctuality and attendance[29].

Substance Use Problems

Compared with other police candidates, the test taker is more likely to have a history of substance use problems[30].

FIGURE 8.2. Ms. Q's MMPI-3 Police Candidate Interpretive Report, continued

Impulse Control Problems

Compared with other police candidates, the test taker is more likely to have a history of anger management problems[31].

She is more likely than most police officers or trainees to exhibit problems reacting to situations with the proper degree of emotional and behavioral restraint and control, and avoiding impulsive and/or unnecessarily risky behavior[32].

ITEM-LEVEL INFORMATION

Unscorable Responses

The test taker produced scorable responses to all the MMPI-3 items.

Critical Responses

Seven MMPI-3 scales—Suicidal/Death Ideation (SUI), Helplessness/Hopelessness (HLP), Anxiety-Related Experiences (ARX), Ideas of Persecution (RC6), Aberrant Experiences (RC8), Substance Abuse (SUB), and Aggression (AGG)—have been designated by the test authors as having critical item content that may require immediate attention and follow-up. Items answered by the individual in the keyed direction (True or False) on a critical scale are listed below if her T score on that scale is 65 or higher. However, any item answered in the keyed direction on SUI is listed.

The test taker has not produced an elevated T score (≥ 65) on any of these scales or answered any SUI items in the keyed direction.

Critical Follow-up Items

This section contains a list of items to which the test taker responded in a manner warranting follow-up. The items were identified by public safety candidate screening experts as having critical content. Clinicians are encouraged to follow up on these statements with the candidate by making related inquiries, rather than reciting the item(s) verbatim. Each item is followed by the candidate's response, the percentage of Police Candidate Comparison Group members who gave this response, and the scale(s) on which the item appears.

> Item number and content omitted. (True; 2.4%; VRIN, TRIN, RC7, ANP)
> Item number and content omitted. (True; 2.3%; ARX)
> Item number and content omitted. (True; 19.4%; BXD, RC9, IMP, DISC)
> Item number and content omitted. (True; 2.0%; ARX)
> Item number and content omitted. (True; 1.4%; VRIN, EID, RC7, ARX, NEGE)
> Item number and content omitted. (True; 12.7%; ARX)
> Item number and content omitted. (True; 5.1%; EID, ARX, NEGE)
> Item number and content omitted. (True; 13.5%; ANP)

FIGURE 8.2. Ms. Q's MMPI-3 Police Candidate Interpretive Report, continued

ENDNOTES

This section lists for each statement in the report the MMPI-3 score(s) that triggered it. In addition, each statement is identified as a <u>Test Response</u>, if based on item content, a <u>Correlate</u>, if based on empirical correlates, or an <u>Inference</u>, if based on the report authors' judgment. (This information can also be accessed on-screen by placing the cursor on a given statement.) For correlate-based statements, research references (Ref. No.) are provided, keyed to the consecutively numbered reference list following the endnotes.

[1] Test Response: K=47
[2] Test Response: EID=55
[3] Test Response: RC7=55; NEGE=54
[4] Test Response: ARX=56
[5] Test Response: STR=53
[6] Test Response: SFD=59
[7] Test Response: SUB=54
[8] Test Response: SHY=61
[9] Correlate: EID=55, Ref. 3, 10; NEGE=54, Ref. 10
[10] Correlate: EID=55, Ref. 3, 10, 12; SFD=59, Ref. 5, 12; STR=53, Ref. 1, 12; NEGE=54, Ref. 1, 3, 10, 12
[11] Correlate: EID=55, Ref. 2, 3, 10
[12] Correlate: EID=55, Ref. 2, 10; SHY=61, Ref. 1, 2
[13] Correlate: RC7=55, Ref. 3, 10; NEGE=54, Ref. 3, 10
[14] Correlate: SFD=59, Ref. 5, 12; NEGE=54, Ref. 3
[15] Correlate: RC7=55, Ref. 2; NEGE=54, Ref. 2
[16] Correlate: EID=55, Ref. 6, 7
[17] Correlate: EID=55, Ref. 10
[18] Correlate: NEGE=54, Ref. 4
[19] Correlate: RC7=55, Ref. 2, 10; SHY=61, Ref. 2, 10
[20] Correlate: EID=55, Ref. 6, 7; ARX=56, Ref. 1
[21] Correlate: EID=55, Ref. 9; NEGE=54, Ref. 6, 10
[22] Correlate: SHY=61, Ref. 2, 3, 10
[23] Correlate: RC7=55, Ref. 2, 10; SHY=61, Ref. 1, 2, 3, 10
[24] Correlate: SHY=61, Ref. 1, 2, 3, 10
[25] Correlate: SFD=59, Ref. 12
[26] Correlate: SHY=61, Ref. 2
[27] Correlate: SUB=54, Ref. 8, 10
[28] Correlate: EID=55, Ref. 2, 7, 10; SHY=61, Ref. 2, 10
[29] Correlate: ARX=56, Ref. 1; SHY=61, Ref. 10; NEGE=54, Ref. 1
[30] Correlate: SUB=54, Ref. 1, 3, 10, 11, 12
[31] Correlate: NEGE=54, Ref. 3, 10
[32] Correlate: EID=55, Ref. 7, 8

FIGURE 8.2. Ms. Q's MMPI-3 Police Candidate Interpretive Report, continued

RESEARCH REFERENCE LIST

The following studies are sources for empirical correlates identified in the Endnotes section of this report.

1. Ben-Porath, Y. S., & Tellegen, A. (2020). *The Minnesota Multiphasic Personality Inventory-3 (MMPI-3): Technical manual.* University of Minnesota Press.

2. Corey, D. M., & Ben-Porath, Y. S. (2022). *Minnesota Multiphasic Personality Inventory-3 (MMPI-3): User's guide for the public safety candidate interpretive reports.* University of Minnesota Press.

3. Detrick, P., Ben-Porath, Y.S., & Sellbom, M. (2016). Associations between MMPI-2-RF (Restructured Form) and Inwald Personality Inventory (IPI) scale scores in a law enforcement preemployment screening sample. *Journal of Police and Criminal Psychology, 31,* 81–95. https://doi.org/10.1007/s11896-015-9172-7

4. Roberts, R. M., Tarescavage, A. M., Ben-Porath, Y. S., & Roberts, M. D. (2018). predicting post-probationary job performance of police officers using CPI and MMPI-2-RF test data obtained during preemployment psychological screening. *Journal of Personality Assessment, 101*(5), 544–555. https://doi.org/10.1080/00223891.2018.1423990

5. Sellbom, M., Corey, D. M., & Ben-Porath, Y. S. (2021). Incremental validity of the Multidimensional Personality Questionnaire in the preemployment assessment of police officer candidates. *Criminal Justice and Behavior.* Advance online publication. https://doi.org/10.1177/00938548211033630

6. Tarescavage, A. M., Brewster, J., Corey, D. M., & Ben-Porath, Y. S. (2015). Use of pre-hire Minnesota Multiphasic Personality Inventory-2-Restructured Form (MMPI-2-RF) police candidate scores to predict supervisor ratings of post-hire performance. *Assessment, 22*(4), 411–428. https://doi.org/10.1177/1073191114548445

7. Tarescavage, A. M., Corey, D. M., & Ben-Porath, Y. S. (2015). Minnesota Multiphasic Personality Inventory-2-Restructured Form (MMPI-2-RF) predictors of police officer problem behavior. *Assessment, 22*(1), 116–132. https://doi.org/10.1177/1073191114534885

8. Tarescavage, A. M., Corey, D. M., & Ben-Porath, Y. S. (2016). A prorating method for estimating MMPI-2-RF scores from MMPI responses: Examination of score fidelity and illustration of empirical utility in the PERSEREC police integrity study sample. *Assessment, 23*(2), 173–190. https://doi.org/10.1177/1073191115575070

9. Tarescavage, A. M., Corey, D. M., Gupton, H. M., & Ben-Porath Y.S. (2015). Criterion validity and practical utility of the Minnesota Multiphasic Personality Inventory-2-Restructured Form (MMPI-2-RF) in assessments of police officer candidates. *Journal of Personality Assessment, 97*(4), 382–394. https://doi.org/10.1080/00223891.2014.995800

10. Tarescavage, A. M., Fischler, G. L., Cappo, B. M., Hill, D. O., Corey, D. M., & Ben-Porath, Y. S. (2015). Minnesota Multiphasic Personality Inventory-2-Restructured Form (MMPI-2-RF) predictors of police officer problem behavior and collateral self-report test scores. *Psychological Assessment, 27*(1), 125–137. https://doi.org/10.1037/pas0000041

11. Whitman, M. R., Corey, D. M., & Ben-Porath, Y. S. (2021). Associations between MMPI-3 and psychosocial history findings obtained in preemployment evaluations of public safety candidates [Manuscript under review].

12. Whitman, M. R., Elias, L. S., Cappo, B. M., & Ben-Porath, Y. S. (2021). Criterion validity of MMPI-3 scores in preemployment evaluations of public safety candidates. *Psychological Assessment.* Advance online publication. https://doi.org/10.1037/pas0001042

End of Report

FIGURE 8.2. Ms. Q's MMPI-3 Police Candidate Interpretive Report, continued

Step 2: Assessing Substantive Scale Findings

Users of the PCIR can see at a glance which MMPI-3 scores are interpreted in the report (Figure 8.2, p. 7) by noting those scales and scores that are printed in **bold font**. Ms. Q's scores on the highlighted Substantive Scales reveal only moderate or subclinical elevations. Although her score on EAT is 65T, this is one of three MMPI-3 substantive scales that does not use 65T as the upper cutoff score for interpretation. Interpretation of the EAT scale begins at 75T, interpretation of SUI begins at 58T, and interpretation of CMP starts at 62T. Ms. Q's moderately elevated scores on the MMPI-3 Substantive Scales fall within three scale domains: Emotional Dysfunction (EID, 55T; RC7, 55T; SFD, 59T; STR, 53T; ARX, 56T; NEGE, 54T), Behavioral Dysfunction (SUB, 54T), and Interpersonal Functioning (SHY, 61T). We will discuss the job-relevant implications of these scale elevations later under "Identifying Relevant Risk Findings." A review of Ms. Q's scores on normal-range testing indicated a tendency to be worry-prone, beset by problems, submissive, guilt-prone, and indecisive.

For some MMPI-3 scales, scores that are quite deviant relative to the comparison group mean still may not be interpreted at their score magnitude. For example, although Ms. Q's score on ANP at 51T is nearly two and a half standard deviations above the mean (40T) for police candidates, and even though 95.9% of the Police Candidate Comparison Group scored below 51T on ANP, no MMPI-3 scale score is interpreted below 53T except for extremely low scores ($\leq 38T$) on designated scales. In other cases, a deviant score may not be interpreted until it reaches a higher level because of a relatively large proportion of the comparison group that scored at or above that level. The reader may recall from our discussion in chapter 7 that MMPI-3 scores are interpreted in the four PSCIRs at cutoffs that occur in less than 8% of comparison group members, most commonly below 4%.

PSCIRs also include Critical Follow-up Items that public safety candidate screening experts identified as having critical content warranting follow-up. Ms. Q responded in the keyed direction to eight of these items (Figure 8.2, p. 11). The item numbers and content appear in the actual report but are omitted here for test security. The parenthetical information that follows each item indicates the candidate's response, the percentage of members of the Police Candidate Comparison Group who gave the same response, and the scale(s) on which the item is scored. The screening professional would want to probe in the interview for information relevant to each item's content but without reading the item verbatim or otherwise alerting the candidate to the fact that the inquiry relates to a test response.

Step 3: Assessing Background Findings

The collateral references interviewed as part of Ms. Q's background investigation were all quite positive, except for the comment from her supervisor that she has trouble following oral instructions and comments from police officers with whom she has gone on ride-alongs and interacted. Whereas the other references described her as thoughtful, compassionate, helpful, welcoming, conscientious, organized, honest, and humble (to name but a few of the adjectives listed), these officers—without denying her positive traits—also observed her to be so preoccupied with "being liked" that they doubted whether she could safely and effectively engage with hostile and resistant subjects. Notably, the administrators at the agency where she worked in a civilian position recommended her quite strongly.

Step 4: Assessing Interview Findings

Ms. Q described growing up in a home with a physically and emotionally abusive father. She said she learned to deal with her father's unpredictable emotional volatility by not doing anything that she thought would provoke his rage, and she carefully observed the things her mother and older sister did that triggered his anger and learned not to repeat them. During the interview, she was quite tearful when discussing her developmental history and acknowledged that she constantly worries about offending or upsetting someone. When asked how she imagined this would play out when enforcing laws with persons who are angry about her stopping them, she said she was confident she could "win them over" through her professionalism. Indeed, Ms. Q said that she considered her anxiety and worry to be qualities that made her a dedicated worker.

Like many who lived with an abusive adult as a child, Ms. Q has also struggled in her relationships with intimate partners. Although she described her husband of six years as her "best supporter," her description of that support made it clear that it comes in the form of consistent messages that she is working below her ability level and ought to do more with her talents. She said she wanted to become a police officer to make her family proud and to give back to her community. Ms. Q reported on her personal history questionnaire and elaborated further in the interview that about two or three times a month, she will drink as many as three alcoholic mixed drinks after her two children are asleep to "de-stress" and "wind down" before bed.

Step 5: Identifying Relevant Risk Findings

a. Considering all risk-related findings from all sources, what evidence-based inferences can be drawn?

TEST FINDINGS
The rarity and risk-related implications of Ms. Q's MMPI-3 scores are described in the Comparison Group Findings section of the PCIR, with each

description annotated with information indicating the scale (and T score) on which the statement is based. In aggregate, these Comparison Group Findings indicate that she reported a comparatively high level of emotional difficulties (EID), particularly negative emotionality (RC7 and NEGE), anxiety (ARX), and stress (STR); a comparatively high level of self-doubt (SFD); a comparatively large number of problems related to misusing substances (SUB); and a comparatively high level of social anxiety (SHY). The base rates associated with her interpreted test scores (i.e., the proportion of Police Candidate Comparison Group members who scored at the same or higher level) ranged from a low of 0.2% (EID) to a high of 3.0% (STR).

The Job-Relevant Correlates (JRC) section of the PCIR contains statements referring to two types of correlates: (a) other self-report measures obtained in police candidate samples that included individuals who were subsequently hired as well as those who were not and (b) outcome data obtained in samples of hired candidates during academy or field training, probation, or the post-probation period. As explained in the italicized boilerplate language at the bottom of page 9 and the top of page 10 of Ms. Q's PCIR, the self-report correlates can be recognized in the report by the statement stem, "Compared with other police candidates," and the outcome correlates will always begin with "[She or he or the candidate] is more likely than most police officers or trainees." Ms. Q's scores produced both types of correlates.

In summary, the self-report correlates describe Ms. Q as worry-prone, lacking in self-confidence, indecisive, ill at ease in dealing with others, and avoiding anything that may prompt scrutiny. These characteristics, along with those identified in the Comparison Group Findings section, are presumed to be associated with the outcome correlates listed in the Job-Relevant Correlates section. These include being more likely than other police officers or trainees to exhibit difficulties applying instructions under stressful conditions and performing under stressful conditions; difficulties carrying out tasks under nonstressful conditions and cognitive adaption problems; multitasking difficulties; difficulties leading to integrity violations and sustained internal affairs investigations; and difficulties with punctuality and attendance. Ms. Q's scores on normal-range testing identified risk-related inferences involving low morale, self-doubt, feelings of alienation, excessive worrying, submissiveness, and indecisiveness.

BACKGROUND FINDINGS

At this stage in the integrative model, the focus is on risk-related findings, not positive attributes and other potentially mitigating findings. Risk-related background findings pertain to her direct supervisor's report that she has difficulty following orally delivered task instructions (possibly resulting from the social anxiety she experiences) and reports from police officers in her employing agency that her preoccupation with potential social disapproval renders her unable to deal effectively with angry and uncooperative citizens.

INTERVIEW FINDINGS

Ms. Q was quite disclosing about the emotional distress and anxieties she experiences on a nearly daily basis, but she regarded them as the inevitable cost of being a conscientious person. She saw no downside to them except in terms of her own suffering; indeed, she saw them as assets, which at least partly explained her relatively nondefensive disclosure both on personality testing and in the clinical interview.

b. What divergent findings might mitigate these inferences?

Ms. Q's work and personal references indicate positive and cooperative relationships with supervisors and coworkers. Arguably, they support Ms. Q's own conclusions about the insignificance and job-irrelevance of her social anxiety and related emotional distress by demonstrating that, despite her symptoms, she is functioning well at work. The fallacy of this argument is that it ignores the association between the risk-related findings and the job to which she is applying and instead focuses on the job she was performing at the time. Proof that Ms. Q is functioning adequately or even well in a clerical role that is unlike the work of a police officer (other than working at a police department) is irrelevant to the prediction of how she will perform as a police officer or trainee. Statements from Ms. Q's references that she is thoughtful, compassionate, helpful, welcoming, conscientious, organized, honest, and humble are not *divergent* findings, they are *complementary* findings. Said another way, Ms. Q has all the listed qualities, **and** she is also anxious, fearful, stressed, and self-medicating with alcohol. Consequently, the screening psychologist reasoned that these findings do not mitigate the risk-related findings.

c. Are any surviving risk-related inferences of sufficient relevance and quality to warrant the candidate's disqualification?

All the risk-related findings cited above are directly relevant to the selection criteria (Table 1.5), particularly Emotional Regulation and Stress Tolerance, Avoidance of Substance Abuse and Other Risk-Taking Behavior, and Assertiveness/Persuasiveness. Their quality is underscored by the fact that the psychological constructs measured by the scales that trigger those job-relevant correlates are evident and reported by the candidate (that is, they are corroborated). In considering the risk-related findings and potentially mitigating evidence, the screening psychologist determined that Ms. Q **does not meet** the criterion standard and is unqualified to be a police officer.

COMPREHENSIVE REVIEW: MR. G, PATROL DEPUTY CANDIDATE

Assessment Issues Presented

- Mitigating significantly negative test findings with significantly positive and reliable background information
- Use of the PCIR

Referral Summary

Mr. G, age 45, is a married male applying for the position of patrol deputy in a large county sheriff's department. At the time of this evaluation, he was working as a drug and alcohol counselor with a county mental health agency. He has a significantly problematic late adolescent and young adult history but a positive adult history.

Data Integration

Step 1: Assessing Protocol Validity

Mr. G's MMPI-3 scores (Figure 8.3) on measures of response consistency (CRIN, VRIN, and TRIN) and overreporting (F, Fp, Fs, FBS, and RBS) are within normal limits (i.e., within or below one standard deviation of their respective Police Candidate Comparison Group means). Mr. G's score on L (44T) is an unusual finding among law enforcement candidates (as seen on p. 2 of Figure 8.3, 22% of comparison group members have a raw score the same as or lower than Mr. G) that raises questions about why he would not attempt to portray himself in a more positive light, as do most individuals under similar circumstances. Mr. G's score on K (62T), on the other hand, is less than one-half a standard deviation below the mean (65T) for the comparison group, thereby indicating that he claims to be about as well-adjusted as does the average police candidate.

As reviewed in chapter 6, Detrick and Chibnall (2014) compared MMPI-2-RF scores of police candidates tested first in a preemployment evaluation (high-demand) context and again for anonymous research purposes after they completed the academy (low-demand context). They reported that, whereas mean L-r and K-r scores were lower in the low-demand context, as were the substantive scale scores, they were not consistently so. The authors found that a lowering of L-r was the sole predictor of increases in the Behavioral/Externalizing domain (BXD, RC4, JCP, and DISC-r), whereas a change in K-r predicted inverse changes in EID, RC7, HLP, BRF, and NEGE-r. Applying this research to

Mr. G's underreporting configuration of low L and moderately high K would lead us to anticipate that any elevations found in the Substantive Scales would likely be on the externalizing behavior scales BXD, RC4, JCP, and DISC.

Step 2: Assessing Substantive Scale Findings

Mr. G's substantive scale scores, with interpretable elevations being on scales BXD (63T), RC4 (74), JCP (74T), AGG (55T), and DISC (60T), are consistent with Detrick and Chibnall's (2014) findings.

The PCIR Clinical Findings section (Figure 8.3, p. 9) includes interpretive statements corresponding to clinically elevated scales ($\geq$ 65T) only, as well as diagnostic considerations associated with RC4. The statements in the Comparison Group Findings section (p. 9) also pertain to scales indicating behavioral/externalizing problems (BXD, RC4, JCP, and DISC).

Mr. G's scores are associated with numerous Job-Relevant Correlates (Figure 8.3, pp. 10–11) within all problem domains (see Table 7.9) except for Decision-Making and Judgment Problems and Assertiveness Problems. Also unusual is the low score on Cynicism (CYN, 32T), indicating that Mr. G describes others as well-intentioned and trustworthy and disavows cynical beliefs about them. His comparatively low scores on other Specific Problems (SP) scales in the Interpersonal Functioning domain (SFI, DOM, DSF, SAV, and SHY), which are generally correlated with CYN (Ben-Porath & Sellbom, 2022), also reflect an absence of social reticence and misanthropy.

A review of scores from normal-range personality testing in this assessment record indicate self-sufficiency, a tendency to trust in the integrity and goodwill of others, and comparatively lower investment in social status and rule-observing behavior.

Step 3: Assessing Background Findings

Mr. G's background reveals two chronologically distinct behavior patterns. In the period up to age 23, his tumultuous upbringing by a single mother and a drug-abusing and largely absent father left him devoid of the support and motivation to perform well in school. During his first two years of high school, he was suspended three times for fighting and truancy, and he dropped out of school altogether after his sophomore year with a grade point average near a D. By the time he turned 18, he had been arrested three times for petty theft and marijuana possession, and it was at the court hearing for his last arrest when the judge urged him to enlist in the military and turn his life around. He obtained a suitability waiver for his juvenile criminal history and enlisted in the U.S. Army shortly before his 19th birthday. Mr. G's military stint did not provide him the discipline the judge had hoped for. He received two disciplinary

Minnesota Multiphasic Personality Inventory®-3

Yossef S. Ben-Porath
Auke Tellegen

MMPI®-3
Police Candidate Interpretive Report
David M. Corey, PhD, & Yossef S. Ben-Porath, PhD

ID Number:	Mr. G
Age:	45
Gender:	Male
Marital Status:	Not reported
Years of Education:	Not reported
Date Assessed:	03/23/2023

Copyright © 2020 by the Regents of the University of Minnesota. All rights reserved. Distributed exclusively under license from the University of Minnesota by NCS Pearson, Inc. Portions reproduced from the *MMPI-3 English Test Booklet*. Copyright © 2020 by the Regents of the University of Minnesota. All rights reserved. Portions excerpted from the *MMPI-3 Manual for Administration, Scoring, and Interpretation*. Copyright © 2020 by the Regents of the University of Minnesota. All rights reserved. Portions excerpted from the *MMPI-3 Technical Manual*. Copyright © 2020 by the Regents of the University of Minnesota. All rights reserved. Used by permission of the University of Minnesota Press.

Minnesota Multiphasic Personality Inventory and **MMPI** are registered trademarks of the Regents of the University of Minnesota. **Pearson** is a trademark, in the US and/or other countries, of Pearson Education, Inc., or its affiliates.

This report contains copyrighted material and trade secrets. Qualified licensees may excerpt portions of this output report, limited to the minimum text necessary to accurately describe their significant core conclusions, for incorporation into a written evaluation of the examinee, in accordance with their profession's citation standards, if any. No adaptations, translations, modifications, or special versions may be made of this report without prior written permission from the University of Minnesota Press.

[1.4 / RE1 / QG1]

ALWAYS LEARNING   **PEARSON**

FIGURE 8.3. Mr. G's MMPI-3 Police Candidate Interpretive Report

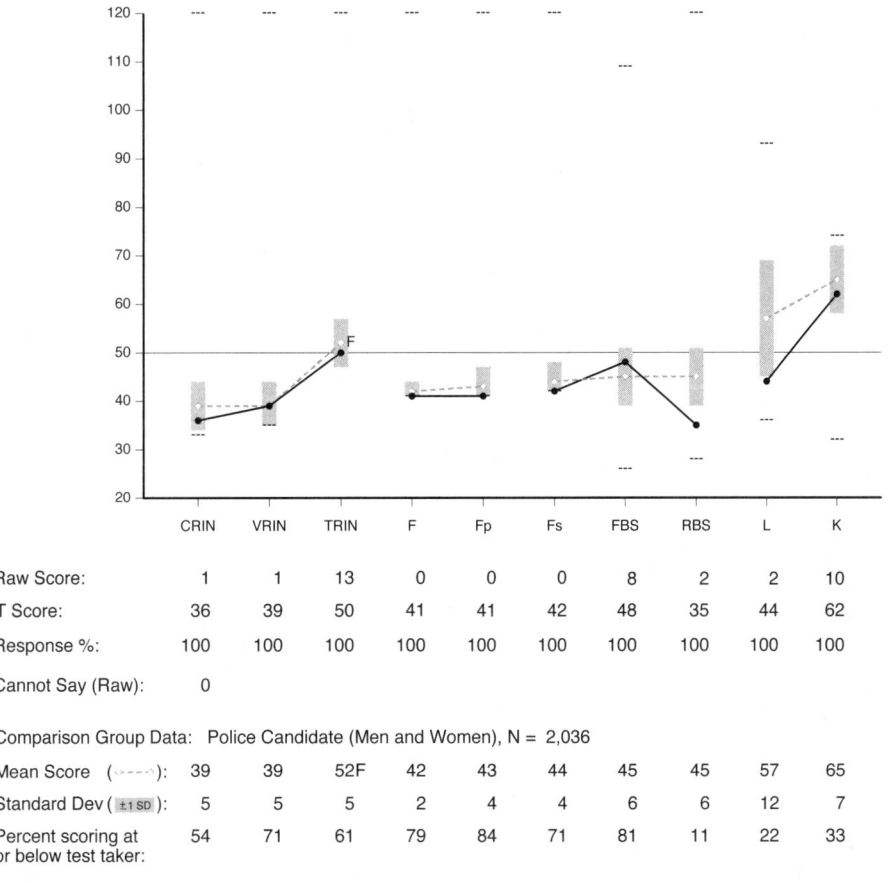

FIGURE 8.3. Mr. G's MMPI-3 Police Candidate Interpretive Report, continued

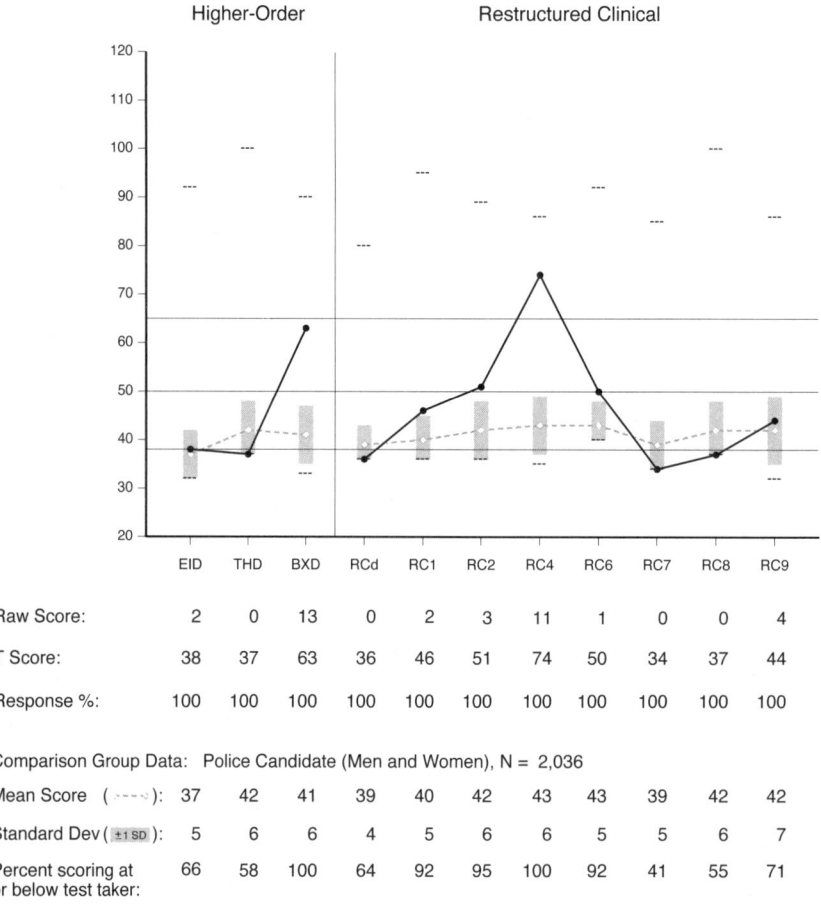

FIGURE 8.3. Mr. G's MMPI-3 Police Candidate Interpretive Report, continued

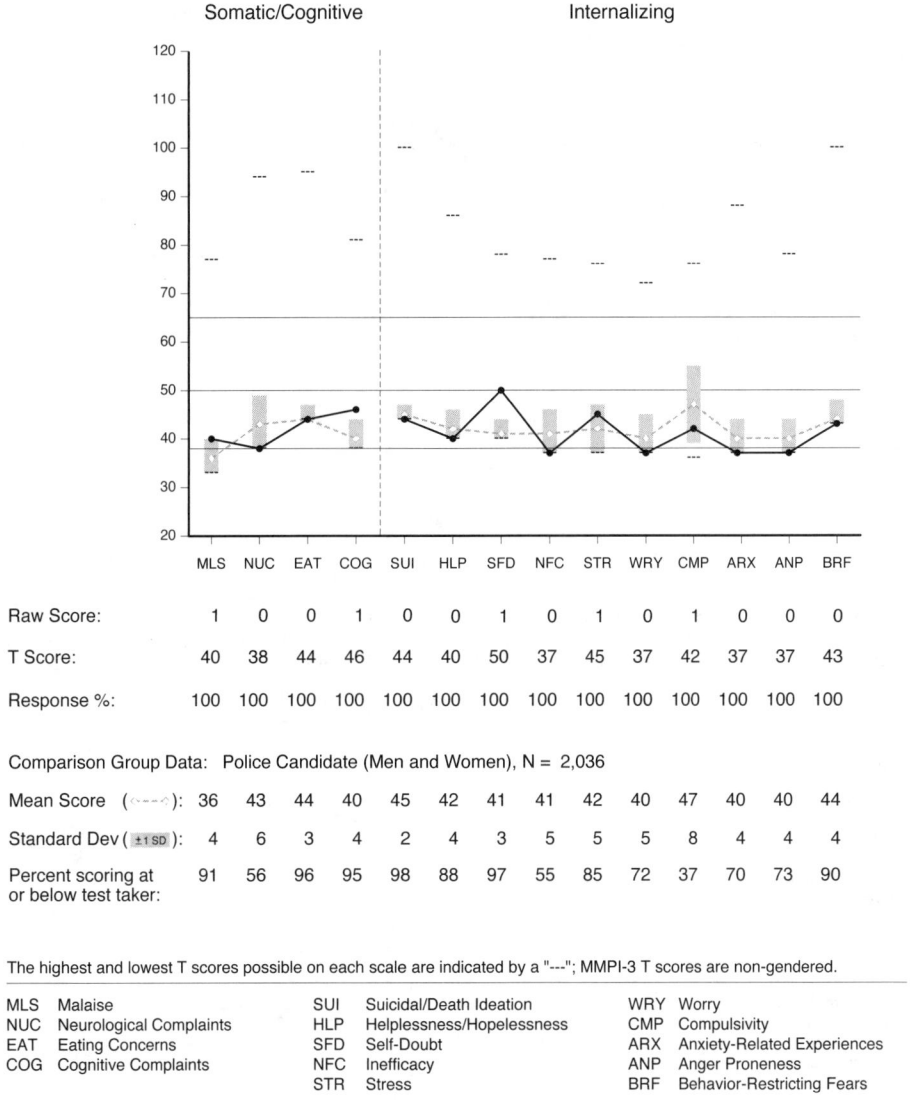

FIGURE 8.3. Mr. G's MMPI-3 Police Candidate Interpretive Report, continued

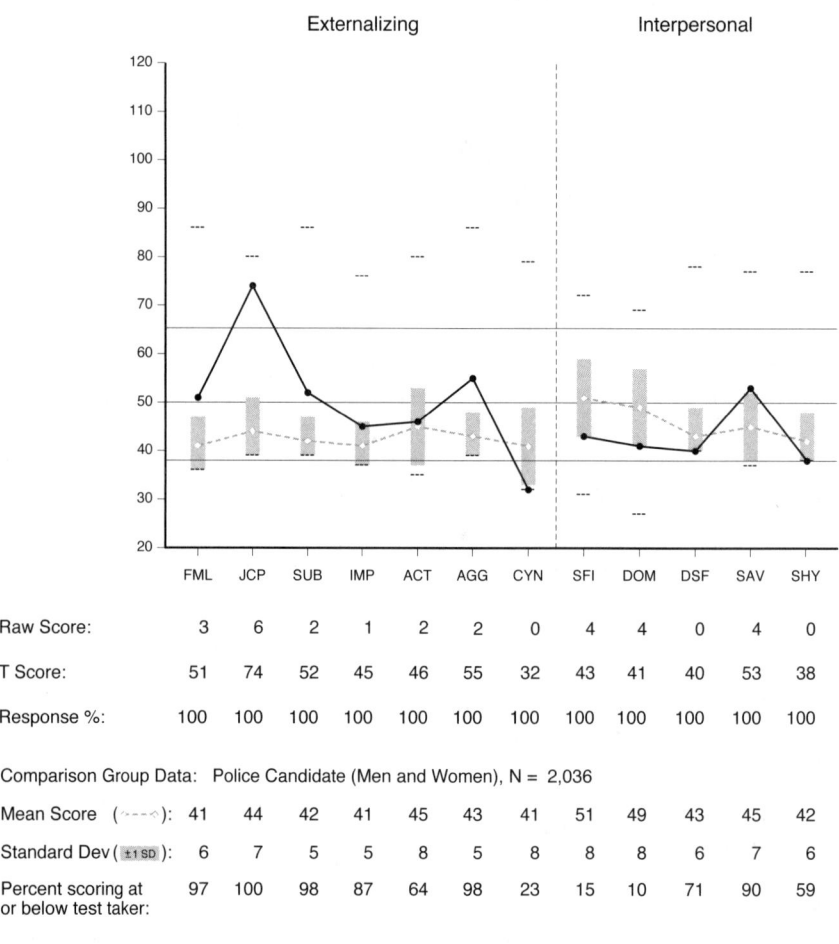

FIGURE 8.3. Mr. G's MMPI-3 Police Candidate Interpretive Report, continued

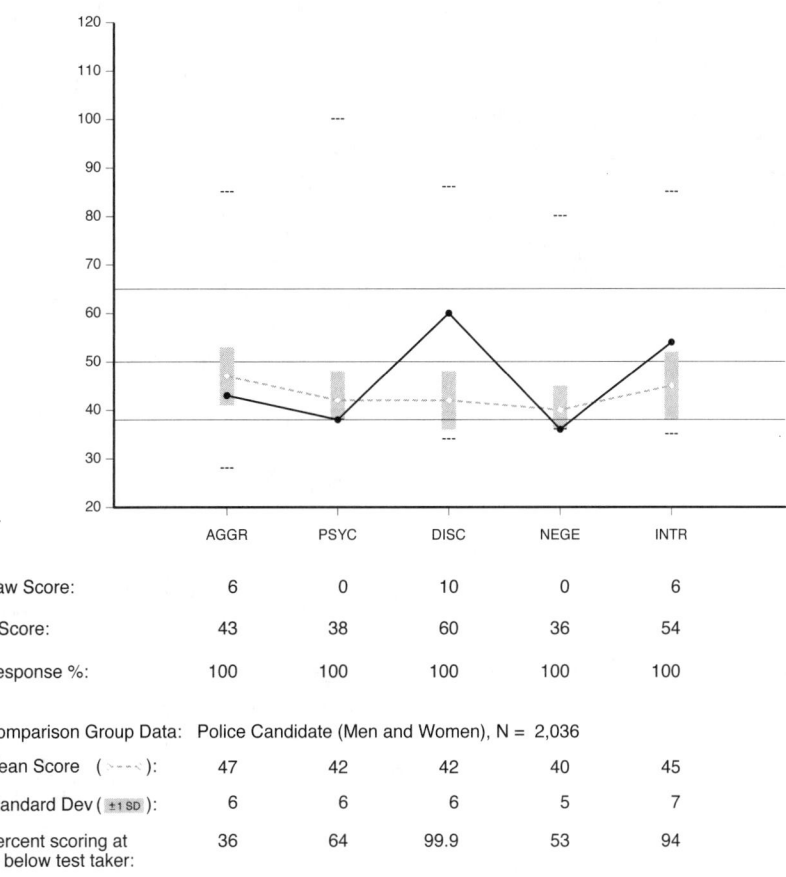

FIGURE 8.3. Mr. G's MMPI-3 Police Candidate Interpretive Report, continued

MMPI®-3 Police Candidate Interpretive Report
03/23/2023, Page 7
ID: Mr. G

MMPI-3 T SCORES (BY DOMAIN)

PROTOCOL VALIDITY

Content Non-Responsiveness	0 CNS	36 CRIN	39 VRIN	50 TRIN		
Over-Reporting	41 F	41 Fp		42 Fs	48 FBS	35 RBS
Under-Reporting	44 L	62 K				

SUBSTANTIVE SCALES

Somatic/Cognitive Dysfunction		46 RC1	40 MLS	38 NUC	44 EAT	46 COG		

Emotional Dysfunction	38 EID	36 RCd	44 SUI	40 HLP	50 SFD	37 NFC		
		51 RC2	54 INTR					
		34 RC7	45 STR	37 WRY	42 CMP	37 ARX	37 ANP	43 BRF	36 NEGE

(Note: last row has 8 columns)

Thought Dysfunction	37 THD	50 RC6
		37 RC8
		38 PSYC

Behavioral Dysfunction	**63** **BXD**	**74** **RC4**	51 FML	**74** **JCP**	52 SUB	
		44 RC9	45 IMP	46 ACT	**55** **AGG**	32 CYN
		60 **DISC**				

Interpersonal Functioning	43 SFI	41 DOM	43 AGGR	40 DSF	53 SAV	38 SHY

Scale scores shown in bold font are interpreted in the report.

Note. This information is provided to facilitate interpretation following the recommended structure for MMPI-3 interpretation in Chapter 5 of the *MMPI-3 Manual for Administration, Scoring, and Interpretation*, which provides details in the text and an outline in Table 5-1.

FIGURE 8.3. Mr. G's MMPI-3 Police Candidate Interpretive Report, continued

MMPI®-3 Police Candidate Interpretive Report
03/23/2023, Page 8

ID: Mr. G

This interpretive report is intended for use by a professional qualified to interpret the MMPI-3 in the context of preemployment psychological evaluations of police and other law enforcement candidates. **It focuses on identifying problems; it does not convey potential strengths.** *The information it contains should be considered in the context of the test taker's background, the demands of the position under consideration, the clinical interview, findings from supplemental tests, and other relevant information.*

The interpretive statements in the Protocol Validity section of the report are based on T scores derived from the general MMPI-3 normative sample, as well as scores obtained by the multisite sample of 2,036 individuals that make up the Police Candidate Comparison Group.

The interpretive statements in the Clinical Findings and Diagnostic Considerations sections of the report are based on T scores derived from the general MMPI-3 normative sample. Following recommended practice, only T scores of 65 and higher (with a few exceptions) are considered clinically significant. Scores at this clinical level are generally rare among police candidates.

Statements in the Comparison Group Findings and Job-Relevant Correlates sections are based on comparisons with scores obtained by the Police Candidate Comparison Group. Statements in these sections may be based on T scores that, although less than 65, are nevertheless uncommon in reference to the comparison group.

The report includes extensive annotation, which appears as superscripts following each statement in the narrative, keyed to Endnotes with accompanying Research References, which appear in the final two sections of the report. Additional information about the annotation features is provided in the headnotes to these sections and in the MMPI-3 User's Guide for the Public Safety Candidate Interpretive Reports.

SYNOPSIS

This is a valid MMPI-3 protocol. Scores on the Substantive Scales indicate clinically significant behavioral dysfunction. Behavioral-externalizing problems include antisocial behavior and juvenile conduct problems.

Comparison group findings point to additional possible concerns about physically aggressive behavior.

Possible job-relevant problems are identified in the following domains: Emotional Control and Stress Tolerance, Routine Task Performance, Decision-Making and Judgment, Feedback Acceptance, Social Competence and Teamwork, Integrity, Conscientiousness and Dependability, Substance Use, and Impulse Control.

PROTOCOL VALIDITY

This is a valid MMPI-3 protocol. There are no problems with unscorable items. The test taker responded to the items relevantly on the basis of their content, and there are no indications of over- or under-reporting.

FIGURE 8.3. Mr. G's MMPI-3 Police Candidate Interpretive Report, continued

CLINICAL FINDINGS

Clinical-level symptoms, personality characteristics, and behavioral tendencies of the test taker are described in this section and organized according to an empirically guided framework. (Please see Chapter 5 of the MMPI-3 Manual for Administration, Scoring, and Interpretation *for details.) Statements containing the word "reports" are based on the item content of MMPI-3 scales, whereas statements that include the word "likely" are based on empirical correlates of scale scores. Specific sources for each statement can be viewed with the annotation features of this report.*

The test taker reports a significant history of acting-out, antisocial behavior[1] and likely has poor impulse control[2], has been involved with the criminal justice system[3], and has difficulties with individuals in positions of authority[4]. He also likely acts out when bored[5] and has antisocial characteristics[6]. More specifically, he reports a history of juvenile conduct problems[7]. He likely has a history of juvenile delinquency and criminal and/or antisocial behavior[8] and experiences conflictual interpersonal relationships[9].

There are no indications of clinically significant somatic, cognitive, emotional, or thought dysfunction in this protocol.

DIAGNOSTIC CONSIDERATIONS

This section provides recommendations for psychodiagnostic assessment based on the test taker's MMPI-3 results. It is recommended that he be evaluated for the following:

Behavioral-Externalizing Disorders
- Antisocial personality disorder, substance-related disorders, and other externalizing disorders[10]

COMPARISON GROUP FINDINGS

This section describes the MMPI-3 substantive scale findings in the context of the Police Candidate Comparison Group. Specific sources for each statement can be accessed with the annotation features of this report.
Job-related correlates of these results, if any, are provided in the subsequent Job-Relevant Correlates section.

Behavioral/Externalizing Problems
The test taker reports a comparatively large number of behavioral problems for a police candidate[11]. Only 0.1% of comparison group members convey this or a greater level of behavioral difficulties. More specifically, his responses indicate a level of antisocial behavior that is likely incompatible with public safety requirements for behavioral control[12]. This level of rule-breaking behavior is uncommon among police candidates. Less than 0.1% of comparison group members give evidence of this level of antisocial behavior. In particular, his responses indicate a history of juvenile conduct problems that may impede conformance with public safety requirements for behavioral control and adherence to rules[13]. This level of juvenile misconduct is uncommon among police candidates. Only 0.2% of comparison group members demonstrate this or a larger number of juvenile conduct problems.

He reports a comparatively high level of physically aggressive behavior for a police candidate[14]. Only 6.0% of comparison group members convey this or a greater level of inappropriately aggressive behavior.

FIGURE 8.3. Mr. G's MMPI-3 Police Candidate Interpretive Report, continued

JOB-RELEVANT CORRELATES

Job-relevant personality characteristics and behavioral tendencies of the test taker are described in this section and organized according to ten problem domains commonly identified in the professional literature as relevant to public safety candidate suitability. (Please see MMPI-3 User's Guide for the Public Safety Candidate Interpretive Reports *for details.) Statements that begin with "Compared with other police candidates" are based on correlations with other self-report measures obtained in police candidate samples that included individuals who were subsequently hired as well as those who were not. Statements that begin with "He is more likely than most police officers or trainees" are based on correlations with outcome data obtained in samples of hired candidates during academy or field training, probation, and/or the postprobation period. Specific sources for each statement can be accessed with the annotation features of this report.*

Emotional Control and Stress Tolerance Problems

Compared with other police candidates, the test taker is more likely to easily become irritated and annoyed by others[15]; to become impatient with others over minor infractions[15]; and to overreact to minor frustrations[16].

Routine Task Performance Problems

Compared with other police candidates, the test taker is more likely to have a history of motor vehicle violations or difficulties[17] and to have a history of job performance problems[18].

Decision-Making and Judgment Problems

The test taker is more likely than most police officers or trainees to exhibit difficulties with performing duties in a manner conducive to the safety of others[19].

Feedback Acceptance Problems

Compared with other police candidates, the test taker is less likely to reflect on his behavior[20] and more likely to brush off criticism and other negative feedback[20].

He is more likely than most police officers or trainees to exhibit difficulties accepting and responding to constructive performance feedback[21].

Social Competence and Teamwork Problems

Compared with other police candidates, the test taker is more likely to be self-centered[22]; to engage in conflicts with authority[23]; and to have a history of problems getting along with others[24]. He is also more likely to be opinionated and outspoken[25] and to fail to consider others' needs and feelings[26].

He is more likely than most police officers or trainees to exhibit difficulties stemming from rude and/or overbearing behavior that results in complaints from the public[27]; cooperating with peers and/or supervisors[28]; and interacting effectively with others in a variety of contexts[19].

Integrity Problems

Compared with other police candidates, the test taker is more likely to fail to integrate ethical considerations into his decision-making[29]; to have a history of conflicts with the law and other violations of social norms[30]; and to have skeptical and/or antisocial views of the world[25]. He is also more likely to lack a commitment to societal rules[31]; to be self-indulgent[31]; and to report a history of committing theft[32]. In addition, he is more likely to be nonconforming[16].

He is more likely than most police officers or trainees to exhibit difficulties leading to integrity violations[33]; sustained internal affairs investigations[34]; and investigations about conduct unbecoming a police officer[35].

Conscientiousness and Dependability Problems

Compared with other police candidates, the test taker is more likely to have a history of absenteeism or tardiness[36] and to have a history of failing to meet obligations[37].

FIGURE 8.3. Mr. G's MMPI-3 Police Candidate Interpretive Report, continued

He is more likely than most police officers or trainees to exhibit difficulties with punctuality and attendance[38].

Substance Use Problems

Compared with other police candidates, the test taker is more likely to have a history of substance use problems[39].

Impulse Control Problems

Compared with other police candidates, the test taker is more likely to behave impulsively or without adequate consideration of the consequences or implications of his actions[40]; to have a history of physical aggression[37]; and to have a history of anger management problems[41]. He is also more likely to be rebellious and lack discipline[16] and to be unpredictable in behavior and attitudes[42].

He is more likely than most police officers or trainees to exhibit problems reacting to situations with the proper degree of emotional and behavioral restraint and control, and avoiding impulsive and/or unnecessarily risky behavior[43]. He is also more likely to exhibit anger management problems[44].

Assertiveness Problems

The candidate's test scores are not associated with problems in this domain.

ITEM-LEVEL INFORMATION

Unscorable Responses

The test taker produced scorable responses to all the MMPI-3 items.

Critical Responses

Seven MMPI-3 scales—Suicidal/Death Ideation (SUI), Helplessness/Hopelessness (HLP), Anxiety-Related Experiences (ARX), Ideas of Persecution (RC6), Aberrant Experiences (RC8), Substance Abuse (SUB), and Aggression (AGG)—have been designated by the test authors as having critical item content that may require immediate attention and follow-up. Items answered by the individual in the keyed direction (True or False) on a critical scale are listed below if his T score on that scale is 65 or higher. However, any item answered in the keyed direction on SUI is listed.

The test taker has not produced an elevated T score (≥ 65) on any of these scales or answered any SUI items in the keyed direction.

Critical Follow-up Items

This section contains a list of items to which the test taker responded in a manner warranting follow-up. The items were identified by public safety candidate screening experts as having critical content. Clinicians are encouraged to follow up on these statements with the candidate by making related inquiries, rather than reciting the item(s) verbatim. Each item is followed by the candidate's response, the percentage of Police Candidate Comparison Group members who gave this response, and the scale(s) on which the item appears.

    Item number and content omitted. (True; 19.4%; BXD, RC9, IMP, DISC)
    Item number and content omitted. (True; 3.0%; VRIN, BXD, RC4, AGG, AGGR)

FIGURE 8.3. Mr. G's MMPI-3 Police Candidate Interpretive Report, continued

ENDNOTES

This section lists for each statement in the report the MMPI-3 score(s) that triggered it. In addition, each statement is identified as a <u>Test Response</u>, if based on item content, a <u>Correlate</u>, if based on empirical correlates, or an <u>Inference</u>, if based on the report authors' judgment. (This information can also be accessed on-screen by placing the cursor on a given statement.) For correlate-based statements, research references (Ref. No.) are provided, keyed to the consecutively numbered reference list following the endnotes.

[1] Test Response: RC4=74
[2] Correlate: RC4=74, Ref. 2, 5, 6, 13, 14, 15, 16, 23, 27, 28, 29, 30, 32, 38, 45, 46, 53
[3] Correlate: RC4=74, Ref. 4, 6, 17, 22, 30, 34, 46
[4] Correlate: RC4=74, Ref. 6, 46
[5] Correlate: RC4=74, Ref. 13, 46
[6] Correlate: RC4=74, Ref. 1, 2, 3, 5, 6, 8, 10, 13, 17, 18, 19, 20, 22, 23, 23, 27, 31, 32, 33, 34, 35, 37, 38, 39, 45, 46, 47, 52
[7] Test Response: JCP=74
[8] Correlate: RC4=74, Ref. 6, 7, 21, 30, 34, 46; JCP=74, Ref. 6, 21, 26
[9] Correlate: RC4=74, Ref. 2, 6, 46; JCP=74, Ref. 6, 46
[10] Correlate: RC4=74, Ref. 3, 6, 9, 18, 25, 32, 36, 38, 46, 48, 51, 52, 54; JCP=74, Ref. 6, 9, 48
[11] Test Response: BXD=63; DISC=60
[12] Inference: RC4=74
[13] Inference: JCP=74
[14] Test Response: AGG=55
[15] Correlate: BXD=63, Ref. 6, 11, 44; RC4=74, Ref. 11
[16] Correlate: RC4=74, Ref. 11
[17] Correlate: BXD=63, Ref. 12, 44; RC4=74, Ref. 12
[18] Correlate: BXD=63, Ref. 12, 44; RC4=74, Ref. 44
[19] Correlate: AGG=55, Ref. 24
[20] Correlate: DISC=60, Ref. 44
[21] Correlate: AGG=55, Ref. 41
[22] Correlate: BXD=63, Ref. 44; RC4=74, Ref. 6
[23] Correlate: BXD=63, Ref. 6, 12, 44; RC4=74, Ref. 6, 12, 44
[24] Correlate: BXD=63, Ref. 6, 12, 44; RC4=74, Ref. 6
[25] Correlate: BXD=63, Ref. 12, 44
[26] Correlate: BXD=63, Ref. 11, 12, 44
[27] Correlate: AGG=55, Ref. 43
[28] Correlate: AGG=55, Ref. 41, 42, 43
[29] Correlate: BXD=63, Ref. 42, 44; RC4=74, Ref. 44
[30] Correlate: BXD=63, Ref. 6, 12, 44, 49; RC4=74, Ref. 6, 12, 44, 49; DISC=60, Ref. 6, 49
[31] Correlate: BXD=63, Ref. 11, 12, 44; RC4=74, Ref. 11, 12, 44
[32] Correlate: BXD=63, Ref. 6, 49; RC4=74, Ref. 6, 49; JCP=74, Ref. 6, 49; DISC=60, Ref. 6, 49
[33] Correlate: BXD=63, Ref. 42, 44; RC4=74, Ref. 42, 44; JCP=74, Ref. 42; DISC=60, Ref. 44
[34] Correlate: BXD=63, Ref. 42, 44; RC4=74, Ref. 42, 44; DISC=60, Ref. 44
[35] Correlate: BXD=63, Ref. 44; JCP=74, Ref. 42
[36] Correlate: BXD=63, Ref. 12, 44; RC4=74, Ref. 12, 44
[37] Correlate: RC4=74, Ref. 6
[38] Correlate: JCP=74, Ref. 44
[39] Correlate: BXD=63, Ref. 6, 12, 40, 44, 49, 50; RC4=74, Ref. 6, 12, 40, 44, 49, 50; DISC=60, Ref. 6, 12, 44, 49, 50
[40] Correlate: RC4=74, Ref. 6, 11, 50; DISC=60, Ref. 11, 12, 44, 50
[41] Correlate: BXD=63, Ref. 6; RC4=74, Ref. 6; DISC=60, Ref. 12, 44
[42] Correlate: RC4=74, Ref. 11, 50; DISC=60, Ref. 11, 50
[43] Correlate: JCP=74, Ref. 40, 42; DISC=60, Ref. 44
[44] Correlate: BXD=63, Ref. 44

FIGURE 8.3. Mr. G's MMPI-3 Police Candidate Interpretive Report, continued

RESEARCH REFERENCE LIST

The following studies are sources for empirical correlates identified in the Endnotes section of this report.

1. Anderson, J. L., & Sellbom, M. (2020). Assessing ICD-11 personality trait domain qualifiers with the MMPI-2-RF. *Journal of Clinical Psychology.* Advance online publication. https://doi.org/10.1002/jclp.23099

2. Anderson, J. L., Sellbom, M., Ayearst, L., Quilty, L. C., Chmielewski, M., & Bagby, R. M. (2015). Associations between DSM-5 Section III personality traits and the Minnesota Multiphasic Personality Inventory 2-Restructured Form (MMPI-2-RF) scales in a psychiatric patient sample. *Psychological Assessment, 27*(3), 801–815. https://doi.org/10.1037/pas0000096

3. Anderson, J. L., Sellbom, M., Pymont, C., Smid, W., De Saeger, H., & Kamphuis, J. H. (2015). Measurement of DSM-5 Section II personality disorder constructs using the MMPI-2-RF in clinical and forensic samples. *Psychological Assessment, 27*(3), 786–800. https://doi.org/10.1037/pas0000103

4. Arbisi, P. A., Sellbom, M., & Ben-Porath, Y. S. (2008). Empirical correlates of the MMPI-2 Restructured Clinical (RC) Scales in psychiatric inpatients. *Journal of Personality Assessment, 90*(2), 122–128. https://doi.org/10.1080/00223890701845146

5. Bagby, R. M., Onno, K. A., Mortezaei, A., & Sellbom, M. (2020). Examining the "Traditional Background Hypothesis" for the MMPI-2-RF L-r Scores in a Muslim Faith-Based Sample. *Psychological Assessment.* Advance online publication. https://doi.org/10.1037/pas0000941

6. Ben-Porath, Y. S., & Tellegen, A. (2020). *The Minnesota Multiphasic Personality Inventory-3 (MMPI-3): Technical manual.* University of Minnesota Press.

7. Binford, A., & Liljequist, L. (2008). Behavioral correlates of selected MMPI-2 Clinical, Content, and Restructured Clinical scales. *Journal of Personality Assessment, 90*(6), 608–614. https://doi.org/10.1080/00223890802388657

8. Bolinskey, P. K., Trumbetta, S. L., Hanson, D. R., & Gottesman, I. I. (2010). Predicting adult psychopathology from adolescent MMPIs: Some victories. *Personality and Individual Differences, 49*(4), 324–330. https://doi.org/10.1016/j.paid.2010.01.026

9. Brown, T. A., & Sellbom, M. (2021). Associations between MMPI-3 scale scores and the DSM-5 personality disorders. *Journal of Clinical Psychology, 77*(12), 2943–2964 https://doi.org/10.1002/jclp.23230

10. Burchett, D. L., & Ben-Porath, Y. S. (2010). The impact of over-reporting on MMPI-2-RF substantive scale score validity. *Assessment, 17*(4), 497–516. https://doi.org/10.1177/1073191110378972

11. Corey, D. M., & Ben-Porath, Y. S. (2022). *Minnesota Multiphasic Personality Inventory-3 (MMPI-3): User's guide for the public safety candidate interpretive reports.* University of Minnesota Press.

12. Detrick, P., Ben-Porath, Y.S., & Sellbom, M. (2016). Associations between MMPI-2-RF (Restructured Form) and Inwald Personality Inventory (IPI) scale scores in a law enforcement preemployment screening sample. *Journal of Police and Criminal Psychology, 31,* 81–95. https://doi.org/10.1007/s11896-015-9172-7

13. Finn, J. A., Ben-Porath, Y. S., & Tellegen, A. (2015). Dichotomous versus polytomous response options in psychopathology assessment: Method or meaningful variance? *Psychological Assessment, 27*(1), 184–193. https://doi.org/10.1037/pas0000044

14. Forbey, J. D., & Ben-Porath, Y. S. (2007). A comparison of the MMPI-2 Restructured Clinical (RC) and Clinical Scales in a substance abuse treatment sample. *Psychological Services, 4*(1), 46–58. https://doi.org/10.1037/1541-1559.4.1.46

FIGURE 8.3. Mr. G's MMPI-3 Police Candidate Interpretive Report, continued

15. Forbey, J. D., & Ben-Porath, Y. S. (2008). Empirical correlates of the MMPI-2 Restructured Clinical (RC) Scales in a non-clinical setting. *Journal of Personality Assessment, 90*(2), 136–141. https://doi.org/10.1080/00223890701845161

16. Forbey, J. D., Ben-Porath, Y. S., & Gartland, D. (2009). Validation of the MMPI-2 Computerized Adaptive version (MMPI-2-CA) in a correctional intake facility. *Psychological Services, 6*(4), 279–292. https://doi.org/10.1037/a0016195

17. Handel, R. W., & Archer, R. P. (2008). An investigation of the psychometric properties of the MMPI-2 Restructured Clinical (RC) Scales with mental health inpatients. *Journal of Personality Assessment, 90*(3), 239–249. https://doi.org/10.1080/00223890701884954

18. Kamphuis, J. H., Arbisi, P. A., Ben-Porath, Y. S., & McNulty, J. L. (2008). Detecting comorbid Axis-II status among inpatients using the MMPI-2 Restructured Clinical Scales. *European Journal of Psychological Assessment, 24,* 157–164. https://doi.org/10.1027/1015-5759.24.3.157

19. Kastner, R. M., Sellbom, M., & Lilienfeld, S. O. (2012). A comparison of the psychometric properties of the Psychopathic Personality Inventory full-length and short-form versions. *Psychological Assessment, 24*(1), 261–267. https://doi.org/10.1037/a0025832

20. Klein Haneveld, E., Kamphuis, J. H., Smid, W., & Forbey, J. D. (2017). Using MMPI-2-RF correlates to elucidate the PCL-R and its four facets in a sample of male forensic psychiatric patients. *Journal of Personality Assessment, 99*(4), 398–407. https://doi.org/10.1080/00223891.2016.1228655

21. Laurinaityte, I., Laurinavicius, A., Ustinaviciute, L., Wygant, D. B., Sellbom, M. (2017). Utility of the MMPI-2 Restructured Form (MMPI-2-RF) in a sample of Lithuanian male offenders. *Law and Human Behavior, 41*(5), 494–505. https://doi.org/10.1037/lhb0000254

22. Menton, W. H., Crighton, A. H., Tarescavage, A. M., Marek, R. J., Hicks, A. D., & Ben-Porath, Y. S. (2019). Equivalence of laptop and tablet administrations of the Minnesota Multiphasic Personality Inventory-2 Restructured Form. *Assessment, 26*(4), 661–669. https://doi.org/10.1177/1073191117714558

23. Phillips, T. R., Sellbom, M., Ben-Porath, Y. S., & Patrick, C. J. (2014). Further development and construct validation of MMPI-2-RF indices of global psychopathy, fearless-dominance, and impulsive-antisociality in a sample of incarcerated women. *Law and Human Behavior, 38*(1), 34–46. https://doi.org/10.1037/lhb0000040

24. Roberts, R. M., Tarescavage, A. M., Ben-Porath, Y. S., & Roberts, M. D. (2018). predicting post-probationary job performance of police officers using CPI and MMPI-2-RF test data obtained during preemployment psychological screening. *Journal of Personality Assessment, 101*(5), 544–555. https://doi.org/10.1080/00223891.2018.1423990

25. Ruiz, M. A., & Dorritie, M. T. (2021). Clinical utility of the Minnesota Multiphasic Personality Inventory-2-Restructured Form (MMPI-2-RF) in a residential treatment program for homeless individuals. *Assessment, 28*(2), 353–366. https://doi.org/10.1177/1073191119899481

26. Sellbom, M. (2016). Elucidating the validity of the externalizing spectrum of psychopathology in correctional, forensic, and community samples. *Journal of Abnormal Psychology, 125*(8), 1027–1038. https://doi.org/10.1037/abn0000171

27. Sellbom, M., Anderson, J. L., & Bagby, R. M. (2013). Assessing DSM-5 Section III personality traits and disorders with the MMPI-2-RF. *Assessment, 20*(6), 709–722. https://doi.org/10.1177/1073191113508808

28. Sellbom, M., & Ben-Porath, Y. S. (2005). Mapping the MMPI-2 Restructured Clinical Scales onto normal personality traits: Evidence of construct validity. *Journal of Personality Assessment, 85*(2), 179–187. https://doi.org/10.1207/s15327752jpa8502_10

FIGURE 8.3. Mr. G's MMPI-3 Police Candidate Interpretive Report, continued

29. Sellbom, M., Ben-Porath, Y. S., & Bagby, R. M. (2008). Personality and psychopathology: Mapping the MMPI-2 Restructured Clinical (RC) Scales onto the five factor model of personality. *Journal of Personality Disorders, 22*(3), 291–312. https://doi.org/10.1521/pedi.2008.22.3.291

30. Sellbom, M., Ben-Porath, Y. S., Baum, L. J., Erez, E., & Gregory, C. (2008). Predictive validity of the MMPI-2 Restructured Clinical (RC) Scales in a batterers' intervention program. *Journal of Personality Assessment, 90*(2), 129–135. https://doi.org/10.1080/00223890701845153

31. Sellbom, M., Ben-Porath, Y. S., & Graham, J. R. (2006). Correlates of the MMPI-2 Restructured Clinical (RC) Scales in a college counseling setting. *Journal of Personality Assessment, 86*(1), 89–99. https://doi.org/10.1207/s15327752jpa8601_10

32. Sellbom, M., Ben-Porath, Y. S., Lilienfeld, S. O., Patrick, C. J., & Graham, J. R. (2005). Assessing psychopathic personality traits with the MMPI-2. *Journal of Personality Assessment, 85,*(3), 334–343. https://doi.org/10.1207/s15327752jpa8503_10

33. Sellbom, M., Ben-Porath, Y. S., Patrick, C. J., Wygant, D. B., Gartland, D. M., & Stafford, K. P. (2012). Development and construct validation of MMPI-2-RF indices of global psychopathy, fearless-dominance, and impulsive-antisociality. *Personality Disorders: Theory, Research, and Treatment, 3*(1), 17–38. https://doi.org/10.1037/a0023888

34. Sellbom, M., Ben-Porath, Y. S., & Stafford, K. P. (2007). A comparison of MMPI-2 measures of psychopathic deviance in a forensic setting. *Psychological Assessment, 19*(4), 430–436. https://doi.org/10.1037/1040-3590.19.4.430

35. Sellbom, M., Graham, J. R., & Schenk, P. W. (2006). Incremental validity of the MMPI-2 Restructured Clinical (RC) Scales in a private practice sample. *Journal of Personality Assessment, 86*(2), 196–205. https://doi.org/10.1207/s15327752jpa8602_09

36. Sellbom, M., & Smith, A. (2017). Assessment of DSM-5 Section II personality disorders with the MMPI-2-RF in a nonclinical sample. *Journal of Personality Assessment, 99*(4), 384–397. https://doi.org/10.1080/00223891.2016.1242074

37. Shkalim, E. (2015). Psychometric evaluation of the MMPI-2/MMPI-2-RF Restructured Clinical Scales in an Israeli sample. *Assessment, 22*(4), 607–618. https://doi.org/10.1177/1073191114555884

38. Simms, L. J., Casillas, A., Clark, L. A., Watson, D., & Doebbeling, B. N. (2005). Psychometric evaluation of the Restructured Clinical Scales of the MMPI-2. *Psychological Assessment, 17*(3), 345–358. https://doi.org/10.1037/1040-3590.17.3.345

39. Sullivan, K. A., Elliott, C. D., Lange, R. T., & Anderson, D. S. (2013). A known-groups evaluation of the Response Bias Scale in a neuropsychological setting. *Applied Neuropsychology: Adult, 20*(1), 20–32. https://doi.org/10.1080/09084282.2012.670149

40. Tarescavage, A. M., Brewster, J., Corey, D. M., & Ben-Porath, Y. S. (2015). Use of pre-hire Minnesota Multiphasic Personality Inventory-2-Restructured Form (MMPI-2-RF) police candidate scores to predict supervisor ratings of post-hire performance. *Assessment, 22*(4), 411–428. https://doi.org/10.1177/1073191114548445

41. Tarescavage, A. M., Corey, D. M., & Ben-Porath, Y. S. (2015). Minnesota Multiphasic Personality Inventory-2-Restructured Form (MMPI-2-RF) predictors of police officer problem behavior. *Assessment, 22*(1), 116–132. https://doi.org/10.1177/1073191114534885

42. Tarescavage, A. M., Corey, D. M., & Ben-Porath, Y. S. (2016). A prorating method for estimating MMPI-2-RF scores from MMPI responses: Examination of score fidelity and illustration of empirical utility in the PERSEREC police integrity study sample. *Assessment, 23*(2), 173–190. https://doi.org/10.1177/1073191115575070

FIGURE 8.3. Mr. G's MMPI-3 Police Candidate Interpretive Report, continued

43. Tarescavage, A. M., Corey, D. M., Gupton, H. M., & Ben-Porath Y.S. (2015). Criterion validity and practical utility of the Minnesota Multiphasic Personality Inventory-2-Restructured Form (MMPI-2-RF) in assessments of police officer candidates. *Journal of Personality Assessment, 97*(4), 382–394. https://doi.org/10.1080/00223891.2014.995800

44. Tarescavage, A. M., Fischler, G. L., Cappo, B. M., Hill, D. O., Corey, D. M., & Ben-Porath, Y. S. (2015). Minnesota Multiphasic Personality Inventory-2-Restructured Form (MMPI-2-RF) predictors of police officer problem behavior and collateral self-report test scores. *Psychological Assessment, 27*(1), 125–137. https://doi.org/10.1037/pas0000041

45. Tarescavage, A. M., & Menton, W. H. (2020). Construct Validity of the Personality Inventory for ICD-11 (PiCD): Evidence from the MMPI-2-RF and CAT-PD-SF. *Psychological Assessment, 32*(9), 889–895. https://doi.org/10.1037/pas0000914

46. Tellegen, A., & Ben-Porath, Y. S. (2008/2011). *Minnesota Multiphasic Personality Inventory-2-Restructured Form (MMPI-2-RF): Technical manual.* University of Minnesota Press.

47. Van der Heijden, P. T., Egger, J. I. M., Rossi, G. M. P., & Derksen, J. J. L. (2012). Integrating psychopathology and personality disorders conceptualized by the MMPI-2-RF and the MCMI-III: A structural validity study. *Journal of Personality Assessment, 4*(4), 345–357. https://doi.org/10.1080/00223891.2012.656861

48. Van der Heijden, P. T., Egger, J. I. M., Rossi, G. M. P., Grundel, G., & Derksen, J. J. L. (2013). The MMPI-2-Restructured Form and the standard MMPI-2 Clinical Scales in relation to DSM-IV. *European Journal of Psychological Assessment, 29*(3), 182–188. https://doi.org/10.1027/1015-5759/a000140

49. Whitman, M. R., Corey, D. M., & Ben-Porath, Y. S. (2021). Associations between MMPI-3 and psychosocial history findings obtained in preemployment evaluations of public safety candidates [Manuscript under review].

50. Whitman, M. R., Elias, L. S., Cappo, B. M., & Ben-Porath, Y. S. (2021). Criterion validity of MMPI-3 scores in preemployment evaluations of public safety candidates. *Psychological Assessment.* Advance online publication. https://doi.org/10.1037/pas0001042

51. Whitman, M. R., Tylicki, J. L., Mascioli, R., Pickle, J., & Ben-Porath, Y. S. (2021). Psychometric properties of the Minnesota Multiphasic Personality Inventory-3 (MMPI-3) in a clinical neuropsychology setting. *Psychological Assessment, 33*(2), 142–155. https://doi.org/10.1037/pas0000969

52. Wolf, E. J., Miller, M. W., Orazem, R. J., Weierich, M. R., Castillo, D. T., Milford, J., Kaloupek, D. G., & Keane, T. M. (2008). The MMPI-2 Restructured Clinical Scales in the assessment of posttraumatic stress disorder and comorbid disorders. *Psychological Assessment, 20*(4), 327–340. https://doi.org/10.1037/a0012948

53. Wygant, D. B., Boutacoff, L. I., Arbisi, P. A., Ben-Porath, Y. S., Kelly, P. H., & Rupp, W. M. (2007). Examination of the MMPI-2 Restructured Clinical (RC) Scales in a sample of bariatric surgery candidates. *Journal of Clinical Psychology in Medical Settings, 14*(3), 197–205. https://doi.org/10.1007/s10880-007-9073-8

54. Zahn, N., Sellbom, M., Pymont, C., & Schenk, P. W. (2017). Associations between MMPI-2-RF scale scores and self-reported personality disorder criteria in a private practice sample. *Journal of Psychopathology and Behavioral Assessment, 39*(4), 723–741. https://doi.org/10.1007/s10862-017-9616-8

End of Report

FIGURE 8.3. Mr. G's MMPI-3 Police Candidate Interpretive Report, continued

actions and a demotion in rank for underage drinking, and he was eventually referred to a military alcohol treatment program. It was there that Mr. G came to understand how out of control his life had become, and he vowed to bring order to it, beginning with his sobriety.

Upon his military discharge at age 23, Mr. G enrolled in a public college under the GI Bill and obtained a bachelor's degree in sociology. While enrolled, he met the woman who would become his wife and a stabilizing and motivating force in his life. At the time Mr. G applied to become a deputy sheriff at the age of 45, he had been sober for 22 years, married for 20 years, and worked as a drug and alcohol treatment specialist for a county agency for 17 years. After an extensive background investigation involving dozens of references, both listed and developed, the background investigator concluded,

> [Mr. G] has been forthright about his past and some poor decisions [he] made over 20 years ago. He has used his past to shape his future and has made positive contributions to those suffering abuse issues. His references consistently speak of his compassion, judgment, and integrity.

Step 4: Assessing Interview Findings

Mr. G avowed a strong commitment to sobriety. He evidenced strong personal insight, self-reflection, and acceptance of personal accountability. No discrepancies between self-reported and collaterally obtained background information were identified. He described his motivation for becoming a deputy sheriff as stemming from his desire to intervene earlier in the cycle of addiction and associated devastation by helping people before their lives become ruined. He said that his daughter, age 14, was also a source of inspiration for him, and he wanted to help to keep his community safe for her.

Step 5: Identifying Relevant Risk Findings

a. Considering all risk-related findings from all sources, what evidence-based inferences can be drawn?

TEST FINDINGS
Mr. G's PCIR identifies multiple Comparison Group Findings that reveal a comparatively high number of reported difficulties that are reported by only 6.0% or less of the Police Candidate Comparison Group. These include behavioral difficulties, poor impulse control, antisocial behavior, juvenile conduct problems, substance use problems, and physically aggressive behavior. The report also indicates a wide range of Job-Relevant Correlates, in comparison both to

police candidates and police officers/trainees, in 8 of the 10 problem domains: Emotional Control and Stress Tolerance Problems, Routine Task Performance Problems, Feedback Acceptance Problems, Social Competence and Teamwork Problems, Integrity Problems, Conscientiousness and Dependability Problems, Substance Use Problems, and Impulse Control Problems. A central feature of the PCIR is its source-annotated identification of risk-related findings associated with MMPI-3 scores and the listing of these annotations in the Endnotes section (Figure 8.3, p. 12). A review of these Endnotes shows that the 39 risk-related statements in Mr. G's PCIR derive from five scales, each associated with the Behavioral Dysfunction domain: BXD (63T), RC4 (74T), JCP (74T), AGG (55T), and DISC (60T). In light of Mr. G's history of alcohol and drug abuse, it may seem curious that his score on SUB was only 52T (raw score of 2). This score is nearly a standard deviation and a half above the mean for the comparison group, with 98% of the comparison group scoring at or below that level. For persons with Mr. G's substance use history, it is important to confirm that their responses to the nine items on the SUB scale are honest. As shown on page 11 of Mr. G's PCIR (Figure 8.3), the screening psychologist chose to print these responses (their numbers and content have been redacted in Figure 8.3 for test security) to confirm his candor. In doing so, he noted that the two SUB items Mr. G answered in the keyed direction (having to do with the historical use of alcohol and drugs) were truthful, as were the items answered in the nonkeyed direction (having to do with past and current alcohol and drug use problems). Indeed, a person who, like Mr. G, has sustained sobriety following a period of substance abuse in their youth can never produce a raw score of 0 (39T) on SUB and is unlikely to score at or above 65T, unless the prior period of abuse included polydrug use.

Mr. G's score on normal-range personality testing were entirely within normal limits compared to the general adult normative sample but outside them for police candidates on a scale assessing potential impulse control, substance use, and aggression problems. It is important to keep in mind that personality test scores within normal limits for the general population normative group are never to be interpreted as indicating the construct-related problems measured by the scale *except when empirical evidence supports such inferences*. The corresponding T scores on Mr. G's normal-range personality test were within normal limits for the normative sample, and no empirical research has been published that validates inferences on this scale for police candidates at this T-score level. Therefore, no risk-related inferences can be drawn from the score, notwithstanding its deviance (93rd percentile) from the comparison group mean.

BACKGROUND FINDINGS

Mr. G's behavioral problems identified from the background investigation occurred before the age of 23 and involve many of the problems associated with his psychological test results. These include multiple arrests for petty theft and drug possession, failure to complete high school, military disciplinary action (including demotion), and substance use problems. (Note that, at this step, we are focused solely on risk-related findings; positive findings from psychological testing, background investigation, and the interview will be addressed at the next step, which deals with divergent findings that might mitigate these inferences.)

INTERVIEW FINDINGS

There are no risk-related findings from Mr. G's interview other than those that are associated with his background. His self-reported history during the interview was entirely consistent with the collateral evidence, and no new risk-related findings were identified.

b. What divergent findings might mitigate these inferences?

TEST FINDINGS

A user-designated feature of the various MMPI-3 reports, including the PCIR, is the option to set the T-score level at which the report prints, for any given scale, the items that the candidate answered in the keyed direction. Figure 8.3 shows an example of this feature for the SUB scale (p. 11). Were the items for the other externalizing scales (BXD, RC4, JCP, AGG, and DISC) to be printed here (test security precludes printing the items in this publicly accessible volume), the reader would see that most items that Mr. G answered in the keyed direction on each of the Behavioral Dysfunction scales pertain to his behavior before the age of 23. This alone does not mitigate the risks associated with these scale scores, but it does illustrate that a candidate like Mr. G, whose juvenile history is replete with rule-breaking and norm-violating behavior and who honestly responds to these items, will inevitably produce similar scores that reflect that history even when it is followed by a substantial and sustained period of prosocial behavior and rehabilitation. To be clear, the mere fact that the items giving rise to a scale's elevation pertain to past conduct, as opposed to current symptoms and behavior, does not itself mitigate the risk-related findings supported by empirical research. Indeed, a significant body of evidence demonstrates the strong predictive relationship between past and future behavior (Corey et al., 2018; Golder et al., 2014; Jager et al., 2015; Tackett et al., 2016; Woodhams & Toye, 2007). However, when past behavior has been followed by a stable, substantial, and verified period of opposing behavior and by persuasive evidence of changes in personal attributes (e.g., cognitive, clinical, social, personality, and moral) presumed necessary to sustain the contemporary behavior, that predictive relationship is weakened, as discussed next.

BACKGROUND FINDINGS

It is not just past behavior that predicts future behavior. Risk factors are generally sorted as either *static risk markers* or *dynamic risk factors* (Kraemer et al., 1997). Static risk markers refer to past factors correlated with a future adverse behavior, event, or condition that cannot change and are not subject to intervention. Examples of static risk markers include adverse childhood experiences (Briggs et al., 2021) a history of arrest, dropping out of college, having been fired from a job, and having been divorced. In contrast, dynamic or variable risk factors refer to behaviors, conditions, or traits associated with future problems that can be altered or ameliorated by treatment or intervention. Examples of dynamic risk factors include the amount and frequency of substance use, severity of mental health symptoms, attitudes, certain personality constructs, and the degree of conflict experienced in a romantic relationship. Dynamic risk factors often account for the greatest variance in the prediction of future problems even after controlling for static markers (see, for example, Wilson et al., 2013).

Mr. G's background reveals multiple static risk markers (e.g., multiple arrests, fighting, substance use problems, and military disciplinary history) that are reflected in his MMPI-3 scores and background findings, but no evidence of dynamic risk factors (e.g., stable problems associated with substance use, antisocial conduct or attitudes, affiliation with problematic peers, marital problems, or occupational problems). Furthermore, there is good evidence to indicate that Mr. G's behavior and adaptation over the 22 years preceding the evaluation were consistently prosocial, norm-conforming, and consistent with his self-reported rehabilitation.

Blumstein and Nakamura (2009) introduced the concept of a "redemption period" following a criminal offender's last offense. They observed that many ex-offenders seeking employment "could be haunted by a stale record" (p. 327). Using data from a state criminal history repository, they estimated for various crime types and ages the declining hazard of rearrest with time "clean." Blumstein and Nakamura concluded that, for many crimes, there exists a redemption period after which a person with a criminal record, who remained free of further contact with the criminal justice system, is of no greater risk than a nonoffender of the same age—"an indication of redemption from the mark of crime" (p. 327). The structural life changes leading to this redemption period are conceptualized as "desistance to crime" (Laub & Sampson, 2001), resulting from cognitive changes in the previously offending person (Nakamura & Bucklen, 2014). Similarly, some police candidates with problematic juvenile or early adult histories demonstrate a sufficiently reliable and well-documented redemption period, and accompanying shifts in cognition and identity, to justify reducing the weight ordinarily assigned to these static risk markers.

INTERVIEW FINDINGS

When determining whether static risk markers from a candidate's relatively distant past and behavioral dysfunction scale score elevations based on them warrant mitigation, attention should be paid not simply to the presence or absence of dynamic risk factors but also to evidence of *protective factors* that serve to reduce future risk (see Heffernan & Ward, 2017). Gaspar and colleagues (2015) concluded from a series of innovative experiments that the predictive power of a static marker involving a prior immoral act (e.g., stealing, lying, or driving intoxicated) is mediated by how the individual thinks about their immoral behavior. They found that persons who reflected counterfactually on their prior moral lapses (i.e., they falsely minimized their own culpability, opportunities to have made more responsible choices, and accountability) were much more likely to engage in future counterproductive behavior (e.g., lying on unrelated tasks with real monetary stakes) than those who reflected factually.

Considering this, it is important to note that Mr. G's reflection on his past behavior during the interview was entirely factual and demonstrated clear evidence of acceptance of his culpability, identification of alternative choices he failed to make, and acceptance of personal accountability. He made no effort to engage in moral rationalization of his past misconduct. He established a clear line of demarcation between his past antisocial behavior and his commitment to prosocial conduct, which was confirmed by the collateral references in the background investigation. Thus, there was substantial evidence of a sustained change in Mr. G's behavior over the prior 22 years that, in combination with the protective factor observed in the interview (factual reflection), supported mitigation of the risk-related findings.

c. Are any surviving risk-related inferences of sufficient relevance and quality to warrant the candidate's disqualification?

Risk mitigation does not equal risk elimination. The many job-relevant correlates observed in the empirical literature between scales in the Behavioral Dysfunction domain and later counterproductive behavior as a police officer were documented without regard to other mitigating factors. In the final analysis, screening professionals are not expected to be flawless in their decisions; rather, they are expected to apply the level of care at which an ordinary and prudent professional, with the same training and experience in good standing in the same or a similar community, would practice under the same or similar circumstances. Spilberg and Corey (2020) present the case that screening psychologists are the "risk assessors," but the employer is the "risk manager." As such, they argue that in cases where a psychologist believes that evidence-based risk is appropriately mitigated by other evidence, it is generally prudent to confer with the hiring agency concerning the employer's tolerance for taking on the risk. When doing so, providing a clear and rational argument for why and how risk mitigation is warranted by other relevant findings—in a conversation with the employer or in the body of the written report—both aids the employer's decision and helps document the psychologist's rationale in the event the evaluation comes under review.

In the case of Mr. G, the examining psychologist determined, in consultation with the hiring agency, that the well-documented redemption period and strong evidence of protective factors warranted mitigation of the risks associated with his test results. Therefore, the screening psychologist determined that Mr. G **does meet** the criterion standard and is qualified to be a deputy sheriff.

COMPREHENSIVE REVIEW: MR. K, CORRECTIONAL DEPUTY CANDIDATE

Assessment Issues Presented

- An MMPI-3 protocol with a single clinically elevated scale and multiple moderate (< 65T) scale elevations

Referral Summary

Mr. K is a 24-year-old single male seeking a position as a correctional deputy with a rural county sheriff's office. At the time of evaluation, Mr. K had been employed for three years as a correctional deputy in another rural county that was a three-hour drive from the home he shared with his parents since birth. He told the background investigator that he sought the new position in hopes of serving his ultimate ambition of becoming a patrol deputy and because he did not enjoy supervising inmates who were often his neighbors and acquaintances.

Data Integration

Step 1: Assessing Protocol Validity

As noted in the CCIR (Figure 8.4, p. 8), "This is a valid MMPI-3 protocol. There are no problems with unscorable items. The test taker responded to the items relevantly on the basis of their content, and there are no indications of over- or under-reporting." Validity measures from normal-range personality testing also indicated the absence of over- and underreporting.

Minnesota Multiphasic Personality Inventory®-3

Yossef S. Ben-Porath
Auke Tellegen

MMPI®-3
Correctional Candidate Interpretive Report
David M. Corey, PhD, & Yossef S. Ben-Porath, PhD

ID Number:	Mr. K
Age:	24
Gender:	Male
Marital Status:	Not reported
Years of Education:	Not reported
Date Assessed:	05/06/2023

Copyright © 2022 by the Regents of the University of Minnesota. All rights reserved. Distributed exclusively under license from the University of Minnesota by NCS Pearson, Inc. Portions reproduced from the *MMPI-3 English Test Booklet*. Copyright © 2020 by the Regents of the University of Minnesota. All rights reserved. Portions excerpted from the *MMPI-3 Manual for Administration, Scoring, and Interpretation*. Copyright © 2020 by the Regents of the University of Minnesota. All rights reserved. Portions excerpted from the *MMPI-3 Technical Manual*. Copyright © 2020 by the Regents of the University of Minnesota. All rights reserved. Used by permission of the University of Minnesota Press.

Minnesota Multiphasic Personality Inventory and **MMPI** are registered trademarks of the Regents of the University of Minnesota. **Pearson** is a trademark, in the US and/or other countries, of Pearson Education, Inc., or its affiliates.

This report contains copyrighted material and trade secrets. Qualified licensees may excerpt portions of this output report, limited to the minimum text necessary to accurately describe their significant core conclusions, for incorporation into a written evaluation of the examinee, in accordance with their profession's citation standards, if any. No adaptations, translations, modifications, or special versions may be made of this report without prior written permission from the University of Minnesota Press.

[1.4 / RE1 / QG1]

ALWAYS LEARNING   PEARSON

FIGURE 8.4. Mr. K's MMPI-3 Correctional Candidate Interpretive Report

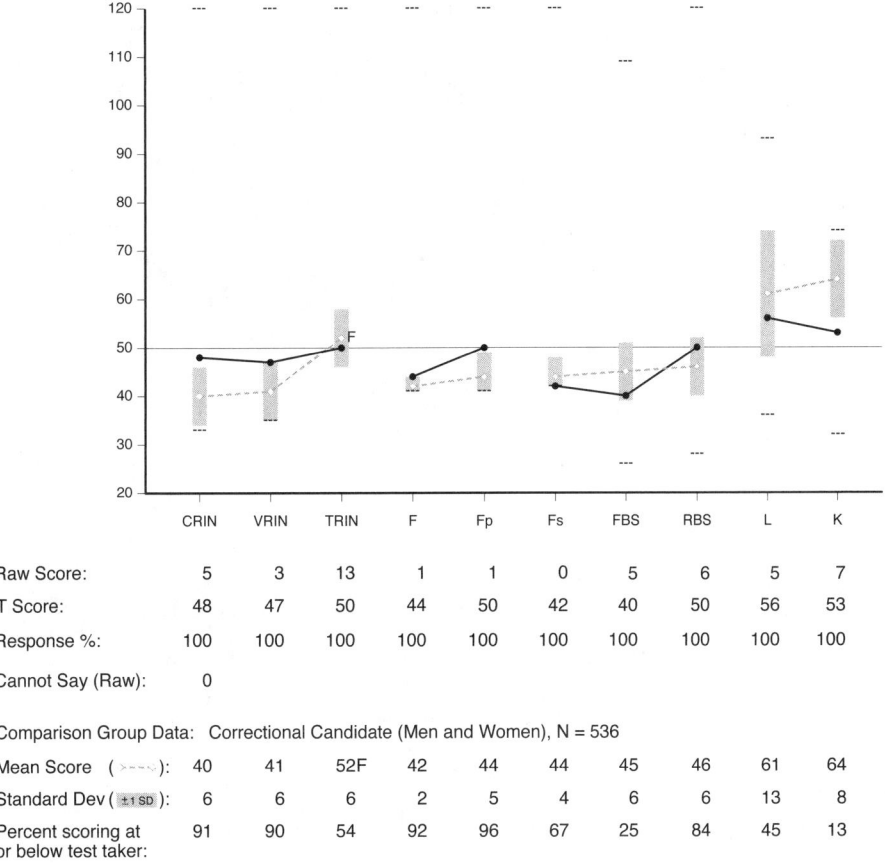

FIGURE 8.4. Mr. K's MMPI-3 Correctional Candidate Interpretive Report, continued

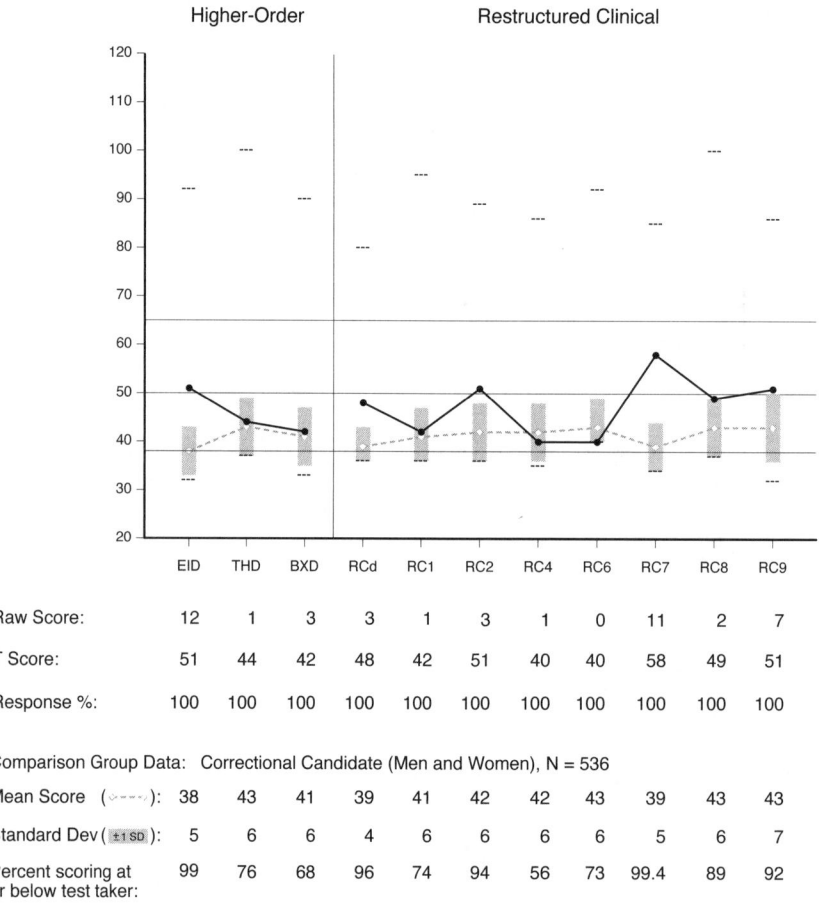

FIGURE 8.4. Mr. K's MMPI-3 Correctional Candidate Interpretive Report, continued

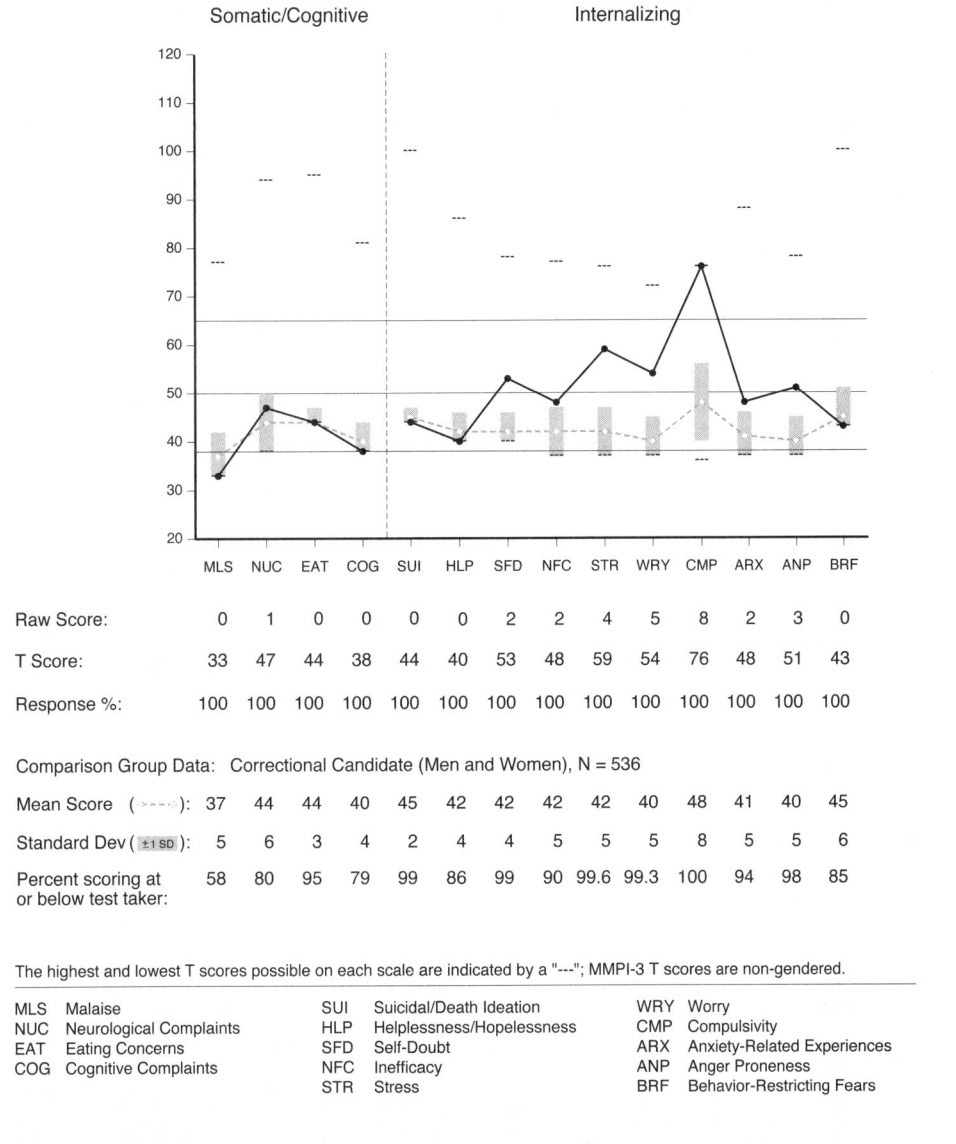

FIGURE 8.4. Mr. K's MMPI-3 Correctional Candidate Interpretive Report, continued

MMPI®-3 Correctional Candidate Interpretive Report
05/06/2023, Page 5

ID: Mr. K

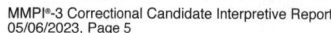

MMPI-3 Externalizing and Interpersonal Scales

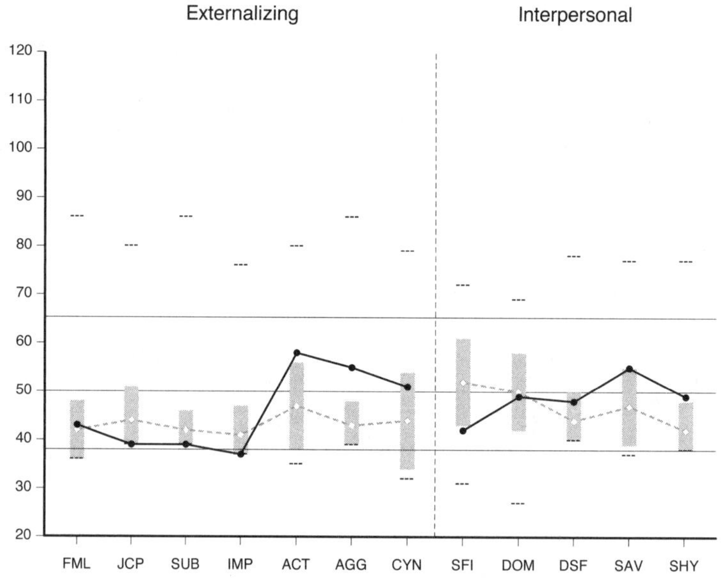

	FML	JCP	SUB	IMP	ACT	AGG	CYN	SFI	DOM	DSF	SAV	SHY
Raw Score:	1	0	0	0	5	2	8	3	7	1	5	2
T Score:	43	39	39	37	58	55	51	42	49	48	55	49
Response %:	100	100	100	100	100	100	100	100	100	100	100	100

Comparison Group Data: Correctional Candidate (Men and Women), N = 536

	FML	JCP	SUB	IMP	ACT	AGG	CYN	SFI	DOM	DSF	SAV	SHY
Mean Score (- - - -):	42	44	42	41	47	43	44	52	50	44	47	42
Standard Dev (±1 SD):	6	7	4	6	9	5	10	9	8	6	8	6
Percent scoring at or below test taker:	76	55	74	58	94	98	85	6	66	84	94	91

The highest and lowest T scores possible on each scale are indicated by a "---"; MMPI-3 T scores are non-gendered.

FML Family Problems
JCP Juvenile Conduct Problems
SUB Substance Abuse
IMP Impulsivity
ACT Activation
AGG Aggression
CYN Cynicism
SFI Self-Importance
DOM Dominance
DSF Disaffiliativeness
SAV Social Avoidance
SHY Shyness

FIGURE 8.4. Mr. K's MMPI-3 Correctional Candidate Interpretive Report, continued

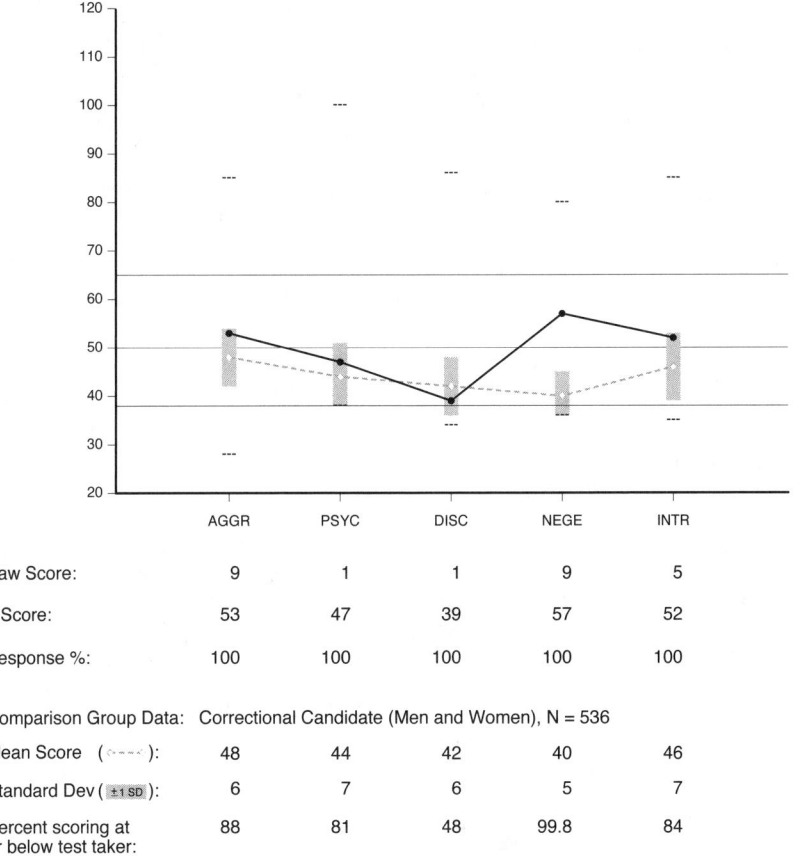

FIGURE 8.4. Mr. K's MMPI-3 Correctional Candidate Interpretive Report, continued

MMPI-3 T SCORES (BY DOMAIN)

PROTOCOL VALIDITY

Content Non-Responsiveness:
- CNS: 0
- CRIN: 48
- VRIN: 47
- TRIN: 50

Over-Reporting:
- F: 44
- Fp: 50
- Fs: 42
- FBS: 40
- RBS: 50

Under-Reporting:
- L: 56
- K: 53

SUBSTANTIVE SCALES

Somatic/Cognitive Dysfunction:
- RC1: 42
- MLS: 33
- NUC: 47
- EAT: 44
- COG: 38

Emotional Dysfunction:
- EID: 51
- RCd: 48
- SUI: 44
- HLP: 40
- **SFD: 53**
- NFC: 48
- RC2: 51
- INTR: 52
- **RC7: 58**
- **STR: 59**
- **WRY: 54**
- **CMP: 76**
- ARX: 48
- ANP: 51
- BRF: 43
- **NEGE: 57**

Thought Dysfunction:
- THD: 44
- RC6: 40
- RC8: 49
- PSYC: 47

Behavioral Dysfunction:
- BXD: 42
- RC4: 40
- FML: 43
- JCP: 39
- SUB: 39
- RC9: 51
- IMP: 37
- ACT: 58
- **AGG: 55**
- CYN: 51
- DISC: 39

Interpersonal Functioning:
- SFI: 42
- DOM: 49
- AGGR: 53
- DSF: 48
- SAV: 55
- SHY: 49

Scale scores shown in bold font are interpreted in the report.

Note. This information is provided to facilitate interpretation following the recommended structure for MMPI-3 interpretation in Chapter 5 of the *MMPI-3 Manual for Administration, Scoring, and Interpretation*, which provides details in the text and an outline in Table 5-1.

FIGURE 8.4. Mr. K's MMPI-3 Correctional Candidate Interpretive Report, continued

This interpretive report is intended for use by a professional qualified to interpret the MMPI-3 in the context of preemployment psychological evaluations of correctional officers and other related law enforcement personnel in institutional settings. **It focuses on identifying problems; it does not convey potential strengths.** The information it contains should be considered in the context of the test taker's background, the demands of the position under consideration, the clinical interview, findings from supplemental tests, and other relevant information.

The interpretive statements in the Protocol Validity section of the report are based on T scores derived from the general MMPI-3 normative sample, as well as scores obtained by the multisite sample of 536 individuals that make up the Correctional Candidate Comparison Group.

The interpretive statements in the Clinical Findings and Diagnostic Considerations sections of the report are based on T scores derived from the general MMPI-3 normative sample. Following recommended practice, only T scores of 65 and higher (with a few exceptions) are considered clinically significant. Scores at this clinical level are generally rare among correctional candidates.

Statements in the Comparison Group Findings and Job-Relevant Correlates sections are based on comparisons with scores obtained by the Correctional Candidate Comparison Group. Statements in these sections may be based on T scores that, although less than 65, are nevertheless uncommon in reference to the comparison group.

The report includes extensive annotation, which appears as superscripts following each statement in the narrative, keyed to Endnotes with accompanying Research References, which appear in the final two sections of the report. Additional information about the annotation features is provided in the headnotes to these sections and in the MMPI-3 User's Guide for the Public Safety Candidate Interpretive Reports.

SYNOPSIS

This is a valid MMPI-3 protocol. Scores on the Substantive Scales indicate clinically significant emotional dysfunction. Emotional-internalizing findings relate to compulsivity.

Comparison group findings point to additional possible concerns about self-doubt, negative emotions, stress, worry, and physically aggressive behavior.

Possible job-relevant problems are identified in the following domains: Emotional Control and Stress Tolerance, Decision-Making and Judgment, and Assertiveness.

PROTOCOL VALIDITY

This is a valid MMPI-3 protocol. There are no problems with unscorable items. The test taker responded to the items relevantly on the basis of their content, and there are no indications of over- or under-reporting.

FIGURE 8.4. Mr. K's MMPI-3 Correctional Candidate Interpretive Report, continued

CLINICAL FINDINGS

Clinical-level symptoms, personality characteristics, and behavioral tendencies of the test taker are described in this section and organized according to an empirically guided framework. (Please see Chapter 5 of the MMPI-3 Manual for Administration, Scoring, and Interpretation *for details.) Statements containing the word "reports" are based on the item content of MMPI-3 scales, whereas statements that include the word "likely" are based on empirical correlates of scale scores. Specific sources for each statement can be viewed with the annotation features of this report.*

The test taker reports engaging in compulsive behavior, including repetitive checking and counting, and making sure things are in place[1]. He indeed very likely engages in compulsive behavior such as repeated checking[2], experiences obsessions[2], and is rigid and perfectionistic[2].

There are no indications of clinically significant somatic, cognitive, thought, or behavioral dysfunction in this protocol.

DIAGNOSTIC CONSIDERATIONS

This section provides recommendations for psychodiagnostic assessment based on the test taker's MMPI-3 results. It is recommended that he be evaluated for the following:

Emotional-Internalizing Disorders
- Obsessive-compulsive disorder[3]

COMPARISON GROUP FINDINGS

This section describes the MMPI-3 substantive scale findings in the context of the Correctional Candidate Comparison Group. Specific sources for each statement can be accessed with the annotation features of this report. **Job-related correlates of these results, if any, are provided in the subsequent Job-Relevant Correlates section.**

Emotional/Internalizing Problems
The test taker reports a comparatively high level of negative emotions for a correctional candidate[4]. Only 0.6% of comparison group members convey this or a greater level of negative emotionality. More specifically, he reports a relatively high level of problems with stress for a correctional candidate[5]. Only 0.9% of comparison group members convey this or a greater level of stress. He also reports a comparatively high level of worries for a correctional candidate[6]. Only 2.0% of comparison group members convey this or a greater level of stress reactivity. His responses indicate a level of compulsivity that may be incompatible with public safety requirements for good emotional adjustment and behavioral adaptability[3]. This level of compulsive behavior is uncommon among correctional candidates. Only 0.7% of comparison group members give evidence of this level of compulsivity.

He reports a comparatively high level of self-doubt for a correctional candidate[7]. Only 5.0% of comparison group members convey this or a greater lack of confidence.

Behavioral/Externalizing Problems
The test taker reports a comparatively high level of physically aggressive behavior for a correctional candidate[8]. Only 5.0% of comparison group members convey this or a greater level of inappropriately aggressive behavior.

FIGURE 8.4. Mr. K's MMPI-3 Correctional Candidate Interpretive Report, continued

JOB-RELEVANT CORRELATES

Job-relevant personality characteristics and behavioral tendencies of the test taker are described in this section and organized according to ten problem domains commonly identified in the professional literature as relevant to public safety candidate suitability. (Please see MMPI-3 User's Guide for the Public Safety Candidate Interpretive Reports *for details.) Statements that begin with "Compared with other correctional candidates" are based on correlations with other self-report measures obtained in correctional candidate samples that included individuals who were subsequently hired as well as those who were not.*

Emotional Control and Stress Tolerance Problems

Compared with other correctional candidates, the test taker is more likely to have difficulty coping with stress[9]; to worry about problems and be uncertain about how to deal with them[10]; and to develop physical symptoms in response to stress and worry about his health[11]. He is also more likely to experience negative emotions[12].

Decision-Making and Judgment Problems

Compared with other correctional candidates, the test taker is more likely to avoid making decisions, fail to take action, or do anything that may prompt scrutiny from others[13]. He is also more likely to be rigid and inflexible[14].

Assertiveness Problems

Compared with other correctional candidates, the test taker is more likely to feel inadequate[13] and to lack assertiveness[11].

The candidate's test scores are not associated with problems in the following domains:

- Routine Task Performance
- Feedback Acceptance
- Social Competence and Teamwork
- Integrity
- Conscientiousness and Dependability
- Substance Use
- Impulse Control

ITEM-LEVEL INFORMATION

Unscorable Responses

The test taker produced scorable responses to all the MMPI-3 items.

Critical Responses

Seven MMPI-3 scales—Suicidal/Death Ideation (SUI), Helplessness/Hopelessness (HLP), Anxiety-Related Experiences (ARX), Ideas of Persecution (RC6), Aberrant Experiences (RC8), Substance Abuse (SUB), and Aggression (AGG)—have been designated by the test authors as having critical item content that may require immediate attention and follow-up. Items answered by the individual in the keyed direction (True or False) on a critical scale are listed below if his T score on that scale is 65 or higher. However, any item answered in the keyed direction on SUI is listed.

The test taker has not produced an elevated T score (≥ 65) on any of these scales or answered any SUI items in the keyed direction.

FIGURE 8.4. Mr. K's MMPI-3 Correctional Candidate Interpretive Report, continued

Critical Follow-up Items

This section contains a list of items to which the test taker responded in a manner warranting follow-up. The items were identified by public safety candidate screening experts as having critical content. Clinicians are encouraged to follow up on these statements with the candidate by making related inquiries, rather than reciting the item(s) verbatim. Each item is followed by the candidate's response, the percentage of Correctional Candidate Comparison Group members who gave this response, and the scale(s) on which the item appears.

  Item number and content omitted. (True; 6.2%; RBS, RC8)
  Item number and content omitted. (True; 2.2%; VRIN, EID, RC7, ARX, NEGE)
  Item number and content omitted. (True; 4.9%; WRY, NEGE)
  Item number and content omitted. (True; 7.3%; EID, ARX, NEGE)

FIGURE 8.4. Mr. K's MMPI-3 Correctional Candidate Interpretive Report, continued

ENDNOTES

This section lists for each statement in the report the MMPI-3 score(s) that triggered it. In addition, each statement is identified as a <u>Test Response</u>, if based on item content, a <u>Correlate</u>, if based on empirical correlates, or an <u>Inference</u>, if based on the report authors' judgment. (This information can also be accessed on-screen by placing the cursor on a given statement.) For correlate-based statements, research references (Ref. No.) are provided, keyed to the consecutively numbered reference list following the endnotes.

[1] Test Response: CMP=76
[2] Correlate: CMP=76, Ref. 1
[3] Inference: CMP=76
[4] Test Response: RC7=58; NEGE=57
[5] Test Response: STR=59
[6] Test Response: WRY=54
[7] Test Response: SFD=53
[8] Test Response: AGG=55
[9] Correlate: SFD=53, Ref. 3, 4; STR=59, Ref. 4; WRY=54, Ref. 4; NEGE=57, Ref. 4
[10] Correlate: WRY=54, Ref. 2
[11] Correlate: SFD=53, Ref. 4
[12] Correlate: RC7=58, Ref. 2; WRY=54, Ref. 2; NEGE=57, Ref. 2
[13] Correlate: RC7=58, Ref. 2
[14] Correlate: CMP=76, Ref. 2

FIGURE 8.4. Mr. K's MMPI-3 Correctional Candidate Interpretive Report, continued

RESEARCH REFERENCE LIST

The following studies are sources for empirical correlates identified in the Endnotes section of this report.

1. Ben-Porath, Y. S., & Tellegen, A. (2020). *The Minnesota Multiphasic Personality Inventory-3 (MMPI-3): Technical manual.* University of Minnesota Press.

2. Corey, D. M., & Ben-Porath, Y. S. (2022). *Minnesota Multiphasic Personality Inventory-3 (MMPI-3): User's guide for the public safety candidate interpretive reports.* University of Minnesota Press.

3. Sellbom, M., Corey, D. M., & Ben-Porath, Y. S. (2021). Incremental validity of the Multidimensional Personality Questionnaire in the preemployment assessment of police officer candidates. *Criminal Justice and Behavior.* Advance online publication. https://doi.org/10.1177/00938548211033630

4. Whitman, M. R., Elias, L. S., Cappo, B. M., & Ben-Porath, Y. S. (2021). Criterion validity of MMPI-3 scores in preemployment evaluations of public safety candidates. *Psychological Assessment.* Advance online publication. https://doi.org/10.1037/pas0001042

End of Report

FIGURE 8.4. Mr. K's MMPI-3 Correctional Candidate Interpretive Report, continued

Step 2: Assessing Substantive Scale Findings

A review of the scores printed in bold font on the "MMPI-3 T Scores (By Domain)" page of Mr. K's CCIR (Figure 8.4, p. 7) shows that seven scales in his protocol are interpreted in the report: six scales (RC7, 58T; STR, 59T; WRY, 54T; CMP, 76T; SFD, 53T; and NEGE, 57T) in the Emotional Dysfunction domain and one moderately elevated scale (AGG, 55T) in the Behavioral Dysfunction domain. Mr. K's scores on normal-range personality testing indicated a tendency to be tense and nervous; to be sensitive; and to feel vulnerable, worried, and anxious.

The comparison group finding associated with Mr. K's RC7 score is listed under the "Emotional/Internalizing Problems" domain heading. (Note that p. 7 of any PSCIR lists each of the Substantive Scales by their associated construct domain, with the Higher-Order scale appearing to the left of the bracket, followed by the associated RC scale to the right, and then a listing of the remaining substantive scales [Specific Problems and PSY-5 scales] associated with that RC scale. Any scale interpreted in the Comparison Group Findings section will always be listed under the same domain label that appears on this page.) The Comparison Group Findings statement indicates, "The test taker reports a comparatively high level of negative emotions for a correctional candidate. Only 0.6% of comparison group members convey this or a greater level of negative emotionality" (Figure 8.4, p. 9). At this moderate level of elevation, RC7 would not be interpreted as indicating clinically significant problems with anxiety, anger, or fear, but this is a much higher than normal level of negative emotionality for a correctional candidate.

As facets of RC7, the Specific Problems scales STR, WRY, and CMP are interpreted next in the report, followed by SFD. As noted on page 9 of Figure 8.4, Mr. K's comparatively rare scores on these scales indicate higher than normal stress (STR = 59T, 0.6%), worry (WRY = 54T, 2.0%), and compulsivity (CMP = 76T, 0.7%), for a correctional candidate. Only 5.0% of the comparison group members convey the same or higher level of self-doubt (SFD = 53T). Because the PSY-5 scale NEGE measures a construct so similar to RC7 (in the normative sample, the scales correlate at .82 for men and .87 for women), NEGE is not interpreted separately when both RC7 and NEGE reach interpretive thresholds.

Mr. K's score on AGG (55T) is interpreted in the Behavioral/Externalizing Problems domain. The narrative states, "The test taker reports a comparatively high level of physically aggressive behavior for a correctional candidate. Only 5.0% of comparison group members convey this or a greater level of inappropriately aggressive behavior" (Figure 8.4, p. 9). Each of the scores interpreted in the Comparison Group Findings section of Mr. K's CCIR is associated with one or more Job-Relevant Correlates in 3 of the 10 problem domains, which are reported on page 10 of the report (Figure 8.4).

Step 3: Assessing Background Findings

Mr. K's background is entirely "clean"—that is, free of negative references, legal problems, negative juvenile history, substance use problems, and so on. The background investigator concluded that he was "universally regarded by his associates, supervisors, and his peers, both personally and professionally." His immediate supervisor at the jail where he worked for three years told the background investigator that Mr. K "gets anxious" in high-stress situations, "but then he analyzes the situation, makes a plan, and does whatever it takes—as quickly as possible—to resolve the cause of his anxiety." Superiors and fellow correctional deputies alike reported him to be reliable and effective. One fellow deputy described him as tending "to be a little hard on himself when he isn't performing to his own expectations, but he gets over it." One reference outside of the sheriff's department reported that he can be "very much a rule follower but is sometimes too black-and-white." Another stated that he "sometimes is too lacking in self-confidence but is more self-confident" since becoming a correctional deputy.

Step 4: Assessing Interview Findings

Mr. K presented in the interview as stoic and rigid, as evidenced by a speaking style that often mimicked the classic narrative of a police report. For example, when asked about an incident at work in which he had raised his voice to a coworker during a disagreement, he replied, "Yes, we had a verbal altercation resulting from disagreement over a procedure, but I had no malice toward him. We agreed to disagree, and the issue was resolved. We had no further incidents."

Regulations from several jurisdictions (e.g., California, Texas, and Washington) require that the psychological interview in a suitability assessment of a peace officer be conducted after reviewing the results of psychological testing and the background investigation. This is because the interview is intended to help clarify information derived from these sources, in addition to other purposes explained by Corey and Zelig (2020) as follows:

> Viewing the interview as something that is *constructed*, rather than passively and unwaveringly carried out in the same way for all candidates, enables evaluations to harness its unique benefits and features. One of these is the opportunity it offers to investigate questions generated by a review of the

psychological testing and personal history. Another is the ability to observe the candidate engaged in decision-making, judgment under stress, reasoning, self-reflection, and social interaction—each relevant to the criterion standards used to evaluate the suitability of a police candidate. (p. 177)

After reviewing the findings from Mr. K's psychological testing and background investigation, the screening psychologist constructed an interview to explore the moderate levels of negative emotionality, stress, worry, and aggression reported by Mr. K, in addition to the clinically significant compulsivity indicated by his score on CMP. Although the background findings were broadly positive, several collateral sources reported observing traits and behaviors consistent with these findings (e.g., becoming anxious under high-stress conditions, too hard on himself, and rigid), and the examining psychologist solicited Mr. K's insight into these traits.

Mr. K's initial responses to the psychologist's questions were characterized by the stoicism and officiousness he exhibited at the start of the interview. This soon gave way to more spontaneous and insightful responses when the psychologist provided the candidate with reflective but supportive feedback and explained that, while the test results and background investigation tell part of the candidate's life story, it is up to him to fill in the details. Mr. K explained that his father retired after a 30-year career with the state police, and as he started his own public safety career, he always felt he was being compared to his father and feared falling short of others' expectations. Indeed, part of his motivation for leaving the small county where his father had been stationed as a state trooper was to establish his own identity apart from his father's legacy. He acknowledged that these stressors and concomitant anxieties were largely self-imposed, and although he considered himself to be increasingly effective in managing them, he wanted to work in an environment in which he believed he was being evaluated on his own merits. He agreed that working in the shadow of his father has undermined his self-confidence.

As for Mr. K's insight into his compulsivity, he acknowledged that he is very focused on following established procedures in the jail to not compromise security or his reputation. He denied repetitive behaviors or mental acts that he feels driven to perform in response to an obsession or according to rules that must be applied rigidly, with the exception to adherence to workplace rules. However, it was evident in the interview that the behaviors he performs compulsively are aimed at preventing or reducing anxiety and negative judgments about his work performance. Concerning aggression (AGG = 55T), he denied ever engaging in a physical altercation outside of his duties as a correctional deputy, but a review of AGG items he answered in the keyed direction indicate aggressive impulses.

Step 5: Identifying Relevant Risk Findings

a. Considering all risk-related findings from all sources, what evidence-based inferences can be drawn?

TEST FINDINGS

Mr. K's scores on RC7, STR, WRY, CMP, SFD, AGG, and NEGE are unusually elevated relative to other correctional candidates. His score on CMP is clinically elevated (76T, which is the ceiling on this scale). Although research to date does not reveal any performance-based correlates, this level of elevation is associated with repetitive checking behavior, experiencing obsessions, and being rigid and perfectionistic (Ben-Porath & Tellegen, 2020a).

His moderate-level scores on RC7, STR, WRY, SFD, AGG, and NEGE are associated with several job-relevant correlates in correctional candidates in 3 of the 10 problem domains: Emotional Control and Stress Tolerance Problems, Decision-Making and Judgment Problems, and Assertiveness Problems. The specific job-relevant correlates—that is, the empirically derived risks—associated with his scale scores are listed on page 10 (Figure 8.4) of his CCIR. Each of these risks is associated with a psychological screening dimension listed in Table 1.5 and, therefore, they "map onto" the criterion standard for the position.

BACKGROUND FINDINGS

Although Mr. K's background was largely, if not globally, nonproblematic, both coworkers and others reported observing his tendencies to be anxious under stress, rigid and "black-and-white" in conforming to rules, and self-doubting.

INTERVIEW FINDINGS

Findings from the interview with Mr. K were generally confirming of those from the background investigation and from the MMPI-3 and normal-range personality testing. However, he also demonstrated insight into many of the environmental and cognitive dynamics that give rise to his worries and associated negative emotionality.

b. What divergent findings might mitigate these inferences?

Although the risk-related findings support the hypothesis that Mr. K may be unsuited for a correctional officer position, the absence of any significant performance deficits and other background findings associated with Mr. K's three years as a correctional deputy in another sheriff's department, particularly in combination with interview findings, may lead the examiner to mitigate these risks. When deciding whether extratest data justify mitigation of risk-related findings from psychological testing, it is important to consider that background investigations are retrospective summaries of a person's functioning in particular contexts and time periods, which vary in their degree of fidelity to the present time and the context of the new position. Mr. K was assessed to have performed well—notwithstanding collateral reports of anxiety under stress, rigidity, compulsivity, and self-doubt—as a correctional deputy in a community where his father was a revered state trooper for 30 years, while living at home with his parents. He now seeks to work in a new and larger agency while living three hours from the town where his entire support system resides. At the same time, he asserts that it is his intention to establish his own identity in a new setting. Whether these considerations are sufficient to mitigate the risk-related findings associated with his test scores is a central decision point in the integrative model (Table 8.1). Indeed, according to Corey and Zelig (2020),

> it is the role of the screening psychologist, armed with a more expansive set of collateral data, to judge whether the construct measured by a particular scale (along with its component risks) can justifiably be ascribed to the particular candidate. (p. 200)

c. Are any surviving risk-related inferences of sufficient relevance and quality to warrant the candidate's disqualification?

Mr. K has applied to an agency where correctional deputies are certified as law enforcement officers and assigned to patrol duties as warranted by their performance. Those who do not meet performance expectations as patrol deputies but who perform well as correctional deputies are permitted to continue in the latter role. The examiner discussed the identified risks with the hiring authority (as well as the likelihood that any significant difficulties would almost certainly be exhibited during academy and field training), who determined that they were within acceptable limits. Consequently, after conferring with the hiring authority, the examiner determined that Mr. K **does meet** the criterion standard and is qualified to be a correctional deputy in the agency to which he applied.

Conferring With the Hiring Authority When Determining Suitability

Some examiners may resist conferring with the hiring authority when deciding whether one or more risk-related findings is disqualifying, but even in jurisdictions where the screening psychologist is explicitly tasked with making the determination (which, as reported by Corey et al. [2023], is the norm in the United States), such collaboration is expected. In discussing California's mandate that the screening psychologist is responsible for determining whether a candidate meets the hiring agency's screening criteria, Spilberg and Corey (2022) noted the importance of this dialogue:

> In evaluating psychological suitability, the screening psychologist is, in effect, determining whether the candidate falls within or outside the parameters of tolerable risk. The psychologist's role is therefore one of *risk assessor*. Establishing the parameters of acceptable risk—*risk management*—is the purview of state law, POST regulations, and the hiring authority. (p. 159)

Whereas some psychologists may consider the determination of a candidate's psychological suitability to be the "ultimate opinion" about whether the candidate is eligible to be a police officer, Corey and Zelig (2020) argue that it is the *penultimate opinion*. "The psychologist respects the employer's role as the ultimate decision maker, not by avoiding a penultimate opinion, but by *educating* the employer about the meaning and significance of the clinical findings" (p. 213). In some jurisdictions, the employer's role in considering the opinion of, but not abdicating to, the examining psychologist is made more explicit. For example, in Washington State, findings from the psychological evaluation "shall be used by the employer to determine the applicant's suitability for employment as a fully commissioned peace officer or reserve officer" (RCW 43.101.070[19]). In Oregon, the employer's prerogative is stated even more succinctly:

> Hiring decisions are the responsibility of each law enforcement unit. The law enforcement hiring unit hiring the police officer or reserve officer maintains the discretion to determine how the information provided in a psychological screening report impacts the hiring decision. (OAR 259-008-0019[19][g])

BRIEF REVIEW: MR. B, POLICE CANDIDATE

Assessment Issues Presented

- An MMPI-3 protocol with both clinically significant and moderately elevated substantive scale scores
- Integration of risk-related MMPI-3 findings with positive background information having low relevance and reliability

Referral Summary

Mr. B is a 30-year-old divorced male seeking a first-time appointment as a police officer with a large urban police department. At the time of the evaluation, Mr. B worked as a debt collector for a national collection agency where he had been employed for two years after relocating to another state. He lives alone and telecommutes from home. He attended college, earning a bachelor's degree in finance eight years earlier. During the six years after college and before starting his current position, he held a series of temporary jobs assisting accountants with tax return preparation and bookkeeping.

The references interviewed during the background investigation included his immediate supervisor (as a telecommuter, he had no coworkers), accountants for whom he had previously worked, family members, and former college instructors and classmates, the latter being his only social network, with whom he interacted mostly via online videogaming. No reference gave a negative assessment of the candidate. Although Mr. B received multiple complaints from persons he contacted to collect debts, his supervisor said that such complaints are common and Mr. B was never disciplined. Mr. B dated briefly but had no sustained romantic relationships.

Assessing Protocol Validity

As shown in Figure 8.5, Mr. B's MMPI-3 protocol is valid with no unscorable items. He "responded to the items relevantly on the basis of their content, and there are no indications of over- or under-reporting" (p. 8).

Substantive Scale Findings

Two of the scales in Mr. B's MMPI-3 protocol reached clinically significant levels (≥ 65T), both of which are in the Behavioral Dysfunction domain: RC9 (76T) and ACT (65T). These scales are interpreted in the Clinical Findings section of Mr. B's PCIR (Figure 8.5, p. 9):

> The test taker reports many behaviors and experiences associated with hypomanic activation, such as excitability, impulsivity, and elevated mood. He is very likely to be restless and become bored and to be acutely over-activated as manifested in poor impulse control, mood instability, euphoria, and excitability. More specifically, he reports episodes of heightened excitation and energy level and may have a history of symptoms associated with manic or hypomanic episodes.

As seen on page 4 of his PCIR, Mr. B's score on SFD (53T) is only 3 T-score points above the normative sample mean, but it is 12 points above the Police Candidate Comparison Group mean. As noted in the Comparison Group Findings (p. 9), this level (or higher) of self-doubt and lack of confidence is reported by only 3.0% of the Police Candidate Comparison Group members. Three scales in the Thought Dysfunction domain, Higher-Order scale THD (60T), Restructured Clinical scale 6 (60T), and PSY-5 scale PSYC (59T), reached interpretable thresholds. When a Higher-Order scale is interpreted in the Comparison Group Findings section of the PCIR, as seen in Mr. B's MMPI-3 protocol,

Minnesota Multiphasic Personality Inventory®-3

Yossef S. Ben-Porath
Auke Tellegen

MMPI®-3
Police Candidate Interpretive Report
David M. Corey, PhD, & Yossef S. Ben-Porath, PhD

ID Number:	Mr. B
Age:	30
Gender:	Male
Marital Status:	Not reported
Years of Education:	Not reported
Date Assessed:	10/24/2022

Copyright © 2020 by the Regents of the University of Minnesota. All rights reserved. Distributed exclusively under license from the University of Minnesota by NCS Pearson, Inc. Portions reproduced from the *MMPI-3 English Test Booklet*. Copyright © 2020 by the Regents of the University of Minnesota. All rights reserved. Portions excerpted from the *MMPI-3 Manual for Administration, Scoring, and Interpretation*. Copyright © 2020 by the Regents of the University of Minnesota. All rights reserved. Portions excerpted from the *MMPI-3 Technical Manual*. Copyright © 2020 by the Regents of the University of Minnesota. All rights reserved. Used by permission of the University of Minnesota Press.

Minnesota Multiphasic Personality Inventory and **MMPI** are registered trademarks of the Regents of the University of Minnesota. **Pearson** is a trademark, in the US and/or other countries, of Pearson Education, Inc., or its affiliates.

This report contains copyrighted material and trade secrets. Qualified licensees may excerpt portions of this output report, limited to the minimum text necessary to accurately describe their significant core conclusions, for incorporation into a written evaluation of the examinee, in accordance with their profession's citation standards, if any. No adaptations, translations, modifications, or special versions may be made of this report without prior written permission from the University of Minnesota Press.

[1.4 / RE1 / QG1]

ALWAYS LEARNING   PEARSON

FIGURE 8.5. Mr. B's MMPI-3 Police Candidate Interpretive Report

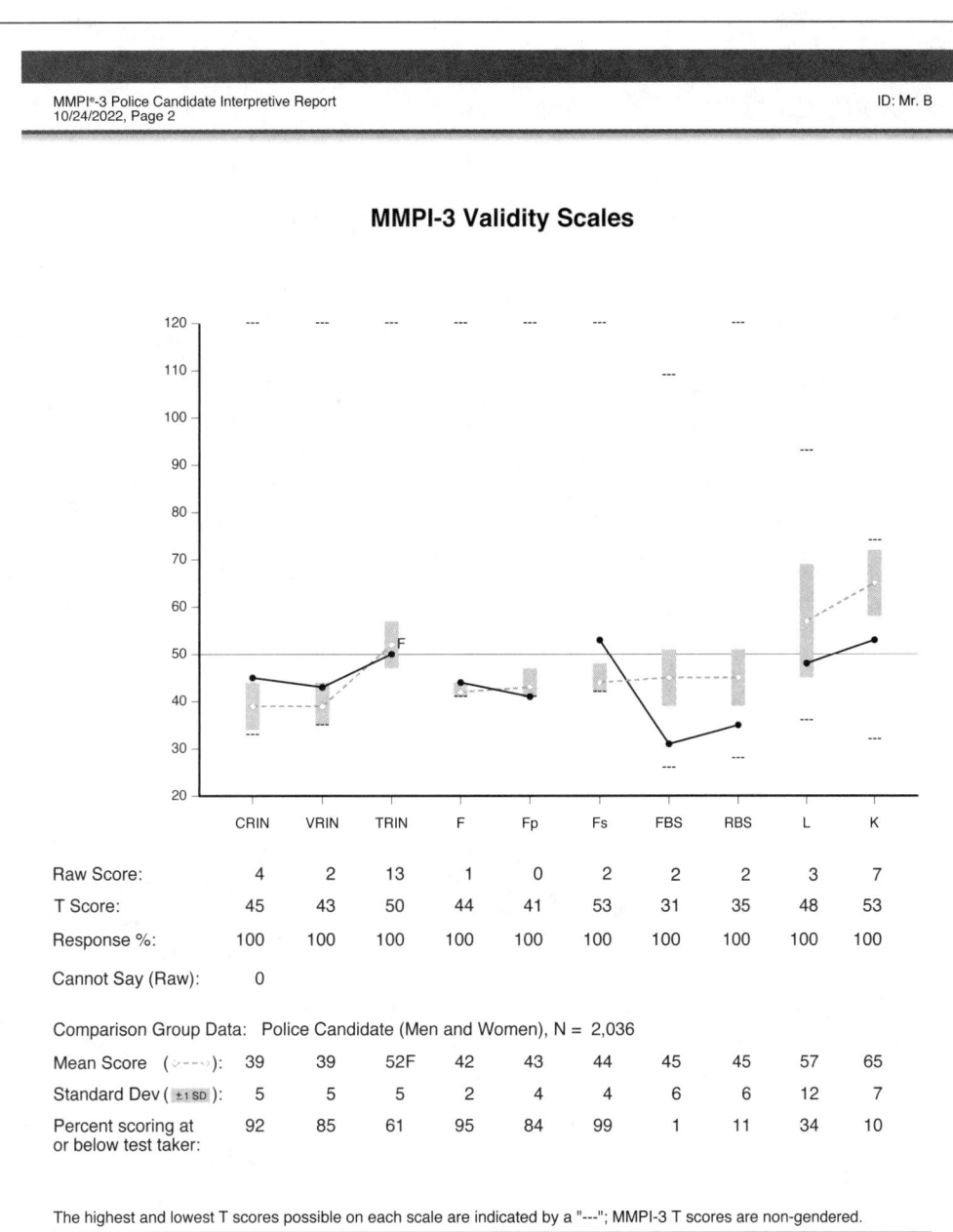

FIGURE 8.5. Mr. B's MMPI-3 Police Candidate Interpretive Report, continued

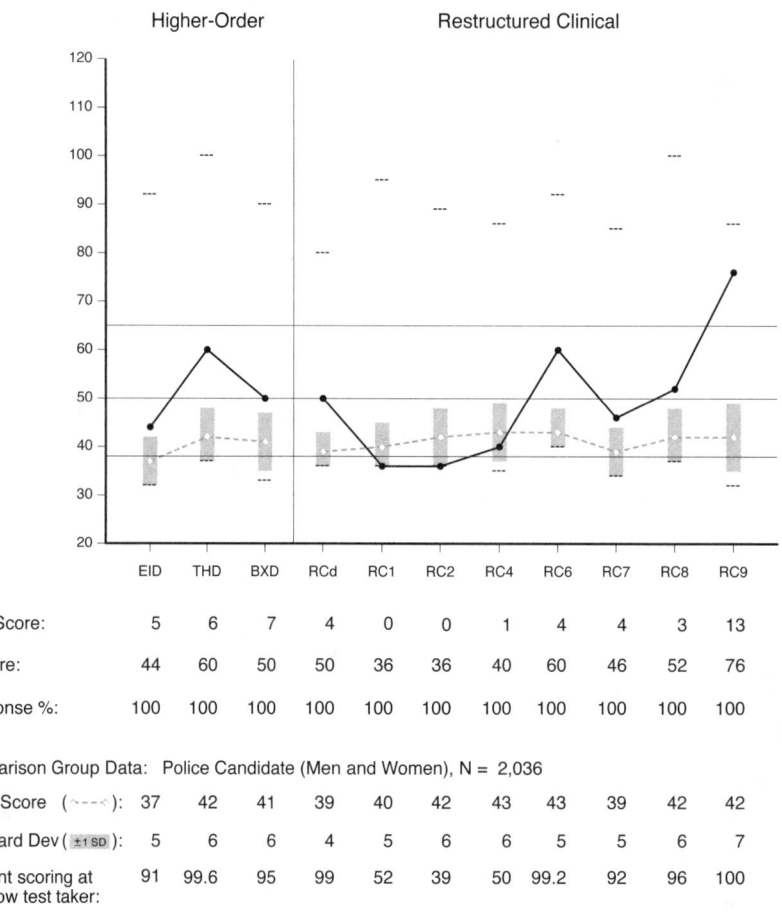

FIGURE 8.5. Mr. B's MMPI-3 Police Candidate Interpretive Report, continued

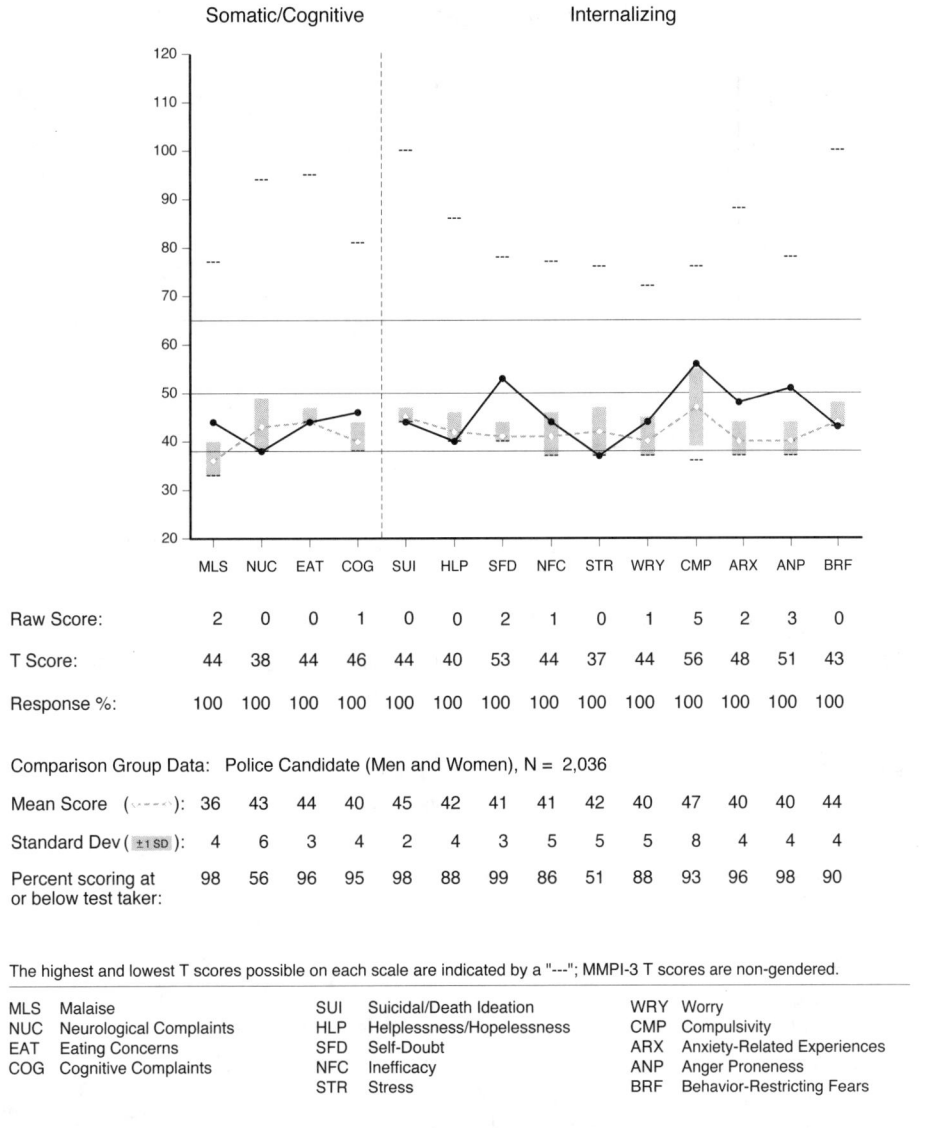

FIGURE 8.5. Mr. B's MMPI-3 Police Candidate Interpretive Report, continued

MMPI-3 Externalizing and Interpersonal Scales

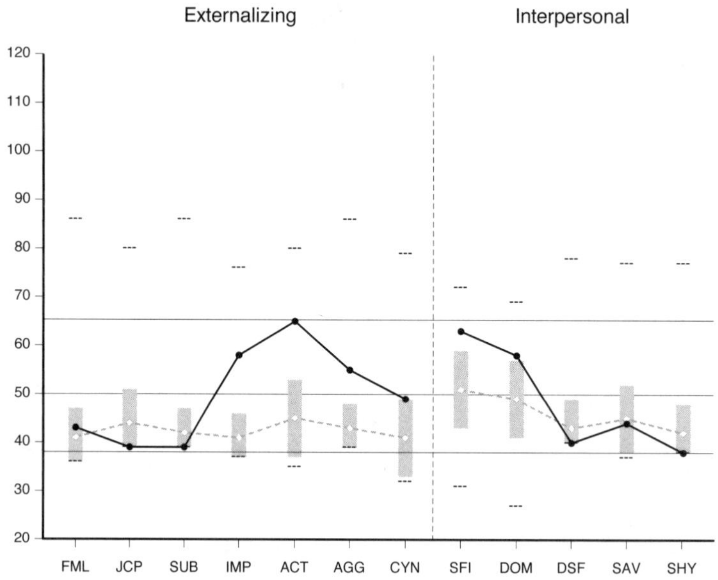

	FML	JCP	SUB	IMP	ACT	AGG	CYN	SFI	DOM	DSF	SAV	SHY
Raw Score:	1	0	0	4	6	2	7	9	8	0	1	0
T Score:	43	39	39	58	65	55	49	63	58	40	44	38
Response %:	100	100	100	100	100	100	100	100	100	100	100	100

Comparison Group Data: Police Candidate (Men and Women), N = 2,036

	FML	JCP	SUB	IMP	ACT	AGG	CYN	SFI	DOM	DSF	SAV	SHY
Mean Score:	41	44	42	41	45	43	41	51	49	43	45	42
Standard Dev (±1 SD):	6	7	5	5	8	5	8	8	8	6	7	6
Percent scoring at or below test taker:	78	53	67	99.6	99	98	87	95	94	71	51	59

The highest and lowest T scores possible on each scale are indicated by a "---"; MMPI-3 T scores are non-gendered.

FML	Family Problems	ACT	Activation	SFI Self-Importance
JCP	Juvenile Conduct Problems	AGG	Aggression	DOM Dominance
SUB	Substance Abuse	CYN	Cynicism	DSF Disaffiliativeness
IMP	Impulsivity			SAV Social Avoidance
				SHY Shyness

FIGURE 8.5. Mr. B's MMPI-3 Police Candidate Interpretive Report, continued

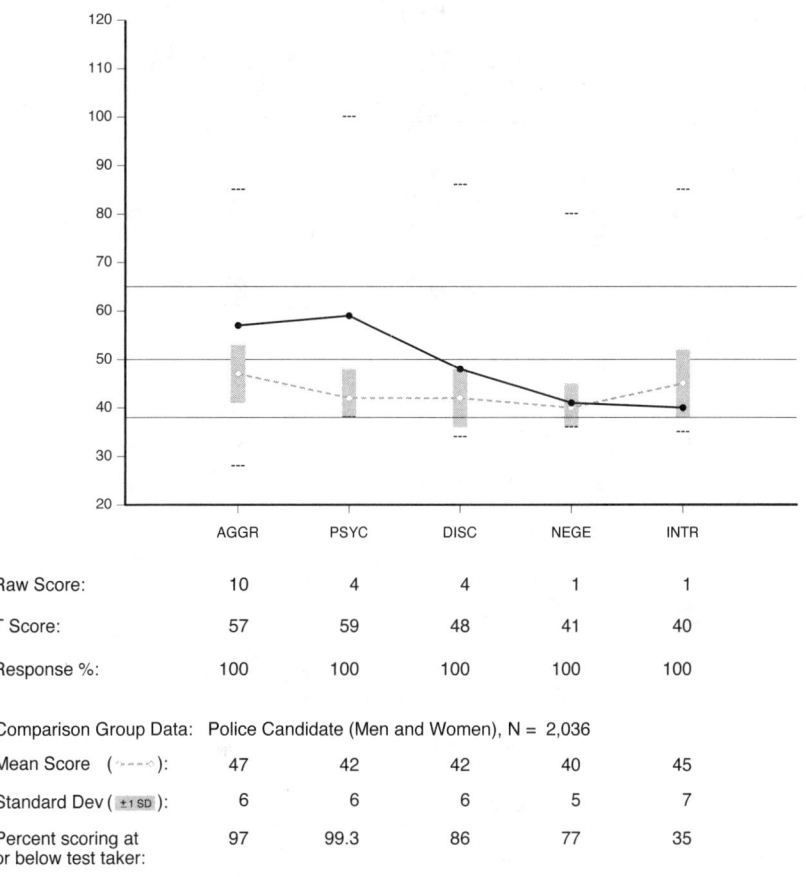

FIGURE 8.5. Mr. B's MMPI-3 Police Candidate Interpretive Report, continued

MMPI-3 T SCORES (BY DOMAIN)

PROTOCOL VALIDITY

Content Non-Responsiveness	0 CNS	45 CRIN	43 VRIN	50 TRIN		
Over-Reporting	44 F	41 Fp		53 Fs	31 FBS	35 RBS
Under-Reporting	48 L	53 K				

SUBSTANTIVE SCALES

Somatic/Cognitive Dysfunction		36 RC1	44 MLS	38 NUC	44 EAT	46 COG			
Emotional Dysfunction	44 EID	50 RCd	44 SUI	40 HLP	**53 SFD**	44 NFC			
		36 RC2	40 INTR						
		46 RC7	37 STR	44 WRY	56 CMP	48 ARX	51 ANP	43 BRF	41 NEGE
Thought Dysfunction	**60 THD**	**60 RC6**							
		52 RC8							
		59 PSYC							
Behavioral Dysfunction	50 BXD	40 RC4	43 FML	39 JCP	39 SUB				
		76 RC9	**58 IMP**	**65 ACT**	**55 AGG**	49 CYN			
		48 DISC							
Interpersonal Functioning		63 SFI	58 DOM	57 AGGR	40 DSF	44 SAV	38 SHY		

Scale scores shown in bold font are interpreted in the report.

Note. This information is provided to facilitate interpretation following the recommended structure for MMPI-3 interpretation in Chapter 5 of the *MMPI-3 Manual for Administration, Scoring, and Interpretation*, which provides details in the text and an outline in Table 5-1.

FIGURE 8.5. Mr. B's MMPI-3 Police Candidate Interpretive Report, continued

This interpretive report is intended for use by a professional qualified to interpret the MMPI-3 in the context of preemployment psychological evaluations of police and other law enforcement candidates. **It focuses on identifying problems; it does not convey potential strengths.** *The information it contains should be considered in the context of the test taker's background, the demands of the position under consideration, the clinical interview, findings from supplemental tests, and other relevant information.*

The interpretive statements in the Protocol Validity section of the report are based on T scores derived from the general MMPI-3 normative sample, as well as scores obtained by the multisite sample of 2,036 individuals that make up the Police Candidate Comparison Group.

The interpretive statements in the Clinical Findings and Diagnostic Considerations sections of the report are based on T scores derived from the general MMPI-3 normative sample. Following recommended practice, only T scores of 65 and higher (with a few exceptions) are considered clinically significant. Scores at this clinical level are generally rare among police candidates.

Statements in the Comparison Group Findings and Job-Relevant Correlates sections are based on comparisons with scores obtained by the Police Candidate Comparison Group. Statements in these sections may be based on T scores that, although less than 65, are nevertheless uncommon in reference to the comparison group.

The report includes extensive annotation, which appears as superscripts following each statement in the narrative, keyed to Endnotes with accompanying Research References, which appear in the final two sections of the report. Additional information about the annotation features is provided in the headnotes to these sections and in the MMPI-3 User's Guide for the Public Safety Candidate Interpretive Reports.

SYNOPSIS

This is a valid MMPI-3 protocol. Scores on the Substantive Scales indicate clinically significant behavioral dysfunction. Behavioral-externalizing problems include hypomanic experiences and excessive activation.

Comparison group findings point to additional possible concerns about self-doubt, persecutory beliefs, impulsivity, and physically aggressive behavior.

Possible job-relevant problems are identified in the following domains: Emotional Control and Stress Tolerance, Routine Task Performance, Decision-Making and Judgment, Feedback Acceptance, Assertiveness, Social Competence and Teamwork, Integrity, Conscientiousness and Dependability, and Impulse Control.

PROTOCOL VALIDITY

This is a valid MMPI-3 protocol. There are no problems with unscorable items. The test taker responded to the items relevantly on the basis of their content, and there are no indications of over- or under-reporting.

FIGURE 8.5. Mr. B's MMPI-3 Police Candidate Interpretive Report, continued

CLINICAL FINDINGS

Clinical-level symptoms, personality characteristics, and behavioral tendencies of the test taker are described in this section and organized according to an empirically guided framework. (Please see Chapter 5 of the MMPI-3 Manual for Administration, Scoring, and Interpretation *for details.) Statements containing the word "reports" are based on the item content of MMPI-3 scales, whereas statements that include the word "likely" are based on empirical correlates of scale scores. Specific sources for each statement can be viewed with the annotation features of this report.*

The test taker reports many behaviors and experiences associated with hypomanic activation, such as excitability, impulsivity, and elevated mood[1]. He is very likely to be restless and become bored[2] and to be acutely over-activated as manifested in poor impulse control[3], mood instability[4], euphoria[5], and excitability[6]. More specifically, he reports episodes of heightened excitation and energy level[7] and may have a history of symptoms associated with manic or hypomanic episodes[8].

There are no indications of clinically significant somatic, cognitive, emotional, or thought dysfunction in this protocol.

DIAGNOSTIC CONSIDERATIONS

This section provides recommendations for psychodiagnostic assessment based on the test taker's MMPI-3 results. It is recommended that he be evaluated for the following:

Emotional-Internalizing Disorders
- Manic or hypomanic episode[9]
- Cycling mood disorder[10]

COMPARISON GROUP FINDINGS

This section describes the MMPI-3 substantive scale findings in the context of the Police Candidate Comparison Group. Specific sources for each statement can be accessed with the annotation features of this report.
Job-related correlates of these results, if any, are provided in the subsequent Job-Relevant Correlates section.

Emotional/Internalizing Problems
The test taker reports a comparatively high level of self-doubt for a police candidate[11]. Only 3.0% of comparison group members convey this or a greater lack of confidence.

Unusual Thoughts, Perceptions, and Beliefs
The test taker reports a comparatively high level of unusual thinking for a police candidate[12]. Only 1.0% of comparison group members convey such thoughts at this or a higher level. More specifically, he reports a relatively high level of persecutory beliefs for a police candidate[13]. Only 2.0% of comparison group members convey this or a greater level of persecutory thinking.

Behavioral/Externalizing Problems
The test taker's responses indicate a level of energy, aggression, and impulsivity that is very likely incompatible with public safety requirements for behavioral control[14]. This level of excitability is uncommon among police candidates. No comparison group members give evidence of this level of over-stimulation. In particular, his responses indicate a level of over-activation that may impede conformance with public safety requirements for behavioral control and sound judgment[15]. This level of excitability is uncommon among police candidates. Only

FIGURE 8.5. Mr. B's MMPI-3 Police Candidate Interpretive Report, continued

4.0% of comparison group members demonstrate this or a greater level of activation. He reports a comparatively high level of impulsive behavior for a police candidate[16]. Only 2.0% of comparison group members convey this or a greater level of impulsivity. He also reports a relatively high level of physically aggressive behavior for a police candidate[17]. Only 6.0% of comparison group members convey this or a greater level of inappropriately aggressive behavior.

JOB-RELEVANT CORRELATES

Job-relevant personality characteristics and behavioral tendencies of the test taker are described in this section and organized according to ten problem domains commonly identified in the professional literature as relevant to public safety candidate suitability. (Please see MMPI-3 User's Guide for the Public Safety Candidate Interpretive Reports *for details.) Statements that begin with "Compared with other police candidates" are based on correlations with other self-report measures obtained in police candidate samples that included individuals who were subsequently hired as well as those who were not. Statements that begin with "He is more likely than most police officers or trainees" are based on correlations with outcome data obtained in samples of hired candidates during academy or field training, probation, and/or the postprobation period. Specific sources for each statement can be accessed with the annotation features of this report.*

Emotional Control and Stress Tolerance Problems

Compared with other police candidates, the test taker is more likely to have difficulty coping with stress[18]; to develop physical symptoms in response to stress and worry about his health[18]; and to believe he has been mistreated[19].

He is more likely than most police officers or trainees to exhibit difficulties performing under stressful conditions[20].

Routine Task Performance Problems

The test taker is more likely than most police officers or trainees to exhibit report writing problems[21].

Decision-Making and Judgment Problems

Compared with other police candidates, the test taker is more likely to have thoughts, perceptions, and/or experiences that are rarely reported[22] and to exhibit difficulty with decision-making and judgment[23].

He is more likely than most police officers or trainees to exhibit difficulties prioritizing multiple and essential functions of the job and performing them in quick succession while maintaining good environmental awareness of vital information (in other words, multi-tasking)[21]. He is also more likely to exhibit difficulties with effective decision-making[20] and with performing duties in a manner conducive to the safety of others[24].

Feedback Acceptance Problems

The test taker is more likely than most police officers or trainees to exhibit difficulties accepting and responding to constructive performance feedback[25].

Assertiveness Problems

Compared with other police candidates, the test taker is more likely to avoid situations that others generally view as benign and non-intimidating[26] and to lack assertiveness[27].

Social Competence and Teamwork Problems

Compared with other police candidates, the test taker is more likely to be self-centered[28]; to have a history of problems getting along with others[29]; and to be opinionated and outspoken[30]. He is also more likely to be demanding[30]; to have difficulty trusting others[31]; and to feel maligned by others[19]. In addition, he is more likely to have problems with social competence[23] and to have difficulties with teamwork[32].

FIGURE 8.5. Mr. B's MMPI-3 Police Candidate Interpretive Report, continued

He is more likely than most police officers or trainees to exhibit difficulties stemming from rude and/or overbearing behavior that results in complaints from the public[33]; cooperating with peers and/or supervisors[34]; and interacting effectively with others in a variety of contexts[24].

Integrity Problems

Compared with other police candidates, the test taker is more likely to have skeptical and/or antisocial views of the world[30] and to be nonconforming[35].

He is more likely than most police officers or trainees to exhibit difficulties leading to sustained internal affairs investigations[36]; complaints from the public[37]; and investigations about conduct unbecoming a police officer[37].

Conscientiousness and Dependability Problems

The test taker is more likely than most police officers or trainees to exhibit difficulties with initiative and drive, such as obtaining information and evidence needed to solve crimes and explain incidents[38]. He is also more likely to exhibit difficulties reliably attending court[39]; with punctuality and attendance[40]; and with conscientiousness[41].

Impulse Control Problems

Compared with other police candidates, the test taker is more likely to behave impulsively or without adequate consideration of the consequences or implications of his actions[42]; to have a history of anger management problems[43]; and to be nonplanful[35].

He is more likely than most police officers or trainees to exhibit problems reacting to situations with the proper degree of emotional and behavioral restraint and control, and avoiding impulsive and/or unnecessarily risky behavior[44]. He is also more likely to exhibit conduct unbecoming a police officer[28].

Substance Use Problems

The candidate's test scores are not associated with problems in this domain.

ITEM-LEVEL INFORMATION

Unscorable Responses

The test taker produced scorable responses to all the MMPI-3 items.

Critical Responses

Seven MMPI-3 scales—Suicidal/Death Ideation (SUI), Helplessness/Hopelessness (HLP), Anxiety-Related Experiences (ARX), Ideas of Persecution (RC6), Aberrant Experiences (RC8), Substance Abuse (SUB), and Aggression (AGG)—have been designated by the test authors as having critical item content that may require immediate attention and follow-up. Items answered by the individual in the keyed direction (True or False) on a critical scale are listed below if his T score on that scale is 65 or higher. However, any item answered in the keyed direction on SUI is listed.

The test taker has not produced an elevated T score ($\geq$ 65) on any of these scales or answered any SUI items in the keyed direction.

Critical Follow-up Items

This section contains a list of items to which the test taker responded in a manner warranting follow-up. The items were identified by public safety candidate screening experts as having critical content. Clinicians are encouraged to follow up on these statements with the candidate by making related inquiries, rather than reciting the item(s) verbatim. Each item is followed by the candidate's response, the percentage of Police Candidate Comparison Group members who gave this response, and the scale(s) on which the item appears.

FIGURE 8.5. Mr. B's MMPI-3 Police Candidate Interpretive Report, continued

Item number and content omitted. (True; 5.1%; BXD, RC9, IMP, DISC)
Item number and content omitted. (True; 19.4%; BXD, RC9, IMP, DISC)
Item number and content omitted. (True; 12.7%; ARX)
Item number and content omitted. (True; 1.5%; VRIN, F, THD, RC6, PSYC)
Item number and content omitted. (True; 5.0%; VRIN, BXD, RC9, IMP, DISC)
Item number and content omitted. (True; 13.5%; ANP)

FIGURE 8.5. Mr. B's MMPI-3 Police Candidate Interpretive Report, continued

ENDNOTES

This section lists for each statement in the report the MMPI-3 score(s) that triggered it. In addition, each statement is identified as a <u>Test Response</u>, if based on item content, a <u>Correlate</u>, if based on empirical correlates, or an <u>Inference</u>, if based on the report authors' judgment. (This information can also be accessed on-screen by placing the cursor on a given statement.) For correlate-based statements, research references (Ref. No.) are provided, keyed to the consecutively numbered reference list following the endnotes.

[1] Test Response: RC9=76
[2] Correlate: RC9=76, Ref. 23
[3] Correlate: RC9=76, Ref. 2, 6, 7, 8, 9, 10, 15, 18, 23
[4] Correlate: RC9=76, Ref. 1, 3, 12, 17, 23
[5] Correlate: RC9=76, Ref. 12, 23
[6] Correlate: RC9=76, Ref. 1, 2, 3, 6, 11, 15, 23
[7] Test Response: ACT=65
[8] Correlate: RC9=76, Ref. 1, 2, 17, 23, 26; ACT=65, Ref. 1, 2, 12, 23, 24, 26
[9] Correlate: RC9=76, Ref. 2, 26; ACT=65, Ref. 14, 24, 26
[10] Correlate: ACT=65, Ref. 24
[11] Test Response: SFD=53
[12] Test Response: THD=60; PSYC=59
[13] Test Response: RC6=60
[14] Inference: RC9=76
[15] Inference: ACT=65
[16] Test Response: IMP=58
[17] Test Response: AGG=55
[18] Correlate: SFD=53, Ref. 16, 25
[19] Correlate: RC6=60, Ref. 4
[20] Correlate: PSYC=59, Ref. 2
[21] Correlate: ACT=65, Ref. 2
[22] Correlate: THD=60, Ref. 22; PSYC=59, Ref. 5, 22
[23] Correlate: THD=60, Ref. 25; RC6=60, Ref. 25
[24] Correlate: AGG=55, Ref. 13
[25] Correlate: AGG=55, Ref. 19
[26] Correlate: PSYC=59, Ref. 5
[27] Correlate: SFD=53, Ref. 25
[28] Correlate: RC9=76, Ref. 2
[29] Correlate: RC9=76, Ref. 2, 5, 22
[30] Correlate: RC9=76, Ref. 5, 22
[31] Correlate: RC9=76, Ref. 5, 22; PSYC=59, Ref. 5, 22
[32] Correlate: RC6=60, Ref. 25
[33] Correlate: RC9=76, Ref. 22; AGG=55, Ref. 21
[34] Correlate: AGG=55, Ref. 19, 20, 21
[35] Correlate: IMP=58, Ref. 4
[36] Correlate: PSYC=59, Ref. 22
[37] Correlate: RC6=60, Ref. 20, 22
[38] Correlate: PSYC=59, Ref. 19, 21
[39] Correlate: THD=60, Ref. 20, 22; PSYC=59, Ref. 20, 22
[40] Correlate: THD=60, Ref. 2, 13; PSYC=59, Ref. 2, 13
[41] Correlate: THD=60, Ref. 2; PSYC=59, Ref. 2
[42] Correlate: RC9=76, Ref. 2, 4, 5, 22; IMP=58, Ref. 4
[43] Correlate: RC9=76, Ref. 2, 5, 22; IMP=58, Ref. 2
[44] Correlate: RC9=76, Ref. 22

FIGURE 8.5. Mr. B's MMPI-3 Police Candidate Interpretive Report, continued

RESEARCH REFERENCE LIST

The following studies are sources for empirical correlates identified in the Endnotes section of this report.

1. Bagby, R. M., Onno, K. A., Mortezaei, A., & Sellbom, M. (2020). Examining the "Traditional Background Hypothesis" for the MMPI-2-RF L-r Scores in a Muslim Faith-Based Sample. *Psychological Assessment*. Advance online publication. https://doi.org/10.1037/pas0000941

2. Ben-Porath, Y. S., & Tellegen, A. (2020). *The Minnesota Multiphasic Personality Inventory-3 (MMPI-3): Technical manual.* University of Minnesota Press.

3. Burchett, D. L., & Ben-Porath, Y. S. (2010). The impact of over-reporting on MMPI-2-RF substantive scale score validity. *Assessment, 17*(4), 497–516. https://doi.org/10.1177/1073191110378972

4. Corey, D. M., & Ben-Porath, Y. S. (2022). *Minnesota Multiphasic Personality Inventory-3 (MMPI-3): User's guide for the public safety candidate interpretive reports.* University of Minnesota Press.

5. Detrick, P., Ben-Porath, Y.S., & Sellbom, M. (2016). Associations between MMPI-2-RF (Restructured Form) and Inwald Personality Inventory (IPI) scale scores in a law enforcement preemployment screening sample. *Journal of Police and Criminal Psychology, 31,* 81–95. https://doi.org/10.1007/s11896-015-9172-7

6. Finn, J. A., Ben-Porath, Y. S., & Tellegen, A. (2015). Dichotomous versus polytomous response options in psychopathology assessment: Method or meaningful variance? *Psychological Assessment, 27*(1), 184–193. https://doi.org/10.1037/pas0000044

7. Forbey, J. D., & Ben-Porath, Y. S. (2007). A comparison of the MMPI-2 Restructured Clinical (RC) and Clinical Scales in a substance abuse treatment sample. *Psychological Services, 4*(1), 46–58. https://doi.org/10.1037/1541-1559.4.1.46

8. Forbey, J. D., & Ben-Porath, Y. S. (2008). Empirical correlates of the MMPI-2 Restructured Clinical (RC) Scales in a non-clinical setting. *Journal of Personality Assessment, 90*(2), 136–141. https://doi.org/10.1080/00223890701845161

9. Forbey, J. D., Ben-Porath, Y. S., & Arbisi, P. A. (2012). The MMPI-2 computer adaptive version (MMPI-2-CA) in a Veterans Administration medical outpatient facility. *Psychological Assessment, 24*(3), 628–639. https://doi.org/10.1037/a0026509

10. Forbey, J. D., Ben-Porath, Y. S., & Gartland, D. (2009). Validation of the MMPI-2 Computerized Adaptive version (MMPI-2-CA) in a correctional intake facility. *Psychological Services, 6*(4), 279–292. https://doi.org/10.1037/a0016195

11. Handel, R. W., & Archer, R. P. (2008). An investigation of the psychometric properties of the MMPI-2 Restructured Clinical (RC) Scales with mental health inpatients. *Journal of Personality Assessment, 90*(3), 239–249. https://doi.org/10.1080/00223890701884954

12. Menton, W. H., Crighton, A. H., Tarescavage, A. M., Marek, R. J., Hicks, A. D., & Ben-Porath, Y. S. (2019). Equivalence of laptop and tablet administrations of the Minnesota Multiphasic Personality Inventory-2 Restructured Form. *Assessment, 26*(4), 661–669. https://doi.org/10.1177/1073191117714558

13. Roberts, R. M., Tarescavage, A. M., Ben-Porath, Y. S., & Roberts, M. D. (2018). predicting post-probationary job performance of police officers using CPI and MMPI-2-RF test data obtained during preemployment psychological screening. *Journal of Personality Assessment, 101*(5), 544–555. https://doi.org/10.1080/00223891.2018.1423990

FIGURE 8.5. Mr. B's MMPI-3 Police Candidate Interpretive Report, continued

14. Sellbom, M., Bagby, R. M., Kushner, S., Quilty, L. C., & Ayearst, L. E. (2011). Diagnostic construct validity of the MMPI-2 Restructured Form (MMPI-2-RF) scale scores. *Assessment, 19*(2), 176–186. https://doi.org/10.1177/1073191111428763

15. Sellbom, M., Ben-Porath, Y. S., & Bagby, R. M. (2008). Personality and psychopathology: Mapping the MMPI-2 Restructured Clinical (RC) Scales onto the five factor model of personality. *Journal of Personality Disorders, 22*(3), 291–312. https://doi.org/10.1521/pedi.2008.22.3.291

16. Sellbom, M., Corey, D. M., & Ben-Porath, Y. S. (2021). Incremental validity of the Multidimensional Personality Questionnaire in the preemployment assessment of police officer candidates. *Criminal Justice and Behavior*. Advance online publication. https://doi.org/10.1177/00938548211033630

17. Sellbom, M., Graham, J. R., & Schenk, P. W. (2006). Incremental validity of the MMPI-2 Restructured Clinical (RC) Scales in a private practice sample. *Journal of Personality Assessment, 86*(2), 196–205. https://doi.org/10.1207/s15327752jpa8602_09

18. Simms, L. J., Casillas, A., Clark, L. A., Watson, D., & Doebbeling, B. N. (2005). Psychometric evaluation of the Restructured Clinical Scales of the MMPI-2. *Psychological Assessment, 17*(3), 345–358. https://doi.org/10.1037/1040-3590.17.3.345

19. Tarescavage, A. M., Corey, D. M., & Ben-Porath, Y. S. (2015). Minnesota Multiphasic Personality Inventory-2-Restructured Form (MMPI-2-RF) predictors of police officer problem behavior. *Assessment, 22*(1), 116–132. https://doi.org/10.1177/1073191114534885

20. Tarescavage, A. M., Corey, D. M., & Ben-Porath, Y. S. (2016). A prorating method for estimating MMPI-2-RF scores from MMPI responses: Examination of score fidelity and illustration of empirical utility in the PERSEREC police integrity study sample. *Assessment, 23*(2), 173–190. https://doi.org/10.1177/1073191115575070

21. Tarescavage, A. M., Corey, D. M., Gupton, H. M., & Ben-Porath Y.S. (2015). Criterion validity and practical utility of the Minnesota Multiphasic Personality Inventory-2-Restructured Form (MMPI-2-RF) in assessments of police officer candidates. *Journal of Personality Assessment, 97*(4), 382–394. https://doi.org/10.1080/00223891.2014.995800

22. Tarescavage, A. M., Fischler, G. L., Cappo, B. M., Hill, D. O., Corey, D. M., & Ben-Porath, Y. S. (2015). Minnesota Multiphasic Personality Inventory-2-Restructured Form (MMPI-2-RF) predictors of police officer problem behavior and collateral self-report test scores. *Psychological Assessment, 27*(1), 125–137. https://doi.org/10.1037/pas0000041

23. Tellegen, A., & Ben-Porath, Y. S. (2008/2011). *Minnesota Multiphasic Personality Inventory-2-Restructured Form (MMPI-2-RF): Technical manual*. University of Minnesota Press.

24. Watson, C., Quilty, L. C., & Bagby, R. M. (2011). Differentiating bipolar disorder from major depressive disorder using the MMPI-2-RF: A receiver operating characteristics (ROC) analysis. *Journal of Psychopathology and Behavioral Assessment, 33*(3), 368–374. https://doi.org/10.1007/s10862-010-9212-7

25. Whitman, M. R., Elias, L. S., Cappo, B. M., & Ben-Porath, Y. S. (2021). Criterion validity of MMPI-3 scores in preemployment evaluations of public safety candidates. *Psychological Assessment*. Advance online publication. https://doi.org/10.1037/pas0001042

26. Whitman, M. R., Tylicki, J. L., Mascioli, R., Pickle, J., & Ben-Porath, Y. S. (2021). Psychometric properties of the Minnesota Multiphasic Personality Inventory-3 (MMPI-3) in a clinical neuropsychology setting. *Psychological Assessment, 33*(2), 142–155. https://doi.org/10.1037/pas0000969

End of Report

FIGURE 8.5. Mr. B's MMPI-3 Police Candidate Interpretive Report, continued

interpretation of its corresponding PSY-5 scale—in this case, PSYC—is suppressed to avoid overweighting two highly intercorrelated scales and conceptually similar constructs (THD and PSYC are correlated in the normative sample at $r = .92$ among men and $r = .93$ among women). As noted on page 9 of the narrative, only 1.0% of the comparison group members reported the same or higher level of unusual thinking (THD), and only 2.0% reported the same or greater level of persecutory thinking (RC6).

The two clinically elevated scales in the Behavioral Dysfunction, RC9 and ACT, are shown in the Comparison Group Findings section of Mr. B's PCIR (Figure 8.5, p. 9) to be rare for police candidates. As stated in the report,

> The test taker's responses indicate a level of energy, aggression, and impulsivity that is very likely incompatible with public safety requirements for behavioral control. This level of excitability is uncommon among police candidates. No comparison group members give evidence of this level of over-stimulation. In particular, his responses indicate a level of over-activation that may impede conformance with public safety requirements for behavioral control and sound judgment. This level of heightened excitation is very uncommon among police candidates. Only 4.0% of comparison group members demonstrate this or a greater level of activation. He reports a comparatively high level of impulsive behavior for a police candidate.

Two other substantive scale scores in the Behavioral Dysfunction domain, IMP and AGG, are moderately elevated. Mr. B's PCIR (Figure 8.5, p. 10) notes that only 2.0% of the comparison group members obtained a score on IMP $\geq 58T$, and only 6.0% obtained a score $\geq 55T$ on AGG, indicating a comparatively rare level of impulsivity and aggressive behavior, respectively.

Discussion

Mr. B's scores on RC9 and ACT are clinically significant, and together, they are associated with nine job-relevant correlates. Combined with inferences supported by his moderately elevated scale scores on THD, RC6, SFD, IMP, AGG, and PSYC, his MMPI-3 protocol is associated with 27 job-relevant correlates in 9 of the 10 problem domains. In addition, he responded in the keyed direction to six Critical Follow-up Items.

Step 5 of the integrative model (Table 8.1) contains three components involving the identification and determination of: (a) evidence-based, risk-related findings from all sources; (b) divergent findings of sufficient relevance, reliability, and validity to mitigate any of the risk-related findings; and (c) whether the nonmitigated risks are of sufficient relevance and quality to warrant the candidate's disqualification. It is the second component—mitigation—that presents the greatest challenge when assessing Mr. B's suitability.

Although Mr. B's background investigation revealed no significantly negative information, the references are of questionable relevance and reliability. The integrative model gives primacy to data with the highest known validity (e.g., risk-related findings supported by peer-reviewed studies) while recognizing that any identified risks could be mitigated by other data sources if deemed sufficiently relevant and reliable. In Mr. B's case, however, his positive references are derived from persons who had no direct, day-to-day contact with him; consequently, their reliability is insufficient to mitigate the known risks associated with his test scores across a wide range of constructs, particularly in light of the warranted clinical inference that Mr. B may be experiencing a mood-cycling disorder.

In addition to concerns about the reliability of the background investigation findings, Mr. B's references are based on interactions with little relevance to the demands of a law enforcement career. Debt collection certainly involves interacting with a wide range of persons, some of whom are undoubtedly distressed and resistant, but it is not clear from the references whether the multiple complaints generated by his debt collection efforts may have been warranted. The performance metrics valued by his employer centered on successful collections, notwithstanding the debtor's experience.

Although most of the risk-related findings from Mr. B's MMPI-3 protocol derive from scales in the Behavioral Dysfunction domain (RC9, IMP, ACT, and AGG), his scores in the Thought Dysfunction domain (THD, RC6, and PSYC) are also associated with 13 job-relevant correlates across multiple problem domains. At the moderate T-score levels produced by his responses, no inferences can be drawn concerning psychotic or disordered thinking, including paranoia. However, even these moderate elevations are rare for police candidates ($\leq 2\%$). The items from these scales that Mr. B answered in the keyed direction can be printed as part of the PCIR (see *MMPI-3 User's Guide for the Public Safety Candidate Interpretive Reports*), and a review of those items reveals the content of Mr. B's unusual thinking. (For test security, the actual item content is not included in Figure 8.5.) Indeed, when considering the cognitive distortions required for a candidate to respond to these items in the keyed direction, it is not surprising that these scales predict the broad range of police performance problems reported by Ben-Porath and Tellegen (2020b); Tarescavage and colleagues (2016); and Tarescavage, Fischler, and colleagues (2015).

Considering the objective findings from the evaluation, including the risk-related inferences associated with Mr. B's MMPI-3 scores, the examiner determined that the candidate **does not meet** the hiring agency's criterion standard.

COMPREHENSIVE REVIEW: MR. M, POLICE CANDIDATE

Assessment Issues Presented

- Invalid MMPI-3 protocol
- Reliance on collateral data
- Consideration of an indeterminate or indeterminable suitability rating

Referral Summary

Mr. M is a 28-year-old, married, male police candidate who was honorably discharged from the U.S. Marine Corps two and a half years before applying to be an entry-level police officer with a small rural police department. During his eight years of military service, he was deployed to combat zones in Afghanistan and Iraq, where he performed minesweeping duties.

Data Integration

Step 1: Assessing Protocol Validity

Mr. M's PCIR (Figure 8.6) includes a narrative interpretation of protocol validity (p. 8). The Protocol Validity section begins with the following statement: "This MMPI-3 protocol is invalid and uninterpretable owing to inconsistent responding. Details are provided below." The details that follow indicate that Mr. M's responses show evidence of excessive inconsistency because of fixed False responding to the MMPI-3 items (TRIN = 85F) and that "this level of inconsistency most likely reflects a non-cooperative test-taking approach."

The interpretive statement just quoted reflects guidance in the *MMPI-3 Manual for Administration, Scoring, and Interpretation,* which lists two possible reasons for a TRIN 85F T score: an uncooperative test-taking approach and difficulties with double negatives. The latter is most likely to apply in cases where the test taker has significant language comprehension deficits or is a non-native English speaker. Neither of these alternatives applies in Mr. M's case, leaving an uncooperative test-taking approach characterized by inconsistent False responding as the most likely explanation for his invalid MMPI-3 protocol.

A protocol rendered invalid by content nonresponsiveness **cannot be interpreted** beyond a review of the three response consistency scales (CRIN, VRIN, and TRIN), including inferring meaning from the overreporting and underreporting scales, moderately elevated substantive scale scores (e.g., Mr. M's RC2 score of 60T), and low scores that would be interpretable in a valid protocol (e.g., his CYN score of 32T). Mr. M's scores from normal-range personality

Minnesota Multiphasic Personality Inventory®-3

Yossef S. Ben-Porath
Auke Tellegen

MMPI®-3
Police Candidate Interpretive Report
David M. Corey, PhD, & Yossef S. Ben-Porath, PhD

ID Number:	Mr. M
Age:	28
Gender:	Male
Marital Status:	Not reported
Years of Education:	Not reported
Date Assessed:	09/26/2022

Copyright © 2020 by the Regents of the University of Minnesota. All rights reserved. Distributed exclusively under license from the University of Minnesota by NCS Pearson, Inc. Portions reproduced from the *MMPI-3 English Test Booklet*. Copyright © 2020 by the Regents of the University of Minnesota. All rights reserved. Portions excerpted from the *MMPI-3 Manual for Administration, Scoring, and Interpretation*. Copyright © 2020 by the Regents of the University of Minnesota. All rights reserved. Portions excerpted from the *MMPI-3 Technical Manual*. Copyright © 2020 by the Regents of the University of Minnesota. All rights reserved. Used by permission of the University of Minnesota Press.

Minnesota Multiphasic Personality Inventory and **MMPI** are registered trademarks of the Regents of the University of Minnesota. **Pearson** is a trademark, in the US and/or other countries, of Pearson Education, Inc., or its affiliates.

This report contains copyrighted material and trade secrets. Qualified licensees may excerpt portions of this output report, limited to the minimum text necessary to accurately describe their significant core conclusions, for incorporation into a written evaluation of the examinee, in accordance with their profession's citation standards, if any. No adaptations, translations, modifications, or special versions may be made of this report without prior written permission from the University of Minnesota Press.

[1.4 / RE1 / QG1]

ALWAYS LEARNING   PEARSON

FIGURE 8.6. Mr. M's MMPI-3 Police Candidate Interpretive Report

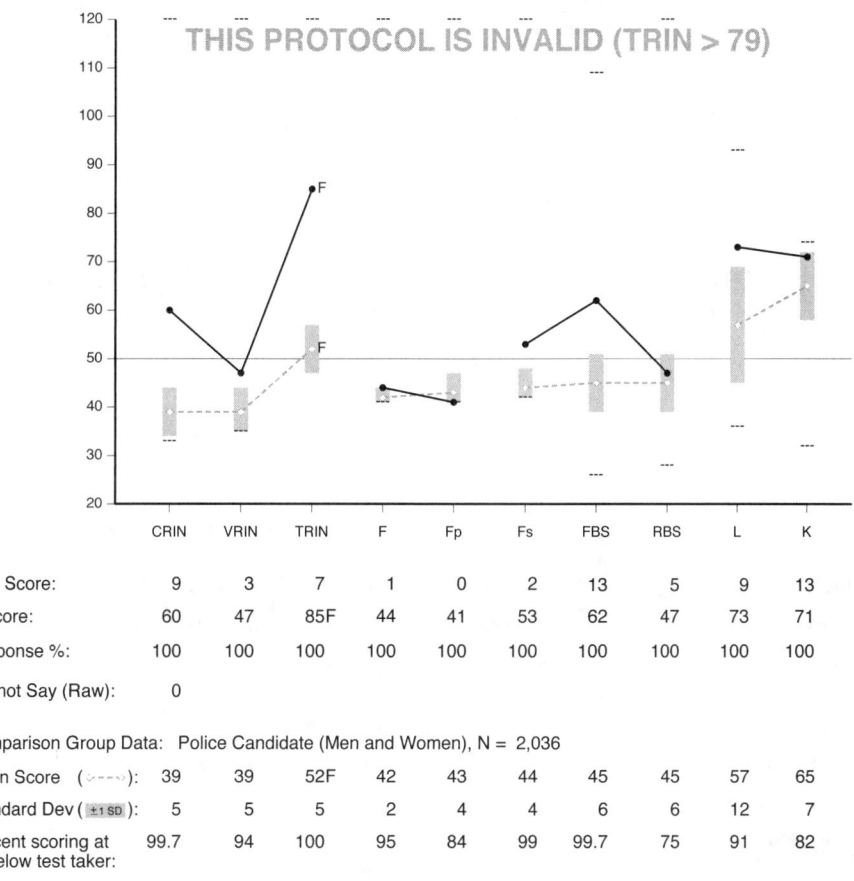

FIGURE 8.6. Mr. M's MMPI-3 Police Candidate Interpretive Report, continued

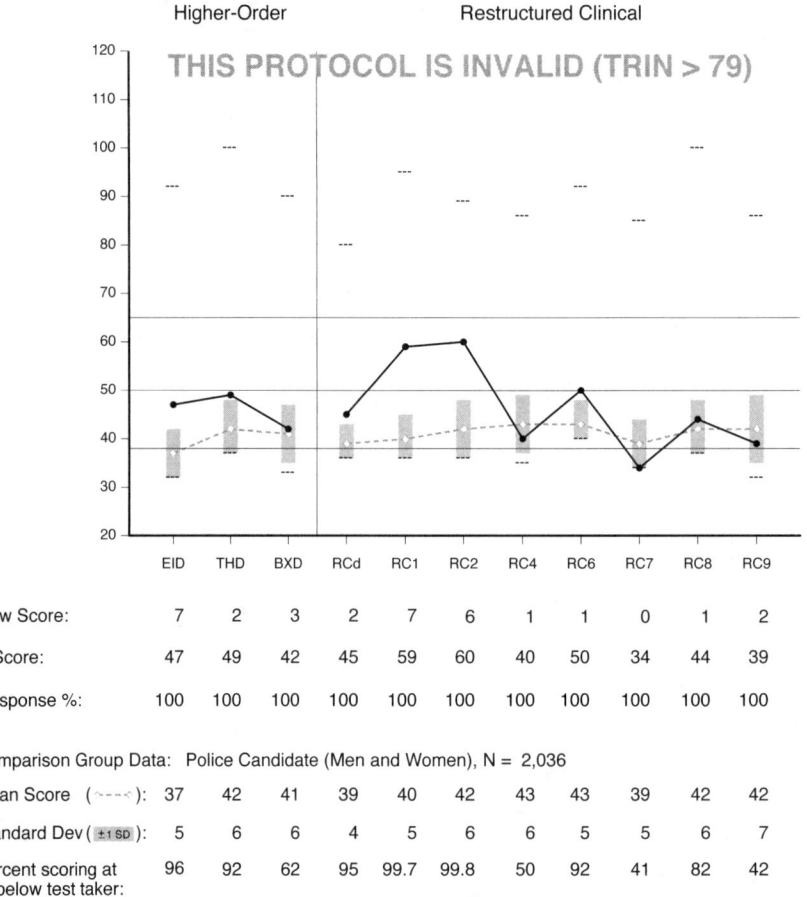

FIGURE 8.6. Mr. M's MMPI-3 Police Candidate Interpretive Report, continued

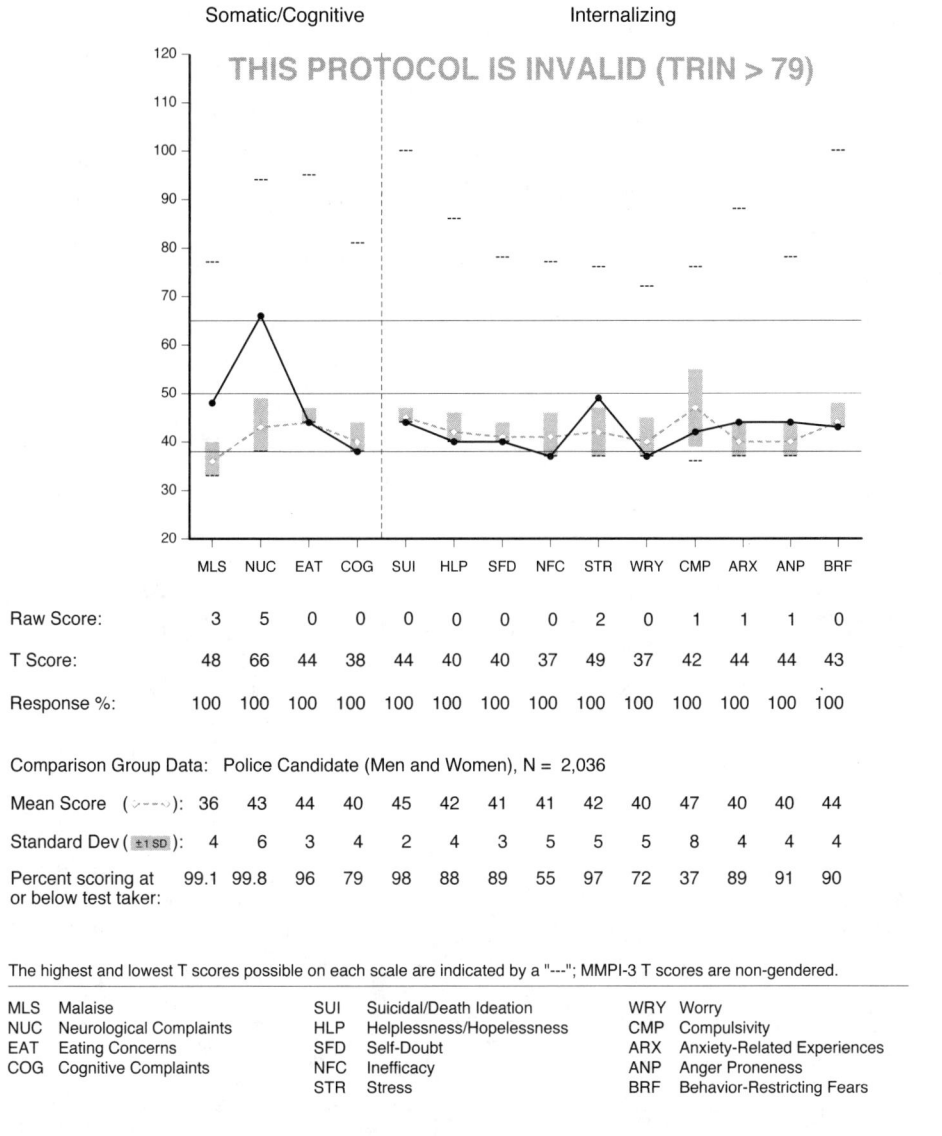

FIGURE 8.6. Mr. M's MMPI-3 Police Candidate Interpretive Report, continued

FIGURE 8.6. Mr. M's MMPI-3 Police Candidate Interpretive Report, continued

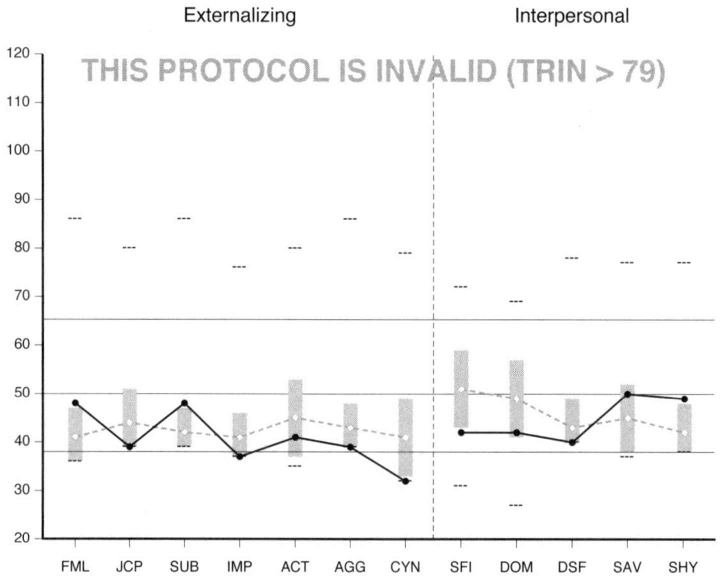

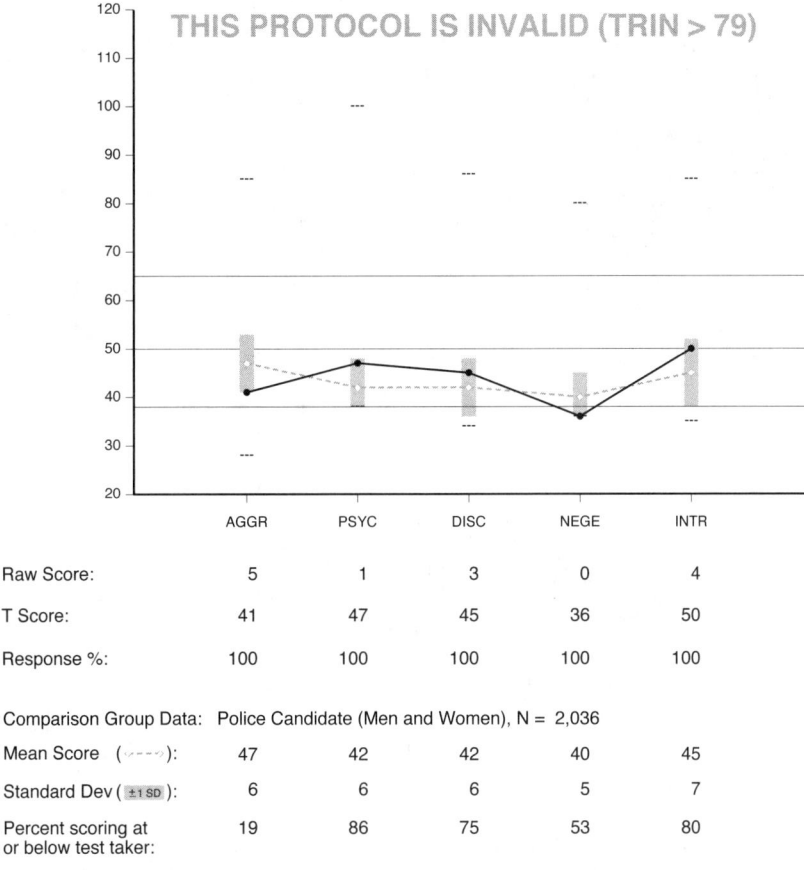

FIGURE 8.6. Mr. M's MMPI-3 Police Candidate Interpretive Report, continued

MMPI-3 T SCORES (BY DOMAIN)

THIS PROTOCOL IS INVALID (TRIN > 79)

PROTOCOL VALIDITY

Content Non-Responsiveness	0 CNS	60 CRIN	47 VRIN	**85 F TRIN**			
Over-Reporting	44 F	41 Fp		53 Fs	62 FBS	47 RBS	
Under-Reporting	73 L	71 K					

SUBSTANTIVE SCALES

Somatic/Cognitive Dysfunction		59 RC1	48 MLS	66 NUC	44 EAT	38 COG			
Emotional Dysfunction	47 EID	45 RCd	44 SUI	40 HLP	40 SFD	37 NFC			
		60 RC2	50 INTR						
		34 RC7	49 STR	37 WRY	42 CMP	44 ARX	44 ANP	43 BRF	36 NEGE
Thought Dysfunction	49 THD	50 RC6							
		44 RC8							
		47 PSYC							
Behavioral Dysfunction	42 BXD	40 RC4	48 FML	39 JCP	48 SUB				
		39 RC9	37 IMP	41 ACT	39 AGG	32 CYN			
		45 DISC							
Interpersonal Functioning		42 SFI	42 DOM	41 AGGR	40 DSF	50 SAV	49 SHY		

Scale scores shown in bold font are interpreted in the report.

Note. This information is provided to facilitate interpretation following the recommended structure for MMPI-3 interpretation in Chapter 5 of the *MMPI-3 Manual for Administration, Scoring, and Interpretation*, which provides details in the text and an outline in Table 5-1.

FIGURE 8.6. Mr. M's MMPI-3 Police Candidate Interpretive Report, continued

This interpretive report is intended for use by a professional qualified to interpret the MMPI-3 in the context of preemployment psychological evaluations of police and other law enforcement candidates. **It focuses on identifying problems; it does not convey potential strengths.** The information it contains should be considered in the context of the test taker's background, the demands of the position under consideration, the clinical interview, findings from supplemental tests, and other relevant information.

The interpretive statements in the Protocol Validity section of the report are based on T scores derived from the general MMPI-3 normative sample, as well as scores obtained by the multisite sample of 2,036 individuals that make up the Police Candidate Comparison Group.

The interpretive statements in the Clinical Findings and Diagnostic Considerations sections of the report are based on T scores derived from the general MMPI-3 normative sample. Following recommended practice, only T scores of 65 and higher (with a few exceptions) are considered clinically significant. Scores at this clinical level are generally rare among police candidates.

Statements in the Comparison Group Findings and Job-Relevant Correlates sections are based on comparisons with scores obtained by the Police Candidate Comparison Group. Statements in these sections may be based on T scores that, although less than 65, are nevertheless uncommon in reference to the comparison group.

The report includes extensive annotation, which appears as superscripts following each statement in the narrative, keyed to Endnotes with accompanying Research References, which appear in the final two sections of the report. Additional information about the annotation features is provided in the headnotes to these sections and in the MMPI-3 User's Guide for the Public Safety Candidate Interpretive Reports.

PROTOCOL VALIDITY

This MMPI-3 protocol is invalid and uninterpretable owing to inconsistent responding. Details are provided below.

Content Non-Responsiveness

Unscorable Responses

The test taker produced scorable responses to all the MMPI-3 items.

Inconsistent Responding

There is evidence of excessive inconsistency because of fixed False responding to the MMPI-3 items[1]. Therefore, this protocol is invalid and uninterpretable[2]. This level of inconsistency most likely reflects a non-cooperative test-taking approach.

Critical Follow-up Items

This section contains a list of items to which the test taker responded in a manner warranting follow-up. The items were identified by public safety candidate screening experts as having critical content. Clinicians are encouraged to follow up on these statements with the candidate by making related inquiries, rather than reciting the item(s) verbatim. Each item is followed by the candidate's response, the percentage of Police Candidate Comparison Group members who gave this response, and the scale(s) on which the item appears.

    Item number and content omitted. (False; 2.1%; TRIN, STR)

FIGURE 8.6. Mr. M's MMPI-3 Police Candidate Interpretive Report, continued

ENDNOTES

This section lists for each statement in the report the MMPI-3 score(s) that triggered it. In addition, each statement is identified as a Test Response, if based on item content, a Correlate, if based on empirical correlates, or an Inference, if based on the report authors' judgment. (This information can also be accessed on-screen by placing the cursor on a given statement.) For correlate-based statements, research references (Ref. No.) are provided, keyed to the consecutively numbered reference list following the endnotes.

[1] Test Response: TRIN=85F
[2] Correlate: TRIN=85F, Ref. 1, 2, 3

FIGURE 8.6. Mr. M's MMPI-3 Police Candidate Interpretive Report, continued

RESEARCH REFERENCE LIST

The following studies are sources for empirical correlates identified in the Endnotes section of this report.

1. Burchett, D., Dragon, W. R., Smith Holbert, A. M., Tarescavage, A. M., Mattson, C. A., Handel, R. W., & Ben-Porath, Y. S. (2016). "False feigners": Examining the impact of non-content-based invalid responding on the Minnesota Multiphasic Personality Inventory-2 Restructured Form content-based invalid responding indicators. *Psychological Assessment, 28*(5), 458–470. https://doi.org/10.1037/pas0000205

2. Gervais, R. O., Tarescavage, A. M., Greiffenstein, M. F., Wygant, D. B., Deslauriers, C., & Arends, P. (2018). Inconsistent responding on the MMPI-2-RF and uncooperative attitude: Evidence from cognitive performance validity measures. *Psychological Assessment, 30*(3), 410–415. https://doi.org/10.1037/pas0000506

3. Handel, R. W., Ben-Porath, Y. S., Tellegen, A., & Archer, R. P. (2010). Psychometric functioning of the MMPI-2-RF VRIN-r and TRIN-r scales with varying degrees of randomness, acquiescence, and counter-acquiescence. *Psychological Assessment, 22*(1), 87–95. https://doi.org/10.1037/a0017061

End of Report

FIGURE 8.6. Mr. M's MMPI-3 Police Candidate Interpretive Report, continued

testing indicated possible underreporting, but the test contained no measures of response inconsistency. It is possible that, as in the case of Mr. M's elevated L and K scores on the MMPI-3, the indication of underreporting on his normal-range personality testing also reflected a nay-saying response set.

Step 2: Assessing Substantive Scale Findings

Because Mr. M's MMPI-3 protocol is invalid, no attempt is made to interpret the substantive scale scores.

Step 3: Assessing Background Findings

Mr. M enlisted in the U.S. Marine Corps immediately after graduating high school and served for 8 years as a combat engineer. Upon receiving an honorable discharge at the rank of corporal (E-4), he used his GI Bill benefits to attend classes at his local community college. His references, consisting mostly of fellow Marines and family members, were entirely positive.

On a written personal history questionnaire that he filled out when he completed his written psychological testing, Mr. M stated that he had no history of disciplinary actions or problems with the law, finances, or driving history. He also stated that he had no history of mental health problems and never filed a claim for compensation related to his mental health.

Step 4: Assessing Interview Findings

In our earlier review of Mr. D's MMPI-3 results, we discussed the importance of using findings from the background and psychological testing to "construct" the interview; that is, to test hypotheses, clarify information, and gather additional information. A review of Mr. M's MMPI-3 results left the screening psychologist with no usable information about the candidate's psychological adjustment and the potential presence of psychopathology or personality problems. This necessitated a particularly well-planned, probing interview.

It is generally less productive to ask candidates questions already answered, even when the credibility of a response is suspect. A more fruitful approach is to ask related questions that are more specific. Mr. M had already stated in his written personal history questionnaire that he had never filed a claim related to his mental health, but the screening psychologist asked in the interview if he had ever filed a claim for disability compensation through the U.S. Department of Veterans Affairs (VA). He answered that he was not sure. "I was asked a lot of health questions when I was discharged." Deciding to skip to a defining question and then work backward if necessary, the examiner asked

Mr. M if he was receiving compensation from the VA for a service-connected disability of any kind. Mr. M answered that he was receiving compensation for a traumatic brain injury. The examiner then asked what "disability rating" he was awarded (the VA pays compensation to injured veterans based on the magnitude of impairment resulting from each disability, which is measured in a percentage rating of 0% to 100%, with higher percentage awards equating to higher monetary compensation). Mr. M said he was awarded a 60% disability rating. Finally, the examiner asked if any portion of the disability award was for a mental injury such as PTSD, depression, or adjustment disorder (the three most common service-connected mental injuries).[2] He said that he received a 50% rating for PTSD.

This iterative inquiry process is necessary with candidates who give brief, sometimes one-word answers to the interview questions or choose not to disclose the full facts from the start of an inquiry. The examiner informed Mr. M that before a suitability determination could be made, it would be necessary for the candidate to provide a copy of the VA Rating Decision, which lists each of the injuries claimed by the veteran, what rating decision the VA reached regarding each claim, what symptoms claimed by the veteran supported the decision, and why the next higher rating did not apply. In the remainder of the interview, the candidate denied ongoing symptoms of traumatic brain injury or PTSD, and he said he had never received treatment for either.

Medical Records Findings

Public safety employers are often pressed to fill open positions and to confirm the new hire's enrollment in the training academy, which in many jurisdictions cannot happen until evidence of successful completion of the psychological evaluation has been provided. But that pressure should not compel the screening professional to truncate procedures necessary for making a reliable determination of the candidate's psychological suitability for the position. In discussing the importance of obtaining copies of VA Rating Decision letters, Corey and Zelig (2020) observed, "requesting these or other mental health records necessarily delays the suitability determination until after the documents are received and reviewed, but failing to obtain them can result in serious error that cannot later be undone" (pp. 175–176). This is especially true when, as with Mr. M, the available information is contradictory and unreliable.

Quite often, a veteran has filed the VA Rating Decision letter in a readily accessible location and can fax or email it to the screening professional shortly after the interview's conclusion. Mr. M sent over the document within two days. The letter indicated that he had, in fact, received a 50% disability rating for PTSD based on a "compensation and pension evaluation" (using VA parlance) conducted about two years before the preemployment psychological evaluation. The VA assigned the rating based on Mr. M's report of

> weekly panic attacks, difficulty in adapting to stressful circumstances, difficulty in adapting to work, suspiciousness, depressed mood, disturbances of motivation and mood, difficulty in adapting to a work-like setting, anxiety, difficulty in establishing and maintaining effective work and social relationships, chronic sleep impairment, and occupational and social impairment with reduced reliability and productivity.

In addition, the decision letter indicated that a previously awarded 10% rating for traumatic brain injury had been reduced to 0% because of improvement in that condition.

Step 5: Identifying Relevant Risk Findings

a. Considering all risk-related findings from all sources, what evidence-based inferences can be drawn?

TEST FINDINGS
MMPI-3 validity scale findings identified an invalidating nay-saying response style that most likely reflected an uncooperative test-taking approach. Substantive scale findings could not be considered because of this invalidating test-taking approach. Findings from normal-range personality testing, which contained no measure of content responsiveness, were interpretable but of questionable reliability. In any event, they yielded no risk-related findings.

BACKGROUND FINDINGS
Mr. M's background investigation provided positive references and no indications of behavioral problems.

INTERVIEW FINDINGS
Risk-related findings from the interview pertained primarily to the emotional control and stress resilience domain and secondarily to the integrity domain.

MEDICAL RECORDS FINDINGS
The VA Rating Decision letter revealed evidence of marked impairment, assessed about two years before the current evaluation, due to PTSD. Mr. M said he had not received subsequent treatment because his symptoms had remitted, and his condition was resolved.

b. What divergent findings might mitigate these inferences?

Mr. M's positive references cannot mitigate the medical record findings, even though they diverge, because symptoms of mental health problems are often not observed (or observable) by others. Mr. M's denial of problems in the interview and written personal history questionnaire also could not mitigate the risk-related findings, because his answers to several questions were untrue (e.g., he answered on the personal history questionnaire that he had never filed a claim for compensation based on mental health issues), and he initially stated that he was receiving compensation only for traumatic brain injury when, in fact, he was receiving compensation only for service-connected PTSD.

Had Mr. M produced a valid MMPI-3 protocol, along with responses to personal history and interview questions that were not contradicted by collateral facts, he may have been able to make the case for what he insisted was true: that he once suffered symptoms of PTSD but no longer does. Although some screening professionals might argue that receiving compensation for a disability that is no longer active is, itself, an integrity violation or moral lapse, there is no clear legal obligation on a veteran's part to report symptom improvement to the VA. Indeed, penalizing a nonsymptomatic veteran merely for receiving disability compensation may violate the Uniformed Services Employment and Reemployment Rights Act (USERRA). Still, the most reliable contemporary evidence available to the screening psychologist is that Mr. M is, in fact, suffering from a mental health condition with symptoms that are both job-relevant and job-limiting for a police officer.

c. Are any surviving risk-related inferences of sufficient relevance and quality to warrant the candidate's disqualification?

The quality of the risk-related inferences pertaining to Mr. M's mental health problems was high, because the source of it was his own self-report shortly after leaving military service. In the absence of potentially mitigating information—a factor resulting largely from the candidate's inconsistent responding to the MMPI-3 items and the test's resulting invalidity—the examiner was left with a choice: (a) to rate Mr. M as psychologically unqualified for a police officer position based on substantial deficits in emotional control and stress resilience (as evidenced by his self-reported symptoms documented in the VA Rating Decision letter) or (b) to rate Mr. M as "indeterminate" or "indeterminable" due to the combination of a two-year-old medical record of a mental health disability (which the candidate claims has been resolved) and invalid, uninterpretable test scores resulting from the candidate's excessively inconsistent responding. In many jurisdictions, these choices produce the same outcome: without a determination by the screening psychologist that the candidate meets the suitability criteria, the candidate cannot be hired. But in other jurisdictions where the hiring decision belongs to the hiring authority, a judgment that the assessment data are too unreliable to make a suitability determination could conceivably lead to the candidate being hired.

In light of the objective findings from the medical records, the examiner concluded that Mr. M **does not meet** the hiring agency's criterion standard, citing the most reliable evidence of the candidate's deficits in the emotional control and stress resilience domain. The examiner considered other findings in this assessment that suggested additional deficits in the integrity domain but decided that these would only "gild the lily" and potentially undermine the defensibility of the determination made based on the most reliable and compelling evidence.

BRIEF REVIEW: MS. P, DISPATCHER CANDIDATE

Assessment Issues Presented

- Use of the MMPI-3 Dispatcher Candidate Interpretive Report (DCIR) in evaluating a dispatcher candidate with prior experience in a related position
- An MMPI-3 protocol with clinically elevated scores in the Somatic/Cognitive domain

Referral Summary

Ms. P is a 23-year-old unmarried woman seeking a position as a 911 dispatcher in a large urban emergency communications center responsible for police, fire, and emergency medical dispatching. At the time of the evaluation, Ms. P had worked for three years as a 911 call taker at a smaller facility.

Assessing Protocol Validity

As shown in Ms. P's DCIR (Figure 8.7, p. 2), she produced a valid and interpretable protocol. However, her score on VRIN (55T), measuring variable response inconsistency, is anomalous in personnel settings in which test takers are normally quite attentive to item content. Although her score is not high enough to indicate an invalid protocol, it falls more than two standard deviations above the Dispatcher Candidate Comparison Group mean (40T, $SD = 6$; see Table 6.5), and her score on CRIN (57T) measuring combined response inconsistency is three standard deviations above the comparison group mean (39T, $SD = 6$). These findings should alert the examiner to look for other evidence indicating inattention or carelessness.

Also notable among the validity scale scores in Ms. P's MMPI-3 protocol are her unusual scores on the over- and underreporting scales. Although her overreporting scale scores do not invalidate the protocol, 2% or less of the comparison group produced scores at or above hers on these scales. Combined with her low underreporting scale scores, this raises questions as to why she is reporting uncommon problems and claiming so little virtue and positive adjustment.

Minnesota Multiphasic Personality Inventory®-3

Yossef S. Ben-Porath
Auke Tellegen

MMPI®-3
Dispatcher Candidate Interpretive Report
David M. Corey, PhD, & Yossef S. Ben-Porath, PhD

ID Number:	Ms. P
Age:	23
Gender:	Female
Marital Status:	Not reported
Years of Education:	Not reported
Date Assessed:	09/27/2022

Copyright © 2022 by the Regents of the University of Minnesota. All rights reserved. Distributed exclusively under license from the University of Minnesota by NCS Pearson, Inc. Portions reproduced from the *MMPI-3 English Test Booklet.* Copyright © 2020 by the Regents of the University of Minnesota. All rights reserved. Portions excerpted from the *MMPI-3 Manual for Administration, Scoring, and Interpretation.* Copyright © 2020 by the Regents of the University of Minnesota. All rights reserved. Portions excerpted from the *MMPI-3 Technical Manual.* Copyright © 2020 by the Regents of the University of Minnesota. All rights reserved. Used by permission of the University of Minnesota Press.

Minnesota Multiphasic Personality Inventory and **MMPI** are registered trademarks of the Regents of the University of Minnesota. **Pearson** is a trademark, in the US and/or other countries, of Pearson Education, Inc., or its affiliates.

This report contains copyrighted material and trade secrets. Qualified licensees may excerpt portions of this output report, limited to the minimum text necessary to accurately describe their significant core conclusions, for incorporation into a written evaluation of the examinee, in accordance with their profession's citation standards, if any. No adaptations, translations, modifications, or special versions may be made of this report without prior written permission from the University of Minnesota Press.

[1.4 / RE1 / QG1]

ALWAYS LEARNING   **PEARSON**

FIGURE 8.7. Ms. P's MMPI-3 Dispatcher Candidate Interpretive Report

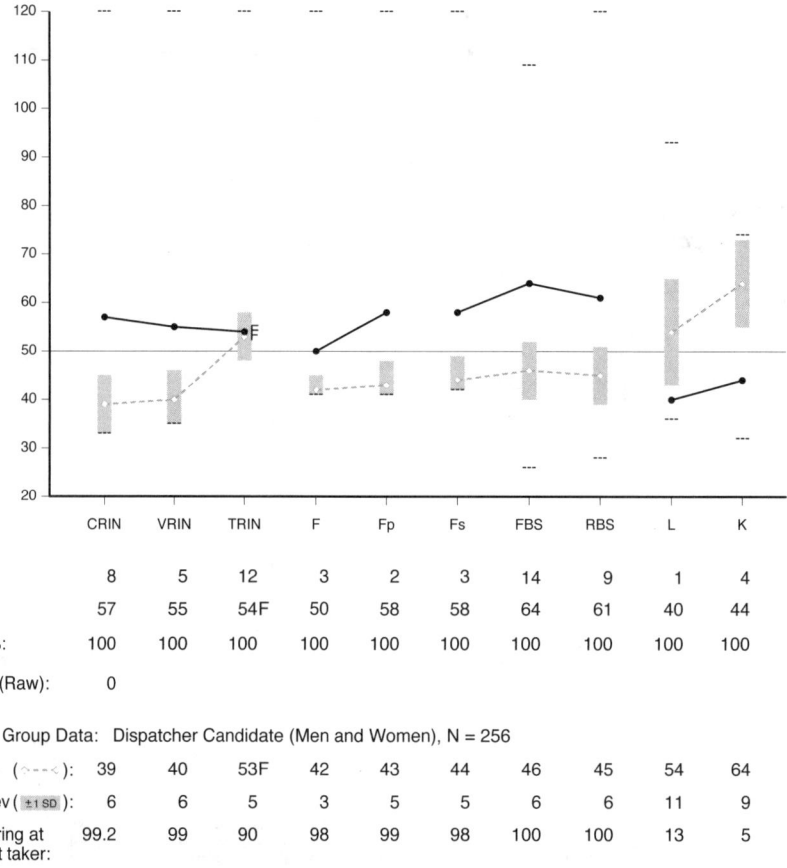

FIGURE 8.7. Ms. P's MMPI-3 Dispatcher Candidate Interpretive Report, continued

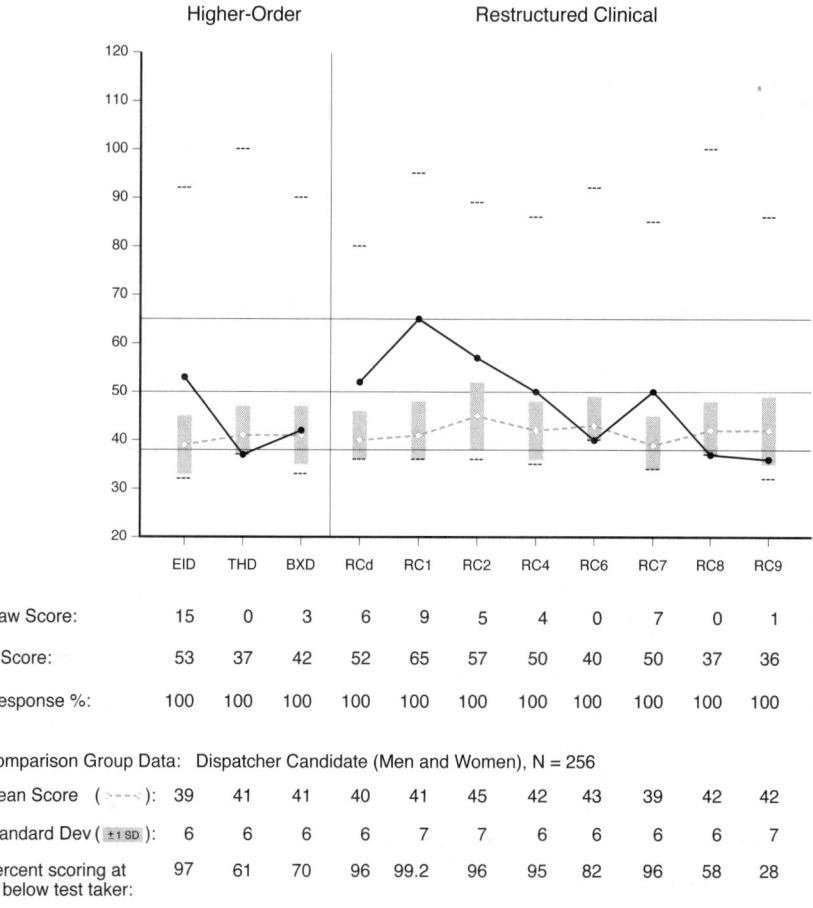

FIGURE 8.7. Ms. P's MMPI-3 Dispatcher Candidate Interpretive Report, continued

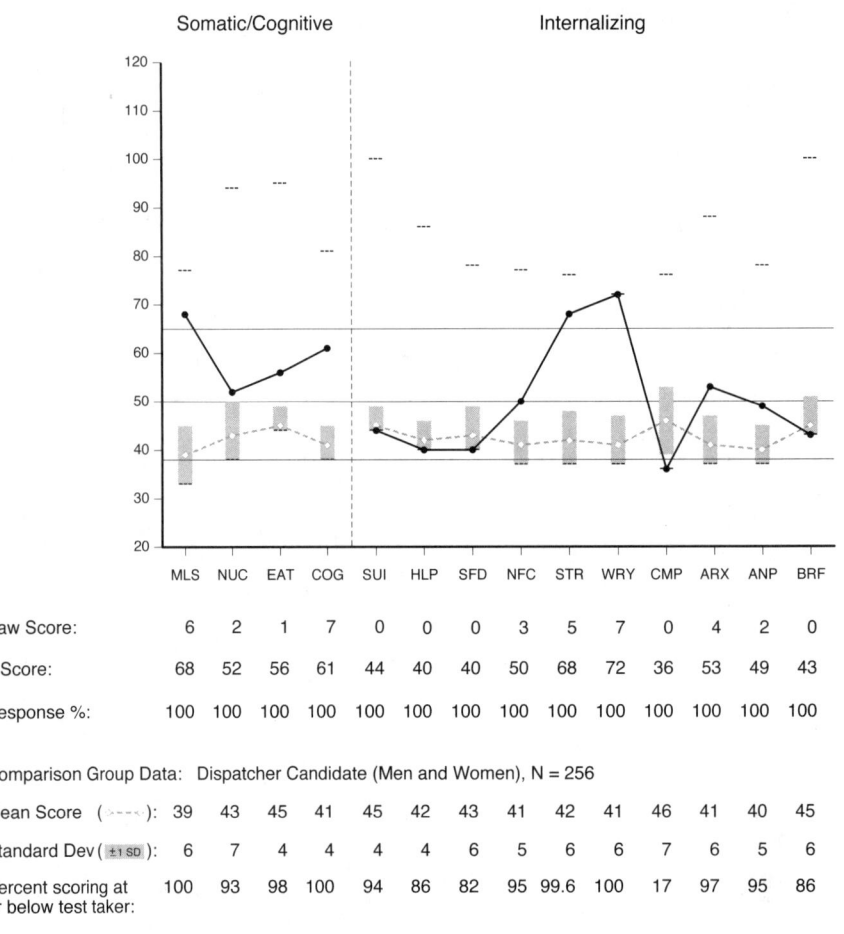

FIGURE 8.7. Ms. P's MMPI-3 Dispatcher Candidate Interpretive Report, continued

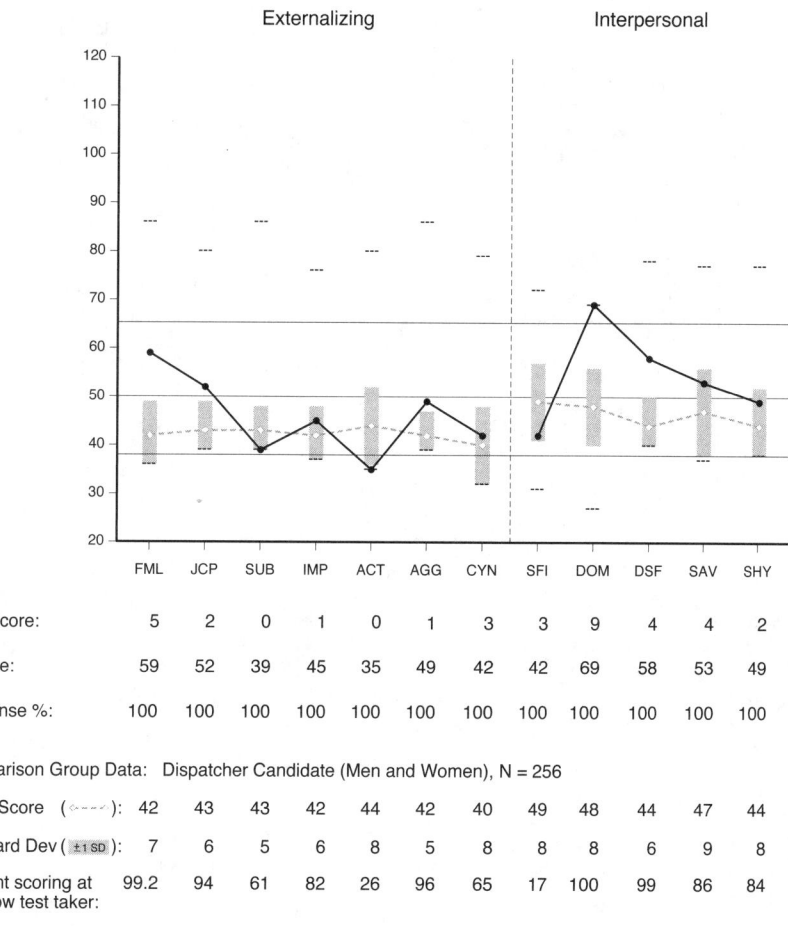

FIGURE 8.7. Ms. P's MMPI-3 Dispatcher Candidate Interpretive Report, continued

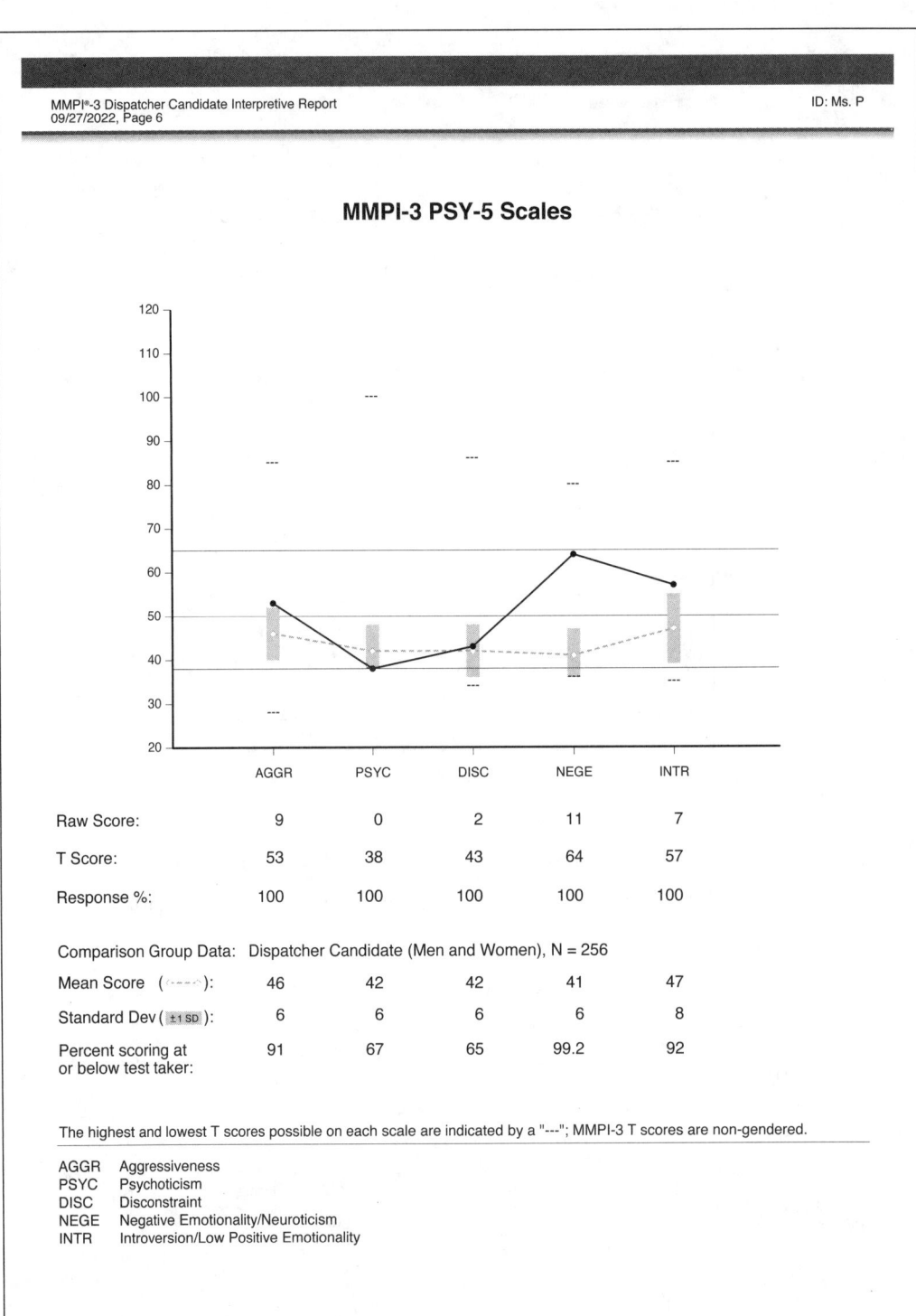

FIGURE 8.7. Ms. P's MMPI-3 Dispatcher Candidate Interpretive Report, continued

MMPI-3 T SCORES (BY DOMAIN)

PROTOCOL VALIDITY

Content Non-Responsiveness

0	57	55	54 F
CNS	CRIN	VRIN	TRIN

Over-Reporting

50	58	58	64	61
F	Fp	Fs	FBS	RBS

Under-Reporting

40	44
L	**K**

SUBSTANTIVE SCALES

Somatic/Cognitive Dysfunction

65	**68**	52	56	**61**
RC1	**MLS**	NUC	EAT	**COG**

Emotional Dysfunction

53	52	44	40	40	50		
EID	RCd	SUI	HLP	SFD	NFC		
	57	57					
	RC2	INTR					
	50	**68**	**72**	36	53	49	43	**64**
	RC7	**STR**	**WRY**	CMP	ARX	ANP	BRF	**NEGE**

Thought Dysfunction

37	40
THD	RC6
	37
	RC8
	38
	PSYC

Behavioral Dysfunction

42	50	**59**	52	39
BXD	RC4	**FML**	JCP	SUB
	36	45	35	49	42
	RC9	IMP	ACT	AGG	CYN
	43				
	DISC				

Interpersonal Functioning

42	**69**	53	**58**	53	49
SFI	**DOM**	AGGR	**DSF**	SAV	SHY

Scale scores shown in bold font are interpreted in the report.

Note. This information is provided to facilitate interpretation following the recommended structure for MMPI-3 interpretation in Chapter 5 of the *MMPI-3 Manual for Administration, Scoring, and Interpretation*, which provides details in the text and an outline in Table 5-1.

FIGURE 8.7. Ms. P's MMPI-3 Dispatcher Candidate Interpretive Report, continued

This interpretive report is intended for use by a professional qualified to interpret the MMPI-3 in the context of preemployment psychological evaluations of emergency communications dispatchers, call-takers, and other positions in public safety answering points. **It focuses on identifying problems; it does not convey potential strengths.** *The information it contains should be considered in the context of the test taker's background, the demands of the position under consideration, the clinical interview, findings from supplemental tests, and other relevant information.*

The interpretive statements in the Protocol Validity section of the report are based on T scores derived from the general MMPI-3 normative sample, as well as scores obtained by the multisite sample of 256 individuals that make up the Dispatcher Candidate Comparison Group.

The interpretive statements in the Clinical Findings and Diagnostic Considerations sections of the report are based on T scores derived from the general MMPI-3 normative sample. Following recommended practice, only T scores of 65 and higher (with a few exceptions) are considered clinically significant. Scores at this clinical level are generally rare among dispatcher candidates.

Statements in the Comparison Group Findings and Job-Relevant Correlates sections are based on comparisons with scores obtained by the Dispatcher Candidate Comparison Group. Statements in these sections may be based on T scores that, although less than 65, are nevertheless uncommon in reference to the comparison group.

The report includes extensive annotation, which appears as superscripts following each statement in the narrative, keyed to Endnotes with accompanying Research References, which appear in the final two sections of the report. Additional information about the annotation features is provided in the headnotes to these sections and in the MMPI-3 User's Guide for the Public Safety Candidate Interpretive Reports.

SYNOPSIS

This is a valid MMPI-3 protocol. Scores on the Substantive Scales indicate clinically significant somatic complaints and emotional and interpersonal dysfunction. Somatic complaints include preoccupation with poor health and malaise. Emotional-internalizing findings include stress and worry. Interpersonal difficulties relate to overly domineering behavior.

Comparison group findings point to additional possible concerns about cognitive complaints, negative emotions, family conflict, and disaffiliativeness.

Possible job-relevant problems are identified in the following domains: Emotional Control and Stress Tolerance, Routine Task Performance, Decision-Making and Judgment, Assertiveness, Social Competence and Teamwork, and Conscientiousness and Dependability.

PROTOCOL VALIDITY

This is a valid MMPI-3 protocol. There are no problems with unscorable items. The test taker responded to the items relevantly on the basis of their content, and there are no indications of over- or under-reporting.

It is worth noting that the test taker reported being much less well-adjusted than a typical dispatcher candidate[1]. Only 5% of members of the Dispatcher Candidate Comparison Group reported this or a lower level of psychological adjustment. As detailed later in this report, her scores on the Substantive Scales do indeed raise significant concerns about the candidate's psychological adjustment.

FIGURE 8.7. Ms. P's MMPI-3 Dispatcher Candidate Interpretive Report, continued

CLINICAL FINDINGS

Clinical-level symptoms, personality characteristics, and behavioral tendencies of the test taker are described in this section and organized according to an empirically guided framework. (Please see Chapter 5 of the MMPI-3 Manual for Administration, Scoring, and Interpretation for details.) Statements containing the word "reports" are based on the item content of MMPI-3 scales, whereas statements that include the word "likely" are based on empirical correlates of scale scores. Specific sources for each statement can be viewed with the annotation features of this report.

The test taker reports multiple somatic complaints including gastrointestinal symptoms and head pain complaints[2]. She likely is prone to developing physical symptoms in response to stress[3] and perceives her physical problems as life-interfering[4]. She also reports experiencing poor health and feeling weak or tired[5]. Indeed she is likely preoccupied with poor health[6] and complains of sleep disturbance[7], fatigue[8], low energy[9], and sexual dysfunction[9].

The test taker reports excessive worry, including worries about misfortune and finances, as well as preoccupation with disappointments[10]. She indeed likely worries excessively[11] and ruminates[12]. She also reports an above average level of stress[13]. She likely complains about stress[14] and feels incapable of controlling her anxiety level[15].

The test taker describes herself as having strong opinions, as standing up for herself, as assertive and direct, and as able to lead others[16]. She likely believes she has leadership capabilities, but is viewed by others as overly domineering[17].

There are no indications of clinically significant cognitive, thought, or behavioral dysfunction in this protocol.

DIAGNOSTIC CONSIDERATIONS

This section provides recommendations for psychodiagnostic assessment based on the test taker's MMPI-3 results. It is recommended that she be evaluated for the following:

Somatic/Cognitive Disorders
- Somatic symptom disorder, if physical origin for malaise has been ruled out[18]

Emotional-Internalizing Disorders
- Disorders involving excessive worry[19]
- Generalized anxiety disorder[15]

Interpersonal Disorders
- Disorders characterized by excessively domineering behavior[20]

COMPARISON GROUP FINDINGS

This section describes the MMPI-3 substantive scale findings in the context of the Dispatcher Candidate Comparison Group. Specific sources for each statement can be accessed with the annotation features of this report. **Job-related correlates of these results, if any, are provided in the subsequent Job-Relevant Correlates section.**

Somatic/Cognitive Complaints
The test taker's responses indicate a level of somatic complaints that may be incompatible with public safety requirements for good psychological adjustment[21]. This level of diffuse health complaints is uncommon among dispatcher candidates. Only 1.0% of comparison group members give evidence of this or a greater level of

FIGURE 8.7. Ms. P's MMPI-3 Dispatcher Candidate Interpretive Report, continued

somatic complaints. More specifically, her responses indicate a level of malaise that may impede conformance with public safety requirements for good psychological adjustment[22]. This level of self-perceived physical debilitation and poor health is uncommon among dispatcher candidates. Only 0.4% of comparison group members demonstrate this level of perceived poor health.

She reports a comparatively high level of cognitive complaints for a dispatcher candidate[23]. Only 0.8% of comparison group members convey this number of cognitive problems.

Emotional/Internalizing Problems

The test taker reports a comparatively large number of emotional problems for a dispatcher candidate[24]. Only 5.0% of comparison group members convey this or a greater level of emotional difficulties. In particular, she reports a relatively high level of negative emotions for a dispatcher candidate[25]. Only 1.0% of comparison group members convey this or a greater level of negative emotionality. More specifically, her responses indicate a level of worry that may be incompatible with public safety requirements for good emotional adjustment and resilience[19]. This level of preoccupation with worries is uncommon among dispatcher candidates. Only 1.0% of comparison group members give evidence of this level of rumination. Her responses also indicate a level of stress that may impede conformance with public safety requirements for good emotional adjustment and resilience[26]. This stress level is uncommon among dispatcher candidates. Only 0.8% of comparison group members demonstrate this or a greater level of stress-related problems.

Interpersonal Problems

The test taker reports a comparatively high level of family conflict for a dispatcher candidate[27]. Only 3.0% of comparison group members convey this or a greater level of family problems. She also reports a relatively high level of disaffiliativeness for a dispatcher candidate[28]. Only 4.0% of comparison group members convey this or a greater level of disinterest in interacting with others.

JOB-RELEVANT CORRELATES

Job-relevant personality characteristics and behavioral tendencies of the test taker are described in this section and organized according to ten problem domains commonly identified in the professional literature as relevant to public safety candidate suitability. (Please see MMPI-3 User's Guide for the Public Safety Candidate Interpretive Reports for details.) Statements that begin with "Compared with other dispatcher candidates" are based on correlations with other self-report measures obtained in dispatcher candidate samples that included individuals who were subsequently hired as well as those who were not.

Emotional Control and Stress Tolerance Problems

Compared with other dispatcher candidates, the test taker is more likely to have difficulty coping with stress[29]; to worry about problems and be uncertain about how to deal with them[30]; and to behave in a self-defeating fashion[31]. She is also more likely to develop physical symptoms in response to stress and worry about her health[32]; to experience negative emotions[33]; and to have a history of adverse childhood experiences[34].

Routine Task Performance Problems

Compared with other dispatcher candidates, the test taker is more likely to be lacking in confidence in her own abilities[31].

Decision-Making and Judgment Problems

Compared with other dispatcher candidates, the test taker is more likely to be made anxious by change and uncertainty[31].

Assertiveness Problems

Compared with other dispatcher candidates, the test taker is more likely to be ill at ease in dealing with others[35].

FIGURE 8.7. Ms. P's MMPI-3 Dispatcher Candidate Interpretive Report, continued

Social Competence and Teamwork Problems

Compared with other dispatcher candidates, the test taker is more likely to have a limited social support network[35]; to prefer to work out problems alone[35]; and to be seen by others as socially detached and emotionally distant[35]. She is also more likely to have problems with social competence[36].

Conscientiousness and Dependability Problems

Compared with other dispatcher candidates, the test taker is more likely to give up easily and not persevere in the face of challenges[31].

The candidate's test scores are not associated with problems in the following domains:
- Feedback Acceptance
- Integrity
- Substance Use
- Impulse Control

ITEM-LEVEL INFORMATION

Unscorable Responses

The test taker produced scorable responses to all the MMPI-3 items.

Critical Responses

Seven MMPI-3 scales—Suicidal/Death Ideation (SUI), Helplessness/Hopelessness (HLP), Anxiety-Related Experiences (ARX), Ideas of Persecution (RC6), Aberrant Experiences (RC8), Substance Abuse (SUB), and Aggression (AGG)—have been designated by the test authors as having critical item content that may require immediate attention and follow-up. Items answered by the individual in the keyed direction (True or False) on a critical scale are listed below if her T score on that scale is 65 or higher. However, any item answered in the keyed direction on SUI is listed.

The test taker has not produced an elevated T score ($\geq$ 65) on any of these scales or answered any SUI items in the keyed direction.

Critical Follow-up Items

This section contains a list of items to which the test taker responded in a manner warranting follow-up. The items were identified by public safety candidate screening experts as having critical content. Clinicians are encouraged to follow up on these statements with the candidate by making related inquiries, rather than reciting the item(s) verbatim. Each item is followed by the candidate's response, the percentage of Dispatcher Candidate Comparison Group members who gave this response, and the scale(s) on which the item appears.

> Item number and content omitted. (True; 2.0%; VRIN, COG)
> Item number and content omitted. (True; 4.3%; VRIN, TRIN, EID, STR)
> Item number and content omitted. (True; 0.4%; Fs, ARX)
> Item number and content omitted. (True; 1.2%; VRIN, COG)
> Item number and content omitted. (True; 3.5%; VRIN, EID, RC7, ARX, NEGE)
> Item number and content omitted. (True; 3.9%; WRY, NEGE)
> Item number and content omitted. (True; 6.6%; EID, ARX, NEGE)
> Item number and content omitted. (True; 1.2%; VRIN, COG)
> Item number and content omitted. (True; 17.2%; ANP)

FIGURE 8.7. Ms. P's MMPI-3 Dispatcher Candidate Interpretive Report, continued

ENDNOTES

This section lists for each statement in the report the MMPI-3 score(s) that triggered it. In addition, each statement is identified as a <u>Test Response</u>, if based on item content, a <u>Correlate</u>, if based on empirical correlates, or an <u>Inference</u>, if based on the report authors' judgment. (This information can also be accessed on-screen by placing the cursor on a given statement.) For correlate-based statements, research references (Ref. No.) are provided, keyed to the consecutively numbered reference list following the endnotes.

[1] Test Response: K=44
[2] Test Response: RC1=65
[3] Correlate: RC1=65, Ref. 11, 24
[4] Correlate: RC1=65, Ref. 3
[5] Test Response: MLS=68
[6] Correlate: RC1=65, Ref. 2, 3, 5, 6, 9, 10, 11, 12, 17, 19, 21, 22, 24, 25, 29; MLS=68, Ref. 3, 5
[7] Correlate: MLS=68, Ref. 3, 23
[8] Correlate: RC1=65, Ref. 4, 23, 24; MLS=68, Ref. 3, 17, 23
[9] Correlate: MLS=68, Ref. 3
[10] Test Response: WRY=72
[11] Correlate: WRY=72, Ref. 3
[12] Correlate: WRY=72, Ref. 3, 14
[13] Test Response: STR=68
[14] Correlate: STR=68, Ref. 2, 3, 14
[15] Correlate: STR=68, Ref. 3
[16] Test Response: DOM=69
[17] Correlate: DOM=69, Ref. 1, 3, 8, 13, 17, 24
[18] Correlate: RC1=65, Ref. 15, 16, 18, 26, 29; MLS=68, Ref. 15, 18, 29
[19] Inference: WRY=72
[20] Inference: DOM=69
[21] Inference: RC1=65
[22] Inference: MLS=68
[23] Test Response: COG=61
[24] Test Response: EID=53
[25] Test Response: NEGE=64
[26] Inference: STR=68
[27] Test Response: FML=59
[28] Test Response: DSF=58
[29] Correlate: EID=53, Ref. 28; RC1=65, Ref. 20, 28; STR=68, Ref. 28; WRY=72, Ref. 28; NEGE=64, Ref. 28
[30] Correlate: EID=53, Ref. 7; WRY=72, Ref. 7
[31] Correlate: EID=53, Ref. 7
[32] Correlate: RC1=65, Ref. 28
[33] Correlate: WRY=72, Ref. 7; NEGE=64, Ref. 7
[34] Correlate: FML=59, Ref. 27
[35] Correlate: DSF=58, Ref. 7
[36] Correlate: DSF=58, Ref. 28

FIGURE 8.7. Ms. P's MMPI-3 Dispatcher Candidate Interpretive Report, continued

RESEARCH REFERENCE LIST

The following studies are sources for empirical correlates identified in the Endnotes section of this report.

1. Ayearst, L. E., Sellbom, M., Trobst, K. K., & Bagby, R. M. (2013). Evaluating the interpersonal content of the MMPI-2-RF Interpersonal Scales. *Journal of Personality Assessment, 95*(2), 187–196. https://doi.org/10.1080/00223891.2012.730085

2. Bagby, R. M., Onno, K. A., Mortezaei, A., & Sellbom, M. (2020). Examining the "Traditional Background Hypothesis" for the MMPI-2-RF L-r Scores in a Muslim Faith-Based Sample. *Psychological Assessment.* Advance online publication. https://doi.org/10.1037/pas0000941

3. Ben-Porath, Y. S., & Tellegen, A. (2020). *The Minnesota Multiphasic Personality Inventory-3 (MMPI-3): Technical manual.* University of Minnesota Press.

4. Benitez, A., & Gunstad, J. (2012). Poor sleep quality diminishes cognitive functioning independent of depression and anxiety in healthy young adults. *The Clinical Neuropsychologist, 26*(2), 214–223. https://doi.org/10.1080/13854046.2012.658439

5. Block, A. R., Ben-Porath, Y. S., & Marek, R. J. (2013). Psychological risk factors for poor outcome of spine surgery and spinal cord stimulator implant: A review of the literature and their assessment with the MMPI-2-RF. *The Clinical Neuropsychologist, 27*(1), 81–107. https://doi.org/10.1080/13854046.2012.721007

6. Burchett, D. L., & Ben-Porath, Y. S. (2010). The impact of over-reporting on MMPI-2-RF substantive scale score validity. *Assessment, 17*(4), 497–516. https://doi.org/10.1177/1073191110378972

7. Corey, D. M., & Ben-Porath, Y. S. (2022). *Minnesota Multiphasic Personality Inventory-3 (MMPI-3): User's guide for the public safety candidate interpretive reports.* University of Minnesota Press.

8. Cox, A., Courrégé, S. C., Feder, A. H., & Weed, N. C. (2017). Effects of augmenting response options of the MMPI-2-RF: An extension of previous findings. *Cogent Psychology, 4*(1), 1323988. https://doi.org/10.1080/23311908.2017.1323988

9. Forbey, J. D., & Ben-Porath, Y. S. (2008). Empirical correlates of the MMPI-2 Restructured Clinical (RC) Scales in a non-clinical setting. *Journal of Personality Assessment, 90*(2), 136–141. https://doi.org/10.1080/00223890701845161

10. Forbey, J. D., Ben-Porath, Y. S., & Arbisi, P. A. (2012). The MMPI-2 computer adaptive version (MMPI-2-CA) in a Veterans Administration medical outpatient facility. *Psychological Assessment, 24*(3), 628–639. https://doi.org/10.1037/a0026509

11. Forbey, J. D., Ben-Porath, Y. S., & Gartland, D. (2009). Validation of the MMPI-2 Computerized Adaptive version (MMPI-2-CA) in a correctional intake facility. *Psychological Services, 6*(4), 279–292. https://doi.org/10.1037/a0016195

12. Handel, R. W., & Archer, R. P. (2008). An investigation of the psychometric properties of the MMPI-2 Restructured Clinical (RC) Scales with mental health inpatients. *Journal of Personality Assessment, 90*(3), 239–249. https://doi.org/10.1080/00223890701884954

13. Kastner, R. M., Sellbom, M., & Lilienfeld, S. O. (2012). A comparison of the psychometric properties of the Psychopathic Personality Inventory full-length and short-form versions. *Psychological Assessment, 24*(1), 261–267. https://doi.org/10.1037/a0025832

14. Kremyar, A. J., & Lee, T. T. C. (2021). MMPI-3 predictors of anxiety sensitivity and distress intolerance. *Assessment.* Advance online publication. https://doi.org/10.1177/10731911211001948

FIGURE 8.7. Ms. P's MMPI-3 Dispatcher Candidate Interpretive Report, continued

15. Locke, D. E. C., Kirlin, K. A., Thomas, M. L., Osborne, D., Hurst, D. F., Drazkowsi, J. F., Sirven, J. I., & Noe, K. H. (2010). The Minnesota Multiphasic Personality Inventory-2-Restructured Form in the epilepsy monitoring unit. *Epilepsy & Behavior, 17*(2), 252–258. https://doi.org/10.1016/j.yebeh.2009.12.004

16. Locke, D. E. C., Kirlin, K. A., Wershba, R., Osborne, D., Drazkowski, J. F., Sirven, J. I., & Noe, K. H. (2011). Randomized comparison of the Personality Assessment Inventory and the Minnesota Multiphasic Personality Inventory-2 in the epilepsy monitoring unit. *Epilepsy & Behavior, 21*(4), 397–401. https://doi.org/10.1016/j.yebeh.2011.05.023

17. Menton, W. H., Crighton, A. H., Tarescavage, A. M., Marek, R. J., Hicks, A. D., & Ben-Porath, Y. S. (2019). Equivalence of laptop and tablet administrations of the Minnesota Multiphasic Personality Inventory-2 Restructured Form. *Assessment, 26*(4), 661–669. https://doi.org/10.1177/1073191117714558

18. Mickens, L. D., Nghiem, D. M., Wygant, D. B., Umlauf, R. L., & Marek, R. J. (2021). Validity of the Somatic Complaints Scales of the MMPI-2-RF in an outpatient chronic pain clinic. *Journal of Clinical Psychology in Medical Settings*. Advance online publication. https://doi.org/10.1007/s10880-021-09766-4

19. Sellbom, M., Ben-Porath, Y. S., & Graham, J. R. (2006). Correlates of the MMPI-2 Restructured Clinical (RC) Scales in a college counseling setting. *Journal of Personality Assessment, 86*(1), 89–99. https://doi.org/10.1207/s15327752jpa8601_10

20. Sellbom, M., Corey, D. M., & Ben-Porath, Y. S. (2021). Incremental validity of the Multidimensional Personality Questionnaire in the preemployment assessment of police officer candidates. *Criminal Justice and Behavior*. Advance online publication. https://doi.org/10.1177/00938548211033630

21. Sellbom, M., Graham, J. R., & Schenk, P. W. (2006). Incremental validity of the MMPI-2 Restructured Clinical (RC) Scales in a private practice sample. *Journal of Personality Assessment, 86*(2), 196–205. https://doi.org/10.1207/s15327752jpa8602_09

22. Shkalim, E. (2015). Psychometric evaluation of the MMPI-2/MMPI-2-RF Restructured Clinical Scales in an Israeli sample. *Assessment, 22*(4), 607–618. https://doi.org/10.1177/1073191114555884

23. Tarescavage, A. M., Scheman, J., & Ben-Porath, Y. S. (2015). Reliability and validity of the Minnesota Multiphasic Personality Inventory-2-Restructured Form (MMPI-2-RF) in evaluations of chronic low back pain patients. *Psychological Assessment, 27*(2), 433–446. https://doi.org/10.1037/pas0000056

24. Tellegen, A., & Ben-Porath, Y. S. (2008/2011). *Minnesota Multiphasic Personality Inventory-2-Restructured Form (MMPI-2-RF): Technical manual*. University of Minnesota Press.

25. Thomas, M. L., & Locke, D. E. C. (2010). Psychometric properties of the MMPI-2-RF Somatic Complaints (RC1) Scale. *Psychological Assessment, 22*(3), 492–503. https://doi.org/10.1037/a0019229

26. Van der Heijden, P. T., Egger, J. I. M., Rossi, G. M. P., Grundel, G., & Derksen, J. J. L. (2013). The MMPI-2-Restructured Form and the standard MMPI-2 Clinical Scales in relation to DSM-IV. *European Journal of Psychological Assessment, 29*(3), 182–188. https://doi.org/10.1027/1015-5759/a000140

27. Whitman, M. R., Corey, D. M., & Ben-Porath, Y. S. (2021). Associations between MMPI-3 and psychosocial history findings obtained in preemployment evaluations of public safety candidates [Manuscript under review].

28. Whitman, M. R., Elias, L. S., Cappo, B. M., & Ben-Porath, Y. S. (2021). Criterion validity of MMPI-3 scores in preemployment evaluations of public safety candidates. *Psychological Assessment*. Advance online publication. https://doi.org/10.1037/pas0001042

29. Whitman, M. R., Tylicki, J. L., Mascioli, R., Pickle, J., & Ben-Porath, Y. S. (2021). Psychometric properties of the Minnesota Multiphasic Personality Inventory-3 (MMPI-3) in a clinical neuropsychology setting. *Psychological Assessment, 33*(2), 142–155. https://doi.org/10.1037/pas0000969

End of Report

FIGURE 8.7. Ms. P's MMPI-3 Dispatcher Candidate Interpretive Report, continued

Substantive Scale Findings

Ms. P's scores on two Somatic/Cognitive domain scales, RC1 (65T) and MLS (68T), are clinically significant. Interpretive inferences and correlates for these clinically elevated MMPI-3 scales are reported in the Clinical Findings section of her DCIR (Figure 8.7, p. 9). A review of the nine RC1 items that Ms. P answered in the keyed direction (printable as a user-designated option but not reproduced here to protect test security) reveals that she reported all three symptom groups measured by this scale: head pain, neurological symptoms, and gastrointestinal symptoms. As seen in the bottom row on page 3 of Ms. P's DCIR (Figure 8.7), only 0.8% of the Dispatcher Candidate Comparison Group scored higher on this scale.

Ms. P's score on MLS (Figure 8.7, p. 4) is also clinically significant (68T), with no comparison group members scoring higher. As noted in Clinical Findings, this level of self-reported poor health and feeling weak or tired is correlated with preoccupation with poor health, complaints of sleep disturbance, fatigue, low energy, and sexual dysfunction.

Ms. P's DCIR (Figure 8.7, p. 4) also shows clinically elevated scores on two Internalizing domain scales, STR (68T) and WRY (72T), indicating reports of an above-average level of stress and worry, respectively, as discussed in Clinical Findings (p. 9). Finally, Ms. P's score on DOM (69T), which is in the Interpersonal Functioning domain, indicates a self-description of (a) having strong opinions, (b) standing up for herself, (c) being assertive and direct, and (d) being able to lead others, and is associated with a likelihood of being viewed as overly domineering.

Comparison Group Findings (pp. 9–10) show that these clinically elevated scale scores are quite rare for dispatcher candidates, with only 1% or fewer Dispatcher Candidate Comparison Group members producing scores as high or higher. Also discussed in this section are the implications of her uncommon but only moderately elevated scores on EID (53T, 5.0%), COG (61T, 0.8%), FML (59T, 3.0%), DSF (58T, 4.0%), and NEGE (64T, 1.0%).

These moderate and clinically-elevated scores are also associated with a wide range of job-relevant correlates (pp. 10–11) in 6 of the 10 problem domains (i.e., Emotional Control and Stress Tolerance Problems, Routine Task Performance Problems, Decision-Making and Judgment Problems, Assertiveness Problems, Social Competence and Teamwork Problems, and Conscientiousness and Dependability Problems).

Background Findings

The background investigation revealed that Ms. P is perceived by some coworkers as "bossy" and "pushy" and by others as having "high standards."

She applied for an open position as a dispatcher with her current employer but was unsuccessful. Although her supervisor described her as a competent call taker (who receives information from a 911 caller and routes the call to a police, fire, or emergency medical dispatcher) and opined that she would make a good dispatcher, she told the background investigator that she did not consider Ms. P to be "a good fit" with the smaller agency where she worked at the time. She said she thought Ms. P needed "a fresh start," because many of her coworkers had already formed opinions about her based on their initial interactions. She said that in the past year, Ms. P has avoided gossiping and no longer openly criticizes other call takers and dispatchers. Ms. P had one letter of counseling in her file for excessive use of sick leave about six months ago.

Interview Findings

Ms. P presented in the interview as stressed and anxious, which conforms to expectations based on her clinically elevated MMPI-3 scores. When the examiner commented on this, she became tearful and explained that she "really needs this job" because she is in the process of finalizing a contentious divorce and has to support herself. Ms. P asserted that she is "doing the job already," although when challenged by the examiner, she conceded that a call taker is not the same as an emergency dispatcher, who communicates with both the 911 caller and emergency response personnel.

Ms. P explained her anxiety and physical distress as stemming from her negative interactions with her coworkers, which she attributed to "weak management" and "social cliques" that ostracized new employees. She said that her coworkers "eat their young," referring to the bullying initiation that new call takers and dispatchers sometimes endure from their more experienced coworkers. She acknowledged that she had begun to experience physical problems, including headaches, gastrointestinal distress, and neurological symptoms, in response to the hazing and negative interaction. She said she was confident that these problems—which she said she never had before working there—would vanish as soon as she found new work.

Discussion

Ms. P's high level of stress and worry manifested in substantial physical distress. This carries a high risk of undermining the emotional control, stress resilience, and adaptability/flexibility required for successful performance in the public safety dispatcher position. In addition, the agency to which she applied is an extremely busy public safety answering point with a very high number of calls for service—more than five times the volume in her current position. The position of police/fire dispatcher would require that she learn many new codes and procedures that she did not learn in her role as a call taker, and her training performance would also likely be challenged by the high level of stress and physical symptoms she was experiencing at the time. Ms. P believed that her coworkers, management, and a dysfunctional work culture were responsible for her problems and absolved herself of any responsibility for the workplace dynamics. She believed her interpersonal dominance was a protective factor that kept her from being entirely defeated. If so, it had little efficacy given the degree of somatic and emotional distress she experienced. But even if Ms. P's assessment and optimism had merit, there is little reason to expect that the new workplace would respond differently to her highly assertive and domineering behavior, arguably only compounding her symptoms. In any event, a current assessment of Ms. P's functioning indicates that she lacks the requisite stress resilience *at this time*. Therefore, in consideration of these facts, the examiner concluded that Ms. P **does not meet** the agency's criterion standard.

BRIEF REVIEW: MR. H, CORRECTIONAL CANDIDATE

Assessment Issues Presented

- An MMPI-3 Correctional Candidate Interpretive Report (CCIR) with a single clinically elevated score on SUB and several moderately elevated substantive scale scores

Referral Summary

Mr. H is a 23-year-old unmarried male seeking a position as a correctional deputy in a moderate-size county sheriff's department. At the time of the evaluation, Mr. H had worked for 3 years as a self-employed mobile car detailer after completing an associate degree in business.

Assessing Protocol Validity

As shown in Mr. H's CCIR (Figure 8.8, p. 2), he produced a valid and interpretable protocol. There are no problems with unscorable items, and he responded to the MMPI-3 in a remarkably consistent manner with a deliberate approach to the assessment. There are no clear indications of over- or underreporting. Although he presented himself as very well-adjusted (K = 71), this finding is relatively common among correctional candidates, with a mean K score of 64T ($SD = 8$) and 16% of the members of the Correctional Candidate Comparison Group scoring at the ceiling (74T) on K. As always in the case of elevated K, if there is collateral evidence that the test taker is not well-adjusted, any absence of elevation on the Substantive Scales should be interpreted with caution, and elevated scores on the Substantive Scales may underestimate the problems assessed by those scales.

Minnesota Multiphasic Personality Inventory®-3

Yossef S. Ben-Porath
Auke Tellegen

MMPI®-3
Correctional Candidate Interpretive Report
David M. Corey, PhD, & Yossef S. Ben-Porath, PhD

ID Number:	Mr. H
Age:	23
Gender:	Male
Marital Status:	Not reported
Years of Education:	Not reported
Date Assessed:	11/23/2022

Copyright © 2022 by the Regents of the University of Minnesota. All rights reserved. Distributed exclusively under license from the University of Minnesota by NCS Pearson, Inc. Portions reproduced from the *MMPI-3 English Test Booklet*. Copyright © 2020 by the Regents of the University of Minnesota. All rights reserved. Portions excerpted from the *MMPI-3 Manual for Administration, Scoring, and Interpretation*. Copyright © 2020 by the Regents of the University of Minnesota. All rights reserved. Portions excerpted from the *MMPI-3 Technical Manual*. Copyright © 2020 by the Regents of the University of Minnesota. All rights reserved. Used by permission of the University of Minnesota Press.

Minnesota Multiphasic Personality Inventory and **MMPI** are registered trademarks of the Regents of the University of Minnesota. **Pearson** is a trademark, in the US and/or other countries, of Pearson Education, Inc., or its affiliates.

This report contains copyrighted material and trade secrets. Qualified licensees may excerpt portions of this output report, limited to the minimum text necessary to accurately describe their significant core conclusions, for incorporation into a written evaluation of the examinee, in accordance with their profession's citation standards, if any. No adaptations, translations, modifications, or special versions may be made of this report without prior written permission from the University of Minnesota Press.

[1.4 / RE1 / QG1]

ALWAYS LEARNING   **PEARSON**

FIGURE 8.8. Mr. H's MMPI-3 Correctional Candidate Interpretive Report

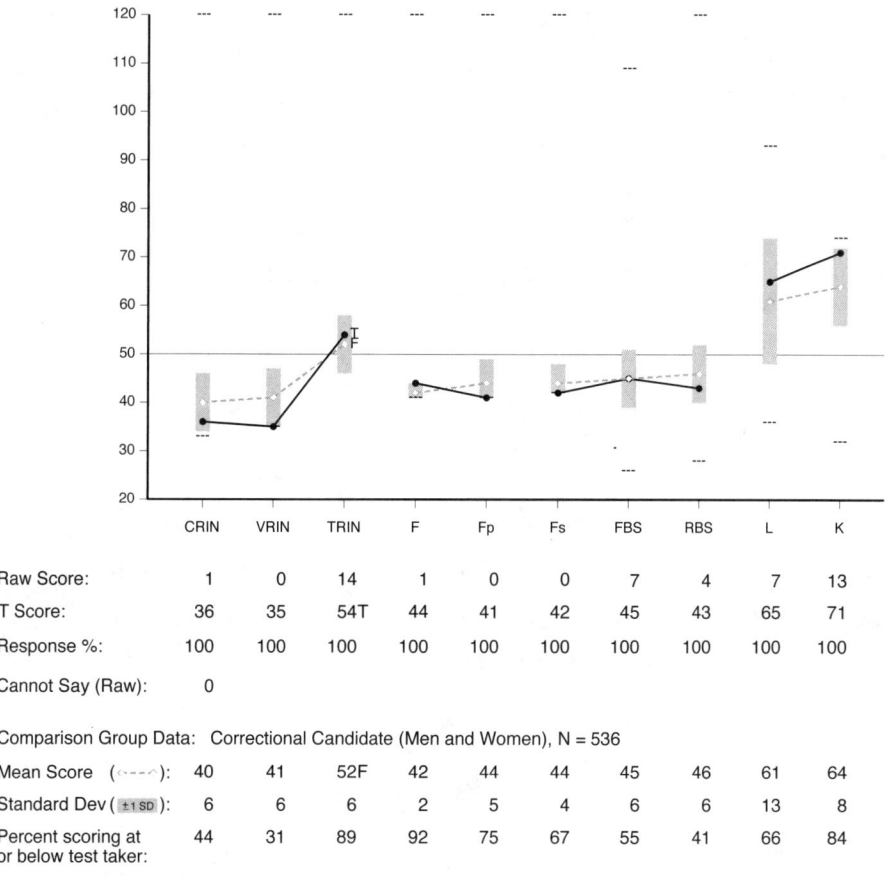

FIGURE 8.8. Mr. H's MMPI-3 Correctional Candidate Interpretive Report, continued

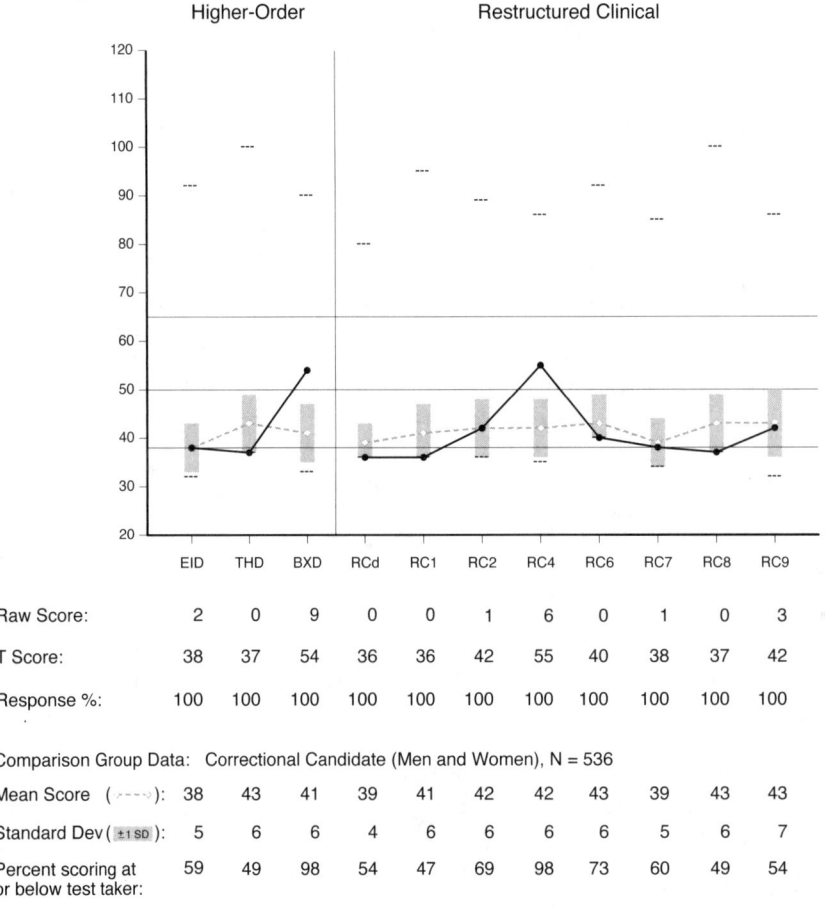

FIGURE 8.8. Mr. H's MMPI-3 Correctional Candidate Interpretive Report, continued

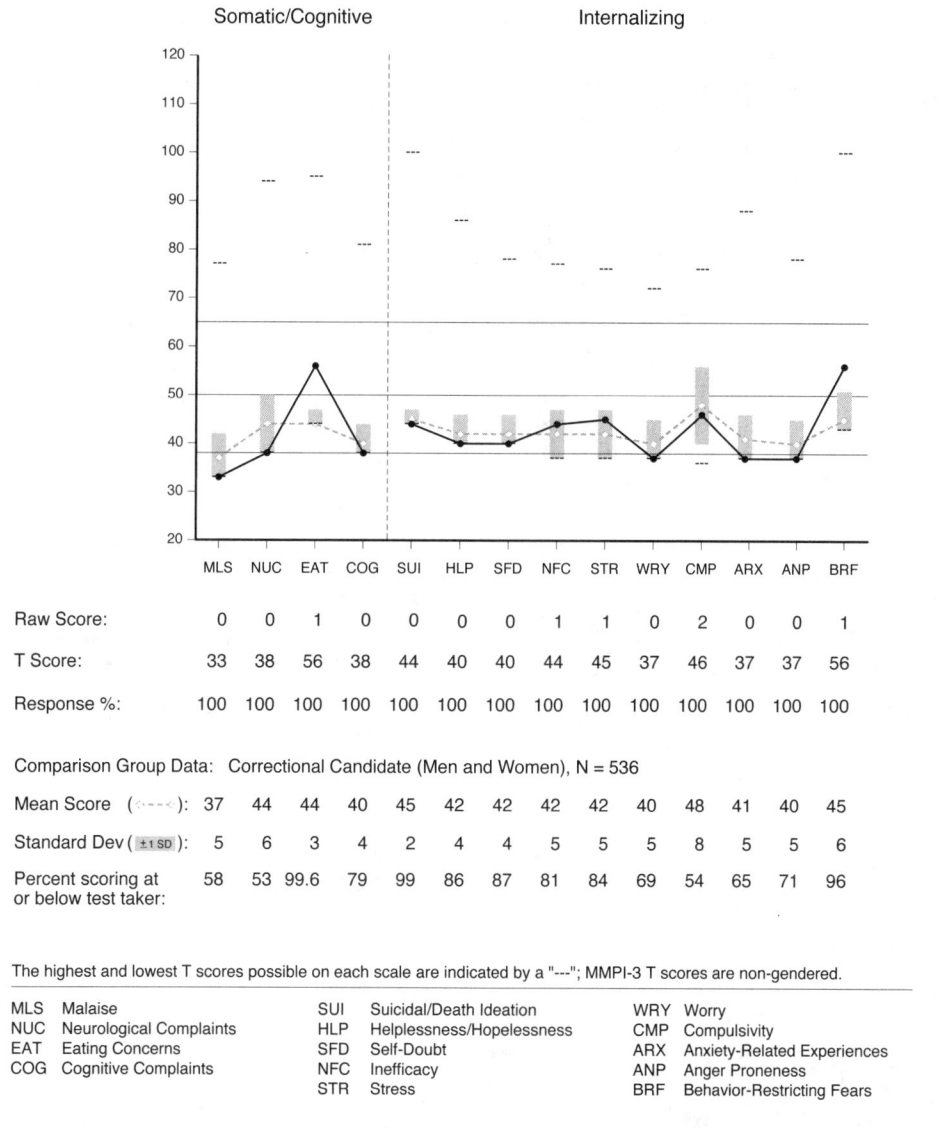

FIGURE 8.8. Mr. H's MMPI-3 Correctional Candidate Interpretive Report, continued

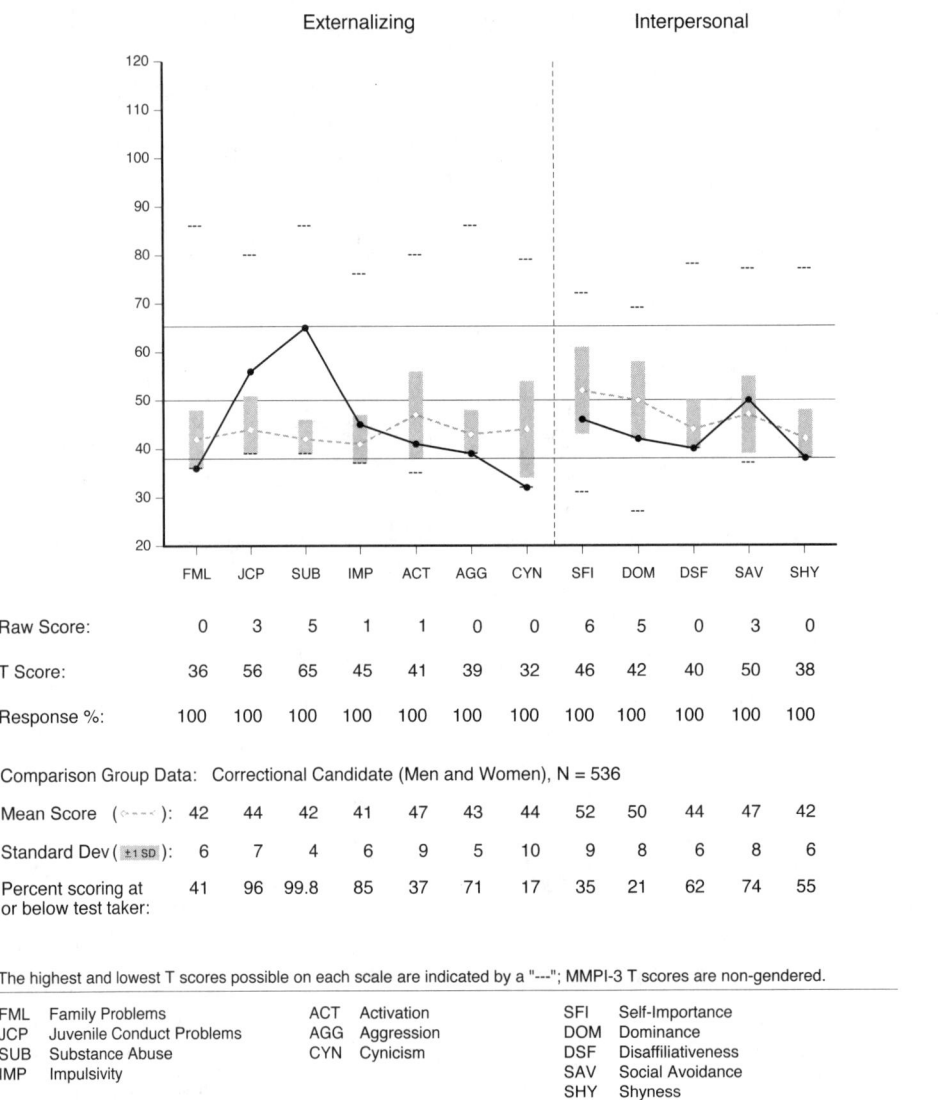

FIGURE 8.8. Mr. H's MMPI-3 Correctional Candidate Interpretive Report, continued

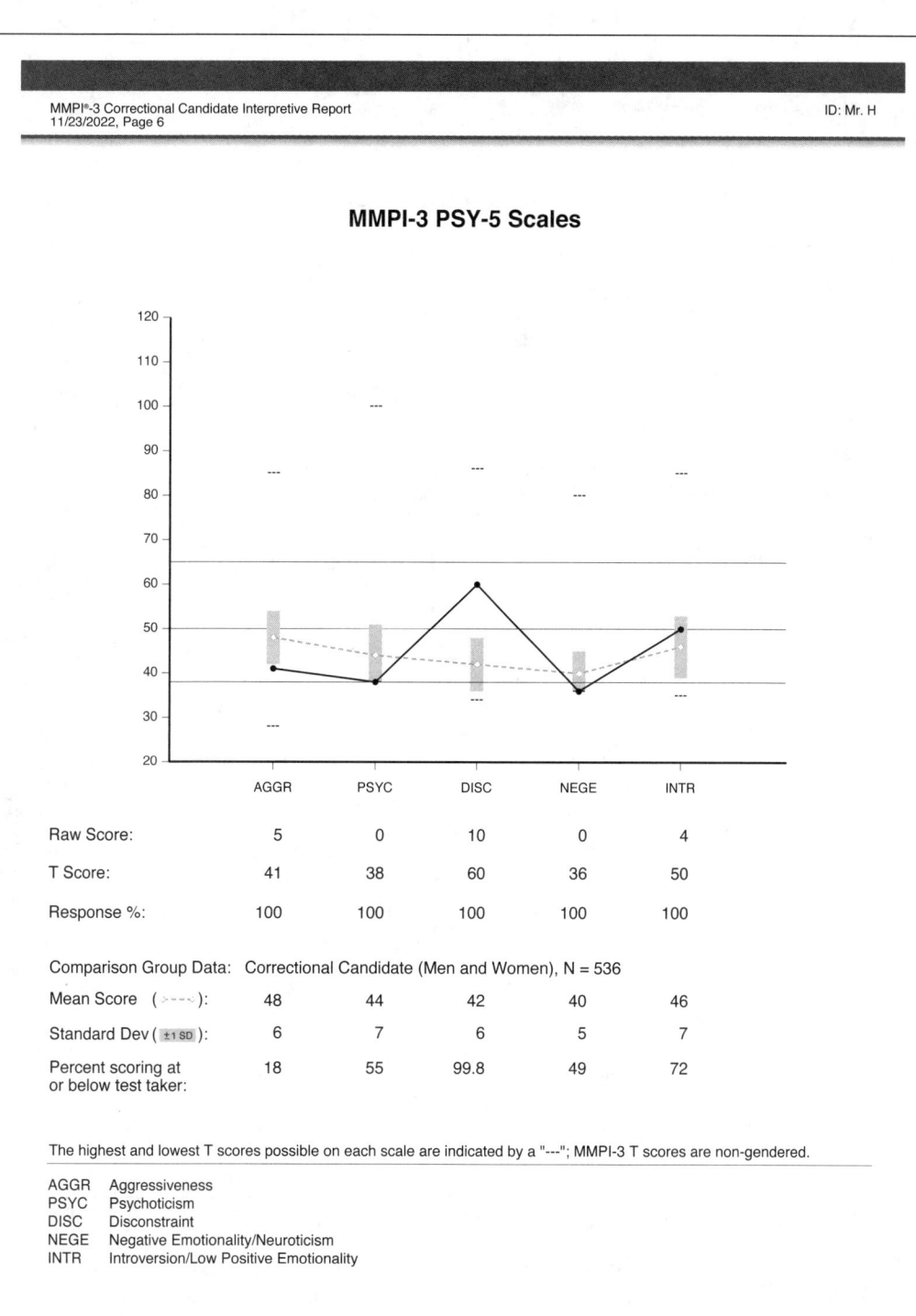

FIGURE 8.8. Mr. H's MMPI-3 Correctional Candidate Interpretive Report, continued

MMPI-3 T SCORES (BY DOMAIN)

PROTOCOL VALIDITY

Content Non-Responsiveness

0	36	35	54 T
CNS	CRIN	VRIN	TRIN

Over-Reporting

44	41		42	45	43
F	Fp		Fs	FBS	RBS

Under-Reporting

65	**71**
L	**K**

SUBSTANTIVE SCALES

Somatic/Cognitive Dysfunction

36	33	38	56	38
RC1	MLS	NUC	EAT	COG

Emotional Dysfunction

38					
EID					

36	44	40	40	44
RCd	SUI	HLP	SFD	NFC

42	50
RC2	INTR

38	45	37	46	37	37	56	36
RC7	STR	WRY	CMP	ARX	ANP	BRF	NEGE

Thought Dysfunction

37
THD

40
RC6

37
RC8

38
PSYC

Behavioral Dysfunction

54
BXD

55	36	56	**65**
RC4	FML	JCP	**SUB**

42	45	41	39	32
RC9	IMP	ACT	AGG	CYN

60
DISC

Interpersonal Functioning

46	42	41	40	50	38
SFI	DOM	AGGR	DSF	SAV	SHY

Scale scores shown in bold font are interpreted in the report.

Note. This information is provided to facilitate interpretation following the recommended structure for MMPI-3 interpretation in Chapter 5 of the *MMPI-3 Manual for Administration, Scoring, and Interpretation*, which provides details in the text and an outline in Table 5-1.

FIGURE 8.8. Mr. H's MMPI-3 Correctional Candidate Interpretive Report, continued

This interpretive report is intended for use by a professional qualified to interpret the MMPI-3 in the context of preemployment psychological evaluations of correctional officers and other related law enforcement personnel in institutional settings. **It focuses on identifying problems; it does not convey potential strengths.** The information it contains should be considered in the context of the test taker's background, the demands of the position under consideration, the clinical interview, findings from supplemental tests, and other relevant information.

The interpretive statements in the Protocol Validity section of the report are based on T scores derived from the general MMPI-3 normative sample, as well as scores obtained by the multisite sample of 536 individuals that make up the Correctional Candidate Comparison Group.

The interpretive statements in the Clinical Findings and Diagnostic Considerations sections of the report are based on T scores derived from the general MMPI-3 normative sample. Following recommended practice, only T scores of 65 and higher (with a few exceptions) are considered clinically significant. Scores at this clinical level are generally rare among correctional candidates.

Statements in the Comparison Group Findings and Job-Relevant Correlates sections are based on comparisons with scores obtained by the Correctional Candidate Comparison Group. Statements in these sections may be based on T scores that, although less than 65, are nevertheless uncommon in reference to the comparison group.

The report includes extensive annotation, which appears as superscripts following each statement in the narrative, keyed to Endnotes with accompanying Research References, which appear in the final two sections of the report. Additional information about the annotation features is provided in the headnotes to these sections and in the MMPI-3 User's Guide for the Public Safety Candidate Interpretive Reports.

SYNOPSIS

This is a valid MMPI-3 protocol. Scores on the Substantive Scales indicate clinically significant behavioral dysfunction. Behavioral-externalizing problems relate to substance abuse.

Comparison group findings point to additional possible concerns about irresponsible behavior.

Possible job-relevant problems are identified in the following domains: Emotional Control and Stress Tolerance, Social Competence and Teamwork, Integrity, Substance Use, and Impulse Control.

PROTOCOL VALIDITY

This is a valid MMPI-3 protocol. There are no problems with unscorable items. The test taker responded to the MMPI-3 in a remarkably consistent manner[1]. He was deliberate in his approach to the assessment. There are no clear indications of over- or under-reporting.

However, the test taker presented himself as very well-adjusted[2]. This reported level of psychological adjustment is relatively rare in the general population but rather common among correctional candidates. If there is collateral evidence that this individual is not well-adjusted, any absence of elevation on the Substantive Scales should be interpreted with caution[3]. Elevated scores on the Substantive Scales may underestimate the problems assessed by those scales[4].

FIGURE 8.8. Mr. H's MMPI-3 Correctional Candidate Interpretive Report, continued

CLINICAL FINDINGS

Clinical-level symptoms, personality characteristics, and behavioral tendencies of the test taker are described in this section and organized according to an empirically guided framework. (Please see Chapter 5 of the MMPI-3 Manual for Administration, Scoring, and Interpretation for details.) Statements containing the word "reports" are based on the item content of MMPI-3 scales, whereas statements that include the word "likely" are based on empirical correlates of scale scores. Specific sources for each statement can be viewed with the annotation features of this report.

The test taker reports significant past and current substance abuse[5], and indeed likely has a history of problematic use of alcohol or drugs, including misuse of prescription medication[6], is sensation-seeking[7], and has had legal problems as a result of substance abuse[8].

There are no indications of clinically significant somatic, cognitive, emotional, or thought dysfunction in this protocol.

DIAGNOSTIC CONSIDERATIONS

This section provides recommendations for psychodiagnostic assessment based on the test taker's MMPI-3 results. It is recommended that he be evaluated for the following:

Behavioral-Externalizing Disorders
- Substance-related disorders[9]

COMPARISON GROUP FINDINGS

This section describes the MMPI-3 substantive scale findings in the context of the Correctional Candidate Comparison Group. Specific sources for each statement can be accessed with the annotation features of this report. **Job-related correlates of these results, if any, are provided in the subsequent Job-Relevant Correlates section.**

Behavioral/Externalizing Problems
The test taker reports a comparatively high level of disconstraint for a correctional candidate[10]. Only 0.4% of comparison group members convey this or a greater level of disconstrained behavior. More specifically, he reports a relatively high level of irresponsible behavior for a correctional candidate[11]. Only 4.0% of comparison group members convey this or a greater level of acting out. In particular, his responses indicate past and/or current substance use that may be incompatible with public safety requirements for refraining from substance misuse[12]. This level of alcohol and possible drug use is uncommon among correctional candidates. Only 0.2% of comparison group members give evidence of this or a greater level of substance use.

JOB-RELEVANT CORRELATES

Job-relevant personality characteristics and behavioral tendencies of the test taker are described in this section and organized according to ten problem domains commonly identified in the professional literature as relevant to public safety candidate suitability. (Please see MMPI-3 User's Guide for the Public Safety Candidate Interpretive Reports for details.) Statements that begin with "Compared with other correctional candidates" are based on correlations with other self-report measures obtained in correctional candidate samples that included individuals who were subsequently hired as well as those who were not.

FIGURE 8.8. Mr. H's MMPI-3 Correctional Candidate Interpretive Report, continued

Emotional Control and Stress Tolerance Problems

Compared with other correctional candidates, the test taker is more likely to easily become irritated and annoyed by others[13]; to become impatient with others over minor infractions[14]; and to overreact to minor frustrations[13].

Social Competence and Teamwork Problems

Compared with other correctional candidates, the test taker is more likely to fail to consider others' needs and feelings[15].

Integrity Problems

Compared with other correctional candidates, the test taker is more likely to have a history of conflicts with the law and other violations of social norms[16]; to lack a commitment to societal rules[14]; and to be self-indulgent[14]. He is also more likely to report a history of committing theft[16] and to be nonconforming[13].

Substance Use Problems

Compared with other correctional candidates, the test taker is more likely to have a history of substance use problems[17].

Impulse Control Problems

Compared with other correctional candidates, the test taker is more likely to behave impulsively or without adequate consideration of the consequences or implications of his actions[18]; to be rebellious and lack discipline[13]; and to be unpredictable in behavior and attitudes[18].

The candidate's test scores are not associated with problems in the following domains:
- Routine Task Performance
- Decision-Making and Judgment
- Feedback Acceptance
- Assertiveness
- Conscientiousness and Dependability

ITEM-LEVEL INFORMATION

Unscorable Responses

The test taker produced scorable responses to all the MMPI-3 items.

Critical Responses

Seven MMPI-3 scales—Suicidal/Death Ideation (SUI), Helplessness/Hopelessness (HLP), Anxiety-Related Experiences (ARX), Ideas of Persecution (RC6), Aberrant Experiences (RC8), Substance Abuse (SUB), and Aggression (AGG)—have been designated by the test authors as having critical item content that may require immediate attention and follow-up. Items answered by the individual in the keyed direction (True or False) on a critical scale are listed below if his T score on that scale is 65 or higher. However, any item answered in the keyed direction on SUI is listed. The percentage of the MMPI-3 normative sample (NS) and of the Correctional Candidate Comparison Group (CG) that answered each item in the keyed direction are provided in parentheses following the item content.

Substance Abuse (SUB, T Score = 65)
    Item number and content omitted. (True; NS 21.7%, CG 0.9%)
    Item number and content omitted. (True; NS 43.0%, CG 7.3%)
    Item number and content omitted. (True; NS 38.2%, CG 12.7%)
    Item number and content omitted. (False; NS 31.9%, CG 9.3%)
    Item number and content omitted. (True; NS 14.4%, CG 0.9%)

FIGURE 8.8. Mr. H's MMPI-3 Correctional Candidate Interpretive Report, continued

Critical Follow-up Items

This section contains a list of items to which the test taker responded in a manner warranting follow-up. The items were identified by public safety candidate screening experts as having critical content. Clinicians are encouraged to follow up on these statements with the candidate by making related inquiries, rather than reciting the item(s) verbatim. Each item is followed by the candidate's response, the percentage of Correctional Candidate Comparison Group members who gave this response, and the scale(s) on which the item appears.

    Item number and content omitted. (True; 0.0%; VRIN, F, EAT)
    Item number and content omitted. (True; 0.9%; BXD, SUB, DISC)

FIGURE 8.8. Mr. H's MMPI-3 Correctional Candidate Interpretive Report, continued

ENDNOTES

This section lists for each statement in the report the MMPI-3 score(s) that triggered it. In addition, each statement is identified as a <u>Test Response</u>, if based on item content, a <u>Correlate</u>, if based on empirical correlates, or an <u>Inference</u>, if based on the report authors' judgment. (This information can also be accessed on-screen by placing the cursor on a given statement.) For correlate-based statements, research references (Ref. No.) are provided, keyed to the consecutively numbered reference list following the endnotes.

[1] Test Response: CRIN=36; VRIN=35
[2] Test Response: K=71
[3] Correlate: K=71, Ref. 4, 7, 11, 15, 22
[4] Correlate: K=71, Ref. 2, 8, 15, 17, 22
[5] Test Response: SUB=65
[6] Correlate: SUB=65, Ref. 1, 2, 3, 5, 9, 10, 12, 13, 14, 16, 18, 23
[7] Correlate: SUB=65, Ref. 2
[8] Correlate: SUB=65, Ref. 2, 17, 23
[9] Correlate: SUB=65, Ref. 2, 3, 13, 19, 23
[10] Test Response: BXD=54; DISC=60
[11] Test Response: RC4=55
[12] Inference: SUB=65
[13] Correlate: RC4=55, Ref. 6
[14] Correlate: BXD=54, Ref. 6; RC4=55, Ref. 6
[15] Correlate: BXD=54, Ref. 6
[16] Correlate: BXD=54, Ref. 20; RC4=55, Ref. 20; DISC=60, Ref. 20
[17] Correlate: BXD=54, Ref. 20, 21; RC4=55, Ref. 20, 21; SUB=65, Ref. 20, 21; DISC=60, Ref. 20, 21
[18] Correlate: RC4=55, Ref. 6, 21; DISC=60, Ref. 6, 21

FIGURE 8.8. Mr. H's MMPI-3 Correctional Candidate Interpretive Report, continued

RESEARCH REFERENCE LIST

The following studies are sources for empirical correlates identified in the Endnotes section of this report.

1. Bagby, R. M., Onno, K. A., Mortezaei, A., & Sellbom, M. (2020). Examining the "Traditional Background Hypothesis" for the MMPI-2-RF L-r Scores in a Muslim Faith-Based Sample. *Psychological Assessment.* Advance online publication. https://doi.org/10.1037/pas0000941

2. Ben-Porath, Y. S., & Tellegen, A. (2020). *The Minnesota Multiphasic Personality Inventory-3 (MMPI-3): Technical manual.* University of Minnesota Press.

3. Block, A. R., Ben-Porath, Y. S., & Marek, R. J. (2013). Psychological risk factors for poor outcome of spine surgery and spinal cord stimulator implant: A review of the literature and their assessment with the MMPI-2-RF. *The Clinical Neuropsychologist, 27*(1), 81–107. https://doi.org/10.1080/13854046.2012.721007

4. Brown, T. A., & Sellbom, M. (2020). The utility of the MMPI-2-RF validity scales in detecting underreporting. *Journal of Personality Assessment, 102*(1), 66–74. https://doi.org/10.1080/00223891.2018.1539003

5. Burchett, D. L., & Ben-Porath, Y. S. (2010). The impact of over-reporting on MMPI-2-RF substantive scale score validity. *Assessment, 17*(4), 497–516. https://doi.org/10.1177/1073191110378972

6. Corey, D. M., & Ben-Porath, Y. S. (2022). *Minnesota Multiphasic Personality Inventory-3 (MMPI-3): User's guide for the public safety candidate interpretive reports.* University of Minnesota Press.

7. Crighton, A. H., Marek, R. J., Dragon, W. R., & Ben-Porath, Y. S. (2017). Utility of the MMPI-2-RF Validity Scales in detection of simulated underreporting: Implications of incorporating a manipulation check. *Assessment, 24*(7), 853–864. https://doi.org/10.1177/1073191115627011

8. Forbey, J. D., Lee, T. T. C., Ben-Porath, Y. S., Arbisi, P. A., & Gartland, D. (2013). Associations between MMPI-2-RF validity scale scores and extra-test measures of personality and psychopathology. *Assessment, 20*(4), 448–461. https://doi.org/10.1177/1073191113478154

9. Laurinaityte, I., Laurinavicius, A., Ustinaviciute, L., Wygant, D. B., Sellbom, M. (2017). Utility of the MMPI-2 Restructured Form (MMPI-2-RF) in a sample of Lithuanian male offenders. *Law and Human Behavior, 41*(5), 494–505. https://doi.org/10.1037/lhb0000254

10. Lincourt, T. M., Tarescavage, A. M., Burchett, D., & Glassmire, D. M. (2020). Association Between MMPI-2-RF SUB Items/Scale and Interview-Reported Substance Abuse History Among Forensic Psychiatric Inpatients. *Psychological Assessment, 32*(2), 132–139. https://doi.org/10.1037/pas0000769

11. Marion, B. E., Sellbom, M., Salekin, R. T., Toomey, J. A., Kucharski, L. T., & Duncan, S. (2013). An examination of the association between psychopathy and dissimulation using the MMPI-2-RF Validity Scales. *Law and Human Behavior, 37*(4), 219–230. https://doi.org/10.1037/lhb0000008

12. Menton, W. H., Crighton, A. H., Tarescavage, A. M., Marek, R. J., Hicks, A. D., & Ben-Porath, Y. S. (2019). Equivalence of laptop and tablet administrations of the Minnesota Multiphasic Personality Inventory-2 Restructured Form. *Assessment, 26*(4), 661–669. https://doi.org/10.1177/1073191117714558

13. Ruiz, M. A., & Dorritie, M. T. (2021). Clinical utility of the Minnesota Multiphasic Personality Inventory-2-Restructured Form (MMPI-2-RF) in a residential treatment program for homeless individuals. *Assessment, 28*(2), 353–366. https://doi.org/10.1177/1073191119899481

14. Sellbom, M. (2016). Elucidating the validity of the externalizing spectrum of psychopathology in correctional, forensic, and community samples. *Journal of Abnormal Psychology, 125*(8), 1027–1038. https://doi.org/10.1037/abn0000171

FIGURE 8.8. Mr. H's MMPI-3 Correctional Candidate Interpretive Report, continued

15. Sellbom, M., & Bagby, R. M. (2008). Validity of the MMPI-2-RF (Restructured Form) L-r and K-r scales in detecting under-reporting in clinical and non-clinical samples. *Psychological Assessment, 20*(4), 370–376. https://doi.org/10.1037/a0012952

16. Tarescavage, A. M., Scheman, J., & Ben-Porath, Y. S. (2015). Reliability and validity of the Minnesota Multiphasic Personality Inventory-2-Restructured Form (MMPI-2-RF) in evaluations of chronic low back pain patients. *Psychological Assessment, 27*(2), 433–446. https://doi.org/10.1037/pas0000056

17. Tellegen, A., & Ben-Porath, Y. S. (2008/2011). *Minnesota Multiphasic Personality Inventory-2-Restructured Form (MMPI-2-RF): Technical manual.* University of Minnesota Press.

18. Thornton, V. A., Dodd, C. G., & Weed, N. C. (2020). Assessment of prescription stimulant misuse among college students using the MMPI-2-RF. *Addictive Behaviors, 110.* https://doi.org/10.1016/j.addbeh.2020.106511

19. Van der Heijden, P. T., Egger, J. I. M., Rossi, G. M. P., Grundel, G., & Derksen, J. J. L. (2013). The MMPI-2-Restructured Form and the standard MMPI-2 Clinical Scales in relation to DSM-IV. *European Journal of Psychological Assessment, 29*(3), 182–188. https://doi.org/10.1027/1015-5759/a000140

20. Whitman, M. R., Corey, D. M., & Ben-Porath, Y. S. (2021). Associations between MMPI-3 and psychosocial history findings obtained in preemployment evaluations of public safety candidates [Manuscript under review].

21. Whitman, M. R., Elias, L. S., Cappo, B. M., & Ben-Porath, Y. S. (2021). Criterion validity of MMPI-3 scores in preemployment evaluations of public safety candidates. *Psychological Assessment.* Advance online publication. https://doi.org/10.1037/pas0001042

22. Whitman, M. R., Tylicki, J. L., & Ben-Porath, Y. S. (2021). Utility of the MMPI-3 Validity Scales for detecting overreporting and underreporting and their effects on substantive scale validity: A simulation study. *Psychological Assessment, 33*(5), 411–426. https://doi.org/10.1037/pas0000988

23. Whitman, M. R., Tylicki, J. L., Mascioli, R., Pickle, J., & Ben-Porath, Y. S. (2021). Psychometric properties of the Minnesota Multiphasic Personality Inventory-3 (MMPI-3) in a clinical neuropsychology setting. *Psychological Assessment, 33*(2), 142–155. https://doi.org/10.1037/pas0000969

End of Report

FIGURE 8.8. Mr. H's MMPI-3 Correctional Candidate Interpretive Report, continued

Substantive Scale Findings

Mr. H's protocol reveals moderate elevations on three Behavioral/Externalizing scales, BXD (54T), RC4 (55T), and DISC (60T). As discussed, when scores on both a Higher-Order scale and a related PSY-5 scale meet or exceed interpretable levels (see Tables 7.1 and 7.3), only the Higher-Order scale is interpreted to avoid producing redundant statements—this is illustrated in Mr. H's protocol. As described in the Comparison Group Findings section of his CCIR (Figure 8.8, p. 9), Mr. H's scores (or higher) on BXD and RC4 were produced by only 0.4% and 4.0%, respectively, of the Correctional Candidate Comparison Group members. Only 0.2% of the comparison group members produced as high a score (65T) or higher on the SUB scale. The five SUB items that Mr. H answered in the keyed direction (Figure 8.8, p. 10, redacted for test security) reveal both alcohol and polydrug use problems.

Findings contained in the Job-Relevant Correlates section of Mr. H's CCIR describe potential problems in 5 of the 10 problem domains (Emotional Control and Stress Tolerance Problems, Social Competence and Teamwork Problems, Integrity Problems, Substance Use Problems, and Impulse Control Problems).

Background Findings

The background investigation documented Mr. H's juvenile drug use, including a high school suspension for marijuana possession and conviction and deferment of a criminal charge for minor in possession of alcohol at the age of 19. Mr. H told the background investigator and polygrapher that he had stopped using all illegal drugs (and prescription drugs prescribed to others) at age 19.

Interview Findings

Mr. H presented in the interview as pleasant, outgoing, and engaging. He reported an uncomplicated developmental history except for being the only child of two professionals in an intact marriage, whose devotion to their work left him with little guidance and oversight.

Mr. H reported in his written personal history questionnaire that he consumes alcohol most days of the week, with an average of two to three drinks on weekdays and six or more on weekend days. He reported occasionally (approximately four times in the past year) going to work hungover, missing work or other obligations while recovering from the effects of alcohol use, and being unable to recall portions of the previous evening after heavy drinking. The examiner asked whether he considered his use excessive, and he said no. He reasoned that he has never driven drunk, never been in trouble with the law because of his drinking (other than for drinking underage), never gotten into a fight while intoxicated, and never experienced other negative consequences associated with alcohol use.

Discussion

As noted in the case illustration for Ms. Q, the National Institute on Alcohol Abuse and Alcoholism (2023) defines heavy alcohol use for men as more than four drinks on any day or 15 or more per week. The Substance Abuse and Mental Health Services Administration (SAMSHA) defines binge drinking as five or more alcoholic drinks for men and four or more for women on the same occasion (i.e., at the same time or within a couple of hours) on at least one day in the past month (National Institute on Alcohol Abuse and Alcoholism, 2023). Thus, Mr. H's alcohol use pattern constitutes both heavy alcohol use and binge drinking, which markedly increase his risk for development of a more serious alcohol use disorder, legal problems, injuries, accidents, and sexual assaults.

It is difficult to predict the trajectory of a young person who binge drinks. Although many gradually reduce their consumption as they age, often stopping altogether or drinking only moderately and infrequently, others develop more serious problems. Because Mr. H's job description involves the requirement to carry a firearm to work (for correctional personnel assigned to the secure areas of the jail, their firearms are stored in gun lockers, but they are re-armed when they leave the facility or participate in transports), and after conferring with the hiring agency, the examiner concluded that Mr. H **does not meet** the agency's criterion standard.

BRIEF REVIEW: MR. Z, FIREFIGHTER/MEDIC CANDIDATE

Assessment Issues Presented

- Use of the Firefighter Candidate Interpretive Report (FCIR) in evaluating an entry-level firefighter/medic candidate with no clinically elevated H-O or RC scales, but with a single clinically significant low score (DOM = 27T) in the Interpersonal Functioning domain

Referral Summary

Mr. Z is a 29-year-old, never married male seeking an entry-level position as a firefighter/medic in a small rural fire protection district where he has served for four years as a volunteer firefighter.

Assessing Protocol Validity

As shown in Mr. Z's FCIR (Figure 8.9, p. 2), Mr. Z's validity scale scores indicate that he attended carefully to item content. The protocol reveals no

Minnesota Multiphasic Personality Inventory®-3

Yossef S. Ben-Porath
Auke Tellegen

MMPI®-3

Firefighter Candidate Interpretive Report

David M. Corey, PhD, & Yossef S. Ben-Porath, PhD

ID Number:	Mr. Z
Age:	29
Gender:	Male
Marital Status:	Not reported
Years of Education:	Not reported
Date Assessed:	10/28/2022

Copyright © 2022 by the Regents of the University of Minnesota. All rights reserved. Distributed exclusively under license from the University of Minnesota by NCS Pearson, Inc. Portions reproduced from the *MMPI-3 English Test Booklet*. Copyright © 2020 by the Regents of the University of Minnesota. All rights reserved. Portions excerpted from the *MMPI-3 Manual for Administration, Scoring, and Interpretation*. Copyright © 2020 by the Regents of the University of Minnesota. All rights reserved. Portions excerpted from the *MMPI-3 Technical Manual*. Copyright © 2020 by the Regents of the University of Minnesota. All rights reserved. Used by permission of the University of Minnesota Press.

Minnesota Multiphasic Personality Inventory and **MMPI** are registered trademarks of the Regents of the University of Minnesota. **Pearson** is a trademark, in the US and/or other countries, of Pearson Education, Inc., or its affiliates.

This report contains copyrighted material and trade secrets. Qualified licensees may excerpt portions of this output report, limited to the minimum text necessary to accurately describe their significant core conclusions, for incorporation into a written evaluation of the examinee, in accordance with their profession's citation standards, if any. No adaptations, translations, modifications, or special versions may be made of this report without prior written permission from the University of Minnesota Press.

[1.4 / RE1 / QG1]

ALWAYS LEARNING   **PEARSON**

FIGURE 8.9. Mr. Z's MMPI-3 Firefighter Candidate Interpretive Report

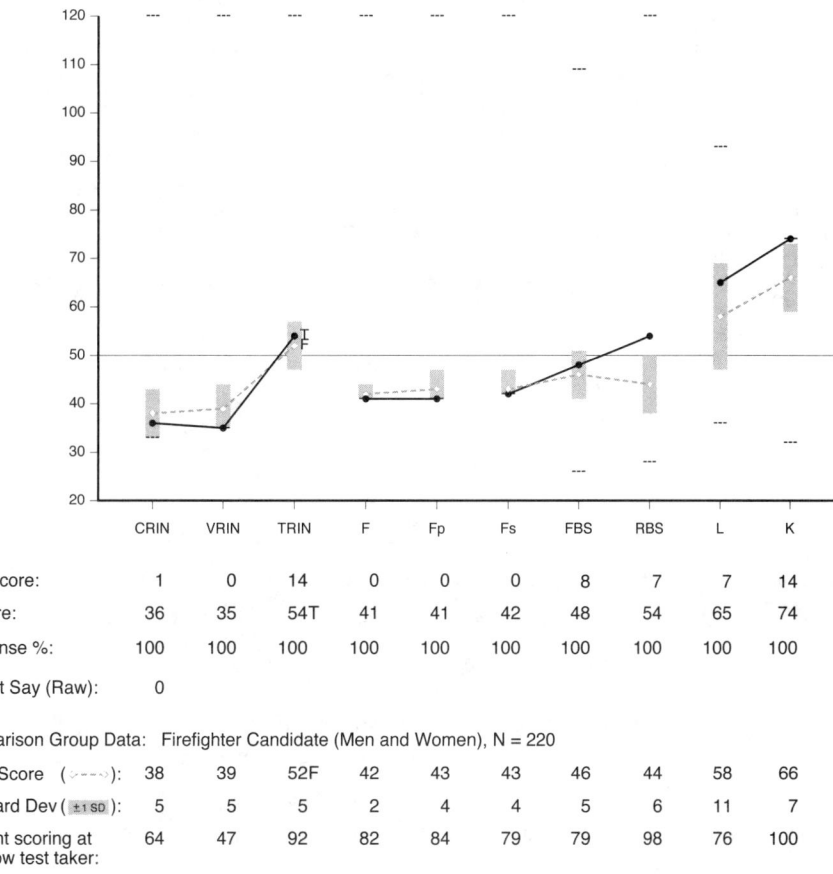

FIGURE 8.9. Mr. Z's MMPI-3 Firefighter Candidate Interpretive Report, continued

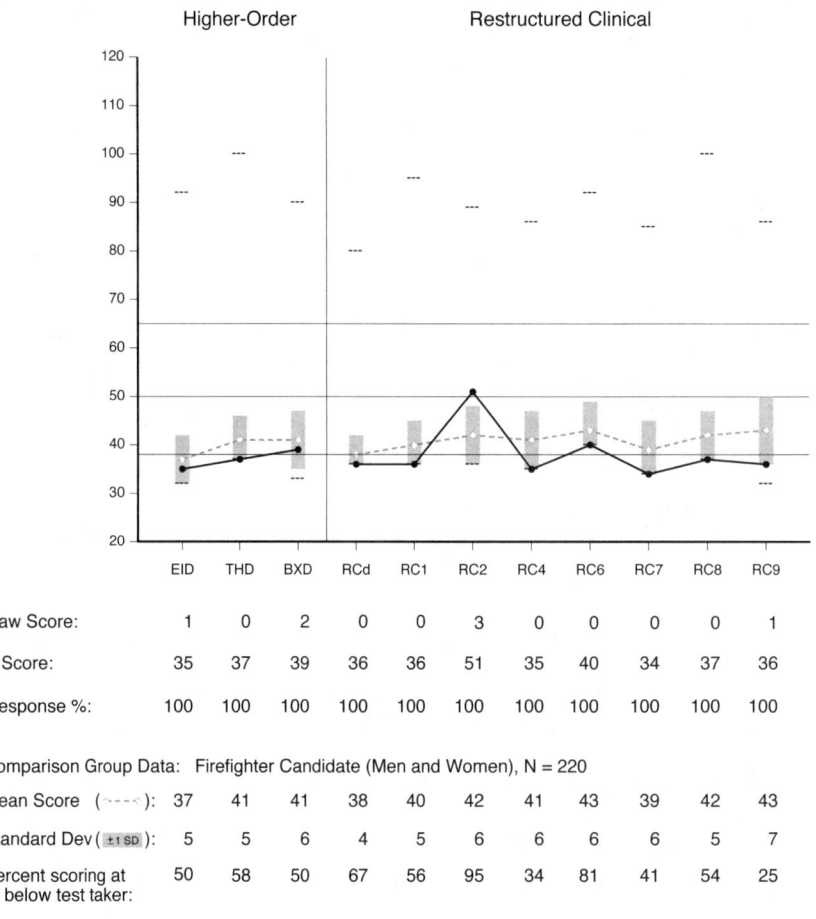

FIGURE 8.9. Mr. Z's MMPI-3 Firefighter Candidate Interpretive Report, continued

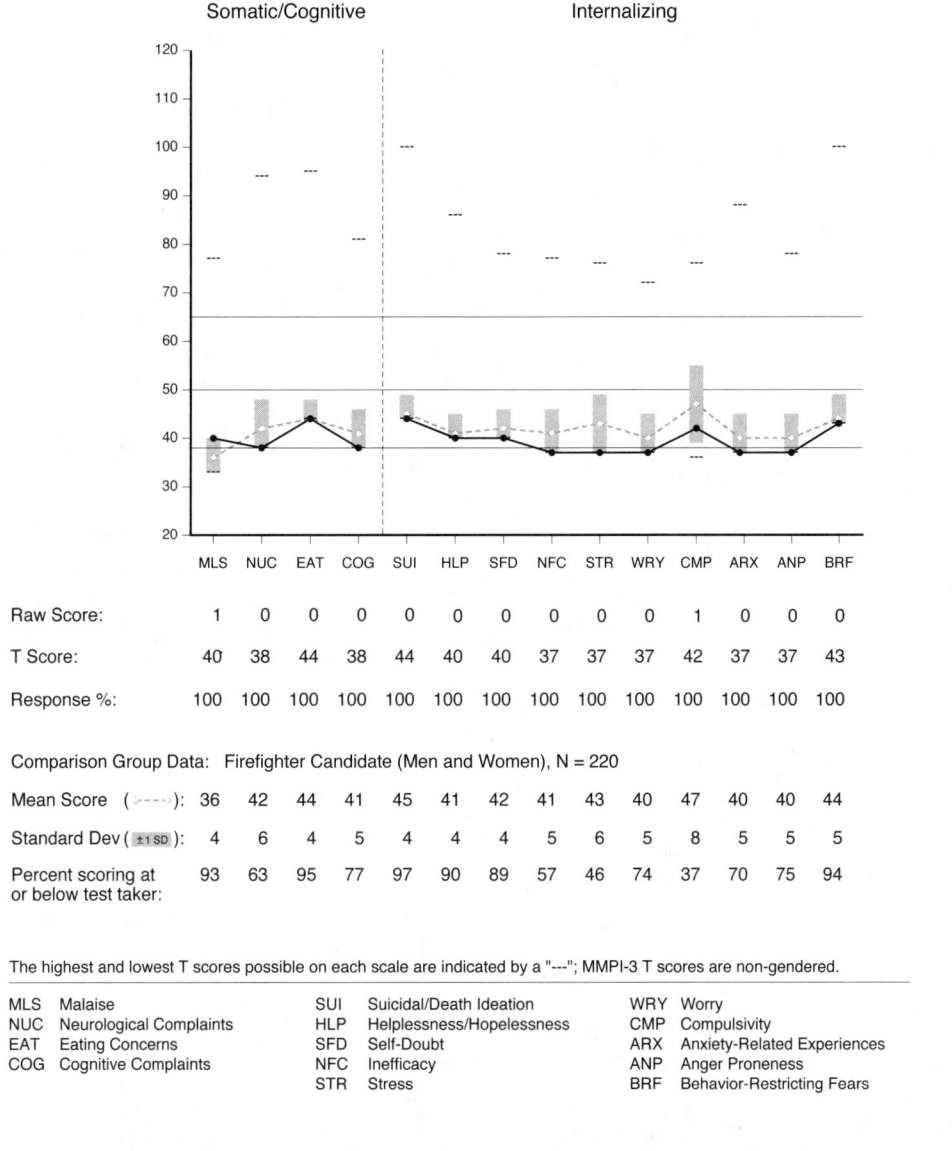

FIGURE 8.9. Mr. Z's MMPI-3 Firefighter Candidate Interpretive Report, continued

MMPI-3 Externalizing and Interpersonal Scales

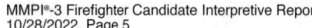

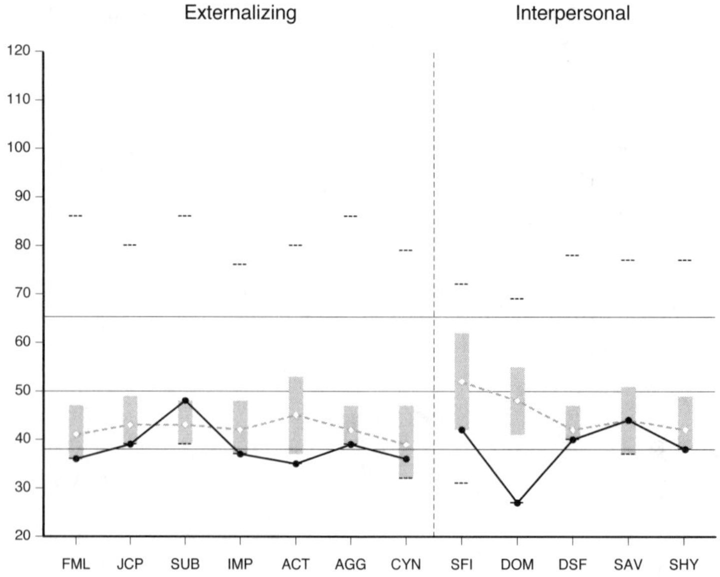

	FML	JCP	SUB	IMP	ACT	AGG	CYN	SFI	DOM	DSF	SAV	SHY
Raw Score:	0	0	1	0	0	0	1	3	0	0	1	0
T Score:	36	39	48	37	35	39	36	42	27	40	44	38
Response %:	100	100	100	100	100	100	100	100	100	100	100	100

Comparison Group Data: Firefighter Candidate (Men and Women), N = 220

	FML	JCP	SUB	IMP	ACT	AGG	CYN	SFI	DOM	DSF	SAV	SHY
Mean Score (◇---◇):	41	43	43	42	45	42	39	52	48	42	44	42
Standard Dev (±1 SD):	6	6	5	6	8	5	8	10	7	5	7	7
Percent scoring at or below test taker:	51	65	89	53	24	80	53	9	0	77	58	64

The highest and lowest T scores possible on each scale are indicated by a "---"; MMPI-3 T scores are non-gendered.

FML Family Problems
JCP Juvenile Conduct Problems
SUB Substance Abuse
IMP Impulsivity
ACT Activation
AGG Aggression
CYN Cynicism
SFI Self-Importance
DOM Dominance
DSF Disaffiliativeness
SAV Social Avoidance
SHY Shyness

FIGURE 8.9. Mr. Z's MMPI-3 Firefighter Candidate Interpretive Report, continued

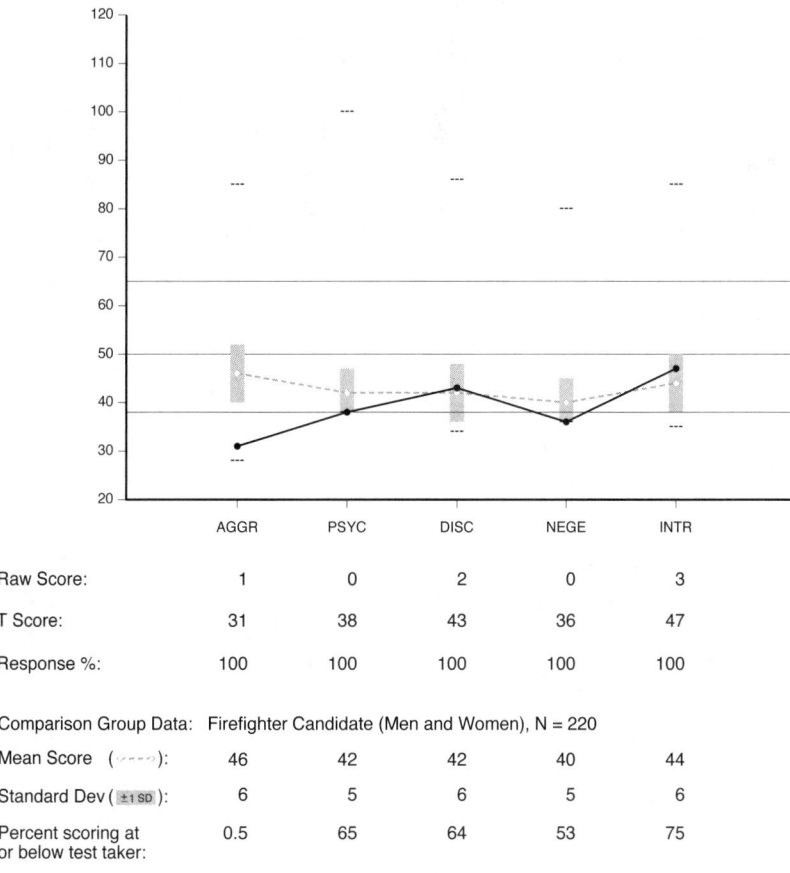

FIGURE 8.9. Mr. Z's MMPI-3 Firefighter Candidate Interpretive Report, continued

MMPI-3 T SCORES (BY DOMAIN)

PROTOCOL VALIDITY

Content Non-Responsiveness

0	36	35	54 T
CNS	CRIN	VRIN	TRIN

Over-Reporting

41	41		42	48	54
F	Fp		Fs	FBS	RBS

Under-Reporting

65	**74**
L	**K**

SUBSTANTIVE SCALES

Somatic/Cognitive Dysfunction

36	40	38	44	38
RC1	MLS	NUC	EAT	COG

Emotional Dysfunction

35					
EID					

36	44	40	40	37
RCd	SUI	HLP	SFD	NFC

51	47
RC2	INTR

34	37	37	42	37	37	43	36
RC7	STR	WRY	CMP	ARX	ANP	BRF	NEGE

Thought Dysfunction

37
THD

40
RC6

37
RC8

38
PSYC

Behavioral Dysfunction

39
BXD

35	36	39	48
RC4	FML	JCP	SUB

36	37	35	39	36
RC9	IMP	ACT	AGG	CYN

43
DISC

Interpersonal Functioning

42	**27**	31	40	44	38
SFI	**DOM**	AGGR	DSF	SAV	SHY

Scale scores shown in bold font are interpreted in the report.

Note. This information is provided to facilitate interpretation following the recommended structure for MMPI-3 interpretation in Chapter 5 of the *MMPI-3 Manual for Administration, Scoring, and Interpretation*, which provides details in the text and an outline in Table 5-1.

FIGURE 8.9. Mr. Z's MMPI-3 Firefighter Candidate Interpretive Report, continued

MMPI®-3 Firefighter Candidate Interpretive Report
ID: Mr. Z

This interpretive report is intended for use by a professional qualified to interpret the MMPI-3 in the context of preemployment psychological evaluations of firefighters, emergency medical technicians, paramedics, and other fire and medical emergency personnel. **It focuses on identifying problems; it does not convey potential strengths.** *The information it contains should be considered in the context of the test taker's background, the demands of the position under consideration, the clinical interview, findings from supplemental tests, and other relevant information.*

The interpretive statements in the Protocol Validity section of the report are based on T scores derived from the general MMPI-3 normative sample, as well as scores obtained by the multisite sample of 220 individuals that make up the Firefighter Candidate Comparison Group.

The interpretive statements in the Clinical Findings and Diagnostic Considerations sections of the report are based on T scores derived from the general MMPI-3 normative sample. Following recommended practice, only T scores of 65 and higher (with a few exceptions) are considered clinically significant. Scores at this clinical level are generally rare among firefighter/medic candidates.

Statements in the Comparison Group Findings and Job-Relevant Correlates sections are based on comparisons with scores obtained by the Firefighter Candidate Comparison Group. Statements in these sections may be based on T scores that, although less than 65, are nevertheless uncommon in reference to the comparison group.

The report includes extensive annotation, which appears as superscripts following each statement in the narrative, keyed to Endnotes with accompanying Research References, which appear in the final two sections of the report. Additional information about the annotation features is provided in the headnotes to these sections and in the MMPI-3 User's Guide for the Public Safety Candidate Interpretive Reports.

SYNOPSIS

Scores on the MMPI-3 Validity Scales raise concerns about the possible impact of under-reporting on the validity of this protocol. With that caution noted, there are no indications of clinically significant somatic or cognitive complaints, or of clinically significant emotional, thought, behavioral, or interpersonal dysfunction.

Comparison group findings point to possible concerns about interpersonal passivity.

Possible job-relevant problems are identified in the following domains: Emotional Control and Stress Tolerance, Routine Task Performance, Decision-Making and Judgment, and Assertiveness.

PROTOCOL VALIDITY

Content Non-Responsiveness

The test taker produced scorable responses to all the MMPI-3 items. He also responded in a remarkably consistent manner[1]. He was deliberate in his approach to the assessment.

Over-Reporting

There are no indications of over-reporting in this protocol.

FIGURE 8.9. Mr. Z's MMPI-3 Firefighter Candidate Interpretive Report, continued

Under-Reporting

The test taker presented himself as remarkably well-adjusted[2]. This reported level of psychological adjustment is rare in the general population and somewhat uncommon among firefighter/medic candidates. This level of good psychological adjustment was reported by 17% of comparison group members. Any absence of elevation on the Substantive Scales should be interpreted with caution[3]. Elevated scores on the Substantive Scales may underestimate the problems assessed by those scales[4].

CLINICAL FINDINGS

The following interpretation needs to be considered in light of cautions noted about the possible impact of under-reporting (of psychological problems) on the validity of this protocol.

There are no indications of clinically significant somatic, cognitive, emotional, thought, or behavioral dysfunction in this protocol. However, because of indications of under-reporting described earlier, such problems cannot be ruled out.

DIAGNOSTIC CONSIDERATIONS

No specific psychodiagnostic recommendations are indicated by this MMPI-3 protocol. However, this finding needs to be considered in light of cautions noted earlier about possible under-reporting.

COMPARISON GROUP FINDINGS

This section describes the MMPI-3 substantive scale findings in the context of the Firefighter Candidate Comparison Group. Specific sources for each statement can be accessed with the annotation features of this report. **Job-related correlates of these results, if any, are provided in the subsequent Job-Relevant Correlates section.**

In light of earlier-described evidence of under-reporting, the comparison group findings discussed below may not identify, or may underestimate, psychological problems that could impede the candidate's ability to perform the duties of a firefighter/medic.

Interpersonal Problems

The test taker's responses indicate a level of interpersonal passivity that is very likely incompatible with public safety requirements for assertiveness[5]. This level of passive behavior is uncommon in firefighter/medic candidates. No comparison group members give evidence of this level of passive, submissive behavior.

JOB-RELEVANT CORRELATES

Job-relevant personality characteristics and behavioral tendencies of the test taker are described in this section and organized according to ten problem domains commonly identified in the professional literature as relevant to public safety candidate suitability. (Please see MMPI-3 User's Guide for the Public Safety Candidate Interpretive Reports *for details.) Statements that begin with "Compared with other firefighter/medic candidates" are based on correlations with other self-report measures obtained in firefighter/medic candidate samples that included individuals who were subsequently hired as well as those who were not.*

In light of earlier-described evidence of under-reporting, the job-relevant correlates described in this section may not identify, or may underestimate, problematic tendencies that could impede the

FIGURE 8.9. Mr. Z's MMPI-3 Firefighter Candidate Interpretive Report, continued

candidate's ability to perform the duties of a firefighter/medic.

Emotional Control and Stress Tolerance Problems
Compared with other firefighter/medic candidates, the test taker is more likely to behave in a self-defeating fashion[6].

Routine Task Performance Problems
Compared with other firefighter/medic candidates, the test taker is more likely to be lacking in confidence in his own abilities[6].

Decision-Making and Judgment Problems
Compared with other firefighter/medic candidates, the test taker is more likely to avoid making decisions, fail to take action, or do anything that may prompt scrutiny from others[6].

Assertiveness Problems
Compared with other firefighter/medic candidates, the test taker is more likely to feel inadequate[6]; to lack assertiveness[6]; and to dislike leadership roles[6].

The candidate's test scores are not associated with problems in the following domains:
- Feedback Acceptance
- Social Competence and Teamwork
- Integrity
- Conscientiousness and Dependability
- Substance Use
- Impulse Control

ITEM-LEVEL INFORMATION

Unscorable Responses
The test taker produced scorable responses to all the MMPI-3 items.

Critical Responses
Seven MMPI-3 scales—Suicidal/Death Ideation (SUI), Helplessness/Hopelessness (HLP), Anxiety-Related Experiences (ARX), Ideas of Persecution (RC6), Aberrant Experiences (RC8), Substance Abuse (SUB), and Aggression (AGG)—have been designated by the test authors as having critical item content that may require immediate attention and follow-up. Items answered by the individual in the keyed direction (True or False) on a critical scale are listed below if his T score on that scale is 65 or higher. However, any item answered in the keyed direction on SUI is listed.

The test taker has not produced an elevated T score (≥ 65) on any of these scales or answered any SUI items in the keyed direction.

Critical Follow-up Items
This section contains a list of items to which the test taker responded in a manner warranting follow-up. The items were identified by public safety candidate screening experts as having critical content. Clinicians are encouraged to follow up on these statements with the candidate by making related inquiries, rather than reciting the item(s) verbatim. Each item is followed by the candidate's response, the percentage of Firefighter Candidate Comparison Group members who gave this response, and the scale(s) on which the item appears.

The test taker did not respond to any critical follow-up items in the keyed direction.

FIGURE 8.9. Mr. Z's MMPI-3 Firefighter Candidate Interpretive Report, continued

ENDNOTES

This section lists for each statement in the report the MMPI-3 score(s) that triggered it. In addition, each statement is identified as a <u>Test Response</u>, if based on item content, a <u>Correlate</u>, if based on empirical correlates, or an <u>Inference</u>, if based on the report authors' judgment. (This information can also be accessed on-screen by placing the cursor on a given statement.) For correlate-based statements, research references (Ref. No.) are provided, keyed to the consecutively numbered reference list following the endnotes.

[1] Test Response: CRIN=36; VRIN=35
[2] Test Response: K=74
[3] Correlate: K=74, Ref. 2, 4, 6, 7, 9
[4] Correlate: K=74, Ref. 1, 5, 7, 8, 9
[5] Inference: DOM=27; AGGR=31
[6] Correlate: DOM=27, Ref. 3

FIGURE 8.9. Mr. Z's MMPI-3 Firefighter Candidate Interpretive Report, continued

RESEARCH REFERENCE LIST

The following studies are sources for empirical correlates identified in the Endnotes section of this report.

1. Ben-Porath, Y. S., & Tellegen, A. (2020). *The Minnesota Multiphasic Personality Inventory-3 (MMPI-3): Technical manual.* University of Minnesota Press.

2. Brown, T. A., & Sellbom, M. (2020). The utility of the MMPI-2-RF validity scales in detecting underreporting. *Journal of Personality Assessment, 102*(1), 66–74. https://doi.org/10.1080/00223891.2018.1539003

3. Corey, D. M., & Ben-Porath, Y. S. (2022). *Minnesota Multiphasic Personality Inventory-3 (MMPI-3): User's guide for the public safety candidate interpretive reports.* University of Minnesota Press.

4. Crighton, A. H., Marek, R. J., Dragon, W. R., & Ben-Porath, Y. S. (2017). Utility of the MMPI-2-RF Validity Scales in detection of simulated underreporting: Implications of incorporating a manipulation check. *Assessment, 24*(7), 853–864. https://doi.org/10.1177/1073191115627011

5. Forbey, J. D., Lee, T. T. C., Ben-Porath, Y. S., Arbisi, P. A., & Gartland, D. (2013). Associations between MMPI-2-RF validity scale scores and extra-test measures of personality and psychopathology. *Assessment, 20*(4), 448–461. https://doi.org/10.1177/1073191113478154

6. Marion, B. E., Sellbom, M., Salekin, R. T., Toomey, J. A., Kucharski, L. T., & Duncan, S. (2013). An examination of the association between psychopathy and dissimulation using the MMPI-2-RF Validity Scales. *Law and Human Behavior, 37*(4), 219–230. https://doi.org/10.1037/lhb0000008

7. Sellbom, M., & Bagby, R. M. (2008). Validity of the MMPI-2-RF (Restructured Form) L-r and K-r scales in detecting under-reporting in clinical and non-clinical samples. *Psychological Assessment, 20*(4), 370–376. https://doi.org/10.1037/a0012952

8. Tellegen, A., & Ben-Porath, Y. S. (2008/2011). *Minnesota Multiphasic Personality Inventory-2-Restructured Form (MMPI-2-RF): Technical manual.* University of Minnesota Press.

9. Whitman, M. R., Tylicki, J. L., & Ben-Porath, Y. S. (2021). Utility of the MMPI-3 Validity Scales for detecting overreporting and underreporting and their effects on substantive scale validity: A simulation study. *Psychological Assessment, 33*(5), 411–426. https://doi.org/10.1037/pas0000988

End of Report

FIGURE 8.9. Mr. Z's MMPI-3 Firefighter Candidate Interpretive Report, continued

indications of overreporting. His score on K (74T) indicates a very high level of self-reported adjustment relative to the normative sample (for which the mean is always 50T), but one that is more common for a firefighter (the mean T score on K for the Firefighter Candidate Comparison Group is 66, $SD = 7$; for L it is 58, $SD = 11$). Taken as a whole, this protocol is valid and interpretable; however, because of possible underreporting, his scores on the Substantive Scales may underestimate the problems they assess.

Substantive Scale Findings

Mr. Z's scores on the H-O and RC scales are not clinically elevated (Figure 8.9, p. 3). In comparison to the Firefighter Candidate Comparison Group, his score on RC2 (51T) lies more than one standard deviation above the mean, as shown in Figure 8.9 (p. 3). However, as shown in Tables 7.1 and 7.3, RC2 is not interpreted in either the Comparison Group Findings or Job-Relevant Correlates sections of the report until the score exceeds 56T. As displayed on page 7 of Mr. Z's FCIR, only one of the substantive scale scores, DOM (27T), is interpretable (DOM is one of several Specific Problems scales that is interpreted at both high and low levels), and it is three standard deviations below the mean for the comparison group (48T, $SD = 7$). No member of the Firefighter Candidate Comparison Group produced a score below 34T.

Findings in the Job-Relevant Correlates section indicate risks associated with 4 of the 10 problem domains (Emotional Control and Stress Tolerance Problems, Routine Task Performance Problems, Decision-Making and Judgment Problems, and Assertiveness Problems), all of which derive from Mr. Z's low score on DOM, which, as described in the Comparison Group Findings sections, indicates "a level of interpersonal passivity that is very likely incompatible with public safety requirements for assertiveness" (p. 9).

Background Findings

The background investigation revealed that Mr. Z is well regarded by the hiring agency based on his performance over the course of 4 years as a volunteer firefighter. During this time, he also performed as a "sleeper" (working 24-hour shifts alongside paid professional firefighters/medics) while completing his studies and practicum for his paramedic certificate, which he finished 1 month prior. Notably, several references who worked beside Mr. Z at the fire district cited his ability to engage people, confront them when necessary, and gain their compliance. He has no history of disciplinary action or counterproductive behavior on or off the job, and there were no other adverse findings reported from the background investigation.

Interview Findings

Mr. Z presented as reserved and quiet, but not shy. He maintained good eye contact throughout the interview and engaged the examiner appropriately. Consistent with the advice provided in this book to not ask the candidate to explain item responses associated with an elevated scale (at least not by reciting an item verbatim), the examiner explained to Mr. Z that his test results suggest that he sees himself as being unassertive and asked the candidate to talk about how that is manifested both at and away from work. Mr. Z explained that he is "low-key" and is comfortable deferring to the wants and interests of others in his personal life, because most things "just don't matter as much to me as they seem to matter to others." As an example, he said that he defers to his girlfriend to choose restaurants, movies, weekend activities, and so on, because she has strong opinions about what she likes, and he does not care as much. On the other hand, he said that when it comes to issues about which he either feels strongly or over which he has responsibility, he is not passive but also not authoritarian or abrasive in presenting his position. He appeared in the interview to be self-reflective and nondefensive.

Discussion

Practice guidance (e.g., IACP, 2020) cautions against making suitability determinations based on a single test score or any other single data source, unless justified. Throughout this book, we have emphasized the importance of weighing findings from all data sources before reaching a suitability determination. In the current case involving Mr. Z, only his low score on DOM is interpretable. There are potential implications for low dominance/high passivity in public safety personnel, but the base rate of low dominance in public safety personnel is quite low (only 0.5% of the members of the Firefighter Candidate Comparison Group scored in the interpretable low range [< 39T] and none produced a score as low as Mr. Z), thereby inhibiting the identification of any performance correlations. Moreover, to the extent that Mr. Z's DOM score may be more a reflection of a disinclination to persuade or control rather than a preference for not asserting his opinion when it is needed, it is worth noting that persuasiveness is not a highly weighted characteristic in firefighters, in contrast to police and correctional officers (see chapter 1). Finally, Mr. Z's background informants reported no problems with assertiveness as a volunteer (and part-time paid) firefighter over a period of 4 years in the same agency to which he is now applying. Thus, applying Step 5b of our integrative model (Table 8.1)—consideration of divergent data that might mitigate the risk-related findings—the background information carries significant weight because of its relevance and reliability. In consideration of these facts, the examiner concluded that Mr. Z **meets** the agency's criterion standard.

EVIDENCE-BASED REPORT WRITING USING THE PSCIRS

The prospective audiences of a written report documenting the findings and suitability determination from a preemployment psychological evaluation are many and varied. In addition to the hiring agency, future readers may include the candidate, a second-opinion psychologist or other expert reviewer, legal counsel for the employer or plaintiff, a civil service commission or appeal board, the court of ultimate jurisdiction, and the psychologist's licensing board and professional ethics committee. In the unfortunate event of a serious future adverse event after a candidate is hired, the report may be read by a host of others responding to or adjudicating the event. To some degree, the report reflects how the writer considers the interests of each of these potential audiences. Collectively, these audiences coalesce to underscore three important functions of a written preemployment psychological evaluation report.

Functions of a Written Report

Reaching and Documenting the Suitability Determination

When writing a report using the data integration model as a framework, the screening psychologist describes the job-relevant, risk-related findings from the psychological testing, personal history, and clinical interview; describes any mitigating facts supported by the evidence and how they weigh against some or all of these risks; and then explains their rationale for the opinion that the aggregate findings warrant qualification or disqualification. This written analytic process is essentially "thinking out loud" and serves both to facilitate the formation of the suitability determination and to document it for the hiring agency and other prospective readers.

Explaining the Evidentiary Support and Rationale for the Suitability Determination

"Explanations, not opinions, are the reason one is an expert" (Grisso, 2008, p. 33). Even if the screening psychologist were able to work through the data integration process and make a suitability judgment without a written report, it is still necessary to explain the evidence relied on for that judgment, as well as how the assessor arrived at the determination. Otto and colleagues (2014) observe, "the only time the expert is in complete control of the information that is and is not presented is when writing the report" (p. 12). The attentive screening psychologist will include in the report those risk-related findings and inferences that are consequential and relevant to the selection criteria.

A well-written report "connects the dots," shows what the evaluator thinks and why, and explains the evaluator's rejection of other possible opinions and conclusions. Grisso (2008) regards the act of writing one's conclusions in a psychological assessment report as a form of hypothesis testing. Having formed a general idea of the conclusion, Grisso contends that writing the explanation for that conclusion "forces us to lay the foundation for how we got there; having to describe that foundation in detail inevitably identifies challenges to our conclusion; and usually this will (or should) modify our thinking" (p. 67).

Dissuading Challenges and Repelling Criticism

In addition to helping reach and document the suitability determination and explaining the evidentiary support and rationale, a third function of the written report is to provide prospective challengers and critics of the evaluation (e.g., civil service commissioners, plaintiff's attorney, second-opinion evaluator, licensing board, or ethics panel) with a clear and compelling testimonial record. The quality of a preemployment psychological screening report is ultimately judged not by whether only one suitability determination could have been reached from the data but, rather, by whether the suitability determination was justified based on valid, reliable, and job-relevant data. In other words, assuming that the evaluation was performed using proper procedures and methods, the important consideration is not whether the report writer "got it right" but rather whether other reasonable experts could have reached the same conclusions. The evaluator is best positioned to articulate how and why the suitability judgment was made, and the best opportunity to make the case is when the facts and rationale are fresh in the assessor's mind. As Appelbaum (2010) observed, "the quality of our reports is often the most tangible and visible measure of our professionalism" (p. 43), and is the single best—indeed, perhaps even the only—opportunity to produce an extemporaneous record of the examiner's rationale for their opinion. The report serves to dissuade potential challenges and repel criticism, and it also creates a testimonial record of how the psychologist integrated the assessment data to form their suitability determination and why they rejected alternative interpretations and inferences.

Minimum Elements of a Written Report

In a preemployment psychological evaluation of a police or other public safety candidate, no single format is required except when mandated by law, regulation, or the hiring authority. The IACP Police Psychological Services Section's Preemployment Psychological Evaluation Guidelines (IACP, 2020) recommend that, at a minimum, written reports (a) include a "clear determination of the candidate's psychological suitability for employment based upon an analysis of all psychological assessment materials, including background information, test data, and interview results" (Guideline 11.1); (b) include ratings or recommendations expressly linked to the selection criteria for the position (11.2); and (c) focus "on the individual candidate's ability to safely and effectively perform the essential functions of the position under consideration" (11.3). The evidence-based findings from a PSCIR can contribute to each of these three elements.

Provides General Guidance

Because the written report has both an immediate audience (the hiring agency) and prospective audiences, care must be taken to ensure that the testimonial record clearly states and adequately explains the examiner's determination and contains nothing to unnecessarily undermine confidence in that decision. These objectives are best met by a narrative that clearly states the examiner's opinions and is well written, error free, jargon free, precise, internally consistent (i.e., contains no contradictions), and objective. Otto and colleagues (2014) and Corey and Zelig (2020) provide valuable advice for writing psychological reports (including suitability and fitness-for-duty evaluation reports) that meet each of these objectives.

Using Findings From the PSCIR

We developed the four PSCIRs so that the evidence-based, risk-related statements could be incorporated easily into a screening professional's written report. Although the PSCIRs are protected by copyright law, the fair use doctrine allows users to extract text from a PSCIR and insert it into their written report as they deem appropriate. When doing so, it is necessary that the examiner decide first that the evidence-based inference is supported by the MMPI-3 score when considered in the context of the other assessment data, as illustrated throughout this chapter.

In the following example involving Mr. N, a 28-year-old male police candidate, the evaluation was based on findings from the MMPI-3 PCIR (Figure 8.10), normal personality testing, self-reported personal history, the hiring agency's background information, and clinical interview. Using the data integrative model, the screening psychologist wrote the following report narrative:

> The findings from this assessment appear to be reliable and reveal no evidence of a psychological disorder that would preclude safe and effective performance as a police officer. However, Mr. N's responses to personality testing produced valid findings characterized by significant deviations from police candidate norms. He reported a variety of problems and experiences that are reported, on average, by fewer than 4.0% of police candidates, including self-doubt, behavior-restricting fears, disconstrained behavior, poor

impulse control, family conflict, and social inhibition. In addition, he reported a comparatively high level of irresponsible behavior for a police candidate, with only 3.0% of police candidates on average conveying this level or greater of acting out. He also reported a relatively high level of disaffiliativeness for a police candidate; only 2.0% of police candidates report this or a greater level of disinterest in interacting with others. These test scores correspond with empirical research findings that indicate he is more likely than other police candidates to be self-defeating, lack confidence in his own abilities, have a history of job performance problems, brush-off criticism, be unsure and act hesitantly, and to be self-indulgent, among other behavioral characteristics.

The test results also place him at elevated risk for a wide range of counterproductive behaviors as a police officer, including: difficulties performing under stressful conditions and cognitive adaptation problems; difficulties engaging or confronting subjects in circumstances in which an officer would normally approach or intervene; difficulties demonstrating a command presence and controlling situations requiring order or resolution; difficulties cooperating with peers or supervisors; difficulties leading to integrity violations, sustained internal affairs investigations, complaints from the public, and investigations about conduct unbecoming a police officer; difficulties with punctuality and attendance, and with reliable work behavior and dependable follow-through; and problems reacting to situations with the proper degree of emotional and behavior restraint and control, and avoiding impulsive or unnecessarily risky behavior.

When judging the validity of test-based predictions, a source of data normally relied upon—although not dispositive—is contemporary evidence of performance in other situations, particularly in situations similar to those in a job candidate's targeted position. In that regard, it is compelling to note that both of Mr. N's current supervisors reported negative information concerning his performance. One supervisor reported that Mr. N's work productivity was dramatically below par for a worker with his level of experience and that he had difficulty performing without direct supervision. This supervisor attributed Mr. N's performance problems to difficulty making decisions on his own. Another supervisor reported that Mr. N "has had trouble focusing on his work, making mistakes more frequently," and "does not seem to care as much about working hard or the quality of his work as he used to." This same supervisor said that Mr. N "takes criticism personally" and "sometimes gets defensive about it," including being "in a bad mood the rest of the day." Finally, he noted that Mr. N "gets easily flustered or frustrated when either they have a large amount of work to be done or something comes up unexpectedly. He said this has been true of [Mr. N] the entire time he has been employed" at Acme Consulting. Neither supervisor recommended Mr. N for a law enforcement officer position.

These collateral reports of employment-related problems are consistent with the findings from personality testing that show a tendency to be lacking in self-confidence, socially inhibited, and irresponsible. In addition, Mr. N's test results that indicate a comparatively high level of antisocial behavior for a police candidate are particularly problematic in light of the background investigation report of a domestic assault six years ago in which he slapped a previous girlfriend in the face when he learned she was involved romantically with another person.

Although there are attributes of Mr. N that render him an attractive candidate for a law enforcement position (e.g., he presented as polite, considerate, and well-mannered in the interview; he was professional and thoughtful in his answers; and he communicated effectively), the consistency between test result findings and his background (both recent and remote) produce a compelling basis for concluding that he is at high risk for similar kinds of counterproductive behavior in a law enforcement position, particularly with respect to problems in emotional control and stress tolerance, impulse control and attention to safety, and decision-making and judgment. In addition, I found no persuasive evidence that mitigates or outweighs the risk-related findings. Therefore, in consideration of the full range of assessment and supplemental data available to me, I conclude that Mr. N **does not meet** the criterion standard for psychological qualification as a police officer with the Acme Police Department.

In this example, the examiner used the base-rate information contained in the Comparison Group Findings section of the PCIR (Figure 8.10, pp. 9–10) both to describe the problematic personality findings and to show how unusual they are for police candidates. The examiner then used the findings from the Job-Relevant Correlates section (Figure 8.10, pp. 10–11) to describe how these problematic traits are likely to manifest as a police officer or trainee and in what problem domains they are likely to occur. The examiner's use of the content in the Comparison Group Findings and Job-Relevant Correlates sections of the PCIR contributed to an explanatory report narrative that anchored the determination (unqualified) to the candidate's personality traits and to risk-related findings. This occurred both retrospectively by linking the test results with past problems identified in the background investigation and prospectively by linking them to likely future counterproductive behavior as a police officer or trainee. Finally, the examiner explained the rejection of alternative interpretations of the evidence.

The written narrative also reflects the examiner's use of the integrative model. It begins with consideration of the validity and reliability of the assessment findings; proceeds to a discussion of job-relevant, risk-related findings

Minnesota Multiphasic Personality Inventory®-3

Yossef S. Ben-Porath
Auke Tellegen

MMPI®-3
Police Candidate Interpretive Report
David M. Corey, PhD, & Yossef S. Ben-Porath, PhD

ID Number:	Mr. N
Age:	28
Gender:	Male
Marital Status:	Not reported
Years of Education:	Not reported
Date Assessed:	12/13/2022

Copyright © 2020 by the Regents of the University of Minnesota. All rights reserved. Distributed exclusively under license from the University of Minnesota by NCS Pearson, Inc. Portions reproduced from the *MMPI-3 English Test Booklet.* Copyright © 2020 by the Regents of the University of Minnesota. All rights reserved. Portions excerpted from the *MMPI-3 Manual for Administration, Scoring, and Interpretation.* Copyright © 2020 by the Regents of the University of Minnesota. All rights reserved. Portions excerpted from the *MMPI-3 Technical Manual.* Copyright © 2020 by the Regents of the University of Minnesota. All rights reserved. Used by permission of the University of Minnesota Press.

Minnesota Multiphasic Personality Inventory and **MMPI** are registered trademarks of the Regents of the University of Minnesota. **Pearson** is a trademark, in the US and/or other countries, of Pearson Education, Inc., or its affiliates.

This report contains copyrighted material and trade secrets. Qualified licensees may excerpt portions of this output report, limited to the minimum text necessary to accurately describe their significant core conclusions, for incorporation into a written evaluation of the examinee, in accordance with their profession's citation standards, if any. No adaptations, translations, modifications, or special versions may be made of this report without prior written permission from the University of Minnesota Press.

[1.4 / RE1 / QG1]

ALWAYS LEARNING   PEARSON

FIGURE 8.10. Mr. N's MMPI-3 Police Candidate Interpretive Report

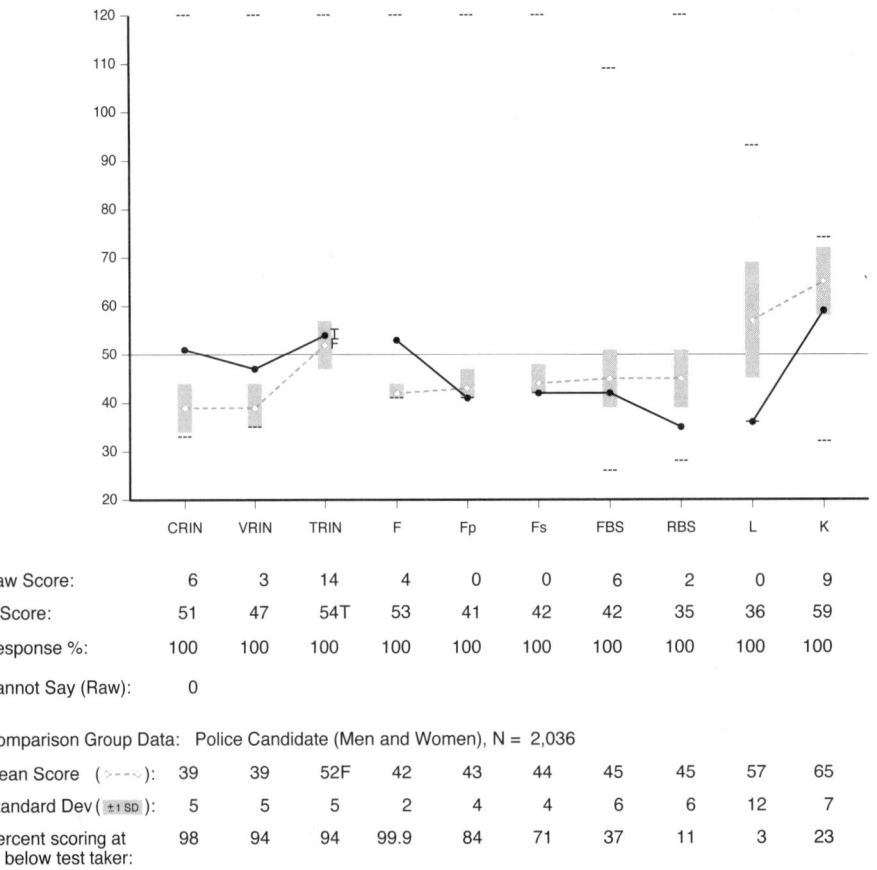

FIGURE 8.10. Mr. N's MMPI-3 Police Candidate Interpretive Report, continued

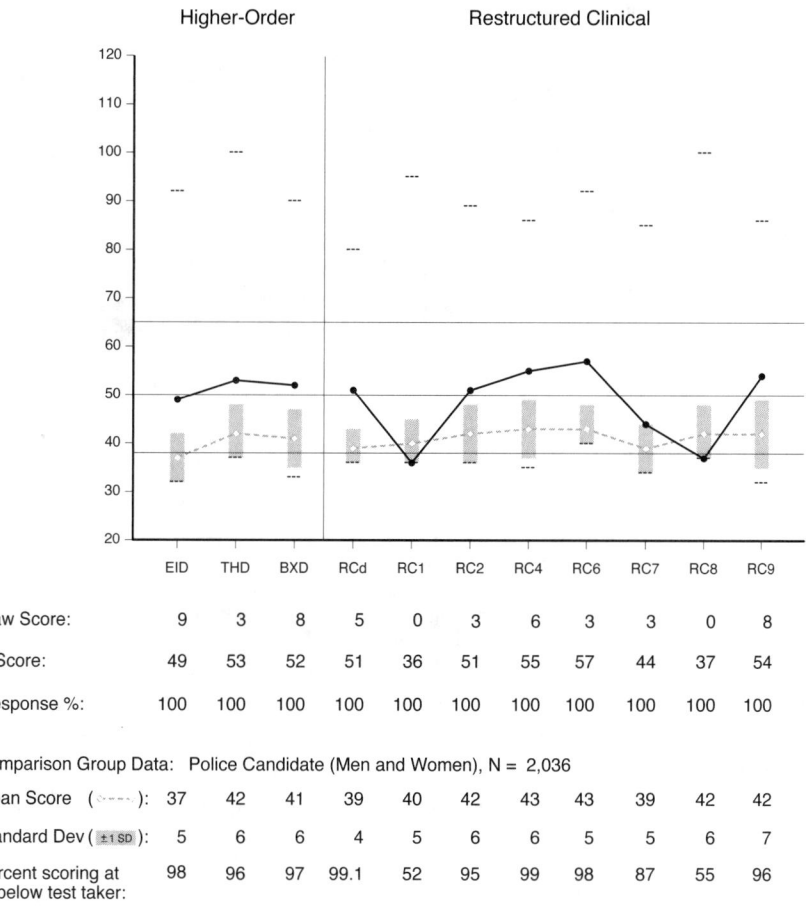

FIGURE 8.10. Mr. N's MMPI-3 Police Candidate Interpretive Report, continued

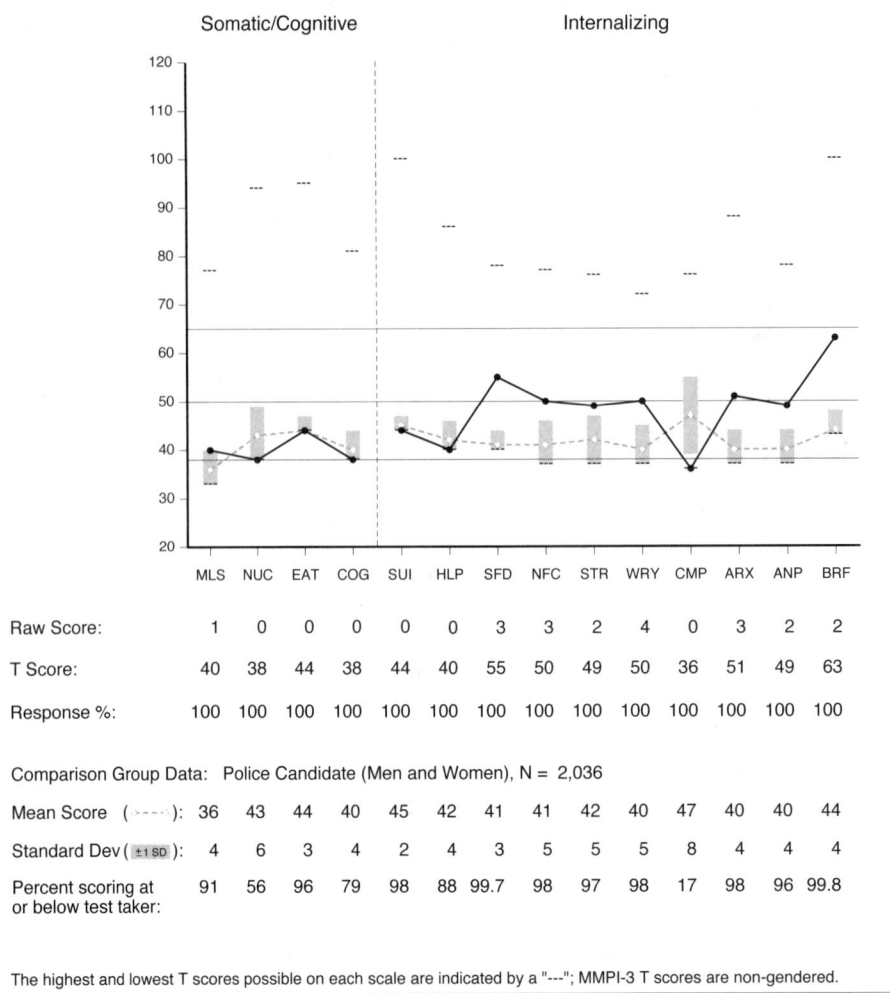

FIGURE 8.10. Mr. N's MMPI-3 Police Candidate Interpretive Report, continued

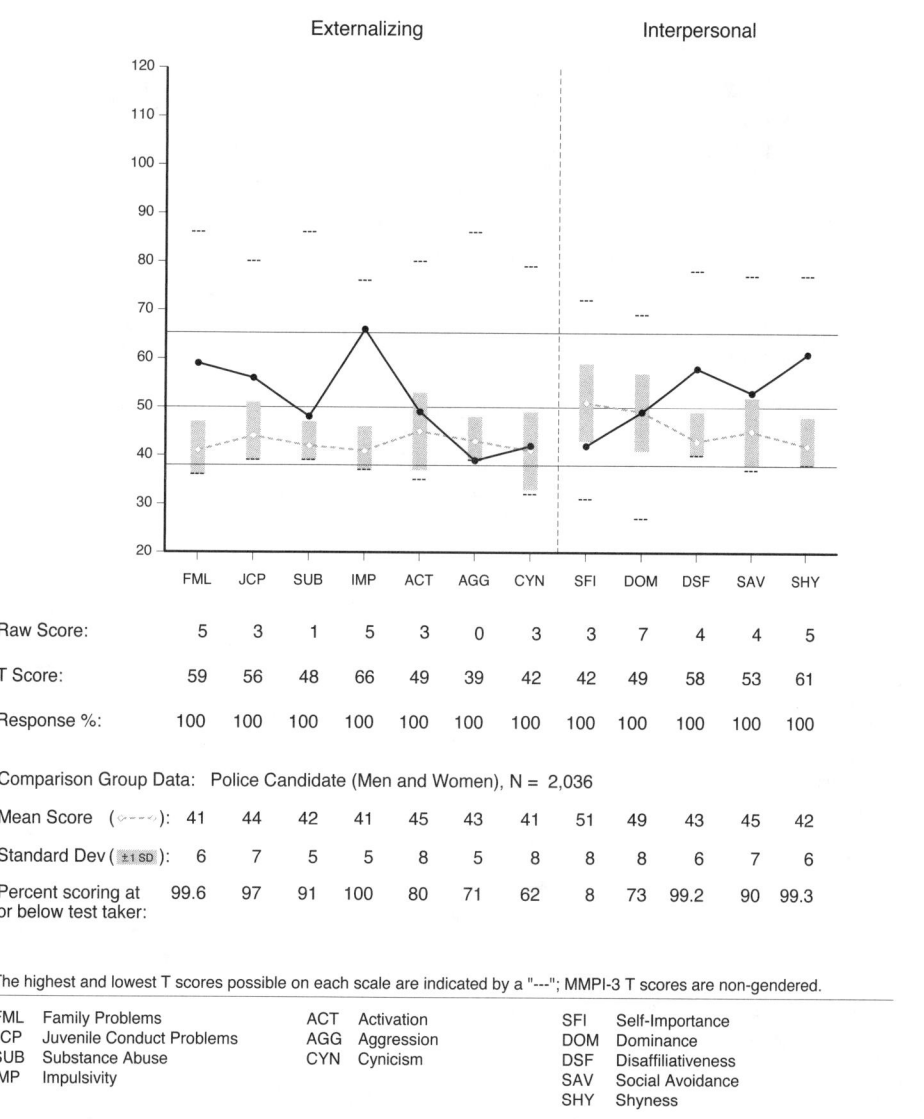

FIGURE 8.10. Mr. N's MMPI-3 Police Candidate Interpretive Report, continued

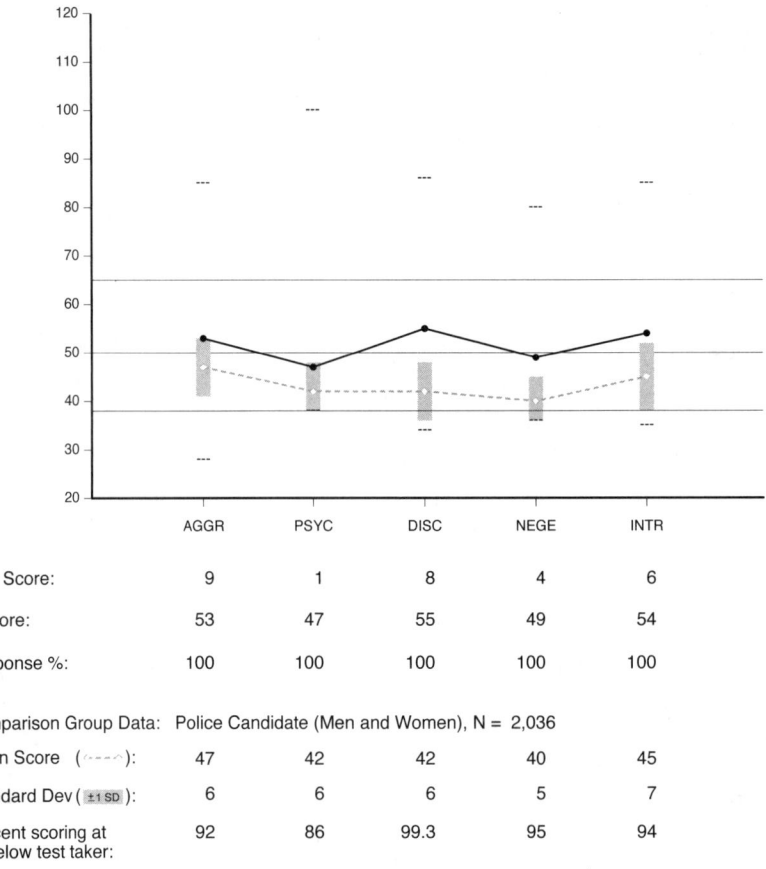

FIGURE 8.10. Mr. N's MMPI-3 Police Candidate Interpretive Report, continued

MMPI-3 T SCORES (BY DOMAIN)

PROTOCOL VALIDITY

Content Non-Responsiveness

0	51	47	54 T
CNS	CRIN	VRIN	TRIN

Over-Reporting

53	41		42	42	35
F	Fp		Fs	FBS	RBS

Under-Reporting

36	59
L	K

SUBSTANTIVE SCALES

Somatic/Cognitive Dysfunction

	36	40	38	44	38
	RC1	MLS	NUC	EAT	COG

Emotional Dysfunction

49	51	44	40	**55**	50		
EID	RCd	SUI	HLP	**SFD**	NFC		
	51	54					
	RC2	INTR					
	44	49	50	36	51	49	**63**	49
	RC7	STR	WRY	CMP	ARX	ANP	**BRF**	NEGE

Thought Dysfunction

53	**57**
THD	**RC6**
	37
	RC8
	47
	PSYC

Behavioral Dysfunction

52	**55**	**59**	56	48
BXD	**RC4**	**FML**	JCP	SUB
	54	**66**	49	39	42
	RC9	**IMP**	ACT	AGG	CYN
	55				
	DISC				

Interpersonal Functioning

	42	49	53	**58**	53	**61**
	SFI	DOM	AGGR	**DSF**	SAV	**SHY**

Scale scores shown in bold font are interpreted in the report.

Note. This information is provided to facilitate interpretation following the recommended structure for MMPI-3 interpretation in Chapter 5 of the *MMPI-3 Manual for Administration, Scoring, and Interpretation*, which provides details in the text and an outline in Table 5-1.

FIGURE 8.10. Mr. N's MMPI-3 Police Candidate Interpretive Report, continued

This interpretive report is intended for use by a professional qualified to interpret the MMPI-3 in the context of preemployment psychological evaluations of police and other law enforcement candidates. **It focuses on identifying problems; it does not convey potential strengths.** The information it contains should be considered in the context of the test taker's background, the demands of the position under consideration, the clinical interview, findings from supplemental tests, and other relevant information.

The interpretive statements in the Protocol Validity section of the report are based on T scores derived from the general MMPI-3 normative sample, as well as scores obtained by the multisite sample of 2,036 individuals that make up the Police Candidate Comparison Group.

The interpretive statements in the Clinical Findings and Diagnostic Considerations sections of the report are based on T scores derived from the general MMPI-3 normative sample. Following recommended practice, only T scores of 65 and higher (with a few exceptions) are considered clinically significant. Scores at this clinical level are generally rare among police candidates.

Statements in the Comparison Group Findings and Job-Relevant Correlates sections are based on comparisons with scores obtained by the Police Candidate Comparison Group. Statements in these sections may be based on T scores that, although less than 65, are nevertheless uncommon in reference to the comparison group.

The report includes extensive annotation, which appears as superscripts following each statement in the narrative, keyed to Endnotes with accompanying Research References, which appear in the final two sections of the report. Additional information about the annotation features is provided in the headnotes to these sections and in the MMPI-3 User's Guide for the Public Safety Candidate Interpretive Reports.

SYNOPSIS

This is a valid MMPI-3 protocol. Scores on the Substantive Scales indicate clinically significant behavioral dysfunction. Behavioral-externalizing problems relate to impulsivity.

Comparison group findings point to additional possible concerns about self-doubt, persecutory beliefs, irresponsible behavior, family conflict, disaffiliativeness, and shyness.

Possible job-relevant problems are identified in the following domains: Emotional Control and Stress Tolerance, Routine Task Performance, Decision-Making and Judgment, Feedback Acceptance, Assertiveness, Social Competence and Teamwork, Integrity, Conscientiousness and Dependability, Substance Use, and Impulse Control.

PROTOCOL VALIDITY

This is a valid MMPI-3 protocol. There are no problems with unscorable items. The test taker responded to the items relevantly on the basis of their content, and there are no indications of over- or under-reporting.

It is worth noting that the test taker claimed no uncommon virtues[1]. This very rare pattern of responding is found in only 3% of the Police Candidate Comparison Group members.

FIGURE 8.10. Mr. N's MMPI-3 Police Candidate Interpretive Report, continued

CLINICAL FINDINGS

Clinical-level symptoms, personality characteristics, and behavioral tendencies of the test taker are described in this section and organized according to an empirically guided framework. (Please see Chapter 5 of the MMPI-3 Manual for Administration, Scoring, and Interpretation *for details.) Statements containing the word "reports" are based on the item content of MMPI-3 scales, whereas statements that include the word "likely" are based on empirical correlates of scale scores. Specific sources for each statement can be viewed with the annotation features of this report.*

The test taker reports engaging in problematic impulsive behavior[2]. He indeed likely engages in non-planful behavior[3] and has poor impulse control and a history of hyperactive behavior[3].

There are no indications of clinically significant somatic, cognitive, emotional, or thought dysfunction in this protocol.

DIAGNOSTIC CONSIDERATIONS

This section provides recommendations for psychodiagnostic assessment based on the test taker's MMPI-3 results. It is recommended that he be evaluated for the following:

Behavioral-Externalizing Disorders

- Impulse-control disorders[4]

COMPARISON GROUP FINDINGS

This section describes the MMPI-3 substantive scale findings in the context of the Police Candidate Comparison Group. Specific sources for each statement can be accessed with the annotation features of this report.
Job-related correlates of these results, if any, are provided in the subsequent Job-Relevant Correlates section.

Emotional/Internalizing Problems

The test taker reports a comparatively high level of behavior-restricting fears for a police candidate[5]. Only 1.0% of comparison group members convey this or a greater level of fears that restrict normal behavior.

He reports a comparatively high level of self-doubt for a police candidate[6]. Only 1.0% of comparison group members convey this or a greater lack of confidence.

Unusual Thoughts, Perceptions, and Beliefs

The test taker reports a comparatively high level of persecutory beliefs for a police candidate[7]. Only 4.0% of comparison group members convey this or a greater level of persecutory thinking.

Behavioral/Externalizing Problems

The test taker reports a comparatively high level of disconstraint for a police candidate[8]. Only 2.0% of comparison group members convey this or a greater level of disconstrained behavior. More specifically, he reports a relatively high level of irresponsible behavior for a police candidate[9]. Only 3.0% of comparison group members convey this or a greater level of acting out.

His responses indicate a level of impulsive behavior that may be incompatible with public safety requirements for behavioral control[4]. This level of impulsivity is uncommon among police candidates. Only 0.4% of comparison group members give evidence of this or a greater level of poor impulse control.

FIGURE 8.10. Mr. N's MMPI-3 Police Candidate Interpretive Report, continued

Interpersonal Problems

The test taker reports a comparatively high level of family conflict for a police candidate[10]. Only 1.0% of comparison group members convey this or a greater level of family problems. He also reports a relatively high level of disaffiliativeness for a police candidate[11]. Only 2.0% of comparison group members convey this or a greater level of disinterest in interacting with others. In addition, he reports a comparatively high level of social anxiety for a police candidate[12]. Only 2.0% of comparison group members convey this or a greater level of shyness and inhibition.

JOB-RELEVANT CORRELATES

Job-relevant personality characteristics and behavioral tendencies of the test taker are described in this section and organized according to ten problem domains commonly identified in the professional literature as relevant to public safety candidate suitability. (Please see MMPI-3 User's Guide for the Public Safety Candidate Interpretive Reports *for details.) Statements that begin with "Compared with other police candidates" are based on correlations with other self-report measures obtained in police candidate samples that included individuals who were subsequently hired as well as those who were not. Statements that begin with "He is more likely than most police officers or trainees" are based on correlations with outcome data obtained in samples of hired candidates during academy or field training, probation, and/or the postprobation period. Specific sources for each statement can be accessed with the annotation features of this report.*

Emotional Control and Stress Tolerance Problems

Compared with other police candidates, the test taker is more likely to have difficulty coping with stress[13]; to behave in a self-defeating fashion[14]; and to easily become irritated and annoyed by others[15]. He is also more likely to become impatient with others over minor infractions[15]; to have trouble tolerating ambiguous, confusing, and unstructured environments[16]; and to develop physical symptoms in response to stress and worry about his health[17]. In addition, he is more likely to believe he has been mistreated[18]; to have a history of adverse childhood experiences[19]; and to overreact to minor frustrations[15].

He is more likely than most police officers or trainees to exhibit difficulties performing under stressful conditions[20].

Routine Task Performance Problems

Compared with other police candidates, the test taker is more likely to be lacking in confidence in his own abilities[14]; to have a history of motor vehicle violations or difficulties[21]; and to have a history of job performance problems[22].

He is more likely than most police officers or trainees to exhibit cognitive adaptation problems[20].

Decision-Making and Judgment Problems

Compared with other police candidates, the test taker is more likely to avoid making decisions, fail to take action, or do anything that may prompt scrutiny from others[23]. He is also more likely to be made anxious by change and uncertainty[14] and to exhibit difficulty with decision-making and judgment[24].

Feedback Acceptance Problems

Compared with other police candidates, the test taker is less likely to reflect on his behavior[25] and more likely to brush off criticism and other negative feedback[25].

Assertiveness Problems

Compared with other police candidates, the test taker is more likely to be ill at ease in dealing with others[26]; to feel inadequate[27]; and to be unsure and act hesitantly[27]. He is also more likely to lack assertiveness[17].

He is more likely than most police officers or trainees to exhibit difficulties engaging or confronting subjects in circumstances in which an officer would normally approach or intervene[28]. He is also more likely to exhibit

FIGURE 8.10. Mr. N's MMPI-3 Police Candidate Interpretive Report, continued

difficulties in demonstrating a command presence and controlling situations requiring order or resolution[29].

Social Competence and Teamwork Problems
Compared with other police candidates, the test taker is more likely to be self-centered[30]; to engage in conflicts with authority[31]; and to have a history of problems getting along with others[32]. He is also more likely to have difficulty creating and sustaining mutually satisfying relationships[33]; to have a limited social support network[34]; and to prefer to work out problems alone[35]. In addition, he is more likely to be seen by others as socially detached and emotionally distant[35]; to feel maligned by others[18]; and to have problems with social competence[36]. He is more likely to have difficulties with teamwork[24].

He is more likely than most police officers or trainees to exhibit difficulties cooperating with peers and/or supervisors[20].

Integrity Problems
Compared with other police candidates, the test taker is more likely to fail to integrate ethical considerations into his decision-making[22]; to have a history of conflicts with the law and other violations of social norms[37]; and to lack a commitment to societal rules[38]. He is also more likely to be self-indulgent[38]; to report a history of committing theft[39]; and to be nonconforming[40].

He is more likely than most police officers or trainees to exhibit difficulties leading to integrity violations[41]; sustained internal affairs investigations[41]; and complaints from the public[42]. He is also more likely to exhibit difficulties leading to investigations about conduct unbecoming a police officer[42].

Conscientiousness and Dependability Problems
Compared with other police candidates, the test taker is more likely to give up easily and not persevere in the face of challenges[23]; to have a history of absenteeism or tardiness[43]; and to have a history of failing to meet obligations[44].

He is more likely than most police officers or trainees to exhibit difficulties with punctuality and attendance[45] and with reliable work behavior and dependable follow-through[29].

Substance Use Problems
Compared with other police candidates, the test taker is more likely to have a history of substance use problems[46].

Impulse Control Problems
Compared with other police candidates, the test taker is more likely to behave impulsively or without adequate consideration of the consequences or implications of his actions[47]; to have a history of physical aggression[44]; and to have a history of anger management problems[48]. He is also more likely to be rebellious and lack discipline[15]; to be nonplanful[49]; and to be unpredictable in behavior and attitudes[50].

He is more likely than most police officers or trainees to exhibit problems reacting to situations with the proper degree of emotional and behavioral restraint and control, and avoiding impulsive and/or unnecessarily risky behavior[25].

ITEM-LEVEL INFORMATION

Unscorable Responses
The test taker produced scorable responses to all the MMPI-3 items.

FIGURE 8.10. Mr. N's MMPI-3 Police Candidate Interpretive Report, continued

Critical Responses

Seven MMPI-3 scales—Suicidal/Death Ideation (SUI), Helplessness/Hopelessness (HLP), Anxiety-Related Experiences (ARX), Ideas of Persecution (RC6), Aberrant Experiences (RC8), Substance Abuse (SUB), and Aggression (AGG)—have been designated by the test authors as having critical item content that may require immediate attention and follow-up. Items answered by the individual in the keyed direction (True or False) on a critical scale are listed below if his T score on that scale is 65 or higher. However, any item answered in the keyed direction on SUI is listed.

The test taker has not produced an elevated T score (≥ 65) on any of these scales or answered any SUI items in the keyed direction.

Critical Follow-up Items

This section contains a list of items to which the test taker responded in a manner warranting follow-up. The items were identified by public safety candidate screening experts as having critical content. Clinicians are encouraged to follow up on these statements with the candidate by making related inquiries, rather than reciting the item(s) verbatim. Each item is followed by the candidate's response, the percentage of Police Candidate Comparison Group members who gave this response, and the scale(s) on which the item appears.

Item number and content omitted. (True; 5.1%; BXD, RC9, IMP, DISC)
Item number and content omitted. (True; 2.3%; ARX)
Item number and content omitted. (True; 19.4%; BXD, RC9, IMP, DISC)
Item number and content omitted. (True; 2.1%; IMP)
Item number and content omitted. (True; 2.0%; ARX)
Item number and content omitted. (True; 2.8%; WRY, NEGE)
Item number and content omitted. (True; 12.7%; ARX)
Item number and content omitted. (True; 1.5%; VRIN, F, THD, RC6, PSYC)
Item number and content omitted. (True; 5.0%; VRIN, BXD, RC9, IMP, DISC)
Item number and content omitted. (True; 13.5%; ANP)

FIGURE 8.10. Mr. N's MMPI-3 Police Candidate Interpretive Report, continued

ENDNOTES

This section lists for each statement in the report the MMPI-3 score(s) that triggered it. In addition, each statement is identified as a <u>Test Response</u>, if based on item content, a <u>Correlate</u>, if based on empirical correlates, or an <u>Inference</u>, if based on the report authors' judgment. (This information can also be accessed on-screen by placing the cursor on a given statement.) For correlate-based statements, research references (Ref. No.) are provided, keyed to the consecutively numbered reference list following the endnotes.

[1] Test Response: L=36
[2] Test Response: IMP=66
[3] Correlate: IMP=66, Ref. 1, 2
[4] Inference: IMP=66
[5] Test Response: BRF=63
[6] Test Response: SFD=55
[7] Test Response: RC6=57
[8] Test Response: DISC=55
[9] Test Response: RC4=55
[10] Test Response: FML=59
[11] Test Response: DSF=58
[12] Test Response: SHY=61
[13] Correlate: SFD=55, Ref. 5, 11
[14] Correlate: SHY=61, Ref. 2, 3
[15] Correlate: RC4=55, Ref. 3
[16] Correlate: BRF=63, Ref. 9
[17] Correlate: SFD=55, Ref. 11
[18] Correlate: RC6=57, Ref. 3
[19] Correlate: FML=59, Ref. 10
[20] Correlate: DSF=58, Ref. 2
[21] Correlate: RC4=55, Ref. 4
[22] Correlate: RC4=55, Ref. 9
[23] Correlate: SHY=61, Ref. 3, 9
[24] Correlate: RC6=57, Ref. 11
[25] Correlate: DISC=55, Ref. 9
[26] Correlate: DSF=58, Ref. 2, 3; SHY=61, Ref. 3, 4, 9
[27] Correlate: SHY=61, Ref. 2, 3, 4, 9
[28] Correlate: DSF=58, Ref. 7
[29] Correlate: DSF=58, Ref. 6, 7
[30] Correlate: RC4=55, Ref. 2; FML=59, Ref. 2
[31] Correlate: RC4=55, Ref. 2, 4, 9
[32] Correlate: RC4=55, Ref. 2; DSF=58, Ref. 9
[33] Correlate: SHY=61, Ref. 3
[34] Correlate: DSF=58, Ref. 3, 9
[35] Correlate: DSF=58, Ref. 3
[36] Correlate: RC6=57, Ref. 11; DSF=58, Ref. 11
[37] Correlate: RC4=55, Ref. 2, 4, 9, 10; DISC=55, Ref. 2, 10
[38] Correlate: RC4=55, Ref. 3, 4, 9
[39] Correlate: RC4=55, Ref. 2, 10; DISC=55, Ref. 2, 10
[40] Correlate: RC4=55, Ref. 3; IMP=66, Ref. 3
[41] Correlate: RC4=55, Ref. 8, 9; DISC=55, Ref. 9
[42] Correlate: RC6=57, Ref. 8, 9
[43] Correlate: RC4=55, Ref. 4, 9
[44] Correlate: RC4=55, Ref. 2
[45] Correlate: SHY=61, Ref. 9
[46] Correlate: RC4=55, Ref. 2, 4, 6, 9, 10, 11; DISC=55, Ref. 2, 4, 9, 10, 11

FIGURE 8.10. Mr. N's MMPI-3 Police Candidate Interpretive Report, continued

[47] Correlate: RC4=55, Ref. 2, 3, 11; IMP=66, Ref. 3; DISC=55, Ref. 3, 4, 9, 11
[48] Correlate: RC4=55, Ref. 2; IMP=66, Ref. 2; DISC=55, Ref. 4, 9
[49] Correlate: IMP=66, Ref. 3
[50] Correlate: RC4=55, Ref. 3, 11; DISC=55, Ref. 3, 11

FIGURE 8.10. Mr. N's MMPI-3 Police Candidate Interpretive Report, continued

RESEARCH REFERENCE LIST

The following studies are sources for empirical correlates identified in the Endnotes section of this report.

1. Bagby, R. M., Onno, K. A., Mortezaei, A., & Sellbom, M. (2020). Examining the "Traditional Background Hypothesis" for the MMPI-2-RF L-r Scores in a Muslim Faith-Based Sample. *Psychological Assessment.* Advance online publication. https://doi.org/10.1037/pas0000941

2. Ben-Porath, Y. S., & Tellegen, A. (2020). *The Minnesota Multiphasic Personality Inventory-3 (MMPI-3): Technical manual.* University of Minnesota Press.

3. Corey, D. M., & Ben-Porath, Y. S. (2022). *Minnesota Multiphasic Personality Inventory-3 (MMPI-3): User's guide for the public safety candidate interpretive reports.* University of Minnesota Press.

4. Detrick, P., Ben-Porath, Y.S., & Sellbom, M. (2016). Associations between MMPI-2-RF (Restructured Form) and Inwald Personality Inventory (IPI) scale scores in a law enforcement preemployment screening sample. *Journal of Police and Criminal Psychology, 31,* 81–95. https://doi.org/10.1007/s11896-015-9172-7

5. Sellbom, M., Corey, D. M., & Ben-Porath, Y. S. (2021). Incremental validity of the Multidimensional Personality Questionnaire in the preemployment assessment of police officer candidates. *Criminal Justice and Behavior.* Advance online publication. https://doi.org/10.1177/00938548211033630

6. Tarescavage, A. M., Brewster, J., Corey, D. M., & Ben-Porath, Y. S. (2015). Use of pre-hire Minnesota Multiphasic Personality Inventory-2-Restructured Form (MMPI-2-RF) police candidate scores to predict supervisor ratings of post-hire performance. *Assessment, 22*(4), 411–428. https://doi.org/10.1177/1073191114548445

7. Tarescavage, A. M., Corey, D. M., & Ben-Porath, Y. S. (2015). Minnesota Multiphasic Personality Inventory-2-Restructured Form (MMPI-2-RF) predictors of police officer problem behavior. *Assessment, 22*(1), 116–132. https://doi.org/10.1177/1073191114534885

8. Tarescavage, A. M., Corey, D. M., & Ben-Porath, Y. S. (2016). A prorating method for estimating MMPI-2-RF scores from MMPI responses: Examination of score fidelity and illustration of empirical utility in the PERSEREC police integrity study sample. *Assessment, 23*(2), 173–190. https://doi.org/10.1177/1073191115575070

9. Tarescavage, A. M., Fischler, G. L., Cappo, B. M., Hill, D. O., Corey, D. M., & Ben-Porath, Y. S. (2015). Minnesota Multiphasic Personality Inventory-2-Restructured Form (MMPI-2-RF) predictors of police officer problem behavior and collateral self-report test scores. *Psychological Assessment, 27*(1), 125–137. https://doi.org/10.1037/pas0000041

10. Whitman, M. R., Corey, D. M., & Ben-Porath, Y. S. (2021). Associations between MMPI-3 and psychosocial history findings obtained in preemployment evaluations of public safety candidates [Manuscript under review].

11. Whitman, M. R., Elias, L. S., Cappo, B. M., & Ben-Porath, Y. S. (2021). Criterion validity of MMPI-3 scores in preemployment evaluations of public safety candidates. *Psychological Assessment.* Advance online publication. https://doi.org/10.1037/pas0001042

End of Report

FIGURE 8.10. Mr. N's MMPI-3 Police Candidate Interpretive Report, continued

from psychological testing, background, and interview; considers potentially mitigating information; analyzes the relevance of the unmitigated risk-related findings to the suitability criterion for the position; and concludes with the examiner's opinion concerning whether the candidate meets the psychological qualification standards. Thus, the integrative model facilitated the examiner's integration and interpretation of data from each of the assessment sources as well as the communication of those findings in a manner expected to be relevant to the employer and other potential readers.

9

Foundational Requirements for Fitness-for-Duty Evaluations

All public safety personnel have the potential to cause serious harm when they are unable to perform the job's essential functions safely and effectively—a status commonly referred to as being "unfit for duty" (Corey & Borum, 2013; Corey & Zelig, 2020; Rostow & Davis, 2004; Stone, 2000). When, based on objective evidence, it is reasonably suspected that a public safety employee is unfit for duty because of a mental health condition, an employer is both permitted and obligated to require the employee to submit to a psychological fitness-for-duty evaluation (FFDE; see, e.g., Corey & Zelig, 2020; Mayer & Corey, 2017).

Case law across the United States is replete with examples of courts having decided that an FFDE is permissible when public safety, including the safety of coworkers, is at risk. This applies equally to police officers (*Brownfield v. City of Yakima*, 2010; *Conte v. Horcher*, 1977; *Krocka v. City of Chicago*, 2000; *Watson v. City of Miami Beach*, 1999), correctional officers (*Colon v. City of Newark*, 2006; *Flynn v. Sandahl*, 1995; *Rice v. City of Oakland*, 1999), dispatchers (*Wisbey v. City of Lincoln*, 2009), and firefighters/medics (*Aldrup v. Caldera*, 2001; *Coffman v. Indianapolis Fire Department*, 2009; *Jenkins v. City of Sandusky*, 2008).

In this chapter, we discuss (a) the professional practice guidelines that inform how fitness evaluations are conducted, (b) how the fitness criterion standard is determined, (c) the legal foundations for conducting fitness evaluations, (d) guidance for conducting fitness evaluations in the absence of legal standards, (e) the use of psychological testing and collateral data in assessing fitness, and (f) reporting findings and opinions from fitness evaluations.

PROFESSIONAL PRACTICE GUIDELINES

Two sources of professional practice guidance are available to psychologists who conduct FFDEs of police officers and other public safety personnel. These are the APA's (2018) *Professional Practice Guidelines for Occupationally Mandated Psychological Evaluations* (OMPE Guidelines) discussed in chapter 1 (see Table 1.6 for a listing of the guideline statements), and the IACP-PPSS *Fitness-for-Duty Evaluation Guidelines* (IACP, 2018; FFDE Guidelines). In addition to underscoring the broad principles of ethical practice applied to these evaluations, both sets of guidelines emphasize the importance of ensuring that the criterion for assessing fitness is identified and that an FFDE is justified by law and institutional policy; that multiple sources of relevant and valid data are used; and that findings, opinions, and conclusions are properly and narrowly communicated. We next turn to a discussion of each of these topics.

IDENTIFYING THE FITNESS CRITERION

As in any forensic mental health assessment, an FFDE begins with an understanding of the psycholegal question(s) underlying the referral (APA, 2018; Corey & Zelig, 2020; Heilbrun et al., 2009). How is fitness or, alternatively, unfitness defined under the terms of law, regulation, administrative rule, and institutional policy? Without an understanding of the fitness criterion provided by the answer to this question, evaluators cannot decide what to evaluate, what to make of their findings, or even assess their own competency to conduct the evaluation. Without a criterion standard, a fitness examiner is flying blind.

For purposes of an FFDE of a public safety employee, two primary sources establish the fitness criterion in the United States. The first is the collective body of statutory, regulatory, and case law pertaining to the Americans With Disabilities Act, as amended (ADA, 1991; ADAAA, 2008) and its state progeny, which may be even more (but cannot be less) restrictive. The second source is federal and state laws pertaining to the position. We summarize next how these laws interweave to inform both procedures and standards for conducting FFDEs of public safety employees. We also discuss several landmark cases that illustrate how courts interpret and apply these statutes in the context of litigation involving FFDEs of police officers and other public safety employees. Our discussion of the legal issues underlying an FFDE is not exhaustive and is limited primarily to United States federal laws and case law pertaining to them. Decisions by federal circuit courts are not precedential in other circuits and, as a result, the interpretation of federal laws and regulatory guidance may differ across jurisdictions. Consequently, readers are advised to consult with local legal professionals to determine what laws apply to FFDEs in their locations.

LEGAL FOUNDATIONS FOR FITNESS-FOR-DUTY EVALUATIONS

Under the ADA (1991), an employer who requires an employee to submit to an evaluation of their physical or mental ability to perform the job must first justify that evaluation as being "job-related and consistent with business necessity" (42 U.S.C. §12112[d][4][A]; 29 C.F.R. §1630.14[c]). The Equal Employment Opportunity Commission (EEOC, 2000) regards this threshold as having been met when an employer "has a reasonable belief, based on objective evidence, that (a) an employee's ability to perform essential job functions will be impaired by a medical condition; or (b) an employee will pose a direct threat due to a medical condition" (EEOC, Question 5, p. 7).

In short, legal justification for a compulsory mental health examination of an employee generally requires objective evidence of job-related performance problems or safety threats *and* a known or reasonably suspected mental condition. One of these elements in the absence of the other represents an insufficient basis for an FFDE (Gold & Shuman, 2009, p. 244). But when an employee's essential job functions implicate public safety, the threshold for satisfying the "business necessity standard" is lowered, although not entirely ignored (see Mayer & Corey, 2017).

In *Brownfield v. City of Yakima* (9th Cir. 2010), the court held that an employee who is exhibiting behavior that gives rise to reasonable concerns about mental fitness but who has not exhibited impaired work performance may, nevertheless, be ordered to submit to a "prophylactic" FFDE (that is, *before* there is objective evidence of impaired performance), "particularly when the employee is engaged in dangerous work" (slip op. at 10825; see also *Cody v. Cigna Healthcare of St. Louis,* 1998; *Watson v. City of Miami Beach,* 1999). Thus, although the business necessity standard "is quite high and is not to be confused with mere expediency" (*Cripe v. City of San Jose,* 2001, p. 890), the standard may be met even in the absence of known medical problems or observed deterioration in the employee's job performance. Fitness-for-duty examiners are well advised to confer with the employer or other referral source to understand the rationale for the mandated evaluation (see Corey & Zelig, 2020 for a discussion of the benefits and importance of this prereferral consultation). However, employers who refer public safety employees for psychological FFDEs are given broad leeway and deference by the courts in light of the potential for serious harm to the employee, coworkers, or others when the employee's ability to perform public safety functions is impaired. Indeed, the long arc of case law in this area makes clear that when a public safety employer has an objective and reasonable basis for suspecting that an employee in a safety-sensitive position is unable to perform their essential functions safely or effectively, the employer not only has a legal right but, in many cases, also an obligation to mandate an FFDE.

In *Thomas v. Johnson* (1968), the federal district court held that a "municipal employer will generally be held liable where it has retained an agent whose past history did in fact, or should have, put the municipality on notice of the agent's propensity for violence or instability" (p. 1031). The *Johnson* court further stated that "if negligence in the selection of unfit persons or *retention of known incompetents* [emphasis added] can be shown on the part of members of the appointing authority, recovery of damages against the municipality will follow" (p. 1031). Indeed, when the head of a law enforcement agency has knowledge of a subordinate officer with "questionable mental stability" or the administrator "is under some [other] affirmative duty to act and he fails to act accordingly, he may be held negligently responsible for his omission" (p. 845). See Mayer and Corey (2017) for further discussion of this topic.

The ADA's business necessity standard also has implications for determining the criterion standard to be used in an FFDE. As noted, the ADA requires that a medical or psychological evaluation of an employee be predicated on business necessity. This means that the evaluation must be justified by objective evidence giving rise to reasonable concerns that the employee has a medical or mental health condition that may impair their ability to perform the essential job functions or pose a direct threat to the employee or others. Therefore, the ADA's two-pronged business necessity standard implies a similar fitness criterion: an employee is medically or psychologically unfit for duty when (a) the employee has a mental, emotional, or psychological impairment and (b) that condition limits their ability to perform the essential job functions or poses a direct threat to the employee or others.[1]

Central to an understanding of the fitness standard is whether the employee's condition must satisfy either the definition of a disability under the ADA (1990 *et seq.*) or meet recognized diagnostic criteria (e.g., using current versions of the *Diagnostic and Statistical Manual for Mental Disorders* [DSM] or the International Classification of Diseases [ICD]) in order to find an employee unfit for duty. Several federal and state courts suggest that it is not a diagnosis per se that renders an employee unfit for duty but rather the impact of the symptom or symptoms (which may not rise to a magnitude warranting diagnosis) on the employee's ability to properly perform the duties of the position. In *Watson v. City of Miami Beach* (1999), Watson, a police officer, maintained that he did not have a mental impairment but, rather, that the employer erroneously "regarded" him as having one and that this entitled him to sue under the ADA for discrimination on the basis of a perceived disability. The appeals court disagreed, noting that the FFDE mandate need not be conditioned on the employer having a reasonable belief that a *mental impairment* exists, but rather only that a *mental condition* exists that may render the employee unable to perform their job duties safely or effectively. The court concluded,

> In any case where a police department reasonably perceives an officer to be even mildly paranoid, hostile, or oppositional, a fitness for duty examination is job related and consistent with business necessity. Police departments place armed officers in positions where they can do tremendous harm if they act irrationally. Contrary to Watson's contention, the ADA does not, indeed cannot, require a police department to forgo a fitness for duty examination to wait until a perceived threat becomes real or questionable behavior results in injuries. (p. 935)

That a mental condition need not meet the diagnostic criteria for a mental disorder is also supported by the California Court of Appeal in *Sager v. County of Yuba* (2007). The psychologist retained by the employer to evaluate Sager, a deputy sheriff, found her unfit for duty based on problematic personality traits. But in a significant clarification of the standard for judging an employee to be unfit for duty, the court ruled that "Sager's fitness for duty did not have to be shown entirely by testimony of a mental health expert" (p. 4). Indeed, the court held that the sheriff, as a law enforcement expert who knew Sager well, was able to opine "that Sager was not mentally fit to work as a peace officer because she could not 'be a team player, who is able to look at things abstractly and not take everything personally, not to be upset when one is criticized, and to work in a team environment'" (p. 4). Although the court observed that the employer was justified in relying on the opinion of its psychologist, it was also entitled to consider and weigh that opinion against its own experiences with the employee over the course of her employment.

It is important to note that the *Sager* court ruled that the *preemployment standards* for qualifying a peace officer candidate in California (see chapter 5 for a full discussion of these suitability standards) apply "throughout a peace officer's career," not merely for purposes of initial hiring, and are properly used to evaluate an incumbent officer's psychological fitness for duty (see also *Brown v. Sandy City Appeal Board* [2014], in which the Utah Court of Appeals held that California's preemployment standards may also be used to assist in evaluating the psychological fitness for duty of an incumbent Utah police officer). The *Sager* court concluded, "if the evidence shows she is not able to maintain *mental fitness,* that is, control her anger, work with other officers, and make sound judgments, then she is not performing the duties [of a peace officer] *in the proper manner*" (p. 8).

This reliance on a broader range of personality-related traits—not just diagnosed disorders—to assess a peace officer's psychological fitness is also consistent with the guidance of the California POST Commission:

> In earlier versions of POST regulations, the stated purpose of the psychological evaluation was limited to ruling out candidates with mental or emotional disorders and/or job-relevant psychopathology (i.e., psychological *stability*). In 2009, [POST Commission] Regulation 1955 formally expanded the role of peace officer psychological screening to include the assessment of both psychological stability *and* normal-range personality traits and characteristics (i.e., psychological *suitability*). This change was made in recognition that personality traits encompass both normal and abnormal personality, and that personality disorders are actually extreme and inflexible manifestations of these otherwise normal traits. The peace officer psychological evaluation is, in effect, an assessment of the influence of personality traits—both normal and abnormal—on job-related behaviors. (Spilberg & Corey, 2022, p. 2)

When evaluating United States federal employees whose access to sensitive and classified information puts national security interests at stake, the criteria used for evaluating eligibility for continued access to such sensitive and classified information are listed in the "adjudicative guidelines" of the Security Executive Agent Directive 4 (SEAD-4) (Office of the Director of National Intelligence, 2017), which includes the following clarification:

> Certain emotional, mental, and personality conditions can impair judgment, reliability, or trustworthiness. *A formal diagnosis of a disorder is not required for there to be a concern under this guideline* [emphasis added]. A duly qualified mental health professional (e.g., clinical psychologist or psychiatrist) employed by, or acceptable to and approved by the U.S. Government, should be consulted when evaluating potentially disqualifying and mitigating information under this guideline. (p. 19)

That a formal diagnosis is not required when identifying a disqualifying psychological condition under SEAD-4 also aligns with the text of the *DSM-5*, which notes that many individuals present with symptoms that do not meet the full criteria for a diagnosis but who nevertheless demonstrate a clear need for treatment or care. The OMPE Guidelines (APA, 2018) also emphasize that "it is not *per se* the diagnosis or mental health condition of an . . . employee that is occupationally relevant, but rather the impact of that diagnosis or condition on the individual's ability to perform the duties of the position in a safe, effective, and/or efficient manner" (p. 191).

For United States federal employees who are required to meet certain medical standards, or for positions subject to medical evaluation programs, the proper standard for evaluating fitness for duty is, in most cases, 5 C.F.R. § 339 (e.g., *Slater v. Department of Homeland Security*, 2008). Under this federal regulation, a history of a particular medical problem may be the basis of a medical disqualification

> only if the condition at issue is itself disqualifying, recurrence of the condition is based on reasonable medical judgment, and the duties of the position are such that a recurrence of the condition would pose a significant risk of substantial harm to the health and safety of the applicant or employee or others that cannot be eliminated or reduced by reasonable accommodation or any other agency efforts to mitigate risk (§ 339.206).

Thus, in both state and federal contexts in the United States, a currently disabling condition does not have to be diagnosed for an employee to be deemed unfit for duty. Instead, it is necessary for an individualized evaluation to document evidence of a mental or emotional condition that is functionally linked to the employee's inability to perform their essential job functions, to perform them in the proper manner, or to perform them without posing a direct threat to the employee or others. Merely having a mental health diagnosis does not necessarily render an employee unfit for duty if it does not also substantially limit the employee's ability to perform their job duties safely and effectively. In positions for which the consequences of failure to perform job duties properly may be catastrophic, the magnitude of the impairment required to find the employee unfit for duty is commensurately lower (e.g., *EEOC v. Amego, Inc.*, 1997; *Lassiter v. Department of Justice*, 1993).

GUIDANCE IN THE ABSENCE OF LEGAL STANDARDS

As discussed, the legal standard for psychological fitness for duty is well established for many public safety positions. This is especially true for law enforcement and other "peace officer" positions. For some public safety positions (e.g., firefighters), guidance on the permissible scope of fitness evaluations is provided by case law and industry standards.

For example, in a landmark case, *McKenna v. Fargo* (1978), the U.S. District Court for the District of New Jersey was asked to decide whether Jersey City's use of psychological testing to select firefighters invaded the candidates' constitutional rights to privacy. Observing that "the task of fighting fires is no ordinary job in difficulty or importance" and that "success depends critically on the psychological capabilities of fire[fighters]," the court held that the requirement was constitutional (p. 1355). Importantly, the court observed that the assessment focused on screening out applicants whose psychological traits undermined one or more of six requirements for safe and effective performance as a firefighter: (a) able to adjust well to close community living; (b) able to follow orders explicitly; (c) able to withstand substantial stress and tension as generated by life-endangering circumstances encountered in fire-fighting situations, where circumstances beyond the individual's control are operative; (d) able to make decisions under stress; (e) able to take calculated but not any unnecessary risks; and (f) free of abnormal fears related to firefighting duties, such as fear of heights or enclosed spaces.

As discussed in chapter 5, the nonprofit National Fire Protection Association (NFPA) produces more than 300 consensus standards relied upon by municipal and state fire departments around the world, among which is the "Standard on Comprehensive Occupational Medical Program for Fire Departments" (NFPA Standard 1582). Section 6.1 of Standard 1582 pertains to medical evaluations conducted prior to a firefighter's participation in training programs or in departmental emergency response activities. Subsection 6.23.1 of these standards stipulates that "any psychiatric condition that results in a person not being able to safely perform essential job tasks" is disqualifying, as is "a history of [a] psychiatric condition or substance abuse problem" or a "requirement for medications that increase an individual's risk of heat stress, or other interference with the ability to safely perform essential job tasks." Thus, even in the absence of a legal requirement for psychological evaluations of emergency personnel, a broad range of other authorities may provide important guidance for establishing fitness standards.

THE USE OF PSYCHOLOGICAL TESTING AND COLLATERAL DATA IN ASSESSING FITNESS FOR DUTY

In the *McKenna v. Fargo* (1978) decision, the court conceded that "there is good reason to scrutinize a government requirement which joins the words psychology and testing" (p. 1357). Nevertheless, the court found the assessment program—which included use of the original MMPI—to be constitutional in large part because of its reliance on tests selected based on a rational nexus to the psychological requirements of the position and supported by literature.

As in all high-stakes psychological assessments, decisions about the choice and use of a test should rest on several considerations, including (a) peer-reviewed research evidence indicating that one or more scales on the test validly measure constructs pertinent to the evaluation criteria; (b) commercial availability of the test; (c) availability of a comprehensive technical manual or equivalent documentation; (d) evidence of adequate levels of reliability; (e) the test's inclusion of measures of test-taking orientation (e.g., content responsiveness, overreporting, and underreporting); and (f) validity evidence that supports the test's use for the intended purpose, setting, and population (Ackerman, 2010; APA, 2018; Corey & Zelig, 2020; Melton et al., 2007; Otto et al., 2000; Spilberg & Corey, 2022). Of course, the test user must also have the qualifications necessary to use the instrument and be adequately trained in its administration, scoring, and interpretation.

Because the evaluation of a police officer's or other public safety employee's psychological fitness for duty is fundamentally an assessment of the degree to which their work performance is, or is likely to become, impaired by a psychological condition, a fitness-for-duty evaluation is partly concerned with dysfunction in emotion, thought, behavior, interpersonal functioning, and somatic adaptation to stress. These psychological domains are indeed the focus of the MMPI-3, but like all psychological assessments, determinations of fitness for duty depend on multiple sources of information about functioning in these domains, including employment records, collateral interviews, mental health records, clinical interview, and psychological testing. Indeed, for an FFDE to meet U.S. federal requirements as a "thorough medical assessment" that can be relied on by an employer for making employment decisions, it must be conducted by an examiner who is familiar with the relevant job duties; obtains relevant, individualized information about the employee's medical condition; has current knowledge of the employee's medical condition; examines the employee in person; and reviews the records of the employee's other treating health care provider(s). (See Mayer & Corey, 2017, for a discussion of this topic.)

As a validated, broadband instrument for measuring personality and psychopathology, the MMPI-3 is well suited to contribute to an assessment of an employee's fitness for duty. It satisfies each of the above-listed criteria for using a test in a high-stakes evaluation, and it provides "much individualized information" as required by federal courts (see *Michael v. City of Troy Police Department,* 2014). In particular, the instrument's hierarchical structure, which focuses on five domains of psychological dysfunction (Somatic/Cognitive, Emotional, Thought, Behavioral, and Interpersonal) and specific problems within each, aids the examiner in understanding how identified problems are likely to manifest on and off the job.

Owing in large part to the preselection and selection factors discussed in chapter 6, police and other public safety *candidates* who complete the MMPI-3 constitute a fairly homogeneous group with generally good psychological adjustment. In contrast, individuals who take the test in an FFDE context—that is, *incumbent employees* for whom there are objective concerns about psychological fitness—are comparatively heterogeneous: some have significant psychopathology, some have none, and others exhibit varying degrees of dysfunction that may be revealed on psychological testing at levels below clinical significance.

Just as with the assessment of a candidate's psychological suitability at the preemployment stage, the valid assessment of an incumbent employee's fitness requires reliance on multiple sources of data pertinent to the individual's job performance problems and any suspected job-limiting mental condition. As described in the FFDE Guidelines (IACP, 2018; Guideline 7.4), these collateral data sources include job class specifications or job descriptions, performance evaluations, previous remediation efforts, commendations, testimonials, internal affairs investigations, formal citizen/public complaints, use-of-force incidents, reports of duty-related trauma exposure, civil claims, disciplinary actions, incident reports of any triggering events, medical and mental health treatment records, and prior psychological evaluations. These collateral sources are needed for a valid assessment for the same reasons as in preemployment screening (discussed in chapter 5): to aid in affirming findings from psychological testing, to protect against the possibility of an examinee's deceptive efforts, to assess how and to what degree the constructs measured by psychological testing are reflected in the examinee's behavior, and under what contexts or environmental conditions psychological functioning varies.

The OMPE Guidelines (APA, 2018) stress the importance of selecting assessment tools that produce reliable data supporting valid inferences pertinent to the referral question(s). In the context of psychological testing, the guidelines note that reliability "implies a precise estimate of the targeted construct," whereas when applied to nontest information, reliability refers to "accuracy" (p. 193). Relying on multiple sources of collateral data reduces the chances that a single inaccurate item of information will have an unwarranted influence on the assessment.

REPORTING FFDE FINDINGS AND OPINIONS

In an FFDE, the "ultimate question" is often phrased in shorthand: Is the employee psychologically "fit for duty"? However, the ADA enforcement guidance makes clear that, in the final analysis, this and all other employment decisions stemming from a medical evaluation (e.g., whether reasonable accommodation may be made to enable a qualified employee with a disability to perform essential job functions) is a matter to be decided by the employer, not the fitness examiner. As stated by the EEOC (2000), when communicating the results of a compulsory medical evaluation, the employer is entitled "to the information necessary to determine whether the employee can do the essential functions of the job or work without posing a direct threat" but no more information than necessary to make that determination (Question 13). A simple statement from the examiner indicating "fit for duty" or "unfit for duty" would deprive the employer of the information needed to meet its obligation. An adequate disclosure of medical information may also be necessary for an employer to determine whether the examination constitutes "a thorough medical assessment," as required by the ADA (*Michael v. City of Troy Police Department*, 2014; see also *Jennings v. Dow Corning Corp.*, 2013; *Wurzel v. Whirlpool Corp.*, 2012).

In seeming opposition to this position, several state and federal courts have held that an employer who mandates a fitness evaluation is entitled only to the examiner's "ultimate fitness determination" (*Sangirardi v. Village of Stickney,* 2003; see also *McGreal v. Ostrov,* 2004; *Pettus v. Cole,* 1996). But careful analysis of these decisions reveals that this restriction was necessitated by the examiners' failure to obtain authorization to disclose their assessment findings using a state-compliant form that is required when disclosing individually identifiable medical information. Absent specific authorization, the holder of the medical information is restricted under most state laws from disclosing "anything other than the fitness for duty determination" (*McGreal v. Ostrov,* 2004). With proper authorization, no such restrictions apply.

On one point involving the content of an FFDE report, both the law and standard of practice are in complete agreement: "When the referral source or another party is responsible for determining the ultimate issue in a referral, psychologists strive to educate and inform rather than answer the ultimate issue" (APA, 2018, p. 195). Examiners who opine on a topic not solicited by the referral source, whether it is within the examiner's clinical expertise or not (e.g., reasonable accommodation, treatment recommendations, or prognosis for recovery) "are acting outside of their contractual role and do a disservice to the referring party" (Mayer & Corey, 2017, p. 109).

As discussed in chapter 5, the Genetic Information Nondiscrimination Act of 2008 (GINA), Title II, prohibits gathering, inquiring about, or using information about the manifestation of a disease or disorder in an individual's family members (i.e., family medical history) when making employment decisions in the United States. This applies equally to both suitability (i.e., preemployment) and fitness evaluations. When requesting medical records from health care providers, it is important to include an admonishment instructing the records custodian not to disclose family medical information using the "GINA warning" (or similar language) provided in chapter 5.

The importance of restricting the report of findings and opinions to those that are pertinent to the referral question(s) and not addressing an ultimate question that belongs to the employer has particular implications for how the fitness determination is framed. Some practitioners advocate for the inclusion of fitness determinations that reflect a fit-for-duty status conditioned on one or more contingencies, such as limited or restricted work activities (i.e., fit for light or modified duty). When doing so, care should be taken to confirm with the referring party that the proposed duty restrictions are realistic and do not impose an undue hardship on the employer; otherwise, the recommendation can become a point of contention or cause for litigation. An even more hazardous contingency is one that conditions fitness for duty on entering or continuing in some course of remediation or treatment. Corey (2011) advised against this approach:

> When such a condition is stipulated, it typically is rationalized in one of two ways: either because the examiner believes the employee's current fitness is

unlikely to be sustained without additional or ongoing treatment, or because the employee's current unfitness results from a minor impairment expected to respond quickly to treatment. In cases of the former, if the employee's current fitness is so fragile or unstable as to be undone in the foreseeable future without the benefit of ongoing treatment, the examiner should reconsider whether the . . . fit-for-duty conclusion [is warranted]. . . . In cases where the employee is judged currently unfit for duty due to a remediable condition, it is usually more prudent to acknowledge the current unfit status and not address recommendations designed to restore fitness unless requested by the referring party. (p. 288)

In the next chapter, we discuss the implications of contextual factors, particularly the motivation to be seen as fit or unfit, on MMPI-3 scores in fitness evaluations. We also consider the appropriateness of considering moderately elevated scales (i.e., scores below 65T) for evaluating psychological fitness of persons whose work has substantial public safety implications. Finally, we present a model for integrating data to reach a fitness determination, and we explicate the model with a variety of illustrative cases.

Using the MMPI-3 to Assess Fitness for Duty

Case Illustrations

As detailed in chapter 9, identification of psychological conditions and symptoms that may limit public safety employees' ability to perform their essential job functions is a critical component of fitness-for-duty evaluations (FFDEs). In essence, an FFDE is a clinical evaluation triggered by specific concerns about an employee's psychological functioning. Consequently, the literature on the MMPI-3 as a measure of personality and psychopathology (which includes the broad literature on the MMPI-2-RF) guides its use in FFDEs. This is fortunate because, contrary to the substantial literature on using the test in preemployment evaluations (reviewed in chapter 6), there remains a dearth of empirical research on using the MMPI or other psychological measures to evaluate fitness for duty. This may be a function of unique aspects of these evaluations, including (a) the heterogeneous nature of the referral issues, which precludes obtaining uniform data sets; (b) legal, regulatory, and logistical constraints pertaining to the availability of collateral (i.e., non-test) data for such research; and (c) a lack of information pertaining to the outcome of FFDEs other than the assessor's opinion, which is likely to be contaminated by test findings. In this chapter, we review the limited research findings relevant to conducting fitness evaluations using the MMPI instruments, introduce a data integration model for determining fitness, and provide case examples to illustrate the use of the MMPI-3 when applying the model.

In the case illustrations, we show how MMPI-3 score information can be integrated with position information (i.e., working conditions, essential job functions, and job demands), collateral information about the examinee, interview findings, and other test data to evaluate psychological fitness in all four public safety job categories: police officer, correctional officer, dispatcher, and firefighter/medic. We include test protocols showing clinically significant elevations as well as those with moderate scale elevations, illustrating how both can be integrated with other data to inform judgments about fitness in public safety positions.

MMPI FFDE RESEARCH

Focusing on motivational factors in FFDEs, Walfish (2010) reported the results of a study on reducing MMPI underreporting in a sample of professionals undergoing an FFDE. The premise of this research was that professionals undergoing mandated psychological evaluations that could result in the loss of their license to practice would be motivated to underreport, similar to preemployment evaluees. The author sought to document the rate of underreported MMPI-2 protocols in such evaluations and to examine whether providing feedback to those who showed evidence of extreme underreporting would result in reduced underreporting if they were then retested. The 53 participants in this study included physicians (64%), dentists (11%), attorneys (9%), nurses (6%), pharmacists (4%), chiropractors (2%), optometrists (2%), and physician assistants (2%). Those with T scores at or above 65 on L or 70 on K were deemed "faking good" and were provided feedback that their test results were invalid because of underreporting. They were asked to retake the MMPI-2 with a "mindset of rigorous openness and honesty on a conscious basis" (Walfish, 2010, p. 77).

Walfish (2010) reported that 31 (59%) of the FFDE participants met criteria for underreporting and were retested with the instructions just noted. All but three scored below the designated underreporting cutoffs in the second testing. A comparison of the first and second test protocols for these individuals showed marked reductions in scores on the MMPI-2 underreporting scales (e.g., L was reduced from a mean T score of 62.26 to 47.81 following feedback), whereas F scores increased (though not to an interpretable level), as did scores on some of the MMPI-2 clinical scales. It is important to note that a similar pattern of increase was observed on other measures administered as part of the FFDE. For example, the initial mean Beck Depression Inventory-II (BDI-II) score for underreporting evaluees was 4.87 ($SD = 5.77$), increasing to 11.58 (8.54) at retest. The greater dispersion of BDI-II scores in retesting is noteworthy, likely reflecting that some test takers changed their response pattern substantially, whereas others did not.

Based on his findings, Walfish (2010) recommended that fitness evaluees who produce an underreported MMPI-2 protocol be retested. Butcher and colleagues (1997) made similar recommendations for preemployment evaluations following a similarly designed study of airline pilot applicants. Like Walfish (2010), they (1997) found that retesting following altered instructions substantially changed substantive scale findings. For example, 12% of those retested produced clinically elevated content scales scores.

Although the findings reported in both studies are informative, we strongly recommend against the practice of retesting with altered instructions for the following reasons. The instructions accompanying retesting necessarily require the examiner to provide a rationale for readministering the test (as Walfish did in his FFDE retesting instructions). Instructions altered in this manner deviate from the standard administration procedures used to develop, norm, and validate MMPI scales. Their use threatens the validity and interpretability of the resulting test scores. In addition, this approach may inadvertently "coach" evaluees on how to respond not only during the current evaluation but also in possible future assessments, where the examiner would not know that a test taker had been subjected previously to nonstandard instructions. Moreover, the implications of the resulting scores, particularly if demonstrating significant psychopathology (as in the Butcher et al., 1997 study), are ambiguous. Nevertheless, Walfish's (2010) results demonstrate that underreporting can be a significant concern in fitness evaluation, that it serves to lower scores on substantive scales when it occurs (as also shown by Detrick and Chibnall [2014] in the context of suitability evaluations), and that this pattern generalizes to other measures (e.g., the BDI-II) administered as part of an FFDE.

Grossman and colleagues (1990) examined the sensitivity of the original MMPI Validity Scales to motivational factors in the psychological evaluations of police officers. They compared MMPI validity scale scores of 20 officers undergoing an FFDE who expressed a desire *not* to return to work with those of 20 officers (matched for age, race, and sex) also undergoing a fitness evaluation but who expressed a desire to return to work. They also compared another sample of 20 similarly matched officers who were not undergoing an FFDE and were actively working. The authors' underlying assumption was that the officers not desiring to return to work might be motived to overreport problems, whereas the sample wishing to return to work might be motivated to underreport. Further, because members of the control group were told that the test results would have no bearing on their employment, members of that group would have no motivation to either over- or underreport.

Grossman and colleagues (1990) compared mean scores for the three groups on the original MMPI F and L scales along with several nonstandard validity scales that are not part of the MMPI-3 and not covered here. Consistent with expectations, the group presumably motivated to over-report scored higher on F than did members of the other two groups, but there were no significant differences on L. Unfortunately, data were not reported for K, which, as discussed later, appears to be more sensitive to the kind of underreporting seen in fitness evaluations. These findings highlight the need to examine MMPI-3 FFDE protocols for threats to protocol validity involving both over- and underreporting because either motivational set may be present in a case.

MMPI-2-RF FFDE FINDINGS

To facilitate use of the MMPI-2-RF in fitness evaluations, Corey and Ben-Porath (2018) assembled a sample of 709 protocols (some administered originally as MMPI-2s and later converted to MMPI-2-RFs) of public safety employees referred for an FFDE. The sample included individuals employed by public safety agencies in Hawaii and in the western, northwestern, southeastern, and northeastern regions of the United States. The sample included 556 men and 153 women, with a mean age of 38.6 years ($SD = 9.1$). Of these, 559 evaluees were law enforcement officers (448 men and 111 women), and 150 were employed either as correctional officers (54 men and 24 women), firefighters/medics (44 and 6), and dispatchers (10 and 12).

Table 10.1 lists the means and standard deviations of the MMPI-2-RF protocols for the 709 public safety employees in the FFDE sample reported by Corey and Ben-Porath (2018). No practically meaningful mean score differences (i.e., greater than 5 T-score points) were found between law enforcement and nonlaw enforcement participants and between male and female participants. Table 10.1 also lists the means and standard deviations of an additional set of 140 public safety employees referred for an FFDE; 47 were administered the MMPI-3 and the remaining 93 completed the MMPI-2-RF-EX (discussed in chapter 2), thereby permitting their protocols to be scored both as an MMPI-2-RF and as an MMPI-3. For the current analyses, law enforcement and nonlaw enforcement participants as well as male and female participants also were combined.

As seen in Table 10.1, there is considerable similarity in the means and standard deviations across samples and test versions. Only two scales, MLS and NUC, produced practically meaningful differences between MMPI-2-RF and MMPI-3 scores. These findings are unsurprising, because they are consistent with normative shifts reported in the *MMPI-3 Technical Manual* (Ben-Porath & Tellegen, 2020). MLS and NUC showed the greatest score increases in comparisons of the MMPI-2-RF and MMPI-3 normative samples. The comparability of MMPI-2-RF MLS and NUC T scores reported in Table 10.1 for the 2018 and current samples indicate that the lower MMPI-3 T scores on these scales are indeed a product of changes in the standard T scores rather than differences across samples. These normative differences notwithstanding, the overall pattern indicates that, by and large, MMPI-2-RF and MMPI-3 scores are comparable for police officers and other public safety employees undergoing FFDEs.

As with the MMPI-2-RF, fitness-for-duty evaluees who completed the MMPI-3 tended generally to score within normal limits on measures of noncontent-based invalid responding and overreporting; on average, they scored

TABLE 10.1. Public Safety Fitness-for-Duty Evaluation (FFDE) Descriptive Statistics

	MMPI-2-RF scores				MMPI-3 scores	
	COREY & BEN-PORATH (2018) SAMPLE (N = 709)		PRESENT SAMPLE (N = 93)		PRESENT SAMPLE (N = 140)	
	M	SD	M	SD	M	SD
CRIN	-	-	-	-	43	8
VRIN/-r	45	9	46	10	44	8
TRIN/-r	51F	8	52F	7	54F	7
F/-r	50	12	52	14	47	9
Fp/-r	46	8	47	8	43	5
Fs	49	10	51	15	47	9
FBS/-r	55	12	57	13	53	10
RBS	51	11	52	11	49	9
L/-r	54	11	53	12	52	11
K/-r	57	11	58	11	58	11
EID	46	12	47	14	46	12
THD	47	9	46	8	43	8
BXD	48	8	47	8	44	7
RCd	48	11	48	13	45	11
RC1	48	12	50	13	46	10
RC2	49	12	51	14	49	11
RC4	48	9	50	9	46	7
RC6	53	11	52	10	48	10
RC7	43	10	44	11	44	10
RC8	46	8	46	8	43	7
RC9	44	8	41	7	43	7
MLS	51	11	53	12	44	10
GIC	52	12	53	14	-	-
HPC	50	11	50	9	-	-
NUC	50	10	53	12	46	10
EAT	-	-	-	-	46	5
COG	47	11	49	12	46	11
SUI	49	11	50	11	49	10
HLP	46	10	46	10	44	7
SFD	48	10	49	11	46	10

(*continued on next page*)

TABLE 10.1, continued

	MMPI-2-RF scores				MMPI-3 scores	
	COREY & BEN-PORATH (2018) SAMPLE (N = 709)		PRESENT SAMPLE (N = 93)		PRESENT SAMPLE (N = 140)	
	M	SD	M	SD	M	SD
NFC	44	9	44	11	43	9
STR/STW	48	10	49	12	48	10
WRY/STW	48	10	49	12	46	11
CMP	-	-	-	-	47	9
ARX/AXY	50	12	52	14	48	12
ANP	45	9	44	9	44	9
BRF	46	7	48	9	47	7
MSF	47	8	45	7	-	-
FML	45	9	45	9	44	8
JCP	50	9	51	11	48	9
SUB	48	8	48	8	46	7
IMP	-	-	-	-	44	7
ACT	43	9	43	10	44	8
AGG	45	8	44	7	45	8
CYN/RC3	45	10	43	10	41	9
SFI	-	-	-	-	48	9
DOM/IPP	48	8	49	8	48	8
DSF	48	9	49	11	46	9
SAV	52	12	54	13	51	12
SHY	45	9	44	8	45	9
AES	42	9	43	9	-	-
MEC	57	10	56	10	-	-
AGGR/-r	50	8	48	7	46	7
PSYC/-r	45	9	44	8	43	7
DISC/-r	50	8	51	8	46	7
NEGE/-r	46	11	46	13	46	11
INTR/-r	53	11	55	13	52	12

about a half standard deviation above the general population mean on the underreporting indicators, with mean K scores a half a standard deviation higher than those found for L. Considering the ADA requirement that public safety employees be reasonably suspected of having a job-limiting psychological condition to be referred for a fitness evaluation in the United States, it is unlikely that the higher K (Adjustment Validity) scores reflect better than average adjustment. More likely, they are an indication of underreporting. As reviewed in chapter 3, Detrick and Chibnall (2014) found that higher K scores are associated with underreporting of emotional dysfunction. As seen in Table 10.1, mean scores on the MMPI-3 Substantive Scales, as with the MMPI-2-RF, also fell mainly within normal limits.

Table 10.2 displays the rates at which fitness evaluees exceeded designated MMPI-3 validity scale cutoffs, including a comparison to the Corey and Ben-Porath (2018) sample and the subset of MMPI-2-RF protocols from the present sample. Very few test takers showed any evidence of non-content-based invalid responding, reflecting the care with which fitness evaluees approach this high-stakes task. Similarly small proportions of evaluees exceeded minimal interpretive cutoffs on the MMPI-3 overreporting indicators. As expected, the most common findings were scores exceeding interpretation cutoffs on the underreporting scales. The elevation rates reflected in the MMPI-3 (and MMPI-2-RF) analyses were comparable to the MMPI-2 findings reported by Walfish (2010), indicating that between one-third to one-half of the fitness evaluees in these samples show some evidence of underreporting.

Of note in this context is the general caution that a finding of underreporting does not itself indicate that the test results are invalid. As Ben-Porath and Tellegen (2020a) instruct, when underreporting is observed in an MMPI-3 protocol, nonelevated and, in particular, low scores on the Substantive Scales cannot be interpreted as reflecting the absence of problems they are used to assess, and elevated substantive scale scores may not fully reflect the magnitude or severity of associated problems. However, clinically elevated substantive scale scores can be interpreted with the understanding that they may underestimate the problems assessed by those scales.

Table 10.3 lists the rates at which fitness evaluees exceeded designated MMPI-3 (and MMPI-2-RF) substantive scale cutoffs. Generally, a substantive scale cutoff of 65 should be used in fitness evaluations in light of the absence of research that supports using lower cutoffs and given the clinical focus of these evaluations. However, Corey and Ben-Porath (2018) showed that mean MMPI-2-RF substantive scale T scores of individuals found unfit for duty generally fell well below 65. This likely reflects both the confound of the motivation to appear high functioning and the fact that problems measured at levels below 65T can be sufficient to render a public safety employee unfit for duty—a finding consistently reported in studies of police candidates who were administered the

TABLE 10.2. Public Safety Fitness-for-Duty Evaluation (FFDE) Validity Scale Elevation Rates

CRITERIA	MMPI-2-RF scores		MMPI-3 scores
	COREY & BEN-PORATH (2018) SAMPLE (N = 709)	PRESENT SAMPLE (N = 93)	PRESENT SAMPLE (N = 140)
CRIN ≥ 70	-	-	0.0
CRIN ≥ 65	-	-	2.1
CRIN ≥ 60	-	-	3.6
CRIN ≥ 55	-	-	9.3
VRIN/-r ≥ 70	8.9	2.2	0.0
VRIN/-r ≥ 65	3.0	4.3	2.1
VRIN/-r ≥ 60	6.3	10.8	7.1
VRIN/-r ≥ 55	13.1	15.1	14.3
TRIN/-r ≥ 70	1.8	2.2	2.9
TRIN/-r ≥ 65	12.3	11.8	6.4
TRIN/-r ≥ 60	12.3	11.8	17.1
TRIN/-r ≥ 55	52.0	50.5	17.1
F/-r ≥ 80	3.0	7.5	0.7
F/-r ≥ 75	4.8	9.7	2.1
F/-r ≥ 70	8.9	14.0	5.0
F/-r ≥ 65	11.8	14.0	9.3
F/-r ≥ 60	15.9	18.3	10.7
F/-r ≥ 55	23.0	25.8	12.9
Fp/-r ≥ 80	0.3	0.0	0.0
Fp/-r ≥ 75	1.3	3.2	0.0
Fp/-r ≥ 70	1.3	3.2	0.0
Fp/-r ≥ 65	4.5	7.5	1.4
Fp/-r ≥ 60	4.5	7.5	1.4
Fp/-r ≥ 55	10.7	9.7	5.7
Fs ≥ 80	2.3	7.5	2.1
Fs ≥ 75	2.3	7.5	3.6
Fs ≥ 70	4.5	8.6	3.6
Fs ≥ 65	10.0	14.0	5.7
Fs ≥ 60	10.0	14.0	7.1
Fs ≥ 55	21.9	23.7	11.4
FBS/-r ≥ 80	5.6	8.6	2.1
FBS/-r ≥ 75	7.8	11.8	5.7
RBS/-r ≥ 80	3.7	2.2	0.0
RBS/-r ≥ 75	4.8	4.3	0.7
RBS/-r ≥ 70	12.4	9.7	2.9
RBS/-r ≥ 65	10.7	10.8	10.7

	MMPI-2-RF scores		MMPI-3 scores
CRITERIA	COREY & BEN-PORATH (2018) SAMPLE (N = 709)	PRESENT SAMPLE (N = 93)	PRESENT SAMPLE (N = 140)
RBS/-r ≥ 60	14.7	17.2	12.9
RBS/-r ≥ 55	21.6	28.0	18.6
L/-r ≥ 80	3.1	3.2	2.1
L/-r ≥ 75	5.8	4.3	4.3
L/-r ≥ 70	10.0	6.5	6.4
L/-r ≥ 65	17.1	10.8	13.6
L/-r ≥ 60	27.8	21.5	22.1
L/-r ≥ 55	42.3	38.7	31.4
K/-r ≥ 70	8.6	5.4	12.1
K/-r ≥ 65	34.8	35.5	36.4
K/-r ≥ 60	46.3	54.8	47.1
K/-r ≥ 55	65.9	74.2	63.6

MMPI-3 and MMPI-2-RF in preemployment contexts (see chapter 6 for a review of these studies).

Roughly 10% of each of the three samples displayed in Table 10.3 produced clinically elevated EID scores, with considerably smaller proportions scoring 65T or higher on THD or BXD. Among the MMPI-3 RC Scales, RCd, RC1, RC2, RC6, and RC7 were most likely to be clinically elevated. On the MMPI-3 Specific Problems (SP) Scales, SUI, STR, WRY, CMP, AXY, SAV, and INTR were most likely to be elevated, reflecting more commonly occurring difficulties with demoralization, stress and anxiety, compulsivity, and interpersonal functioning. Overall, 55% of the MMPI-3 FFDE sample produced at least one clinically significant elevation on a substantive scale.

Based on the currently available data, we recommend limiting substantive scale interpretation in FFDEs to clinically elevated (65 and higher, except for SUI, for which the clinically elevated T-score cutoff is 58) T scores. However, slightly lower scores may be useful in identifying potential problem areas that can be assessed by extratest data, including clinical interview, employment records, treatment records, and collateral interviews. Evidence of the generalizability of MMPI-2-RF validity and substantive scale findings to the MMPI-3 (discussed in chapter 2), provides a solid foundation for using the MMPI-3 as an empirically supported and informative data source, combined with other sources, to make fitness for duty determinations.

TABLE 10.3. Public Safety Fitness-for-Duty Evaluation (FFDE) Substantive Scale Elevation Rates

	MMPI-2-RF scores				MMPI-3 scores	
	COREY & BEN-PORATH (2018) SAMPLE (N = 709)		PRESENT SAMPLE (N = 93)		PRESENT SAMPLE (N = 140)	
Criteria	>60	>65	>60	>65	>60	>65
EID	14.7	10.0	19.4	14.0	10.7	9.3
THD	10.7	2.7	7.5	1.1	5.7	2.1
BXD	8.9	2.5	6.5	1.1	1.4	0.0
RCd	16.5	10.9	20.4	14.0	12.9	9.3
RC1	15.5	10.0	23.7	14.0	7.9	7.1
RC2	16.1	11.3	17.2	15.1	12.9	10.0
RC4	8.5	5.9	11.8	6.5	2.1	0.7
RC6	27.5	16.9	29.0	12.9	11.4	6.4
RC7	7.2	5.1	10.8	7.5	9.3	4.3
RC8	4.8	2.8	4.3	1.1	1.4	0.7
RC9	4.9	2.3	1.1	0.0	4.3	0.7
MLS	20.3	12.0	17.2	9.7	6.4	6.4
GIC	22.6	12.6	22.6	17.2	-	-
HPC	13.8	13.8	11.8	11.8	-	-
NUC	11.4	11.4	15.1	15.1	8.6	5.7
EAT	-	-	-	-	3.6	3.6
COG	10.2	6.8	16.1	11.8	12.1	8.6
SUI	14.1	14.1	18.3	18.3	12.9	12.9
HLP	13.4	6.3	14.0	6.5	2.9	2.9
SFD	12.8	12.8	18.3	18.3	8.6	8.6
NFC	5.5	2.8	7.5	7.5	7.1	5.0
STR/STW	12.1	12.1	11.8	11.8	10.0	10.0
WRY/STW	12.1	12.1	11.8	11.8	12.9	12.9
CMP	-	-	-	-	11.4	11.4
ARX/AXY	13.1	13.1	16.1	16.1	12.9	10.0
ANP	8.3	8.3	7.5	7.5	8.6	5.7
BRF	5.2	1.7	12.9	4.3	7.1	1.4
MSF	4.5	4.5	2.2	2.2	-	-
FML	6.9	3.7	6.5	1.1	2.9	2.9
JCP	14.2	5.1	20.4	9.7	9.3	5.0
SUB	7.8	3.9	10.8	3.2	2.9	2.9

	MMPI-2-RF scores				MMPI-3 scores	
	COREY & BEN-PORATH (2018) SAMPLE (N = 709)		PRESENT SAMPLE (N = 93)		PRESENT SAMPLE (N = 140)	
Criteria	>60	>65	>60	>65	>60	>65
IMP	-	-	-	-	2.1	2.1
ACT	3.5	3.5	6.5	6.5	5.7	5.7
AGG	7.1	3.2	5.4	1.1	6.4	1.4
CYN/RC3	9.9	6.2	9.7	6.5	6.4	2.9
SFI	-	-	-	-	14.3	4.3
DOM/IPP	10.6	6.2	11.8	4.3	5.0	5.0
DSF	6.5	6.5	11.8	11.8	6.4	6.4
SAV	18.9	18.9	25.8	25.8	23.6	18.6
SHY	6.1	6.1	4.3	4.3	10.0	4.3
AES	5.1	2.3	8.6	3.2	-	-
MEC	46.1	32.0	40.9	30.1	-	-
AGGR/-r	16.1	8.2	6.5	5.4	4.3	1.4
PSYC/-r	5.1	2.8	1.1	1.1	1.4	0.7
DISC/-r	7.8	5.4	10.8	6.5	4.3	0.7
NEGE/-r	9.4	6.3	15.1	11.8	14.3	6.4
INTR/-r	25.2	14.5	29.0	21.5	22.1	17.9

IMPORTANT CONSIDERATIONS WHEN USING THE MMPI-3 IN FFDES OF PUBLIC SAFETY EMPLOYEES

In the previous chapter, we noted that fitness evaluations constitute forensic assessments because they are mandated by a third party, are often conducted in anticipation of litigation, and are not focused on assessing the needs of, or providing mental health services to, the evaluee. Legal and procedural implications of this distinction are discussed there. Here, it is important to emphasize a general principle of using the MMPI-3 in forensic mental health evaluations: There is no empirical basis for reaching "ultimate issue" inferences based on MMPI-3 findings alone. Just as there is no MMPI-3 (or other MMPI version) "profile" that differentiates defendants who are competent versus incompetent to stand trial, or disability claimants who are disabled versus not disabled because of a work accident, or which of two parents disputing custody of their children would better meet the children's needs, MMPI-3 findings alone are not dispositive on the matter of fitness for duty. They are, nonetheless, quite relevant and should be given due weight in the context of an integrated assessment, but the matter of fitness is ultimately an administrative question informed by a well-constructed and communicated forensic mental health assessment.

AN INTEGRATIVE MODEL FOR FFDES

Heilbrun and colleagues (2009) highlighted the benefits of relying on a model to guide data gathering, data interpretation, and communication of results in forensic mental health evaluations. As discussed, fitness evaluations are mental health assessments carried out in contemplation of potential litigation in which an employee's property right to the position, constitutional right to privacy, and statutory rights to nondiscrimination (based on disability, perceived disability, or a record of disability) and accommodation are at issue. In chapter 8, we presented an integrative model for use in suitability evaluations, and we demonstrated its use in several case examples. Next, we now do the same for fitness evaluations.

The integrative model discussed in chapter 8 is grounded in the risk-based nature of preemployment psychological screening. Because candidates are screened out *only* when risk-related findings indicate an unacceptable risk for counterproductive behavior in the position—whether the risks derive from a mental condition, from problematic personality traits, or from behavioral propensities—the integrative model focuses on an evidence-based assessment of these risks. In contrast, determinations of fitness for duty derive from a different analytic framework. In chapter 9, we discussed the ADA's two-pronged "business necessity standard" for justifying any medical evaluation of an employee; namely, there must be an objective and reasonable basis for believing that (a) the employee has a mental, emotional, or psychological condition and (b) the condition limits the employee's ability to perform their essential job functions or poses a direct threat to the employee or others. This standard also provides examiners with a model for assessing fitness. Bifurcating the second prong of the ADA business necessity standard into current and reasonably anticipated impairment, the standard can be viewed as a three-step model for integrating data across sources of assessment information. The analytic steps of this model involve three sequential questions:

Step 1. Is there evidence of an emotional, cognitive, behavioral, thought, interpersonal, or other psychological condition? If yes, proceed to Step 2. (If no condition exists, the employee does not meet the foundational criterion necessary to be deemed psychologically unfit for duty, even if the employee is clearly otherwise problematic.)

Step 2. Does the identified condition substantially limit the employee's **current** ability to perform the essential job functions, to perform them properly, or to perform them without posing a direct threat to the employee or others?

Step 3. If the employee has a mental health condition that is currently nonlimiting, is the employee's fitness sustainable upon return to duty?

THREE-STEP MODEL FOR INTEGRATING ASSESSMENT DATA

Assessing for a Psychological Condition

As with all mental health assessments, the determination of whether an employee has a psychological condition does not rely solely on psychological testing, but it can be meaningfully and uniquely informed by it. Just as a test score in the clinical range (i.e., ≥ 65T) implies but does not establish the presence of psychopathology, so too can a score in the moderate range reflect a comparatively high magnitude of problems that, in the context of a safety-sensitive position, may limit job functioning to a degree warranting the conclusion that the employee is psychologically unfit for duty. Nevertheless, this decision should also be informed by psychological testing but not determined by it. Findings from other assessment data sources, such as employment records, collateral reports, treatment records, and clinical interview, must always be considered when carrying out the three steps of the integrative process.

Evidence of an existing psychological condition may not always be apparent in psychological testing or in the clinical interview when examinees are highly guarded or determined to present themselves as psychologically fit for duty. In such cases, employees may understate or deny problems. Conversely, some employees who may be motivated to appear impaired for purposes of some anticipated secondary gain, such as a medical retirement, may present with feigned problems. For these reasons, forensic mental health evaluations always involve a review of multiple sources of relevant information to maximize reliability and validity (Heilbrun et al., 2009), as do all occupationally mandated psychological evaluations (APA, 2018). This is also why using psychological tests such as the MMPI-3, with well-validated response bias indictors, is a critical component of the FFDE.

Any existing mental health condition currently in remission, or the symptoms of which are ameliorated by treatment, also may not be apparent from a review of psychological test findings. Here, too, collateral information—including mental health treatment records—will prove vital in carrying out the integrative model. This is especially important because, under the ADA Amendments Act (ADAAA, 2008), consideration of the ameliorative effects of treatment is prohibited when determining whether a mental health condition is disabling.

Some problems that lead to fitness evaluations are the result of interpersonal rivalries, motivational deficits, retribution, misunderstandings, or poor judgment and can occur even in the absence of an underlying psychological condition. In the case illustrations that follow, we demonstrate for the reader how MMPI-3 findings can be integrated with other nontest information to aid in differentiating these contextual and relationship-specific problems from emotional or mental conditions that are the proper focus of clinical attention.

Assessing for a Substantially Limiting Impairment

Fitness evaluations can be thought of as another form of a competency evaluation—in this case, competency to perform the duties of a particular position. Grisso and colleagues (2003) effectively argue that all competency evaluations necessarily involve an analysis of the *interaction* between an individual's psychological functioning and environmental demands. For example, psychologists performing a parenting competency evaluation would consider not only the parent's emotional, behavioral, cognitive, and personality functioning but also the needs of the child or children. A parent with only episodic and moderate depressive symptoms may lack the competency to provide for the needs of a young child with serious medical, behavioral or psychological needs, or multiple older children with similar needs, whereas a parent with significant and chronic depressive symptoms may still be competent to parent an independent, well-adjusted, and high-functioning teenager. In the same way, evaluating an individual's fitness (competency) for duty requires an understanding of the position's specific job demands, the working conditions in which they occur, and the consequences of an impaired ability to perform the essential functions of the position. This information can be acquired through a combination of a review of the formal job description, interviews with supervisors and incumbent employees, and on-site observations, among other methods.

Assessing the Sustainability of Fitness

Although the future course of a mental health condition can be viewed as an aspect of the second integrative step (i.e., an assessment of current *and* anticipated impairment), contemporary thinking (e.g., Corey & Zelig, 2020; Mayer & Corey, 2017) regards it as a separate step in the analysis. This derives in part from how the ADAAA (2008) broadens the definition of disability. The ADAAA stipulates that some disorders

> may constitute substantially limiting impairments if they are substantially limiting when active or have a high likelihood of recurrence in substantially limiting forms. For some individuals, psychiatric impairments such as

bipolar disorder, major depression, and schizophrenia may remit and intensify, sometimes repeatedly, over the course of several months or several years. (EEOC, 1997/2009, at Question 8)

As such, an individual with a currently nonsymptomatic condition that is episodic or chronically relapsing may still be substantially impaired (and disabled), just as a person with a currently remitted substance use disorder may, under the law, still be regarded as engaged in "current use" if the last use is recent enough to suggest that it is ongoing (i.e., relapsing). Various courts have interpreted the period following symptom remission, during which a condition may be considered still active, to comprise weeks, months, or longer, depending on the condition (*Salley v. Circuit City Stores, Inc.*, 1998; *Shafer v. Preston Memorial Hospital Corp.*, 1997; *Zenor v. El Paso Healthcare Systems, Ltd.*, 1999). Thus, even when psychological test results indicate the absence of current, clinically significant dysfunction, other assessment data may nonetheless indicate otherwise or may support the conclusion that the current fitness is likely unsustainable upon returning to duty. We illustrate such cases in this chapter.

ABOUT THE CASE STUDIES

The following cases involve employees in all four public safety job categories: police officer, correctional officer, dispatcher, and firefighter/medic. Although the historical information in each case study reflects the facts in the assessment record, details that might reveal identities have been altered. None of these alterations meaningfully changes the record.

As with the preemployment case studies presented in chapter 8, because of space limitations, we have not reproduced the full set of assessment data (e.g., complete employment and medical records, findings from other psychological assessment instruments, and the examiner's notes from the mental status examination and clinical interview). Instead, we have selected data from these various sources as appropriate to illustrate a particular case and to show how that information may be integrated with MMPI-3 findings to reach a fitness determination. And, as with the cases presented in chapter 8, some readers may arrive at different conclusions about an employee's fitness (or unfitness) for duty based on the findings presented in these case illustrations. Here, too, our goal is not to point to a single "right" conclusion in any case but, rather, to enhance readers' understanding of how the integrative model can be applied to arrive at a well-reasoned fitness determination, to spur discussion of other related guidance, and to communicate the rationale for the fitness determination to the various stakeholders.

Readers, particularly those who wish to delve more thoroughly into the process of data integration in public safety fitness evaluations, will benefit from reviewing all cases, not just those from specific job categories. The material we discuss in each is germane to all fitness evaluations, and all the cases share the same assessment components and integrative steps.

The MMPI-3 report used in all seven cases is the Interpretive Report for Clinical Settings. Although it was developed primarily for use in clinical assessments conducted in the context of diagnosis and treatment planning, it is appropriate and can be helpful in fitness evaluations because of its empirically based focus on psychological dysfunction. The report and its elements are described in detail by Ben-Porath and Tellegen (2020c). Briefly, it consists of all the elements of the MMPI-3 Score Report (consisting of scale scores and item-level information) and an automated, annotated, and empirically grounded interpretation of the results. The major elements/sections of the clinical interpretive report include the Synopsis, summarizing the main findings in an MMPI-3 protocol; Protocol Validity, identifying potential threats to protocol validity discussed in chapter 2; and Substantive Scale Interpretation, reporting findings related to Somatic/Cognitive Dysfunction, Emotional Dysfunction, Thought Dysfunction, Behavioral Dysfunction, and Interpersonal Functioning scales. Diagnostic Considerations and Treatment Considerations sections are followed by one that provides Item-Level Information. As with the PSCIRs (described in chapter 7), the clinical interpretive report is fully annotated, meaning that the origin of (i.e., scale scores leading to) every statement in the report is identified and characterized as either being content based, empirically derived, or an inference of the report authors. Correlate-based statements are linked to specific publications that support them and can be accessed via hyperlinks. A primary advantage of this report is that it integrates a vast amount of information in a comprehensive, efficient, transparent, and consistent manner.

Use of the MMPI-3 Public Safety Candidate Interpretive Reports in FFDEs

It is never appropriate to use a PSCIR in an FFDE of any public safety employee. This is largely because (a) the demand characteristics and contexts under which both the PSCIR comparison group members and the candidates in the related validity studies took the test were different from those in an FFDE and (b) at the time of their suitability evaluation referral, all members of the PSCIR comparison groups were presumed free of psychopathology, in contrast to persons referred for an FFDE. Consequently, the base rates for scale elevations among public safety candidates in suitability evaluations are substantially lower than for fitness examinees. For example, Corey and Ben-Porath (2020) reported that only 0.3% of the MMPI-2-RF Police Candidate Comparison Group members scored at or above 55T on the EID scale. On the other hand, in a sample of

$N = 448$ male and $N = 111$ female law enforcement officers evaluated in an FFDE, the proportions scoring at or above 55T on EID were 12.1% and 18.0%, respectively (Corey & Ben-Porath, 2018). Thus, the use of a PSCIR is contraindicated in fitness evaluations.

MR. S, POLICE OFFICER

Assessment Issues Presented

- Prominent indications of underreporting combined with a pattern of problematic off-duty behavior
- Integration of moderately elevated substantive scales measuring psychopathology with collateral evidence related to future risk

Referral Summary

Mr. S is a 44-year-old, divorced police officer with 13 years of service in law enforcement, all with his current employer. He was referred for an FFDE after his intimate partner of 7 years filed a criminal complaint alleging that Mr. S had been harassing her. He allegedly sent repeated and unwanted text messages; had arrived at her home late at night, uninvited and intoxicated, demanding to be let in after she had informed him by text that she wanted no more contact; and had tried to choke her 2 months prior to this event during an intense verbal altercation—an incident that led her to end their relationship. She also provided copies of email messages in which he threatened suicide if she did not agree to a reconciliation. After notifying the police, she filed a petition for a restraining order against Mr. S, which he contested and the court denied due to insufficient evidence. For the same reason, no criminal indictment was filed against Mr. S.

After Mr. S was cleared of criminal charges, his employer conducted an internal affairs investigation, which found that Mr. S had engaged in behavior unbecoming a police officer. He served a 2-week unpaid suspension, after which the employer referred Mr. S for an FFDE. The referral letter stated that the purpose of the evaluation was to provide opinions concerning (a) any functional limitations in his ability to perform the essential functions of his position and (b) whether Mr. S posed a direct threat to himself or others as a result of a mental condition.

The employer reported that there had been no prior disciplinary actions or citizen complaints. During the 4 months between the index incident and the fitness evaluation, Mr. S was assigned to his home on paid administrative leave, except for the 2 weeks when he served his suspension.

Assessment Findings

Employment Records

A review of Mr. S's employment records, including his complete personnel file and employee medical file, confirmed the absence of prior disciplinary actions. All the performance evaluations for the previous 13 years contained positive ratings ("meets" or "exceeds" performance standards).

Findings from the internal affairs investigation, on the other hand, document two important facts. (See Corey and Borum [2013] and Corey and Zelig [2020] for a discussion of the importance, whenever possible, of conducting an FFDE only when internal affairs or other administrative investigations have concluded and findings are available for review by the fitness examiner.) First, Mr. S had not only sent 75 texts to his former romantic partner in the hours before he showed up uninvited at her home, but in the 3 months prior, he had sent her nearly 3,000 text messages; she had sent him fewer than 100, most of which were replies. His assertion that he did not know his texts were unwanted because he had blocked her phone was unconvincing. He claimed to have blocked her messages 2 days before she sent her cease-and-desist demand, yet many of his subsequent messages included pleas for her to reply and queries as to why she was not responding. A second piece of undisputed evidence was the email message he sent her threatening suicide if she continued to refuse reconciliation, notwithstanding his characterization of the threat as empty.

Mental Status Examination

Mr. S's appearance was unremarkable with regard to grooming, dress, and other features of his appearance. His speech displayed normal rate, intelligibility, volume, quality, and quantity. His affective expression was normal, and his mood was euthymic. Mr. S displayed no abnormalities with respect to his perception, thought process, or sensorium and cognition. His insight and judgment appeared impaired, as evidenced by his consistent denial of facts established by the internal affairs investigation. He denied past or current suicidal and homicidal ideation, as well as suicidal threats, notwithstanding his email message to his former romantic partner in which he threatened suicide unless she agreed to reconcile their relationship. His attitude toward the examiner was characterized by flippancy and arrogance.

Clinical Interview

Mr. S had a ready answer for every incriminating fact in the record. He admitted that he sent the barrage of text messages to his former partner, but he had "blocked her on my phone so I never received her message" demanding that he stop texting her. He said he came uninvited to his former romantic partner's home late at night and asked ("I never demanded") to be let in, because "in our 7-year relationship this kind of thing happened all the time and we always wound-up making up." He said the email message in which he threatened suicide was "just an effort to get her attention" and had never seriously considered killing himself. He also denied being intoxicated and challenged the credibility of his former partner's allegation that he had been drinking because she never opened her door and, therefore, could not have known. (She reported that she based her assessment on his loud voice and slurred speech—a pattern she said she had witnessed many times over the years of his allegedly heavy drinking.)

Mr. S reported that he was depressed when his partner announced that she wanted to end their relationship, but after he went to her home and she "made it crystal clear" that "she wanted nothing to do with me anymore," he accepted her refusal and "moved on." He said he has not been depressed since, except for brief periods during the internal affairs investigation when he worried that he might be fired. He denied a history of alcohol abuse. When asked if he had ever been in therapy, Mr. S declined to answer, stating that he considers his interactions with personal health care providers to be private information that is irrelevant to the purpose of this evaluation.

Medical Records

Mr. S's effort to evade disclosing his mental health treatment records was ultimately unsuccessful. He had placed these records "at issue" by presenting a letter from his therapist to his employer for mitigation purposes at the conclusion of the internal affairs investigation but before a final disciplinary decision had been made; therefore, they were no longer subject to the protections against compulsory disclosure normally afforded psychotherapy records (e.g., *Flora v. Hamilton*, 1978; *Thomas v. Corwin*, 2007; *Thompson v. City of Arlington*, 1993; see also Corey & Zelig, 2020 and Mayer & Corey, 2017). Under orders from his employer, Mr. S authorized the release of his mental health treatment records to the fitness examiner, after which the examiner had a brief phone consultation with the therapist.

The records revealed that Mr. S had reported to his treating therapist that he had long struggled with binge drinking in response to personal crises—a pattern Mr. S referred to as "self-medicating." The therapist's mitigation letter prepared for the employer discussed only Mr. S's history of depression and nothing more. During a subsequent phone conference with the fitness examiner, the treating therapist said that he included in the mitigation letter only the information that Mr. S authorized him to disclose.

The treatment records also contained the therapist's opinion that Mr. S had established an entrenched pattern of intense, unstable interpersonal relationships that resulted in emotional dysregulation and threats to his identity, which, *in more than one previous relationship,* had resulted in suicidal threats in an attempt to restore the status quo.

MMPI-3 Findings

Mr. S's MMPI-3 Interpretive Report for Clinical Settings is presented in Figure 10.1. An interpretation of Mr. S's MMPI-3 results begins with an examination of his unscorable responses and validity scale scores. He responded to all but one of the MMPI-3 items, which, as seen on page 2 of Figure 10.1 (at the row labeled "Response %"), is scored only on the CRIN, VRIN, and FBS scales. Nonetheless, his validity scale scores indicate that he responded to the remaining items in a relevant and consistent manner. Indeed, he was unusually attentive to response consistency, as indicated by his score of 39T on TRIN. In addition, there is no evidence of overreporting.

As described in the Protocol Validity section of Mr. S's report (Figure 10.1), his score on the Adjustment Validity scale (K = 68T) indicates that he "presented himself as very well-adjusted" and "any absence of elevation on the Substantive Scales should be interpreted with caution" if there is evidence that the test taker "is not especially well-adjusted" (p. 8). Ample evidence supports such a cautionary stance when interpreting Mr. S's substantive scale scores, all of which are < 60T. Notable among these scores is a T score of 58 on SUI (Figure 10.1, p. 4), which is considered clinically elevated. The SUI item that Mr. S responded to in the keyed direction is printed on page 10 of the report (but is redacted in Figure 10.1 for test security) and indicates a history of suicidal thoughts.

Data Integration

Step 1: Assessing for a Mental Health Condition

The first step in the integrative process is to assess for evidence indicating the presence of a mental health condition. As discussed, findings from psychological tests, although not dispositive of a diagnosis, help inform that assessment. In forensic contexts, when interpreting an MMPI-3 protocol in which a test taker's overreporting or underreporting scores are elevated but not invalidating, it is important to consider possible motives, particularly involving secondary gain for either feigning a disability or concealing problems, respectively. Although Mr. S made no substantial claim of moral virtuousness (i.e., L = 48T), his claim of positive psychological adjustment is contradicted by information contained in the psychotherapy notes and his documented recent behavior. Due

Interpretive Report: Clinical Settings

MMPI®-3
Minnesota Multiphasic Personality Inventory®-3
Yossef S. Ben-Porath, PhD, & Auke Tellegen, PhD

ID Number:	Mr. S
Age:	44
Gender:	Male
Marital Status:	Not reported
Years of Education:	Not reported
Date Assessed:	07/18/2021

Copyright © 2020 by the Regents of the University of Minnesota. All rights reserved. Distributed exclusively under license from the University of Minnesota by NCS Pearson, Inc. Portions reproduced from the *MMPI-3 English Test Booklet.* Copyright © 2020 by the Regents of the University of Minnesota. All rights reserved. Portions excerpted from the *MMPI-3 Manual for Administration, Scoring, and Interpretation.* Copyright © 2020 by the Regents of the University of Minnesota. All rights reserved. Portions excerpted from the *MMPI-3 Technical Manual.* Copyright © 2020 by the Regents of the University of Minnesota. All rights reserved. Used by permission of the University of Minnesota Press.

Minnesota Multiphasic Personality Inventory and **MMPI** are registered trademarks of the Regents of the University of Minnesota. **Pearson** is a trademark, in the US and/or other countries, of Pearson Education, Inc., or its affiliates.

This report contains copyrighted material and trade secrets. Qualified licensees may excerpt portions of this output report, limited to the minimum text necessary to accurately describe their significant core conclusions, for incorporation into a written evaluation of the examinee, in accordance with their profession's citation standards, if any. No adaptations, translations, modifications, or special versions may be made of this report without prior written permission from the University of Minnesota Press.

[1.0 / 19 / QG]

ALWAYS LEARNING   PEARSON

FIGURE 10.1. Mr. S's MMPI-3 Clinical Settings Interpretive Report

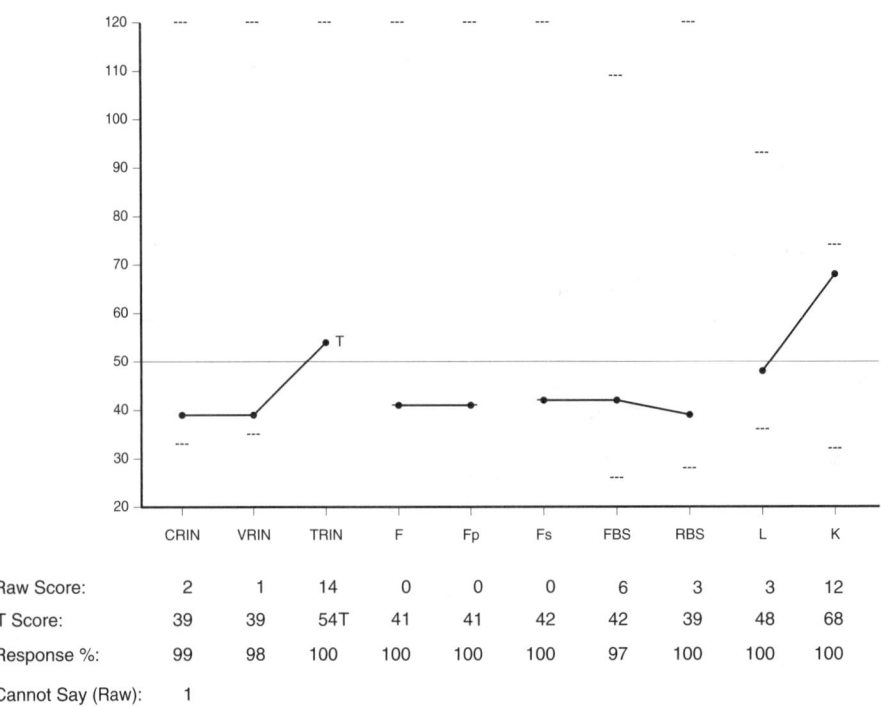

FIGURE 10.1. Mr. S's MMPI-3 Clinical Settings Interpretive Report, continued

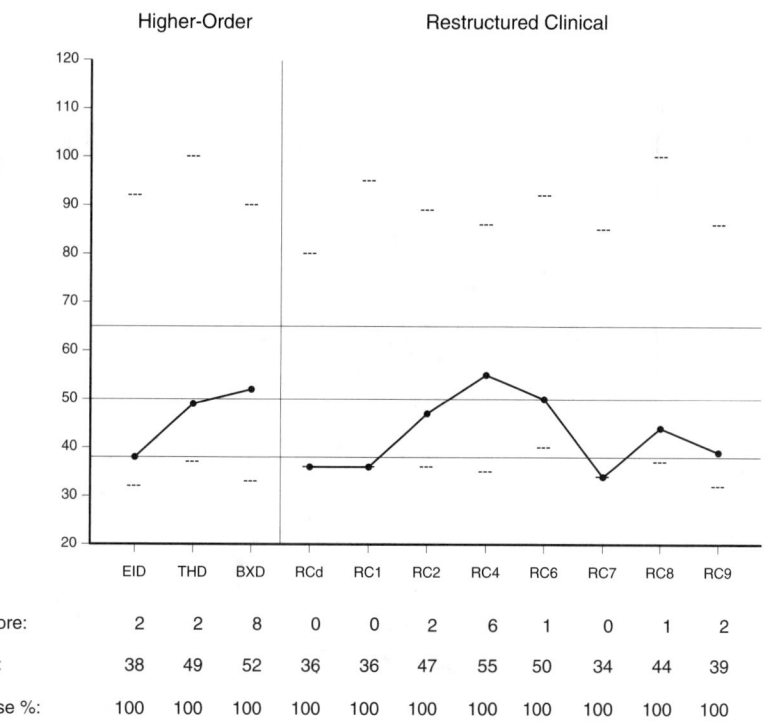

FIGURE 10.1. Mr. S's MMPI-3 Clinical Settings Interpretive Report, continued

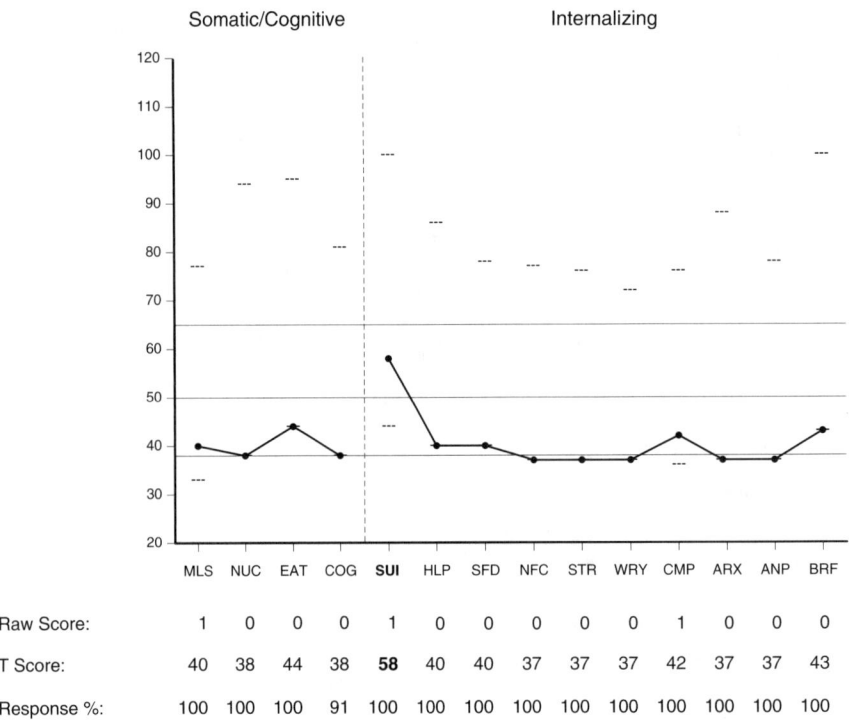

FIGURE 10.1. Mr. S's MMPI-3 Clinical Settings Interpretive Report, continued

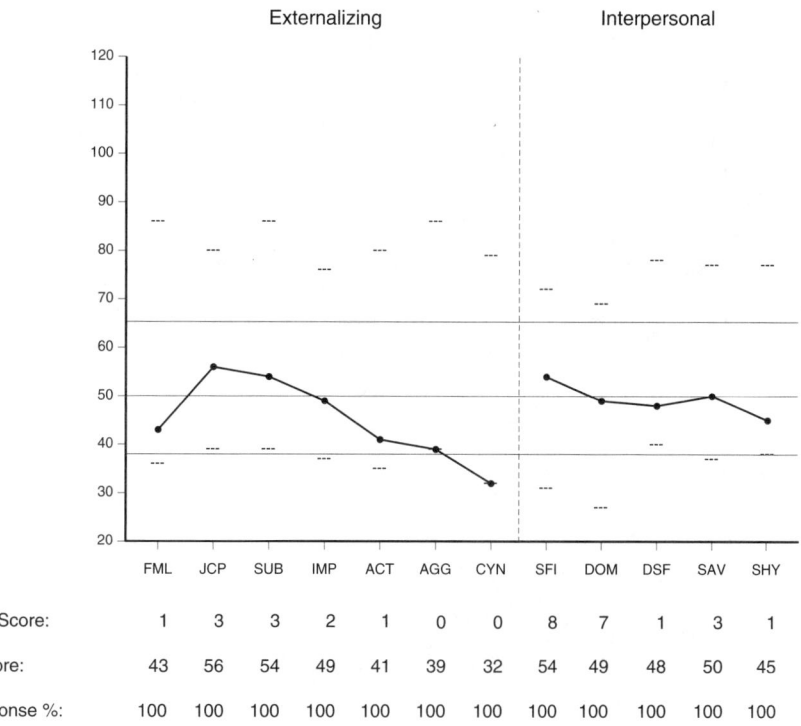

FIGURE 10.1. Mr. S's MMPI-3 Clinical Settings Interpretive Report, continued

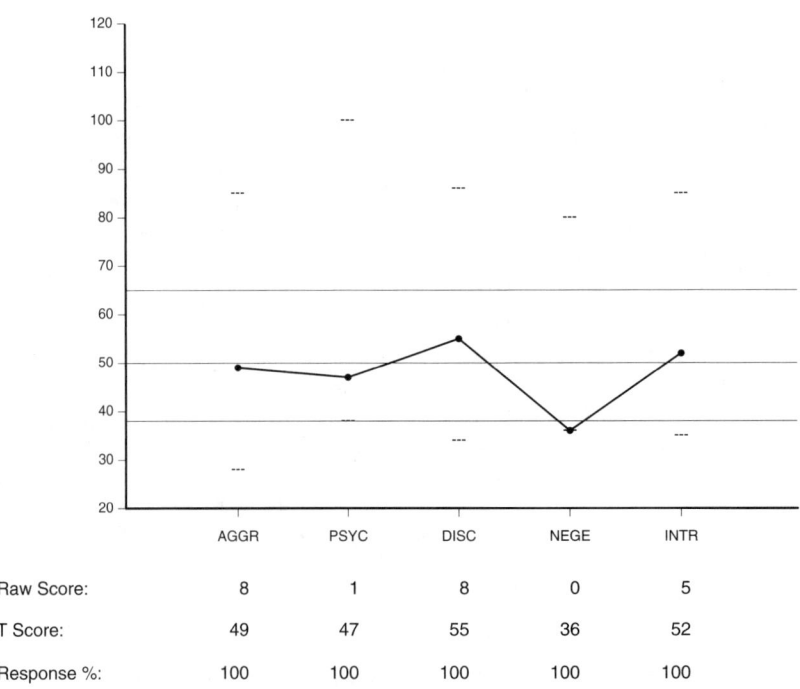

FIGURE 10.1. Mr. S's MMPI-3 Clinical Settings Interpretive Report, continued

MMPI®-3 Interpretive Report: Clinical Settings
07/18/2021, Page 7
ID: Mr. S

MMPI-3 T SCORES (BY DOMAIN)

PROTOCOL VALIDITY

Content Non-Responsiveness		1 CNS	39 CRIN	39 VRIN	54 T TRIN		
Over-Reporting		41 F	41 Fp		42 Fs	42 FBS	39 RBS
Under-Reporting		48 L	**68** **K**				

SUBSTANTIVE SCALES

Somatic/Cognitive Dysfunction		36 RC1	40 MLS	38 NUC	44 EAT	38 COG			
Emotional Dysfunction	38 EID	36 RCd	**58** **SUI**	40 HLP	40 SFD	37 NFC			
		47 RC2	**52** **INTR**						
		34 RC7	37 STR	37 WRY	42 CMP	37 ARX	37 ANP	43 BRF	36 NEGE
Thought Dysfunction	49 THD	50 RC6							
		44 RC8							
		47 PSYC							
Behavioral Dysfunction	52 BXD	55 RC4	43 FML	56 JCP	54 SUB				
		39 RC9	49 IMP	41 ACT	39 AGG	32 CYN			
		55 DISC							
Interpersonal Functioning		54 SFI	49 DOM	49 AGGR	48 DSF	50 SAV	45 SHY		

Scale scores shown in bold font are interpreted in the report.

Note. This information is provided to facilitate interpretation following the recommended structure for MMPI-3 interpretation in Chapter 5 of the *MMPI-3 Manual for Administration, Scoring, and Interpretation*, which provides details in the text and an outline in Table 5-1.

FIGURE 10.1. Mr. S's MMPI-3 Clinical Settings Interpretive Report, continued

This interpretive report is intended for use by a professional qualified to interpret the MMPI-3. The information it contains should be considered in the context of the test taker's background, the circumstances of the assessment, and other available information.

The report includes extensive annotation, which appears as superscripts following each statement in the narrative, keyed to Endnotes with accompanying Research References, which appear in the final two sections of the report. Additional information about the annotation features is provided in the headnotes to these sections and in the MMPI-3 User's Guide for the Score and Clinical Interpretive Reports.

SYNOPSIS

Scores on the MMPI-3 Validity Scales raise concerns about the possible impact of under-reporting on the validity of this protocol. With that caution noted, scores on the Substantive Scales indicate emotional dysfunction. Emotional-internalizing findings relate to **suicidal ideation**.

PROTOCOL VALIDITY

Content Non-Responsiveness

The test taker answered at least 90% of the items on each of the MMPI-3 scales. He also responded relevantly to the items on the basis of their content.

Over-Reporting

There are no indications of over-reporting in this protocol.

Under-Reporting

The test taker presented himself as very well-adjusted[1]. This reported level of psychological adjustment is relatively rare in the general population. If there is evidence that this individual is not especially well-adjusted, any absence of elevation on the Substantive Scales should be interpreted with caution[2]. Elevated scores on the Substantive Scales may underestimate the problems assessed by those scales[3].

SUBSTANTIVE SCALE INTERPRETATION

Clinical symptoms, personality characteristics, and behavioral tendencies of the test taker are described in this section and organized according to an empirically guided framework. (Please see Chapter 5 of the MMPI-3 Manual for Administration, Scoring, and Interpretation *for details.) Statements containing the word "reports" are based on the item content of MMPI-3 scales, whereas statements that include the word "likely" are based on empirical correlates of scale scores. Specific sources for each statement can be viewed with the annotation features of this report.*

In light of earlier-described evidence of under-reporting (of psychological problems), the following statements may not identify, or may underestimate, the test taker's psychological issues.

FIGURE 10.1. Mr. S's MMPI-3 Clinical Settings Interpretive Report, continued

Somatic/Cognitive Dysfunction

There are no indications of somatic or cognitive dysfunction in this protocol. However, because of indications of under-reporting described earlier, such problems cannot be ruled out.

Emotional Dysfunction

The test taker responded to one of the seven Suicidal/Death Ideation (SUI) scale items in the keyed direction. The content of this item is provided in the Critical Responses section later in this report[4]. He may be at risk for self-harm[5], preoccupied with suicide and death[6], and at risk for current suicidal ideation and attempts[7].

Thought Dysfunction

There are no indications of disordered thinking in this protocol. However, because of indications of under-reporting described earlier, such problems cannot be ruled out.

Behavioral Dysfunction

There are no indications of maladaptive externalizing behavior in this protocol. However, because of indications of under-reporting described earlier, such problems cannot be ruled out.

Interpersonal Functioning Scales

These scales provide no further evidence of dysfunction.

DIAGNOSTIC CONSIDERATIONS

No specific psychodiagnostic recommendations are indicated by this MMPI-3 protocol. However, this finding needs to be considered in light of cautions noted earlier about possible under-reporting.

TREATMENT CONSIDERATIONS

This section provides inferential treatment-related recommendations based on the test taker's MMPI-3 scores. **The following recommendation needs to be considered in light of cautions noted earlier about possible threats to protocol validity.**

Areas for Further Evaluation

- <u>Risk for suicide</u> should be assessed immediately[8].

ITEM-LEVEL INFORMATION

Unscorable Responses

Following is the item to which the test taker did not provide a scorable response. Unanswered or double answered (both True and False) items are unscorable. The scale(s) on which the item appears are in parentheses following the item content.

    Item number and content omitted. (VRIN, FBS, COG)

Critical Responses

Seven MMPI-3 scales—Suicidal/Death Ideation (SUI), Helplessness/Hopelessness (HLP), Anxiety-Related Experiences (ARX), Ideas of Persecution (RC6), Aberrant Experiences (RC8), Substance Abuse (SUB), and Aggression (AGG)—have been designated by the test authors as having critical item content that may require immediate attention and follow-up. Items answered by the individual in the keyed direction (True or False) on a

FIGURE 10.1. Mr. S's MMPI-3 Clinical Settings Interpretive Report, continued

critical scale are listed below if his T score on that scale is 65 or higher. However, any item answered in the keyed direction on SUI is listed. The percentage of the MMPI-3 normative sample that answered each item in the keyed direction is provided in parentheses following the item content.

Suicidal/Death Ideation (SUI, T Score = 58)
    Item number and content omitted. (True, 22.2%)

FIGURE 10.1. Mr. S's MMPI-3 Clinical Settings Interpretive Report, continued

ENDNOTES

This section lists for each statement in the report the MMPI-3 score(s) that triggered it. In addition, each statement is identified as a <u>Test Response</u>, if based on item content, a <u>Correlate</u>, if based on empirical correlates, or an <u>Inference</u>, if based on the report authors' judgment. (This information can also be accessed on-screen by placing the cursor on a given statement.) For correlate-based statements, research references (Ref. No.) are provided, keyed to the consecutively numbered reference list following the endnotes.

[1] Test Response: K=68
[2] Correlate: K=68, Ref. 3, 4, 9, 13
[3] Correlate: K=68, Ref. 2, 5, 13, 16
[4] Test Response: SUI=58
[5] Correlate: SUI=58, Ref. 2, 8, 11
[6] Correlate: SUI=58, Ref. 1, 2, 6, 7, 10, 11, 12, 14, 16
[7] Correlate: SUI=58, Ref. 1, 2, 6, 7, 11, 14, 15, 16
[8] Inference: SUI=58

FIGURE 10.1. Mr. S's MMPI-3 Clinical Settings Interpretive Report, continued

RESEARCH REFERENCE LIST

The following studies are sources for empirical correlates identified in the Endnotes section of this report.

1. Anestis, J. C., Finn, J. A., Gottfried, E. D., Hames, J. L., Bodell, L. P., Hagan, C. R., Arnau, R. C., Anestis, M. D., Arbisi, P. A., & Joiner, T. E. (2018). Burdensomeness, belongingness, and capability: Assessing the interpersonal-psychological theory of suicide with MMPI-2-RF scales. *Assessment, 25*(4), 415–431. https://doi.org/10.1177/1073191116652227

2. Ben-Porath, Y. S., & Tellegen, A. (2020). *The Minnesota Multiphasic Personality Inventory-3 (MMPI-3): Technical manual.* University of Minnesota Press.

3. Brown, T. A., & Sellbom, M. (2020). The utility of the MMPI-2-RF validity scales in detecting underreporting. *Journal of Personality Assessment, 102*(1), 66–74. https://doi.org/10.1080/00223891.2018.1539003

4. Crighton, A. H., Marek, R. J., Dragon, W. R., & Ben-Porath, Y. S. (2017). Utility of the MMPI-2-RF Validity Scales in detection of simulated underreporting: Implications of incorporating a manipulation check. *Assessment, 24*(7), 853–864. https://doi.org/10.1177/1073191115627011

5. Forbey, J. D., Lee, T. T. C., Ben-Porath, Y. S., Arbisi, P. A., & Gartland, D. (2013). Associations between MMPI-2-RF validity scale scores and extra-test measures of personality and psychopathology. *Assessment, 20*(4), 448–461. https://doi.org/10.1177/1073191113478154

6. Glassmire, D. M, Tarescavage, A. M., Burchett, D., Martinez, J., & Gomez, A. (2016). Clinical utility of the MMPI-2-RF SUI items and scale in a forensic inpatient setting: Association with interview self-reports and future suicidal behavior. *Psychological Assessment, 28*(11), 1502–1509. https://doi.org/10.1037/pas0000220

7. Gottfried, E., Bodell, L., Carbonell, J., & Joiner, T. (2014). The clinical utility of the MMPI-2-RF Suicidal/Death Ideation Scale. *Psychological Assessment, 26*(4), 1205–1211. https://doi.org/10.1037/pas0000017

8. Laurinaityte, I., Laurinavicius, A., Ustinaviciute, L., Wygant, D. B., Sellbom, M. (2017). Utility of the MMPI-2 Restructured Form (MMPI-2-RF) in a sample of Lithuanian male offenders. *Law and Human Behavior, 41*(5), 494–505. https://doi.org/10.1037/lhb0000254

9. Marion, B. E., Sellbom, M., Salekin, R. T., Toomey, J. A., Kucharski, L. T., & Duncan, S. (2013). An examination of the association between psychopathy and dissimulation using the MMPI-2-RF Validity Scales. *Law and Human Behavior, 37*(4), 219–230. https://doi.org/10.1037/lhb0000008

10. Menton, W. H., Crighton, A. H., Tarescavage, A. M., Marek, R. J., Hicks, A. D., & Ben-Porath, Y. S. (2019). Equivalence of laptop and tablet administrations of the Minnesota Multiphasic Personality Inventory-2 Restructured Form. *Assessment, 26*(4), 661–669. https://doi.org/10.1177/1073191117714558

11. Miller, S. N., Bozzay, M. L., Ben-Porath, Y. S., & Arbisi, P. A. (2019). Distinguishing levels of suicide risk in depressed male veterans: The role of internalizing and externalizing psychopathology as measured by the MMPI-2-RF. *Assessment, 26*(1), 85–98. https://doi.org/10.1177/1073191117743787

12. Rogers, M. L., Anestis, J. C., Harrop, T. M., Schneider, M., Bender, T. W., Ringer, F. B., & Joiner, T. E. (2017). Examination of MMPI-2-RF substantive scales as indicators of acute suicidal affective disturbance components. *Journal of Personality Assessment, 99*(4), 424–434. https://doi.org/10.1080/00223891.2016.1222393

13. Sellbom, M., & Bagby, R. M. (2008). Validity of the MMPI-2-RF (Restructured Form) L-r and K-r scales in detecting under-reporting in clinical and non-clinical samples. *Psychological Assessment, 20*(4), 370–376. https://doi.org/10.1037/a0012952

FIGURE 10.1. Mr. S's MMPI-3 Clinical Settings Interpretive Report, continued

14. Stanley, I. H., Yancey, J. R., Patrick, C. J., & Joiner, T. E. (2018). A distinct configuration of MMPI-2-RF scales RCd and RC9/ACT is associated with suicide attempt risk among suicide ideators in a psychiatric outpatient sample. *Psychological Assessment, 30*(9), 1249–1254. https://doi.org/10.1037/pas0000588

15. Tarescavage, A. M., Glassmire, D. M., & Burchett, D. (2018). Minnesota Multiphasic Personality Inventory-2-Restructured Form markers of future suicidal behavior in a forensic psychiatric hospital. *Psychological Assessment, 30*(2), 170–178. https://doi.org/10.1037/pas0000463

16. Tellegen, A., & Ben-Porath, Y. S. (2008/2011). *Minnesota Multiphasic Personality Inventory-2-Restructured Form (MMPI-2-RF): Technical manual.* University of Minnesota Press.

End of Report

FIGURE 10.1. Mr. S's MMPI-3 Clinical Settings Interpretive Report, continued

to the discrepancies between Mr. S's claims of positive adjustment and other collateral information, the absence of elevation in Mr. S's MMPI-3 substantive scale scores cannot be interpreted as indicating the absence of the problems they measure, particularly in the Emotional/Internalizing domain (Detrick & Chibnall, 2014).

Setting aside the allegations that Mr. S denied, evidence indicating the possibility of a mental health condition exists from these undisputed facts: (a) the more than 3,000 texts he sent his former romantic partner in the last 3 months of their relationship (including 75 on the last day), representing more than a 30:1 ratio of sent/received messages; (b) his noncredible assertion that he was unaware of her demand that he stop communicating with her (it was his persistent unwanted communications that formed the basis for the employer's finding of conduct unbecoming an officer and its imposition of a 2-week suspension); (c) his emailed suicide threat; and (d) psychotherapy records documenting his history of binge drinking, prior suicide threats, and persistent dysthymia.

Step 2: Assessing for Current Work Impairment

The second step in the integrative process addresses whether Mr. S's condition substantially limits his *current* ability to perform his essential job functions, to perform them properly, or to perform them without posing a direct threat to himself or others. We begin this analysis with the behavior that led to Mr. S's 2-week suspension (i.e., his excessive, unwanted communications with his former romantic partner). In every fitness evaluation in which the referral was precipitated by the employer's (a) conclusion that the employee engaged in impermissible behavior and (b) belief that it may be caused by a mental health condition, the most parsimonious path in this second analytical step is to assess whether the identified condition is causally linked to the problem behavior and, if unresolved, likely to lead to the same or similar behavior, or a direct threat to himself or others, in the foreseeable future.

Findings from extratest data establish a clear pattern of impaired functioning in emotion regulation, intimate relationships, and self-identity. Although this trio of symptoms is characteristic of borderline personality disorder, the examiner declined to diagnose a personality disorder or to make any other precise diagnosis considering Mr. S's noncredible responding throughout the assessment. Instead, the examiner documented these functional limitations and their nexus to the index incident. Although Mr. S had initiated psychotherapy, the examiner concluded from a review of treatment records that insufficient therapeutic progress had been made to warrant the expectation that the functional limitations have been resolved. Assessing the nexus between a mental health condition and work impairment requires an understanding of both the natural course of the condition (i.e., how it typically manifests, what systems are typically affected by it, symptom intransigence, and treatment effectiveness) and how it interacts with the individual's personality, life circumstances, and treatment engagement.

The clinical evidence in this case establishes a compelling nexus between Mr. S's symptoms (i.e., emotional dysregulation, unstable self-identity and associated suicidal ideation, impaired interpersonal functioning in his intimate relationships, and binge drinking) and the index incident. Furthermore, there is no clinical basis for believing that Mr. S's symptoms are now sufficiently controlled as to make it more likely than not that the same or similar response to provocation would be inhibited. Said another way, the probability of recurrence remains high. The parsimony of this analysis lies in linking the employee's condition to a recurrence of the index incident rather than speculating about what other essential job functions might be impaired by it. This is not to say that such speculation is never appropriate or needed in some situations. But when, as in this case, the behavior precipitating the FFDE referral is both causally linked to the employee's mental health condition and already identified by the employer as incompatible with acceptable job performance, the fitness analysis does not require more.

Nevertheless, the referral also asked the examiner to determine whether Mr. S posed a direct threat to himself or others in his capacity as a police officer. Assessing for direct threat requires an individualized examination of what is commonly referred to as the four *Arline factors,* so-named after a landmark decision by the U.S. Supreme Court (*School Board of Nassau County v. Arline,* 1987). These consist of (a) the nature of the risk, (b) the duration of the risk, (c) the severity of the risk, and (d) the probability that harm will occur. When, as here, the examinee's position implicates others' safety with potentially severe harm or is engaged in dangerous work in which the consequences of impaired functioning can be catastrophic, even a low probability of harm may be sufficient to establish a direct threat (see, e.g., *Brownfield v. Yakima,* 2010; *Butler v. Thornburgh,* 1990; *Hogarth v. Thornburgh,* 1993; *Myers v. Hose,* 1995). Concerns about the prospect of suicide by Mr. S are reinforced by indications of "thwarted belongingness" (Chu et al., 2017), components of which include living alone, a nonintact family, and relationship conflict, among others (Van Orden et al., 2010).

Step 3: Assessing for Sustainability of Fitness

The third step in the integrative process is required only in cases where the employee's episodic mental health condition is currently nonlimiting. Given the fact that Mr. S's condition substantially limits his current occupational functioning and poses a direct threat of self-harm, this step is moot.

Conclusion

The aggregate evidence derived from all sources indicates that Mr. S was experiencing substantial impairment at the time of the evaluation, including occupational impairment (i.e., the ongoing risk of conduct unbecoming a police officer), as a result of a current mental health condition that causes dysregulation of his mood, behavior, and interpersonal functioning. His condition substantially limited his functioning on the dimensions of Emotional Regulation and Stress Tolerance, Impulse Control/Attention to Safety, and Decision-Making and Judgment. His risk of self-harm also posed a direct threat to himself (and, in the capacity of a police officer, to others). Thus, the examiner determined that Mr. S was *unfit for duty*.

MR. R, DEPUTY SHERIFF

Assessment Issues Presented

- A law enforcement officer who, while intoxicated, became despondent, crashed his vehicle, and was arrested for drunk driving
- Integration of moderately elevated scores on substantive scales measuring psychopathology with collateral evidence related to future risk

Referral Summary

Mr. R is a 25-year-old unmarried man who, at the time of this fitness evaluation, had been employed for 4 years as a deputy sheriff in a rural county. During a 3-day camping trip with fellow deputies and their spouses or partners, Mr. R became extremely intoxicated. He began making sexual overtures—all verbal—to several women in the group, and these comments persisted even after it was made clear by the women and their partners that they were unwanted and needed to stop. Eventually, several of his fellow deputies pulled him aside and told him to return to his tent to "sleep it off." Instead, Mr. R took his loaded firearm and drove off in his vehicle. Once his direction was established, his fellow deputies called 911 to arrange for his vehicle to be stopped and for Mr. R to be taken into safe custody. He was arrested for drunk driving and released to the custody of his parents. While being processed for his arrest, he made statements that reasonably led witnesses to believe he may have been suicidal. Following an internal affairs investigation, adjudication of his drunk driving offense, and completion of his 2-week unpaid suspension, he was referred for evaluation of his fitness for duty.

Assessment Findings

Employment Records

A review of Mr. R's employment records, including his complete personnel file and employee medical file, confirmed the absence of prior disciplinary actions. The available annual performance reviews reflected a positive performance record and a strong reputation for reliability, work ethic, and an absence of citizen complaints. The records contained several commendations for exemplary service.

Mental Status Examination

Mr. R's appearance was unremarkable with regard to grooming, dress, weight, movement, and other features. His behavior also was unremarkable. His speech was normal, as indicated by its rate, intelligibility, volume, quality, and quantity. His affective expression was normal, and his mood was euthymic. Mr. R displayed no abnormalities with respect to his perception, thought process, sensorium and cognition, judgment, insight, or reliability.

Clinical Interview

The fitness evaluation took place slightly more than 3 months after Mr. R's arrest. During that time, he completed a court-ordered substance abuse evaluation and a 30-day inpatient treatment, followed by intensive outpatient treatment, which included counseling focused on relapse prevention. Throughout the clinical interview, Mr. R was straightforward in acknowledging his offenses, involving both his behavior at the campsite and his decision to drive while intoxicated. He said he had limited memory of the evening, including his sexual comments to the women at the campsite, his drunk driving, and statements that implied an intent to kill himself, but he also said that all of the witnesses to these alleged behaviors are credible and he did not deny the behaviors or attempt to minimize their significance.

Mr. R said that he has "never been a drinker" and "had no business drinking so much," especially since he has always had a low tolerance for alcohol. He said that he has a clear memory of feeling "like a fifth wheel" at the campground, because all his friends came with a spouse or partner. He said he was feeling "a bit depressed" and now realized how alcohol only deepened his depressed state. He said he was now committed to sobriety and has no intention of drinking again, "at least for a while." He displayed a good understanding of relapse management and relapse triggers unique to him.

Medical Records

A review of the records from Mr. R's inpatient and outpatient substance use treatment revealed a high level of sustained engagement and continued sobriety (as evidenced by random screening). Clinical summaries noted his cooperation, completion of all assigned tasks (e.g., daily journaling and participation in sobriety-maintenance group meetings), and positive prognosis.

MMPI-3 Findings

Mr. R's MMPI-3 Interpretive Report for Clinical Settings is reproduced in Figure 10.2. The report indicates that there are no unscorable items, and Mr. R responded to the MMPI-3 in a remarkably consistent manner, as indicated by his CRIN, VRIN, and TRIN scale scores (36T, 35T, and 54T, respectively). There are no indications of overreporting in the protocol, and he claimed few uncommon virtues (48T). However, consistent with his self-report in the clinical interview, he presented himself as well-adjusted (K = 65T). In light of the collateral records and findings from the clinical interview, his self-reported level of adjustment appeared to be valid. His scores on the Substantive Scales were all in the moderate, nonclinical range, which, as summarized in the Substantive Scale Interpretation section of the report, indicate the absence "of somatic, cognitive, emotional, thought, or behavioral dysfunction in this protocol" (p. 8), with the caveat that "because of indications of underreporting described earlier, such problems cannot be ruled out." Importantly, a review of his responses to the items on the SUB scale were consistent with his known history of alcohol use problems; he had no known history of other substance use problems.

Data Integration

Step 1: Assessing for a Mental Health Condition

The aggregate evidence indicates an unspecified alcohol use disorder characterized by clinically significant impairment in important areas of functioning but without indications of a problematic pattern of alcohol use. No other mental health conditions were identified, and his depressed mood at the time of the index incident appeared to be situationally induced and chemically exacerbated.

Step 2: Assessing for Current Work Impairment

The clinical evidence suggests that Mr. R's sobriety, although still in the early stages, has been sustained for 3 months. His insight and therapeutic engagement support a positive prognosis for full recovery and continued sobriety, at

Minnesota Multiphasic Personality Inventory®-3

Interpretive Report: Clinical Settings

MMPI®-3
Minnesota Multiphasic Personality Inventory®-3
Yossef S. Ben-Porath, PhD, & Auke Tellegen, PhD

ID Number:	Mr. R
Age:	25
Gender:	Male
Marital Status:	Not reported
Years of Education:	Not reported
Date Assessed:	12/26/2020

Copyright © 2020 by the Regents of the University of Minnesota. All rights reserved. Distributed exclusively under license from the University of Minnesota by NCS Pearson, Inc. Portions reproduced from the *MMPI-3 English Test Booklet*. Copyright © 2020 by the Regents of the University of Minnesota. All rights reserved. Portions excerpted from the *MMPI-3 Manual for Administration, Scoring, and Interpretation*. Copyright © 2020 by the Regents of the University of Minnesota. All rights reserved. Portions excerpted from the *MMPI-3 Technical Manual*. Copyright © 2020 by the Regents of the University of Minnesota. All rights reserved. Used by permission of the University of Minnesota Press.

Minnesota Multiphasic Personality Inventory and **MMPI** are registered trademarks of the Regents of the University of Minnesota. **Pearson** is a trademark, in the US and/or other countries, of Pearson Education, Inc., or its affiliates.

This report contains copyrighted material and trade secrets. Qualified licensees may excerpt portions of this output report, limited to the minimum text necessary to accurately describe their significant core conclusions, for incorporation into a written evaluation of the examinee, in accordance with their profession's citation standards, if any. No adaptations, translations, modifications, or special versions may be made of this report without prior written permission from the University of Minnesota Press.

[1.0 / 19 / QG]

ALWAYS LEARNING PEARSON

FIGURE 10.2. Mr. R's MMPI-3 Clinical Settings Interpretive Report

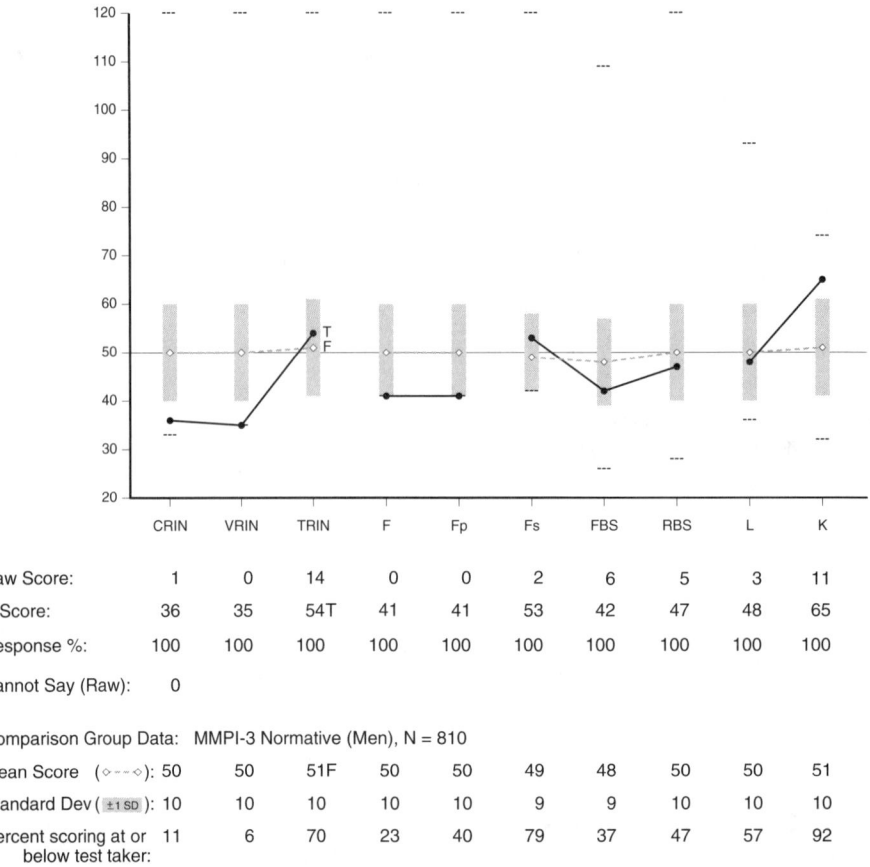

FIGURE 10.2. Mr. R's MMPI-3 Clinical Settings Interpretive Report, continued

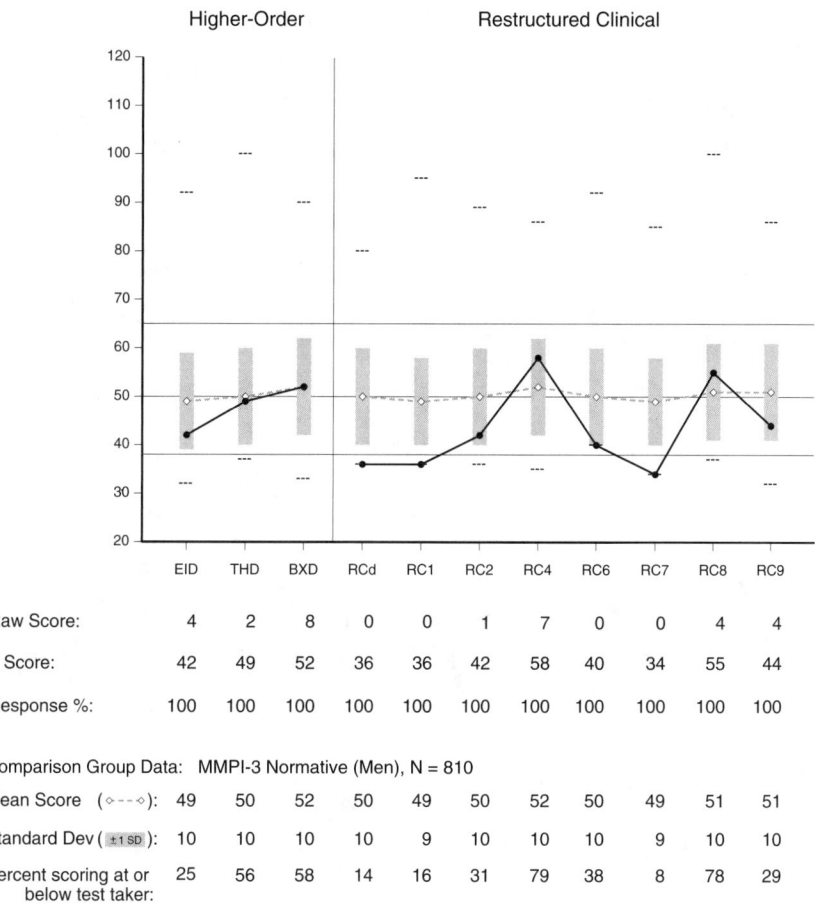

FIGURE 10.2. Mr. R's MMPI-3 Clinical Settings Interpretive Report, continued

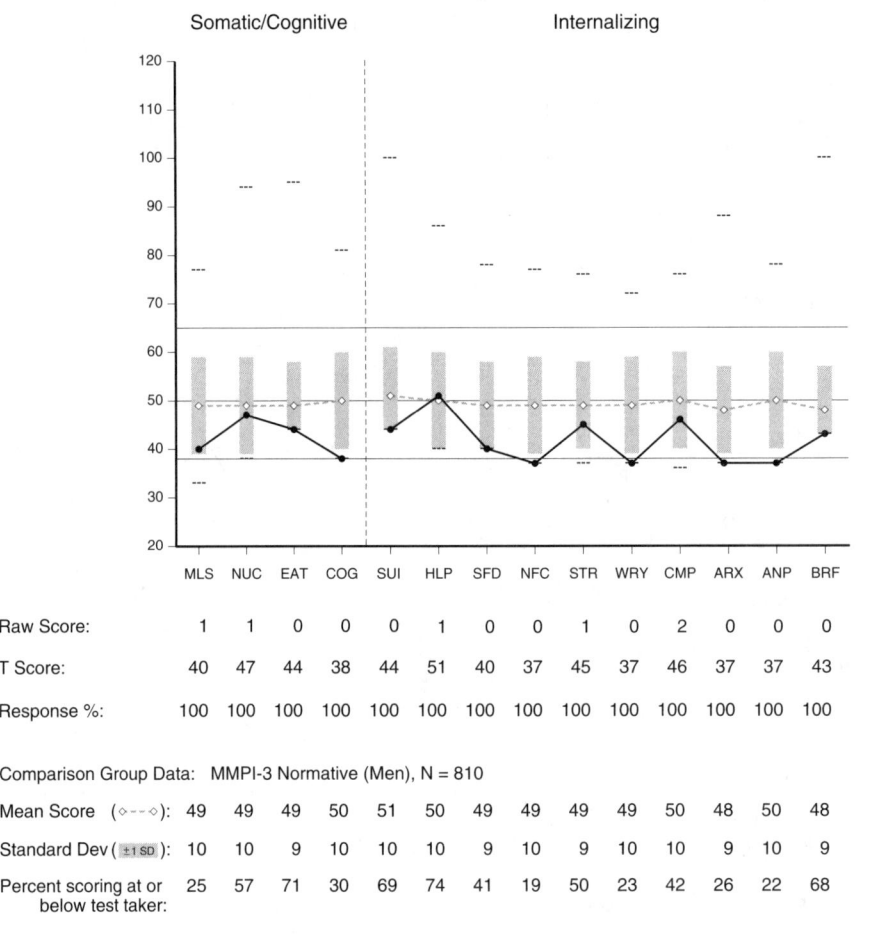

FIGURE 10.2. Mr. R's MMPI-3 Clinical Settings Interpretive Report, continued

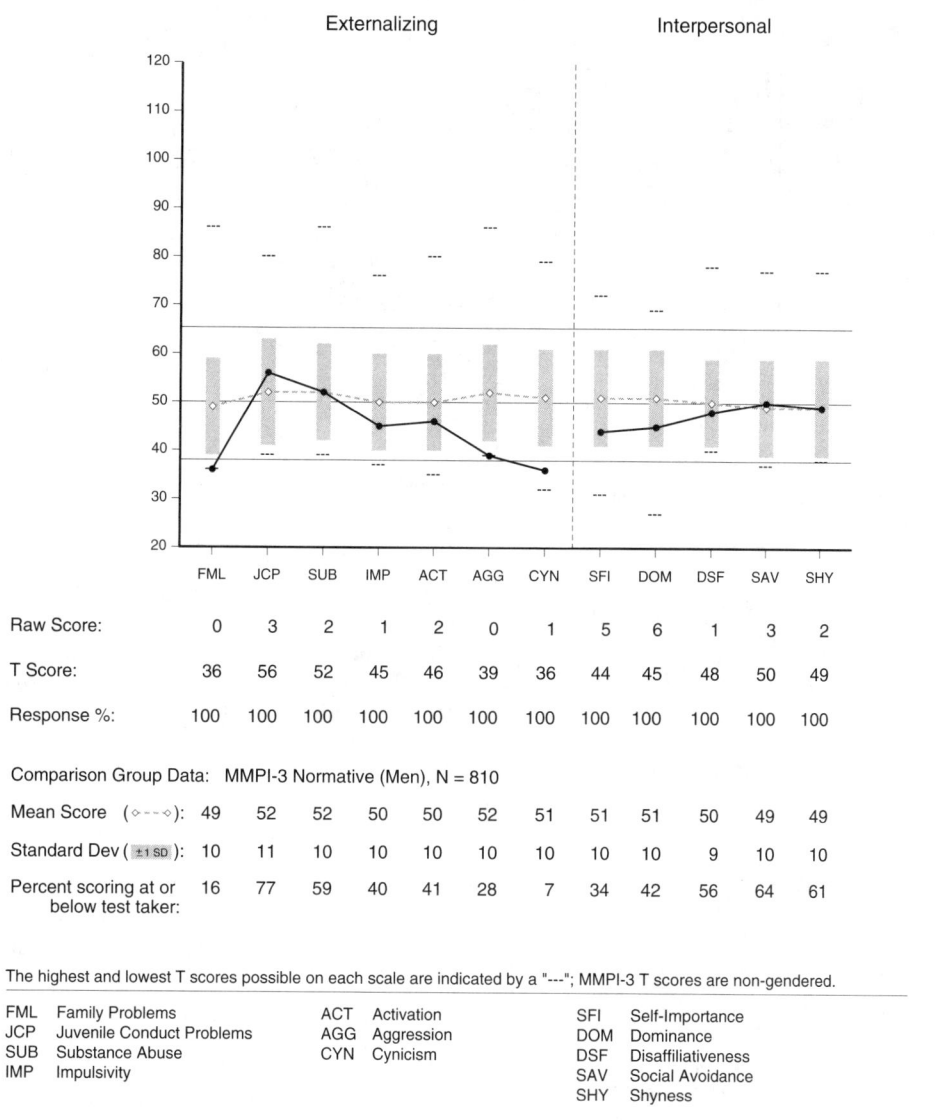

FIGURE 10.2. Mr. R's MMPI-3 Clinical Settings Interpretive Report, continued

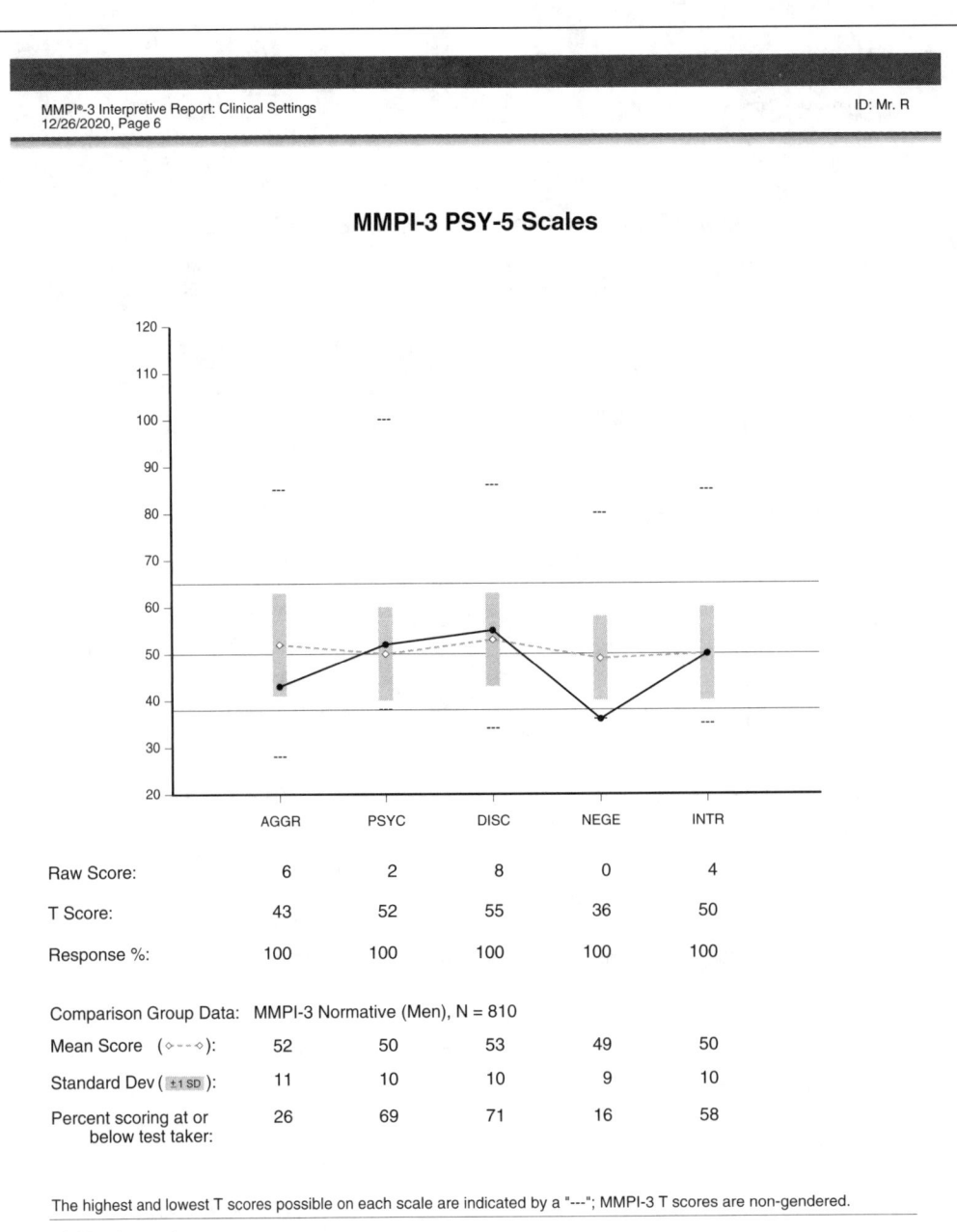

FIGURE 10.2. Mr. R's MMPI-3 Clinical Settings Interpretive Report, continued

MMPI-3 T SCORES (BY DOMAIN)

PROTOCOL VALIDITY

Content Non-Responsiveness

0	36	35	54 T
CNS	CRIN	VRIN	TRIN

Over-Reporting

41	41	53	42	47
F	Fp	Fs	FBS	RBS

Under-Reporting

48	**65**
L	K

SUBSTANTIVE SCALES

Somatic/Cognitive Dysfunction

36	40	47	44	38
RC1	MLS	NUC	EAT	COG

Emotional Dysfunction

42	36	44	51	40	37		
EID	RCd	SUI	HLP	SFD	NFC		
	42	50					
	RC2	INTR					
	34	45	37	46	37	37	43	36
	RC7	STR	WRY	CMP	ARX	ANP	BRF	NEGE

Thought Dysfunction

49	40
THD	RC6
	55
	RC8
	52
	PSYC

Behavioral Dysfunction

52	58	36	56	52
BXD	RC4	FML	JCP	SUB
	44	45	46	39	36
	RC9	IMP	ACT	AGG	CYN
	55				
	DISC				

Interpersonal Functioning

44	45	43	48	50	49
SFI	DOM	AGGR	DSF	SAV	SHY

Scale scores shown in bold font are interpreted in the report.

Note. This information is provided to facilitate interpretation following the recommended structure for MMPI-3 interpretation in Chapter 5 of the *MMPI-3 Manual for Administration, Scoring, and Interpretation*, which provides details in the text and an outline in Table 5-1.

FIGURE 10.2. Mr. R's MMPI-3 Clinical Settings Interpretive Report, continued

This interpretive report is intended for use by a professional qualified to interpret the MMPI-3. The information it contains should be considered in the context of the test taker's background, the circumstances of the assessment, and other available information.

The report includes extensive annotation, which appears as superscripts following each statement in the narrative, keyed to Endnotes with accompanying Research References, which appear in the final two sections of the report. Additional information about the annotation features is provided in the headnotes to these sections and in the MMPI-3 User's Guide for the Score and Clinical Interpretive Reports.

SYNOPSIS

Scores on the MMPI-3 Validity Scales raise concerns about the possible impact of under-reporting on the validity of this protocol. With that caution noted, there are no indications of somatic or cognitive complaints, or of emotional, thought, behavioral, or interpersonal dysfunction.

PROTOCOL VALIDITY

Content Non-Responsiveness

The test taker produced scorable responses to all the MMPI-3 items. He also responded in a remarkably consistent manner[1]. He was deliberate in his approach to the assessment.

Over-Reporting

There are no indications of over-reporting in this protocol.

Under-Reporting

The test taker presented himself as well-adjusted[2]. If there is evidence that this individual is not well-adjusted, any absence of elevation on the Substantive Scales should be interpreted with caution[3]. Elevated scores on the Substantive Scales may underestimate the problems assessed by those scales[4].

SUBSTANTIVE SCALE INTERPRETATION

Clinical symptoms, personality characteristics, and behavioral tendencies of the test taker are described in this section and organized according to an empirically guided framework. (Please see Chapter 5 of the MMPI-3 Manual for Administration, Scoring, and Interpretation *for details.) Statements containing the word "reports" are based on the item content of MMPI-3 scales, whereas statements that include the word "likely" are based on empirical correlates of scale scores. Specific sources for each statement can be viewed with the annotation features of this report.*

The following interpretation needs to be considered in light of cautions noted about the possible impact of under-reporting (of psychological problems) on the validity of this protocol.

Somatic/Cognitive, Emotional, Thought, and Behavioral Dysfunction

There are no indications of somatic, cognitive, emotional, thought, or behavioral dysfunction in this protocol. However, because of indications of under-reporting described earlier, such problems cannot be ruled out.

FIGURE 10.2. Mr. R's MMPI-3 Clinical Settings Interpretive Report, continued

Interpersonal Functioning Scales

These scales provide no evidence of dysfunction.

DIAGNOSTIC CONSIDERATIONS

No specific psychodiagnostic recommendations are indicated by this MMPI-3 protocol. However, this finding needs to be considered in light of cautions noted earlier about possible under-reporting.

TREATMENT CONSIDERATIONS

No specific recommendations for treatment are indicated by this MMPI-3 protocol. However, this finding needs to be considered in light of cautions noted earlier about possible under-reporting.

ITEM-LEVEL INFORMATION

Unscorable Responses

The test taker produced scorable responses to all the MMPI-3 items.

Critical Responses

Seven MMPI-3 scales—Suicidal/Death Ideation (SUI), Helplessness/Hopelessness (HLP), Anxiety-Related Experiences (ARX), Ideas of Persecution (RC6), Aberrant Experiences (RC8), Substance Abuse (SUB), and Aggression (AGG)—have been designated by the test authors as having critical item content that may require immediate attention and follow-up. Items answered by the individual in the keyed direction (True or False) on a critical scale are listed below if his T score on that scale is 65 or higher. However, any item answered in the keyed direction on SUI is listed.

The test taker has not produced an elevated T score ($\geq$ 65) on any of these scales or answered any SUI items in the keyed direction.

FIGURE 10.2. Mr. R's MMPI-3 Clinical Settings Interpretive Report, continued

ENDNOTES

This section lists for each statement in the report the MMPI-3 score(s) that triggered it. In addition, each statement is identified as a <u>Test Response</u>, if based on item content, a <u>Correlate</u>, if based on empirical correlates, or an <u>Inference</u>, if based on the report authors' judgment. (This information can also be accessed on-screen by placing the cursor on a given statement.) For correlate-based statements, research references (Ref. No.) are provided, keyed to the consecutively numbered reference list following the endnotes.

[1] Test Response: CRIN=36; VRIN=35
[2] Test Response: K=65
[3] Correlate: K=65, Ref. 2, 3, 5, 6
[4] Correlate: K=65, Ref. 1, 4, 6, 7

FIGURE 10.2. Mr. R's MMPI-3 Clinical Settings Interpretive Report, continued

RESEARCH REFERENCE LIST

The following studies are sources for empirical correlates identified in the Endnotes section of this report.

1. Ben-Porath, Y. S., & Tellegen, A. (2020). *The Minnesota Multiphasic Personality Inventory-3 (MMPI-3): Technical manual.* University of Minnesota Press.

2. Brown, T. A., & Sellbom, M. (2020). The utility of the MMPI-2-RF validity scales in detecting underreporting. *Journal of Personality Assessment, 102*(1), 66–74. https://doi.org/10.1080/00223891.2018.1539003

3. Crighton, A. H., Marek, R. J., Dragon, W. R., & Ben-Porath, Y. S. (2017). Utility of the MMPI-2-RF Validity Scales in detection of simulated underreporting: Implications of incorporating a manipulation check. *Assessment, 24*(7), 853–864. https://doi.org/10.1177/1073191115627011

4. Forbey, J. D., Lee, T. T. C., Ben-Porath, Y. S., Arbisi, P. A., & Gartland, D. (2013). Associations between MMPI-2-RF validity scale scores and extra-test measures of personality and psychopathology. *Assessment, 20*(4), 448–461. https://doi.org/10.1177/1073191113478154

5. Marion, B. E., Sellbom, M., Salekin, R. T., Toomey, J. A., Kucharski, L. T., & Duncan, S. (2013). An examination of the association between psychopathy and dissimulation using the MMPI-2-RF Validity Scales. *Law and Human Behavior, 37*(4), 219–230. https://doi.org/10.1037/lhb0000008

6. Sellbom, M., & Bagby, R. M. (2008). Validity of the MMPI-2-RF (Restructured Form) L-r and K-r scales in detecting under-reporting in clinical and non-clinical samples. *Psychological Assessment, 20*(4), 370–376. https://doi.org/10.1037/a0012952

7. Tellegen, A., & Ben-Porath, Y. S. (2008/2011). *Minnesota Multiphasic Personality Inventory-2-Restructured Form (MMPI-2-RF): Technical manual.* University of Minnesota Press.

End of Report

FIGURE 10.2. Mr. R's MMPI-3 Clinical Settings Interpretive Report, continued

least in the near term. However, because alcohol use disorders are characterized by relapse and remission, the duration of risk is ongoing, as discussed next.

Step 3: Assessing for Sustainability of Fitness

The third step in the integrative process is reserved for cases in which the employee's episodic mental health condition is currently not job-limiting. When an employee's only mental health condition involves substance use and the individual is sober at the time of the evaluation, the sustainability of fitness is unknown. The absence of an established pattern of alcohol use problems in Mr. R's history presents a basis for optimism about sustained sobriety, but care must be taken to not overstate confidence in that optimism. Although Mr. R said that he was committed to sobriety, he also equivocated by adding, "at least for a while." The sustainability of his fitness for duty is indeed threatened if he resumes alcohol use in any amount; however, concluding that relapse is more likely than not would be highly speculative and arguably unwarranted by the collective facts.

Conclusion

The aggregate clinical evidence derived from all sources indicates that Mr. R was currently *fit for duty*. The examiner summarized her conclusions and recommendation in this way:

> As long as Mr. R remains sober, the findings from this evaluation indicate that he poses a low risk of impaired performance in his job and a low risk of harm to himself or others. However, because of the demonstrated deleterious effects of alcohol on Mr. R's emotion regulation and decision making, these risks quickly rise when he is intoxicated. Because Mr. R has not established a pattern of alcohol use problems, and this evaluation has not identified any additional mental health conditions or aggravating factors, there is good reason to hope that this is a one-time incident that will not be repeated. However, it is too early to tell. He stated that he intends to not drink at all ("at least for a while"), and if he does drink again he intends to consume no more than two drinks. To aid Mr. R in his commitment to sobriety or responsible, controlled drinking, it may prove useful to provide him with a clear written statement of the consequences for a recurrence of alcohol-related misconduct.

As noted by the examiner, the sustainability of Mr. R's fitness for duty depends entirely on his ability to remain sober. If enforced, a written last-chance agreement governing his return to work could play an important role in motivating and enforcing his continued commitment to sobriety and mental health treatment.

MR. J, FIREFIGHTER

Assessment Issues Presented

- Indications of acute and sustained distress six months after failed efforts to save an infant in a residential house fire
- Multiple clinically elevated substantive scale scores

Referral Summary

Mr. J is a 53-year-old married man with 22 years of experience as a firefighter in an urban fire department. Approximately 6 months before being referred for this fitness evaluation, Mr. J was part of a crew that responded to an alarm of an early-morning house fire. Neighbors informed the arriving firefighters that a couple and their newborn infant lived in the house that was completely engulfed in a raging fire. Mr. J was one of two firefighters directed to the nursery, but a collapsing ceiling prevented them from entering the structure. When the fire was suppressed enough to allow safe entry, all three inhabitants were found dead, huddled together in a bathtub.

Immediately following the incident, Mr. J and his fellow firefighters were provided access to a regional peer support team and a mental health professional who conducted a critical incident debriefing. He also sought counseling from a therapist affiliated with the city's employee assistance program, who submitted paperwork indicating that Mr. J had developed a serious health condition requiring temporary medical leave under the Family Medical Leave Act. With the approval of his therapist, he returned to work about 5 weeks after the incident.

Changes in Mr. J's behavior and work performance were apparent to his station captain and fellow firefighters within days of his return to duty. In contrast to his normally gregarious, affable, and active nature, he now appeared despondent, sullen, and self-isolating; he retreated to his room during downtimes; he frequently called in sick without giving adequate notice; he arrived to work disheveled and fatigued; and, when confronted with concerns about these observations, he responded either tearfully or with uncharacteristic hostility. Although his captain and battalion chief initially took a hands-off approach in hopes that he would rebound, growing concerns about his mental fitness among his fellow firefighters led them to recommend a mandatory fitness evaluation.

Assessment Findings

Employment Records

Mr. J's employment records confirmed the absence of prior disciplinary actions and a track record of exemplary attendance and work performance.

Mental Status Examination

Mr. J's appearance was remarkably unkempt. His mood was despondent, he responded to questions only after a long delay, he had difficulty maintaining eye contact, and he frequently cried when discussing the fatal residential fire, his own family, and his obvious difficulties adapting to the psychological sequelae. He reported fleeting thoughts of suicide without a specific plan, although he said he would not act on these thoughts because of the impact it would have on his wife and children. He reported sleeping only 2 to 3 hours a night, along with distressing dreams several nights a week.

Clinical Interview

Mr. J made no effort to dismiss or minimize the concerns of his supervisors and fellow firefighters. He said he was "ashamed" for "being weak," noting that he had no more of a connection to the deceased family than the other members of the crew who experienced the same trauma. He was distraught over his inability to "pull myself together" and "get over" the incident. In addition to the insomnia, nightmares, and night terrors, he reported hypervigilance, substantial depression described as "incredible sadness," anhedonia, irritability, unsuccessful efforts to avoid thinking about the trauma, intrusive recollections of images of the dead family (particularly the scene of the man holding his wife, who cradled their infant child), guilt over his inability to rescue the family, social isolation, and poor concentration. At times, he wept uncontrollably, describing himself as "a wreck" and expressing disbelief that after a 22-year career in the fire service, during which time he has witnessed many deaths from house fires, he was unable to rebound from this one.

Medical Records

Records from Mr. J's employee assistance counselor documented his self-reported symptoms and therapeutic efforts, which included EMDR and cognitive restructuring.

MMPI-3 Findings

Mr. J's MMPI-3 Interpretive Report for Clinical Settings is reproduced in Figure 10.3. It is a valid protocol with no unscorable items. There are no indications of over- or underreporting in this protocol.

Mr. J's MMPI-3 scores reveal an array of clinically significant findings, which are particularly concerning considering his disclosure of recent suicidal ideation. Mr. J reports having had recent thoughts of killing himself

Interpretive Report: Clinical Settings

MMPI®-3
Minnesota Multiphasic Personality Inventory®-3
Yossef S. Ben-Porath, PhD, & Auke Tellegen, PhD

ID Number:	Mr. J
Age:	53
Gender:	Male
Marital Status:	Not reported
Years of Education:	Not reported
Date Assessed:	12/02/2020

Copyright © 2020 by the Regents of the University of Minnesota. All rights reserved. Distributed exclusively under license from the University of Minnesota by NCS Pearson, Inc. Portions reproduced from the *MMPI-3 English Test Booklet*. Copyright © 2020 by the Regents of the University of Minnesota. All rights reserved. Portions excerpted from the *MMPI-3 Manual for Administration, Scoring, and Interpretation*. Copyright © 2020 by the Regents of the University of Minnesota. All rights reserved. Portions excerpted from the *MMPI-3 Technical Manual*. Copyright © 2020 by the Regents of the University of Minnesota. All rights reserved. Used by permission of the University of Minnesota Press.

Minnesota Multiphasic Personality Inventory and **MMPI** are registered trademarks of the Regents of the University of Minnesota. **Pearson** is a trademark, in the US and/or other countries, of Pearson Education, Inc., or its affiliates.

This report contains copyrighted material and trade secrets. Qualified licensees may excerpt portions of this output report, limited to the minimum text necessary to accurately describe their significant core conclusions, for incorporation into a written evaluation of the examinee, in accordance with their profession's citation standards, if any. No adaptations, translations, modifications, or special versions may be made of this report without prior written permission from the University of Minnesota Press.

[1.0 / 19 / QG]

ALWAYS LEARNING   PEARSON

FIGURE 10.3. Mr. J's MMPI-3 Clinical Settings Interpretive Report

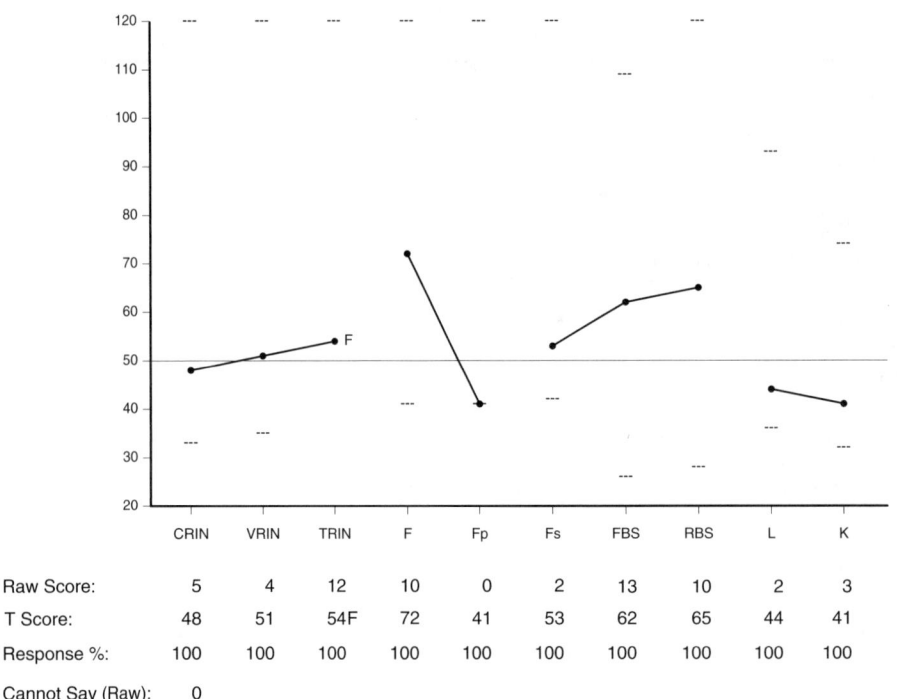

FIGURE 10.3. Mr. J's MMPI-3 Clinical Settings Interpretive Report, continued

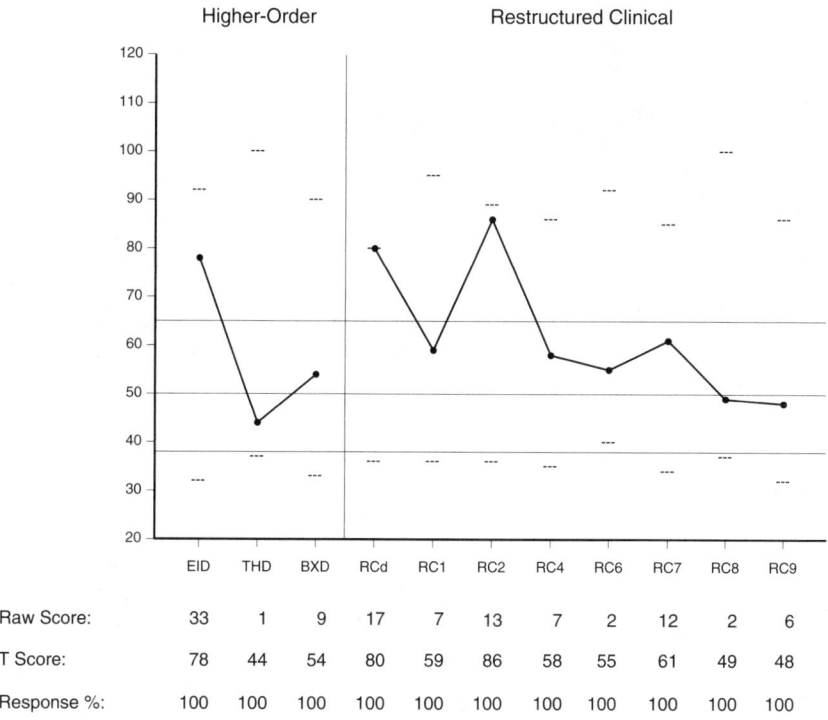

FIGURE 10.3. Mr. J's MMPI-3 Clinical Settings Interpretive Report, continued

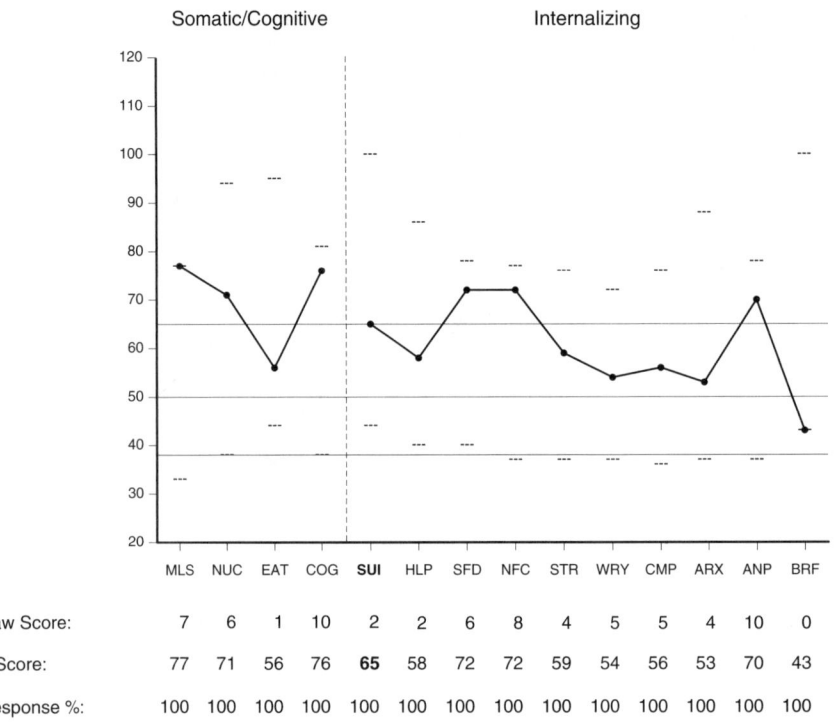

FIGURE 10.3. Mr. J's MMPI-3 Clinical Settings Interpretive Report, continued

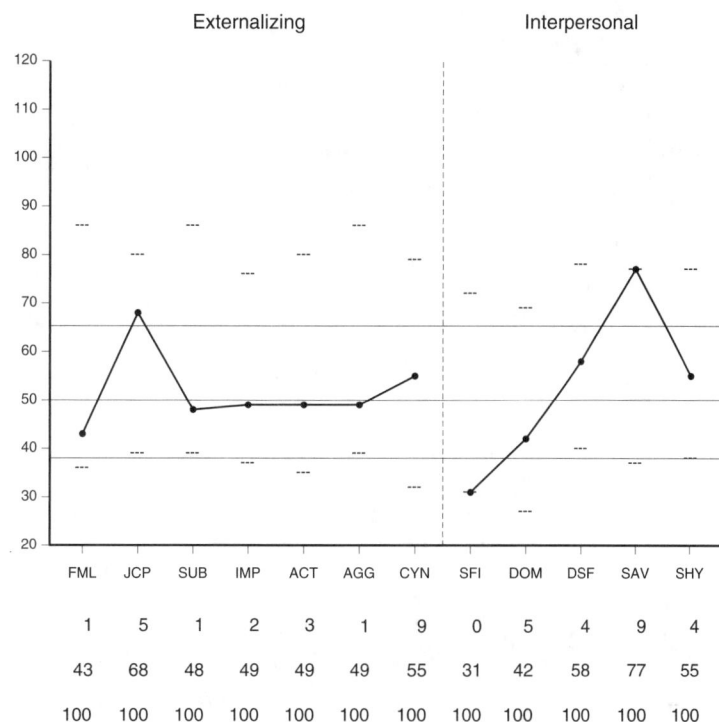

FIGURE 10.3. Mr. J's MMPI-3 Clinical Settings Interpretive Report, continued

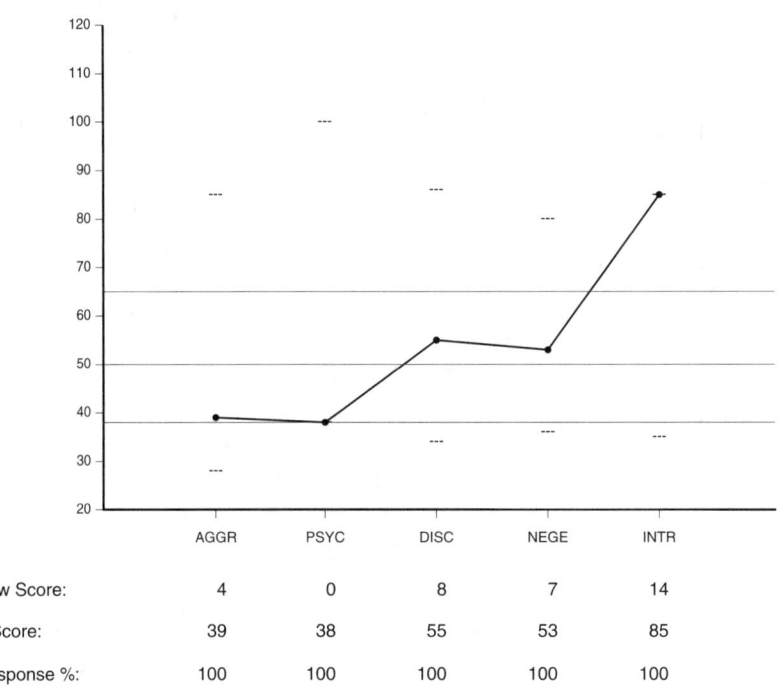

FIGURE 10.3. Mr. J's MMPI-3 Clinical Settings Interpretive Report, continued

MMPI-3 T SCORES (BY DOMAIN)

PROTOCOL VALIDITY

Content Non-Responsiveness

0	48	51	54 F
CNS	CRIN	VRIN	TRIN

Over-Reporting

72	41		53	62	65
F	Fp		Fs	FBS	RBS

Under-Reporting

44	41
L	K

SUBSTANTIVE SCALES

Somatic/Cognitive Dysfunction

59	**77**	71	56	**76**
RC1	**MLS**	**NUC**	EAT	**COG**

Emotional Dysfunction

78	**80**	65	58	**72**	**72**		
EID	**RCd**	**SUI**	HLP	**SFD**	**NFC**		
	86	85					
	RC2	**INTR**					
	61	59	54	56	53	**70**	43	53
	RC7	STR	WRY	CMP	ARX	**ANP**	BRF	NEGE

Thought Dysfunction

44	55
THD	RC6
	49
	RC8
	38
	PSYC

Behavioral Dysfunction

54	58	43	**68**	48	
BXD	RC4	FML	**JCP**	SUB	
	48	49	49	49	55
	RC9	IMP	ACT	AGG	CYN
	55				
	DISC				

Interpersonal Functioning

31	42	39	58	**77**	55
SFI	DOM	AGGR	DSF	**SAV**	SHY

Scale scores shown in bold font are interpreted in the report.

Note. This information is provided to facilitate interpretation following the recommended structure for MMPI-3 interpretation in Chapter 5 of the *MMPI-3 Manual for Administration, Scoring, and Interpretation*, which provides details in the text and an outline in Table 5-1.

FIGURE 10.3. Mr. J's MMPI-3 Clinical Settings Interpretive Report, continued

This interpretive report is intended for use by a professional qualified to interpret the MMPI-3. The information it contains should be considered in the context of the test taker's background, the circumstances of the assessment, and other available information.

The report includes extensive annotation, which appears as superscripts following each statement in the narrative, keyed to Endnotes with accompanying Research References, which appear in the final two sections of the report. Additional information about the annotation features is provided in the headnotes to these sections and in the MMPI-3 User's Guide for the Score and Clinical Interpretive Reports.

SYNOPSIS

This is a valid MMPI-3 protocol. Scores on the Substantive Scales indicate somatic and cognitive complaints, and emotional, behavioral, and interpersonal dysfunction. Somatic complaints include malaise and neurological symptoms. Cognitive complaints include difficulties in memory and concentration. Emotional-internalizing findings include **suicidal ideation**, demoralization, lack of positive emotions, self-doubt, perceived inefficacy, and anger. Behavioral-externalizing problems relate to juvenile conduct problems. Interpersonal difficulties include lack of self-esteem and social avoidance.

PROTOCOL VALIDITY

This is a valid MMPI-3 protocol. There are no problems with unscorable items. The test taker responded to the items relevantly on the basis of their content, and there are no indications of over- or under-reporting.

SUBSTANTIVE SCALE INTERPRETATION

Clinical symptoms, personality characteristics, and behavioral tendencies of the test taker are described in this section and organized according to an empirically guided framework. (Please see Chapter 5 of the MMPI-3 Manual for Administration, Scoring, and Interpretation *for details.) Statements containing the word "reports" are based on the item content of MMPI-3 scales, whereas statements that include the word "likely" are based on empirical correlates of scale scores. Specific sources for each statement can be viewed with the annotation features of this report.*

Somatic/Cognitive Dysfunction

The test taker reports a general sense of malaise manifested in poor health, and feeling tired, weak, and incapacitated[1]. Indeed he is very likely preoccupied with poor health[2] and complains of sleep disturbance[3], fatigue[4], low energy[5], and sexual dysfunction[5]. He also reports vague neurological complaints[6] and likely presents with multiple somatic complaints[7] and is prone to developing physical symptoms in response to stress[8].

He reports a diffuse pattern of cognitive difficulties including memory problems, difficulties with attention and concentration, and possible confusion[9]. Indeed he very likely complains about memory problems[10], does not cope well with stress[11], and experiences difficulties in attention and/or concentration[12].

Emotional Dysfunction

The test taker reports a history of suicidal/death ideation and/or past suicide attempts, as well as having made a plan for killing himself[13]. He likely is at risk for self-harm[14], is preoccupied with suicide and death[15], and is at risk for current suicidal ideation and attempts[16].

FIGURE 10.3. Mr. J's MMPI-3 Clinical Settings Interpretive Report, continued

His responses indicate significant emotional distress[17]. More specifically, he reports a significant lack of positive emotional experiences and a marked lack of interest[18]. He very likely presents with anhedonia[19] and displays vegetative symptoms of depression[20].

The test taker reports experiencing significant demoralization, feeling overwhelmed, and being extremely unhappy, sad, and dissatisfied with his life[21]. He very likely complains about significant depression[22] and experiences sadness and despair[23]. In particular, he reports self-doubt and futility[24] and likely is prone to rumination, feels insecure and inferior, and is self-disparaging and intropunitive[25]. He also reports being indecisive and inefficacious[26]. He likely experiences subjective incompetence and shame[27] and lacks perseverance and self-reliance[28].

He reports being anger-prone[29]. He indeed likely has problems with anger, irritability, and low tolerance for frustration[30]; holds grudges[31]; has temper tantrums[32]; and is hostile, argumentative, and abusive[32].

Thought Dysfunction
There are no indications of disordered thinking in this protocol.

Behavioral Dysfunction
The test taker reports a history of juvenile conduct problems[33]. He likely has a history of juvenile delinquency and criminal and/or antisocial behavior[34], experiences conflictual interpersonal relationships[35], engages in acting-out behavior[35], and has difficulties with individuals in positions of authority[35].

Interpersonal Functioning Scales
The test taker describes himself as lacking in positive qualities[36].

He reports not enjoying social events and avoiding social situations, including parties and other events where crowds are likely to gather[37]. He very likely is socially introverted[38], has difficulty forming close relationships[39], and is emotionally restricted[40].

DIAGNOSTIC CONSIDERATIONS

This section provides recommendations for psychodiagnostic assessment based on the test taker's MMPI-3 results. It is recommended that he be evaluated for the following:

Somatic/Cognitive Disorders
- Somatic symptom disorder, if physical origins for malaise[41] and neurological complaints[42] have been ruled out
- Disorders related to attention difficulties[43]

Emotional-Internalizing Disorders
- Major depression and other anhedonia-related disorders[44]
- Anger-related disorders[45]

Behavioral-Externalizing Disorders
- Externalizing disorders, particularly antisocial personality disorder[46]

Interpersonal Disorders
- Features of personality disorders involving detachment[47]
- Disorders associated with social avoidance such as avoidant personality disorder[48]

FIGURE 10.3. Mr. J's MMPI-3 Clinical Settings Interpretive Report, continued

TREATMENT CONSIDERATIONS

This section provides inferential treatment-related recommendations based on the test taker's MMPI-3 scores.

Areas for Further Evaluation
- **Risk for suicide** should be assessed immediately[49].
- May require inpatient treatment because of significant depression[50].
- Need for antidepressant medication[51].
- Origin of malaise complaints[52].
- Extent to which genuine physical health problems contribute to the score on the Neurological Complaints (NUC) scale[42].
- Origin of cognitive complaints[43]. May require a neuropsychological evaluation.

Psychotherapy Process Issues
- Malaise may impede his willingness or ability to engage in treatment[52].
- Likely to reject psychological interpretations of somatic complaints[42].
- Serious emotional difficulties may motivate him for treatment[53].
- Indecisiveness may interfere with establishing treatment goals and progress in treatment[54].

Possible Targets for Treatment
- Demoralization as an initial target[55]
- Pronounced anhedonia[56]
- Low self-esteem and other manifestations of self-doubt[57]
- Anger management[45]
- Difficulties associated with social avoidance[58]

ITEM-LEVEL INFORMATION

Unscorable Responses

The test taker produced scorable responses to all the MMPI-3 items.

Critical Responses

Seven MMPI-3 scales—Suicidal/Death Ideation (SUI), Helplessness/Hopelessness (HLP), Anxiety-Related Experiences (ARX), Ideas of Persecution (RC6), Aberrant Experiences (RC8), Substance Abuse (SUB), and Aggression (AGG)—have been designated by the test authors as having critical item content that may require immediate attention and follow-up. Items answered by the individual in the keyed direction (True or False) on a critical scale are listed below if his T score on that scale is 65 or higher. However, any item answered in the keyed direction on SUI is listed. The percentage of the MMPI-3 normative sample that answered each item in the keyed direction is provided in parentheses following the item content.

Suicidal/Death Ideation (SUI, T Score = 65)
    Item number and content omitted. (True, 22.2%)
    Item number and content omitted. (True, 4.1%)

FIGURE 10.3. Mr. J's MMPI-3 Clinical Settings Interpretive Report, continued

ENDNOTES

This section lists for each statement in the report the MMPI-3 score(s) that triggered it. In addition, each statement is identified as a <u>Test Response</u>, if based on item content, a <u>Correlate</u>, if based on empirical correlates, or an <u>Inference</u>, if based on the report authors' judgment. (This information can also be accessed on-screen by placing the cursor on a given statement.) For correlate-based statements, research references (Ref. No.) are provided, keyed to the consecutively numbered reference list following the endnotes.

[1] Test Response: MLS=77
[2] Correlate: MLS=77, Ref. 6, 9; NUC=71, Ref. 6, 10
[3] Correlate: MLS=77, Ref. 6, 47
[4] Correlate: MLS=77, Ref. 6, 32, 47
[5] Correlate: MLS=77, Ref. 6
[6] Test Response: NUC=71
[7] Correlate: NUC=71, Ref. 6, 10, 32
[8] Correlate: NUC=71, Ref. 12
[9] Test Response: COG=76
[10] Correlate: COG=76, Ref. 6, 10, 20, 32
[11] Correlate: RCd=80, Ref. 48; COG=76, Ref. 48
[12] Correlate: COG=76, Ref. 6, 10, 32
[13] Test Response: SUI=65
[14] Correlate: SUI=65, Ref. 6, 27, 33
[15] Correlate: SUI=65, Ref. 3, 6, 21, 22, 32, 33, 34, 45, 48
[16] Correlate: SUI=65, Ref. 3, 6, 21, 22, 33, 45, 46, 48
[17] Correlate: EID=78, Ref. 6, 26, 35, 48
[18] Test Response: RC2=86; INTR=85
[19] Correlate: RC2=86, Ref. 6, 48; INTR=85, Ref. 6, 48
[20] Correlate: RC2=86, Ref. 4, 6, 48; INTR=85, Ref. 6
[21] Test Response: RCd=80
[22] Correlate: RCd=80, Ref. 1, 4, 6, 8, 9, 10, 13, 14, 15, 16, 17, 24, 25, 31, 32, 37, 39, 40, 41, 43, 44, 47, 48, 49, 50, 52, 53; RC2=86, Ref. 1, 4, 6, 8, 9, 10, 15, 16, 17, 24, 25, 37, 39, 40, 41, 43, 44, 48, 49, 50, 52, 53; INTR=85, Ref. 6, 48
[23] Correlate: RCd=80, Ref. 6
[24] Test Response: SFD=72
[25] Correlate: SFD=72, Ref. 6, 48
[26] Test Response: NFC=72
[27] Correlate: NFC=72, Ref. 6
[28] Correlate: NFC=72, Ref. 10
[29] Test Response: ANP=70
[30] Correlate: ANP=70, Ref. 1, 6, 10, 14, 18, 32, 34, 37
[31] Correlate: ANP=70, Ref. 48
[32] Correlate: ANP=70, Ref. 32
[33] Test Response: JCP=68
[34] Correlate: JCP=68, Ref. 6, 27, 36
[35] Correlate: JCP=68, Ref. 6, 48
[36] Test Response: SFI=31
[37] Test Response: SAV=77
[38] Correlate: SAV=77, Ref. 1, 2, 5, 6, 14, 19
[39] Correlate: SAV=77, Ref. 1, 6, 7, 11, 18
[40] Correlate: SAV=77, Ref. 6, 48
[41] Correlate: MLS=77, Ref. 29
[42] Inference: NUC=71
[43] Inference: COG=76
[44] Correlate: RCd=80, Ref. 6, 23, 28, 30, 38, 44, 48, 51; RC2=86, Ref. 6, 23, 28, 30, 38, 44, 48, 51

FIGURE 10.3. Mr. J's MMPI-3 Clinical Settings Interpretive Report, continued

[45] Inference: ANP=70
[46] Correlate: JCP=68, Ref. 6, 42
[47] Inference: INTR=85
[48] Correlate: SAV=77, Ref. 6, 42, 51
[49] Inference: SUI=65
[50] Inference: RC2=86
[51] Correlate: RC2=86, Ref. 6
[52] Inference: MLS=77
[53] Inference: EID=78; RCd=80
[54] Inference: NFC=72
[55] Inference: RCd=80
[56] Inference: RC2=86; INTR=85
[57] Inference: SFD=72
[58] Inference: SAV=77

FIGURE 10.3. Mr. J's MMPI-3 Clinical Settings Interpretive Report, continued

RESEARCH REFERENCE LIST

The following studies are sources for empirical correlates identified in the Endnotes section of this report.

1. Anderson, J. L., Sellbom, M., Ayearst, L., Quilty, L. C., Chmielewski, M., & Bagby, R. M. (2015). Associations between DSM-5 Section III personality traits and the Minnesota Multiphasic Personality Inventory 2-Restructured Form (MMPI-2-RF) scales in a psychiatric patient sample. *Psychological Assessment, 27*(3), 801–815. https://doi.org/10.1037/pas0000096

2. Anderson, J. L., Sellbom, M., Pymont, C., Smid, W., De Saeger, H., & Kamphuis, J. H. (2015). Measurement of DSM-5 Section II personality disorder constructs using the MMPI-2-RF in clinical and forensic samples. *Psychological Assessment, 27*(3), 786–800. https://doi.org/10.1037/pas0000103

3. Anestis, J. C., Finn, J. A., Gottfried, E. D., Hames, J. L., Bodell, L. P., Hagan, C. R., Arnau, R. C., Anestis, M. D., Arbisi, P. A., & Joiner, T. E. (2018). Burdonesomeness, belongingness, and capability: Assessing the interpersonal-psychological theory of suicide with MMPI-2-RF scales. *Assessment, 25*(4), 415–431. https://doi.org/10.1177/1073191116652227

4. Arbisi, P. A., Sellbom, M., & Ben-Porath, Y. S. (2008). Empirical correlates of the MMPI-2 Restructured Clinical (RC) Scales in psychiatric inpatients. *Journal of Personality Assessment, 90*(2), 122–128. https://doi.org/10.1080/00223890701845146

5. Ayearst, L. E., Sellbom, M., Trobst, K. K., & Bagby, R. M. (2013). Evaluating the interpersonal content of the MMPI-2-RF Interpersonal Scales. *Journal of Personality Assessment, 95*(2), 187–196. https://doi.org/10.1080/00223891.2012.730085

6. Ben-Porath, Y. S., & Tellegen, A. (2020). *The Minnesota Multiphasic Personality Inventory-3 (MMPI-3): Technical manual.* University of Minnesota Press.

7. Bianchini, K. J., Aguerrevere, L. E., Curtis, K. L., Roebuck-Spencer, T. M., Frey, F. C., Greve, K. W., & Calamia, M. (2018). Classification accuracy of the Minnesota Multiphasic Personality Inventory-2 (MMPI-2)-Restructured Form Validity Scales in detecting malingered pain-related disability. *Psychological Assessment, 30*(7), 857–869. https://doi.org/10.1037/pas0000532

8. Binford, A., & Liljequist, L. (2008). Behavioral correlates of selected MMPI-2 Clinical, Content, and Restructured Clinical scales. *Journal of Personality Assessment, 90*(6), 608–614. https://doi.org/10.1080/00223890802388657

9. Block, A. R., Ben-Porath, Y. S., & Marek, R. J. (2013). Psychological risk factors for poor outcome of spine surgery and spinal cord stimulator implant: A review of the literature and their assessment with the MMPI-2-RF. *The Clinical Neuropsychologist, 27*(1), 81–107. https://doi.org/10.1080/13854046.2012.721007

10. Burchett, D. L., & Ben-Porath, Y. S. (2010). The impact of over-reporting on MMPI-2-RF substantive scale score validity. *Assessment, 17*(4), 497–516. https://doi.org/10.1177/1073191110378972

11. Cox, A., Courrégé, S. C., Feder, A. H., & Weed, N. C. (2017). Effects of augmenting response options of the MMPI-2-RF: An extension of previous findings. *Cogent Psychology, 4*(1), 1323988. https://doi.org/10.1080/23311908.2017.1323988

12. Duncan, C. J., Roberts, N. A., Kirlin, K. A., Parkhurst, D., Burleson, M. H., Drazkowski, J. F., Sirven, J. I., Noe, K. H., Crepeau, A. Z., Hoerth, M. T., Locke, D. E. C. (2018). Diagnostic utility of the Minnesota Multiphasic Personality Inventory-2 Restructured Form in the epilepsy monitoring unit: Considering sex differences. *Epilepsy and Behavior, 88,* 117–122. https://doi.org/10.1016/j.yebeh.2018.08.033

FIGURE 10.3. Mr. J's MMPI-3 Clinical Settings Interpretive Report, continued

13. Erbes, C. R., Polusny, M. A., Arbisi, P. A., & Koffel, E. (2012). PTSD symptoms in a cohort of National Guard Soldiers deployed to Iraq: Evidence for nonspecific and specific components. *Journal of Affective Disorders, 142*(1–3), 269–274. https://doi.org/10.1016/j.jad.2012.05.013

14. Finn, J. A., Ben-Porath, Y. S., & Tellegen, A. (2015). Dichotomous versus polytomous response options in psychopathology assessment: Method or meaningful variance? *Psychological Assessment, 27*(1), 184–193. https://doi.org/10.1037/pas0000044

15. Forbey, J. D., & Ben-Porath, Y. S. (2008). Empirical correlates of the MMPI-2 Restructured Clinical (RC) Scales in a non-clinical setting. *Journal of Personality Assessment, 90*(2), 136–141. https://doi.org/10.1080/00223890701845161

16. Forbey, J. D., Ben-Porath, Y. S., & Arbisi, P. A. (2012). The MMPI-2 computer adaptive version (MMPI-2-CA) in a Veterans Administration medical outpatient facility. *Psychological Assessment, 24*(3), 628–639. https://doi.org/10.1037/a0026509

17. Forbey, J. D., Ben-Porath, Y. S., & Gartland, D. (2009). Validation of the MMPI-2 Computerized Adaptive version (MMPI-2-CA) in a correctional intake facility. *Psychological Services, 6*(4), 279–292. https://doi.org/10.1037/a0016195

18. Forbey, J. D., Lee, T. T. C., & Handel, R. W. (2010). Correlates of the MMPI-2-RF in a college setting. *Psychological Assessment, 22*(4), 737–744. https://doi.org/10.1037/a0020645

19. Franz, A. O., Harrop, T. M., & McCord, D. M. (2017). Examining the construct validity of the MMPI-2-RF Interpersonal Functioning Scales using the Computerized Adaptive Test of Personality Disorder as a comparative framework. *Journal of Personality Assessment, 99*(4), 416–423. https://doi.org/10.1080/00223891.2016.1222394

20. Gervais, R. O., Ben-Porath, Y. S., & Wygant, D. B. (2009). Empirical correlates and interpretation of the MMPI-2-RF Cognitive Complaints (COG) scale. *The Clinical Neuropsychologist, 23*(6), 996–1015. https://doi.org/10.1080/13854040902748249

21. Glassmire, D. M, Tarescavage, A. M., Burchett, D., Martinez, J., & Gomez, A. (2016). Clinical utility of the MMPI-2-RF SUI items and scale in a forensic inpatient setting: Association with interview self-reports and future suicidal behavior. *Psychological Assessment, 28*(11), 1502–1509. https://doi.org/10.1037/pas0000220

22. Gottfried, E., Bodell, L., Carbonell, J., & Joiner, T. (2014). The clinical utility of the MMPI-2-RF Suicidal/Death Ideation Scale. *Psychological Assessment, 26*(4), 1205–1211. https://doi.org/10.1037/pas0000017

23. Haber, J. C., & Baum, L. J. (2014). Minnesota Multiphasic Personality Inventory-2 Restructured Form (MMPI-2-RF) Scales as predictors of psychiatric diagnoses. *South African Journal of Psychology, 44*(4), 439–453. https://doi.org/10.1177/0081246314532788

24. Handel, R. W., & Archer, R. P. (2008). An investigation of the psychometric properties of the MMPI-2 Restructured Clinical (RC) Scales with mental health inpatients. *Journal of Personality Assessment, 90*(3), 239–249. https://doi.org/10.1080/00223890701884954

25. Kamphuis, J. H., Arbisi, P. A., Ben-Porath, Y. S., & McNulty, J. L. (2008). Detecting comorbid Axis-II status among inpatients using the MMPI-2 Restructured Clinical Scales. *European Journal of Psychological Assessment, 24*, 157–164. https://doi.org/10.1027/1015-5759.24.3.157

26. Lanyon, R. I., & Thomas, M. L. (2013). Assessment of global psychiatric categories: The PSI/PSI-2 and the MMPI-2-RF. *Psychological Assessment, 25*(1), 227–232. https://doi.org/10.1037/a0030313

FIGURE 10.3. Mr. J's MMPI-3 Clinical Settings Interpretive Report, continued

27. Laurinaityte, I., Laurinavicius, A., Ustinaviciute, L., Wygant, D. B., Sellbom, M. (2017). Utility of the MMPI-2 Restructured Form (MMPI-2-RF) in a sample of Lithuanian male offenders. *Law and Human Behavior, 41*(5), 494–505. https://doi.org/10.1037/lhb0000254

28. Lee, T. T. C., Graham, J. R., & Arbisi, P. A. (2018). The utility of MMPI-2-RF scale scores in the differential diagnosis of schizophrenia and major depressive disorder. *Journal of Personality Assessment, 100*(3), 305–312. https://doi.org/10.1080/00223891.2017.1300906

29. Locke, D. E. C., Kirlin, K. A., Thomas, M. L., Osborne, D., Hurst, D. F., Drazkowsi, J. F., Sirven, J. I., & Noe, K. H. (2010). The Minnesota Multiphasic Personality Inventory-2-Restructured Form in the epilepsy monitoring unit. *Epilepsy & Behavior, 17*(2), 252–258. https://doi.org/10.1016/j.yebeh.2009.12.004

30. McCord, D. M., & Drerup, L. C. (2011). Relative practical utility of the Minnesota Multiphasic Personality Inventory-2 Restructured Clinical Scales versus the Clinical Scales in a chronic pain patient sample. *Journal of Clinical and Experimental Neuropsychology, 33*(1), 140–146. https://doi.org/10.1080/13803395.2010.495056

31. McDevitt-Murphy, M. E., Weathers, F. W., Flood, A. M., Eakin, D. E., & Benson, T. A. (2007). The utility of the PAI and the MMPI-2 for discriminating PTSD, depression, and social phobia in trauma-exposed college students. *Assessment, 14*(2), 181–195. https://doi.org/10.1177/1073191106295914

32. Menton, W. H., Crighton, A. H., Tarescavage, A. M., Marek, R. J., Hicks, A. D., & Ben-Porath, Y. S. (2019). Equivalence of laptop and tablet administrations of the Minnesota Multiphasic Personality Inventory-2 Restructured Form. *Assessment, 26*(4), 661–669. https://doi.org/10.1177/1073191117714558

33. Miller, S. N., Bozzay, M. L., Ben-Porath, Y. S., & Arbisi, P. A. (2019). Distinguishing levels of suicide risk in depressed male veterans: The role of internalizing and externalizing psychopathology as measured by the MMPI-2-RF. *Assessment, 26*(1), 85–98. https://doi.org/10.1177/1073191117743787

34. Rogers, M. L., Anestis, J. C., Harrop, T. M., Schneider, M., Bender, T. W., Ringer, F. B., & Joiner, T. E. (2017). Examination of MMPI-2-RF substantive scales as indicators of acute suicidal affective disturbance components. *Journal of Personality Assessment, 99*(4), 424–434. https://doi.org/10.1080/00223891.2016.1222393

35. Romero, I. E., Toorabally, N., Burchett, D., Tarescavage, A. M., & Glassmire, D. M. (2017). Mapping the MMPI-2-RF substantive scales onto, internalizing, externalizing, and thought dysfunction dimensions in a forensic inpatient setting. *Journal of Personality Assessment, 99*(4), 351–362. https://doi.org/10.1080/00223891.2016.1223681

36. Sellbom, M. (2016). Elucidating the validity of the externalizing spectrum of psychopathology in correctional, forensic, and community samples. *Journal of Abnormal Psychology, 125*(8), 1027–1038. https://doi.org/10.1037/abn0000171

37. Sellbom, M., Anderson, J. L., & Bagby, R. M. (2013). Assessing DSM-5 Section III personality traits and disorders with the MMPI-2-RF. *Assessment, 20*(6), 709–722. https://doi.org/10.1177/1073191113508808

38. Sellbom, M., Bagby, R. M., Kushner, S., Quilty, L. C., & Ayearst, L. E. (2011). Diagnostic construct validity of the MMPI-2 Restructured Form (MMPI-2-RF) scale scores. *Assessment, 19*(2), 176–186. https://doi.org/10.1177/1073191111428763

39. Sellbom, M., Ben-Porath, Y. S., & Bagby, R. M. (2008). On the hierarchical structure of mood and anxiety disorders: Confirmatory evidence and elaboration of a model of temperament markers. *Journal of Abnormal Psychology, 117*(3), 576–590. https://doi.org/10.1037/a0012536

40. Sellbom, M., Ben-Porath, Y. S., & Graham, J. R. (2006). Correlates of the MMPI-2 Restructured Clinical (RC) Scales in a college counseling setting. *Journal of Personality Assessment, 86*(1), 89–99. https://doi.org/10.1207/s15327752jpa8601_10

FIGURE 10.3. Mr. J's MMPI-3 Clinical Settings Interpretive Report, continued

41. Sellbom, M., Graham, J. R., & Schenk, P. W. (2006). Incremental validity of the MMPI-2 Restructured Clinical (RC) Scales in a private practice sample. *Journal of Personality Assessment, 86*(2), 196–205. https://doi.org/10.1207/s15327752jpa8602_09

42. Sellbom, M., & Smith, A. (2017). Assessment of DSM-5 Section II personality disorders with the MMPI-2-RF in a nonclinical sample. *Journal of Personality Assessment, 99*(4), 384–397. https://doi.org/10.1080/00223891.2016.1242074

43. Shkalim, E. (2015). Psychometric evaluation of the MMPI-2/MMPI-2-RF Restructured Clinical Scales in an Israeli sample. *Assessment, 22*(4), 607–618. https://doi.org/10.1177/1073191114555884

44. Simms, L. J., Casillas, A., Clark, L. A., Watson, D., & Doebbeling, B. N. (2005). Psychometric evaluation of the Restructured Clinical Scales of the MMPI-2. *Psychological Assessment, 17*(3), 345–358. https://doi.org/10.1037/1040-3590.17.3.345

45. Stanley, I. H., Yancey, J. R., Patrick, C. J., & Joiner, T. E. (2018). A distinct configuration of MMPI-2-RF scales RCd and RC9/ACT is associated with suicide attempt risk among suicide ideators in a psychiatric outpatient sample. *Psychological Assessment, 30*(9), 1249–1254. https://doi.org/10.1037/pas0000588

46. Tarescavage, A. M., Glassmire, D. M., & Burchett, D. (2018). Minnesota Multiphasic Personality Inventory-2-Restructured Form markers of future suicidal behavior in a forensic psychiatric hospital. *Psychological Assessment, 30*(2), 170–178. https://doi.org/10.1037/pas0000463

47. Tarescavage, A. M., Scheman, J., & Ben-Porath, Y. S. (2015). Reliability and validity of the Minnesota Multiphasic Personality Inventory-2-Restructured Form (MMPI-2-RF) in evaluations of chronic low back pain patients. *Psychological Assessment, 27*(2), 433–446. https://doi.org/10.1037/pas0000056

48. Tellegen, A., & Ben-Porath, Y. S. (2008/2011). *Minnesota Multiphasic Personality Inventory-2-Restructured Form (MMPI-2-RF): Technical manual.* University of Minnesota Press.

49. Tellegen, A., Ben-Porath, Y. S., Sellbom, M., Arbisi, P. A., McNulty, J. L., & Graham, J. R. (2006). Further evidence on the validity of the MMPI-2 Restructured Clinical (RC) Scales: Addressing questions raised by Rogers, Sewell, Harrison, and Jordan and Nichols. *Journal of Personality Assessment, 87*,(2), 148–171. https://doi.org/10.1207/s15327752jpa8702_04

50. Vachon, D. D., Sellbom, M., Ryder, A. G., Miller, J. D., & Bagby, R. M. (2009). A five-factor model description of depressive personality disorder. *Journal of Personality Disorders, 23*(5), 447–465. https://doi.org/10.1521/pedi.2009.23.5.447

51. Van der Heijden, P. T., Egger, J. I. M., Rossi, G. M. P., Grundel, G., & Derksen, J. J. L. (2013). The MMPI-2-Restructured Form and the standard MMPI-2 Clinical Scales in relation to DSM-IV. *European Journal of Psychological Assessment, 29*(3), 182–188. https://doi.org/10.1027/1015-5759/a000140

52. Wolf, E. J., Miller, M. W., Orazem, R. J., Weierich, M. R., Castillo, D. T., Milford, J., Kaloupek, D. G., & Keane, T. M. (2008). The MMPI-2 Restructured Clinical Scales in the assessment of posttraumatic stress disorder and comorbid disorders. *Psychological Assessment, 20*(4), 327–340. https://doi.org/10.1037/a0012948

53. Wygant, D. B., Boutacoff, L. I., Arbisi, P. A., Ben-Porath, Y. S., Kelly, P. H., & Rupp, W. M. (2007). Examination of the MMPI-2 Restructured Clinical (RC) Scales in a sample of bariatric surgery candidates. *Journal of Clinical Psychology in Medical Settings, 14*(3), 197–205. https://doi.org/10.1007/s10880-007-9073-8

End of Report

FIGURE 10.3. Mr. J's MMPI-3 Clinical Settings Interpretive Report, continued

(Figure 10.3, p. 4; SUI = 65T). Concerns over the risk of suicide are especially warranted by Mr. J's self-reported demoralization (RCd = 80T) and associated feelings of sadness, a general dissatisfaction with his life circumstances, and his report on the MMPI-3 of having made a plan for killing himself (which he disavowed in the interview). Additionally, he reported self-doubt (SFD = 72T), which is associated with rumination, feelings of insecurity and inferiority, self-disparaging and intropunitive tendencies, a lack of confidence, and feeling worthless. Mr. J's self-doubt, combined with being indecisive and inefficacious (NFC = 72T), are likely contributors to his demoralization and potential targets for therapeutic intervention. Mr. J's score on ARX (53T) does not reach a level of clinical significance; however, his reports of anxiety-related experiences mainly pertaining to reexperiencing the traumatic event—which can be identified by printing item-level information but which is not shown in Mr. J's report—provide valuable information for further exploration in the clinical interview and potentially for use by Mr. J's treatment provider. Mr. J's report of anger proneness (ANP = 70T) is also consistent with his coworkers' observations of easy irritability, hostility, and low tolerance for frustration.

The MMPI-3 scores in the behavioral dysfunction and interpersonal functioning domains provide no indications of pervasive, clinically significant problems, but they do alert the test user to areas of potential concern warranting further clinical assessment (e.g., a history of substantial juvenile conduct problems, which may correspond with adverse childhood experiences that may comprise a static risk for posttraumatic adaptation problems [see, e.g., Briggs et al., 2021]).

Considering Mr. J's MMPI-3 scores in the emotional dysfunction domain, the item-level information contained in the report, and his disclosures during the clinical interview, the examiner also administered the Detailed Assessment of Posttraumatic Stress (DAPS; Briere, 2001), which produced valid results with no indications of over- or underreporting of symptoms, and the Clinician-Administered PTSD Scale for DSM-5 (CAPS-5; Weathers et al., 2013), both of which indicated symptoms associated with PTSD, particularly symptoms involving avoidance and reexperiencing the traumatic event.

Data Integration

Step 1: Assessing for a Mental Health Condition

As we have noted throughout this book, the diagnosis of a mental health condition is made based on a thorough, comprehensive assessment, not merely on the MMPI-3 or any other assessment tool alone. These data together provide the diagnosis with convergent and discriminant validity that no single instrument can give. Collectively, the data persuaded the examiner that Mr. J suffered from PTSD-related symptoms that produce both clinically significant emotional distress and occupational impairment and that he needed mental health treatment—a need underscored by his self-reported suicidal ideation. In a fitness evaluation, an examiner need not arrive at a level of diagnostic certainty required in other contexts (e.g., worker's compensation, nonindustrial disability). The analytical focus at Step 1 of the FFDE data integration model is whether there is sufficient evidence of a mental or emotional condition, not its precise diagnostic classification. (Thus, the possibility that early developmental trauma may have contributed to the etiology of his symptoms is immaterial in an FFDE, although it may be of material significance in a worker's compensation evaluation.) As Corey and Zelig (2020) noted,

> diagnostic reliability is hampered by efforts to conceal symptoms that make up the diagnostic criteria, and many examinees in fitness evaluations fear (usually unnecessarily) that an honest acknowledgment of their symptoms will lead to job termination. Consequently, they sometimes work hard to keep the examiner from discovering their problems. (p. 202)

Although Mr. J made no apparent effort to conceal his distress and impairment, it is important to keep in mind that diagnostic certainty is not always possible in an FFDE.

Step 2: Assessing for Current Work Impairment

Mr. J's work performance problems were well documented at the time of the evaluation. It is notable that none of the observations reported by his station captain and crew members involved behavior on the fireground or in another emergency response. However, it is an established legal principle that public safety employers need not wait for such problems to arise before referring an employee for a fitness evaluation (e.g., *Brownfield v. Yakima*, 2010). Further, fitness examiners need not await such evidence before determining that an employee's psychological condition poses a substantial risk of problems in the absence of effective therapeutic intervention.

Step 3: Assessing for Sustainability of Fitness

It is arguable that the examiner has sufficient clinical data to support finding Mr. J unfit for duty simply based on his reported symptoms and job performance. However, the reasonably anticipated trajectory of his functioning, given his diagnosis and the absence of follow-up treatment, led the examiner to conduct the third step in the data integration analysis. Left untreated, the course of trauma-related conditions is quite variable, but the risks are especially pernicious in a suicidal individual who is experiencing marked distress from reexperiencing and avoidance symptom clusters (as his MMPI-3 item-level information revealed). For this reason, the examiner concluded that even if Mr. J were able to improve in the short term through heightened motivation and self-monitoring, such improvement would likely not be sustainable without effective treatment. (This is not to say that Mr. J's therapy was deficient in any way but, rather, that it had not yet achieved therapeutic efficacy.)

Conclusion

The aggregate clinical evidence derived from all sources indicated that Mr. J was currently experiencing substantial emotional distress and occupational impairment because of trauma-related symptoms. His condition substantially limited his functioning on the dimension of Emotional Regulation and Stress Tolerance. The examiner determined that Mr. J was *unfit for duty*.

MR. W, CORRECTIONAL OFFICER (INITIAL EVALUATION)

Assessment Issues Presented

- Initial fitness evaluation of a correctional officer in acute distress

Referral Summary

Mr. W is a 22-year-old, unmarried, male correctional officer who was referred for evaluation after only 18 months of employment in a state correctional institution. The referral was prompted by an acute stress reaction in response to an inmate who hanged himself in his cell on Mr. W's watch. Mr. W was the first officer to find the inmate, and despite Mr. W's efforts to resuscitate him, the inmate died. Mr. W was observed to be extremely distraught when the inmate was pronounced dead, and he called in sick on the next 3 scheduled workdays before his weekend. Upon returning to work on his next scheduled shift, he worked 3 hours before experiencing a debilitating panic attack (which he initially mistook for a heart attack but which a prison nurse ruled out) and being sent home on administrative leave pending the results of a fitness evaluation.

Assessment Findings

Employment Records

Due to the brevity of Mr. W's employment, the records provided by the employer contained little information other than a summary of the facts leading to the referral. The employer did not require preemployment psychological screening of its correctional officers, so there were no psychological records indicating his functioning at the time of hire.

Medical Records

The examiner received records from the prison infirmary and Mr. W's primary care physician, both of which ruled out a physical explanation for his symptoms.

Mental Status Examination

Mr. W's appearance was unremarkable with respect to his grooming and dress. However, his speech was slow and muted, as indicated by its rate, volume, quality, and quantity. His affective expression was dysthymic, and he reported his mood similarly. He displayed no abnormalities in perception, thought process, sensorium and cognition, judgment, or insight. His attitude toward the examiner was cooperative.

Clinical Interview

Mr. W reported that he was extremely upset when the inmate hanged himself and could not be revived. He said the inmate was similar to him in age, and he had a conversation with him earlier in the shift that led him to believe that the inmate had a good chance of "making something of his life" and diverting from the criminal path he was on—a path largely pursued to support a chronic drug addiction. Mr. W said he took several days off work after the incident to "get [his] head together," and he thought he was fine when he returned to work after his weekend. He and his girlfriend live with her parents, who he said are very supportive and nurturing, and he felt he had processed the incident well and was ready to resume his duties.

The panic attack Mr. W had at work was prototypical: an abrupt surge of intense discomfort that reached a peak within minutes and included palpitations and a fast, pounding heartbeat; sweating, shortness of breath, and a sensation of smothering; chest discomfort; light-headedness; and a fear of dying. He notified his supervisor when the symptoms failed to dissipate, and he was sent to the infirmary for evaluation, fearing that he was having a heart attack despite his young age. (The mean age at onset for panic attacks in the United States is approximately 22–23 years among adults [American Psychiatric Association, 2022].) A heart attack was ruled out by a prison nurse who evaluated him shortly after the onset of his symptoms.

Mr. W said that he initially did not accept that his symptoms were produced by a panic attack, and he saw his primary care physician afterward to confirm the diagnosis. In retrospect, he said he believed that his panic attack was triggered by seeing a new inmate, of similar age and appearance, in the cell where the suicide occurred. In the first week of being placed on administrative leave, he said he had fleeting thoughts of taking his own life, primarily because he believed that he would now be regarded by his coworkers as mentally unstable and his career would be ruined.

As discussed earlier in this chapter, individuals who undergo fitness evaluations are much more heterogeneous in comparison to candidates who undergo preemployment suitability evaluations. Many are defensive and motivated to deny problems for fear of losing their jobs; others, like Mr. W (and Mr. J in the previous case), have good insight into their problems and recognize their need for intervention. In Mr. W's case, that insight was reinforced by a caring family who encouraged him to prioritize his health over his job. Thus, he made no effort to conceal or minimize his distress, which at the time of the evaluation (2 weeks following the traumatic event), included negative mood, as well as intrusion, dissociative, avoidance, and arousal symptoms characteristic of acute stress disorder.

MMPI-3 Findings

Mr. W's MMPI-3 Interpretive Report for Clinical Settings is reproduced in Figure 10.4. A review of his validity scale scores (p. 2) indicates that there are no unscorable items, but there is "some evidence of inconsistency because of fixed True responding to the MMPI-3 items" (TRIN = 73T; p. 8). There are no indications of over- or underreporting in the protocol, but as noted in the Protocol Validity summary, although this level of inconsistency does not invalidate the test protocol, scores on the remaining Validity and Substantive Scales "should be interpreted with some caution" (p. 8). Indeed, as indicated by his score on K (35T), he presented himself as quite poorly adjusted at the time—a finding consistent with the objective evidence.

Mr. W's substantive scale scores indicate a clinically significant (65T) score on EID and moderate but nonclinically elevated scores on the RC Scales (Figure 10.4, p. 4); clinically elevated scores on three Internalizing domain scales (STR = 68T, WRY = 65T, ARX = 73T); and a clinically interpretable low score (33T) on BXD. The Substantive Scale Interpretation section of the report provides a narrative summary of interpretable findings organized by five functional domains: Somatic/Cognitive Dysfunction, Emotional Dysfunction, Thought Dysfunction, Behavioral Dysfunction, and Interpersonal Functioning. In Mr. W's report, the summary under Emotional Dysfunction focuses first on his response in the keyed direction to one of the seven SUI (58T) scale items and its association with a risk of self-harm, preoccupation with suicide and death, and current suicidal ideation and attempts. The narrative continues with interpretations related to the other clinically elevated scores in the Emotional Dysfunction domain (EID, STR, WRY, and ARX).

Interpretive Report: Clinical Settings

MMPI®-3
Minnesota Multiphasic Personality Inventory®-3
Yossef S. Ben-Porath, PhD, & Auke Tellegen, PhD

ID Number:	Mr. W
Age:	22
Gender:	Male
Marital Status:	Not reported
Years of Education:	Not reported
Date Assessed:	11/17/2020

Copyright © 2020 by the Regents of the University of Minnesota. All rights reserved. Distributed exclusively under license from the University of Minnesota by NCS Pearson, Inc. Portions reproduced from the *MMPI-3 English Test Booklet*. Copyright © 2020 by the Regents of the University of Minnesota. All rights reserved. Portions excerpted from the *MMPI-3 Manual for Administration, Scoring, and Interpretation*. Copyright © 2020 by the Regents of the University of Minnesota. All rights reserved. Portions excerpted from the *MMPI-3 Technical Manual*. Copyright © 2020 by the Regents of the University of Minnesota. All rights reserved. Used by permission of the University of Minnesota Press.

Minnesota Multiphasic Personality Inventory and **MMPI** are registered trademarks of the Regents of the University of Minnesota. **Pearson** is a trademark, in the US and/or other countries, of Pearson Education, Inc., or its affiliates.

This report contains copyrighted material and trade secrets. Qualified licensees may excerpt portions of this output report, limited to the minimum text necessary to accurately describe their significant core conclusions, for incorporation into a written evaluation of the examinee, in accordance with their profession's citation standards, if any. No adaptations, translations, modifications, or special versions may be made of this report without prior written permission from the University of Minnesota Press.

[1.0 / 19 / QG]

ALWAYS LEARNING   PEARSON

FIGURE 10.4. Mr. W's MMPI-3 Clinical Settings Interpretive Report (Initial)

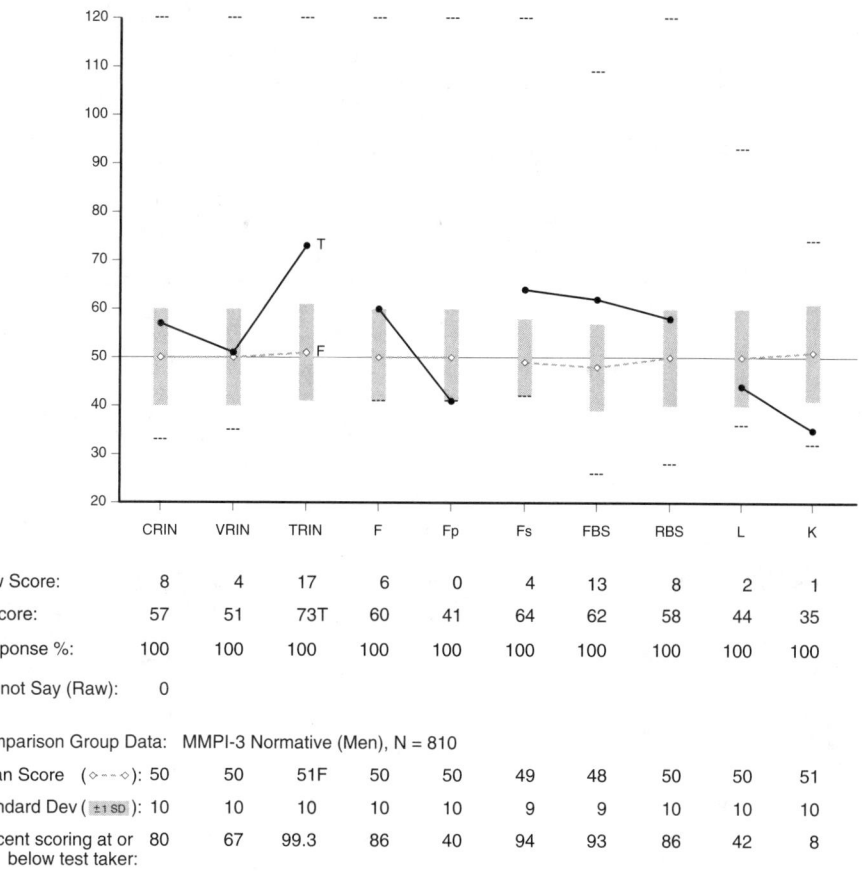

FIGURE 10.4. Mr. W's MMPI-3 Clinical Settings Interpretive Report (Initial), continued

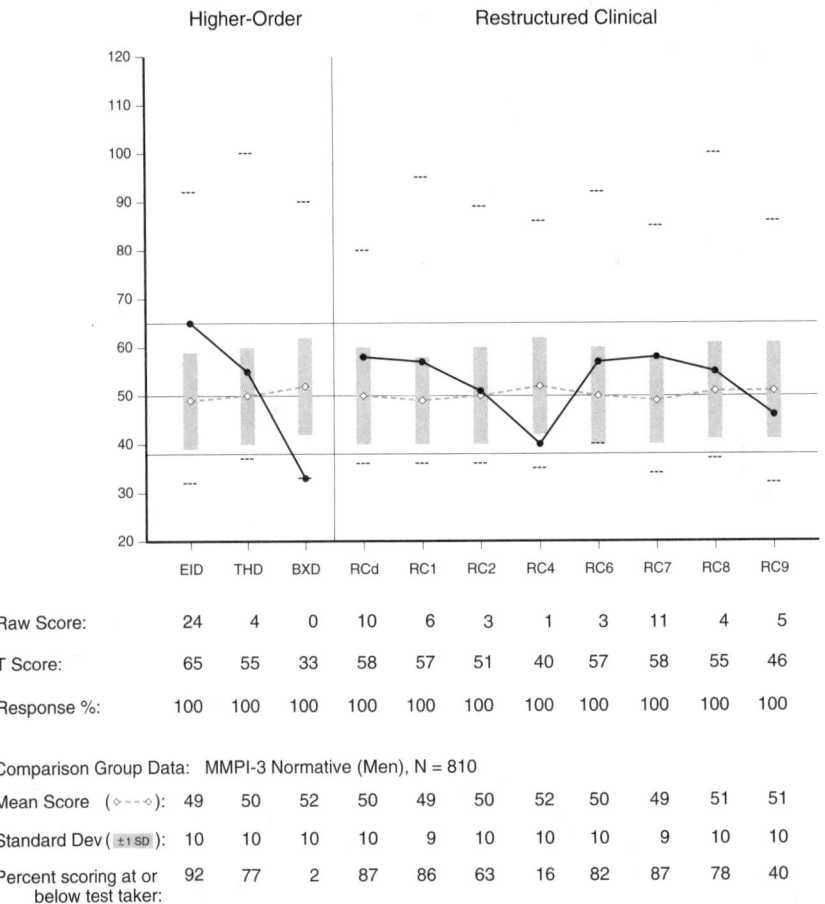

FIGURE 10.4. Mr. W's MMPI-3 Clinical Settings Interpretive Report (Initial), continued

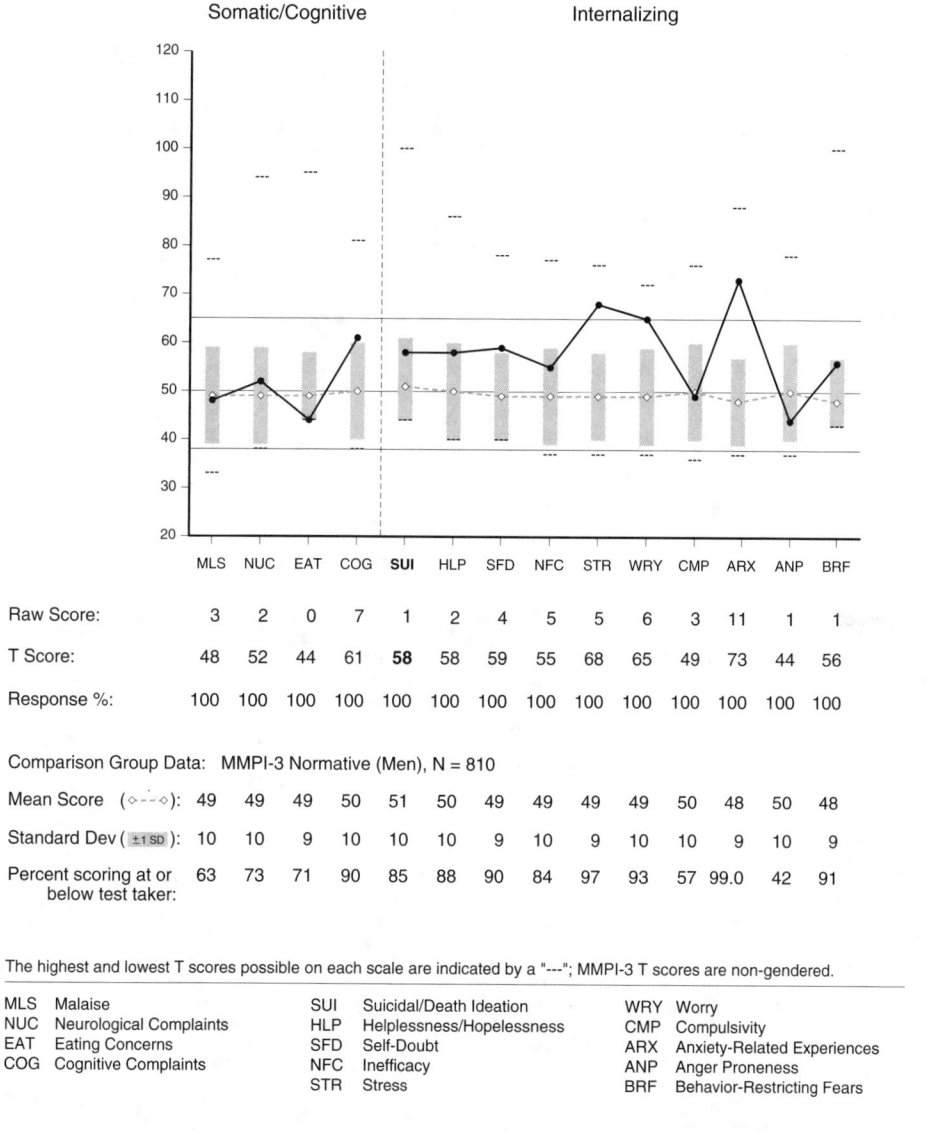

FIGURE 10.4. Mr. W's MMPI-3 Clinical Settings Interpretive Report (Initial), continued

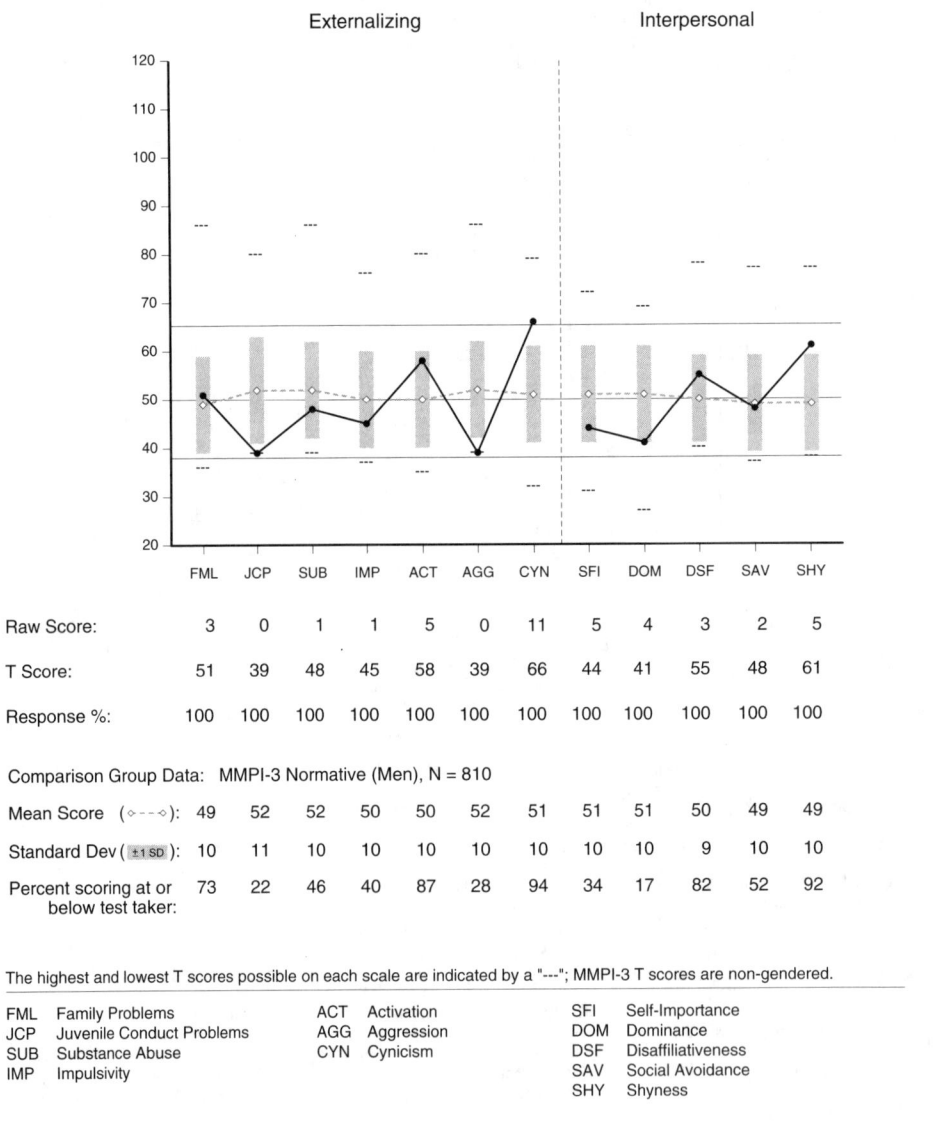

FIGURE 10.4. Mr. W's MMPI-3 Clinical Settings Interpretive Report (Initial), continued

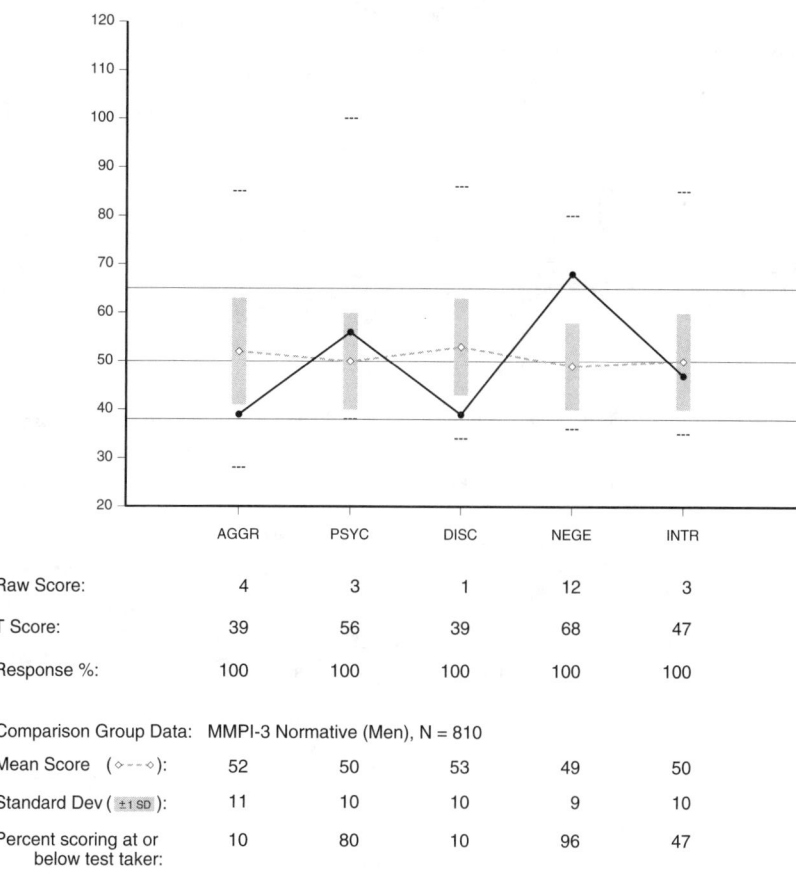

FIGURE 10.4. Mr. W's MMPI-3 Clinical Settings Interpretive Report (Initial), continued

MMPI-3 T SCORES (BY DOMAIN)

PROTOCOL VALIDITY

Content Non-Responsiveness

CNS	CRIN	VRIN	TRIN
0	57	51	**73 T**

Over-Reporting

F	Fp	Fs	FBS	RBS
60	41	64	62	58

Under-Reporting

L	K
44	35

SUBSTANTIVE SCALES

Somatic/Cognitive Dysfunction

RC1	MLS	NUC	EAT	COG
57	48	52	44	61

Emotional Dysfunction

EID: 65

RCd	SUI	HLP	SFD	NFC
58	**58**	58	59	55

RC2	INTR
51	47

RC7	STR	WRY	CMP	ARX	ANP	BRF	NEGE
58	**68**	**65**	49	**73**	44	56	**68**

Thought Dysfunction

THD: 55

RC6	RC8	PSYC
57	55	56

Behavioral Dysfunction

BXD: 33

RC4	FML	JCP	SUB
40	51	39	48

RC9	IMP	ACT	AGG	CYN
46	45	58	39	**66**

DISC
39

Interpersonal Functioning

SFI	DOM	AGGR	DSF	SAV	SHY
44	41	39	55	48	61

Scale scores shown in bold font are interpreted in the report.

Note. This information is provided to facilitate interpretation following the recommended structure for MMPI-3 interpretation in Chapter 5 of the *MMPI-3 Manual for Administration, Scoring, and Interpretation*, which provides details in the text and an outline in Table 5-1.

FIGURE 10.4. Mr. W's MMPI-3 Clinical Settings Interpretive Report (Initial), continued

This interpretive report is intended for use by a professional qualified to interpret the MMPI-3. The information it contains should be considered in the context of the test taker's background, the circumstances of the assessment, and other available information.

The report includes extensive annotation, which appears as superscripts following each statement in the narrative, keyed to Endnotes with accompanying Research References, which appear in the final two sections of the report. Additional information about the annotation features is provided in the headnotes to these sections and in the MMPI-3 User's Guide for the Score and Clinical Interpretive Reports.

SYNOPSIS

Scores on the MMPI-3 Validity Scales raise concerns about the possible impact of inconsistent responding on the validity of this protocol. With that caution noted, scores on the Substantive Scales indicate emotional and behavioral dysfunction. Emotional-internalizing findings include **suicidal ideation**, negative emotionality, stress, worry, and anxiety. Behavioral-externalizing problems relate to cynicism.

PROTOCOL VALIDITY

Content Non-Responsiveness

Unscorable Responses
The test taker produced scorable responses to all the MMPI-3 items.

Inconsistent Responding
There is some evidence of inconsistency because of fixed True responding to the MMPI-3 items[1]. This level of inconsistency does not invalidate the test protocol. However, scores on the remaining Validity and Substantive Scales should be interpreted with some caution[2].

Over-Reporting

There are no indications of over-reporting in this protocol.

Under-Reporting

There are no indications of under-reporting in this protocol.

SUBSTANTIVE SCALE INTERPRETATION

Clinical symptoms, personality characteristics, and behavioral tendencies of the test taker are described in this section and organized according to an empirically guided framework. (Please see Chapter 5 of the MMPI-3 Manual for Administration, Scoring, and Interpretation for details.) Statements containing the word "reports" are based on the item content of MMPI-3 scales, whereas statements that include the word "likely" are based on empirical correlates of scale scores. Specific sources for each statement can be viewed with the annotation features of this report.

FIGURE 10.4. Mr. W's MMPI-3 Clinical Settings Interpretive Report (Initial), continued

The following interpretation needs to be considered in light of cautions noted about the possible impact of inconsistent responding on the validity of this protocol.

Somatic/Cognitive Dysfunction
There are no indications of somatic or cognitive dysfunction in this protocol.

Emotional Dysfunction
The test taker responded to one of the seven Suicidal/Death Ideation (SUI) scale items in the keyed direction. The content of this item is provided in the Critical Responses section later in this report[3]. He may be at risk for self-harm[4], preoccupied with suicide and death[5], and at risk for current suicidal ideation and attempts[6].

His responses indicate significant emotional distress[7]. He also reports experiencing an elevated level of negative emotionality[8] and indeed likely experiences various negative emotions[9]. More specifically, he reports multiple anxiety-related experiences, including generalized anxiety and reexperiencing and/or panic[10]. He indeed likely experiences significant anxiety and anxiety-related problems[11], PTSD features including intrusive ideation and nightmares[12], and panic[13]. He also reports an above average level of stress[14]. He likely complains about stress[15] and feels incapable of controlling his anxiety level[15]. In addition, he reports excessive worry, including worries about misfortune and finances, as well as preoccupation with disappointments[16]. He indeed likely worries excessively[17] and ruminates[17].

Thought Dysfunction
There are no indications of disordered thinking in this protocol.

Behavioral Dysfunction
The test taker reports having cynical beliefs, distrust of others, and believing others look out only for their own interests[18]. He likely is hostile toward others[19] and feels alienated from them[20]; is distrustful, self-centered, and lacking in empathy[21]; and has negative interpersonal experiences as a result of his cynical beliefs, self-centeredness, and hostility[22].

However, his responses indicate a higher than average level of behavioral constraint[23]. He is unlikely to engage in externalizing, acting-out behavior[24].

Interpersonal Functioning Scales
These scales provide no further evidence of dysfunction.

DIAGNOSTIC CONSIDERATIONS

*This section provides recommendations for psychodiagnostic assessment based on the test taker's MMPI-3 results. It is recommended that he be evaluated for the following, **bearing in mind possible threats to protocol validity noted earlier in this report**:*

Emotional-Internalizing Disorders
- Features of personality disorders involving negative emotionality such as Dependent[25]
- Anxiety-related disorders[13] including generalized anxiety disorder[15] and PTSD[26]
- Disorders involving excessive worry[27]

Behavioral-Externalizing Disorders
- Personality disorders involving mistrust of and hostility toward others[28]

FIGURE 10.4. Mr. W's MMPI-3 Clinical Settings Interpretive Report (Initial), continued

TREATMENT CONSIDERATIONS

This section provides inferential treatment-related recommendations based on the test taker's MMPI-3 scores. **The following recommendations need to be considered in light of cautions noted earlier about possible threats to protocol validity.**

Areas for Further Evaluation

- <u>Risk for suicide</u> should be assessed immediately[29].

Psychotherapy Process Issues

- Emotional difficulties may motivate him for treatment[30].
- Cynicism may interfere with seeking or forming a therapeutic relationship[31].
- Cynical beliefs may result in treatment non-compliance[32].

Possible Targets for Treatment

- Anxiety[33]
- Developing stress management skills[34]
- Excessive worry and rumination[27]
- Lack of interpersonal trust[28]

ITEM-LEVEL INFORMATION

Unscorable Responses

The test taker produced scorable responses to all the MMPI-3 items.

Critical Responses

Seven MMPI-3 scales—Suicidal/Death Ideation (SUI), Helplessness/Hopelessness (HLP), Anxiety-Related Experiences (ARX), Ideas of Persecution (RC6), Aberrant Experiences (RC8), Substance Abuse (SUB), and Aggression (AGG)—have been designated by the test authors as having critical item content that may require immediate attention and follow-up. Items answered by the individual in the keyed direction (True or False) on a critical scale are listed below if his T score on that scale is 65 or higher. However, any item answered in the keyed direction on SUI is listed. The percentage of the MMPI-3 normative sample (NS) and of the MMPI-3 Normative (Men) Comparison Group (CG) that answered each item in the keyed direction are provided in parentheses following the item content.

Suicidal/Death Ideation (SUI, T Score = 58)

    Item number and content omitted. (True; NS 8.1%, CG 9.6%)

Anxiety-Related Experiences (ARX, T Score = 73)

    Item number and content omitted. (True; NS 31.2%, CG 26.7%)
    Item number and content omitted. (True; NS 31.4%, CG 30.9%)
    Item number and content omitted. (True; NS 16.9%, CG 11.0%)
    Item number and content omitted. (True; NS 10.9%, CG 10.0%)
    Item number and content omitted. (True; NS 4.7%, CG 3.8%)
    Item number and content omitted. (True; NS 28.6%, CG 26.5%)
    Item number and content omitted. (True; NS 26.0%, CG 22.5%)
    Item number and content omitted. (True; NS 41.7%, CG 37.5%)
    Item number and content omitted. (True; NS 35.8%, CG 30.9%)
    Item number and content omitted. (True; NS 8.6%, CG 7.0%)
    Item number and content omitted. (True; NS 15.2%, CG 10.4%)

FIGURE 10.4. Mr. W's MMPI-3 Clinical Settings Interpretive Report (Initial), continued

ENDNOTES

This section lists for each statement in the report the MMPI-3 score(s) that triggered it. In addition, each statement is identified as a <u>Test Response</u>, if based on item content, a <u>Correlate</u>, if based on empirical correlates, or an <u>Inference</u>, if based on the report authors' judgment. (This information can also be accessed on-screen by placing the cursor on a given statement.) For correlate-based statements, research references (Ref. No.) are provided, keyed to the consecutively numbered reference list following the endnotes.

[1] Test Response: TRIN=73T
[2] Correlate: TRIN=73T, Ref. 9, 14, 18
[3] Test Response: SUI=58
[4] Correlate: SUI=58, Ref. 7, 21, 23
[5] Correlate: SUI=58, Ref. 3, 7, 15, 17, 22, 23, 24, 30, 32
[6] Correlate: SUI=58, Ref. 3, 7, 15, 17, 23, 30, 31, 32
[7] Correlate: EID=65, Ref. 7, 20, 25, 32
[8] Test Response: NEGE=68
[9] Correlate: NEGE=68, Ref. 7
[10] Test Response: ARX=73
[11] Correlate: ARX=73, Ref. 1, 7, 8, 16, 22, 24, 28; NEGE=68, Ref. 7
[12] Correlate: ARX=73, Ref. 7, 16, 22; NEGE=68, Ref. 7, 32
[13] Correlate: ARX=73, Ref. 7
[14] Test Response: STR=68
[15] Correlate: STR=68, Ref. 7
[16] Test Response: WRY=65
[17] Correlate: WRY=65, Ref. 7
[18] Test Response: CYN=66
[19] Correlate: CYN=66, Ref. 1, 6, 7, 11, 13, 19, 22, 27, 32
[20] Correlate: CYN=66, Ref. 7, 10, 19, 26, 32
[21] Correlate: CYN=66, Ref. 32
[22] Correlate: CYN=66, Ref. 7, 12, 22, 32
[23] Correlate: BXD=33, Ref. 7, 20, 25, 32
[24] Correlate: BXD=33, Ref. 7, 20, 32
[25] Correlate: NEGE=68, Ref. 2, 7, 29
[26] Correlate: ARX=73, Ref. 4, 7, 28, 32
[27] Inference: WRY=65
[28] Inference: CYN=66
[29] Inference: SUI=58
[30] Inference: EID=65; NEGE=68
[31] Correlate: CYN=66, Ref. 5, 33
[32] Correlate: CYN=66, Ref. 33
[33] Inference: ARX=73
[34] Inference: STR=68

FIGURE 10.4. Mr. W's MMPI-3 Clinical Settings Interpretive Report (Initial), continued

RESEARCH REFERENCE LIST

The following studies are sources for empirical correlates identified in the Endnotes section of this report.

1. Anderson, J. L., Sellbom, M., Ayearst, L., Quilty, L. C., Chmielewski, M., & Bagby, R. M. (2015). Associations between DSM-5 Section III personality traits and the Minnesota Multiphasic Personality Inventory 2-Restructured Form (MMPI-2-RF) scales in a psychiatric patient sample. *Psychological Assessment, 27*(3), 801–815. https://doi.org/10.1037/pas0000096

2. Anderson, J. L., Wood, M. E., Tarescavage, A. M., Burchett, D., & Glassmire, D. M. (2018). The role of dimensional personality psychopathology in a forensic inpatient psychiatric setting. *Journal of Personality Disorders, 32*(4), 447–464. https://doi.org/10.1521/pedi_2017_31_301

3. Anestis, J. C., Finn, J. A., Gottfried, E. D., Hames, J. L., Bodell, L. P., Hagan, C. R., Arnau, R. C., Anestis, M. D., Arbisi, P. A., & Joiner, T. E. (2018). Burdensomeness, belongingness, and capability: Assessing the interpersonal-psychological theory of suicide with MMPI-2-RF scales. *Assessment, 25*(4), 415–431. https://doi.org/10.1177/1073191116652227

4. Arbisi, P. A., Polusny, M. A., Erbes, C. R., Thuras, P., & Reddy, M. K. (2011). The Minnesota Multiphasic Personality Inventory-2 Restructured Form in National Guard soldiers screening positive for posttraumatic stress disorder and mild traumatic brain injury. *Psychological Assessment, 23*(1), 203–214. https://doi.org/10.1037/a0021339

5. Arbisi, P. A., Rusch, L., Polusny, M. A., Thuras, P., & Erbes, C. R. (2013). Does cynicism play a role in failure to obtain needed care? Mental health service utilization among returning U.S. National Guard soldiers. *Psychological Assessment, 25*(3), 991–996. https://doi.org/10.1037/a0032225

6. Ayearst, L. E., Sellbom, M., Trobst, K. K., & Bagby, R. M. (2013). Evaluating the interpersonal content of the MMPI-2-RF Interpersonal Scales. *Journal of Personality Assessment, 95*(2), 187–196. https://doi.org/10.1080/00223891.2012.730085

7. Ben-Porath, Y. S., & Tellegen, A. (2020). *The Minnesota Multiphasic Personality Inventory-3 (MMPI-3): Technical manual.* University of Minnesota Press.

8. Block, A. R., Ben-Porath, Y. S., & Marek, R. J. (2013). Psychological risk factors for poor outcome of spine surgery and spinal cord stimulator implant: A review of the literature and their assessment with the MMPI-2-RF. *The Clinical Neuropsychologist, 27*(1), 81–107. https://doi.org/10.1080/13854046.2012.721007

9. Burchett, D., Dragon, W. R., Smith Holbert, A. M., Tarescavage, A. M., Mattson, C. A., Handel, R. W., & Ben-Porath, Y. S. (2016). "False feigners": Examining the impact of non-content-based invalid responding on the Minnesota Multiphasic Personality Inventory-2 Restructured Form content-based invalid responding indicators. *Psychological Assessment, 28*(5), 458–470. https://doi.org/10.1037/pas0000205

10. Cox, A, Pant, H., Gilson, A. N., Rodriguez, J. L., Young, K. R., Kwon, S., & Weed, N. C., (2012). Effects of augmenting response options on MMPI-2 RC Scale psychometrics. *Journal of Personality Assessment, 94*(6), 613–619. https://doi.org/10.1080/00223891.2012.700464

11. Forbey, J. D., & Ben-Porath, Y. S. (2008). Empirical correlates of the MMPI-2 Restructured Clinical (RC) Scales in a non-clinical setting. *Journal of Personality Assessment, 90*(2), 136–141. https://doi.org/10.1080/00223890701845161

12. Forbey, J. D., Ben-Porath, Y. S., & Arbisi, P. A. (2012). The MMPI-2 computer adaptive version (MMPI-2-CA) in a Veterans Administration medical outpatient facility. *Psychological Assessment, 24*(3), 628–639. https://doi.org/10.1037/a0026509

FIGURE 10.4. Mr. W's MMPI-3 Clinical Settings Interpretive Report (Initial), continued

13. Franz, A. O., Harrop, T. M., & McCord, D. M. (2017). Examining the construct validity of the MMPI-2-RF Interpersonal Functioning Scales using the Computerized Adaptive Test of Personality Disorder as a comparative framework. *Journal of Personality Assessment, 99*(4), 416–423. https://doi.org/10.1080/00223891.2016.1222394

14. Gervais, R. O., Tarescavage, A. M., Greiffenstein, M. F., Wygant, D. B., Deslauriers, C., & Arends, P. (2018). Inconsistent responding on the MMPI-2-RF and uncooperative attitude: Evidence from cognitive performance validity measures. *Psychological Assessment, 30*(3), 410–415. https://doi.org/10.1037/pas0000506

15. Glassmire, D. M, Tarescavage, A. M., Burchett, D., Martinez, J., & Gomez, A. (2016). Clinical utility of the MMPI-2-RF SUI items and scale in a forensic inpatient setting: Association with interview self-reports and future suicidal behavior. *Psychological Assessment, 28*(11), 1502–1509. https://doi.org/10.1037/pas0000220

16. Gottfried, E. D., Anestis, J. C., Dillon, K. H., & Carbonell, J. L. (2016). The associations between Minnesota Multiphasic Personality Inventory-2-Restructured Form and self-reported physical and sexual abuse and posttraumatic symptoms in a sample of incarcerated women. *International Journal of Forensic Mental Health, 15*(4), 323–332. https://doi.org/10.1080/14999013.2016.1228088

17. Gottfried, E., Bodell, L., Carbonell, J., & Joiner, T. (2014). The clinical utility of the MMPI-2-RF Suicidal/Death Ideation Scale. *Psychological Assessment, 26*(4), 1205–1211. https://doi.org/10.1037/pas0000017

18. Handel, R. W., Ben-Porath, Y. S., Tellegen, A., & Archer, R. P. (2010). Psychometric functioning of the MMPI-2-RF VRIN-r and TRIN-r scales with varying degrees of randomness, acquiescence, and counter-acquiescence. *Psychological Assessment, 22*(1), 87–95. https://doi.org/10.1037/a0017061

19. Ingram, P. B., Kelso, K. M., & McCord, D. M. (2011). Empirical correlates and expanded interpretation of the MMPI-2-RF Restructured Clinical Scale 3 (Cynicism). *Assessment, 18*(1), 95–101. https://doi.org/10.1177/1073191110388147

20. Lanyon, R. I., & Thomas, M. L. (2013). Assessment of global psychiatric categories: The PSI/PSI-2 and the MMPI-2-RF. *Psychological Assessment, 25*(1), 227–232. https://doi.org/10.1037/a0030313

21. Laurinaityte, I., Laurinavicius, A., Ustinaviciute, L., Wygant, D. B., Sellbom, M. (2017). Utility of the MMPI-2 Restructured Form (MMPI-2-RF) in a sample of Lithuanian male offenders. *Law and Human Behavior, 41*(5), 494–505. https://doi.org/10.1037/lhb0000254

22. Menton, W. H., Crighton, A. H., Tarescavage, A. M., Marek, R. J., Hicks, A. D., & Ben-Porath, Y. S. (2019). Equivalence of laptop and tablet administrations of the Minnesota Multiphasic Personality Inventory-2 Restructured Form. *Assessment, 26*(4), 661–669. https://doi.org/10.1177/1073191117714558

23. Miller, S. N., Bozzay, M. L., Ben-Porath, Y. S., & Arbisi, P. A. (2019). Distinguishing levels of suicide risk in depressed male veterans: The role of internalizing and externalizing psychopathology as measured by the MMPI-2-RF. *Assessment, 26*(1), 85–98. https://doi.org/10.1177/1073191117743787

24. Rogers, M. L., Anestis, J. C., Harrop, T. M., Schneider, M., Bender, T. W., Ringer, F. B., & Joiner, T. E. (2017). Examination of MMPI-2-RF substantive scales as indicators of acute suicidal affective disturbance components. *Journal of Personality Assessment, 99*(4), 424–434. https://doi.org/10.1080/00223891.2016.1222393

25. Romero, I. E., Toorabally, N., Burchett, D., Tarescavage, A. M., & Glassmire, D. M. (2017). Mapping the MMPI-2-RF substantive scales onto, internalizing, externalizing, and thought dysfunction dimensions in a forensic inpatient setting. *Journal of Personality Assessment, 99*(4), 351–362. https://doi.org/10.1080/00223891.2016.1223681

FIGURE 10.4. Mr. W's MMPI-3 Clinical Settings Interpretive Report (Initial), continued

26. Sellbom, M., & Ben-Porath, Y. S. (2005). Mapping the MMPI-2 Restructured Clinical Scales onto normal personality traits: Evidence of construct validity. *Journal of Personality Assessment, 85*(2), 179–187. https://doi.org/10.1207/s15327752jpa8502_10

27. Sellbom, M., Ben-Porath, Y. S., & Bagby, R. M. (2008). Personality and psychopathology: Mapping the MMPI-2 Restructured Clinical (RC) Scales onto the five factor model of personality. *Journal of Personality Disorders, 22*(3), 291–312. https://doi.org/10.1521/pedi.2008.22.3.291

28. Sellbom, M., Lee, T. T. C., Ben-Porath, Y. S., Arbisi, P. A., & Gervais, R. O. (2012). Differentiating PTSD symptomatology with the MMPI-2-RF (Restructured Form) in a forensic disability sample. *Psychiatry Research, 197*(1–2), 172–179. https://doi.org/10.1016/j.psychres.2012.02.003

29. Sellbom, M., & Smith, A. (2017). Assessment of DSM-5 Section II personality disorders with the MMPI-2-RF in a nonclinical sample. *Journal of Personality Assessment, 99*(4), 384–397. https://doi.org/10.1080/00223891.2016.1242074

30. Stanley, I. H., Yancey, J. R., Patrick, C. J., & Joiner, T. E. (2018). A distinct configuration of MMPI-2-RF scales RCd and RC9/ACT is associated with suicide attempt risk among suicide ideators in a psychiatric outpatient sample. *Psychological Assessment, 30*(9), 1249–1254. https://doi.org/10.1037/pas0000588

31. Tarescavage, A. M., Glassmire, D. M., & Burchett, D. (2018). Minnesota Multiphasic Personality Inventory-2-Restructured Form markers of future suicidal behavior in a forensic psychiatric hospital. *Psychological Assessment, 30*(2), 170–178. https://doi.org/10.1037/pas0000463

32. Tellegen, A., & Ben-Porath, Y. S. (2008/2011). *Minnesota Multiphasic Personality Inventory-2-Restructured Form (MMPI-2-RF): Technical manual.* University of Minnesota Press.

33. Tylicki, J. L., Martin-Fernandez, K. W., & Ben-Porath, Y. S. (2019). Predicting therapist ratings of treatment progress and outcomes with the MMPI-2-RF. *Journal of Clinical Psychology, 75*(9), 1673–1683. https://doi.org/10.1002/jclp.22795

End of Report

FIGURE 10.4. Mr. W's MMPI-3 Clinical Settings Interpretive Report (Initial), continued

Consistent with the interpretive guidance provided by Ben-Porath and Tellegen (2020a), the report is organized by the MMPI-3's hierarchical structure, first with interpretation of Mr. W's clinically elevated H-O scale (EID = 65T), indicating significant emotional distress. An interpretation of any clinically elevated RC scale would follow, but in the absence of an RC scale elevation ≥ 65T, the report narrative moves next to a discussion of Mr. W's clinically elevated scores on the other substantive scales, beginning with the finding that he "reports experiencing an elevated level of negative emotionality and indeed likely experiences various negative emotions" (p. 9; NEGE = 68T), followed by more specific interpretations related to multiple anxiety-related experiences (ARX = 73T), an above average level of stress (STR = 68T), and excessive worry (WRY = 65T).

In the Behavioral Dysfunction subsection, the interpretation is focused on the one clinically elevated score in this domain, CYN, which at 66T is associated with "having cynical beliefs, distrust of others, and believing others look out only for their own interests" (Figure 10.4, p. 9). However, because of his interpretable low score on BXD (33T), it is noted that "his responses indicate a higher than average level of behavioral constraint" and that "he is unlikely to engage in externalizing, acting-out behavior" (p. 9).

Data Integration

Step 1: Assessing for a Mental Health Condition

Mr. W's anxiety and mood symptoms first appeared within a day following exposure to the suicide of an inmate on his watch and his unsuccessful efforts to resuscitate him. The symptoms are characteristic of acute stress disorder and span all five categories of the diagnosis (negative mood and intrusion, dissociative, avoidance, and arousal symptoms). As discussed in the context of Mr. J, diagnostic precision is not the primary objective in a fitness evaluation, although diagnostic accuracy is always desirable and facilitates more accurate projections of fitness restoration and maintenance. It is certainly possible that a preexisting mood or personality disorder may also contribute to Mr. W's clinical picture, but when, as here, the symptoms and their progression are amply accounted for by a less speculative diagnosis, no further analysis is required at this step in the integrative model. It is clear that Mr. W has a trauma- and stressor-related disorder requiring treatment. The next step in the model is to assess whether that condition currently impairs his work functioning.

Step 2: Assessing for Current Work Impairment

At this step in the model, the principal question is whether Mr. W's symptoms are reasonably expected to substantially limit his ability to perform one or more of his essential job functions, which include but are not limited to:

- Observes prisoners' or detainees' activities to detect unusual or prohibited behavior, which might be a threat to the security of the facility or the safety of prisoners, detainees, employees, or visitors.
- Observes and appropriately responds to such "critical incidents" as assaults on employees, prisoners, or detainees; prisoner or detainee disturbances; or other situations threatening to the security of the facility and prepares written reports. Appropriate response may include the use of firearms.
- Responds quickly to calls for assistance in other areas of the prison as directed by the control center or shift supervisor. Assists in controlling disturbances and isolating instigators.

Mr. W experienced a panic attack during his most recent shift—a little more than a week prior to the fitness evaluation—that substantially limited his ability to perform each of the essential job functions just listed. He also remained in active distress and, although he was scheduled to be seen by a psychiatric-mental health nurse practitioner, he had not yet started treatment. Therefore, the fitness examiner concluded that Mr. W's condition remained substantially job-limiting.

Step 3: Assessing for Sustainability of Fitness

This step in the integrative model is moot when, as in Mr. W's case, the employee's condition is active and precludes safe and effective job performance.

Conclusion

The aggregate clinical evidence derived from all sources indicated Mr. W had an active trauma- and stressor-related disorder that the examiner determined to be substantially job-limiting at the time of this initial evaluation. Therefore, Mr. W was assessed to be psychologically *unfit for duty* pending treatment of his condition and restoration of his fitness.

MR. W, CORRECTIONAL OFFICER (FOLLOW-UP EVALUATION)

Assessment Issues Presented

- Fitness evaluation of a correctional officer earlier determined to be psychologically unfit for duty
- Follow-up evaluation after 3 months of treatment

Referral Summary

Within a week after the fitness evaluation, Mr. W was placed on family medical leave following certification by his primary care physician that he had a serious health condition and was unable to work even in a limited capacity. Following approximately 12 weeks of mental health treatment, including medication (prazosin and sertraline) and cognitive processing therapy, his primary care physician certified Mr. W as ready to return to work. Consistent with the provisions of the federal Family Medical Leave Act, Mr. W was immediately returned to paid status and placed on administrative leave pending an independent evaluation of his fitness for duty (see, e.g., *White v. County of Los Angeles*, 2014).

Assessment Findings

Medical Records

Records from Mr. W's primary care physician, psychiatric-mental health nurse practitioner, and mental health counselor documented their diagnosis (acute stress disorder), treatment, his engagement and therapeutic progress, and his providers' respective opinions that his symptoms were sufficiently in remission to warrant reevaluation of his fitness for duty.

Mental Status Examination

In contrast to Mr. W's initial evaluation, he presented with a euthymic mood and a normal rate and rhythm of speech. He evidenced no abnormalities in perception, thought process, sensorium and cognition, judgment, or insight, and he remained cooperative with the examiner.

Clinical Interview

Mr. W reported that he felt completely ready to return to work. He had gained substantial skill in identifying, clarifying, and modifying his cognitive distortions concerning the suicide, his role in it, and the potential for recurrence in a high-security prison. He reported a high level of confidence in his ability to apply his newly developed coping strategies in the face of either new traumatic events or a reemergence of anxiety symptoms. He said that prazosin helped reduce his disturbing dreams, sertraline had effectively eliminated his anxiety symptoms and negative mood, and he slept normally and awakened rested. Consistent with the reports of his health care providers, he said he intended to continue in treatment at a reduced frequency for no less than 6 months after returning to work. He said he felt ready to resume his duties and had confidence in his ability to monitor and address his anxiety level to avert a future panic attack.

MMPI-3 Findings

Mr. W's second MMPI-3 Interpretive Report for Clinical Settings is reproduced in Figure 10.5. The Protocol Validity summary (p. 8) indicates that his responses produced a valid MMPI-3 protocol, there were no problems with unscorable items, he responded to the items relevantly based on their content, and there were no indications of over- or underreporting.

A review of Mr. W's substantive scale scores reveals no indications of somatic/cognitive or thought dysfunction. His score on SUI (at 65T in contrast to his previous score of 58T) reflect both his acknowledgment of having previously considered killing himself as well as having thought about how he might do it. SUI items are automatically printed when they are answered in the keyed direction. This information led the examiner to inquire about when these thoughts occurred. Mr. W clarified that they occurred both before the first fitness evaluation and shortly thereafter but before he began treatment. He said that his treatment providers quickly led him to be optimistic that he could recover and resume his career, and his suicidal thoughts stopped.

Mr. W's score on CYN (32T) also contrasts significantly from the first evaluation (68T). He initially reported having cynical beliefs, being distrustful of others, and believing that others look out only for their own interests. In the second evaluation, he described others as well-intentioned and trustworthy, and he disavowed cynical beliefs about them. Inasmuch as low CYN has been shown to be associated with higher scores on measures of self-efficacy, optimism, and empathy (Ben-Porath & Tellegen, 2020b), Mr. W's lower CYN score is likely a product of therapeutic growth, as with his low score on IMP (37T), indicating a below average level of impulsive behavior. (Note: Mr. W's IMP score at the first evaluation was 45T, which is equivalent to a raw score of 1. A score of 37T results from a raw score of 1. Consequently, care should be taken to not place undue weight on this score change.)

Data Integration

Step 1: Assessing for a Mental Health Condition

The first evaluation led to a provisional diagnosis of acute stress disorder, which was affirmed by Mr. W's treating health care providers. As previously discussed, diagnostic precision is often difficult to achieve in fitness evaluations, particularly when they are adversarial. Arguably, once his symptoms persisted

Interpretive Report: Clinical Settings

MMPI®-3
Minnesota Multiphasic Personality Inventory®-3
Yossef S. Ben-Porath, PhD, & Auke Tellegen, PhD

ID Number:	Mr. W
Age:	23
Gender:	Male
Marital Status:	Not reported
Years of Education:	Not reported
Date Assessed:	02/19/2021

FIGURE 10.5. Mr. W's MMPI-3 Clinical Settings Interpretive Report (Follow-up)

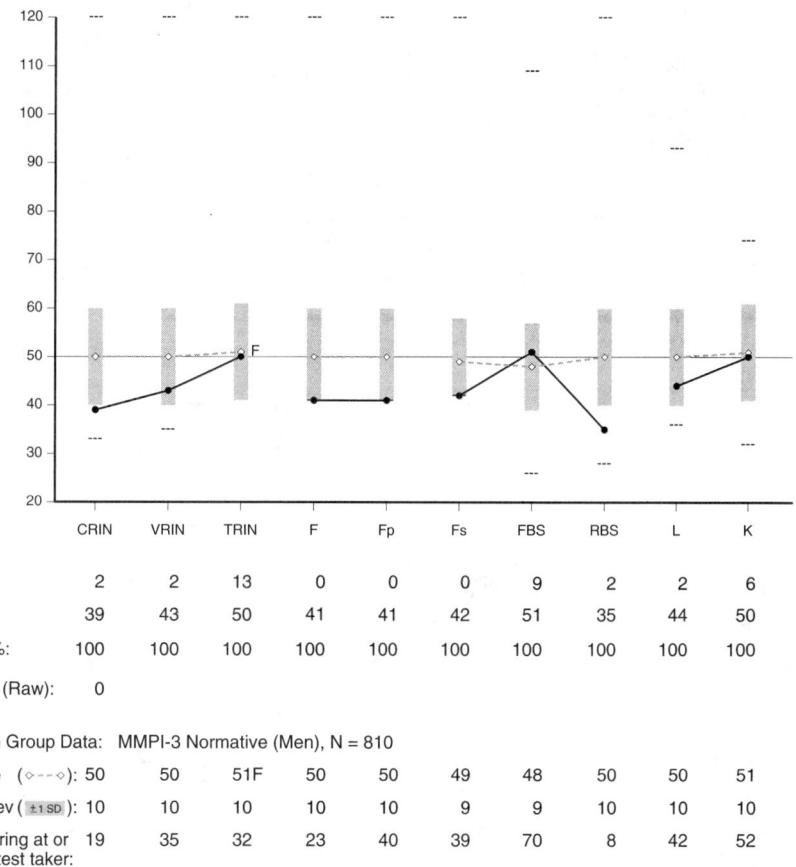

FIGURE 10.5. Mr. W's MMPI-3 Clinical Settings Interpretive Report (Follow-up), continued

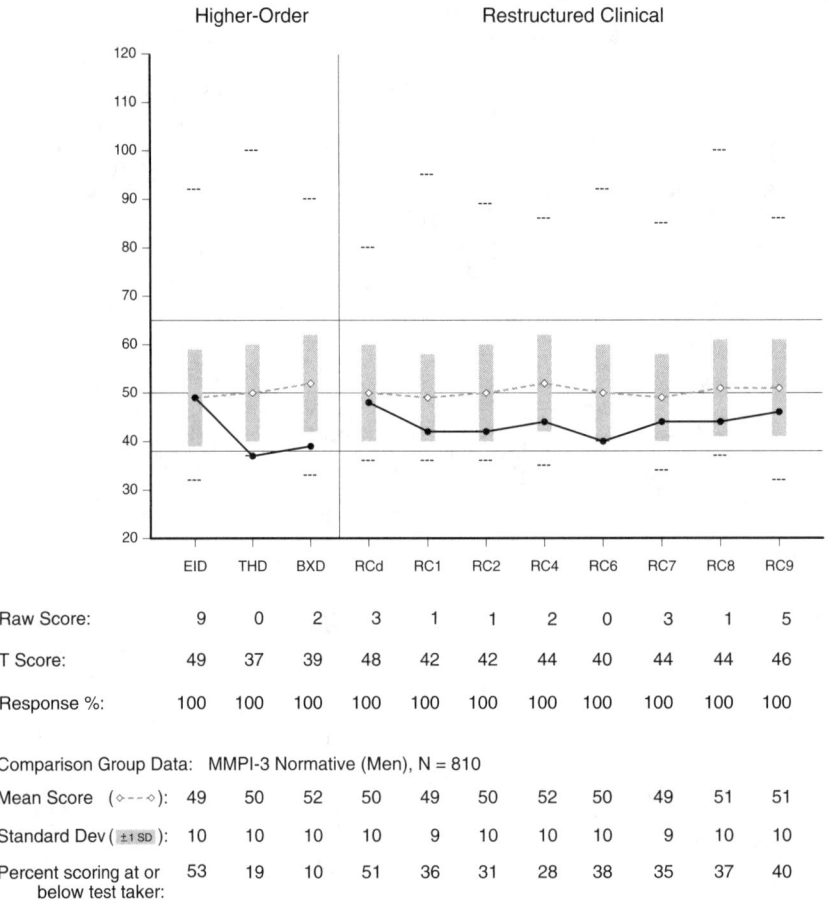

FIGURE 10.5. Mr. W's MMPI-3 Clinical Settings Interpretive Report (Follow-up), continued

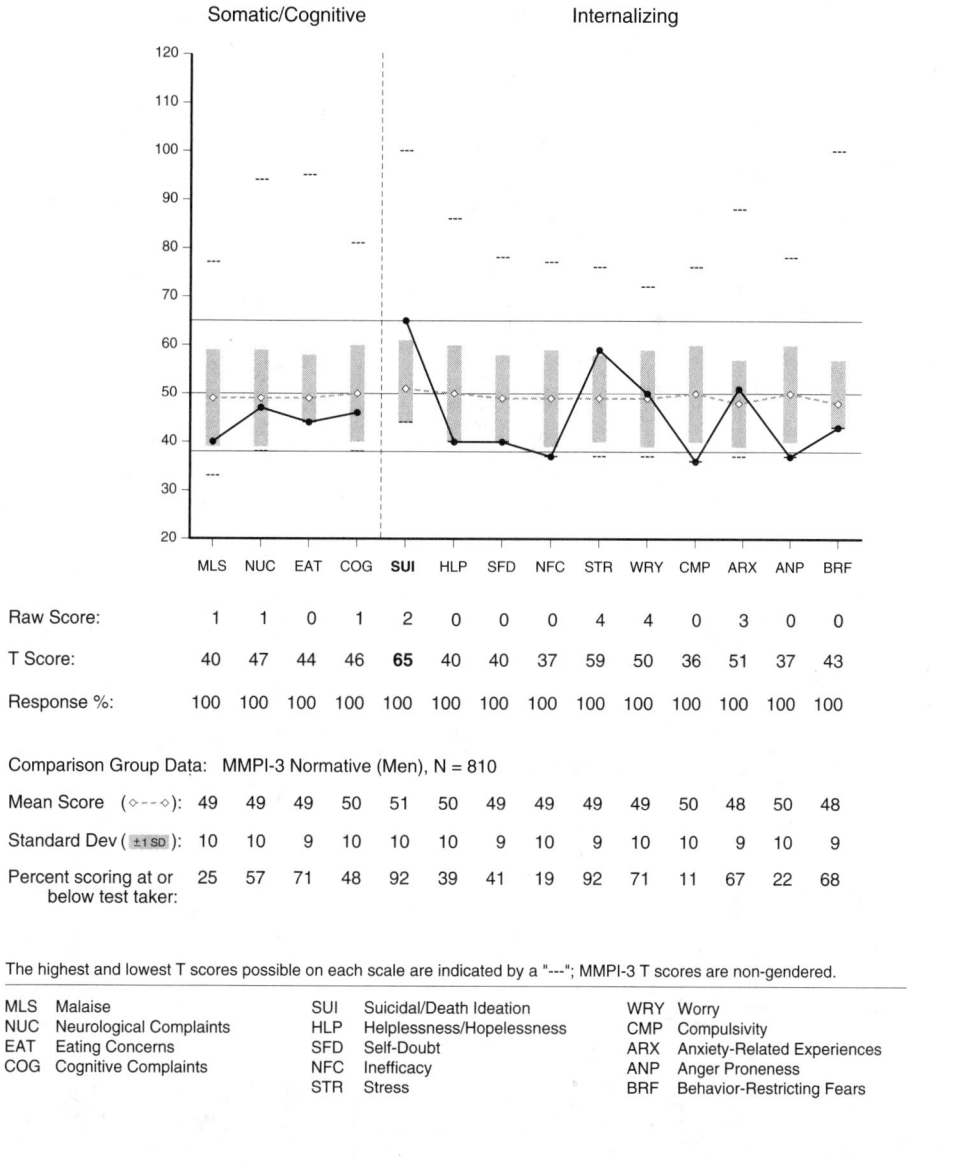

FIGURE 10.5. Mr. W's MMPI-3 Clinical Settings Interpretive Report (Follow-up), continued

FIGURE 10.5. Mr. W's MMPI-3 Clinical Settings Interpretive Report (Follow-up), continued

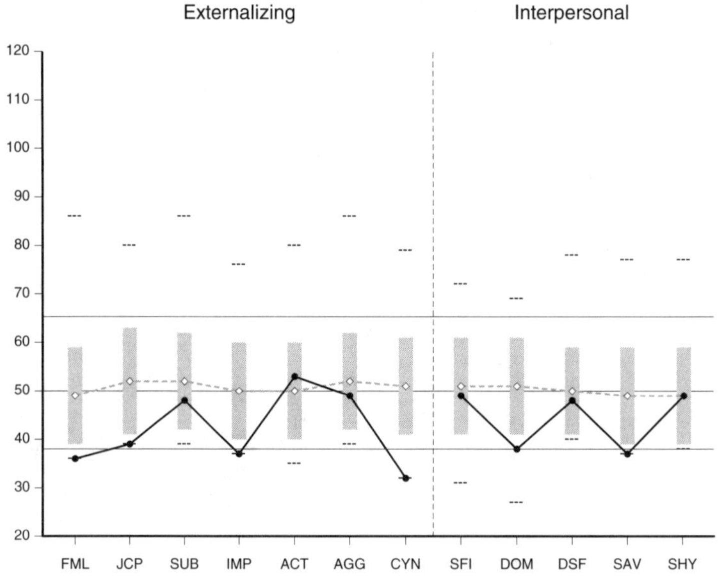

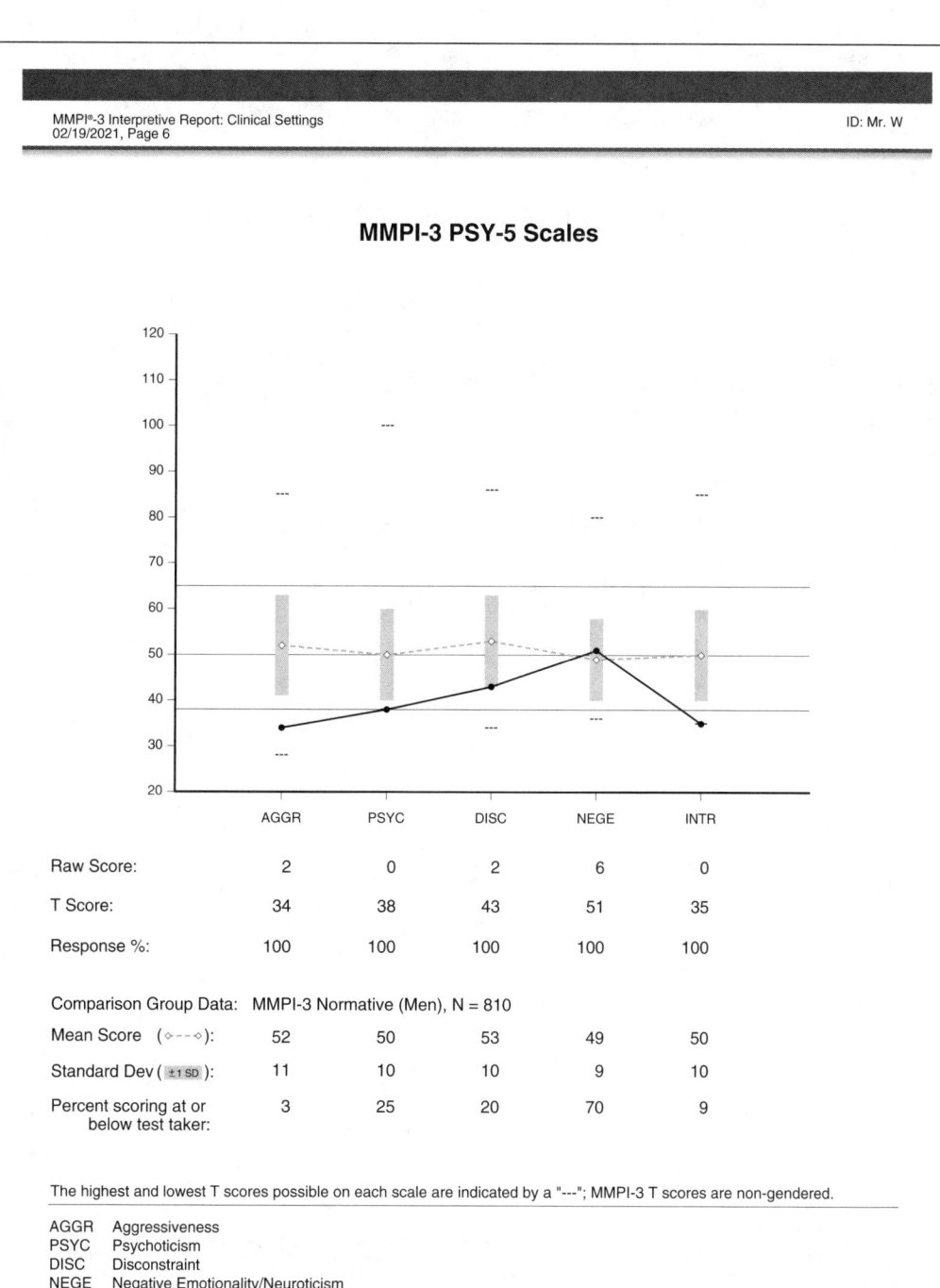

FIGURE 10.5. Mr. W's MMPI-3 Clinical Settings Interpretive Report (Follow-up), continued

MMPI-3 T SCORES (BY DOMAIN)

PROTOCOL VALIDITY

Content Non-Responsiveness

CNS	CRIN	VRIN	TRIN
0	39	43	50

Over-Reporting

F	Fp	Fs	FBS	RBS
41	41	42	51	35

Under-Reporting

L	K
44	50

SUBSTANTIVE SCALES

Somatic/Cognitive Dysfunction

RC1	MLS	NUC	EAT	COG
42	40	47	44	46

Emotional Dysfunction

EID	RCd	SUI	HLP	SFD	NFC
49	48	**65**	40	40	37

RC2	INTR
42	35

RC7	STR	WRY	CMP	ARX	ANP	BRF	NEGE
44	59	50	36	51	37	43	51

Thought Dysfunction

THD	RC6
37	40

RC8
44

PSYC
38

Behavioral Dysfunction

BXD	RC4	FML	JCP	SUB
39	44	36	39	48

RC9	IMP	ACT	AGG	CYN
46	**37**	53	49	**32**

DISC
43

Interpersonal Functioning

SFI	DOM	AGGR	DSF	SAV	SHY
49	38	34	48	**37**	49

Scale scores shown in bold font are interpreted in the report.

Note. This information is provided to facilitate interpretation following the recommended structure for MMPI-3 interpretation in Chapter 5 of the *MMPI-3 Manual for Administration, Scoring, and Interpretation*, which provides details in the text and an outline in Table 5-1.

FIGURE 10.5. Mr. W's MMPI-3 Clinical Settings Interpretive Report (Follow-up), continued

This interpretive report is intended for use by a professional qualified to interpret the MMPI-3. The information it contains should be considered in the context of the test taker's background, the circumstances of the assessment, and other available information.

The report includes extensive annotation, which appears as superscripts following each statement in the narrative, keyed to Endnotes with accompanying Research References, which appear in the final two sections of the report. Additional information about the annotation features is provided in the headnotes to these sections and in the MMPI-3 User's Guide for the Score and Clinical Interpretive Reports.

SYNOPSIS

This is a valid MMPI-3 protocol. Scores on the Substantive Scales indicate emotional dysfunction. Emotional-internalizing findings relate to **suicidal ideation**.

PROTOCOL VALIDITY

This is a valid MMPI-3 protocol. There are no problems with unscorable items. The test taker responded to the items relevantly on the basis of their content, and there are no indications of over- or under-reporting.

SUBSTANTIVE SCALE INTERPRETATION

Clinical symptoms, personality characteristics, and behavioral tendencies of the test taker are described in this section and organized according to an empirically guided framework. (Please see Chapter 5 of the MMPI-3 Manual for Administration, Scoring, and Interpretation *for details.) Statements containing the word "reports" are based on the item content of MMPI-3 scales, whereas statements that include the word "likely" are based on empirical correlates of scale scores. Specific sources for each statement can be viewed with the annotation features of this report.*

Somatic/Cognitive Dysfunction
There are no indications of somatic or cognitive dysfunction in this protocol.

Emotional Dysfunction
The test taker reports a history of suicidal/death ideation and/or past suicide attempts[1]. He likely is at risk for self-harm[2], is preoccupied with suicide and death[3], and is at risk for current suicidal ideation and attempts[4].

Thought Dysfunction
There are no indications of disordered thinking in this protocol.

Behavioral Dysfunction
There are no indications of maladaptive externalizing behavior in this protocol. The test taker reports a below average level of impulsive behavior[5]. In addition, he describes others as well-intentioned and trustworthy and disavows cynical beliefs about them[6]. He is possibly overly trusting[7].

FIGURE 10.5. Mr. W's MMPI-3 Clinical Settings Interpretive Report (Follow-up), continued

Interpersonal Functioning Scales

The test taker reports enjoying social situations and events[8], and likely is perceived as outgoing and gregarious[9].

DIAGNOSTIC CONSIDERATIONS

No specific psychodiagnostic recommendations are indicated by this MMPI-3 protocol.

TREATMENT CONSIDERATIONS

This section provides inferential treatment-related recommendations based on the test taker's MMPI-3 scores.

Areas for Further Evaluation
- <u>Risk for suicide</u> should be assessed immediately[10].

ITEM-LEVEL INFORMATION

Unscorable Responses

The test taker produced scorable responses to all the MMPI-3 items.

Critical Responses

Seven MMPI-3 scales—Suicidal/Death Ideation (SUI), Helplessness/Hopelessness (HLP), Anxiety-Related Experiences (ARX), Ideas of Persecution (RC6), Aberrant Experiences (RC8), Substance Abuse (SUB), and Aggression (AGG)—have been designated by the test authors as having critical item content that may require immediate attention and follow-up. Items answered by the individual in the keyed direction (True or False) on a critical scale are listed below if his T score on that scale is 65 or higher. However, any item answered in the keyed direction on SUI is listed. The percentage of the MMPI-3 normative sample (NS) and of the MMPI-3 Normative (Men) Comparison Group (CG) that answered each item in the keyed direction are provided in parentheses following the item content.

Suicidal/Death Ideation (SUI, T Score = 65)
    Item number and content omitted. (True; NS 22.2%, CG 24.4%)
    Item number and content omitted. (True; NS 8.1%, CG 9.6%)

FIGURE 10.5. Mr. W's MMPI-3 Clinical Settings Interpretive Report (Follow-up), continued

ENDNOTES

This section lists for each statement in the report the MMPI-3 score(s) that triggered it. In addition, each statement is identified as a <u>Test Response</u>, if based on item content, a <u>Correlate</u>, if based on empirical correlates, or an <u>Inference</u>, if based on the report authors' judgment. (This information can also be accessed on-screen by placing the cursor on a given statement.) For correlate-based statements, research references (Ref. No.) are provided, keyed to the consecutively numbered reference list following the endnotes.

[1] Test Response: SUI=65
[2] Correlate: SUI=65, Ref. 3, 8, 10
[3] Correlate: SUI=65, Ref. 1, 3, 6, 7, 9, 10, 11, 14, 16
[4] Correlate: SUI=65, Ref. 1, 3, 6, 7, 10, 14, 15, 16
[5] Test Response: IMP=37
[6] Test Response: CYN=32
[7] Correlate: CYN=32, Ref. 12, 13, 16
[8] Test Response: SAV=37
[9] Correlate: SAV=37, Ref. 2, 3, 4, 5, 9; INTR=35, Ref. 3
[10] Inference: SUI=65

FIGURE 10.5. Mr. W's MMPI-3 Clinical Settings Interpretive Report (Follow-up), continued

RESEARCH REFERENCE LIST

The following studies are sources for empirical correlates identified in the Endnotes section of this report.

1. Anestis, J. C., Finn, J. A., Gottfried, E. D., Hames, J. L., Bodell, L. P., Hagan, C. R., Arnau, R. C., Anestis, M. D., Arbisi, P. A., & Joiner, T. E. (2018). Burdonesomeness, belongingness, and capability: Assessing the interpersonal-psychological theory of suicide with MMPI-2-RF scales. *Assessment, 25*(4), 415–431. https://doi.org/10.1177/1073191116652227

2. Ayearst, L. E., Sellbom, M., Trobst, K. K., & Bagby, R. M. (2013). Evaluating the interpersonal content of the MMPI-2-RF Interpersonal Scales. *Journal of Personality Assessment, 95*(2), 187–196. https://doi.org/10.1080/00223891.2012.730085

3. Ben-Porath, Y. S., & Tellegen, A. (2020). *The Minnesota Multiphasic Personality Inventory-3 (MMPI-3): Technical manual.* University of Minnesota Press.

4. Finn, J. A., Ben-Porath, Y. S., & Tellegen, A. (2015). Dichotomous versus polytomous response options in psychopathology assessment: Method or meaningful variance? *Psychological Assessment, 27*(1), 184–193. https://doi.org/10.1037/pas0000044

5. Franz, A. O., Harrop, T. M., & McCord, D. M. (2017). Examining the construct validity of the MMPI-2-RF Interpersonal Functioning Scales using the Computerized Adaptive Test of Personality Disorder as a comparative framework. *Journal of Personality Assessment, 99*(4), 416–423. https://doi.org/10.1080/00223891.2016.1222394

6. Glassmire, D. M, Tarescavage, A. M., Burchett, D., Martinez, J., & Gomez, A. (2016). Clinical utility of the MMPI-2-RF SUI items and scale in a forensic inpatient setting: Association with interview self-reports and future suicidal behavior. *Psychological Assessment, 28*(11), 1502–1509. https://doi.org/10.1037/pas0000220

7. Gottfried, E., Bodell, L., Carbonell, J., & Joiner, T. (2014). The clinical utility of the MMPI-2-RF Suicidal/Death Ideation Scale. *Psychological Assessment, 26*(4), 1205–1211. https://doi.org/10.1037/pas0000017

8. Laurinaityte, I., Laurinavicius, A., Ustinaviciute, L., Wygant, D. B., Sellbom, M. (2017). Utility of the MMPI-2 Restructured Form (MMPI-2-RF) in a sample of Lithuanian male offenders. *Law and Human Behavior, 41*(5), 494–505. https://doi.org/10.1037/lhb0000254

9. Menton, W. H., Crighton, A. H., Tarescavage, A. M., Marek, R. J., Hicks, A. D., & Ben-Porath, Y. S. (2019). Equivalence of laptop and tablet administrations of the Minnesota Multiphasic Personality Inventory-2 Restructured Form. *Assessment, 26*(4), 661–669. https://doi.org/10.1177/1073191117714558

10. Miller, S. N., Bozzay, M. L., Ben-Porath, Y. S., & Arbisi, P. A. (2019). Distinguishing levels of suicide risk in depressed male veterans: The role of internalizing and externalizing psychopathology as measured by the MMPI-2-RF. *Assessment, 26*(1), 85–98. https://doi.org/10.1177/1073191117743787

11. Rogers, M. L., Anestis, J. C., Harrop, T. M., Schneider, M., Bender, T. W., Ringer, F. B., & Joiner, T. E. (2017). Examination of MMPI-2-RF substantive scales as indicators of acute suicidal affective disturbance components. *Journal of Personality Assessment, 99*(4), 424–434. https://doi.org/10.1080/00223891.2016.1222393

12. Sellbom, M., Ben-Porath, Y. S., & Bagby, R. M. (2008). Personality and psychopathology: Mapping the MMPI-2 Restructured Clinical (RC) Scales onto the five factor model of personality. *Journal of Personality Disorders, 22*(3), 291–312. https://doi.org/10.1521/pedi.2008.22.3.291

FIGURE 10.5. Mr. W's MMPI-3 Clinical Settings Interpretive Report (Follow-up), continued

13. Simms, L. J., Casillas, A., Clark, L. A., Watson, D., & Doebbeling, B. N. (2005). Psychometric evaluation of the Restructured Clinical Scales of the MMPI-2. *Psychological Assessment, 17*(3), 345–358. https://doi.org/10.1037/1040-3590.17.3.345

14. Stanley, I. H., Yancey, J. R., Patrick, C. J., & Joiner, T. E. (2018). A distinct configuration of MMPI-2-RF scales RCd and RC9/ACT is associated with suicide attempt risk among suicide ideators in a psychiatric outpatient sample. *Psychological Assessment, 30*(9), 1249–1254. https://doi.org/10.1037/pas0000588

15. Tarescavage, A. M., Glassmire, D. M., & Burchett, D. (2018). Minnesota Multiphasic Personality Inventory-2-Restructured Form markers of future suicidal behavior in a forensic psychiatric hospital. *Psychological Assessment, 30*(2), 170–178. https://doi.org/10.1037/pas0000463

16. Tellegen, A., & Ben-Porath, Y. S. (2008/2011). *Minnesota Multiphasic Personality Inventory-2-Restructured Form (MMPI-2-RF): Technical manual.* University of Minnesota Press.

End of Report

FIGURE 10.5. Mr. W's MMPI-3 Clinical Settings Interpretive Report (Follow-up), continued

beyond one month, his diagnosis would have changed from acute stress disorder to posttraumatic stress disorder. Had that occurred, it would not have changed anything regarding the first step in his fitness-for-duty determination. Mr. W had a mental health condition regardless of the diagnostic category used to describe it, and its state of remission or inactivity also does not change this fact. But when, as here, a condition is in remission or inactive, both of the next two steps are necessary to reach a valid determination of fitness.

Step 2: Assessing for Current Work Impairment

A condition that is in remission (partial or full) or is inactive simply means that the symptoms are insufficient in number or magnitude to meet diagnostic criteria. It does not mean that the person has no symptoms potentially leading to distress or impairment. For example, a PTSD diagnosis using the DSM-5-TR taxonomy (American Psychiatric Association, 2022) requires at least one of several listed intrusion and avoidance symptoms as well as at least two associated with negative alterations in cognitions and mood, and marked alterations in arousal and reactivity, associated with the traumatic event(s). A person whose symptoms fall short of these minimum criteria would not satisfy the diagnostic requirements, but the symptoms that are present may nonetheless be substantially job-limiting. In Mr. W's case, the collective evidence indicated that his symptoms were fully inactive and, therefore, could not impair his occupational functioning. The third step in the integrative model concerns an assessment of the sustainability of that remission once back at work.

Step 3: Assessing for Sustainability of Fitness

Panic attacks are either expected (i.e., attacks for which there is an obvious cue or trigger) or unexpected (e.g., when relaxing or during sleep). Mr. W's panic attack appeared to have been triggered by seeing another inmate, similar in age and appearance, in the cell where the suicide had occurred. Evidence-based treatment provided Mr. W with cognitive-behavioral skills to cope with emerging anxiety. Although there is certainly some risk that he could experience another panic attack upon returning to work, it is mitigated by the evidence of therapeutic efficacy and his prior action in notifying a supervisor within minutes of the onset of the previous attack. Thus, although there is no certainty that Mr. W's fitness will be sustained upon returning to the work environment, the collective evidence suggests that it is more likely than not and that environmental safeguards exist that mitigate the consequences were he to experience a repeat panic attack.

Conclusion

The examiner concluded, based on his reevaluation of Mr. W, that his mental condition was in remission and likely to remain so upon return to work. Therefore, he was assessed to be psychologically *fit for duty*.

MS. U, PUBLIC SAFETY DISPATCHER

Assessment Issues Presented

- Referral to determine whether the employee poses a direct threat to herself or others

Referral Summary

Ms. U is a 46-year-old married woman with 25 years of experience as a public safety dispatcher (6 years with a small agency and the last 19 with the same urban emergency communications center). Following a series of email exchanges with a new supervisor over a 2-week period in which she expressed multiple grievances against them for "petty micromanaging" and "gross incompetence," Ms. U eventually wrote, "if things don't change around here, someone's going to die and it won't be me." Ms. U was called in by the human resources director to discuss the incident. She said that what she wrote was a "true statement" and refused to say any more about it. Ms. U was placed on administrative leave pending a fitness evaluation to determine whether she posed a direct threat to herself or others as a result of a mental condition.

Assessment Findings

Employment Records

Ms. U's employment records documented that she was well-respected by her coworkers and previous supervisors, and she had no prior disciplinary history. Her performance evaluations were all positive. Approximately 4 months before the referral, Ms. U was assigned to a new supervisor who wrote her multiple "counseling memos" (nondisciplinary notices of concern about various aspects of her performance) concerning excessive breaks, talking too much with other dispatchers and first responders, and not being a team player. The counseling memos indicated that the last concern resulted from overhearing Ms. U's conversations with coworkers in which she was critical of her supervisor.

Medical Records

No medical records were provided and no mental health treatment or previous evaluations were disclosed.

Mental Status Examination

Ms. U's appearance was unremarkable with regard to grooming, dress, movement, and other observable features. Her speech was normal, as indicated by its rate, intelligibility, volume, quality, and quantity, although its intensity was consistent with her irritable affective expression. She displayed no abnormalities with respect to her perception, thought process, sensorium and cognition, judgment, insight, or reliability.

Clinical Interview

At the start of the evaluation, Ms. U was hostile toward the examiner and dismissed the evaluation as a "sham" and "an effort to get [her] fired." She denied a history of suicidal or homicidal ideation, and she said she was "offended" by an interpretation of her email as indicating homicidal intent. Indeed, she took offense to any of the examiner's questions about the email, continuing to assert that it "speaks for itself."

When an examinee in a fitness evaluation responds indignantly and uncooperatively, it is often helpful to attempt a reset. One strategy for resetting the interaction is to explain the fitness evaluation process using the three-step data integration model as a structure to help the employee understand what questions the examiner needs to answer and how the employee can be helpful (versus self-defeating) in that process. Employees who have been referred for a fitness or "direct threat" evaluation are often defensive and hostile, particularly when, as in Ms. U's case, they regard the referral as simply one more effort by their supervisor to harass them.

After explaining the model that the examiner will be using to assess the candidate's fitness for duty, it can be useful to ask the employee what they think will happen if they are determined to be unfit for duty. Frequently, but almost always erroneously, employees believe they will be fired. Although it sometimes happens that an employee, particularly a public safety worker employed by a public agency, has a condition that cannot be remediated sufficiently to return to duty, it is a rare occurrence that happens only after substantial remediation efforts. In most cases, an employee who is deemed unfit for duty obtains treatment by a provider of their choosing and eventually returns to duty. Relieving the employee's fear of sudden termination typically contributes to greater cooperation and openness.

After having this discussion with Ms. U, the examiner asked her if she believed that maintaining her hostile attitude in the interview would likely facilitate or harm her interests. She said she was not aware that she was being hostile, so the examiner provided her with several examples. Ms. U apologized and said she was embarrassed that she had not noticed her own irritability. She also spontaneously noted that the same thing probably happened during her meeting with the human resources director. Thus, when offered the opportunity to start fresh, Ms. U said she would be grateful for the opportunity. During the remainder of the evaluation, she was cooperative, even when the interview topic turned to her relationship with her supervisor. When discussing that topic, Ms. U clearly became agitated and irritable, but it remained restricted to that relationship.

One of the challenges of determining whether an employee poses a direct threat to themselves or others is that such referrals often arise from an interpersonal dispute in which one party oversteps civil bounds. Ms. U's email was ambiguous but understandably concerning, and her self-defeating refusal to clarify her intentions when called in to discuss it with the human resources director only aggravated concerns about her risk of harm. Ms. U wanted to spend time justifying her hostility toward her supervisor, but the examiner made clear that they were not evaluating the supervisor. Still, it was important to understand whether Ms. U's perceptions of her supervisor as retaliatory, micromanaging, and petty were based on objective observations (in which case, they would likely be shared by her fellow dispatchers) or idiosyncratic, distorted perceptions. To resolve this question, the examiner called the human resources director and learned that, indeed, Ms. U's coworkers had expressed similar concerns and perceptions about their new supervisor, although none wrote an email with similar content.

To further assess Ms. U's reality testing, the examiner asked her how she thought her statement—that someone would die if things did not change, and it would not be her—*should have been* interpreted by her supervisor. Ms. U explained that the full email thread included her assertion that her supervisor's actions were distracting dispatchers from their core duties and causing undue levels of stress that could affect their work in emergency situations, which always carries the potential for loss of life. She said that this was so obvious to her that she resented having to explain it, but she now understood that her refusal to do so was self-sabotaging.

Ms. U reported that she was eligible for a 25-year retirement but was not able to draw it until she turns 50 in 4 years. She said she was resentful that she might have to endure her supervisor for so long. Outside of work, she said that she had a satisfying marriage of 27 years, a close relationship with her three adult daughters, their partners, and her five grandchildren, and she enjoyed multiple close and longstanding relationships with friends. She said she consumed little alcohol and had no history of alcohol or other substance abuse. She did not have access to firearms and reported no history of mental health problems or treatment.

MMPI-3 Findings

Ms. U's MMPI-3 Interpretive Report for Clinical Settings is reproduced in Figure 10.6. A review of her validity scale scores indicates no unscorable items and that she responded to the items relevantly based on their content. As reflected in her score on K (62T), she presented herself as well-adjusted. The narrative summary in the Substantive Scale Interpretation section of the report (pp. 8–9) states, "there are no indications of somatic, cognitive, emotional, thought, or behavioral dysfunction in this protocol. However, because of indications of under-reporting described earlier, such problems cannot be ruled out." Scores on the Interpersonal Functioning scales provided no evidence of dysfunction in that domain.

Data Integration

Step 1: Assessing for a Mental Health Condition

Findings from this assessment produced no persuasive clinical evidence indicating that Ms. U has a mental condition, although it could be argued that the interpersonal conflict with her supervisor produced an adjustment disorder (i.e., the development of emotional or behavioral symptoms in response to an identifiable stressor occurring within 3 months of the stressor's onset). However, this diagnosis would also require specifying a disturbance in mood, anxiety, or conduct that the examiner determined was not supported by the evidence. Indeed, according to the human resource director, there was no longer any basis for Ms. U to worry about consequences from the supervisor's counseling memos, because none of the conduct issues raised in them were valid. Her supervisor has since been instructed to have all draft counseling memos reviewed by the department director before forwarding them to one of her subordinates. Thus, the examiner determined that Ms. U had no mental health condition.

Steps 2 and 3: Assessing for Current Work Impairment and Sustainability of Fitness

Both steps are moot when it has been determined that the employee does not have a mental health condition.

Conclusion

The examiner concluded that Ms. U did not pose a direct threat (i.e., an imminent risk of serious harm to herself or others as a result of a mental condition

Minnesota Multiphasic Personality Inventory®-3

Interpretive Report: Clinical Settings

MMPI®-3
Minnesota Multiphasic Personality Inventory®-3
Yossef S. Ben-Porath, PhD, & Auke Tellegen, PhD

ID Number:	Ms. U
Age:	46
Gender:	Female
Marital Status:	Not reported
Years of Education:	Not reported
Date Assessed:	07/06/2021

Copyright © 2020 by the Regents of the University of Minnesota. All rights reserved. Distributed exclusively under license from the University of Minnesota by NCS Pearson, Inc. Portions reproduced from the *MMPI-3 English Test Booklet.* Copyright © 2020 by the Regents of the University of Minnesota. All rights reserved. Portions excerpted from the *MMPI-3 Manual for Administration, Scoring, and Interpretation.* Copyright © 2020 by the Regents of the University of Minnesota. All rights reserved. Portions excerpted from the *MMPI-3 Technical Manual.* Copyright © 2020 by the Regents of the University of Minnesota. All rights reserved. Used by permission of the University of Minnesota Press.

Minnesota Multiphasic Personality Inventory and **MMPI** are registered trademarks of the Regents of the University of Minnesota. **Pearson** is a trademark, in the US and/or other countries, of Pearson Education, Inc., or its affiliates.

This report contains copyrighted material and trade secrets. Qualified licensees may excerpt portions of this output report, limited to the minimum text necessary to accurately describe their significant core conclusions, for incorporation into a written evaluation of the examinee, in accordance with their profession's citation standards, if any. No adaptations, translations, modifications, or special versions may be made of this report without prior written permission from the University of Minnesota Press.

[1.0 / 19 / QG]

ALWAYS LEARNING   **PEARSON**

FIGURE 10.6. Ms. U's MMPI-3 Clinical Settings Interpretive Report

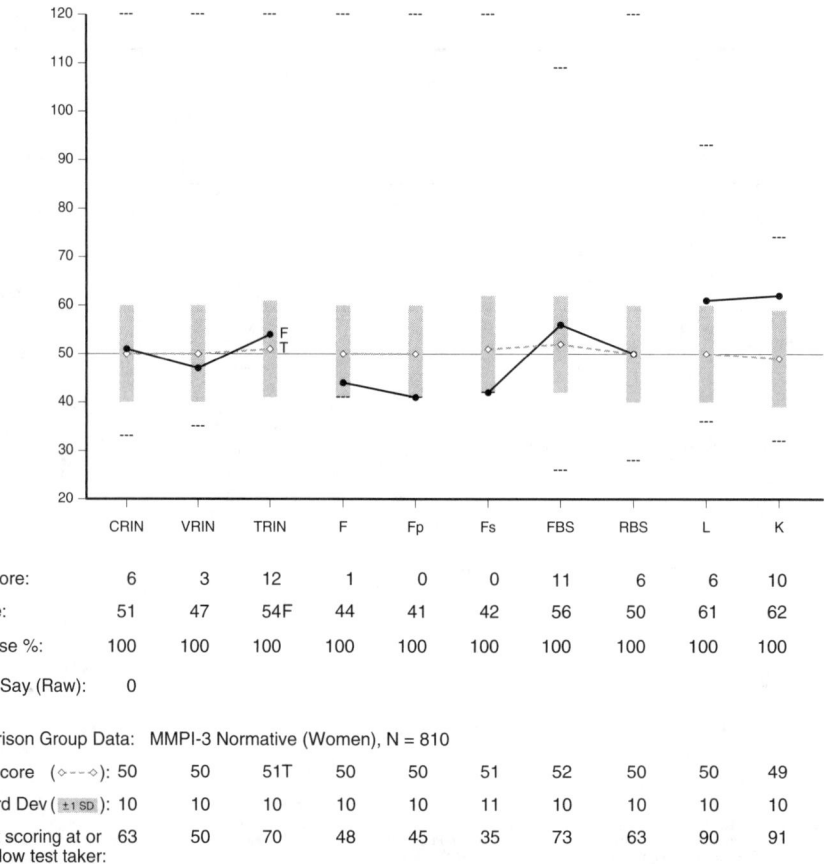

FIGURE 10.6. Ms. U's MMPI-3 Clinical Settings Interpretive Report, continued

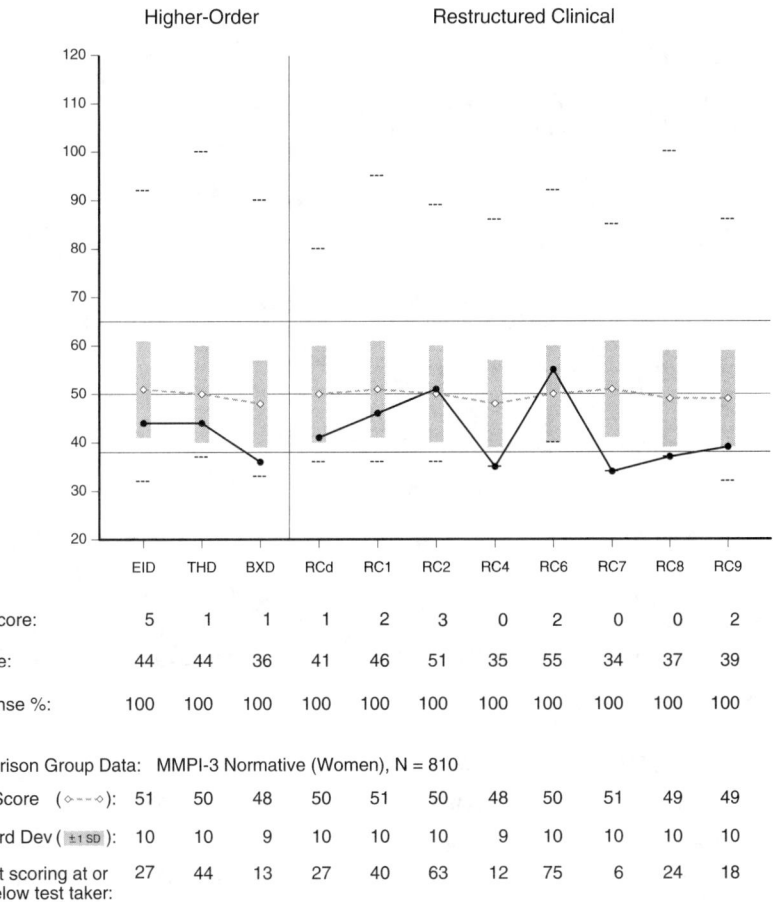

FIGURE 10.6. Ms. U's MMPI-3 Clinical Settings Interpretive Report, continued

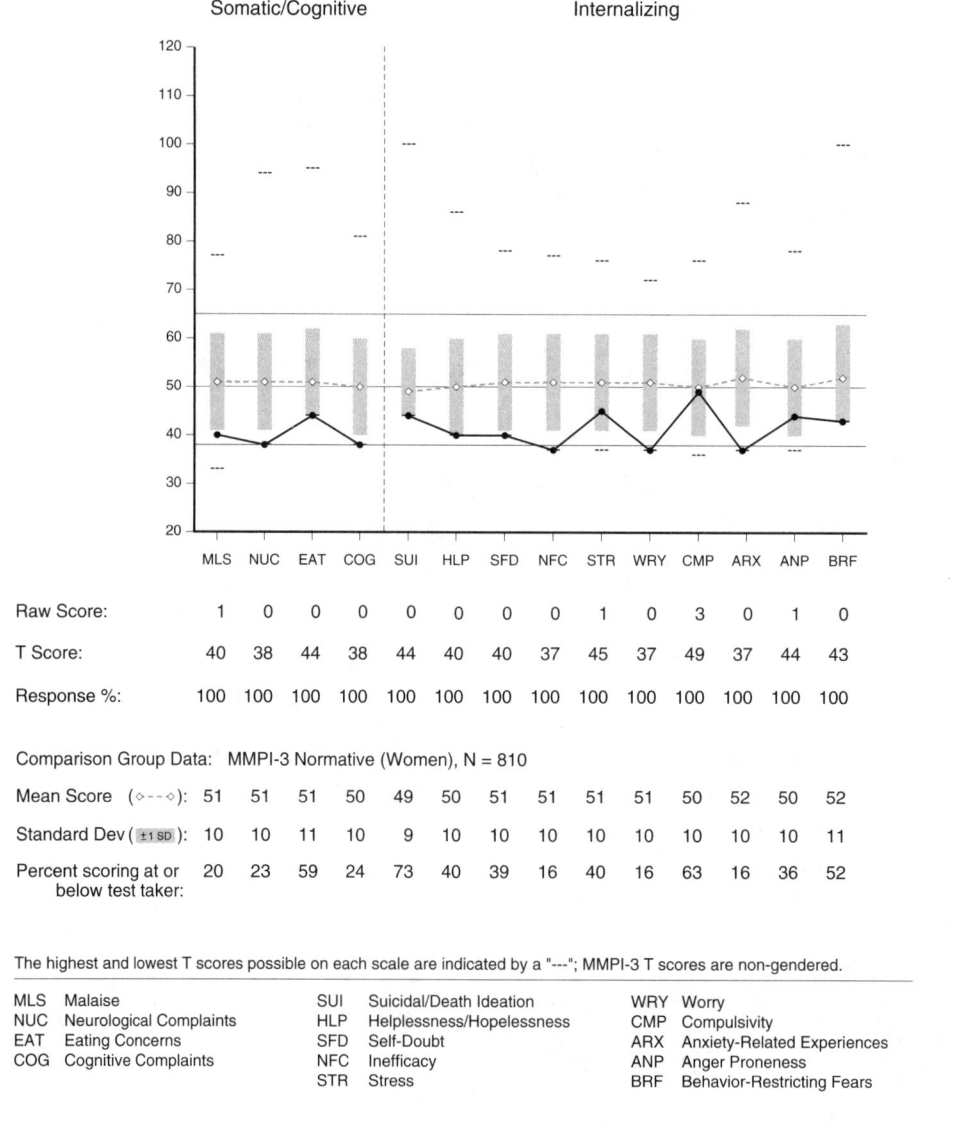

FIGURE 10.6. Ms. U's MMPI-3 Clinical Settings Interpretive Report, continued

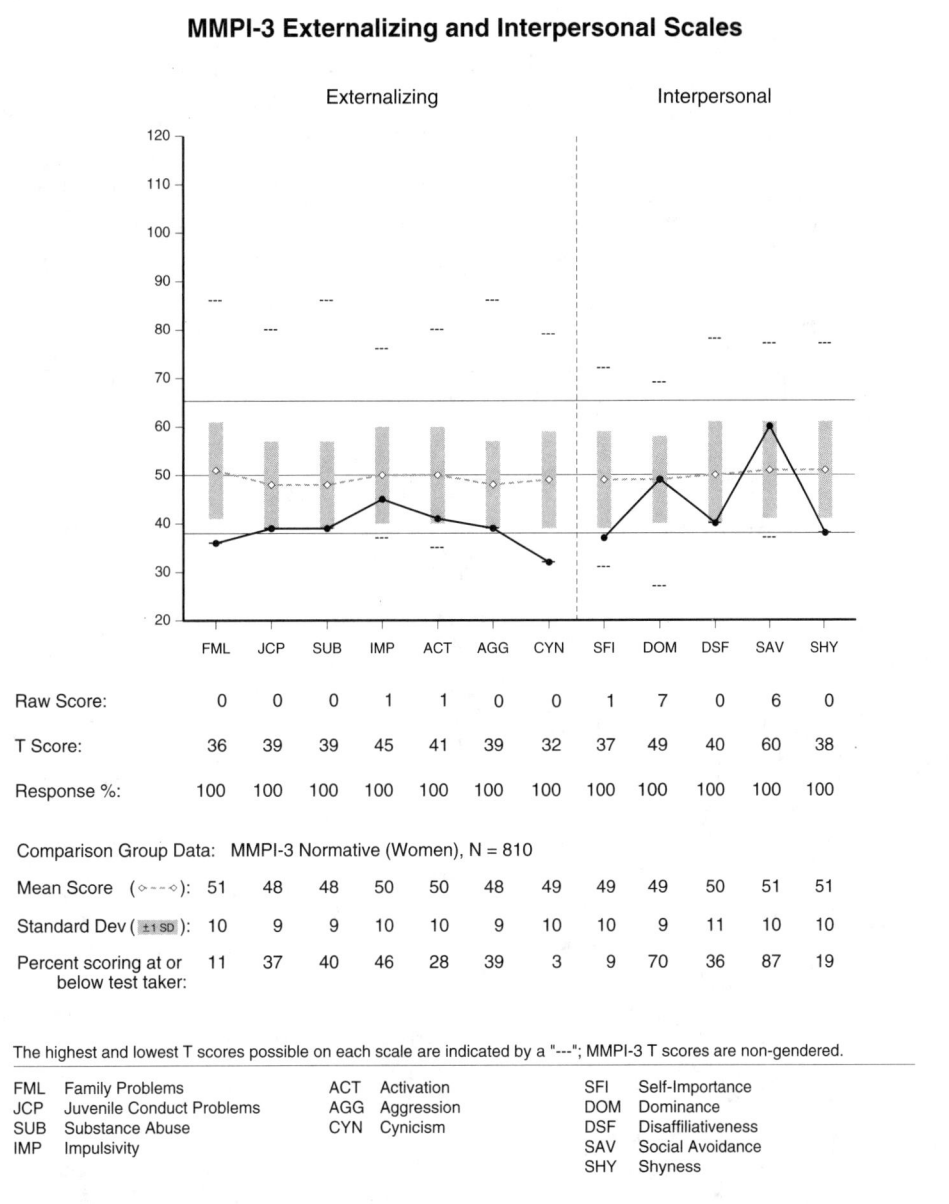

FIGURE 10.6. Ms. U's MMPI-3 Clinical Settings Interpretive Report, continued

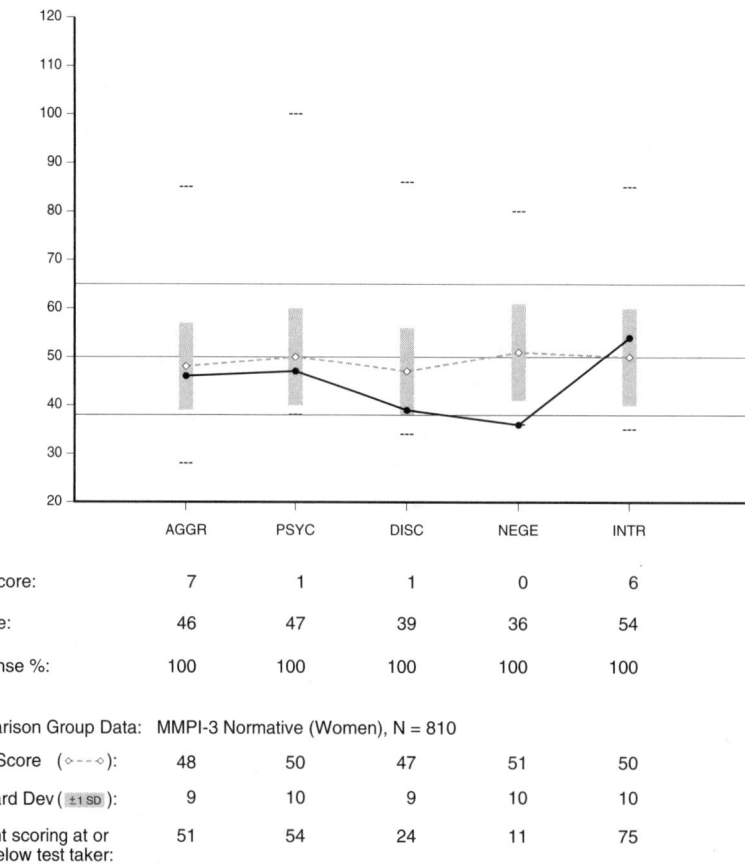

FIGURE 10.6. Ms. U's MMPI-3 Clinical Settings Interpretive Report, continued

MMPI-3 T SCORES (BY DOMAIN)

PROTOCOL VALIDITY

Content Non-Responsiveness

CNS	CRIN	VRIN	TRIN
0	51	47	54 F

Over-Reporting

F	Fp	Fs	FBS	RBS
44	41	42	56	50

Under-Reporting

L	K
61	**62**

SUBSTANTIVE SCALES

Somatic/Cognitive Dysfunction

RC1	MLS	NUC	EAT	COG
46	40	38	44	38

Emotional Dysfunction

EID: 44

RCd	SUI	HLP	SFD	NFC
41	44	40	40	37

RC2	INTR
51	54

RC7	STR	WRY	CMP	ARX	ANP	BRF	NEGE
34	45	37	49	37	44	43	36

Thought Dysfunction

THD: 44

RC6	RC8	PSYC
55	37	47

Behavioral Dysfunction

BXD: 36

RC4	FML	JCP	SUB
35	36	39	39

RC9	IMP	ACT	AGG	CYN
39	45	41	39	32

DISC
39

Interpersonal Functioning

SFI	DOM	AGGR	DSF	SAV	SHY
37	49	46	40	60	38

Scale scores shown in bold font are interpreted in the report.

Note. This information is provided to facilitate interpretation following the recommended structure for MMPI-3 interpretation in Chapter 5 of the *MMPI-3 Manual for Administration, Scoring, and Interpretation*, which provides details in the text and an outline in Table 5-1.

FIGURE 10.6. Ms. U's MMPI-3 Clinical Settings Interpretive Report, continued

This interpretive report is intended for use by a professional qualified to interpret the MMPI-3. The information it contains should be considered in the context of the test taker's background, the circumstances of the assessment, and other available information.

The report includes extensive annotation, which appears as superscripts following each statement in the narrative, keyed to Endnotes with accompanying Research References, which appear in the final two sections of the report. Additional information about the annotation features is provided in the headnotes to these sections and in the MMPI-3 User's Guide for the Score and Clinical Interpretive Reports.

SYNOPSIS

Scores on the MMPI-3 Validity Scales raise concerns about the possible impact of under-reporting on the validity of this protocol. With that caution noted, there are no indications of somatic or cognitive complaints, or of emotional, thought, behavioral, or interpersonal dysfunction.

PROTOCOL VALIDITY

Content Non-Responsiveness

The test taker produced scorable responses to all the MMPI-3 items. She also responded relevantly to the items on the basis of their content.

Over-Reporting

There are no indications of over-reporting in this protocol.

Under-Reporting

The test taker presented herself as well-adjusted[1]. If there is evidence that this individual is not well-adjusted, any absence of elevation on the Substantive Scales should be interpreted with caution[2]. Elevated scores on the Substantive Scales may underestimate the problems assessed by those scales[3].

SUBSTANTIVE SCALE INTERPRETATION

Clinical symptoms, personality characteristics, and behavioral tendencies of the test taker are described in this section and organized according to an empirically guided framework. (Please see Chapter 5 of the MMPI-3 Manual for Administration, Scoring, and Interpretation *for details.) Statements containing the word "reports" are based on the item content of MMPI-3 scales, whereas statements that include the word "likely" are based on empirical correlates of scale scores. Specific sources for each statement can be viewed with the annotation features of this report.*

The following interpretation needs to be considered in light of cautions noted about the possible impact of under-reporting (of psychological problems) on the validity of this protocol.

Somatic/Cognitive, Emotional, Thought, and Behavioral Dysfunction

There are no indications of somatic, cognitive, emotional, thought, or behavioral dysfunction in this protocol. However, because of indications of under-reporting described earlier, such problems cannot be ruled out.

FIGURE 10.6. Ms. U's MMPI-3 Clinical Settings Interpretive Report, continued

Interpersonal Functioning Scales

These scales provide no evidence of dysfunction.

DIAGNOSTIC CONSIDERATIONS

No specific psychodiagnostic recommendations are indicated by this MMPI-3 protocol. However, this finding needs to be considered in light of cautions noted earlier about possible under-reporting.

TREATMENT CONSIDERATIONS

No specific recommendations for treatment are indicated by this MMPI-3 protocol. However, this finding needs to be considered in light of cautions noted earlier about possible under-reporting.

ITEM-LEVEL INFORMATION

Unscorable Responses

The test taker produced scorable responses to all the MMPI-3 items.

Critical Responses

Seven MMPI-3 scales—Suicidal/Death Ideation (SUI), Helplessness/Hopelessness (HLP), Anxiety-Related Experiences (ARX), Ideas of Persecution (RC6), Aberrant Experiences (RC8), Substance Abuse (SUB), and Aggression (AGG)—have been designated by the test authors as having critical item content that may require immediate attention and follow-up. Items answered by the individual in the keyed direction (True or False) on a critical scale are listed below if her T score on that scale is 65 or higher. However, any item answered in the keyed direction on SUI is listed.

The test taker has not produced an elevated T score ($\geq$ 65) on any of these scales or answered any SUI items in the keyed direction.

FIGURE 10.6. Ms. U's MMPI-3 Clinical Settings Interpretive Report, continued

ENDNOTES

This section lists for each statement in the report the MMPI-3 score(s) that triggered it. In addition, each statement is identified as a Test Response, if based on item content, a Correlate, if based on empirical correlates, or an Inference, if based on the report authors' judgment. (This information can also be accessed on-screen by placing the cursor on a given statement.) For correlate-based statements, research references (Ref. No.) are provided, keyed to the consecutively numbered reference list following the endnotes.

[1] Test Response: K=62
[2] Correlate: K=62, Ref. 2, 3, 5, 6
[3] Correlate: K=62, Ref. 1, 4, 6, 7

FIGURE 10.6. Ms. U's MMPI-3 Clinical Settings Interpretive Report, continued

RESEARCH REFERENCE LIST

The following studies are sources for empirical correlates identified in the Endnotes section of this report.

1. Ben-Porath, Y. S., & Tellegen, A. (2020). *The Minnesota Multiphasic Personality Inventory-3 (MMPI-3): Technical manual.* University of Minnesota Press.

2. Brown, T. A., & Sellbom, M. (2020). The utility of the MMPI-2-RF validity scales in detecting underreporting. *Journal of Personality Assessment, 102*(1), 66–74. https://doi.org/10.1080/00223891.2018.1539003

3. Crighton, A. H., Marek, R. J., Dragon, W. R., & Ben-Porath, Y. S. (2017). Utility of the MMPI-2-RF Validity Scales in detection of simulated underreporting: Implications of incorporating a manipulation check. *Assessment, 24*(7), 853–864. https://doi.org/10.1177/1073191115627011

4. Forbey, J. D., Lee, T. T. C., Ben-Porath, Y. S., Arbisi, P. A., & Gartland, D. (2013). Associations between MMPI-2-RF validity scale scores and extra-test measures of personality and psychopathology. *Assessment, 20*(4), 448–461. https://doi.org/10.1177/1073191113478154

5. Marion, B. E., Sellbom, M., Salekin, R. T., Toomey, J. A., Kucharski, L. T., & Duncan, S. (2013). An examination of the association between psychopathy and dissimulation using the MMPI-2-RF Validity Scales. *Law and Human Behavior, 37*(4), 219–230. https://doi.org/10.1037/lhb0000008

6. Sellbom, M., & Bagby, R. M. (2008). Validity of the MMPI-2-RF (Restructured Form) L-r and K-r scales in detecting under-reporting in clinical and non-clinical samples. *Psychological Assessment, 20*(4), 370–376. https://doi.org/10.1037/a0012952

7. Tellegen, A., & Ben-Porath, Y. S. (2008/2011). *Minnesota Multiphasic Personality Inventory-2-Restructured Form (MMPI-2-RF): Technical manual.* University of Minnesota Press.

End of Report

FIGURE 10.6. Ms. U's MMPI-3 Clinical Settings Interpretive Report, continued

and which could not be mitigated by reasonable accommodation). In the absence of a mental health condition, an employee may still be otherwise problematic, disruptive, or inefficient, but such facts alone cannot meet the criteria for being deemed psychologically unfit for duty. As Corey (2011) noted,

> These employees may be ill-suited for continued employment, and an administrative decision to terminate their employment may very well be justified. But the fact that an examinee in an FFD examination is a "bad" employee, perhaps even undeserving of continued employment, does not require—legally or ethically—that it is the examining psychologist who should make that determination. In general, clinical opinions about fitness for duty should rest on evidence that the layperson is not qualified to assess (e.g., signs and symptoms of psychopathology). When judgments about unfitness are based on behaviors and other evidence that an employer, layperson, and psychologist can assess with equal facility—such as in the case of an insubordinate, disruptive, or dishonest police officer whose conduct does not result from a mental health condition—they fall outside the realm of a professional, clinical or "medical" opinion because they are devoid of the special expertise required for such judgments. . . . If examiners conclude or suspect that problematic personality traits; moral turpitude; or deficits in knowledge, skill, practices, or training, unconnected to an underlying psychological condition or disorder, render an employee potentially ineffective, inefficient, or unsafe, they should report this to the referring party and defer any judgments about disposition to the employer. (p. 268; citations removed).

MR. Y, FIREFIGHTER

Assessment Issues Presented

- Manic episode at work, followed by inpatient evaluation and treatment for bipolar I disorder

Referral Summary

Mr. Y is a 31-year-old married man with 3 years of experience as a firefighter in a suburban fire department. About 2 weeks prior to the fitness evaluation, Mr. Y exhibited signs of a manic episode at the station. During dinner, he became highly and uncharacteristically verbose and animated. He displayed an abnormally and persistently elevated and expansive mood, and after his captain and crew went to bed, he woke each of them to continue the debate over a trivial disagreement at dinner about a sports rivalry. His speech was pressured, and he displayed a flight of ideas. His station captain eventually called Mr. Y's wife to take him home.

Mr. Y's wife called the department 3 days later to report that his behavior had become increasingly more agitated after he got home, and he did not sleep for the next 2 days. He eventually began to voice paranoid delusions about his crew members poisoning his food at dinner. Fearful of what was happening to him, she called his parents, and they persuaded him to go to the local hospital for evaluation. He was prescribed a mood stabilizer and, after a day and a half, was released to return to work. His employer placed him on paid administrative leave pending the outcome of a fitness evaluation, which was conducted 10 days after his discharge from the hospital.

Assessment Findings

Employment Records

Mr. Y's employment records confirmed the absence of prior disciplinary actions. All his performance evaluations were positive.

Medical Records

Records from Mr. Y's voluntary hospitalization documented the information provided by his wife and revealed a diagnosis of bipolar I disorder, moderate, with psychotic features.

Mental Status Examination

Mr. Y's appearance was unremarkable with regard to grooming, dress, movement, and other observable features. His speech was rapid but intelligible. His affective expression was normal, and his mood was euphoric and expansive. He displayed no abnormalities with respect to his perception, thought process, sensorium and cognition, judgment, or reliability. However, his insight was poor, inasmuch as he denied having a mental health disorder. His attitude toward the examiner was cooperative and friendly.

Clinical Interview

Mr. Y's assertion that he did not have a mental health condition and, in particular, did not have bipolar I disorder, was itself remarkable in light of the known facts. Asked to explain his reason for believing he had been misdiagnosed, he said that his own research showed that sleep deprivation can cause temporary psychosis, and that there was nothing wrong with him other than a period of insomnia that is now resolved. He said that he was taking the mood stabilizer, sodium valproate, not because he has bipolar I disorder, but because it also has dual efficacy in preventing migraine headaches, which he occasionally has had. He said he is sleeping well but does not need more than 3 hours of sleep to feel fully rested. He was receiving no outpatient treatment but was scheduled to see his primary care physician in a month.

MMPI-3 Findings

Mr. Y's MMPI-3 Interpretive Report for Clinical Settings is reproduced in Figure 10.7. It is a valid protocol with no unscorable items. The Protocol Validity summary on page 8 of his report indicates that he "responded to the MMPI-3 in a remarkably consistent manner," which the Endnotes (p. 10) attribute to CRIN (36T) and VRIN (35T).

A review of the bold-font (i.e., interpretable) scores on page 7 show one clinically elevated score (ACT = 65T) and six interpretable low scores: NFC (37T), WRY (37T), CYN (32T), SAV (37T), and SHY (38T). The Substantive Scale Interpretation section (Figure 10.7, p. 8) interprets the low scores, respectively, as self-reported decisiveness and efficacy; below average worry; disavowal of cynical beliefs and a belief that others are well-intentioned and trustworthy; enjoyment of social situations and events; and absence of social anxiety. His clinically elevated ACT score indicates self-reported episodes of over-activation such as heightened excitation and energy level, and the narrative interpretation notes that he "may have a history of symptoms associated with manic or hypomanic episodes" (p. 8).

Data Integration

Step 1: Assessing for a Mental Health Condition

Mr. Y contends that he does not have a mental health problem and simply suffered from sleep deprivation, which was now resolved. This is a common but erroneous belief among laypersons and professionals alike—that the resolution of symptoms equates to resolution of the underlying disorder. The clinical evidence establishes convincingly that Mr. Y meets the diagnostic criteria for bipolar I disorder, including a distinct period of abnormally and persistently elevated and irritable mood with psychotic features (the duration is irrelevant if hospitalization is necessary), with the following symptoms: decreased need for sleep, more talkative than usual or pressure to keep talking, flight of ideas, distractibility, and psychomotor agitation. Individuals hospitalized for a single manic episode continue to have bipolar I disorder, regardless of their postrecovery status.

Minnesota Multiphasic Personality Inventory®-3

Interpretive Report: Clinical Settings

MMPI®-3
Minnesota Multiphasic Personality Inventory®-3
Yossef S. Ben-Porath, PhD, & Auke Tellegen, PhD

ID Number:	Mr. Y
Age:	31
Gender:	Male
Marital Status:	Not reported
Years of Education:	Not reported
Date Assessed:	10/21/2020

Copyright © 2020 by the Regents of the University of Minnesota. All rights reserved. Distributed exclusively under license from the University of Minnesota by NCS Pearson, Inc. Portions reproduced from the *MMPI-3 English Test Booklet*. Copyright © 2020 by the Regents of the University of Minnesota. All rights reserved. Portions excerpted from the *MMPI-3 Manual for Administration, Scoring, and Interpretation*. Copyright © 2020 by the Regents of the University of Minnesota. All rights reserved. Portions excerpted from the *MMPI-3 Technical Manual*. Copyright © 2020 by the Regents of the University of Minnesota. All rights reserved. Used by permission of the University of Minnesota Press.

Minnesota Multiphasic Personality Inventory and **MMPI** are registered trademarks of the Regents of the University of Minnesota. **Pearson** is a trademark, in the US and/or other countries, of Pearson Education, Inc., or its affiliates.

This report contains copyrighted material and trade secrets. Qualified licensees may excerpt portions of this output report, limited to the minimum text necessary to accurately describe their significant core conclusions, for incorporation into a written evaluation of the examinee, in accordance with their profession's citation standards, if any. No adaptations, translations, modifications, or special versions may be made of this report without prior written permission from the University of Minnesota Press.

[1.0 / 19 / QG]

ALWAYS LEARNING   PEARSON

FIGURE 10.7. Mr. Y's MMPI-3 Clinical Settings Interpretive Report

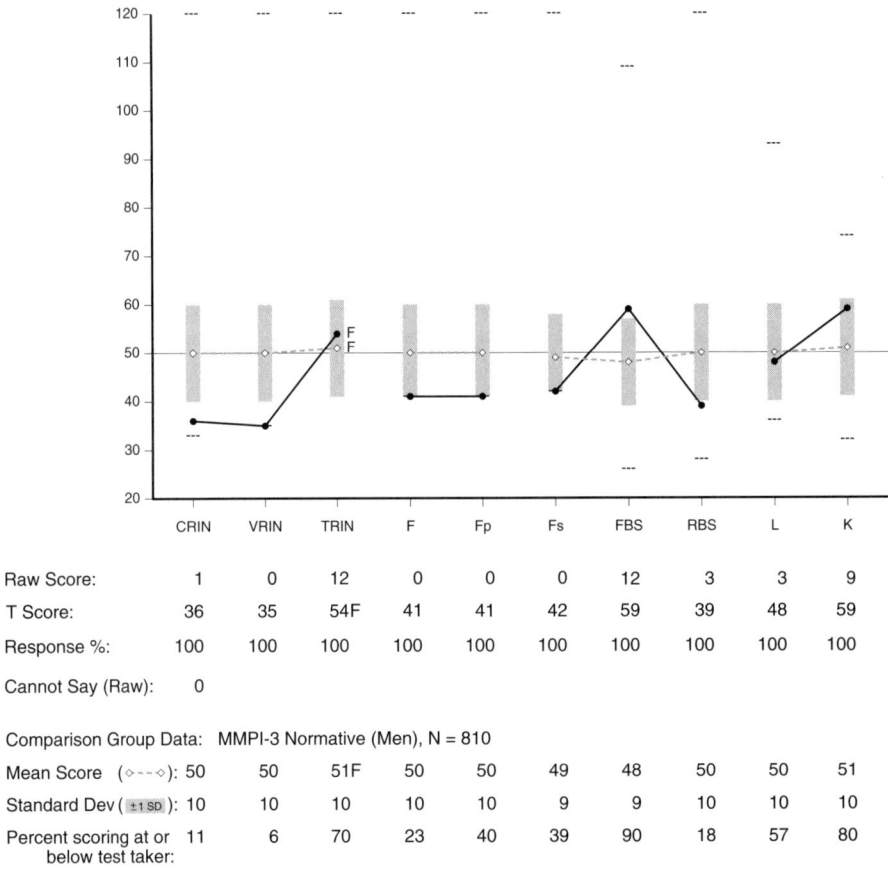

FIGURE 10.7. Mr. Y's MMPI-3 Clinical Settings Interpretive Report, continued

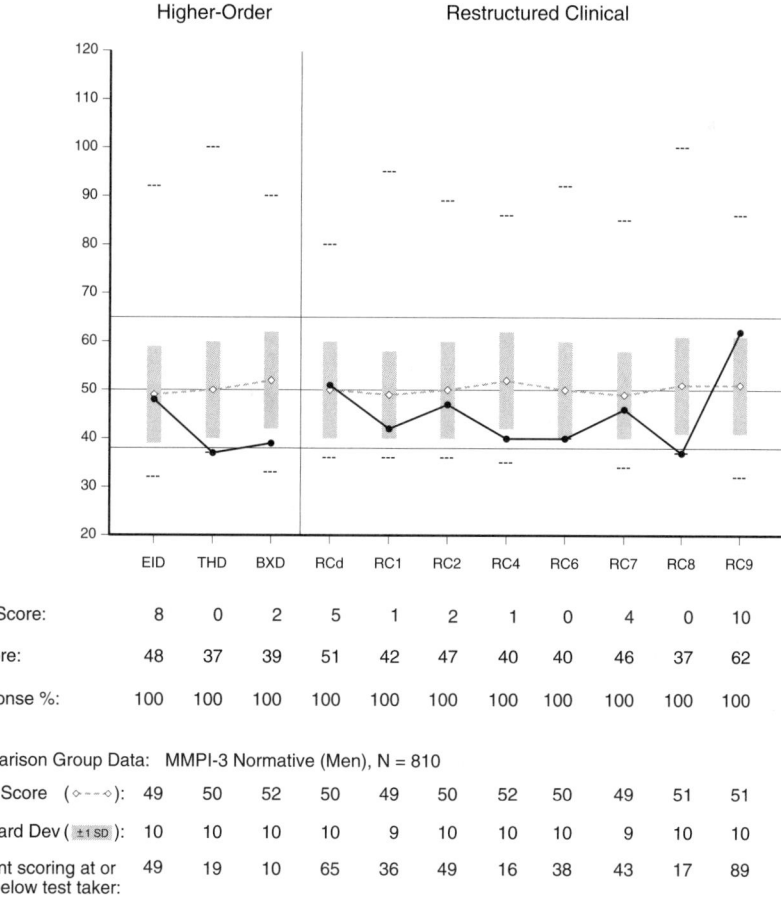

FIGURE 10.7. Mr. Y's MMPI-3 Clinical Settings Interpretive Report, continued

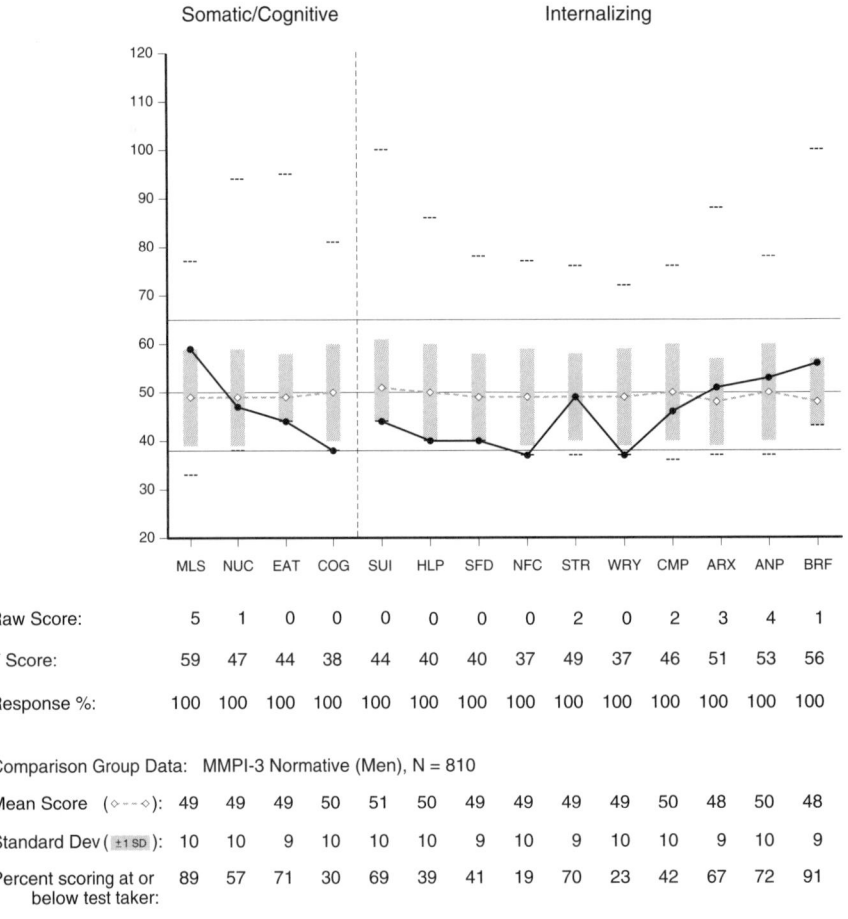

FIGURE 10.7. Mr. Y's MMPI-3 Clinical Settings Interpretive Report, continued

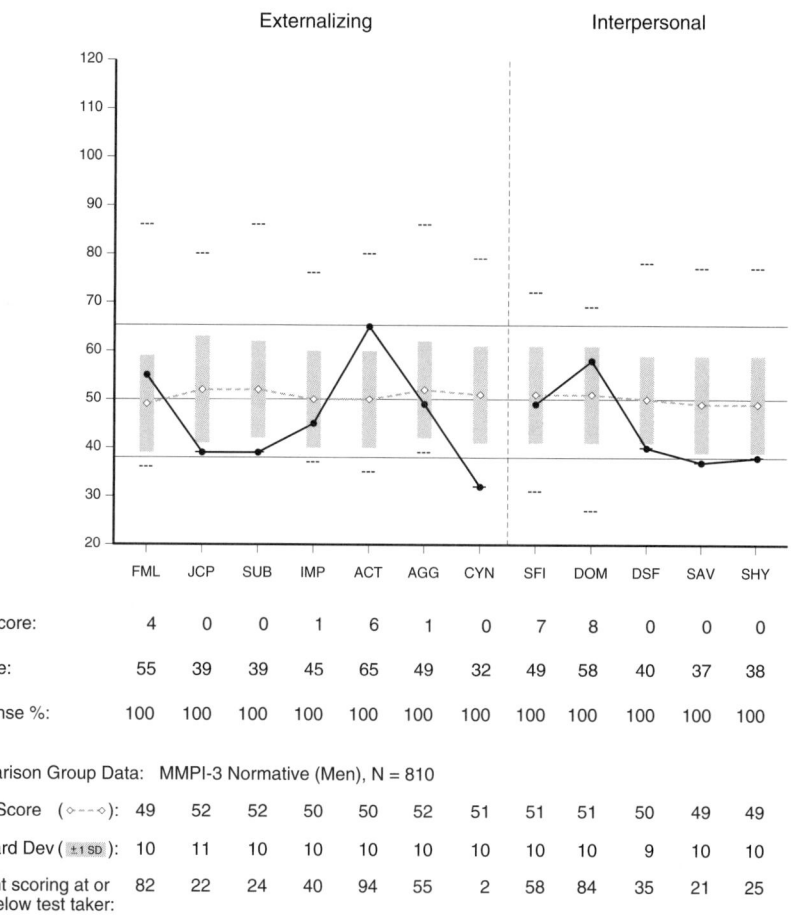

FIGURE 10.7. Mr. Y's MMPI-3 Clinical Settings Interpretive Report, continued

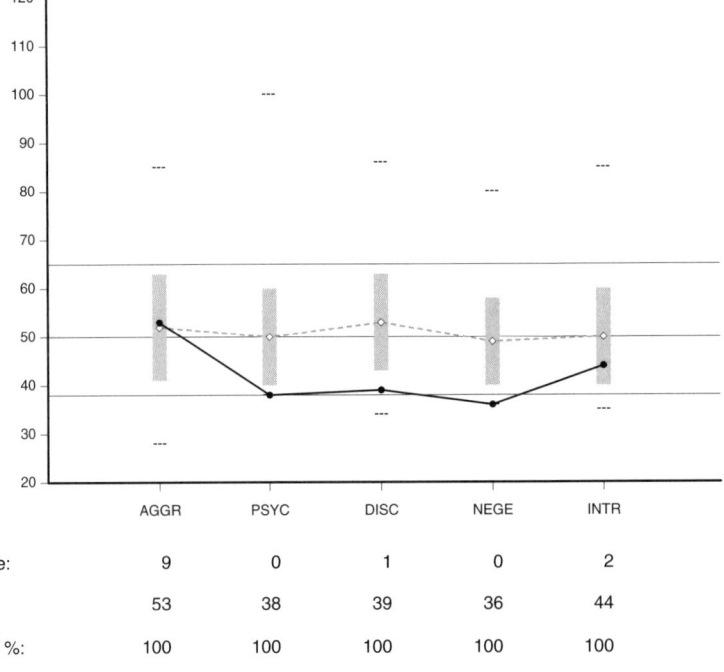

FIGURE 10.7. Mr. Y's MMPI-3 Clinical Settings Interpretive Report, continued

MMPI-3 T SCORES (BY DOMAIN)

PROTOCOL VALIDITY

Content Non-Responsiveness

0	36	35	54 F
CNS	CRIN	VRIN	TRIN

Over-Reporting

41	41	42	59	39
F	Fp	Fs	FBS	RBS

Under-Reporting

48	59
L	K

SUBSTANTIVE SCALES

Somatic/Cognitive Dysfunction

42	59	47	44	38
RC1	MLS	NUC	EAT	COG

Emotional Dysfunction

48							
EID							
	51	44	40	40	**37**		
	RCd	SUI	HLP	SFD	**NFC**		
	47	44					
	RC2	INTR					
	46	49	**37**	46	51	53	56	36
	RC7	STR	**WRY**	CMP	ARX	ANP	BRF	NEGE

Thought Dysfunction

37	
THD	
	40
	RC6
	37
	RC8
	38
	PSYC

Behavioral Dysfunction

39				
BXD				
	40	55	39	39
	RC4	FML	JCP	SUB
	62	45	**65**	49	**32**
	RC9	IMP	**ACT**	AGG	**CYN**
	39				
	DISC				

Interpersonal Functioning

49	58	53	40	**37**	**38**
SFI	DOM	AGGR	DSF	**SAV**	**SHY**

Scale scores shown in bold font are interpreted in the report.

Note. This information is provided to facilitate interpretation following the recommended structure for MMPI-3 interpretation in Chapter 5 of the *MMPI-3 Manual for Administration, Scoring, and Interpretation*, which provides details in the text and an outline in Table 5-1.

FIGURE 10.7. Mr. Y's MMPI-3 Clinical Settings Interpretive Report, continued

MMPI®-3 Interpretive Report: Clinical Settings ID: Mr. Y
10/21/2020, Page 8

This interpretive report is intended for use by a professional qualified to interpret the MMPI-3. The information it contains should be considered in the context of the test taker's background, the circumstances of the assessment, and other available information.

The report includes extensive annotation, which appears as superscripts following each statement in the narrative, keyed to Endnotes with accompanying Research References, which appear in the final two sections of the report. Additional information about the annotation features is provided in the headnotes to these sections and in the MMPI-3 User's Guide for the Score and Clinical Interpretive Reports.

SYNOPSIS

This is a valid MMPI-3 protocol. Scores on the Substantive Scales indicate behavioral dysfunction. Behavioral-externalizing problems relate to excessive activation.

PROTOCOL VALIDITY

This is a valid MMPI-3 protocol. There are no problems with unscorable items. The test taker responded to the MMPI-3 in a remarkably consistent manner[1]. He was deliberate in his approach to the assessment. There are no indications of over- or under-reporting.

SUBSTANTIVE SCALE INTERPRETATION

Clinical symptoms, personality characteristics, and behavioral tendencies of the test taker are described in this section and organized according to an empirically guided framework. (Please see Chapter 5 of the MMPI-3 Manual for Administration, Scoring, and Interpretation *for details.) Statements containing the word "reports" are based on the item content of MMPI-3 scales, whereas statements that include the word "likely" are based on empirical correlates of scale scores. Specific sources for each statement can be viewed with the annotation features of this report.*

Somatic/Cognitive Dysfunction
There are no indications of somatic or cognitive dysfunction in this protocol.

Emotional Dysfunction
There are no indications of emotional-internalizing dysfunction in this protocol. The test taker reports a below average level of worry[2]. He also reports being decisive and efficacious[3] and likely is self-reliant and power-oriented[4].

Thought Dysfunction
There are no indications of disordered thinking in this protocol.

Behavioral Dysfunction
The test taker reports episodes of over-activation such as heightened excitation and energy level[5] and may have a history of symptoms associated with manic or hypomanic episodes[6]. describes others as well-intentioned and trustworthy and disavows cynical beliefs about them[7]. He is possibly overly trusting[8].

FIGURE 10.7. Mr. Y's MMPI-3 Clinical Settings Interpretive Report, continued

Interpersonal Functioning Scales

The test taker reports enjoying social situations and events[9], and likely is perceived as outgoing and gregarious[10]. He also reports little or no social anxiety[11].

DIAGNOSTIC CONSIDERATIONS

This section provides recommendations for psychodiagnostic assessment based on the test taker's MMPI-3 results. It is recommended that he be evaluated for the following:

Emotional-Internalizing Disorders
- Manic or hypomanic episode[12]
- Cycling mood disorder[13]

TREATMENT CONSIDERATIONS

This section provides inferential treatment-related recommendations based on the test taker's MMPI-3 scores.

Psychotherapy Process Issues
- Excessive behavioral activation may interfere with treatment[14].

ITEM-LEVEL INFORMATION

Unscorable Responses

The test taker produced scorable responses to all the MMPI-3 items.

Critical Responses

Seven MMPI-3 scales—Suicidal/Death Ideation (SUI), Helplessness/Hopelessness (HLP), Anxiety-Related Experiences (ARX), Ideas of Persecution (RC6), Aberrant Experiences (RC8), Substance Abuse (SUB), and Aggression (AGG)—have been designated by the test authors as having critical item content that may require immediate attention and follow-up. Items answered by the individual in the keyed direction (True or False) on a critical scale are listed below if his T score on that scale is 65 or higher. However, any item answered in the keyed direction on SUI is listed.

The test taker has not produced an elevated T score (≥ 65) on any of these scales or answered any SUI items in the keyed direction.

FIGURE 10.7. Mr. Y's MMPI-3 Clinical Settings Interpretive Report, continued

ENDNOTES

This section lists for each statement in the report the MMPI-3 score(s) that triggered it. In addition, each statement is identified as a Test Response, if based on item content, a Correlate, if based on empirical correlates, or an Inference, if based on the report authors' judgment. (This information can also be accessed on-screen by placing the cursor on a given statement.) For correlate-based statements, research references (Ref. No.) are provided, keyed to the consecutively numbered reference list following the endnotes.

[1] Test Response: CRIN=36; VRIN=35
[2] Test Response: WRY=37
[3] Test Response: NFC=37
[4] Correlate: NFC=37, Ref. 9
[5] Test Response: ACT=65
[6] Correlate: ACT=65, Ref. 2, 5, 9, 10
[7] Test Response: CYN=32
[8] Correlate: CYN=32, Ref. 7, 8, 9
[9] Test Response: SAV=37
[10] Correlate: SAV=37, Ref. 1, 2, 3, 4, 5
[11] Test Response: SHY=38
[12] Correlate: ACT=65, Ref. 6, 10
[13] Correlate: ACT=65, Ref. 10
[14] Inference: ACT=65

FIGURE 10.7. Mr. Y's MMPI-3 Clinical Settings Interpretive Report, continued

RESEARCH REFERENCE LIST

The following studies are sources for empirical correlates identified in the Endnotes section of this report.

1. Ayearst, L. E., Sellbom, M., Trobst, K. K., & Bagby, R. M. (2013). Evaluating the interpersonal content of the MMPI-2-RF Interpersonal Scales. *Journal of Personality Assessment, 95*(2), 187–196. https://doi.org/10.1080/00223891.2012.730085

2. Ben-Porath, Y. S., & Tellegen, A. (2020). *The Minnesota Multiphasic Personality Inventory-3 (MMPI-3): Technical manual.* University of Minnesota Press.

3. Finn, J. A., Ben-Porath, Y. S., & Tellegen, A. (2015). Dichotomous versus polytomous response options in psychopathology assessment: Method or meaningful variance? *Psychological Assessment, 27*(1), 184–193. https://doi.org/10.1037/pas0000044

4. Franz, A. O., Harrop, T. M., & McCord, D. M. (2017). Examining the construct validity of the MMPI-2-RF Interpersonal Functioning Scales using the Computerized Adaptive Test of Personality Disorder as a comparative framework. *Journal of Personality Assessment, 99*(4), 416–423. https://doi.org/10.1080/00223891.2016.1222394

5. Menton, W. H., Crighton, A. H., Tarescavage, A. M., Marek, R. J., Hicks, A. D., & Ben-Porath, Y. S. (2019). Equivalence of laptop and tablet administrations of the Minnesota Multiphasic Personality Inventory-2 Restructured Form. *Assessment, 26*(4), 661–669. https://doi.org/10.1177/1073191117714558

6. Sellbom, M., Bagby, R. M., Kushner, S., Quilty, L. C., & Ayearst, L. E. (2011). Diagnostic construct validity of the MMPI-2 Restructured Form (MMPI-2-RF) scale scores. *Assessment, 19*(2), 176–186. https://doi.org/10.1177/1073191111428763

7. Sellbom, M., Ben-Porath, Y. S., & Bagby, R. M. (2008). Personality and psychopathology: Mapping the MMPI-2 Restructured Clinical (RC) Scales onto the five factor model of personality. *Journal of Personality Disorders, 22*(3), 291–312. https://doi.org/10.1521/pedi.2008.22.3.291

8. Simms, L. J., Casillas, A., Clark, L. A., Watson, D., & Doebbeling, B. N. (2005). Psychometric evaluation of the Restructured Clinical Scales of the MMPI-2. *Psychological Assessment, 17*(3), 345–358. https://doi.org/10.1037/1040-3590.17.3.345

9. Tellegen, A., & Ben-Porath, Y. S. (2008/2011). *Minnesota Multiphasic Personality Inventory-2-Restructured Form (MMPI-2-RF): Technical manual.* University of Minnesota Press.

10. Watson, C., Quilty, L. C., & Bagby, R. M. (2011). Differentiating bipolar disorder from major depressive disorder using the MMPI-2-RF: A receiver operating characteristics (ROC) analysis. *Journal of Psychopathology and Behavioral Assessment, 33*(3), 368–374. https://doi.org/10.1007/s10862-010-9212-7

End of Report

FIGURE 10.7. Mr. Y's MMPI-3 Clinical Settings Interpretive Report, continued

Step 2: Assessing for Current Work Impairment

It is unclear from the clinical evidence that Mr. Y has fully recovered normal functioning following his index manic episode with psychotic features. But the duration of risk does not end with recovery from a chronic, episodic disorder that is substantially limiting when active and has a high likelihood of recurrence in substantially limiting forms, as discussed next.

Step 3: Assessing for Sustainability of Fitness

The third step in the integrative process is reserved for cases in which the employee's episodic mental health condition is currently nonimpairing. Although bipolar I disorder characteristically involves complete interepisode recovery (that is, a full remission of symptoms between manic episodes), it also has high rates of relapse chronicity (Vieta et al., 2013). Bipolar disorder follows a relapsing course with, on average, approximately eight episodes over the 10 years following diagnosis in hospitalized samples (Goodwin, 2009). The lifetime risk of suicide in individuals with bipolar disorder is estimated to be 20 to 30 times greater than in the general population (*DSM-5-TR;* American Psychiatric Association, 2022, p. 148). Research shows that persons with bipolar disorder experience some degree of disability during the majority of their time in long-term follow-up (54% to 59% of months), including 19% to 23% of months with moderate and 7% to 9% of months with severe overall impairment (Judd et al., 2008).

Despite the development of new medications for bipolar disorder with fewer side effects and greater effectiveness, treatment remains suboptimal, even among patients who adhere consistently to their treatment regimens (Batista et al., 2011). Longitudinal studies indicate that even when patients are protected by state-of-the-art pharmacotherapy, about 40% relapse in 1 year, 60% in 2 years, and 73% over 5 years. Thus, the duration of Mr. Y's risk for bipolar I disorder relapse continues throughout his life, and the risk for harm resulting from his actions as a firefighter when impaired by his condition endures for the remaining term of his career. This risk is exacerbated by Mr. Y's lack of insight into his condition, which can result in discontinuation of medication that may assist with its stabilization. Finally, concerns about the sustainability of Mr. Y's fitness for duty are underscored by the absence of coordinated psychiatric treatment, psychoeducation, and adjunctive psychotherapy.

Conclusion

The aggregate clinical evidence indicates that Mr. Y has partially recovered from a recent manic episode with psychotic features requiring hospitalization. However, he requires long-term treatment for bipolar I disorder, which is an episodic and recurrent mental health condition with a high risk of relapse. When symptomatic, his condition can lead to behavior with catastrophic consequences to him, his fellow firefighters, and the public. His condition impairs his functioning in the Emotional Regulation and Stress Tolerance, Impulse Control/Attention to Safety, and Decision-Making and Judgment dimensions. These risks are aggravated by the fact that Mr. Y is not receiving treatment consistent with best practices (which combines medication management with relapse prevention counseling; see, e.g., Goodwin, 2009), in part because he believes he does not have a mental condition requiring treatment. In consideration of all these facts, the examiner determined that Mr. Y is *unfit for duty*. [Epilogue: Following the fitness evaluation, Mr. Y was placed on medical leave pending initiation of a coordinated treatment plan and consideration of reasonable accommodations. Four months later, he had stopped taking his medication, separated from his wife, and was arrested for burglary, which he carried out to obtain funds to support a newly acquired drug habit. He was subsequently terminated.]

Notes

1. INTRODUCTION TO THE PSYCHOLOGICAL ASSESSMENT OF POLICE AND OTHER PUBLIC SAFETY PERSONNEL

1. We use the labels *police officer, peace officer,* and *law enforcement officer* interchangeably throughout this book. These terms are intended to refer to armed (or armable) public sector employees vested by the legislating jurisdiction with the authority to enforce the law and make or refer arrests for criminal prosecution. Examples include city police officers; reserve police officers; deputy sheriffs; parole and probation officers; sworn personnel of law enforcement subunits of port, transit, and housing authorities; college campus police officers; and federal law enforcement officers.
2. *Correctional officers* consist of public sector employees responsible for the supervision, safety, and security of inmates (adult or juvenile) in a prison, jail, or similar form of secure custody.
3. *Dispatcher* includes the positions of public safety dispatcher, emergency dispatcher, emergency communication (or communications) dispatcher/operator, communications specialist, police dispatcher, 911 dispatcher, 911 operator, telecommunicator, emergency telecommunicator, call-taker, and so on.
4. *Firefighter* includes both full-time and volunteer positions, regardless of the context (e.g., municipal, rural, airport, district, state, or federal) and includes firefighter engineer, inspector, wildland firefighter, airport firefighter, fire investigator, and fire marshal/deputy fire marshal with first responder functions. *Firefighter/medic* refers to firefighter/EMT, firefighter/paramedic, single-role EMT, and single-role paramedic positions working as emergency first-responders in fire rescue settings.
5. Throughout this book, a *candidate* refers to an individual who has received an offer of employment conditioned on the findings of the postoffer psychological evaluation. An *applicant* refers to an individual at the preoffer stage of the application process.

6. See, for example, Texas Administrative Code Title 37, Part 7, Rule § 217.1(b)(12).
7. In some jurisdictions, dispatchers perform many other functions that may also involve processing and storing evidence and seized assets, including money. Additionally, some firefighters, such as those who also perform services as arson investigators, are authorized to use force and enforce laws.
8. The 14 personality traits recommended by Weiner (1997) to "serve as the foundation for the psychological evaluation" (p. 5) are (1) tolerance of stress, (2) integrity, (3) dependability, (4) emotional control (5) tolerance of unpleasant work environment, (6) adaptability, (7) teamwork, (8) maturity, (9) productivity, (10) positive attitude, (11) assertiveness, (12) social concern, (13) motivation, and (14) interpersonal sensitivity.
9. The *hiring agency* is the agency or department in which the candidate has applied to work. The *hiring authority* is responsible for processing the candidate through the application and selection process. These entities are often the same but will differ when, for example, the application process for a police department is administered by a separate human resources department.

5. FOUNDATIONAL REQUIREMENTS FOR PREEMPLOYMENT ASSESSMENTS

1. Throughout this book, we interchangeably use *qualified* and *suitable* to indicate a judgment that a candidate meets the criterion standard, and we use both *unqualified* and *unsuitable* to refer to a determination that a candidate does not meet the criterion standard.
2. In Canada, where there exists no counterpart to the ADA, professional practice guidelines for evaluating the psychological suitability of police candidates nevertheless stipulate that, when the evaluation addresses "potentially sensitive characteristics that may be protected under human rights legislation, such as history of mental illness," such evaluations "should only be conducted once a candidate is being seriously considered for hire and has demonstrated other basic job competencies" (Canadian Psychological Association, 2013, p. 7).
3. The prohibition against communicating the findings from a psychological evaluation conducted for one employer derives from federal law under the ADA [(29 C.F.R. §1630.10[a]) and (2)]. Some state jurisdictions may have laws that run counter to this prohibition. For example, in the state of Washington, administrative code 139-07-030 permits findings from one psychological evaluation of a police candidate to be shared with more than one law enforcement agency under the following circumstances: "(a) the agency that initiated the psychological examination and the qualified professional conducting the examination agreed to share the psychological examination report and recommendations with the other law enforcement agency; (b) the applicant signed a release permitting the other agency to have the psychological examination report; (c) the psychological examination was completed within 6 months of the request by the other law enforcement agency; and (d) the job analyses of the initiating and other law enforcement agencies must be substantially similar." Screening professionals who agree to share an examination report and recommendations with more than one law enforcement agency may wish to consult first with legal counsel to determine how to proceed when state and federal regulations appear to be in opposition to that sharing.

4. This is commonly referred to as the *business necessity standard* and is discussed in greater detail in chapter 9 in the context of fitness-for-duty evaluations. In preemployment evaluations, however, when a person with a disability is not hired because of that disability (and an adverse hiring decision will presumptively result in that conclusion), the business necessity standard requires generally that the exclusionary criterion reasonably achieves the employer's legitimate business interests and that another, less exclusionary alternative would not satisfy those interests. For this reason, criteria used to disqualify police and other public safety candidates in any medical evaluation should be assiduously linked to safety and other essential performance requirements of the position.
5. The Age Discrimination in Employment Act of 1967 provides similar protections for U.S. applicants and employees 40 years of age or older.
6. MMPI-3 standard T-scores are based on combined gender norms derived from an equal number of male and female participants in the normative sample. When a test publisher calculates combined gender norms for a police candidate sample using the naturally occurring distribution of male and female candidates in a pool, the normative sample will, in most cases, be composed of predominantly male participants, because 85.8% of U.S. police officers are male (Data USA, 2022).
7. Reference to *clinical* versus *nonclinical* evaluations is intended to reflect the legal distinction between *medical* examinations or inquiries and procedures or tests generally not considered medical examinations. This use of *clinical evaluations* is consistent with the concept of *medical examinations* under the ADA (1991) in that both terms denote any procedure or test that seeks information about an individual's physical or mental impairments or health and includes, but is not limited to, psychological tests designed to identify a mental disorder or impairment. In contrast, psychological tests that measure only personality traits such as honesty, preferences, and habits would not be considered a medical examination (EEOC, 2000, Question 2).
8. In California, this determination is made by evaluating the condition's impact on the candidate's performance and conduct relevant to the 10 CA-POST Psychological Screening Dimensions.
9. The President's Commission on Law Enforcement and Administration of Justice (1967), whose call for the increased use of psychological testing and interviews of police candidates is widely credited for the nearly universal use of psychological screening today (Trompetter, 2019), also made a plea for higher-quality background investigations. The Commission noted: "If properly conducted a background investigation can provide invaluable information on the character of applicants. . . . In many cities, however, character investigations are extremely limited in scope and investigators seldom probe deeply enough to uncover the information needed for professional evaluation. Few municipal forces have yet devoted enough attention to the character investigation of applicants. Civil Service routines often merely require that the applicant provide character vouchers or 'references' which are accepted without further question. . . . No department should admit any person into the police service until his background has been comprehensively investigated. Trained investigators should examine school, credit, and criminal records; interview persons used as references and other persons in the applicant's neighborhood; and interview past and present employers. The investigative process should extend to

other communities as well, if the applicant has lived elsewhere. . . . Prior convictions, work habits, prejudices, emotional stability, among other characteristics, should be determined to ascertain whether the applicant is fit to perform police work. Since background investigations are expensive, if properly conducted, they should be restricted to those who otherwise have qualified" (p. 129). Fifty years later, the Commission's admonishment is no less fitting. Background investigations vary considerably in quality from agency to agency, and the information provided about a candidate's character and other characteristics from a high-quality investigation contributes immeasurably to the validity of the psychological evaluation.

10. Conducting the interview only after the psychologist has obtained and reviewed findings from psychological testing is a legal requirement in some jurisdictions, including California (11 C.C.R. § 1955[e][4]) and Texas (T.A.C. Title 37, Part 7, Rule §217.1[b][12]).

11. Some states require evaluation of a police candidate's positive traits and characteristics (i.e., assets or strengths). However, this assessment alone does not comprise an adequate preemployment psychological evaluation that, in most jurisdictions, includes the minimum requirement that "the candidate be free from any psychological impairment that might adversely affect the performance of safety-based duties and responsibilities and be capable of withstanding the psychological demands inherent in the prospective position" (IACP, 2020; Guideline 3.2).

7. THE MMPI-3 PUBLIC SAFETY CANDIDATE INTERPRETIVE REPORTS

1. The base rates reflect the percent of individuals who score at or above the test taker on a given scale. If added to the percent scoring at or above the test taker (listed on the profile page below the scale score), the result will exceed 100%. This is because the percent of comparison group test takers who score the same as the test taker is included in both figures.

2. If the test taker defines the gender demographic as anything other than Male or Female, the report will automatically use gender-neutral language as recommended by the *Publication Manual of the American Psychological Association* (7th ed.; APA, 2020). For reports generated using Q Local®, gender-neutral language is triggered if gender is omitted. For reports generated using Q-global®, gender-neutral language is triggered if gender is omitted or is set to Unspecified or Other.

8. USING THE MMPI-3 IN PREEMPLOYMENT ASSESSMENTS OF POLICE AND OTHER PUBLIC SAFETY CANDIDATES

1. When it is legally or institutionally required that the screening psychologist provide a clear determination of a candidate's suitability, stating that the candidate is qualified/unqualified or suitable/unsuitable is necessary. In the absence of such a requirement, some psychologists use a Likert-type rating scale indicating levels of suitability or risk. However, when the rating indicates reservations about an otherwise qualified or suitable

candidate, this carries a risk of rendering the report discoverable in civil or criminal proceedings (see, for example, *Miron v. Town of Stratford,* 1976 F. Supp. 2d 120 [2013]).
2. See https://www.benefits.va.gov/REPORTS/abr/docs/2019-compensation.pdf.

9. FOUNDATIONAL REQUIREMENTS FOR FITNESS-FOR-DUTY EVALUATIONS

1. The Equal Employment Opportunity Commission (EEOC), the federal agency responsible for enforcing the ADA's provisions, provides guidance on what constitutes an essential job function (EEOC, 1992). This guidance includes several reasons why a function could be considered essential, including (1) the position exists to perform the function, (2) there are a limited number of other employees available to perform the function or among whom the function can be distributed, and (3) a function is highly specialized, and the person in the position is hired for special expertise or ability to perform it. The EEOC also provides a nonexhaustive list of several types of evidence an employer may consider in determining whether a function is essential, including the employer's judgment, a written job description prepared before advertising or interviewing applicants, the amount of time spent performing the function, the consequences of not requiring a person in the job to perform the function, the terms of a collective bargaining agreement, work experience of people who have performed the job in the past, work experience of people who currently perform similar jobs, and other relevant factors. For purposes of reaching a fitness for duty determination, professionals generally rely on the employer to distinguish essential from marginal job functions.

References

Achenbach, T. M., & Edelbrock, C. S. (1978). The classification of child psychopathology: A review and analysis of empirical efforts. *Psychological Bulletin, 85*(6), 1275–1301.

Ackerman, M. J. (2010). *Essentials of psychological assessment* (2nd ed.). John Wiley & Sons.

Age Discrimination in Employment Act of 1967, Pub. L. No. 90-202, 29 U.S.C. §§ 621–634. (1967).

Aldrup v. Caldera, #01-50369, 2001 U.S. App. Lexis 26347 (5th Cir. 2001).

Allard, G., & Faust, D. (2000). Errors in scoring objective personality tests. *Assessment, 7*(2), 119–131.

American Board of Police & Public Safety Psychology. (2014). Core scientific knowledge for specialists in police and public safety psychology. Author. https://abpp.org/wp-content/uploads/2022/07/Core-Scientific-Knowledge-Assessment-051015.pdf

American Educational Research Association, American Psychological Association, & National Council on Measurement in Education. (2014). *Standards for educational and psychological testing.* American Educational Research Association.

American Psychiatric Association. (2022). *Diagnostic and statistical manual of mental disorders* (5th ed., text rev.).

American Psychological Association. (2017). Ethical principles of psychologists and code of conduct. https://www.apa.org/ethics/code/ethics-code-2017.pdf

American Psychological Association. (2018). Professional practice guidelines for occupationally mandated psychological evaluations. *American Psychologist, 73*(2), 186–197.

Americans With Disabilities Act, 29 C.F.R. § 1630.9[a] (1991). https://www.govinfo.gov/content/pkg/FR-1991-07-26/pdf/FR-1991-07-26.pdf

Americans With Disabilities Act, 29 C.F.R. §1630.10[a] (1991). https://www.govinfo.gov/content/pkg/FR-1991-07-26/pdf/FR-1991-07-26.pdf

Americans With Disabilities Act, 29 C.F.R. § 1630.14[b] (1991). https://www.govinfo.gov/content/pkg/FR-1991-07-26/pdf/FR-1991-07-26.pdf

Americans With Disabilities Act Amendments Act, Pub. L. No. 110-325 (2008).

Americans With Disabilities Act of 1990, Pub. L. No. 101-336, § 2, 104 Stat. 328 (1991).

Annotated Code of Maryland 12.04.01.04. (2021). Selection standards for provisional certification. http://mdrules.elaws.us/comar/12.04.01.04#:~:text=(2)%20May%20attend%20an%20academy,years%20old%20and%20provisionally%20certified

Appelbaum, K. L. (2010). Commentary: The art of forensic report writing. *Journal of the American Academy of Psychiatry and Law, 38*(1), 43–45.

Azen, S. P., Snibbe, H. M., & Montgomery, H. R. (1973). A longitudinal predictive study of success and performance of law enforcement officers. *Journal of Applied Psychology, 57*(2), 190–192.

Bandura, A. (1994). Social cognitive theory of mass communication. In J. Bryant & D. Zillmann (Eds.), *Media effects: Advances in theory and research* (pp. 61–90). Lawrence Erlbaum Associates.

Bandura, A. (2001). Social cognitive theory: An agentic perspective. *Annual Review of Psychology, 52*, 1–26.

Batista, T. A., Baes, C. V. W., & Juruena, M. F. (2011). Efficacy of psychoeducation in bipolar patients: Systematic review of randomized trials. *Psychology & Neuroscience, 4*(3), 409–416.

Ben-Porath, Y. S., & Butcher, J. N. (1989a). The psychometric stability of rewritten MMPI items. *Journal of Personality Assessment, 53*, 645–653.

Ben-Porath, Y. S., & Butcher, J. N. (1989b). The comparability of MMPI and MMPI-2 scales and profiles. *Psychological Assessment: A Journal of Consulting and Clinical Psychology, 1*, 345–347.

Ben-Porath, Y. S., & Forbey, J. D. (2003). *Non-gendered norms for the MMPI-2*. University of Minnesota Press.

Ben-Porath, Y. S., & Sellbom, M. (2023). *Interpreting the MMPI-3*. University of Minnesota Press.

Ben-Porath, Y. S., & Tellegen, A. (2008/2011). *MMPI-2-RF: Manual for administration, scoring and interpretation*. University of Minnesota Press.

Ben-Porath, Y. S., & Tellegen, A. (2020a). *Minnesota Multiphasic Personality Inventory-3 (MMPI-3): Manual for administration, scoring, and interpretation*. University of Minnesota Press.

Ben-Porath, Y. S., & Tellegen, A. (2020b). *Minnesota Multiphasic Personality Inventory-3 (MMPI-3): Technical manual*. University of Minnesota Press.

Ben-Porath, Y. S., & Tellegen, A. (2020c). *Minnesota Multiphasic Personality Inventory-3 (MMPI-3): User's guide for the score and clinical interpretive reports*. University of Minnesota Press.

Ben-Porath, Y. S., Tellegen, A., & Puente, A. (2020). *Minnesota Multiphasic Personality Inventory-3 (MMPI-3): Manual supplement for the U.S. Spanish translation*. University of Minnesota Press.

Berner, J. (1997). *POST public safety dispatcher psychological assessment resource document*. California Commission on Peace Officer Standards and Training. https://post.ca.gov/Portals/0/Publications/Dispatcher_Psychological_Assessment.pdf?ver=2019-07-12-131117-420

Beutler, L. E., Storm, A., Kirkish, P., Scogin, F., & Gaines, J. A. (1985). Parameters in the prediction of police officer performance. *Professional Psychology: Research and Practice, 16*(2), 324–335.

Bhar, S. S., Ghahramanlou-Holloway, M., Brown, G. K., & Beck, A. T. (2008). Self-esteem and suicide ideation in psychiatric outpatients. *Suicide and Life-Threatening Behavior, 38*(5), 511–516.

Blonigen, D. M., Hicks, B. M., Krueger, R. F., Patrick, C. J., & Iacono, W. G. (2005). Psychopathic personality traits: Heritability and genetic overlap with internalizing and externalizing psychopathology. *Psychological Medicine: A Journal of Research in Psychiatry and the Allied Sciences, 35*(5), 637–648.

Blum, R. H. (1964). *Police selection*. Charles C. Thomas.

Blumstein, A., & Nakamura, K. (2009). Redemption in the presence of widespread criminal background checks. *Criminology, 47*(2), 327–359.

Boes, J. O., Chandler, C. J., & Timm, H. W. (1997). *Police integrity: Use of personality measures to identify corruption-prone officers*. Defense Personnel Security Research Center, Publication No. PERSTR-97–003.

Briere, J. (2001). *Detailed Assessment of Posttraumatic Stress (DAPS)*. Psychological Assessment Resources.

Briggs, E. C., Amaya-Jackson, L., Putnam, K. T., & Putnam, F. W. (2021). All adverse childhood experiences are not equal: The contribution of synergy to adverse childhood experience scores. *American Psychologist, 76*(2), 243.

Brown v. Sandy City Appeal Board, 330 P.3d 767 (Ut. App. 2014).

Brownfield v. City of Yakima, 612 F.3d 1140 (9th Cir. 2010).

Buss, A. H., & Perry, M. (1992). The Aggression Questionnaire. *Journal of Personality and Social Psychology, 63*, 452–459.

Butcher, J. N. (1972). *Objective personality assessment: Changing perspectives*. Academic Press.

Butcher, J. N., Dahlstrom, W. G., Graham, J. R., Tellegen, A., & Kaemmer, B. (1989). *Manual for the restandardized Minnesota Multiphasic Personality Inventory: MMPI-2*. University of Minnesota Press.

Butcher, J. N., Graham, J. R., Ben-Porath, Y. S., Tellegen, A., Dahlstrom, W. G., & Kaemmer, B. (2001). *MMPI-2: Manual for administration and scoring* (Rev. Ed.). University of Minnesota Press.

Butcher, J. N., Graham, J. R., Williams, C. L., & Ben-Porath, Y. S. (1990). *Development and use of the MMPI-2 content scales*. University of Minnesota Press.

Butcher, J. N., Morfitt, R. C., Rouse, S. V., & Holden, R. R. (1997). Reducing MMPI-2 defensiveness: The effect of specialized instructions on test validity in a job applicant sample. *Journal of Personality Assessment, 68*(2), 385–401.

Butcher, J. N., Williams, C. L., Graham, J. R., Archer, R., Tellegen, A., Ben-Porath, Y. S., & Kaemmer, B. (1992). *MMPI-A manual for administration, scoring, and interpretation*. University of Minnesota Press.

Butler v. Thornburgh, 900 F.2d 871, 876 (5th Cir. 1990), cert. denied, 498 U.S. 998 (1990).

Canadian Psychological Association. (2013). *The pre-employment clinical assessment of police candidates: Principles and guidelines for Canadian psychologists*. https://cpa.ca/docs/File/News/2013-07/Police%20assess%20guidelines%20April2013final.pdf

Castaneda, L. W., & Ridgeway, G. (2010). *Today's police and sheriff recruits: Insights from the newest members of America's law enforcement community.* The RAND Corporation.

Chu, C., Buchman-Schmitt, J. M., Stanley, I. H., Hom, M. A., Tucker, R. P., Hagan, C. R., Rogers, M. L., Podlogar, M. C., Chiurliza, B., Ringer, F. B., Michaels, M. S., Patros, C. H. G., & Joiner, T. E., Jr. (2017). The interpersonal theory of suicide: A systematic review and meta-analysis of a decade of cross-national research. *Psychological Bulletin, 143*(12), 1313–1345. https://dx.doi.org/10.1037/bul0000123

Civil Rights Act of 1964, § 7, Pub. L. No. 88-352, 78 Stat. 241 (1964).

Civil Rights Act of 1991, Pub. L. No. 102-166 (1991).

Cleckley, H. (1941). *The mask of sanity: An attempt to reinterpret the so-called psychopathic personality.* Mosby.

Coffman v. Indianapolis Fire Dept., 2009 U.S. App. Lexis 18717 (7th Cir. 2009).

Colon v. City of Newark, 909 A.2d 725, 188 N.J. 489 (2006).

Conte v. Horcher, 365 N.E.2d 567 (Ill. App. 1977).

Corey, D. M. (2011). Principles of fitness-for-duty evaluations for police psychologists. In J. Kitaeff (Ed.), *Handbook of police psychology* (pp. 263–293). Routledge Psychology Press.

Corey, D. M. (2016, October 16). *Assessment protocols, procedures & pass rates for psychological evaluations of police candidates* [Paper presentation]. International Association of Chiefs of Police Conference, San Diego, CA, United States.

Corey, D. M., & Ben-Porath, Y. S. (2014). *User's guide for the MMPI-2-RF Police Candidate Interpretive Report.* University of Minnesota Press.

Corey, D. M., & Ben-Porath, Y. S. (2018). *Assessing police and other public safety personnel using the MMPI-2-RF.* University of Minnesota Press.

Corey, D. M., & Ben-Porath, Y. S. (2020). *Minnesota Multiphasic Personality Inventory-3 (MMPI-3): User's guide for the Police Candidate Interpretive Report.* University of Minnesota Press.

Corey, D. M., & Ben-Porath, Y. S. (2022). *MMPI-3 user's guide for the Public Safety Candidate Interpretive Reports.* University of Minnesota Press.

Corey, D. M., & Borum, R. (2013). Forensic assessment for high-risk occupations. In R. K. Otto & I. B. Weiner (Eds.), *Handbook of psychology: Forensic psychology* (pp. 246–270). John Wiley & Sons.

Corey, D. M., & Detrick, P. (2022). Psychological assessment in public safety personnel screening. In R. M. Bagby and M. Sellbom (Eds.), *Comprehensive clinical psychology* (Vol. 4, Assessment, 2nd ed., pp. 258–284). Elsevier. https://dx.doi.org/10.1016/B978-0-12-818697-8.00200-4

Corey, D. M., McElroy, H. K., & Ben-Porath, Y. S. (2023). Statewide psychological screening mandates for police candidates in the United States: A review and comparison to the standard of practice. *Professional Psychology: Research and Practice, 54*(2), 156–166. https://doi.org/10.1037/pro0000487

Corey, D. M., Sellbom, M., & Ben-Porath, Y. S. (2018). Risks associated with overcontrolled behavior in police officer recruits. *Psychological Assessment, 30*(12), 1691.

Corey, D. M., & Zelig, M. (2020). *Evaluations of police suitability and fitness for duty.* Oxford University Press.

Cuttler, M. J., & Muchinsky, P. M. (2006). Prediction of law enforcement training performance and dysfunctional job performance with general mental ability, personality and life history variables. *Criminal Justice and Behavior, 33*(1), 3–25.

Data USA. (2022). *Police officers: Demographics*. Retrieved February 20, 2024. https://datausa.io/profile/soc/police-officers#demographics

Detrick, P., Ben-Porath, Y. S., & Sellbom, M. (2016). Associations between MMPI-2-RF (Restructured Form) and Inwald Personality Inventory (IPI) scale scores in a law enforcement preemployment screening sample. *Journal of Police and Criminal Psychology, 31*, 81–95.

Detrick, P., & Chibnall, J. T. (2013). Revised NEO Personality Inventory normative data for police officer selection. *Psychological Services, 10*(4), 372–377.

Detrick, P., & Chibnall, J. T. (2014). Underreporting on the MMPI-2-RF in a high-demand police officer selection context: An illustration. *Psychological Assessment, 26*(3), 1044–1049.

Detrick, P., Chibnall, J. T., & Rosso, M. (2001). Minnesota Multiphasic Personality Inventory—2 in police officer selection: Normative data and relation to the Inwald Personality Inventory. *Professional Psychology: Research and Practice, 32*, 484–490.

Dick, D. M. (2007). Identification of genes influencing a spectrum of externalizing psychopathology. *Current Directions in Psychological Science, 16*(6), 331–335.

Dohrenwend, B. P., Shrout, P. E., Egri, G., & Mendelsohn, F. S. (1980). Nonspecific psychological distress and other dimensions of psychopathology. *Archives of General Psychiatry, 37*(11), 1229–1236.

Dunkley, D. M., & Grilo, C. M. (2007). Self-criticism, low self-esteem, depressive symptoms, and over-evaluation of shape and weight in binge eating disorder patients. *Behaviour Research and Therapy, 45*, 139–149.

Duran v. City of Douglas, 904 F.2d 1372 (9th Cir. 1990).

Eckblad, M., & Chapman, L. J. (1986). Development and validation of a scale for hypomanic personality. *Journal of Abnormal Psychology, 95*(3), 214–222.

Eckhardt, C. I., Norlander, B., & Deffenbacher, J. L. (2004). The assessment of anger and hostility: A critical review. *Aggression and Violent Behavior: A Review Journal, 9*, 17–43.

Equal Employment Opportunity Commission. (1979). Adoption of questions and answers to clarify and provide a common interpretation of the Uniform Guidelines on Employee Selection Procedures. *Federal Register, 44*, 11996–12009.

Equal Employment Opportunity Commission. (1992). *Title I technical assistance manual*. https://www.eeoc.gov/laws/guidance/technical-assistance-manual-employment-provisions-title-i-americans-disabilities-act

Equal Employment Opportunity Commission. (1995, October 10). *Enforcement guidance: Preemployment disability-related questions and medical examinations* (Vol. II, Sect. 902, No. 915.002). https://www.eeoc.gov/laws/guidance/enforcement-guidance-preemployment-disability-related-questions-and-medical

Equal Employment Opportunity Commission. (2000, July 27). *Enforcement guidance on disability-related Inquiries and Medical Examinations of Employees Under the Americans with Disabilities Act (ADA)* (Vol. II, No. 915.002). https://www.eeoc.gov/policy/docs/guidance-inquiries.html

Equal Employment Opportunity Commission v. Amego, Inc., 110 F.3d 135 (1st Cir. 1997).

Fernández-Ballesteros, R., De Bruyn, E. E. J., Godoy, A., Hornke, L. F., Ter Laak, J., Vizcarro, C., Westhoff, K., Westmeyer, H., & Zaccagnini, J. L. (2001). Guidelines for the Assessment Process (GAP): A proposal for discussion. *European Journal of Psychological Assessment, 17*(3), 187.

Flynn v. Sandahl, 58 F.3d 283, 10 IER Cases (BNA) 1187, 1995 U.S.App. Lexis 14902 (7th Cir. 1995).

Forbey, J. D., Lee, T. C., Ben-Porath, Y. S., Arbisi, P. A., & Gartland, D. M. (2013). Associations between MMPI-2-RF validity scale scores and extra-test measures of personality and psychopathology. *Assessment, 20*(4), 448–461.

Frances, A. J., Widiger, T. A., & Sabshin, M. (1991). Psychiatric diagnosis and normality. In D. Offer & M. Sabshin (Eds.). *The diversity of normal behavior: Further contributions to normatology* (pp. 3–38). Basic Books.

Frank, J. D. (1974). Psychotherapy: The restoration of morale. *American Journal of Psychiatry, 131,* 271–274.

Frank, J. D. (1985). Further thoughts on the anti-demoralization hypothesis of psychotherapeutic effectiveness. *Integrative Psychiatry, 3,* 17–20.

Gaspar, J. P., Seabright, M. A., Reynolds, S. J., & Yam, K. C. (2015). Counterfactual and factual reflection: The influence of past misdeeds on future immoral behavior. *The Journal of Social Psychology, 155*(4), 370–380.

Genetic Information Nondiscrimination Act of 2008 (GINA), 42 U.S.C. § 2000 (2008).

Genetic Information Nondiscrimination Act of 2008, 29 C.F.R. § 1635.8 (2008). https://www.eeoc.gov/statutes/genetic-information-nondiscrimination-act-2008

Georgia Administrative Rules and Regulations 464-3-.02. Qualifications for certification: Pre-employment requirements. https://rules.sos.state.ga.us/GAC/464-3

Gilberstadt, H., & Duker, J. (1965). *A handbook for clinical and actuarial MMPI interpretation.* Saunders.

Glassmire, D. M., Stolberg, R. A., Greene, R. L., & Bongar, B. (2001). The utility of MMPI-2 suicide items for assessing suicidal potential: Development of a suicidal potential scale. *Assessment, 8*(3), 281–290.

Gold, L. H., & Shuman, D. W. (2009). *Evaluating mental health disability in the workplace.* Springer Science & Business Media.

Golder, S., Hall, M. T., Engstrom, M., Higgins, G. E., & Logan, T. K. (2014). Correlates of recent drug use among victimized women on probation and parole. *Psychology of Addictive Behaviors, 28*(4), 1105–1116.

Goldstein, B. (1975). *Screening for emotional and psychological fitness in correctional officer hiring.* Washington, DC: American Bar Association, Resource Center on Correctional Law and Legal Services.

Goodwin, G. M. (2009). Evidence-based guidelines for treating bipolar disorder: Revised second edition—Recommendations from the British Association for Psychopharmacology. *Journal of Psychopharmacology, 23*(4), 346–388.

Gough, H. G. (1946). Diagnostic patterns on the MMPI. *Journal of Clinical Psychology, 2,* 23–37.

Gough, H. G. (1956). *California Psychological Inventory manual.* Consulting Psychologists Press.

Graham, J. R. (2012). *MMPI-2: Assessing personality and psychopathology.* Oxford University Press.

Gray, J. A. (1970). The psychophysiological basis of introversion-extraversion. *Behaviour Research and Therapy, 8*(3), 249–266.

Green, P., Lees-Halley, P. R., & Allen, L. M. (2002). The Word Memory Test and the validity of neuropsychological test scores. *Journal of Forensic Neuropsychology, 2,* 97–124.

Greene, R. L. (2011). *The MMPI-2/MMPI-2-RF: An interpretive manual* (3rd ed.). Pearson.

Grisso, T. (2008, May 17). *Writing forensic reports.* Paper presented at the American Academy of Forensic Psychology workshop, San Francisco, CA.

Grisso, P., Borum, R., Edens, J. F., Moye, J., & Otto, R. K. (2003). *Evaluating competencies: Forensic assessments and instruments.* Kluwer Academic/Plenum Publishers.

Grossman, L. S., Haywood, T. W., Ostrov, E., Wasyliw, O., & Cavanaugh, J. (1990). Sensitivity of MMPI validity scales to motivational factors in psychological evaluations of police officers. *Journal of Personality Assessment, 55*(3–4), 549–561. https://doi.org/10.1080/00223891.1990.9674090

Gynther, M. D., Altman, H., & Sletten, I. W. (1973). Replicated correlates of MMPI two-point code types: The Missouri actuarial system. *Journal of Clinical Psychology, 29*(3), 263–289.

Hargrave, G. E., Hiatt, D., Ogard, E. M., & Karr, C. (1994). Comparison of the MMPI and the MMP-2 for a sample of peace officers. *Psychological Assessment, 6*(1), 27–32.

Harkness, A. R. (1992). Fundamental topics in the personality disorders: Candidate trait dimensions from lower regions of the hierarchy. *Psychological Assessment, 4,* 251–259.

Harkness, A. R., & McNulty, J. L. (1994). The Personality Psychopathology Five (PSY-5): Issues from the pages of a diagnostic manual instead of a dictionary. In S. E. Strack & M. Lorr (Eds.), *Differentiating normal and abnormal personality* (pp. 291–315). Springer Publishing.

Harkness, A. R., McNulty, J. L., & Ben Porath, Y. S. (1995). The Personality Psychopathology Five (PSY-5): Constructs and MMPI-2 scales. *Psychological Assessment, 7,* 104–114.

Harris, R., & Lingoes, J. (1955). *Subscales for the Minnesota Multiphasic Personality Inventory.* Mimeographed materials, The Langley Porter Clinic.

Hathaway, S. R. (1960). Forward. In W. G. Dahlstrom & G. S. Welsh (Eds.), *An MMPI handbook: A guide to use in clinical practice and research.* University of Minnesota Press.

Hathaway, S. R. (1972). Forward. In W. G. Dahlstrom, G. S. Welsh, & L. E. Dahlstrom (Eds.), *An MMPI handbook: Vol. 1. Clinical interpretation* (pp. vii–xi). University of Minnesota Press.

Hathaway, S. R., & McKinley, J. C. (1940). A multiphasic personality schedule (Minnesota): I. Construction of the schedule. *Journal of Psychology, 10,* 249–254.

Hathaway, S. R., & McKinley, J. C. (1943). *The Minnesota Multiphasic Personality Inventory.* University of Minnesota Press.

Heffernan, R., & Ward, T. (2017). A comprehensive theory of dynamic risk and protective factors. *Aggression and Violent Behavior, 37,* 129–141.

Heilbrun, K., DeMatteo, D., Marczyk, G., & Goldstein, A. M. (2008). Standards of practice and care in forensic mental health assessment: Legal, professional, and principles-based consideration. *Psychology, Public Policy, and Law, 14*(1), 1–26.

Heilbrun, K., Grisso, T., & Goldstein, A. M. (2009). *Foundations of forensic mental health assessment*. Oxford University Press.

Herbig, K. L. (2011). *The evolution of adjudicative guidelines in the Department of Defense*. (Publication No. 11-04). Defense Personnel Security Research Center.

Hicks, B. M., DiRago, A. C., Iacono, W. G., & McGue, M. (2009). Gene-environment interplay in internalizing disorders: Consistent findings across six environmental risk factors. *Journal of Child Psychology and Psychiatry, 50*(10), 1309–1317.

Hoelzle, J. B., & Meyer, G. J. (2009). The invariant component structure of the Personality Assessment Inventory (PAI) full scales. *Journal of Personality Assessment, 91*(2), 175–186.

Hogarth v. Thornburgh, 833 F. Supp. 1077 (SDNY 1993).

Holland, T. R., Helm, R. B., & Holt, N. (1976). Personality patterns among correctional officer applicants. *Journal of Clinical Psychology, 32*(4), 786–791. https://doi.org/10.1002/1097-4679(197610)32:4<786::AID-JCLP2270320409>3.0.CO;2-F

Hough, L. (2016). Community-oriented policing: Hiring in the spirit of service. *Industrial and Organizational Psychology, 9*(3), 573–582.

Hunter, J. E., & Schmidt, F. L. (1990). Dichotomization of continuous variables: The implications for meta-analysis. *Journal of Applied Psychology, 75*(3), 334.

International Association of Chiefs of Police. (2020). *Preemployment psychological evaluation guidelines*. https://www.theiacp.org/sites/default/files/all/p-r/Psych-Preemployment PsychEval1.pdf

Inwald, R. E. (1992). *Inwald Personality Inventory technical manual* (revised). Hilson Research.

Inwald, R., Knatz, H., & Shusman, E. (1982). *Inwald Personality Inventory manual*. Hilson Research.

Jager, J., Keyes, K. M., & Schulenberg, J. E. (2015). Historical variation in young adult binge drinking trajectories and its link to historical variation in social roles and minimum legal drinking age. *Developmental Psychology, 51*(7), 962–974.

James, L., & Taylor, J. (2008). Revisiting the structure of mental disorder: Borderline personality disorder and the internalizing/externalizing spectra. *British Journal of Clinical Psychology, 47*, 361–380.

Jenkins v. City of Sandusky, #E-07-067, 2008 Ohio App. Lexis 3966 (6th App. Dist.).

Johnson, Roberts, & Associates, Inc. (2011). *Psychological History Questionnaire (PsyQ) for law enforcement and other public safety applicants*.

Judd, L. L., Schettler, P. J., Solomon, D. A., Maser, J. D., Coryell, W., Endicott, J., & Akiskal, H. S. (2008). Psychosocial disability and work role function compared across the long-term course of bipolar I, bipolar II and unipolar major depressive disorders. *Journal of Affective Disorders, 73*, 123–131.

Karraker v. Rent-A-Center, Inc., 411 F.3d 831 (7th Cir. 2005).

Kashdan, T. B., Uswatte, G., Steger, M. F., & Julian, T. (2006). Fragile self-esteem and affective instability in posttraumatic stress disorder. *Behaviour Research and Therapy, 44*, 1609–1619.

Klein, D. F. (1974). Endogenomorphic depression. A conceptual and terminological revision. *Arch Gen Psychiatry, 31*, 447–454.

Knatz, H. F., Inwald, R. E., Brockwell, A. L., & Tran, L. N. (1992). IPI and MMPI predictions of counterproductive job behaviors by racial group. *Journal of Business and Psychology, 7*(2), 189–201. https://doi.org/10.1007/BF01013928

Kraemer, H. C., Kazdin, A. E., Offord, D. R., Kessler, R. C., Jensen, P. S., & Kupfer, D. J. (1997). Coming to terms with the terms of risk. *Archives of General Psychiatry, 54*(4), 337–343.

Kraepelin, E. (1921). Ueber entwurtzelung. *Zeitschrift für die Gesamte Neurologie und Psychiatrie, 63,* 1–8.

Kramer, M. D., Krueger, R. F., & Hicks, B. M. (2008). The role of internalizing and externalizing liability factors in accounting for gender differences in the prevalence of common psychopathological syndromes. *Psychological Medicine: A Journal of Research in Psychiatry and the Allied Sciences, 38*(1), 51–61.

Kring, A. M., & Germans, M. K. (2000). Anhedonia. In A. E. Kazdin (Ed.), *Encyclopedia of psychology, Vol. 1* (pp. 174–175). American Psychological Association.

Krocka v. City of Chicago, 203 F.3d 507, 515 (7th Cir. 2000).

Krueger, R. F., Chentsova-Dutton, Y. E., Markon, K. E., Goldberg, D., & Ormel, J. (2003). A cross-cultural study of the structure of comorbidity among common psychopathological syndromes in the general health care setting. *Journal of Abnormal Psychology, 112,* 437–447.

Krueger, R. F., Hicks, B. M., Patrick, C. J., Carlson, S. R., Iacono, W. G., & McGue, M. (2002). Etiologic connections among substance dependence, antisocial behavior and personality: Modeling the externalizing spectrum. *Journal of Abnormal Psychology, 111*(3), 411–424.

Krueger, R. F., & Markon, K. E. (2006). Reinterpreting comorbidity: A model-based approach to understanding and classifying psychopathology. *Annual Review of Clinical Psychology, 2,* 111–133.

Krueger, R. F., Markon, K. E., Patrick, C. J., & Iacono, W. G. (2005). Externalizing psychopathology in adulthood: A dimensional-spectrum conceptualization and its implications for DSM-V. *Journal of Abnormal Psychology, 114,* 537–550.

Kwapil, T. R., Miller, M. B., Zinser, M. C., Chapman, L. J., Chapman, J., & Eckblad, M. (2000). A longitudinal study of high scorers on the Hypomanic Personality Scale. *Journal of Abnormal Psychology, 109,* 222–226.

Kwaske, I. H., & Morris, S. B. (2015). The validity of individual psychological assessments for entry-level police and firefighter positions. *Personnel Assessment and Decisions, 1*(1), 3.

Laguna, L. (2020). [Review of the book *Assessing police and other public safety personnel using the MMPI-2-RF: A practical guide,* by David M. Corey and Yossef Ben-Porath]. *Journal of Criminal Justice Education, 31*(4), 623–626. https://doi.org/10.1080/10511253.2020.1790621

Lamberty, G. (2008). *Understanding somatization in the practice of clinical neuropsychology.* Oxford University Press.

Laub, J. H., & Sampson, R. J. (2001). Understanding desistance from crime. In M. Tonry (Ed.), *Crime and Justice* (pp. 1–69). University of Chicago Press.

Leonel v. American Airlines, Inc., 400 F.3d 702 (9th Cir. 2005).

Lindsey v. Costco Wholesale Corporation, No. 15-cv-03006-WHO (N.D. Cal. 2016).

Lowmaster, S. E., & Morey, L. C. (2012). Predicting law enforcement officer job performance with the Personality Assessment Inventory. *Journal of Police Science and Administration, 94*(3), 254–261.

Lynum, L. I., Wilberg, T., & Karterud, S. (2008). Self-esteem in patients with borderline and avoidant personality disorders. *Scandinavian Journal of Psychology, 49*(5), 469–477.

MacAndrew, C. (1965). The differentiation of male alcoholic out-patients from nonalcoholic psychiatric patients by means of the MMPI. *Quarterly Journal of the Studies on Alcohol, 26,* 238–246.

Marks, P. A., & Seeman, W. (1963). *The actuarial description of abnormal personality: An atlas for use with the MMPI.* The Williams & Wilkins Company.

Marsh, S. H. (1962). Validating the selection of deputy sheriffs. *Public Personnel Review, 23,* 41–44.

Marshall, G. N., Miles, J. N. V., & Stewart, S. H. (2010). Anxiety sensitivity and PTSD symptom severity are reciprocally related: Evidence from a longitudinal study of physical trauma survivors, *Journal of Abnormal Psychology, 119,* 143–150.

Mayer, M. J., & Corey, D. M. (2017). Current issues in psychological fitness-for-duty evaluations of law enforcement officers: Legal and practice implications. In C. L. Mitchell & E. H. Dorian (Eds.), *Police psychology and its growing impact on modern law enforcement* (pp. 93–117). IGI Global.

McGreal v. Ostrov, 368 F.3d 657 (7th Cir. 2004).

McKenna v. Fargo, 451 F.Supp. 1355 (D.N.J. 1978).

McLellan, A. T., Luborsky, L., O'Brien, C. P., & Woody, G. E. (1980). An improved diagnostic instrument for substance abuse patients: The Addiction Severity Index. *Journal of Nervous and Mental Diseases, 168,* 26–33.

Meehl, P. E. (1946). Profile analysis of the MMPI in differential diagnosis. *Journal of Applied Psychology, 30,* 517–524.

Meehl, P. E. (1954). *Clinical versus statistical prediction: A theoretical analysis and a review of the evidence.* University of Minnesota Press.

Meehl, P. E. (1956). Wanted—A good cookbook. *American Psychologist, 11,* 263–272.

Meehl, P. E. (1962). Schizotaxia, schizotypy, schizophrenia. *American Psychologist, 17*(12), 827–838.

Melton, G. B., Petrila, J., Poythress, N. G., & Slobogin, C. (2007). *Psychological evaluations for the courts: A handbook for mental health professionals and lawyers* (3rd ed.). Guilford Press.

Menton, W., Corey, D. M., & Ben-Porath, Y. S. (2022). Evidence for the comparability of local and remote administrations of the MMPI-2-RF in police candidate evaluations. *Psychological Assessment, 34*(1), 98–104.

Meyer, G. J., Finn, S. E., Eyde, L. D., Kay, G. G., Moreland, K. L., Dies, R. R., Eisman, E. J., Kubiszyn, T. W., & Reed, G. M. (2001). Psychological testing and psychological assessment: A review of evidence and issues. *American Psychologist, 56*(2), 128–165.

Miller, M. W., Fogler, J. M., Wolf, E. J., Kaloupek, D. G., & Keane, T. M. (2008). The internalizing and externalizing structure of psychiatric comorbidity in combat veterans. *Journal of Traumatic Stress, 21*(1), 58–65.

Miranda, R., Fontes, M., & Marroquin, B. (2008). Cognitive content-specificity in future expectancies: role of hopelessness and intolerance of uncertainty in depression and GAD symptoms. *Behaviour Research and Therapy, 46,* 1151–1159.

Mitchell, C. L. (2017). Preemployment psychological screening of police officer applicants: Basic considerations and recent advances. In C. L Mitchell & E. H. Dorian (Eds.), *Police psychology and its growing impact on modern law enforcement* (pp. 28–50). IGI Global.

Myers v. Hose, 50 F.3d 278 (4th Cir. 1995).

Nakamura, Y., & Bucklen, K. B. (2014). Recidivism, redemption, and desistance: Understanding continuity and change in criminal offending and implications for interventions. *Sociology Compass, 8*(4), 384–397.

National Conference of State Legislators. (2022). State Bill Tracking Database. https://www.ncsl.org/research/civil-and-criminal-justice/legislative-responses-for-policing.aspx

National Fire Protection Association. (2022). *NFPA Standard 1582: Standard on Comprehensive Occupational Medical Program for Fire Departments.*

National Institute on Alcohol Abuse and Alcoholism. (2023). *Drinking Levels Defined: Heavy Alcohol Use.* Retrieved February 20, 2024. https://www.niaaa.nih.gov/alcohol-health/overview-alcohol-consumption/moderate-binge-drinking#:~:text=NIAAA%20defines%20heavy%20drinking%20as,or%20more%20drinks%20per%20week

National Institute on Alcohol Abuse and Alcoholism. (2023). *Drinking Levels Defined: Binge Drinking.* Retrieved February 20, 2024. https://www.niaaa.nih.gov/alcohol-health/overview-alcohol-consumption/moderate-binge-drinking#:~:text=NIAAA%20defines%20heavy%20drinking%20as,or%20more%20drinks%20per%20week

Novaco, R. W. (1994). *Novaco Anger Scale and Provocation Inventory (NAS-PI).* Western Psychological Services.

Office of the Director of National Intelligence. (2017). National security adjudicative guidelines. Author. https://www.dni.gov/files/NCSC/documents/Regulations/SEAD-4-Adjudicative-Guidelines-U.pdf

Orth, U., Robins, R. W., Trzesniewski, K. H., Maes, J., & Schmitt, M. (2009). Low self-esteem is a risk factor for depressive symptoms from young adulthood to old age. *Journal of Abnormal Psychology, 118,* 472–478.

Otto, R. K., DeMier, R., & Boccaccini, M. (2014). *Forensic reports and testimony: A guide to effective communication for psychologists and psychiatrists.* John Wiley & Sons.

Otto, R. K., Edens, J. F., & Barcus, E. H. (2000). The use of psychological testing in child custody evaluations. *Family & Conciliation Courts Review, 38*(3), 312–340.

Pedersen, S. S., Denollet, J., Erdman, R. A. M., Serruys, P. W., & van Domburg, R. T. (2009). Co-occurrence of diabetes and hopelessness predicts adverse prognosis following percutaneous coronary intervention. *Journal of Behavioral Medicine, 32*(3), 294–301.

Pettus v. Cole, 57 Cal. Rptr. 2d 46 (Cal. App. 1996).

President's Commission on Law Enforcement and Administration of Justice. (1967). *Task force report: The police.* U.S. Government Printing Office.

President's Task Force on 21st Century Policing. (2015). *Final report of the President's Task Force on 21st Century Policing.* Office of Community Oriented Policing Services.

Rado, S. (1956). *Psychoanalysis of behavior; collected papers.* Grune & Stratton.

Reiss, S., & McNally, R. (1985). Expectancy model of fear. In S. Reiss & R. R. Bootzin (Eds.), *Theoretical issues in behavior therapy.* Academic Press.

Rice v. City of Oakland, No. 97-1897, 1999 U.S. Dist. LEXIS 8330 (N.D. Cal. May 24, 1999).

Roberts, M. D., & Johnson, M. (2001). *CPI police and public safety selection report: Technical manual.* Law Enforcement Psychological Services.

Roberts, R. M., Tarescavage, A. M., Ben-Porath, Y. S., & Roberts, M. D. (2019). Predicting postprobationary job performance of police officers using CPI and MMPI–2–RF test data obtained during preemployment psychological screening. *Journal of Personality Assessment, 101*(5), 544–555.

Rostow, C. D., & Davis, R. D. (2004). *A handbook for psychological fitness-for-duty evaluations in law enforcement*. Haworth Press.

Sager v. County of Yuba, 68 Cal. Rptr. 3d 1 (Cal. App. 2007).

Sangirardi v. Village of Stickney, 342 Ill. App. 3d 1 (Ill. App. 2003).

Sarchione, C. D., Cuttler, M. J., Muchinsky, P. M., & Nelson-Gray, R. O. (1998). Prediction of dysfunctional job behaviors among law enforcement officers. *Journal of Applied Psychology, 83*(6), 904–912. https://doi.org/10.1037/0021-9010.83.6.904

Saxe, S. J., & Reiser, M. (1976). A comparison of three police applicant groups using the MMPI. *Journal of Police Science & Administration, 4*(4), 419–425.

Scarpa, A., & Raine, A. (1997). Psychophysiology of anger and violent behavior. *Psychiatric Clinics of North America, 20*, 375–394.

Schinka, J. A., & LaLone, L. (1997). MMPI-2 norms: Comparisons with a census-matched subsample. *Psychological Assessment, 9*, 307–311.

Schmidt, H. O. (1945). Test profiles as a diagnostic aid: the Minnesota Multiphasic Inventory. *Journal of Applied Psychology, 29*, 115–131.

School Board of Nassau County v. Arline, 480 U.S. 273 (1987).

Sellbom, M. (2019). The MMPI-2-Restructured Form (MMPI-2-RF): Assessment of personality and psychopathology in the twenty-first century. *Annual Review of Clinical Psychology, 15*(1), 149–177.

Sellbom, M., Ben-Porath, Y. S., & Bagby, R. M. (2008). On the hierarchical structure of mood and anxiety disorders: Confirmatory evidence and elaboration of a model of temperament markers. *Journal of Abnormal Psychology, 117*, 576–590.

Sellbom, M., Fischler, G. L., & Ben-Porath, Y. S. (2007). Identifying MMPI-2 predictors of police officer integrity and misconduct. *Criminal Justice and Behavior, 34*(8), 985–1004.

Selzer, M. L. (1971). The Michigan Alcoholism Screening Test: The quest for a new diagnostic instrument. *American Journal of Psychiatry, 127*, 1653–1658.

Serafino, G. F. (2010). Fundamental issues in police psychological assessment. In P. A. Weiss (Ed.), *Personality assessment in police psychology: A 21st century perspective* (pp. 29–55). Charles C. Thomas.

Simons, R., Goodard, R., & Patton, W. (2002). Hand-scoring error rates in psychological testing. *Assessment, 9*, 292–300.

Skinner, B. F. (1983). *A matter of consequences*. Knopf.

Skinner, H. A., & Jackson, D. N. (1978). A model of psychopathology based on an integration of MMPI actuarial systems. *Journal of Consulting and Clinical Psychology, 46*, 231–238.

Slater v. Department of Homeland Security, 2008 MSPB 73, Docket No. SF-0752-06-0805-I-2.

Spielberger, C. D., Jacobs, G., Russell, S., & Crane, R. S. (1983). Assessment of anger: The state-trait anger scale. *Advances in Personality Assessment, 2*, 161–189.

Spilberg, S. W., & Corey, D. M. (2022). Peace officer psychological screening manual. California Commission on Peace Officer Standards and Training (POST). https://post.ca.gov/peace-officer-psychological-screening-manual

Stein, L. A. R., Graham, J. R., Ben Porath, Y. S., & McNulty, J. L. (1999). Using the MMPI-2 to detect substance abuse in an outpatient mental health setting. *Psychological Assessment, 11*, 94–100.

Stern, S. L., Dhanda, R., & Hazuda, H. P. (2009). Helplessness predicts the development of hypertension in older Mexican and European Americans. *Journal of Psychosomatic Research, 67,* 333–337.

Stone, A. V. (2000). *Fitness for duty: Principles, methods and legal issues.* CRC Press.

Sundberg, N. D. (1961). The practice of psychological testing in clinical services in the United States. *American Psychologist, 16*(2), 79–83.

Swanson, S. C, Templer, D. I., Thomas-Dobson, S., Cannon, W. G., Streiner, D. L., Reynolds, R. M., & Miller, H. R. (1995). Development of a three-scale MMPI: The MMPI-TRI. *Journal of Clinical Psychology, 51*(3), 361–374.

Tackett, J. L., Herzhoff, K., Kushner, S. C., & Rule, N. (2016). Thin slices of child personality: Perceptual, situational, and behavioral contributions. *Journal of Personality and Social Psychology, 110*(1), 150.

Tarescavage, A. M., Alosco, M. L., Ben-Porath, Y. S., Wood, A., & Luna-Jones, L. (2014). MMPI-2-RF scores generated from the MMPI-2 and MMPI-2-RF test booklets: Comparability in a sample of criminal defendants. *Assessment, 22*(2), 188–197.

Tarescavage, A. M., Brewster, J. A., Corey, D. M., & Ben-Porath, Y. S. (2015). Use of pre-hire MMPI-2-RF police candidate scores to predict supervisor ratings of post-hire performance. *Assessment, 22*(4), 411–428.

Tarescavage, A. M., Corey, D. M., & Ben-Porath, Y. S. (2015). Minnesota Multiphasic Personality Inventory-2-Restructured Form (MMPI-2-RF) predictors of police officer problem behavior. *Assessment, 22*(1), 116–132.

Tarescavage, A. M., Corey, D. M., & Ben-Porath, Y. S. (2016). A prorating method for estimating MMPI-2-RF Scores from MMPI responses: Examination of score fidelity and illustration of empirical utility in the PERSEREC Police Integrity Study sample. *Assessment, 23,* 173–190.

Tarescavage, A. M., Corey, D. M., Gupton, H. M., & Ben-Porath, Y. S. (2015). Criterion validity and practical utility of the Minnesota Multiphasic Personality Inventory-2-Restructured Form (MMPI-2-RF) in assessments of police officer candidates. *Journal of Personality Assessment, 97*(4), 382–394.

Tarescavage, A. M., Fischler, G., Cappo, B., Hill, D., Corey, D. M., & Ben-Porath, Y. S. (2015). Minnesota Multiphasic Personality Inventory-2-Restructured Form (MMPI-2-RF) predictors of police officer problem behavior and collateral self-report test scores. *Psychological Assessment, 27*(1), 125–137.

Tatar, M., & Morgenbesser, L. I. (1993). *Psychological screening program for correction officer applicants.* New York State Department of Correctional Services. https://www.ncjrs.gov/pdffiles1/Digitization/149202NCJRS.pdf

Tellegen, A. (1982). *Brief manual of the Multidimensional Personality Questionnaire.* Unpublished manuscript. University of Minnesota.

Tellegen, A. (1985). Structures of mood and personality and their relevance to assessing anxiety, with an emphasis on self-report. In A. H. Tuma & J. D. Maser (Eds.) *Anxiety and the anxiety disorders* (pp. 681–706). Lawrence Erlbaum Associates.

Tellegen, A., & Ben-Porath, Y. S. (1992). The new uniform T-scores for the MMPI-2: Rationale, derivation, and appraisal. *Psychological Assessment, 4,* 145–155.

Tellegen, A., & Ben-Porath, Y. S. (2008/2011). *The Minnesota Multiphasic Personality Inventory -2 Restructured Form: Technical manual.* University of Minnesota Press.

Tellegen, A., Ben-Porath, Y. S., McNulty, J. L., Arbisi, P. A., Graham, J. R., & Kaemmer, B. (2003). *The MMPI-2 Restructured Clinical Scales: Development, validation, and interpretation.* University of Minnesota Press.

Tellegen, A., Sellbom, M., Kamp, J., & Handel, R. W. (2023). *Multidimensional Personality Questionnaire Manual for administration, scoring, and interpretation.* University of Minnesota Press.

Tellegen, A., & Waller, N. G. (2008). Exploring personality through test construction: Development of the Multidimensional Personality Questionnaire. In G. J. Boyle, G. Matthews, & D. H. Saklofske (Eds.), *The SAGE handbook of personality theory and assessment: Personality measurement and testing* (Vol. 2, pp. 261–292). Sage Publications Ltd.

Thomas v. Johnson, 295 F. Supp. 1025 (D.D.C. 1968).

Trimble, M. (2004). *Somatoform disorders: A medicolegal guide.* Cambridge University Press.

Trompetter, P. S. (2019). A history of police psychology. In *Police science: Breakthroughs in research and practice* (pp. 377–402). IGI Global.

Vaidyanathan, U., Patrick, C., & Cuthbert, B. (2009). Linking dimensional models of internalizing psychopathology to neurobiological systems: Affect-modulated startle as an indicator of fear and distress disorders and affiliated traits. *Psychological Bulletin, 135,* 909–942.

Valtonen, H. M., Suominen, K., Haukka, J., Mantere, O., Arvilommi, P., Leppämäki, S., & Isometsä, E. (2009). Hopelessness across phases of bipolar I or II disorder: A prosepective study. *Journal of Affective Disorders, 115*(1–2), 11–17.

Valtonen, H. M., Suominen, K., Haukka, J., Mantere, O., Leppämäki, S., Arvilommi, P., & Isometsä, E. (2008). Differences in incidence of suicide attempts during phases of bipolar I and II disorders. *Bipolar Disorders, 10,* 588–596.

van der Heijden, P. T., Egger, J. I. M., & Derksen, J. J. L. (2010). Comparability of scores on the MMPI–2–RF scales generated with the MMPI–2 and MMPI–2–RF booklets. *Journal of Personality Assessment, 92*(3), 254–259.

Van Orden, K. A., Witte, T. K., Cukrowicz, K. C., Braithwaite, S. R., Selby, E. A., & Joiner, T. E., Jr. (2010). The interpersonal theory of suicide. *Psychological Review, 117,* 575–600. http://dx.doi.org/10.1037/a0018697

Vieta, E., Langosch, J. M., Figueira, M. L., Souery, D., Blasco-Colmenares, E., Medina, E., Moreno-Manzanaro, M., Gonzalez, M. A., & Bellivier, F. (2013). Clinical management and burden of bipolar disorder: Results from a multinational longitudinal study (WAVE-bd). *International Journal of Neuropsychopharmacology, 16*(8), 1719–1732. https://doi.org/10.1017/S1461145713000278

Walfish, S. (2010). Reducing MMPI-defensiveness in professionals presenting for evaluation. *Journal of Addictive Diseases, 30*(1), 75–80.

Watson v. City of Miami Beach, 177 F.3d 932 (11th Cir. 1999).

Watson, D., & Clark, L. A. (1984). Negative affectivity: The disposition to experience aversive emotional states. *Psychological Bulletin, 96,* 465–490.

Watson, L. C., Quilty, L. C., & Bagby, R. M. (2010). Differentiating bipolar disorder from major depressive disorder using the mmpi-2-rf: a receiver operating characteristics (roc) analysis. *Journal of Psychopathology and Behavioral Assessment, 33,* 368–374.

Weathers, F. W., Blake, D. D., Schnurr, P. P., Kaloupek, D. G., Marx, B. P., & Keane, T. M. (2013). *The Clinician-Administered PTSD Scale for DSM-5 (CAPS-5).* National Center for PTSD.

Webb, J. T., Levitt, E. E., & Rojdev, R. (1993). *After three years: A comparison of the clinical use of the MMPI and MMPI-2* [Paper presentation]. 53rd Annual Meeting of the Society for Personality Assessment, San Francisco, CA.

Weed, N. C., Butcher, J. N., McKenna, T., & Ben-Porath, Y. S. (1992). New measures for assessing alcohol and drug abuse with the MMPI-2: The APS and AAS. *Journal of Personality Assessment, 58*, 389–404.

Weiner, J. A. (1997). *POST Public Safety Dispatcher Psychological Assessment Resource Document*. California Commission on Peace Officer Standards and Training.

Weiss, P. A., & Weiss, W. U. (2010). Using the MMPI-2 in police psychological assessment. In P. A. Weiss (Ed.), *Personality assessment in police psychology* (pp. 59–61). Charles C. Thomas.

Welsh, G. S., & Dahlstrom, W. G. (Eds.). (1956). *Basic readings on the MMPI in psychology and medicine*. University of Minnesota Press.

White v. County of Los Angeles, 225 Cal. App. 4th 690 (Cal. App. 2014).

Whitman, M. R., Corey, D. M., & Ben-Porath, Y. S. (2022). Does prior law enforcement experience affect scores on preemployment psychological testing? An investigation using the MMPI-3. *Psychological Services, 20*(4), 889–898. https://doi.org/10.1037/ser0000679

Whitman, M. R., Corey, D. M., & Ben-Porath, Y. S. (2023). Associations between MMPI-3 and psychosocial history findings obtained in preemployment evaluations of public safety candidates. *Assessment, 30*(7), 2128–2145. https://doi.org/10.1177/10731911221138931

Whitman, M. R., Elias, L. S., Cappo, B. M., & Ben-Porath, Y. S. (2021). Criterion validity of MMPI-3 scores in preemployment evaluations of public safety candidates. *Psychological Assessment, 33*(12), 1169–1180. https://doi.org/10.1037/pas0001042

Widiger, T. A., & Costa, P. T. (2002). Five factor model personality disorder research. In P. T. Costa & T. A. Widiger (Eds.), *Personality disorders and the five factor model of personality* (2nd ed., pp. 59–87). American Psychological Association.

Wiener, D. N., & Harmon, L. R. (1946). *Subtle and obvious keys for the MMPI: Their development*. Minneapolis VA Advisement Bulletin, No. 16.

Wiggins, J. S. (1966). Substantive dimensions of self-report in the MMPI item pool. *Psychological Monographs, 80*(22), 1–42.

Williams, C. B., Galanter, M., Dermatis, H., & Schwartz, V. (2008). The importance of hopelessness among university students seeking psychiatric counseling. *Psychiatric Quarterly, 79*(4), 311–319.

Wilson, C. M., Desmarais, S. L., Nicholls, T. L., Hart, S. D., & Brink, J. (2013). Predictive validity of dynamic factors: Assessing violence risk in forensic psychiatric inpatients. *Law and Human Behavior, 37*(6), 377–388.

Wingate, L., Joiner, T., Walker, R., Rudd, M. D., & Jobes, D. (2004). Empirically informed approaches to topics in suicide risk assessment. *Behavioral Sciences & the Law, 22*, 1–15.

Wisbey v. City of Lincoln, #4:08-CV-3093, 2009 U.S. Dist. Lexis 30819, 21 AD Cases (BNA) 1377 (D. Neb.).

Woodhams, J., & Toye, K. (2007). An empirical test of the assumptions of case linkage and offender profiling with serial commercial robberies. *Psychology, Public Policy, and Law, 13*(1), 59–85.

Wu, C. (2009). Factor analysis of the general self-efficacy scale and its relationship with individualism/collectivism among twenty-five countries: Application of multilevel confirmatory factor analysis. *Personality and Individual Differences, 46*, 699–703.

Index

Aberrant Experiences (RC8), 43, 44, 86, 90, 100, 128, 134; described, 48
Absorption Scale, 48
accountability, personal, 214, 218
Acting-Out, 43
Activation (ACT), 54, 97, 100, 239, 255, 256, 474
acute stress disorder, 403, 423, 425, 443, 456
ADA. *See* Americans With Disabilities Act
ADA Amendments Act (ADAAA) (2008), 63, 365, 366
adaptability, 8, 10, 76, 288, 490n8
Addiction Acknowledgment Scale (AAS), 54
Addiction Severity Index (ASI), 54
adjustment disorders, 269, 460
Adjustment Validity (K) scale, 39, 88, 121, 122, 175, 355; described, 36; scores, 37, 40, 87, 88–89, 113, 196, 197, 268, 289, 318, 354, 359, 460; using, 83
Age Discrimination in Employment Act (1967), 491n5
agency, 52, 69, 73, 176
aggression, 46, 49, 235
Aggression (AGG), 54, 97, 98, 134, 197, 215, 216, 233, 235, 236, 255, 256
Aggressiveness (AGGR), 56–57, 97, 98, 100, 128

alcohol abuse, 54, 91, 215, 305, 390, 402, 460; history of, 371; impact of, 304; treatment for, 214
Aldrup v. Caldera (2001), 31
American Bar Association, 1
American Board of Police & Public Safety Psychology (ABPPSP), 13
American Board of Professional Psychology (ABPP), 13
American Educational Research Association, 66
American Psychiatric Association, 486
American Psychological Association (APA), 13, 42, 66, 342
American Psychological Association (APA) Ethics Code, 13
Americans With Disabilities Act (ADA), 3, 13, 84, 342, 343, 345, 350, 364, 490n2, 490n3, 493n1; business necessity standard of, 344; described, 62–64; medical examinations under, 491n7
AMPD. *See* DSM-5 Alternative Model of Personality Disorders
Anger Proneness (ANP), 53, 100, 192, 421
anhedonia, 46, 404
Annotation (ANP), 135–36
ANP. *See* Anger Proneness

511

Antagonism, 57, 97
Antisocial Behavior (RC4), 43, 44, 49, 53, 54, 86, 96, 97, 100, 196, 197, 215, 216, 304; described, 46–47
antisocial personality disorder (ASPD), 46, 47, 53
anxiety, 48, 57, 94, 194, 195, 234, 235, 288, 421, 440, 443; symptoms of, 442
anxiety disorder, 51, 53
Anxiety-Related (ARX), 52, 53, 134, 192, 194, 361, 421, 425, 440
APA. *See* American Psychological Association
Appelbaum, K. L., 321
Arline factors, 387
ARX. *See* Anxiety-Related
ASPD. *See* antisocial personality disorder
assertiveness, 10, 91, 94, 318
Assertiveness/Persuasiveness, 195
Assertiveness Problems, 132, 197, 236, 287, 318
assessments: competence, 4; conducting, 2; emotional, 71–72; findings, 370–72, 386–88, 389–90, 403–4, 423–25, 442–43, 457–60, 473; information, 364; interviews, 76; issues, 13, 68, 154, 156–57, 178, 196, 219, 238, 257, 272, 289, 304–5, 369, 388, 403, 423, 457, 472; medical, 349, 350; police, 13; preemployment, 58, 86; psychological, 61, 68–69, 71, 74, 76, 153, 155, 348, 349; public safety, 13, 99, 155; testing and, 12–13
Attention to Safety, 10, 388, 487
avoidance, 10, 421, 423, 425, 456; harm, 49; social, 55; symptoms, 440
avoidant personality disorder, 52
AXY. *See* Anxiety-Related
Azen, S. P., 80

background findings, 176, 194–95, 215–16, 217, 236, 270, 287–88, 304; assessing, 173, 192–93, 197–98, 234
background information, 152, 153, 171, 319; collateral, 74–75, 155, 171

background investigations, 3, 75, 174, 216, 318, 491–92n9; discrepancies in, 175; findings from, 173; reliability of, 256
Beck Depression Inventory-II (BDI-II), 354
behavior, 90, 96, 175–76, 216, 235, 270, 349, 366; acting-out, 46–47, 440; aggressive, 46, 233, 255; antisocial, 46–47, 50; assertive, 289; biased, 75; counterproductive, 10, 69, 81–82, 85, 154, 175, 218, 323, 324, 364; disconstrained, 322; domains of, 9; domineering, 55, 289; dramatic, 46; immoral, 218; impulsive, 46, 443; inflexible, 177; irresponsible, 323; negative, 81; observing, 235; off-duty, 369; overcontrolled, 97; positive, 11; predicting, 217; problem, 7, 345, 386; prosocial, 216; questionable, 345; regulating, 76; risk taking, 10; risky, 10, 323; rule-observing, 197; uncontrolled, 44; violent, 54; work, 323, 346
behavioral conditions, 364; identifying, 215–16
Behavioral Dysfunction, 58, 89, 91, 92, 94–95, 172, 192, 218, 233, 239, 255, 256, 368, 425, 440; scales of, 215, 216
Behavioral/Externalizing Dysfunction (BXD), 37, 44, 90, 92, 97, 100, 129, 196, 197, 215, 216, 233, 304, 361, 368, 440
Behavioral Inhibition System, 47
Behavior Restricting Fears (BRF), 53, 94, 100, 196
Ben-Porath, Yossef S., 18, 21, 24, 41, 43, 44, 46, 48, 57, 80, 172, 256, 359, 440; externalizing scales and, 97; fitness evaluations and, 356; integrity violations and, 95–96; MMPI-2-RF scores and, 90–91, 97–98; MMPI-2-RF/CA-POST and, 98; MMPI-3 scores and, 31, 102; predictive validity and, 91–92, 93; research reviewed by, 36; Specific Problem Scales and, 49, 50; Substantive Scales and, 134; test manual and, 25
Beutler, L. E., 81, 82, 84
Bhar, S. S., 52

bias, 75, 81, 171; racial/ethnic, 69; response, 36, 365
Bias Assessment Framework (CA-POST), 75
biodata, 97, 100
bipolar disorder, 49, 367, 472, 473; diagnostic criteria for, 474; treatment for, 486–87
Blum, R. H., 80–81
Blumstein, A., 217
Boes, J. O., 82, 84, 85, 95, 96
borderline personality disorder, 42, 52, 386
Brewster, J., 70, 90–91
BRF. *See* Behavior Restricting Fears
Brownfield v. City of Yakima (2010), 341, 343, 387, 422
Brown v. Sandy City Appeal Board (2014), 3, 12, 345
business necessity standard, 343, 344, 491n4
Buss, A. H., 54
Buss Perry Aggression Questionnaire, 54
Butcher, J. N., 21, 354
Butler v. Thornburgh (1990), 387
BXD. *See* Behavioral/Externalizing Dysfunction

California Code of Regulations, 171
California Commission on Peace Officer Standards and Training (CA-POST), 3, 6–7, 75, 101, 345–46; dimensions of, 11–12; MMPI-2-RF and, 98; Psychological Screening Dimensions of, 9, 71, 90, 131, 491n8; regulations, 238, 346
California Court of Appeal, *Sager* and, 12, 345
California Psychological Inventory (CPI), 42, 93, 97, 99, 131; Involuntary Departure, 100; scales, 94, 103; scores, 94, 100
candidate comparison groups, 105, 106–8, 110–11, 113, 121, 130; age bands and means/standard deviations of, 110 (table); community origin of, 108 (table); education levels, 111 (table); geographic distribution of, 107 (table); means/standard deviations for, 112–13 (table); MMPI-3 Externalizing and Interpersonal Scales Means/Standard Deviations for, 126 (fig.); MMPI-3 Higher-Order (H-O) and Restructured Clinical (RC) Scales Means/Standard Deviations for, 124 (fig.); MMPI-3 PSY-5 Scales Means/Standard Deviations for, 127 (table); MMPI-3 Somatic/Cognitive and Internalizing Scales Means/Standard Deviations for, 125 (fig.); MMPI-3 Validity Scales Means/Standard Deviations for, 123 (fig.); percent scoring at/above designated cutoffs for, 114 (table), 121 (table); race/ethnicity of, 109 (table)
Cannot Say (CNS), 34, 37, 38, 157
Cappo, B., 93, 101–2
cardiovascular disease, 52, 54
case studies, 62, 154–56, 342, 347; pre-employment, 367–69
Castaneda, L. W., 108, 110
CCIR. *See* Correctional Candidate Interpretive Report
Chapman, L. J., 54
Chibnall, J. T., 71, 88, 89, 121, 196, 197, 355, 359
civil litigation, 86, 493n1
Civil Rights Act (1964), 62, 64–65, 83, 152
Civil Rights Act (1991), 62, 65, 107
civil service commission, 320, 321
Clinical Findings, 128, 136, 146 (fig.), 156, 166 (fig.), 187 (fig.), 206 (fig.), 228 (fig.), 239, 248 (fig.), 281 (fig.), 287, 298 (fig.), 314 (fig.), 333 (fig.); described, 129
Clinical Scale 0, 49
Clinical Scale 1, 45, 81
Clinical Scale 2, 45–46, 80, 81, 82, 83
Clinical Scale 3, 45, 51, 82
Clinical Scale 4, 81, 82, 83
Clinical Scale 6, 81, 82
Clinical Scale 7, 43, 47, 81, 82, 83
Clinical Scale 8, 43, 49, 51, 80, 83
Clinical Scale 9, 80, 82, 83

Clinical Scales, 7, 45, 49, 50, 80, 84, 87, 354; improving, 21, 22; interpretation of, 23; original, 17, 18, 20–21, 24, 43; prehire, 86; scores, 82, 83; validity of, 23

Clinician-Administered PTSD Scale for DSM-5 (CAPS-5), 421

CMP. *See* Compulsivity

CNS. *See* Cannot Say

Cody v. Cigna Healthcare of St. Louis (1998), 343

Coffman v. Indianapolis Fire Department (2009), 341

Cognitive Complaints (COG), 50, 51, 92, 100, 287

cognitive conditions, 50, 51, 323, 364

cognitive distortions, identifying/clarifying/modifying, 442

cognitive process therapy, 442

Cohen's *q*, 102

Colon v. City of Newark (2006), 341

Combined Response Inconsistency (CRIN) scale, 34, 38, 113, 157, 177, 196, 257, 272, 372, 474; scores, 39, 390

Comparison Group Findings, 111, 113, 121–22, 128, 135, 136, 146 (fig.), 156, 166 (fig.), 187 (fig.), 193, 194, 197, 206 (fig.), 214, 228 (fig.), 233, 239, 248–49 (fig.), 255, 281–82 (fig.), 287, 298 (fig.), 304, 314 (fig.), 318, 324, 333–34 (fig.); described, 129–30

Compulsivity (CMP), 52, 129, 192, 233, 235, 236, 237, 361

conditional offer of employment (COE), 63

Conduct Disorder, 43

confounds, 121; consideration of, 37–40; extra-test, 39

Conscientiousness, 8, 132, 195, 215, 287

Constraint, 42, 56

Content Scales, 21

Conte v. Horcher (1977), 341

Corey, David M., 64, 70, 71, 73, 74, 103, 153, 174, 218, 237, 238, 269, 322, 359, 368, 472; background information and, 171; on diagnostic reliability, 422; externalizing scales and, 97; fitness evaluations and, 356; integrity violations and, 95–96; interviews and, 234–35; MMPI-2-RF scores and, 90–91; MMPI-2-RF/CA-POST and, 98; MMPI-3 scores and, 102; predictive validity and, 91–92, 93; psychological assessments and, 155

Correctional Candidate Comparison Group, 108, 289, 304

Correctional Candidate Interpretive Report (CCIR), 65, 105, 131, 219, 233–34, 236, 289, 304

correctional officers/jailers, 9, 367, 489n2; essential job functions of, 5 (table); screening, 424

CPI. *See* California Psychological Inventory

criminal activity, 172, 217, 369

criminal history, 84; juvenile, 197

CRIN scale. *See* Combined Response Inconsistency scale

Cripe v. City of San Jose (2001), 343

criterion standards, 61, 101, 121, 237, 272, 342

Critical Follow-up Items, 131, 135, 192, 255

Critical Responses, 131, 135; described, 134

current work impairment, assessing, 386–87, 390, 402, 422, 440–41, 456, 460

cutoffs, 38, 65, 68, 70, 82, 85, 86, 87, 92, 95, 96, 101, 102, 111, 129, 130, 131, 157, 172, 191; alternative, 134, 135; substantive scale, 113, 359; T score, 85, 111, 113, 130 (table), 133 (table), 134, 361; underreported, 354; validity scale, 113, 359

cynicism, 54–55, 89

Cynicism (CYN), 54, 86, 121, 122, 197, 257, 440, 443, 474

Cynicism (RC 3), 27, 44, 53, 54, 86, 97

data: assessment, 155, 156, 271, 321, 322, 364–67; background, 75; collateral, 74, 171, 257, 341, 348–50; collecting, 25, 26, 27, 364; divergent, 319; integration, 155, 157, 170–78, 196–97, 214–19, 233–37, 257, 268–72, 352, 372, 386–88,

390, 402, 421–23, 422, 440–41, 443, 456–57, 460, 474, 486–87; interpreting, 364; psychosocial history, 26; self-report, 75; validation, 26, 172
DCIR. *See* Dispatcher Candidate Interpretive Report
deception, inference of, 177–78
Decision-Making, 10, 93, 132, 157, 197, 236, 287, 318, 324, 388, 487
Demoralization (RCd), 43, 44, 48, 49, 52, 361, 421; described, 45; markers, 23
Department of Veterans Affairs (VA), 270
dependability, 10, 98, 215, 490n8
Dependability Problems, 132, 215, 287
depression, 48, 51, 52, 94, 269, 367, 371; low self-esteem and, 52
Depression, 18, 46
Detachment, 57
Detailed Assessment of Posttraumatic Stress (DAPS), 421
Detrick, P., 71, 83, 87, 88, 89, 90, 94, 121, 196, 197, 355, 359
Diagnostic and Statistical Manual for Mental Disorders (DSM), 344
Diagnostic and Treatment Considerations, 59
Diagnostic Considerations, 58, 128, 146 (fig.), 166 (fig.), 187 (fig.), 206 (fig.), 228 (fig.), 248 (fig.), 298 (fig.), 314 (fig.), 333 (fig.), 368, 381 (fig.), 399 (fig.), 452 (fig.), 469 (fig.), 483 (fig.); described, 129
Diagnostic Findings, 281 (fig.), 413 (fig.), 434 (fig.)
diagnostic tests, 18, 345
disability, 4, 36, 491n4; compensation, 268; defining, 366; discrimination and, 64; mental health, 271; perceived, 364; ratings, 269, 270; service-connected, 268, 269
Disaffiliativeness (DSF), 55, 100, 197, 287
DISC. *See* Disconstraint
disciplinary actions, 95, 96, 350, 369, 389, 473
Disconstraint (DISC), 57, 100, 129, 197, 215, 216, 304

Disconstraint (DISC-r), 92, 94, 97, 98, 196
DISC-r. *See* Disconstraint
discrimination: disability and, 64; evidence of, 65; hiring, 64; intentional, 64
Disinhibition, 57, 97
Dispatcher Candidate Comparison Group, 108, 122, 272, 287
Dispatcher Candidate Interpretive Report (DCIR), 65, 105, 131, 272, 287
dispatchers, 9, 367; essential job functions of, 5 (table); types of, 489n3
disqualification, 177–78, 195, 271, 320; criteria for, 70; medical, 347; psychological, 74
distress, 43, 45, 77; acute, 403, 443, 456; emotional, 195, 289, 423; sustained, 403
Dohrenwend, B. P., 45
Dominance (DOM), 29, 55, 121, 128, 129, 197, 287, 305, 318, 319
drug abuse, 54, 91, 171, 215, 367, 390, 424, 460, 487; frequency of, 217; juvenile, 304; problems with, 234
Drug Abuse Screening Test (DAST), 54
drunk driving, 388, 389
DSF. *See* Disaffiliativeness
DSM-5 Alternative Model of Personality Disorders (AMPD), 42, 57, 346
DSM-5 Personality Disorder Workgroup, 57
DSM-5-TR, 456, 486
DSM-III-R, 56
DSM-III-R Axis II, 55
Duran v. City of Douglas (1990), 1
dysfunction, 52, 53; behavioral, 43, 44, 218, 460; cognitive, 460; emotional, 460; psychological, 39, 47–48, 349; somatic, 460; thought, 460
Dysfunctional Negative Emotions (RC7), 43, 44, 50, 52, 57, 70, 94, 192, 194, 196, 233, 236, 361; described, 47–48

Eating Concerns (EAT), 38, 51, 129, 192
Eckblad, M., 54
Eckhardt, C. I., 53

EEOC. *See* Equal Employment Opportunity Commission
EEOC v. Amego, Inc. (1997), 347
EID. *See* Emotional/Internalizing Dysfunction
Elias, L. S., 101–2
Emotional, 43, 349
emotional conditions, 3, 194, 347, 364, 422
Emotional Control, 91, 93, 132, 215, 236, 270, 271, 287, 288, 304, 318
Emotional Dysfunction, 58, 59, 192, 233, 368, 425; underreporting, 359
emotional dysregulation, 372, 387
emotional functioning, 76, 176
emotional impairment, 73, 344
Emotional/Internalizing Dysfunction (EID), 44, 90, 113, 129, 192, 194, 196, 233, 287, 361, 368, 369, 386, 425, 440
Emotional Regulation, 10, 76, 195, 388, 423, 487
employment records, 177, 370, 389, 403, 423–24, 457, 473
Endnotes, 128, 149, 168, 190, 209, 231, 252, 266, 284, 301, 316, 337, 383, 400, 415, 436, 453, 470, 474, 484; annotation and, 136, 215; described, 136
Endogenomorphic Depression, 46
Equal Employment Opportunity Commission (EEOC), 13, 62, 343, 350, 493n1
Ethical Principles for Psychologists and Code of Conduct (EPPCC), 66
ethics, 10, 13, 67, 94, 98, 176, 177, 320, 321, 342
ethnicity, 4, 103, 107–8
evaluations: follow-up, 441–43, 456–57; initial, 441; medical/psychological, 63, 350. *See also* fitness evaluations; fitness-for-duty Evaluations; preemployment evaluations; psychological evaluations
externalizing disorders, 42
externalizing dysfunction, scores, 94
Externalizing Scales, 27, 53–55, 97, 142 (fig.), 162 (fig.), 183 (fig.), 202 (fig.), 224 (fig.), 244 (fig.), 262 (fig.), 277 (fig.), 294 (fig.), 310 (fig.), 329 (fig.), 377 (fig.), 395 (fig.), 409 (fig.), 430 (fig.), 448 (fig.), 465 (fig.), 479 (fig.)
Externalizing Specific Problems Scales, 27, 53, 54, 86, 97
extra-test factors, 37, 39
Extraversion, 56
Eysenck Personality Questionnaire, 42

factor-analytic studies, 42, 43
False, 35, 39, 133
Family Medical Leave Act, 403, 442
Family Problems (FML), 27, 53, 97, 100, 287
FBS scale. *See* Symptom Validity scale
FCIR. *See* Firefighter Candidate Interpretive Report
fear, 50, 53, 72, 171, 233, 348, 422, 424, 425, 458; behavior-restricting, 322
feedback, 132, 215, 235, 354
Feedback Acceptance Problems, 132, 215
FFDEs. *See* fitness-for-duty evaluations
Field Performance Dimensions, 91, 92
Firefighter Candidate Comparison Group, 318, 319
Firefighter Candidate Interpretive Report (FCIR), 65, 105, 131, 156, 305, 318
firefighters/medics, 9, 367; essential job functions of, 5 (table); types of, 489n1
Fischler, G. L., 70, 93, 100, 103, 256
fitness: criterion, 342; determination of, 364, 367–68, 456; judgments about, 354, 387; psychological, 348–49, 353; restoring, 352; standards, 344, 348; sustainability for, 366–67, 441, 456–57, 486
fitness evaluations, 347, 350–51, 356, 363, 364, 366, 389, 403, 422, 425, 441, 442, 457, 458, 472, 473, 487; findings/opinions from, 341; initial, 423
fitness for duty, 458; assessing, 348–50, 351, 352, 361, 367; evaluating, 4; light/modified, 351; psychological, 347; sustainability of, 402
Fitness-for-Duty Evaluation (FFDE) Guidelines, 350

fitness-for-duty evaluations (FFDEs), 4, 13, 14, 16, 40, 59, 322, 341, 349, 353, 387, 456, 457, 472; basis for, 343; conducting, 342, 363–64; data integration, 422; descriptive statistics, 357–58 (table); evaluation in, 369; examining, 355–56; findings on, 356, 359, 361; integrative model for, 364–65; legal foundations for, 343–47; prophylactic, 343; PSCIRs in, 368–69; psychological, 11–12, 343; reporting findings/opinions of, 350–52; research for, 354–56; substantive scale evaluation rates, 362–63 (table); validity scale elevation rates, 360–61 (table)
fixed responding, 32, 33
flexibility, 10, 77, 288
Flora v. Hamilton (1978), 371
Flynn v. Sandahl (1995), 341
FML. *See* Family Problems
Forbey, J. D., 25
four-fifths rule, 64, 152
Fp scale. *See* Infrequent Psychopathology Responses scale
Frank, J. D., 45
Freud, Sigmund, 47
F scale. *See* Infrequent Responses scale
Fs scale. *See* Infrequent Somatic Responses scale

Gaspar, J. P., 218
gender, 4; analysis by, 88; differences, 42; norms, 491n6
General Performance Dimensions, 91–92
Genetic Information Nondiscrimination Act of 2008 (GINA), 3, 13, 62, 351; described, 65–66
Germans, M. K., 46
GINA. *See* Genetic Information Nondiscrimination Act of 2008
Glassmire, D. M., 51
Gough, H. G., 42
Gray, J. A., 47
Grisso, P., 321, 366

Grossman, L. S., 355
Gupton, H. M., 93

Happy/Unhappy, 45
Hargrave, G. E., 82
Harkness, A. R., 22, 55, 56
harm, 343, 345, 347, 387, 402, 460, 486; avoiding, 49; causing, 341; risk of, 459
Harmon, L. R., 19
Harris, R., 19
Harris–Lingoes Lassitude/Malaise (Hy3) scale, 51
Hathaway, S. R., 18, 19, 22, 31; MMPI and, 17; updating and, 20
health conditions, 40, 46, 343, 350
heart attacks, 423, 424
Heilbrun, K., 364
Helplessness/Hopelessness (HLP), 51–52, 100, 134, 196
Hierarchical Taxonomy of Psychopathology (HiTOP), 42
Higher-Order (H-O) Scales, 24, 28, 41, 42–44, 49, 140 (fig.), 160 (fig.), 181 (fig.), 200 (fig.), 222 (fig.), 233, 239, 242 (fig.), 260 (fig.), 275 (fig.), 292 (fig.), 304, 305, 308 (fig.), 318, 327 (fig.), 375 (fig.), 393 (fig.), 407 (fig.), 428 (fig.), 440, 446 (fig.), 463 (fig.), 477 (fig.)
Hippocrates, 45
hiring agency, 16, 171, 272, 322, 490n9
hiring authority, 237–38, 490n9
history: juvenile, 234; legal, 173; medical, 66, 173, 351; personal, 12, 74, 99, 102, 153, 155, 171–72, 173, 174, 175, 177, 193, 268, 271, 304, 322; psychological, 102, 173; psychosocial, 102; self-reported, 216; work, 136–37, 177
HLP. *See* Helplessness/Hopelessness
Hoelzle, J. B., 43–44
Hogarth v. Thornburgh (1993), 387
Holland, T. R., 81
homicidal intent/ideation, 458
Honolulu Police Department, 93
H-O Scales. *See* Higher-Order Scales
Hough, L., 9

Hunter, J. E., 85, 86
Hypochondriasis, 18
Hypomania, 18, 49, 474
Hypomanic Activation (RC 9), 43, 44, 53, 54, 92, 129, 172, 239, 255, 256; described, 48–49; scores, 173
Hypomanic Personality Scale (HYP), 54
Hysteria, 18, 45

IACP. *See* International Association of Chiefs of Police
IACP-PPSS Fitness-for-Duty Evaluation Guidelines, 342
ICD. *See* International Classification of Diseases
Ideas of Persecution (RC6), 43, 44, 86, 90, 94, 128, 134, 255, 256, 361; described, 47
Identifying Relevant Risk Findings, 192
IMP. *See* Impulsivity
Impression Management, 34
impulse control, 10, 239, 323, 388, 487
Impulse Control Problems, 215, 304
Impulsivity (IMP), 54, 255, 256, 443
Inefficacy (NFC), 52, 100, 421, 474
information: assessment, 173, 364; background, 322; collateral, 152; genetic, 65–66; medical, 63, 66, 350, 351; mitigating, 340; national security, 70; negative, 256; personal history, 3, 97, 153
Infrequent Psychopathology Responses (Fp) scale, 37, 38, 39, 157, 196; described, 36; scores, 113
Infrequent Responses (F) scale, 36, 48, 80, 157, 196, 355; scores, 35, 36, 37, 39, 113, 354
Infrequent Somatic Responses (Fs) scale, 36, 40, 157; scores, 113
integrative model, 174, 237, 324, 456
integrative process, 13, 154, 365
integrity, 8, 10, 178, 490n8; violations, 95–96, 271, 323
Integrity/Ethics, 176
Integrity Problems, 132, 215, 304
Interest Scales, 24–25

internal affairs investigations, 86, 94, 323, 369, 370, 371, 388
Internalizing Scales, 51–53, 141 (fig.), 161 (fig.), 182 (fig.), 201 (fig.), 223 (fig.), 243 (fig.), 261 (fig.), 276 (fig.), 293 (fig.), 309 (fig.), 328 (fig.), 376 (fig.), 394 (fig.), 408 (fig.), 429 (fig.), 447 (fig.), 464 (fig.), 478 (fig.)
Internalizing Specific Problems Scales, 51
International Association of Chiefs of Police (IACP), 69, 73, 74
International Classification of Diseases (ICD), 344
Interpersonal Disorders, 129
Interpersonal Functioning, 58, 59, 76, 129, 137, 176, 192, 305, 368, 460; measures of, 93; scales of, 197
Interpersonal Passivity (IPP), 27, 29, 55, 97
Interpersonal Scales, 27, 29, 142 (fig.), 162 (fig.), 183 (fig.), 202 (fig.), 224 (fig.), 244 (fig.), 262 (fig.), 277 (fig.), 294 (fig.), 310 (fig.), 329 (fig.), 377 (fig.), 395 (fig.), 409 (fig.), 430 (fig.), 448 (fig.), 465 (fig.), 479 (fig.); described, 55
interpretation: framework for, 58, 58 (table); guidelines for, 37
Interpretive Report for Clinical Settings, 372, 390, 404, 425, 443, 460, 474; described, 368
interview findings, 152, 177, 195, 216, 218, 236, 270, 287, 304, 319; assessing, 173–76, 193, 214, 234–35
interviews: clinical, 3, 75–77, 320, 322, 365, 367, 370–71, 389, 404, 424–25, 442–43, 458–60, 473–74; psychological, 234; questions, 76; strategies, 175
Introversion/Low Positive Emotion (INTR), 57, 361
intrusion, 425, 440, 456
invalid responding: content-based, 33–34; non-content-based, 32–33, 34–37
Inwald Personality Inventory (IPI), 81, 83, 90, 93, 94, 131
IPP. *See* Interpersonal Passivity

Item-Level Information, 75, 131, 134–35, 148 (fig.), 167 (fig.), 182, 189 (fig.), 208 (fig.), 229–30 (fig.), 250–51 (fig.), 283 (fig.), 299–300 (fig.), 315 (fig.), 335–36 (fig.), 368, 381–82 (fig.), 399 (fig.), 414 (fig.), 435 (fig.), 452 (fig.), 469 (fig.), 483 (fig.)

Jackson, D. N., 43
JCP. *See* Juvenile Conduct Problems
Jenkins v. City of Sandusky (2008), 341
Jennings v. Dow Corning Corp (2013), 350
job demands: problems with, 6, 7 (table); psychological, 6, 7, 7 (table)
job performance, 91, 343, 386; effective, 2, 441; impairments to, 72; problems with, 6, 6 (table), 349–50; safety in, 347, 348
Job-Relevant Correlates (JRC), 68, 111, 128, 130–31, 135, 136, 147–48 (fig.), 156, 166 (fig.), 187–89 (fig.), 194, 197, 207–8 (fig.), 214, 218, 229 (fig.), 234, 249 (fig.), 282–83 (fig.), 298–99 (fig.), 304, 314–15 (fig.), 324, 328, 334–35 (fig.); MMPI-3 scales/T-score cutoffs for generating statements in/by problem domain, 133 (table)
Johnson, Lyndon B., 1
Johnson, M., 94, 100
JRC. *See* Job-Relevant Correlates
Judgment, 10, 76, 93, 324, 388, 487
Judgment Problems, 132, 197, 236, 287, 318
Juvenile Conduct Problems (JCP), 53, 97–98, 100, 196, 197, 215, 216, 421
juvenile misconduct, 46

Karraker v. Rent-A-Center (2005), 63
Klein, D. F., 46
Knatz, H., 81
Kraepelin, E.: nosology of, 17, 48–49
Kring, A. M., 46
Krocka v. City of Chicago (2000), 341
K scale. *See* Adjustment Validity scale

Lack of Ego Mastery Cognitive, 51
LaLone, L., 20

Lamberty, G., 45
Lassiter v. Department of Justice (1993), 347
law enforcement, 102, 489n1, 490n3; public trust in, 1
legal standards, 72–73; absence of, 347–48
Leonel v. American Airlines, Inc. (2005), 63
Likert-type rating scale, 33, 92, 492n1
Lingoes, J., 19
Los Angeles County Sheriff's Department, 80
Low Positive Emotions (RC2), 43, 44, 47, 49, 57, 74, 93, 257, 318, 361; described, 45–46
low self-esteem, 45, 46, 52
L scales. *See* Uncommon Virtues scale

MacAndrew Alcoholism Scale–Revised, 54
Malaise (MLS), 51, 287, 356
manic episodes, 472, 474, 486
Manual for Administration, Scoring, and Interpretation, 40
Marsh, S. H., 80
Masculinity-Femininity, 18, 25
McGreal v. Ostrov (2004), 351
McKenna v. Fargo (1978), 71, 347, 348
McKinley, J. C., 17, 18, 19, 31
McNally, R., 53
McNulty, J. L., 22, 55, 56
medical records, 3, 290, 371–72, 404, 424, 442, 458, 473; findings from, 269–70
Meehl, P. E., 19, 43, 46
mental health, 25, 27, 35, 55, 77, 403, 486; assessments, 364, 365; counselors, 346, 442; diagnosis, 347; questionable, 344; services, 363
mental health conditions, 3, 36, 46, 270–71, 341, 343, 344–45, 347, 366, 402, 403, 421, 457, 472, 473; assessing, 364, 372, 386, 390, 421–22, 440, 443, 456, 460, 474; fitness for duty and, 365, 456
mental health examinations, 343, 367, 370, 389, 404, 424, 442, 473; forensic, 363
mental health treatment, 350, 371, 402, 442, 458

Meyer, G. J., 13, 43

Michael v. City of Troy Police Department (2014), 349, 350

Michigan Alcoholism Screening Test (MAST), 54

micromanaging, 457, 459

Minnesota Multiphasic Personality Inventory (MMPI): development of, 79; factor analytic studies of, 43; instruments, 14, 16, 17–27, 29–30; original, 17–20, 80–82, 95, 103, 348; research on, 80–87; updating, 20; using, 23, 80

Minnesota Multiphasic Personality Inventory-2 (MMPI-2): described, 20–22; items in, 20, 23, 44; nongendered norms, 83; normative sample, 26; publication of, 82–83; research on, 73, 80–87; scales, 22, 24, 42; scores, 74–75, 82, 83, 85; studies, 43, 83, 85

Minnesota Multiphasic Personality Inventory-2 (MMPI-2) Restandardization Committee, 22

Minnesota Multiphasic Personality Inventory-2 Restructured Form (MMPI-2-RF), 1, 41, 44, 48, 353, 356, 359, 361; development of, 24–26; findings, 102–3; items, 26, 87–88; measurements by, 24; normative sample from, 25, 26, 27, 94; CA-POST and, 98; predictive validity of, 91; preemployment evaluations and, 101; public safety assessments and, 99; RC Scales, 87; research on, 27, 87–95; scales, 50, 54, 87–88, 89–90, 91, 93, 94, 95, 96, 103, 193; scores, 88, 90–91, 92, 93, 94, 96, 97; Specific Problems Scales for, 50; studying, 83, 101; transition from, 27

Minnesota Multiphasic Personality Inventory-2 Restructured Form (MMPI-2-RF) Validity Scales, 25, 99

Minnesota Multiphasic Personality Inventory-2 Restructured Form Extended (MMPI-2-RF-EX), 99, 100, 101, 356; administering, 26–27; data collection with, 27

Minnesota Multiphasic Personality Inventory-3 (MMPI-3): described, 17; findings, 59, 238, 372; items, 26, 134, 170, 173, 174, 175, 176; preemployment evaluations and, 101; protocol, 39, 133, 157, 219, 238, 239, 255, 256, 257; research on, 90–103; scales, 28–29 (table), 51, 100, 111, 134, 193; scores, 16, 89, 102, 121, 153, 192, 193, 256

Minnesota Multiphasic Personality Inventory-3 (MMPI-3) Clinical Interpretive Report, 29

Minnesota Multiphasic Personality Inventory-3 (MMPI-3) Validity Scales, 12, 31, 38 (table), 40, 41–42, 44, 47, 356, 363, 364; assessments with, 2, 103; clinical use of, 58; described, 26–27, 29–30; findings, 122, 155, 156; interpreting, 16, 25, 41, 80, 106; items, 128, 173; normative sample and, 27, 35; public safety assessments and, 99; scales, 14, 17, 103, 106, 122; scores, 29, 103, 157, 172; using, 73, 74, 80, 83, 157

Mitchell, C. L., 9, 74

mitigation, 218–19, 236, 256, 371

MLS. *See* Malaise

MMPI. *See* Minnesota Multiphasic Personality Inventory

MMPI-2. *See* Minnesota Multiphasic Personality Inventory-2

MMPI-2-RF Technical Manual (Tellegen and Ben-Porath), 27, 50, 87, 99, 106, 136

MMPI-3. *See* Minnesota Multiphasic Personality Inventory-3

MMPI-3 Manual for Administration, Scoring, and Interpretation (Ben-Porath and Tellegen), 14–15, 15–16, 27, 39, 40, 41, 45, 57, 134, 172, 257, 789

MMPI-3 Manual Supplement for the U.S. Spanish Translation (Ben-Porath et al.), 27

MMPI-3 Technical Manual (Ben-Porath and Tellegen), 15, 26, 27, 29, 41, 45,

50, 101, 106, 130–31, 136, 356; data reported in, 99
MMPI-3 User's Guide for the Public Safety Candidate Interpretive Reports (Corey and Ben-Porath), 2, 14, 98, 129, 130, 136, 170, 174, 256
model. *See* integrative model
mood-cycling disorder, 256
mood stabilizers, 473, 474
mood symptoms, 239, 440
moral character, 9, 89
moral lapse, 271, 472
Multidimensional Personality Questionnaire (MPQ), 42, 131; Absorption subscales of, 48
Myers v. Hose (1995), 287

Nakamura, K., 217
National Council on Measurement in Education, 66
National Fire Protection Association (NFPA), 61, 72, 348
National Institute on Alcohol Abuse and Alcoholism, 305
National Security Adjudication Guidelines, 70
Negative Affectivity, 47, 57
Negative Emotionality (NEM), 42, 47, 48, 52, 53, 56, 235
Negative Emotionality/Neuroticism (NEGE), 56, 57, 192, 194, 196, 233, 236, 287, 440
Negative Treatment Indicators, 21
NEM. *See* Negative Emotionality
Neurological Complaints (NUC), 51, 356
Neurotic Depression, 46
New York State Department of Correctional Services, 1, 72
NFC. *See* Inefficacy
NFPA. *See* National Fire Protection Association
nonresponding, 32, 34, 37
normal personality, 42, 43, 346; measures of, 155; underreporting and, 171

norms, 27, 35; gender-specific, 25; non-gendered, 25, 65; standardized, 172; successful, 81
Novaco, R. W., 53
NUC. *See* Neurological Complaints

Obama, Barack, 1
obsessions, 76, 90, 235, 236
Occupational Information Network (O*NET), 7, 9
OMPE Guidelines. *See* Professional Practice Guidelines for Occupationally Mandated Psychological Evaluations
Other Risk-Taking Behavior, 195
Otto, R. K., 320, 322
overreporting, 24, 39, 40, 178, 289, 348, 355, 356, 443; indicators, 359; intentional, 33; unintentional, 34

PAI. *See* Personality Assessment Inventory
panic attacks, 423, 424–25, 441, 443, 456
Paranoia, 18, 47, 473
paranoid delusional thought, 47
parenting competency, evaluating, 366
pathology, 77, 365
PCIR. *See* Police Candidate Interpretive Report
Peace Officer Psychological Screening Manual (Spilberg and Corey), 3, 71
peace officers, 347, 489n1
Pearson, 25, 98
PEM. *See* Positive Emotionality
performance problems, 92, 319, 323, 422
Perry, M., 54
personal history questionnaires, 12, 74, 99, 102, 155, 171–72, 173, 174, 175, 177, 193, 268, 271, 304
personality, 23, 24, 42; abnormal, 43, 73, 346; measure of, 17, 19; phobic, 94; psychopathology and, 4, 56; self-report measure of, 31. *See also* normal personality
Personality Assessment Inventory (PAI), 43, 73
personality problems, 57, 70, 80–81, 268

Personality Psychopathology Five (PSY-5) Scales, 25, 41, 143 (fig.), 163 (fig.), 184 (fig.), 203 (fig.), 225 (fig.), 233, 239, 245 (fig.), 255, 263 (fig.), 278 (fig.), 295 (fig.), 304, 311 (fig.), 330 (fig.), 378 (fig.), 396 (fig.), 410 (fig.), 431 (fig.), 449 (fig.), 466 (fig.), 480 (fig.); described, 22, 55–57

personality tests, 19, 74, 236, 268, 322

personality traits, 345; normal/abnormal, 3; normal-range, 346; problematic, 472

personnel screening, standard of practice in, 62–66, 68–69

Petrus v. Cole (1996), 351

Pleasant/Unpleasant, 45

Police Candidate Comparison Group, 89, 91, 92, 94, 96, 103, 107–8, 122, 157, 170, 172, 192, 194, 196, 239, 368

Police Candidate Interpretive Report (PCIR), 65, 101, 105, 128, 130, 131, 134, 135, 137, 138–51 (fig.), 158–69 (fig.), 170, 173, 178, 179–91 (fig.), 192, 193, 194, 196, 198–213 (fig.), 214, 215, 216, 220–32 (fig.), 239, 240–54 (fig.), 255, 256, 257, 258–67 (fig.), 273–86 (fig.), 290–303 (fig.), 306–17 (fig.), 324, 325–39 (fig.), 373–85 (fig.), 391–401 (fig.), 405–20 (fig.), 426–39 (fig.), 444–55 (fig.), 461–71 (fig.), 475–85 (fig.); Clinical Findings, 197

police officers, 9, 367; essential job functions of, 5 (table); term, 489n1

Police Psychological Services Section (IACP), 321

Poor Psychological Suitability, 100

Portland (Oregon) Police Bureau, 70, 91

Positive Emotionality (PEM), 42, 47, 56

Positive Emotions, 74

POST. *See* California Commission on Peace Officer Standards and Training

posttraumatic stress disorder (PTSD), 42, 47, 52, 53, 269, 270, 271, 421, 456

preemployment evaluations, 4, 13, 14, 16, 40, 59, 61, 62, 69, 73, 84, 87, 88, 89, 91, 98, 99, 137, 152, 320, 351, 354, 424, 425; conducting, 106; gender-/race-based norms in, 83; MMPI-3 and, 101; psychological screening dimensions and, 11–12

Preemployment Psychological Evaluation Guidelines (IACP), 69, 70, 72, 73, 74, 75, 321

preemployment screening, 1, 134–35, 350

President's Commission on Law Enforcement and Administration of Justice, 1, 491n9

President's Task Force on 21st Century Policing, 1

Problem Behaviors, 91, 92, 93

professional practice guidelines, 14, 341, 342; described, 68

Professional Practice Guidelines for Occupationally Mandated Psychological Evaluations (OMPE Guidelines), 14, 68, 342, 346, 350

Protocol Validity, 73, 145–46 (fig.), 165–66 (fig.), 186–87 (fig.), 205–6 (fig.), 227–28 (fig.), 247–48 (fig.), 265–66 (fig.), 280–81 (fig.), 297–98 (fig.), 313–14 (fig.), 332–33 (fig.), 356, 368, 372, 380 (fig.), 398 (fig.), 412 (fig.), 425, 433 (fig.), 443, 451 (fig.), 468 (fig.), 474, 482 (fig.); assessing, 31–34, 37–40, 157, 170–72, 178, 196–97, 219, 239, 257, 268, 272, 289, 305, 318; described, 128–29

PSCIRs. *See* Public Safety Candidate Interpretive Reports

PSCIR User's Guide, 134, 135

PSYC. *See* Psychoticism

Psychasthenia, 18

psychiatric conditions, 42, 45, 348, 366

psychological adjustments, 40, 175, 372

psychological conditions, 36, 45, 70, 72, 344, 349, 353, 359, 364, 472, 492n11; assessing, 365–66

psychological evaluations, 16, 48, 61, 69, 73, 84, 89, 99, 174, 238, 320, 346, 348, 355, 365, 424, 490n3, 490n8, 492n9

psychological screening, 1, 10 (table), 72, 75, 76, 236, 491n8, 491n9; ethical standards pertinent to, 67–68 (table);

model of, 153–54, 155, 171; reports, 321; using, 9, 11–12
psychological suitability, 171, 238, 321; assessment of, 349–50; criteria for, 71–73
psychological tests, 3, 13, 68, 73–74, 76, 77, 89, 154, 216, 235, 320, 340, 341, 365, 372; findings from, 236–37; manuals for, 14; results of, 174; review of, 75; using, 348–50
psychology, 347; personality-related, 22; police, 54
psychometrics, 4, 19, 26, 32, 709
Psychoneurosis, 43
Psychopathic Deviate, 18
psychopathology, 1–2, 17, 24, 37, 43, 48, 49, 77, 268, 365, 369; anxiety-related, 47; displaying, 72; domain, 42; genuine, 36, 39–40; indicators of, 33, 472; measuring, 13, 19, 31, 388; models of, 23; personality and, 4, 25, 56; severe, 39; somatoform, 51
psychopathy, 42, 46, 49
Psychosis, 43, 48; temporary, 473–74
psychosocial functioning, assessment of, 74
psychotherapy, 45, 346, 386, 486
psychotic features, 43, 48, 473, 486
Psychoticism (PSYC), 56, 57, 100, 128, 239, 255, 256
PSY-5 Scales. *See* Personality Psychopathology Five Scales
PTSD. *See* posttraumatic stress disorder
Publication Manual of the American Psychological Association, 492n2
public safety, 26; defending, 2–3, 343; implications for, 352
Public Safety Candidate Interpretive Reports (PSCIRs), 2, 16, 30, 34, 64, 65, 68, 79, 102, 111, 153, 170, 192, 233, 368–69; comparison groups, 122; fitness evaluations and, 369; interpretive statements and, 135; preemployment assessments and, 106; problem domains as organizing structure in, 132 (table); report writing using, 105, 320–24, 340; structure/content of, 122, 128–31, 133–36; using findings from, 137, 152, 156, 322–24, 340
public safety classifications, 9; attributes for, 8 (table)
public safety positions: categories of, 367; essential job functions of, 5 (table)

Q-global Remote On-Screen Assessment (ROSA) system, 98, 99

race, 4, 107–8, 193
Rado, S., 46
Raine, A., 53
Random Responding, 32, 39
RBS scale. *See* Response Bias scale
RC Scales. *See* Restructured Clinical Scales
reasonable accommodation, 63–64, 351, 472
redemption period, 217, 218
Referral Summary, 157, 178, 196, 219, 238, 257, 272, 289, 305, 369, 388, 403, 423, 442, 457, 472–73
Reiser, M., 81, 82
Reiss, S., 53
relapse management, 389, 402, 487
relationships, 366, 459; social, 270; stable, 77; unstable interpersonal, 372
relative risk ratios (RRRs), 85, 86, 95
relevant risk findings, identifying, 176–78, 193–95, 214–19, 236–37, 270–72
report writing, evidence-based, 320–24, 340
Research Reference List, 128, 136
Response Bias (RBS) scale, 39, 40, 113, 157, 196; described, 36
Response% statistic, 34, 37, 38
Restandardization Project, 20–21, 22, 50
Restructured Clinical (RC) Scales, 28, 41, 43, 49, 50, 84, 94, 140 (fig.), 160 (fig.), 181 (fig.), 200 (fig.), 222 (fig.), 239, 242 (fig.), 260 (fig.), 275 (fig.), 292 (fig.), 305, 208 (fig.), 318, 327 (fig.), 361, 375 (fig.), 393 (fig.), 407 (fig.), 428 (fig.), 440, 446 (fig.), 463 (fig.), 477 (fig.); described, 22–23, 44–45; developing, 23–24, 44; elevated scores for, 425; including, 87; prehire, 86

Revised NEO Personality Inventory (NEO PI-R), 74
Ribot, T. H., 46
Rice v. City of Oakland (1999), 341
Ridgeway, G., 108, 110
risk mitigation. *See* mitigation
risk-related findings, 174, 177–78, 236–37, 322
risks: elimination of, 218; factors for, 217, 238; identifying, 237; taking, 219
Roberts, R. M., 94, 97–98, 100
ROSA. *See* Q-global Remote On-Screen Assessment system
Routine Task Performance Problems, 93, 132, 215, 287, 318
RRRs. *See* relative risk ratios

Sager v. Yuba County (2007), 12, 345
Salley v. Circuit City Stores, Inc. (1998), 367
SAMSHA. *See* Substance Abuse and Mental Health Services Administration
Sangirardi v. Village of Stickney (2003), 351
SAV. *See* Social Avoidance
Saxe, S. J., 81, 82
scales, 13, 14, 22, 25, 27, 355; cognitive, 28; constructing, 19, 33; externalizing, 29; internalizing, 28–29; interpersonal, 29; original, 18; overreporting, 35; somatic, 28; underreporting, 88–89, 354, 359
scale scores, 27, 58, 87, 355, 368; gender-normed/nongendered, 25; underreporting, 272; validation of, 26
Scarpa, A., 53
Schinka, J. A., 20
schizoid personality disorder, 55
Schizophrenia, 18, 367
Schmidt, H. O., 84, 86
School Board of Nassau County v. Arline (1987), 387
Score Report, 29, 105, 106, 122, 137, 140, 156, 368
screening psychologists, 171, 172, 174, 219, 237, 238, 268, 271, 320, 490n3, 492n1; as risk assessors, 218

Security Executive Agent Directive 4 (SEAD-4), 346
Seed (S) Scales, 23, 49
Selection Validation Survey (SVS), 91, 92, 100, 101
self-confidence, 77, 235, 324
self-doubt, 52, 236, 237, 322
Self-Doubt (SFD), 52, 192, 233, 236, 239, 255, 421
self-identity, 386, 387
Self-Importance (SFI), 55, 121, 197
self-reporting, 31, 51, 76, 177, 194
Sellbom, M., 18, 24, 37, 41, 42, 46, 48, 57, 80, 84, 85, 92, 93, 94, 96; Clinical Scales and, 87; externalizing scales and, 97; MMPI-2-RF/POST and, 98; MMPI-3 and, 31; prehire assessments and, 86; research reviewed by, 36
sexual orientation, 4, 21, 69
SFD. *See* Self-Doubt
SFI. *See* Self-Importance
Shafer v. Preston Memorial Hospital Corp. (1997), 367
Shyness (SHY), 55, 192, 197, 198, 474
Skinner, H. A., 43
Slater v. Department of Homeland Security (2008), 346
sleep deprivation, 270, 473–74
sobriety, commitment to, 390, 402
social anxiety, 194, 474
Social Avoidance (SAV), 55, 57, 197, 361, 474
Social Competence, 10, 76, 93, 132, 215, 287, 304
Social Introversion, 18
socioeconomic status (SES), 20
Somatic Complaints (RC 1), 44, 50, 94, 287, 361; described, 45
Somatic/Cognitive Dysfunction Scales, 58, 129, 141 (fig.), 161 (fig.), 182 (fig.), 201 (fig.), 223 (fig.), 243 (fig.), 261 (fig.), 272, 276 (fig.), 293 (fig.), 309 (fig.), 328 (fig.), 376 (fig.), 349, 368, 394 (fig.), 408 (fig.), 425, 429 (fig.), 447 (fig.), 464 (fig.), 478 (fig.); described, 50–51

somatic concerns, 45, 289
Specific Problems (SP) Scales, 24, 27, 28, 41, 53, 197, 233, 318, 361; demoralization-related, 51; described, 49–50
Spielberger, C. D., 53
Spilberg, S. W., 64, 153, 174, 218; background information and, 171
S Scales. *See* Seed Scales
Standard on Comprehensive Occupational Medical Program(s) for Fire Protection (NFPA), 72, 348
Standards for Educational and Psychological Testing (American Educational Research Association, APA, and National Council on Measurement in Education), 15, 66, 135
STR. *See* Stress
stress, 91, 93, 194, 237, 323, 414, 440; acute, 403, 423, 425, 443, 456; resilience, 171, 270, 288, 289; tolerance of, 490n8
Stress (STR), 52, 100, 192, 194, 233, 235, 236, 287, 361, 425, 440
Stress Tolerance, 8, 10, 132, 195, 215, 236, 270, 271, 287, 288, 304, 318, 388, 423, 487
SUB. *See* Substance Abuse
Subjective Distress, 43
substance abuse, 46, 94, 195, 367, 390, 460, 487; avoidance of, 10; evaluation, 389; frequency of, 217; problems with, 234
Substance Abuse (SUB), 54, 134, 192, 215, 216, 289, 304, 309; prehire, 86
Substance Abuse and Mental Health Services Administration (SAMSHA), 305
Substance Use Problems, 215, 304
substantially limiting impairments, assessing for, 366
Substantive Scale Interpretation, 57–59, 368, 380–81 (fig.), 398–99 (fig.), 412–13 (fig.), 433–34 (fig.), 451–52 (fig.), 460, 468–69 (fig.), 482–83 (fig.), 474
Substantive Scales, 14, 30, 35, 36, 41, 41–47, 42, 43, 58, 89–90, 92, 94, 97, 99, 100, 101, 103, 121, 136, 176, 178, 359, 372, 390, 440; assessing, 172–73, 192, 197, 233–34; findings on, 129, 239, 268–69, 287, 304, 318; scores on, 89, 128, 156, 172, 238, 289, 318, 369, 386, 388, 403, 425; underreporting on, 157; using, 79
Suicidal/Death Ideation (SUI), 51, 129, 134, 192, 361, 372, 425, 443
suicidal ideation, 387, 404, 421, 422
suicide, 51, 404, 423, 425, 442; prospect of, 287; risk of, 421; threatening, 369, 370, 371, 372, 386
suitability determinations, 2, 269, 271, 319; evidentiary support/rationale for, 320–21; hiring authority and, 237–38; reaching/documenting, 320. *See also* psychological suitability
sustainability of fitness, assessing, 387, 402, 422–23, 456–57, 460
SVS. *See* Selection Validation Survey
Swanson, S. C., 43
Sydenham, Thomas, 45
Symptom Validity (FBS) scale, 39, 113, 157, 196, 372; described, 36
Synopsis, described, 128

Tarescavage, A. M., 48, 70, 100, 103, 256; CPI/MMPI-2-RF scores and, 97–98; integrity violations and, 95–96; MMPI-2-F scores and, 90–91; MMPI-2-RF/CPI/IPI and, 93–95; predictive validity and, 91–93
teamwork, 10, 93, 490n8
Teamwork Problems, 132, 215, 287, 304
Tellegen, Auke, 43, 44, 46, 47, 48, 56, 87, 172, 256, 359, 368, 440; Demoralization and, 45; Low Positive Emotions and, 45; MMPI-2 Restandardization Committee and, 22; MPQ and, 42; RC Scales and, 23; Specific Problem Scales and, 49, 50; Substantive Scales and, 134
test findings, 19, 174, 176, 193–94, 214–15, 216, 236, 270; misleading, 34
testing, 33, 73–74, 257; assessment and, 12–13; reality, 459; security for, 16, 135, 256, 287; standardized, 2, 89

test scores, 4, 12, 24, 31, 34, 131, 153, 155, 237, 256, 323, 365; uninterpretable, 271
Texas Administrative Code Title 37, 490n6
THD. *See* Thought Dysfunction
Thomas v. Corwin (2007), 371
Thomas v. Johnson (1968), 344
Thompson v. City of Arlington (1993), 371
Thought Disorders, 129
Thought Dysfunction (THD), 43, 44, 58, 90, 93, 94, 100, 128, 129, 137, 239, 255, 256, 361, 368, 425
trauma-related disorder, 350, 440, 441
traumatic brain injury, 270, 271
Treatment Considerations, 58, 368, 381 (fig.), 399 (fig.), 414 (fig.), 435 (fig.), 452 (fig.), 469 (fig.), 483 (fig.)
TRIN scale. *See* True Response Inconsistency scale
True, 32, 33, 35, 133, 425; protocol, 39; responses, 39
True Response Inconsistency (TRIN) scale, 38, 39, 96, 113, 157, 177, 196, 257, 372, 425; score, 35, 390
T scores, 21, 25, 35, 39, 40, 79, 82, 84, 86, 91, 94, 96, 99, 101, 111, 121, 122, 128, 129, 130, 134, 194, 215, 216, 233, 239, 256, 257, 318, 356, 359; cutoffs for, 113, 130 (table); deviations, 83; mean, 354; standard deviation, 85
T Scores (by Domain), 144 (fig.), 164–65 (fig.), 185–86 (fig.), 204–5 (fig.), 226–27 (fig.), 246–47 (fig.), 264–65 (fig.), 279–80 (fig.), 296–97 (fig.), 312–13 (fig.), 331–32 (fig.), 379–80 (fig.), 397–98 (fig.), 411–12 (fig.), 432–33 (fig.), 450–51 (fig.), 467–68 (fig.), 481–82 (fig.)

Uncommon Virtues (L) scale, 36, 39, 40, 57, 121, 355; scores, 88–89, 113, 121, 157, 170, 197, 268, 359; underreporting, 37
underreporting, 24, 33–34, 36, 37, 39, 121, 157, 170, 176, 178, 197, 268, 272, 289, 318, 348, 354, 355, 356, 443; indicators of, 89; intentional, 34; interpreting, 156; measuring, 172; normal personality and, 171; of scales, 88–89, 354, 359; unintentional, 34
Undue Suspiciousness, 90
unfit for duty, 341, 343, 347, 350, 352, 441, 472, 487; determining, 388
Uniformed Services Employment and Reemployment Rights Act (USERRA), 271
uniform T (UT) scores, 21
University of Minnesota Hospital, 17
University of Minnesota Press, 20, 25, 26, 27
Unscorable Responses, 131, 133–34
Unusual Experiences/Thoughts, 90
U.S. Census Bureau, 108
U.S. Department of Labor/Employment and Training Administration, 7
U.S. Department of Veterans Affairs (VA), 268
U.S. District Court for the District of New Jersey, 347
use of force, 1, 7
User-Designated Item-Level Information, 131, 134–35
Utah Court of Appeals, 12, 345

validity: evidence of, 68; indicators, 37; measures, 101, 219; predictive, 91–92, 93; threats to, 32
Validity Scales, 24, 25, 28, 58, 88, 99, 122, 128, 129, 139 (fig.), 159 (fig.), 180 (fig.), 199 (fig.), 221 (fig.), 241 (fig.), 259 (fig.), 270, 274 (fig.), 291 (fig.), 307 (fig.), 326 (fig.), 374 (fig.), 359, 392 (fig.), 406 (fig.), 425, 427 (fig.), 445 (fig.), 460, 462 (fig.), 476 (fig.); described, 34–40; public safety and, 40; scores on, 305, 355, 372
VA Rating Decision, 269, 270, 271
Variable Response Inconsistency (VRIN) scale, 34, 38, 113, 157, 177, 196, 257, 372, 474; scores, 35, 39, 272, 390

Walfish, S., 354, 355, 359
Watson, L. C., 54, 345
Watson v. City of Miami Beach (1999), 341, 343, 344
Weiner, I. B., 490n8
Weiss, P. A., 87
Weiss, W. U., 87
White v. County of Los Angeles (2014), 442
Whitman, M. R., 101–2, 128
Wiener, D. N., 19
Wiggins, J. S., 19, 21
Wingate, L., 51
Wisbey v. City of Lincoln (2009), 341

Word Memory Test, 36
Worry (WRY), 52, 233, 235, 236, 287, 361, 425, 440, 474
written reports: elements of, 321–22; function of, 320–21
WRY. *See* Worry
Wurzel v. Whirlpool Corp. (2012), 350

Zelig, M., 73, 174, 237, 238, 269, 322; on diagnostic reliability, 422; interviews and, 234–35; psychological assessments and, 155
Zenor v. El Paso Healthcare Systems, Ltd. (1999), 367

DAVID M. COREY, PHD, is a practicing psychologist in Portland, Oregon, with more than 40 years of experience conducting suitability and fitness evaluations for police and other public safety positions. He is the founding president of the American Board of Police & Public Safety Psychology and a fellow of the American Psychological Association. He is board certified in forensic psychology and in police and public safety psychology with the American Board of Professional Psychology.

YOSSEF S. BEN-PORATH, PHD, is professor of psychological sciences at Kent State University. He received his doctoral training at the University of Minnesota and has been involved extensively in MMPI research since 1986. He is a codeveloper of the MMPI-3, MMPI-2-RF, and MMPI-A-RF and coauthor of test manuals, books, book chapters, and articles on the MMPI instruments. Dr. Ben-Porath is a board-certified clinical psychologist (American Board of Professional Psychology-Clinical) whose clinical practice involves supervision of assessments at Kent State's Psychological Clinic, consultation to agencies that screen candidates for public safety positions, and provision of consultation and expert witness services in forensic cases.